South Africa's Radical Tradition: A documentary history

Volume 1: 1907 – 1950

South Africa's Radical Tradition: A documentary history

Volume 1: 1907 – 1950

edited by
ALLISON DREW

Buchu Books: Cape Town
Mayibuye Books: Cape Town
UCT Press: Cape Town

First published 1996
UCT Press, University of Cape Town, Private Bag, 7700 Rondebosch, South Africa,
Buchu Books, P.O. Box 2580, 8000 Cape Town, South Africa and
Mayibuye Books, History and Literature Series no. 59, Mayibuye Centre, University
of the Western Cape, Private Bag X17, 7535 Bellville, South Africa

The Mayibuye Centre for History and Culture in South Africa is based at the University of the Western Cape. Focusing on all aspects of apartheid, resistance, social life and culture in South Africa, its aim is to help recover the rich heritage of all South Africans and to encourage cultural creativity and expression. The Mayibuye History and Literature Series is part of this project. The series editors are Barry Feinberg and André Odendaal.

All rights reserved. No part of this publication may be reproduced, stored in a retrieval system or transmitted, in any form by any means, electronic, mechanical, photocopying, recording or otherwise, without the prior permission of the publishers.

© 1996 Allison Drew

ISBN 0-7992-1613-5

Layout and desktop publishing: birga thomas
Cover design: A. Schultz
Cover photograph: Courtesy Millie Haston

Printed by Formsxpress Retreat

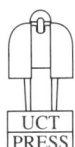

Contents

List of abbreviations 6

Preface 9

Acknowledgements 13

Introduction 15

PART ONE
South African socialists and the racially-divided working class 41

PART TWO
Communists and the national struggle: The Native Republic Thesis 75

PART THREE
The Comintern and the New Line 107

PART FOUR
The origins and development of Trotskyism in South Africa 123

PART FIVE
Building political alliances: Workers' unity and black united fronts 195

PART SIX
World war and the suppression of socialism 331

List of documents 393

Sources 397

Select bibliography 397

Index 401

List of abbreviations

AAC	All African Convention
ACDWU	African Commercial and Distributive Workers' Union
ADP	African Democratic Party
AEU	Amalgamated Engineering Union
AMTU	African Metal Trades Union
AMWU	African Mine Workers' Union
ANC	African National Congress
Anti-CAD	Anti-Coloured Affairs Department
APDUSA	African People's Democratic Union of Southern Africa
APO	African People's Organisation
B-L	Bolshevik-Leninist
BLL	Bolshevist Leninist League
CCATU	Co-ordinating Committee of African Trade Unions
CFLU	Cape Federation of Labour Unions
CLA	Communist League of Africa
CLSA	Communist League of South Africa
CNETU	Council of Non-European Trade Unions
Comintern	Communist International
CPSA	Communist Party of South Africa
CPSU	Communist Party of the Soviet Union
ECCI	Executive Committee of the Communist International
FIOSA	Fourth International Organisation of South Africa
FSU	Friends of the Soviet Union
ICU	Industrial and Commercial Workers' Union
ILP	Independent Labour Party
IS	International Secretariat (Left Opposition)
ISL	International Socialist League
JCATU	Joint Committee of African Trade Unions
LAR	League of African Rights
NEF	New Era Fellowship
NEUF	Non-European United Front
NEUM	Non-European Unity Movement
NIC	Natal Indian Congress
NLL	National Liberation League
NP	National Party

NRC	Natives' Representative Council
PTU	Progressive Trade Union Group
RILU	Red International of Labour Unions
SAFNETU	South African Federation of Non-European Trade Unions
SAIC	South African Indian Congress
SAIF	South African Industrial Federation
SAIRR	South African Institute of Race Relations
SALP	South African Labour Party
SAMWU	South African Mine Workers' Union
SANNC	South African Native National Congress
SASP	South African Socialist Party
SATLC	South African Trades and Labour Council
SATUC	South African Trades Union Congress
SATUCC	South African Trades Union Co-ordinating Council
SWL	Socialist Workers League
TIC	Transvaal Indian Congress
TLSA	Teachers' League of South Africa
UCT	University of Cape Town
UNISA	University of South Africa
UP	United Party
WIL	Workers' International League
WPSA	Workers' Party of South Africa
YCL	Young Communist League

Preface

The compiling and editing of a documentary history raises several interrelated historiographical and methodological issues concerning, firstly, the significance of primary documents for the study and writing of history, and secondly, the methodology of the editor with regards to scope, selection, organisation and editorial style. The first issue raises the question of the relationship between such documents and history, which, in turn, obliges us to address the question, what is history?

It is conventional wisdom to claim that facts speak for themselves, yet as E. H. Carr (1987:10–15) points out, facts are the raw materials of history, and their significance turns on the historian's assessment and interpretation of them. This in no way implies a purely subjective notion of history, Carr adds. History, he writes, "... is a continuous process of interaction between the historian and his facts, an unending dialogue between the present and the past" (1987:30).

In contemporary South Africa, the past is very much part of the present, not only in terms of the legacies which have shaped the present but in terms of the acute controversies which have arisen over conflicting interpretations of the past. Thus, in South Africa one observes the "fetishism of documents" against which Carr (1987:16) cautioned. This fetishism takes two forms. First, it appears in the struggle to establish ideological hegemony through, not merely the adoption, but in some cases the imposition of particular documents on community and trade union organisations, the controversy over the Congress movement's Freedom Charter being the most notable example. Second, it appears in the struggle to establish ideological purity and control by refusing to work with groups which have not adopted particular documents, such as the Non-European Unity Movement's (NEUM) Ten Point Programme.

In addition to these ideological struggles, this fetishism of documents has a historical basis in the lack of a continuous written tradition within the liberation movement and on the left. Not only were many political activists and radical intellectuals, often black, denied access to formal education, but they were subjected to continual state harassment which led them to bury and even burn their own books and documents. Thus, many political documents have been lost or destroyed because of fear of political repression. For political organisations outside the dominant Congress tradition, in particular, the loss of the raw materials from which these organisations could construct a historical record of their own past has exacerbated political defeats and political marginalisation and led to a mystification of missing documents.

But as Carr (1987:16) notes, documents by themselves do not constitute a history:

> No document can tell us more than what the author of the document thought
> – what he thought had happened, what he thought ought to happen or would
> happen, or perhaps only what he wanted others to think he thought, or even
> what he himself thought he thought. None of this means anything until the
> historian has got to work on it and deciphered it.

This raises the question of the scope of this two-volume documentary history and of my methods of selection and organisation of the material (see Kline 1987 for a discussion of these issues). The answer to these questions begins first with a recognition that much documentation of South Africa's liberation movement, particularly private correspondence and unpublished material, has been lost or destroyed; thus, the remaining accessible material is itself only a portion of the original. No documentary history of the South African liberation movement can claim to be exhaustive or comprehensive (Kline 1987:67). These volumes are intended as a selective and authoritative documentary history which will supplement other documentary histories or bibliographic references of the South African liberation movement (see, *inter alia*, Karis and Carter 1973–1977; African National Congress 1977; Bunting 1981; Bhana and Pachai 1984; Dadoo 1990; Bohmer 1986–87).

The selection and organisation of material reflects the multiple aims of this project. Firstly, I hope to demonstrate the existence and indicate the development of a heterogeneous and eclectic radical-left tradition which reflects the articulation of both the socialist and nationalist movements in their international and domestic aspects. The documents are drawn principally from political organisations within this radical tradition. Linked to this, I have attempted to illustrate some of the principal choices, dilemmas and controversies which have confronted South Africa's radical tradition over the twentieth century. As part of this task, I have sought to include documents which indicate the range of positions found within the radical tradition. This is no arcane endeavor as many of the issues and problems debated in these documents continue to confront South Africa in its post-apartheid phase.

Most documentary histories of South Africa's liberation movement, like most histories, have reflected the historical predominance of the African National Congress and its affiliated organisations or allies. This focus on the majority political tendency has had the effect of underestimating the degree of debate and controversy within the liberation movement. Notwithstanding Carr's (1987:50) dictum that "[n]umbers count in history" – that masses of people constitute social forces that can reshape society – minority political tendencies and organisations can have a political significance which transcends their numbers.

For these reasons, although the material in both volumes follows a broadly chronological arrangement, I have organised the documents into thematic or topical subdivisions which illustrate the origins and development of various political concerns and debates over the twentieth century. In other words, because the process of selection and organisation is linked to the above objectives, it is necessarily interpretive (Kline 1987:74–75). In this respect, it must be emphasised that a documentary history is indeed a history, and not simply a collection of documents; as such, it represents the historical interpretations of its editor.

Volume One opens in 1907, when Scottish socialist Keir Hardie, who had supported Afrikaners in their struggle against British imperialism a few years earlier, returned to

South Africa and encountered the virulently racist face of white labour. This volume traces the origins and development of socialism in South Africa until 1950, shortly before the passage of the Suppression of Communism Act which made overt socialist organisation illegal. It covers the dilemmas which socialists faced in confronting a racially-divided working class, their gradual recognition of the national question and their efforts to build political alliances. It also considers the impact of international socialist politics and of World War Two on the South African socialist movement.

Volume Two covers the relationship between socialist currents and the national liberation movement from the 1940s to the early 1960s, addressing some of the main dilemmas facing the national liberation movement – from the perspective of the diverse socialist groups which for much of this period operated in a clandestine and muted manner. It begins in 1943, a focal year for the national liberation movement, which saw the launching of the ANC Youth League, the Anti-CAD movement, the NEUM and the African Democratic Party and, accordingly, the intensification of debates about political alliances, the national question, the agrarian question and the armed struggle which were debated within the national liberation movement, particularly by socialists, during these decades.

Textual treatment

The choice of editorial methodology has political ramifications in the highly-charged South African context. A notable example is Neville Alexander's (1991) essay, "Black Consciousness: A Reactionary Tendency?" Commissioned by an affiliate of the NEUM, and written pseudonymously in 1974 under house arrest, the essay was edited without authorial permission in a manner which transformed its meaning. The magnitude of the transformation, as Alexander (1991:240) notes, was symbolised by the simple elimination of the question mark at the end of the title.

I have opted for a conservative editing approach and have tried to reproduce the original documents as accurately as possible, including stylistic variations and peculiarities, and grammatical, spelling and typographical errors (Kline 1987:90). Most written political discourse in South Africa's liberation movement has been urban-based and written in English. The varied styles reflect both the different organisational homes and social class backgrrounds of the writers, some of whom were highly literate elites who spoke English as a mother tongue, while others had limited formal education and spoke English as a second or third language. All of these details may be of historical interest, providing insights into both the social backgrounds and modes of communication of the authors of these documents (Kline 153–155).

In cases where the original documents or photocopies of the original indicate editorial changes, I have reproduced what appears to be the final corrected version, indicating any substantive changes that are not of a grammatical nature in the notes at the end of each section. In their original form, most of the documents reproduced here were either typed or typeset, and most of the correspondence was originally handwritten. Letterheads are reproduced in italics and centered at the top of the document.

In terms of physical format, I have standardised the following: document titles; the placement of subheadings within documents; the placement of datelines, salutations and closings in correspondence; paragraph indentations; block quotes; and numbered and lettered lists. I have also supplied missing punctuation that is part of a set, such as parentheses or quotation marks, as well as missing terminal punctuation in cases where the author started a new sentence with a capital letter but omitted the preceding closing punctuation. In the rare occasion where words or punctuation have been duplicated in the source text, the duplicated item has been deleted. Hard hyphens have been carried over from the source texts.

Aside from these silent emendations, all other editorial interpolations in the text are indicated in brackets and italicised in order to distinguish such interpolations from the occasional use of brackets by authors of the source material. All other editorial notes are to be found at the end of each section. Unrecoverable gaps in original texts, generally due to the poor physical condition of the source material or to illegible handwriting, are indicated by the use of dashes in italicised brackets; where possible, the number of dashes approximates the number of missing words. Missing lines or sections in the original are noted as such in brackets and italicised. Underlining and other emphasis in the source text are indicated through conventional typesetting symbols, e.g., underlined material in the source text has been italicised, and double underlines are indicated by the use of small capitals. The use of bold and capitalisation in the source text has been reproduced as in the original document. Where I have reproduced an extract of a document, the material omitted has been indicated by ellipses in brackets.

Acknowledgements

My thanks to the many people who have assisted me on this project: to Neville Alexander for suggesting the idea of a documentary history to me while I was engaged in doctoral research; to Karen Press and Venetia Naidoo at Buchu Books; to Barry Feinberg at Mayibuye Books; to Rose Meny-Gibert at UCT Press; to Mary Troost; to Julie Parle; to birga thomas for the German translations and for a colossal typesetting job; and to Leonie Twentyman-Jones for the index. Ronald Kieve's continued friendship has been a source of strength. My biggest thanks go to David Howell for his unflagging encouragement and his help with the endnotes! Any errors are, of course, my own responsibility. The Centre for African Studies at the University of Cape Town kindly provided me with office space for this project while I was in Cape Town. This project was facilitated by a grant from the Lipman Trust in England and by a post-doctoral research fellowship at the Department of Political Studies, University of Natal, Pietermaritzburg.

The material in this documentary history has been collected from libraries and archives and from private parties in South Africa, Britain and the United States, to all of whom I am most appreciative. I would like to particularly acknowledge the assistance of the following institutions: in South Africa, the Historical Papers Library at the University of the Witwatersrand, the Manuscripts and Archives Department of the University of Cape Town Libraries, the Mayibuye Historical Papers at the University of the Western Cape and the South African Reference Library in Cape Town; in Britain, the Communist Party of Great Britain Library and Archive; the Borthwick Institute of Historical Research at the University of York; the British Library in London; the Brynmor Jones Library at the University of Hull; the Institute of Commonwealth Studies at the University of London; the Modern Records Centre at the University of Warwick Library; the National Museum of Labour History in Manchester; the Public Record Office in London and the Working Class Movement Library in Salford; and in the United States, the Hoover Institution Archives at Stanford University; the Houghton Library at Harvard University; the Prometheus Research Library in New York City; the Special Collections at the University Research Library, University of California, Los Angeles; and the Manuscripts and Archives office at Yale University Library.

Every effort has been made by the editor and publishers to obtain permission to reproduce the documents in this volume. Where it has not been possible to trace the copyrightholders of documents, the publishers would be glad to hear from such copyrightholders, so that omissions can be rectified in future editions.

Introduction

South Africa's radical and socialist traditions have been obscured both in popular understanding and in historiography. This marginalisation is the product of political defeats for the left that should be located in the context of South Africa's distinctive development. First, capitalist development itself, based on colonial conquest and then on British imperialism's quest for cheap mine labour, produced national oppression in South Africa before a working class was formed. Second, within the movement for national liberation and democracy which arose in response to this oppression, the black *petite bourgeoisie*, aided by the mission education system, developed as a crystallised and conscious class well before the black proletariat. This black *petite bourgeoisie* has tended to pursue a social vision based on incorporation into the pre-existing system. Prevailing scholarship has generally reinforced this historical development and has presented an oversimplified picture of South Africa's continually developing national liberation movement. This literature rests on two assumptions which are often invalidated by historical developments: that majority political tendencies will remain dominant over time and that minority tendencies have only limited influence. But in fact South Africa's radical and socialist traditions have always had disproportionate influence in shaping debates within the liberation movement. As a result, the liberation movement was pushed further to the left. This documentary history points to some of the many strands that have been woven together to form these traditions, and it highlights their relationship with the broader national liberation movement.

South African socialists and the racially-divided working class

In its origins, South African socialism was foreign-born. As a movement it arose in the early twentieth century from the traditions of skilled British workers and Eastern Europeans fleeing Tsarist repression (Johns 1976; Adler 1979; Adler 1976; Mantzaris 1987). Early Marxist analyses were formulated with direct reference to British and European experience rather than to South Africa's particular conditions of colonial and imperialist domination (Ntsebeza 1988:27-9). Reflecting the social conditions in which it developed, the socialist movement was fragmented along national lines and embued with both white labour chauvinism and male chauvinism. The challenge facing socialists, of which they became increasingly conscious over the decades, was to build a movement which could resonate with the democratic demands of the oppressed majority, and particularly with the demands of the oppressed black working class.

As an organised tendency, South African socialism traces its roots primarily to the white labour movement of the early twentieth century, particularly to the all-white South African Labour Party (SALP), which was a member of the Second Socialist International. Although South African Communist Eddie Roux (Document 25) cited white labour's support for British labour struggles as proof of its internationalism, this support can arguably be seen as proof of its British nationalism. The solidarity of English-speaking white workers in South Africa with those in Britain lay in the fact that most of the former had been born in Britain and still saw themselves as British workers. By contrast, white workers saw Africans, Asians and Chinese as tools of the capitalists who undercut white wages, and they responded with rigid protectionist policies aimed to keep blacks out of the workforce and out of the trade unions (Documents 1, 2). As Scottish socialist Keir Hardie quickly learned on his trip to South Africa in 1907, even raising the possibility of letting blacks join trade unions produced seething anger and violence. The very Afrikaners whose struggle against British imperialism Hardie had championed only a few years earlier during the Anglo-Boer War, now jeered him (Document 1).

This ambivalent relationship with national and international labour was seen also in the early socialist movement, which echoed the issues and debates – syndicalism, the efficacy of electoral politics and attitudes towards war – found in Western socialist movements. Organisationally, the break between the white labour and socialist movements did not occur over the national question of working class unity – the SALP's adoption of a segregationist policy in 1912 did not produce a split – but over the question of international working class unity posed by World War One. In 1915 an anti-war minority in the SALP established itself as an independent body called the International Socialist League (ISL) (Document 3). Like the SALP, it looked to white labour as the working vanguard. But influenced by the thinking of American socialist Daniel DeLeon and by broader syndicalist currents, the ISL adopted the principle of labour solidarity regardless of colour or creed. A minority, including T. W. Thibedi and S. P. Bunting, argued for the organisation of black workers. In 1917 they established the Industrial Workers of Africa (IWA), named after the Industrial Workers of the World, and the first black trade union in South Africa (Ntsebeza 1988:35-7).

Three assumptions percolated, with various permutations, through socialist thinking in the late 1910s and 1920s. The first was an unquestioning acceptance of the biological basis of separate human races which, it was assumed, should quite naturally follow separate paths of development. Linked to this was another assumption that Africans were better off in the rural areas where they were not a threat to urban white workers. But by the late 1910s, the continuing influx of black people to the cities and mines made this deproletarianisation thesis untenable. Now recognising that blacks were a permanent part of the industrial workforce, socialists assumed that capitalist development would immiserate both black and white workers, laying the basis for their common unity. Despite this utopian expectation that objective conditions would equalise blacks and whites, socialists still believed that white labour was the proletarian vanguard and that appeals to white labour's reason could pave the way for working class unity (Documents 4, 5, 7).

Socialists underestimated both the extent to which racial divisions had been structured into the working class through capitalist development and the extent to which racial ideology permeated its outlook (Ntsebeza 1988:33-4). Certainly until the early 1920s they continued to see the colour question as something which distracted from the more fundamental class conflict. Hence, many socialist debates had an abstract quality to them. For example, the Industrial Socialist League, an ephemeral grouplet of 1918–1920, blasted the ISL for participating in the Parliamentary electoral system, which, it argued, obscured the antagonism between capital and labour through the appeal to common citizenship and "one man, one vote" (Document 6).[1] But this argument had little relevance for a society in which the majority was disenfranchised due to colour and gender. This early call to boycott Parliament, quite clearly directed to the white minority, was a far cry from the boycott movement that emerged in the 1930s and '40s which refused on principle to participate in racial structures designed for an inferior "child race". The early boycott call fell on deaf ears, as white labour successfully used its vote to entrench its racial interests. The later call became a rallying cry which mobilised a mass movement and remained a salient factor throughout the apartheid era.

These assumptions influenced the way in which socialists viewed the first wave of collective black working class protest which began in the 1910s and which underlined the fact that black workers were a permanent part of the industrial workforce. In 1913 indentured Indian labour in Natal went on strike. Black mineworkers struck the same year, following a strike of white miners, and again in 1915-16 and 1918. In 1919 the newly-formed Industrial and Commercial Workers' Union (ICU) organised a strike of black dockworkers and Johannesburg municipal workers or "bucket boys" went on strike. These protests culminated with the black mineworkers' strike of 1920.

By all indications these protests were largely self-organised. The 1920 black mineworkers strike paralysed the industry, lasted longer and involved more workers than the better-known 1946 African mineworkers strike. Yet the IWA and the Transvaal Native Congress (precursor to the African National Congress) played only tangential roles (Roux 1964:132-4; Bonner 1979:277; Ntsebeza 1988:39-42), and the ISL was busy contesting elections in the white Parliament (Bunting 1981:53). The event received scant attention in the socialist press, mainly appeals to white workers not to scab. Racial antagonism between black and white workers was seen as a secondary issue which masked the real conflict between capital and labour (Documents 4, 5). As Lungisile Ntsebeza has argued (1988:40), socialists generally did not believe that blacks were sufficiently educated and organised to carry out an effective strike. Socialists might have aspired to lower the barrier dividing black and white, but they presumed that this meant first uplifting blacks to the level of whites.

In July 1921 a number of tiny groupings merged to form the Communist Party of South Africa (CPSA) on the basis of their common acceptance of the 21 points of the Third Communist International.[2] The CPSA's Manifesto combined the rhetoric of internationalism with white labour chauvinism. On the one hand it appealed to black and white workers to unite to overthrow capitalism; on the other, it called to blacks – "cheap docile labour" – to join the working class movement (Bunting 1981:57-65). How were these contradictory principles manifested in practice?

The CPSA's first major test came in early 1922 with the all-white Rand Revolt, which had far greater impact on socialists than did the 1920 black mine workers' strike. As the social historian W. M. MacMillan points out (1922), the Rand Revolt was the first major white mining strike after the entry of unskilled Afrikaners into the mines and, accordingly, the first mining strike led by industrial rather than craft trade unions.[3] Just as craft workers had felt the threat of semi-skilled blacks and unskilled whites fifteen years earlier, now newly proletarianised Afrikaners felt their vulnerability to replacement by cheap labour if the colour bar was modified. Consequently, they were the most militant strikers in 1922. Communists were sympathetic to the vulnerability and poor working conditions of white workers and hoped that their propaganda would push them towards unity with black workers (Documents 7, 8; Bunting 1981:68-9; Hirson 1993b).[4]

But the state's brutal squashing of the Rand Revolt caused profound disillusionment amongst Communists, who turned to the international Communist movement for support. International solidarity resulted in a visit from the renowned English Communist and former syndicalist, Tom Mann, who did, indeed, revive the morale of his South African comrades. Mann, who had previously visited South Africa in 1910 and 1914, arrived in Cape Town in October 1922. His aims were two-fold: to rebuild the demolished trade union movement and promote working class unity under the rubric of the Red International of Labour Unions, and to fight for amnesty for those Rand strikers who had been sentenced to death. Mann was clearly impressed by the level of organisation which he observed at the Third Annual Conference of the ICU, as he saw the industrial organisation of Africans as fundamental to building working class solidarity across the colour line (Documents 9–11; Tsuzuki 1991:209-12).

What lessons did Communists draw from the Rand Revolt? The Comintern still believed in the feasibility of world socialist revolution in the early 1920s, despite the defeat of socialism in Italy and Germany and the failure of the Russian Revolution to internationalise. Seemingly accepting this assumption, S. P. Bunting (Document 8) argued that at that time the greatest obstacle to a South African revolution was discord across the colour line and antagonism between Afrikaners and English, despite their common interests against black competition. Later, Bunting attempted to sketch a line of strategy and tactics for promoting working class unity across colour and national lines which followed the Comintern's 21 principles, particularly point 8 on the national and colonial questions.

Yet the difference between Lenin's and Bunting's arguments for working class internationalism is striking. Lenin (1971) insisted that the right of national self-determination of oppressed peoples was a fundamental democratic principle and a precondition for working class internationalism. His argument that workers in advanced countries must give unconditional support to the struggle against national oppression is reflected in point 8 which, while internationalist, was nonetheless written from a European perspective, in that it dealt with Communist Parties in advanced countries which had colonies, rather than with socialism and labour movements in the colonies themselves. By contrast, Bunting took a tactical approach to the problem of working class internationalism. He argued that the struggle against cheap labour and for equal wages was essentially a movement to make capitalism tolerable and therefore not a Communist principle. Nonetheless, it was a tactical necessity for working class unity: "The point is not equality but solidarity" (Document 8). Communist propaganda needed an atmosphere of co-operation to be effective, he maintained, and that could only develop by fighting inequality and cheap labour policies. Similarly, he continued, national liberation movements often alienate workers of the advanced countries and are relevant for the socialist struggle only in so far as they are composed of exploited workers. But support for national liberation was a tactical necessity to win blacks to the working class movement. The point of contact between blacks and whites was as workers, Bunting concluded; therefore, socialists should organise them on that basis.

This dichotomy between the principles and tactics of working class internationalism is reflected in two significant strands of socialist thought which can be traced in the CPSA through the 1920s. The first, represented by T. W. Thibedi and S. P. Bunting, argued for the importance of work in black organisations like the ICU. This strand became dominant in 1924, when the CPSA's third congress, in a break from previous policy, resolved not to apply for affiliation to the SALP. The second strand, exemplified by W. H. Andrews, continued to see white labour as the working class vanguard.

Communists were well represented at the national leadership level of the ICU, but in 1926, in response to their continued criticism of his alleged reformism and corruption, ICU leader Clements Kadalie expelled those Communists, like Jimmy La Guma, who refused to give up their Party membership.[5] Patronising attitudes towards Kadalie are apparent in the writings of white Communists, and Kadalie, in turn, railed against white Communists (Documents 15–17; Roux 1964:166). Nonetheless, Thibedi's letter to Roux (Document 12) suggests that friction between the ICU and Communists was not solely a question of colour – a number of those expelled were African – but concerned conflict over strategy and tactics, chiefly the use of the strike tactic. That an ICU branch continued to work with Thibedi even after his expulsion suggests a lack of accord between the ICU's national leadership and its local branches.

Like the CPSA, the ICU was caught in a dilemma between class and colour in South Africa: not sufficiently working class and radical for the CPSA; too black for the white labour movement. In 1927, then mainly a rural movement which gave little attention to the needs of urban black workers, the ICU applied for affiliation on the basis of its claimed 100 000 members to the South African Trades Union Co-ordinating Council (SATUCC), a joint body representing the all-white Johannesburg-based South African Trades Union Congress (SATUC) and the Cape Federation of Labour Unions, whose affiliates included some coloured members. The SATUCC responded with the possibility of affiliation on the basis of 5 000 members, which Kadalie rejected. Eddie Roux, then a Communist, evidently presumed that blacks should want unity with whites at any cost (Document 15), and saw Kadalie's refusal as proof of his lack of interest in working class unity (*cf.* Roux 1964:176).

After their expulsion from the ICU, Communists generally viewed it as an organisation manipulated by a corrupt and reformist *petit bourgeois* leadership. By 1928 Roux was arguing that the CPSA should support the ICU in so far as it supported the working class but that the collapse of the ICU would not be against the Party's interests (Document 15). Yet, when Kadalie resigned from the ICU, which brought in the Scotsman William Ballinger from the Motherwell Trades and Labour Council to sort out its financial problems, the CPSA evidently considered reentering the ICU (Document 17; Roux 1964:178-88).

Those Communists in the white trade union movement were able to get leadership positions which enabled them to play a minority role in the SATUC (Document 15). Nonetheless, their optimism about white labour's revolutionary potential was misguided: Communist trade unionists were generally far more radical than the rank and file union members. Almost invariably, through the 1920s and '30s, the few cases of working class solidarity across the colour line were cases where black workers supported white workers. Two contrasting strikes of tailoring and clothing workers in 1928 are cases in point.

In early 1927 socialists Frank Glass and Johnny Gomas had hopes of amalgamating the numerous tailoring unions around the country. Glass was General Secretary of the all-white Witwatersrand Tailors' Association (WTA) until around 1928; Gomas was a tailor himself, who had been politicised by his involvement in this radical industry dominated by ex-slaves, and who organised the Garment Workers' Union in Cape Town (Musson 1989). When the WTA went on strike at Germiston in May 1928, the black Clothing Workers Union (CWU) went on a solidarity strike. But shortly thereafter, when the CWU went on strike in Johannesburg, the WTA refused to call out its members (Documents 13–15; Berger 1992:95-6).

Communists and the national struggle: The Native Republic Thesis

By the late 1920s most Communists were disillusioned by the passivity and bureaucracy of white trade unions under the Pact Government, and they favoured more practical work amongst urban black workers. Several contending conceptions of the path to social revolution can be discerned amongst socialists in the late 1920s. Jimmy La Guma, who, along with Nikolai Bukharin of the Comintern, formulated the Native Republic thesis for South Africa, stressed the revolutionary potential of an anti-imperialist national movement.[6] But until 1928 the majority saw national liberation and democratic rights as reformist goals which were inherently subordinate to the working class struggle (Documents 22, 26, 27). Participation in national liberation organisations was seen as a tactic rather than a democratic principle. This ambivalent attitude on national liberation was challenged by the Comintern, which in 1927 and 1928 agitated for the adoption of the Native Republic thesis in South Africa. This external pressure pushed the CPSA very painfully towards a reinterpretation of the relationship between the national liberation and socialist struggles and between the urban working class and rural majority.

The Native Republic thesis proposed national self-determination through a struggle against British imperialism, but this was an imperialism defined not by its capitalist essence, but by its colonial aspect, which included both foreign and racial domination. From its emphasis on the seemingly colonial character of South African society flowed the belief that, in the absence of a black bourgeoisie, the land-hungry peasantry was the moving force of the South African revolution. By giving primacy to the satisfaction of black land hunger, argued the Comintern, South African Communists would induce rural blacks to align themselves under proletarian leadership, as in the Russian Revolution. The land question, then, was the heart of the South African struggle and laid the parameters for the national question (Document 26; Bunting 1981:94-6). The colonial analogy presumed a two-stage conception of social change and laid the basis for the South African Communist Party's subsequent colonialism of a special type analysis. But these historical documents indicate that the two-stage notion was not readily accepted (Documents 24, 31).

When the draft resolution was first submitted to the South African comrades, the majority immediately rejected it as anti-white and anti-internationalist.[7] It was strikingly close to Marcus Garvey's "Black Republic" and "Africa for the Africans" slogans which the CPSA had campaigned against for several years (Roux 1993:121; Simons 1983:396). This response did not follow colour lines: a number of black Communists, notably Thibedi and, initially, Johnny Gomas, firmly opposed the slogan (Document 29; Roux 1993: 131–3; Musson 1989:48). Roux still believed that white labour could be convinced to unite with black workers (Document 25). Bunting, who believed in the possibility of an uninterrupted transition to socialism, thought the thesis overemphasised the peasantry to the neglect of black and white workers, even claiming, wrongly, that there had not yet been any significant black rural movement (Document 26). Not only had South Africa seen numerous peasant uprisings against taxation and land scarcity; by the late 1920s the ICU had swelled to a mass movement of black sharecroppers and labour-tenants seeking to forestall proletarianisation, and the Western Cape ANC represented farmworkers striving to improve their working conditions (Hofmeyr 1983:26-49 and 1985; Nzula 1979:104, 163, 199-201, 210-11). Factions quickly crystallised within the Party. La Guma was opposed, on the one side, by Thibedi and Bennie Weinbren, who agitated against the thesis amongst their trade union constituency (Documents 29–31). On the other side stood Communists who still worked in the white labour movement, such as T. P. Tinker and W. H. Andrews. But the increased racism and discriminatory legislation of the late 1920s pushed many socialists who had initially rejected the thesis to accept it, and in January 1929, after much acrimony, the CPSA endorsed a version of the thesis which read:

> An Independent South African Native Republic as a stage towards the Workers' and Peasants' Republic, guaranteeing protection and complete equality to all national minorities (Bunting 1981: 104).

The adoption of the Native Republic thesis laid the basis for practical work in the countryside. Hitherto the Party had been urban-based with the significant exception of rural towns like Potchefstroom, where it made contact with farmworkers and labour tenants (Roux 1993:135-40; Simons 1983:411-13). In 1929, under the banner of the Native Republic, the Party established the League of African Rights (LAR), an organisation composed of affiliated local structures around the country, which aimed to unite Africans against the proposed Hertzog bills to curtail their economic and political rights. In structure and aims the LAR was a precursor to the black united fronts of the next decade. That it was able to draw in representatives from the ANC and ICU indicated its catholic appeal, given that both organisations had rejected the Native Republic thesis as too radical (Documents 31–33).

The absence of a black bourgeoisie raised the possibility that the weight of the working class and impoverished rural masses would push the national liberation movement towards socialism. But the Native Republic thesis was premised on a peasant-based colonial model which differed in important respects from South Africa of the late 1920s, and it had limitations as a mobilising device for socialism. Presupposing national self-determination for a predominantly agrarian black colony conquered by white foreigners, its implicit concept of the South African nation was a racial or colour-based one, derived from a colonial model and superimposed on a post-colonial, racial capitalist society. The thesis assumed that Bantu-speaking Africans constituted a homogenous, undifferentiated peasantry. While its proposal to eliminate all social relations and laws which restricted the development of a black farming class would mean the formal dismantling of the reserve system which restricted the amount of land available to black cultivators, the thesis did not address the needs of the large proportion of virtually proletarianised reserve dwellers whose livelihood depended on migrant wage labour and who probably could not afford to buy land, even if a legal option. Nor did it address the needs of farmworkers, who generally responded to those demands specific to their needs as a proletariat seeking control of their working conditions rather than to the demands of an aspirant peasantry (Hofmeyr 1985:321-8).

Moreover, by linking the national and class struggles in a mechanical, linear manner, the thesis tended to polarise the two struggles. It avoided the question of whether capitalist development in South Africa was creating conditions for a nation whose identity was no longer rooted in the period of white colonial conquest of blacks. Only in the late 1930s and '40s did socialists begin to question and reject a colour-based determination of nationhood (see No Sizwe 1979 on evolving conceptions of nationality in South Africa).

Despite these drawbacks, the Native Republic thesis represented a significant advance in South African socialist thinking. For the first time socialists put South Africa's pressing social problems, the national, democratic and land questions, at the top of their political programme, reconciling the slogan with their various scenarios for social revolution.

The Comintern and the New Line

If the Native Republic thesis subordinated the struggle for socialism to a stage following national liberation and bourgeois democracy, the Comintern's sharp left turn of mid-1928 with its New Line began swinging the pendulum back. With fascism dominant in Italy and the left in retreat elsewhere in Europe, the Comintern now argued that the crisis of capitalism had reached its third period, one where the contradictions of the capitalist system were rapidly leading to its collapse. The immiseration of the working class, it was assumed, would lay the conditions for revolutionary proletarian class consciousness. With worldwide Communist revolution imminent, social-democratic and reformist policies were seen as particularly dangerous counter-revolutionary attempts to divert the working class from the struggle against capitalism. The Comintern's slogan, "class against class", referred to the working class struggle against social democracy and its capitalist allies. But if the 1929 Great Depression was seen as confirmation of the third period thesis, subsequent events in Europe and South Africa failed to confirm the Comintern's corollary assumption that deepening economic crisis would radicalise the working class and strengthen Communist support (Braunthal 1967:365; Document 38).

While the New Line can certainly be traced to the domestic policies of the Communist Party of the Soviet Union, it can also be understood in part as a reaction to the growth of right-wing and anti-Communist practices within European trade unions and social-democratic parties. Excluded from united fronts with labour and social-democratic organisations, Communist Parties now hoped to pull workers away from those organisations and form united fronts from below. In South Africa the New Line meant that nationalism and democracy were once again subordinated to the class struggle of black and white workers. But the call for proletarian unity to fight reformism, while seemingly radical, was ill-suited for South Africa's racially-divided class structure. Given the enormity of racial oppression, which stifled the development of even a tiny black bourgeoisie, the leaderships of black democratic organisations were hardly in a position, at that time, to align with or be co-opted by the white bourgeoisie. Their social class position was not analogous to that of the trade union and political party bureaucracies of the West. Furthermore, white labour in South Africa derived economic, political and social benefits from the super-exploitation of black people, meaning that, with rare individual exceptions, working class unity across the colour line was impossible. The only feasible organisational possibilities which did not concede to white chauvinism were the direct organisation of black workers and the alliance of all blacks on a common democratic platform.

By 1930 the South African state had smashed the first wave of collective black working class protest. The ICU, unable to prevent the proletarianisation of its largely rural constituency and not having systematically organised its branches around the country, began disintegrating. The ANC, under pressure of anti-African legislation, and with no counter-pressure from the African working class, distanced itself from the CPSA and elected a new slate of conservative leaders in 1930 (Bradford 1985:418-19; Hofmeyr 1985:289-304; Simons 1983:427-9).

Despite the fact that the mass movement was at a low ebb, the Comintern directed the Party to cease work in so-called reformist organisations. The Party placed the Native Republic thesis, with its focus on democratic reforms, on the back-burner and obediently disbanded the LAR just as it was gaining momentum (Document 34).[8] Anticipating that the poverty of the Depression years would radicalise white workers, the Party now tried to organise unemployed workers across colour lines. Like earlier attempts at joint black-white activity this was unsuccessful. The growing poverty of Afrikaner peasants and workers was not reflected in a non-racial consciousness (Roux 1972:131; Simons 1983:456).

The effect of the New Line was to deplete Party membership and to distance those who remained from the black working-class and reorient them towards the white working class. Roux (1964:269) estimates CPSA membership in 1933 to be no higher than 150. This movement towards white labour accelerated in the mid-1930s, coinciding with CPSA participation in electoral politics. Internally, the Party was wracked by faction fights, as the Comintern's dominant role in the CPSA led to the stifling of internal political debate and the expulsion of dissidents (Documents 35–37, 39; Roux 1993:156–64; Roux 1964:256; Simons 1983:421–25; Bunting 1975:68-9). But despite these expulsions, internal political divisions remained acute.

The origins and development of Trotskyism in South Africa

The Trotskyist tendency emerged in South Africa when the socialist movement itself was at a low ebb (Lee 1970; Southall 1978; Drew 1991a:179-265; Drew 1991b; Hirson 1993a). Three themes illuminate the first few decades of its development. First, its organisational dilemma, which reflected its political isolation and in turn impinged on its practical work; second, its turn to the national question, manifested in its work in black united fronts; third, coinciding with a turn to national liberation politics, a growing aloofness from practical trade union work. Like South African Communists, Trotskyists had difficulty reconciling the class and national struggles in their theory and practical work.

By the early 1930s most socialists who had left or had been expelled from the CPSA were loosely grouping themselves under the banner of Trotskyism. Yet, while deploring the lack of democracy within the Party which resulted from the Comintern's intervention, these early Trotskyists were far from united in their approaches towards the class and national struggles. Indeed, many of their positions were quite close to those of the CPSA, echoing, for instance, many of the earlier Communist debates on the Native Republic thesis.

Like the early socialist movement before the formation of the CPSA, South African Trotskyism emerged as a regionally and organisationally fragmented tendency. The first Trotskyist grouplet to emerge on the Witwatersrand was the ephemeral Communist League of Africa (CLA), formed in 1932 by veteran trade unionist T. W. Thibedi, who had been recently expelled from the CPSA. The CLA was atypical of subsequent Trotskyist groups because of its all-African membership, and the content of its early communications with Leon Trotsky and American socialists of the International Left Opposition indicates that the South African left was still permeated with white chauvinism. But like the series of small Trotskyist groups in Johannesburg which followed the CLA, and unlike most Cape Town-based Trotskyist groups, its concern was to organise the urban black proletariat (Documents 40–46). Two years later the Bolshevist Leninist League picked up the threads left by the CLA, then merged with the majority of the Cape Town-based Lenin Club in 1935 to form the Workers' Party of South Africa (WPSA). The tiny Johannesburg WPSA rapidly dwindled, to be followed over the next few years by other short-lived Trotskyist groups (Documents 47, 61, 62, 65–70).

Trotskyism's strongest base in South Africa has been the Western Cape, where it had a propagandistic orientation. The Lenin Club, formed in 1933 from various socialist grouplets, provided the pattern for South African Trotskyist groups until 1960. Initially, the Lenin Club encouraged political debate, and the intense theoretical discussions amongst Trotskyists in the early 1930s reflected their efforts to forge a programmatic unity based on an analysis of South African political economy. But in 1934 the Lenin Club split into two factions, and the following year this division was formalised when the majority formed the WPSA and established the Spartacus Club – an intellectual and cultural circle with sections in Cape Town and Johannesburg – to rival the Lenin Club. In September 1936 the Lenin Club dissolved itself.

The self-imposed challenge facing South African Trotskyists in the 1930s and '40s was to form a unified organisation as a means to building a working class base. However, in contrast to the CPSA's strong internal control of factions, Trotskyism in South Africa has been characterised by a centrifugal tendency, splitting over theoretical issues which often had no immediate programmatic implications. Like the CPSA's repeated policy oscillations, this weakened the tendency's ability to do effective practical work.

This organisational fragmentation reflected in part the regionalism of South African political economy and the timing of Trotskyism's origins. Born in a period when the black protest movement had recently been crushed for its first efforts at collective class action in the late 1910s and 1920s, and CPSA membership depleted by the ultra-left New Line, Trotskyists had difficulty developing a systematic and sustained relationship with the black working class, as did the CPSA through most of the 1930s. This isolation from the working class simultaneously reflected and accentuated the tendency's organisational instability.

The issues behind the split in the Lenin Club which led to the formation of the Workers' Party and the Communist League of South Africa (CLSA) were mainly theoretical rather than problems of immediate practical concern necessitating programmatic divergences or an organisational break (*cf.* Southall 1978:33-8 and Lee 1970). Both Trotskyist groups concurred that the land and national questions had a common root in British imperialism and that the task of socialists was to demonstrate this common origin to black and white urban workers who would lead the anti-imperialist struggle supported by the rural poor. Like most Communists in the 1930s they believed that South African capitalism was heading towards a crisis which would force the bourgeoisie to break its historic pact with the white working class; that the immiseration of white workers and Afrikaner *bywoners* would lay the material basis for their potential radicalisation and that it was incumbent on socialists to organise poor whites rather than let them succumb to fascist ideology. Consequently, like Bunting and Roux in 1928, they rejected the Native Republic thesis on the grounds that it pandered to black nationalism while alienating white labour (Documents 48–50).

Their difference boiled down to one of emphasis on the nature and degree of peasant consciousness amongst the rural population and the degree of black proletarian development. The Workers' Party believed that social mobilisation must be based on people's perceptions of their problems. The CLSA and its successor, the Fourth International Organisation of South Africa, argued that socio-economic trends like proletarianisation and urbanisation should be the guideline for developing strategy. The difference in emphasis and perspective stemmed from the fact that the two groups were focusing on different aspects of the same broader phenomenon during a period of rapid socio-economic change in which social classes were in a state of flux.

In an argument strikingly similar to the Native Republic thesis, the WPSA took as its point of departure the distorted social relations on the land. The skewed racial distribution of landholdings left most blacks landless, forcing them to labour on mines and white-owned farms. This cheap black labour was then used to threaten white job security and wages. The black majority's extremely low level of economic development restricted the domestic market and stunted industrial development. The WPSA saw rural blacks, including farmworkers, as a landless peasantry, and believed that black land hunger would be the mobilising force and the pivot of a permanent revolution led by a united black and white working class (Document 48).

While the CLSA recognised that rural stagnation was hastening rather than impeding proletarianisation, it nonetheless idealistically maintained that this process would translate into a class consciousness transcending colour divisions. It argued that the solution to South Africa's social problems lay not in agrarian revolution but in the overthrow of British imperialism under working class leadership with rural support. Such rural support would not come from the black peasantry which, like Bunting, the CLSA saw as politically backwards. Instead, the Afrikaner peasantry and bourgeoisie could be mobilised for an anti-imperialist revolution on the basis of their historic, anti-British sentiments. This utopian belief in the progressive potential of Afrikaner nationalism, later rejected by the FIOSA, ignored the class interests of the aspirant Afrikaner bourgeoisie and the depth of racial ideology, mistakenly assuming that anti-British movements were necessarily progressive. Paradoxically, although they looked to different sections of the rural population, both the CLSA and the early WPSA propounded a two-stage conception of revolution in which an anti-imperialist stage preceded a later socialist revolution (Document 49).

Seeking programmatic unity, in 1935 both groups turned to Trotsky and to the International Secretariat (IS) of the International Left Opposition to mediate their differences.[9] Trotsky and the IS both argued that since the South African Trotskyists recognised that the land, national and class struggles had common roots in British imperialism, they should not polarise these struggles but seek socialist solutions which emphasised their common origins. In response to the WPSA's draft theses, Trotsky argued that a party which sought to represent proletarian class interests and build a working-class base must fully support the black majority's democratic demands for and right to self-determination through a Black Republic. But, he pointed out, a socialist solution to the national question must be based on the method of class struggle rather than the "classless" anti-imperialist bloc then being advocated by the Comintern as part of its People's Front policy (Document 51).

The IS's letters were more explicitly programmatic, concerned chiefly with South African Trotskyism's tendency to fragment, which it believed would weaken attempts to build up a working class base. The IS argued that a communist league was a more appropriate form of organisation for the young Trotskyist tendency than a party, which presumed a working class social base. It suggested joint practical and editorial work, as a step towards developing working class support (Documents 52–55).

Trotsky's letter, published as a pamphlet by the Workers' Party, had a significant political impact. Initially, the WPSA was critical of Trotsky's sympathetic stance towards the Native Republic, a reaction which should be understood with reference to ongoing debates within the CPSA on the Native Republic thesis. Although the CPSA had marginalised the thesis around 1930, it briefly resurrected it from 1932 to 1934 to mean a workers' and peasants' government. Two Communists, however, Lazar Bach and L. L. Leepile, put forward a minority position which called "For Independence and Soviet rule and for the voluntary unification of the free Native Republics – Basuto, Bechuana, Swazi, Zulu, Xosa etc. into a Federation of Independent Native Republics" (*Umsebenzi*, 5 May 1934; Simons 1983:473). The minority thesis itself should be viewed as a response to attempts to incorporate the British Protectorates like Bechuanaland into the Union of South Africa. But most socialists, both Communists and Trotskyists, have disagreed with the minority position on the grounds that it would reinforce national fragmentation and impede the building of an anti-imperialist socialist movement. The Workers' Party similarly thought that Trotsky's stress on national self-determination followed the Soviet model too closely, a model which they felt had little relevance for South Africa.[10]

But over the next decade Cape Town Trotskyists used Trotsky's letter to reevaluate the relationship of the land and national struggles to the class struggle. From the late 1930s they increasingly emphasised building a national movement for black unity and democratic rights, which in South Africa were seen as transitional demands. Initially the Workers' Party saw the land question as the key to the political revolution. It now modified its original slogan, "Land to the Native", to "Land and Liberty", to reflect the interrelationship of the land and political struggles. This transposition is seen in the Ten Point Programme of the Non-European Unity Movement, whose formulation in 1943 was strongly influenced by members of the Workers' Party, and which assumes the political question, specifically the franchise (Point One), to be the key to the land question (Point Seven).[11] Similarly, the FIOSA, heir to the CLSA which had downplayed the role of the black rural majority, now admitted the significance of the land question for social mobilisation. M. N. Averbach argued that the struggle for democratic rights, especially property rights, could lay the basis for a permanent revolution. Since implementing the right to own land entailed the expropriation of large landholdings, it was part and parcel of the socialist struggle. Both Trotskyist groups continued to think that the industrial strength of white workers made them strategically necessary for a socialist struggle. Only a strong movement for black democratic rights, they believed, could pull white workers away from their alliance with capital (Documents 64, 75).

But at the practical organisational level, neither Trotskyist faction systematically followed the International Secretariat's recommendations for unity. Aside from the notable exception of their involvement in black united fronts in the late 1930s, Trotskyist groups worked independently of each other despite parallel activities in trade unions and discussion clubs, and at times their relations were even antagonistic. This weakened their effectiveness at countering Communist influence and sustaining the long-term political work needed to build a working class base, and the creative potential seen in their early cultural activities remained latent (Documents 57–74; Roux 1964:312).

Building political alliances

The political implications of Communism and Trotskyism in practice become clearer during the years 1935-45, a period aptly called pivotal in that it saw the birth and convergence of the major political tendencies shaping the liberation movement (No Sizwe 1979:53-4). The mid-1930s saw the beginnings of the first long-term alliance of the black *petite bourgeoisie*, working class and rural masses in South African history, one which attempted to cut across the colour-caste divisions imposed by the state. Proportionately, the black *petite bourgeoisie* was tiny. Its meagre ranks included a few small shopowners, merchant traders, struggling artisans and teachers in which coloureds and Indians predominated. Whites dominated virtually all professions, aside from teaching and religion, and in 1936 less than one per cent of all medical practitioners, advocates, attorneys, dentists, chemists, architects and engineers were black (Van der Horst 1949:113, 122-3). Nonetheless, the black *petite bourgeoisie*'s relative access to education and restricted voting rights had hitherto given it predominance in black political organisations. Now, its movement towards the working class reflected the growing power of urban black workers, a power manifesting itself in militant collective protest. Organisationally, this class alliance took the form of black united fronts like the National Liberation League, the Non-European United Front and the All African Convention.

Alongside the emergent black mass movement, urban and rural whites struggled against unemployment and poverty as the Depression swept rural Afrikaners off the farms and into the cities. By the 1930s, the urban white working class, smashed and co-opted in the 1920s, was economically ravaged. Afrikaner nationalists and fascists sought to capture this social base; socialists, especially Communists, hoped to counteract this.

The emergence of these movements and alliances raised questions concerning the political content of class alliances, the relationship of the working class struggle to the democratic struggle, and the organisational forms, programmes and methods of political struggle. The very recent development of collective black working class action meant that a struggle over the political content of class alliances was taking place for the first time. The growing weight of the urban black working class posed again the issue of working class unity in South Africa. The absence of a black bourgeoisie in the 1930s and '40s meant that the class alliance of the oppressed majority turned entirely on the relationship between *petite bourgeoisie* and proletariat and raised the possibility that this alliance could take an anti-capitalist direction. However, this development did not occur in part because the struggle for hegemony between the black *petite bourgeoisie* and proletariat was embryonic. Socialist organisations interacted with and influenced the political movements and alliances which arose during these years. Communist policy and practice attempted to unite white workers and poor peasants with the black democratic movement into a broad anti-fascist People's Front. Trotskyists directed their efforts to the black united fronts.

Workers' unity and the anti-fascist struggle

The CPSA's reorientation towards mass politics entailed a reversal of its earlier class against class line and, like its other policy shifts, was accompanied by internal turmoil and expulsions. A few Communists had tried, unsuccessfully, to challenge the ultra-left wing policy of the early 1930s. But it was the Comintern's anti-fascist People's Front strategy, unveiled at its Seventh World Congress in August 1935, which finally enabled an internal faction led by Moses Kotane to successfully challenge the Party's isolation from black politics (Roux 1993:170-5; Simons 1983:476; *cf.* Bunting 1975:68). The People's Front aimed to split the social base of the fascist movement in Europe by appealing to the interests of the poorer strata of the *petite bourgeoisie* and peasantry and drawing them into an alliance with working class organisations which were themselves to be aligned in a proletarian united front (Dimitrov 1986:26, 34-6, 48; Claudin 1975:166-242).

The transition to and implementation of the People's Front policy is directly traceable in the CPSA's theoretical and practical work. The Party's renewed interest in mass-based politics coincided with the temporary revival of a revised Native Independent Republic thesis and sparked a heated debate about the existence of an African bourgeoisie (Documents 76, 78, 79, 81–86; Roux 1993:126, 152-3; Simons 1983:476, 491; Legassick 1973:51-2). The revised thesis and the series in *Umsebenzi* are the last significant statements on the Native Republic, which was relegated to obscurity during the People's Front era. The revised thesis can be seen as a transition between the class against class line and the People's Front strategy.

The 1928 Native Republic thesis, recognising that there was then no African bourgeoisie, had envisioned a peasant-based anti-imperialist revolution culminating in a bourgeois democratic republic which would be a stage towards a workers' and peasants' government. In the revised thesis, the Native Independent Republic is seen as the outcome of an anti-imperialist revolution entailing both majority rule and a break from the British empire. In a practical sense this was equated with a workers' and peasants' government which would aim to promote free peasant development and to improve the conditions of the working class, rather than to actively construct socialism. The Party now claimed to find an African bourgeoisie which exploited black workers. While this class would benefit economically with the overthrow of British imperialism, its exploitative relationship with black workers and ambivalent attitude towards the British Empire prevented it from leading an anti-imperialist struggle. Neither was the *petit bourgeois* leadership of the ANC and ICU capable, in the CPSA's view, of leading an anti-imperialist struggle. This was indicated by the fact that neither organisation was then willing to promote the Native Republic slogan. In fact, the revised thesis argued, black workers and peasants had more in common with white workers and poor peasants, who were also exploited by imperialism, than with the African bourgeoisie and *petit bourgeois* classes claiming to lead them. Only a united struggle of all workers and peasants could achieve a Native Independent Republic, the document concludes.

The idea of an African bourgeoisie and the repudiation of work in nationalist organisations were not uncontested. Moses Kotane, for one, warned against analysing South African conditions through a European lens and argued that denouncing popular ANC leaders was tactically unwise (Bunting 1981:120-2). A number of people, including the journalist Gilbert Coka, were expelled for denying the existence of an African bourgeoisie.

The sanguine expectation, seen in the revised Native Independent Republic thesis, that common anti-imperialist interests would unite black and white workers received further support with the Party's speedy endorsement of the People's Front and Proletarian United Front policies (*Umsebenzi*, September 1935). While aiming at working class and popular unity across colour lines, these twin policies ignored the political, economic and social benefits which gave white workers a stake in the racial system. Thus, in practice they reinforced the development of two separate movements in South Africa: one, the anti-fascist movement to protect the existing democratic rights of white South Africans from which blacks were excluded; the other, the movement to gain democratic rights for blacks, represented by the All African Convention, in which whites were virtually absent.

The Proletarian United Front was essentially a continuation of the Party's attempts to organise black and white unemployed workers during the Depression, and it provided the theoretical underpinnings for the Party's reorientation towards white labour (Roux 1972:131). Like all socialist groups in the late 1930s, the CPSA continued to believe that poor whites would eventually recognise their mutual class interests with black workers and that both would unite in a common struggle against fascism. The Party began a propaganda drive to tap this potential audience, appealing to the tradition of the 1922 Rand Revolt (Documents 100, 107). In 1935 it began publishing *Die Arbeider en Arme Boer (Worker and Poor Peasant)*, and the next year *Umsebenzi* was renamed *The South African Worker*, now including Afrikaans articles but curtailing Bantu language news coverage. Moses Kotane, in the meantime, started *Umvikele-Thebe/The African Defender*, the multilingual organ of the Ikaka labaSebenzi (Document 106; Simons 1983:471, 479; Bunting 1975:78-9).

But the Party's increased attention to white workers meant less practical work in black organisations, as white labour adamantly refused to join organisations which called for black democratic rights (Bunting 1981:125-7, 128-30; Simons 1983:478-82). For a short while in 1936 the 1920s debate on whether black or white labour constituted the working class vanguard resurfaced, with arguments that an organisation of both black and white was impractical (Simons 1983:477-80; Southall 1978:67-70). Under the influence of a visiting Comintern representative, the CPSA settled on a "compromise" in which it saw itself as a link between a People's Front against Fascism and War and the newly-formed All African Convention, each specialised along colour lines. This only conceded to racial chauvinism. In 1937, when African-American social scientist Ralph Bunche visited South Africa, Eddie Roux, Sam Kahn, Harry Snitcher and Edwin Mofutsanyana all confided that the Party's overemphasis on whites led to the neglect of blacks (Bunche Collection, boxes 64 and 65, Documents 93–95, 99, 100).

In 1940 the Party's Draft Programme was still anti-imperialist in tone but, not surprisingly, its proposed Independent Republic, now explicitly socialist, made no mention of a Native or Black Republic. Instead, it argued that independence from the British Empire would benefit blacks and whites and that freedom for all national groups depended on the unity of all races and nationalities and could not be achieved by any section alone (Document 120). By 1944 the CPSA dropped its anti-imperialist stance (Lodge 1985:7), hoping to bridge the colour bar by appealing simultaneously to white labour and blacks struggling for democratic rights.

Black united fronts and non-collaboration

Alongside and overshadowing the anti-fascist movement in South Africa, black people, confronted with an onslaught of racially-discriminatory laws which accelerated in the 1930s under the Fusion Government, began to organise across sectional or colour-caste lines, forming alliances based on Non-European unity. Following the tradition established by the first Non-European Conference in 1927, black leaders convened an All African Convention (AAC) to fight the proposed Representation of Natives Bill and the Native Trust and Land Bill, which attacked political and economic rights for Africans. The first bill, while curtailing the Cape African franchise, called for the creation of a Natives' Representative Council (NRC) with solely advisory status on so-called Native issues. The second reasserted the restrictions on black landholding rights to scheduled areas (Karis and Carter 1973:4-5; Lewis 1987:103).

Communists and Trotskyists enthusiastically welcomed the formation of the AAC and envisioned it as a permanent organisation which could fill the organisational vacuum left by the virtually defunct ANC and the fragmented ICU. They vehemently opposed the Hertzog Bills and the formation of the NRC; the CPSA scathingly called it a step towards fascism (Bunting 1981:122-3; Documents 87–92, 98, 99). But they differed in their strategic visions of the AAC. Communists saw it as a cornerstone of a United Front of the People against Imperialism, an alliance which proved impossible in the face of white labour racism (Bunting 1981:126-7). Trotskyists saw in the AAC and other black united fronts an opportunity to apply the method of working class struggle which Trotsky had discussed in his 1935 letter.

In the late 1930s, the black population consisted overwhelmingly of rural cultivators, a migrant labour force whose income was supplemented by subsistence farming and an urban working class. There was no black bourgeoisie and only a tiny *petite bourgeoisie* in which Africans were statistically negligible (Van der Horst 1949:113, 122-3). This coincidence of class and colour suggested to South African Trotskyists that black united fronts could form the basis for a revolutionary alliance of workers and peasants. In this racial society, where the white bourgeoisie prevented the extension of full democratic rights to all, many socialists, especially Trotskyists, argued that the struggle against class collaboration would take the form of non-collaboration and political boycott (Document 104; Alexander 1986:4).

Non-collaboration with racial structures signified both a break from the ANC's petitionist politics which aimed at incorporation in the existing system and a rejection of the state's intensified efforts to co-opt black leadership into government-created racial political structures. In the immediate tactical sense, the boycott of the NRC was seen as a means to resist the government's systematic exclusion of blacks from national political institutions and their segregation into powerless advisory bodies. In the longer term, by confronting state authority, which in South Africa assumed a racial form, the non-collaborationist response raised the possibility that the black working class and rural masses could establish their own institutions and challenge the state through dual power (Tabata [1952]:19, 25-6; Alexander 1986).

Although not as inherently flawed as the People's Front strategy, the promotion of black working class interests through a non-collaborationist policy was far more difficult than anticipated. Socialists generally, and Trotskyists especially, were not successful in linking their vision to an effective set of tactics. While the People's Front strategy foundered on racism, the early Trotskyist vision foundered on class divisions. Despite its statistically minute size, a tiny but influential aspirant bourgeois stratum, eager to develop black business, actively promoted its own class interests within the AAC. By 1937 many socialists were aware that leadership of the united fronts was being hijacked by a group that eschewed militancy for petitionary methods and ended up participating in government structures. Yet they were not successful in restraining this right-wing movement.

The AAC embodied a variety of class and regional interests whose common denominator was the lack of democratic rights. Regionally, it was strongest in the Cape where Africans still retained a qualified franchise. The class interests of privileged Africans were apparent in Convention's endorsement of a civilisation test as a prerequisite for the franchise (Karis and Carter 1973:33). But reflecting the class structure of black society, its social base was composed overwhelmingly of proletarians and land-hungry peasants. The common democratic interest of these different classes was seen at the AAC's inaugural meeting in December 1935 in the unanimous opposition to the Hertzog Bills (Karis and Carter 1973:7; Musson 1989:81; Bunting 1981:128).

But the class divisions became clearer once the Hertzog Bills became law. By the June 1936 conference, although still opposed to the Bills in principle, Convention was unable to agree on a method of protest. Between June 1936 and December 1937 many AAC leaders, including ANC and CPSA representatives, decided unilaterally to participate in the NRC. The AAC had begun with a mandate to reject the NRC; now it became a vehicle for NRC representatives (Karis and Carter 1973:8-11).

Reformist tendencies clearly had the momentum while radicals were unsure how to stop this conservative movement. Former Communists C. B. I. Dladla and Gana Makabeni, critical of conservative African leadership and disillusioned about the prospects of reforming the AAC, argued that building the black trade union movement was the best alternative available to socialists at that time. But other socialists remained in the AAC, forming a left-wing "Rump Parliament" which met on 14 December 1937 after the regular session and criticised Convention's inactivity among the masses. But the Rump Parliament was unsuccessful in preventing what Jimmy La Guma, among others, alleged to be internal sabotage by reformist black leaders unduly influenced by white Native Representatives. When the majority of AAC leaders finally decided to support the NRC, they simply removed Goolam Gool, then a member of the WPSA, from the Central Executive for his vocal advocacy of non-collaboration (Bunche Collection, box 64).

The movement towards participation in the NRC was accompanied by a growing rift between the ANC and the AAC which echoed the division between Communists and Trotskyists. In conception, the AAC was meant to function as a Parliament for all Africans, representing them through their affiliated organisations, rather than through individual membership. But, by April 1936, some ANC leaders, led by Dr P. ka I. Seme, were voicing fears that if the AAC were to become a permanent body it would undermine the ANC. Communists like Edwin Mofutsanyana, who had originally rejected this view, began to sympathise with it, and although the CPSA had wholeheartedly endorsed the AAC's formation, by 1937 it was backing the revival of the ANC and supporting its competition with Convention. By ensuring that Convention met only once every three years and that it endorsed the NRC, the AAC's potential as a representative body was stifled (Documents 99, 108, 110, 111; *South African Worker*, 1 August 1937; 4 September 1937; Bunting 1981:131-2; Bunting 1975:80-3).

Aside from a few Communists like Johnny Gomas, the CPSA, preoccupied in the People's Front period with white labour, supported the movement to participate in the NRC, at first tacitly, then overtly. Once Parliament passed the Hertzog Bills, the Party began arguing that the NRC offered a platform for propaganda; Communists Edwin Mofutsanyana and Hyman Basner were amongst the first to contest seats and participate in the NRC (Basner 1993; Southall 1978:69-70). As the AAC ossified into inactivity, its mass support dwindled (Bunche Collection, box 64).

The National Liberation League (NLL) and Non-European United Front (NEUF) were two short-lived black united fronts which, while similar in aims to the AAC, were more radical in their rhetoric and their espousal of militant tactics. Like the AAC, they fell prey to left-wing schisms over strategy and tactics (Simons 1976:221-3; Hommel 1981:65-71; Lewis 1987:179-206; Everett 1978).

While upholding a long-term goal of working class unity across the colour line, the NLL's emphasis on black leadership, its anti-imperialist stance, and its self-conscious distancing from overtly socialist goals bore the stamp of the Native Republic thesis which La Guma had so actively promoted in the late '20s. Formed in December 1935, the League aimed to organise blacks on the basis of their local needs and link these with broad democratic demands like the abolition of the colour bar, poll taxes and pass laws. Building a black trade union movement was seen as a precondition for pulling white labour from its historic alliance with the bourgeoisie. The NLL quickly attracted a working class base throughout the Western Cape (Document 105). Its organisers were acutely concerned with the problem of linking political analysis and practical work: a manuscript found with NLL papers entitled *How to work among urban Africans* argued that the ICU and ANC had declined due to their failure to develop local structures like trade union branches and residents' associations with which to begin fighting for immediate demands. This insight had limitations when it came to gender: Dr Waradia Abdurahman formed a Women's Bureau to attract women members but, reflecting the historic pattern of women's organisations in the liberation movement, this was seen as an auxiliary to the NLL's national struggle, rather than as a means of mobilising women on the basis of their distinctive needs as an oppressed group. Hawa Ahmed's [Halima Gool] gender analysis of the struggle for the franchise was a significant exception to the general marginalisation of women within the liberation movement (Documents 114, 115; Lewis 1987:180-1; Walker 1991).

By 1936 disputes had arisen over the League's methods of protest. Under the leadership of Cissie Gool, a member of the CPSA, the NLL restricted its work to petitions to government authorities for local reforms. Cissie Gool was ousted in March 1937 by the NLL's left-wing, which included Jimmy La Guma, Johnny Gomas and Goolam Gool, and whose views are found in the short-lived monthly, *The Liberator* (Document 109).

Although the League established several trade unions in 1937-38, largely through the efforts of La Guma and Gomas, the Goolam Gool faction had trouble maintaining the NLL's initial level of mass support, indicated by the fact that none of the League's 12 branches sent delegates to its April 1938 conference. In explaining this, the faction was already polarised between Goolam Gool's argument that education was a precondition for the development of popular political consciousness, and Johnny Gomas' argument that the leadership was pursuing visionary goals while neglecting immediate popular needs (Lewis 1987:187).

In April 1938 the NLL formed the NEUF, headed by Cissie Gool, to fight the proposed Stuttaford Bills. These Bills aimed to enforce segregation in public and residential areas and were part of a broader move to eliminate coloured rights (Hommel 1981:67-8). The NEUF's first major Western Cape campaign culminated in March 1939 in a massive march on Parliament against residential segregation; and even though coloured *petit bourgeois* homeowners had the most to lose from forced relocation, the issue struck an emotive chord amongst working-class people as well (Abrahams 1954:332; *cf.* Lewis 1987:194). This show of strength convinced the government to temporarily back down, and as a result the NLL and NEUF reaped organisational gains with new affiliates springing up around the country. In the Transvaal, the Communist Y. M. Dadoo led the NEUF on vigorous campaigns against support for World War Two (Documents 116–119; Lewis 1987:188-94).

Nonetheless, the NLL and NEUF lost vitality during the war, no doubt in part due to the CPSA's moderate war-time policy. When the CPSA began supporting the government's war efforts following Nazi Germany's invasion of the Soviet Union in June 1941, the NEUF abandoned its anti-war campaigns, indicating the strong presence of Communist leadership (Lodge 1985:3; Swan 1987:200-2; Roux 1964:357-8; Simons 1976:223; Karis and Carter 1973:389-91). In the NLL, divisions between Trotskyists and Communists, often articulated in terms of colour, became more acute. By April

1939 Lewis (1987:34, n. 86) notes, the NLL's leadership was predominantly white, with Communist links. In mid-1939 Goolam Gool's faction was ousted from the NLL in a fight ostensibly over the colour composition of leadership (Documents 112, 113; Lewis 1987:195; Simons 1983: 503). From then on, once again under Cissie Gool's leadership, the NLL concentrated mainly on Communist electoral campaigns. Still radical in rhetoric, by 1942, Lewis (1987:204-6) argues, it was approximating the moderate (coloured) African People's Organisation in its use of the Cape Town City Council to fight local campaigns and its call for quotas for skilled coloureds.[12]

World war and the suppression of socialism

Reflecting its position within the British Empire, South Africa declared war against Germany in September 1939, even though the government's white constituency was sharply divided in its sympathies between the Allied and Axis powers. The war spurred rapid urbanisation and industrial development, especially on the Witwatersrand, which became the most volatile centre of black working class activity. Having lost interest in the AAC, urban blacks protested their working and living conditions through strikes, bus boycotts and squatters' movements. The escalating insurgency in the factories and on the mines could capitalise on years of organising by trade unionists like Max Gordon, Daniel Koza and T. W. Thibedi, all influenced by Trotskyism, and former Communist Gana Makabeni. They, together with others, revived and rebuilt the black trade union movement which had been decimated by the CPSA's left-wing swing in the early 1930s. By 1940, Gordon's Joint Committee of African Trade Unions (JCATU) was the leading trade union group on the Witwatersrand (Roux 1964:326-34; Stein 1978). The mass protest movements of these years jolted national liberation leaders: in 1943 the ANC Youth League, African Democratic Party and Non-European Unity Movement were all launched to capture this social base (Lodge 1983:13-20; Karis and Carter 1973:71-2). The government, demanding greater production of war goods, tried to curtail this militancy. In 1940, Gordon was interned for his opposition to the war. The JCATU lost members and splintered, some of its unions remaining with Koza while others aligned with Makabeni or with the CPSA (Documents 124–126; Hirson 1989a:85-6).

How did the outbreak of World War Two and the Smuts government's domestic war efforts affect the socialist movement and its relationship with the democratic and working class struggles? Until June 1941, when Nazi Germany invaded the Soviet Union, both Communist and Trotskyist currents opposed the war on the grounds that it was an intra-imperialist conflict. Not surprisingly, the peak of the limited Communist and Trotskyist co-operation was reached in the late 1930s in united fronts like the NLL and NEUF. With the assassination of Trotsky in 1940, followed by the CPSA's pro-war stance in 1941, the Communist/Trotskyist divide became more pronounced.

Until June 1941 the CPSA's anti-war policy was based on building a united front against fascism and war which was meant to include both the white labour and the black democratic movements. Almost immediately after Germany's invasion of the Soviet Union, the CPSA joined the war effort, arguing that defence of the Soviet Union was a precondition for the defeat of fascism. Following the Comintern, the CPSA developed a much more elastic conception of the social classes which were potentially anti-fascist and now included some elements of the bourgeoisie. It also saw some progressive potential in the interventionist policies of the war-time state (Bunting 1981: 149-65; Hirson 1989a:84-5). In contrast, Trotskyists remained adamantly opposed to war and the government's war efforts. Their own outlook was influenced by the formation of a Fourth International in 1938. Anticipating that the intra-imperialist conflict would precipitate a post-war collapse of capitalism, Trotskyists hoped that the Fourth International would attract mass support and provide new revolutionary leadership capable of counteracting the reformist effects of Stalinism (Documents 122, 129).

The CPSA's policy reversal meant that it now found itself allied with the government which it had hitherto attacked in its comparison of racial oppression in South Africa with fascism in Europe. Its pro-war position meant an endorsement of the government's domestic war policies which set the Party on a distinctly accommodationist path. The Party gained a dual dividend from its new stance. Its anti-war position had alienated white labour support, and now, like other Communist Parties, it was able to benefit from the pro-war nationalism of sections of the white working class and *petite bourgeoisie* and the black *petite bourgeoisie*. Throughout the war, the Party directed itself to the white electorate, and its biggest recruitment was amongst the white *petite bourgeoisie* (Simons 1983:478-80; Lodge 1985:1-6; Hirson 1989a:85). The Party was no longer at odds with the leaderships of the AAC and ANC over the war, even if most blacks were, as Hirson (1989a:80-2) argues, indifferent to a struggle against fascism in Europe while their own democratic demands remained unmet. Moreover, despite the seeming contradiction between the Party's new stance and the increasing militancy of blacks during the war, the Party emerged at the war's end as the strongest socialist organisation with a firm foothold in the black trade union movement.

What did the CPSA's pro-war stance mean in practical terms? Its support for the national war drive did not mean a drop in its trade union activity. In 1940 the CPSA threw itself with vigour into trade union work on the Rand, and it carried out a number of effective leafleting and propaganda campaigns in the early 1940s which attracted some black members (Documents 127, 128, 130). Despite its efforts to curb strikes following the German invasion of the Soviet Union, the CPSA nonetheless recognised the legitimacy of black working class demands. Thus, when it opposed War Measure 145 of 1942, which outlawed strikes by Africans, it did so on the grounds that better pay and recognition of African trade unions would be more effective means of preventing strikes. However, neither the Party's restraining efforts and its resistance to illegal protest activity nor War Measure 145 failed to stop the wave of organised and spontaneous strikes (Morkel 1942; Lodge 1985:13-15, 23; Hirson 1987:51-2 and 1989a:88-9; Bunting 1981:162; Roux 1964:328, 330-1).

Despite the achievements of individual Trotskyist trade unionists in the late 1930s, the Trotskyist tendency was not able to benefit from the CPSA's accommodationist stance. The organisational fragmentation and regionalism of the Trotskyist tendency left it ill-prepared to combat Communism's moderating influence on the black trade union movement during the '40s. Cape Town Trotskyists had always been geared towards propaganda and education rather than trade union work. While Johannesburg Trotskyists were more oriented towards the black trade union movement, each wave of activity ended in organisational collapse. The tiny Johannesburg WPSA, which included Max Gordon and Fanny Klenerman, who had organised South Africa's first union of women workers, made a few stabs at organising black mineworkers. These efforts dwindled, due both to the difficulties of penetrating mining compounds and to the group's internal dynamics: it was far from whole-hearted in its support for Gordon's systematic shopfloor organising. The Johannesburg WPSA was succeeded by the ephemeral Socialist Workers' League in 1939, which, in turn, was a precursor to the Workers' International League (WIL) of the 1940s.[13] Similarly, in Cape Town, the CLSA was unable to sustain its activities during the war, although it was revived in the 1940s as the Fourth International Organisation of South Africa (FIOSA). And in June 1939, fearing that South Africa was on the verge of fascism, the WPSA went underground and ceased all open activity (Drew 1991a:239-49).[14]

Within a few years of its formation in late 1941, the Council of Non-European Trade Unions (CNETU) was divided between a Communist-influenced leadership urging moderation and the more militant, although bureaucratised, Progressive Trade Unions faction in which Dan Koza and Trotskyists in the WIL figured prominently (Document 132).[15] But the WIL and the Cape Town-based FIOSA found themselves on opposite sides of the CNETU dispute, having failed to achieve organisational unity despite the virtual identity of their programmes, and Communists gained the advantage. Against the background of this intra-left division, the African Mineworkers' Strike of 1946 erupted without adequate preparation when union leaders could no longer control workers' militancy. The strike's defeat aborted the war-time insurgency (Documents 131-134, 137-140; Lodge 1983:20; Lodge 1985:14-15; Hirson 1987:52-3).

At the close of the war, South African socialism was characterised by a paradox. Despite the CPSA's repeated policy oscillations, its continuing efforts to recruit white labour and its efforts to dampen black working class militancy during the war, it nonetheless emerged at the war's end with a foothold in the black trade union movement. In contrast, the Trotskyist groups were fragmented and often scorned immediate struggles, preferring revolutionary propaganda. They were therefore unable to profit from the CPSA's ambiguous and often unenthusiastic response to black workers' protests. Yet the CPSA's advance was both limited and tenuous. It had been unable to resolve the problems posed by the complex relationship between class and nationalist struggles.

South African left orthodoxy has portrayed the post-war period as a stage in the national liberation movement in which the class and the national struggles merged (O'Meara 1975:167). But this merger was an uneasy one, made when organised black labour was at its nadir. After the war, trade union membership declined drastically and the CNETU fell apart from the pressure of a wave of failed strikes and internal political struggles for control of the federation. (Hirson 1987:49*ff.*; Lodge 1983:20). With many of its own class organisations demolished, the black working class moved towards nationalist leadership for direction. As socialist groups disbanded or went underground in anticipation of the 1950 Suppression of Communism Act, building the nation replaced uniting the working class as the first item on the agenda of the new generation of socialists and radicals.

The Trotskyist tendency was in a state of organisational disarray at the war's end. Both the WIL and the FIOSA broke up in the late 1940s. At the request of the Fourth International overseas, which still urged South African Trotskyists to unite, a few FIOSA members joined the WPSA, whose members helped form the NEUM in 1943 and acted as its secret inner core through the 1940s and '50s. Others formed the Forum Club, one of several left-wing discussion clubs, including the New Era Fellowship, Left

Book Club, Africa Club and Modern Youth Society, which flourished in the 1940s and '50s.

Within the international Communist movement, World War Two's victory over fascism was seen as a defeat for international capitalism which tilted the balance of class forces towards the working class, resulting in social democratic electoral victories across Western Europe.[16] Nonetheless, with fascism still considered a potential threat, Communist Parties adapted the war-time People's Front policy to form broad fronts of progressive, anti-fascist forces; in South Africa, the CPSA called for a National Front (Document 135-6). By 1947 and '48, however, the notion of a broad progressive front was no longer seen as viable, either in the West or in South Africa, as Labour and Social Democratic parties became increasingly anti-Communist.

While the CPSA saw the Cold War as a sign of the internationalisation of class conflict, within South Africa it believed that the growth of right-wing influence would exacerbate racial and national rather than class conflict (Bunting 1981:200-11). Yet its own activities followed racial lines: in 1948 the Party contested all-white elections on an anti-fascist platform and supported elections for the NRC even while condemning it. The Party's admission that its own members inevitably grouped themselves along racial and national lines indicates how far it actually was from effecting a merger of class and national struggles. Even after the Nationalist Party's (NP) marginal electoral victory of 1948, the Party optimistically believed that the NP would alienate the white working class once in office, and that repressive conditions would produce a social radicalisation favourable to the Party's growth (Document 141).

The Communist policy of alliance with the national liberation movement, premised theoretically on the CPSA's notion of a two-stage transition to socialism, was endorsed at the Party's last national conference before its dissolution in 1950 (Bunting 1981:200-11). But this was a formal, organisational approach to the national question rather than a political resolution of the tensions between working class interests and nationalism, indicated not only by the Party's internal policies and its practical work, but by its condemnation of the ANC Youth League's call for self-determination as tantamount to apartheid (Bunting 1981:209). In late 1946 the CPSA's Central Executive Committee had been charged with sedition by the state, foreshadowing the 1950s Treason Trial (Bunting 1981:194-6). Expecting further repression, in 1950 the majority of Communists voted to liquidate the Party, a decision which would later be criticised by the reconstituted, underground South Africa Communist Party (Bunting 1981: 213-15; 310).[17]

As the period of legal socialist activity came to an end, the bifurcated socialist movement remained unable to resolve the tension between popular struggles for reforms, articulated in nationalist terms, and its own avowedly revolutionary goals, premised on class struggle. The implications of this dilemma would unfold during the era of apartheid.

NOTES

1. The Industrial Socialist League was formed from a faction within the ISL in May 1918. It eschewed parliamentary politics and advocated industrial unionism and a general strike as the means to revolution. It published *The Bolshevist* in May 1919 and *The Bolshevik* from September 1919 to 1920.
2. In September 1920 the Cape Town and Johannesburg branches of the Industrial Socialist League merged to form the Communist Party of South Africa (see *The Bolshevik*, October 1920, Simons Papers). Initially, the dispute over participation in parliamentary politics was a barrier to broader socialist unity. However, the ISL successfully argued that the question of parliamentary politics was not fundamental in the South African context, where the majority of people were denied the franchise. Thus the Communist Party of South Africa in turn amalgamated with several other organisations, including the ISL, to form a new Communist Party of South Africa (Section of the Communist International) in July 1921. The Simonses (1983:261), however, argue that the new CPSA "... was virtually a continuation of the [*ISL*]", a view reinforced by *South African Communists Speak* (Bunting 1981:1-57).
3. Nonetheless, Macmillan (1949:310) points to an aspect of the strike which most commentators focusing on its working-class character overlooked: "The Rand strike of 1922 was to outward appearance, a rising of the extreme Left. Two or three of the more obscure but vocal leaders were known as 'Communists', and there was certainly much talk of a Republic – ostensibly a Workers' Republic. There is no doubt, however, that the Republic dreamt of by the men who actually took up arms was the Boer Republic of former times." That interpretation is born out by Herd's (1966:31) observation: "... the call to preserve a White South Africa swept through the rural areas where the strikers, not vainly as it proved, had hoped for moral and material support. Food and promises of further aid began flowing in from the Platteland. *Ons Vaderland* reported that the strikers were receiving cattle from the farmers as outright gifts or as purchases on deferred terms. Shopkeepers were allowing them generous credit."
4. The CPSA has been falsely blamed for the notorious slogan, "Workers of the World Fight and Unite for a White S.A.", apparently the only banner noted during the Rand Revolt (*cf.* Saunders 1994a:223). The CPSA neither coined the slogan nor endorsed it. For photographs see [*The Star*] (1922).
5. At its national conference in late 1926, the ICU council resolved, six to five: "No officer of the ICU shall be a member of the Communist Party" (Simons 1983:354). Three Communists on the National Council refused to give up their membership in either organisation and were expelled: Jimmy La Guma, ICU General Secretary, E. J. Khaile, ICU Financial Secretary, and John Gomas, Cape Provincial Secretary. Another Communist, Thomas Mbeki, remained with the ICU. Evidently other Communists in the ICU, like T. W. Thibedi, were also expelled. Former Communist Frank Glass became the ICU's bookkeeper after the expulsions. For CPSA accounts see Bunting (1981:85-7); Roux (1993:108-11); Simons (1983:353-85), Documents 12, 15 and 17. For Kadalie's views see his autobiography (1970:99-100), where he argues that he tried to maintain a middle ground between Communism and African nationalism and that the latter view eventually won in the National Council, and Document 16. Trapido (Kadalie 1970:19-20) notes that much of the tension was due to divergent views over the use of the strike tactic.
6. Along with J. T. Gumede of the ANC and Daniel Colraine of the TUC, in February 1927 La Guma attended the League Against Imperialism conference in Brussels. The conference adopted two resolutions of relevance to South Africa. The first, submitted by the South African delegation, called for "[t]he right of self-determination through the complete overthrow of capitalism and imperial domination". The second, a general resolution on the Negro question, demanded "... full freedom, equality with all other races, and the right to govern Africa" (Simons 1983:389). Later that year La Guma visited Moscow, where he and Bukharin reformulated these resolutions into a draft resolution on South Africa which was sent to the CPSA. See also Roux (1993:7-11).
7. This draft resolution read in part: "The Party must orientate itself chiefly upon the native toiling masses while continuing to work actively among the white workers. The Party leadership must be developed in the same sense. This can only be achieved by bringing the native membership without delay into much more active leadership of the Party both locally and centrally.

    While developing and strengthening the fight against all the customs, laws and regulations which discriminate against the native and coloured population in favour of the white population, the Communist Party of South Africa must combine the fight against all anti-native laws with the general political slogan in the fight against British domination, the slogan of an independent native South African republic as a stage towards a workers' and peasants' republic with full equal rights for all races, black, coloured and white.

    South Africa is a black country, the majority of its population is black and so is the majority of workers and peasants. The bulk of the South African population is the black peasantry, whose land has been expropriated by the white minority. Seven eights of the land is owned by the whites. Hence the national question in South Africa, which is based upon the agrarian question, lies at the foundation of the revolution is South Africa. The black peasantry constitutes the basic moving force of the revolution in alliance with and under the leadership of the working class" (quoted in Roux 1993:7).

8 *Umsebenzi*, the CPSA paper, had decidedly fewer references to the Native Republic thesis in the early 1930s, compared to the late 1920s or the mid-1930s. By mid-1932 the slogan *"Mayibuye"* (Let Africa Return) was dropped from the paper's masthead, leaving only the slogan "Workers of all Lands Unite" and hammer and sickle (*Umsebenzi*, 12 and 19 December 1930 and 11 May 1932).

9 A Left Opposition, in which Leon Trotsky became the principal figure, formed within the Communist Party of the Soviet Union in 1923 to contest Stalin's policies and his growing influence in the Party. The Left Opposition became international around 1929/30 during Trotsky's exile on Prinkipo. The Nazis took power in Germany in January 1933; the same year, the International Left Opposition (Bolshevik-Leninist) became the International Communist League (Bolshevik-Leninist), and Trotsky (1975:429–47) argued for the need to break from the Third International. Debate ensued over the merits of forming a new International or a looser network of socialist groupings. In 1938 a Fourth International was formed.

10 Interview with R. O. Dudley, Cape Town, April 1988.

11 For the Ten Point Programme see *South Africa's Radical Tradition*, Volume 2.

12 Hommel (1981:81) argues that in the early 1940s neither the NLL nor NEUF was able to form an effective opposition to the government's proposed Coloured Advisory Council, another move to curtail coloured voting rights; hence the formation of the Anti-Coloured Affairs Department (Anti-CAD).

13 The Socialist Workers' League saw the WPSA as black nationalist and the CPSA as white chauvinist. But its own programme echoed views held by the CPSA's right wing in mid-1936: "Our road can only lie in the steady and patient organisation in parallel lines of both sections of the population, drawing them ever closer as objective conditions make this possible, and in the steady spread amongst *both* sections of our revolutionary propaganda and agitation on the basis of the class struggle." It justified this proposal on the grounds that "... we are compelled to compromise in our tactics of approach [*to white workers*] in order that we may at least get a hearing, that we may be able to put our point of view." See *Statement of Policy and Programme of Work for South Africa and Rules and Regulations of the Socialist Workers League submitted for joint discussion*, [c. 1939], Trotsky Archives, item 16596, Houghton Library, Harvard University.

14 Thus, in its last issue, the editors of *The Spark* wrote: "The position is clear. From one side comes the war danger, to be followed immediately by martial law; on the other side the Press law makes the existence of a revolutionary organ like the 'Spark' impossible as a legal paper. It will have to go the way of the revolutionary press in Tsarist Russia 50 years ago, [...] the period of legal existence in bourgeois democracy is over." See "The Workers' movement faces a new road", *The Spark*, 5, 6, June 1939, South African Reference Library.

15 Within the WIL there was much internal criticism of its top-down approach to trade union organisation via the PTU secretaries, suggesting that WIL's rank and file strength remained weak, despite its support for the pro-strike sentiment of the rank and file (Workers' International League 1946).

16 The Comintern dissolved itself in May 1943, calling upon its supporters to give all their energies to the war against fascism (Bunting 1981:177-183).

17 In May 1950 the Government attempted to pass the Unlawful Organisations Bill as a means to proscribe the CPSA. This was opposed on the grounds that it did not specifically mention the CPSA and thus could be applied to all opposition groups. The Government then introduced the seemingly more precise Suppression of Communism Act which in practice was used to target both Communists and non-Communists.

Part One

South African socialists and the racially-divided working class

EDITOR'S NOTE
The central theme of Part One is the attempts of socialists, both South African-born and from overseas, to come to terms with the problems posed by racial and national divisions within the working class. These difficulties were acute for socialists from all traditions, whether those schooled in the ethical socialism of the British ILP, syndicalists or those who took their guidance from Moscow. The emerging hegemony of the Bolshevik model is increasingly clear. This is evidenced in the transformation of the South African Left into a Communist Party, in the growing links with socialists in the international Communist movement and in the growing centrality of Comintern decisions to South African socialist debate.

Document 1
Keir Hardie, "Stoned in South Africa", 1907[1]

I landed at Durban, and was, of course, soon being interviewed by the Press. Then, as now, the racial question was acute, and the Unions were alarmed at the manner in which the coloured people were supplanting them, even in the skilled trades. To meet this competition, the Unions refused to admit the coloured races to membership, which, of course, only aggravated the evil. My suggestion was that the Unions should be thrown open to the coloured men, and that, as they would then claim the same pay as the whites, a thing they were anxious to do, their competition as cheap workers would end. It will scarcely be credited by those not on the spot, but this produced as much sensation as though I had proposed to cut the throat of every white man in South Africa. The capitalist Press simply howled with rage – there were, of course, exceptions – and at Ladysmith a mob, led by a local lawyer, wrecked the windows of the hotel in which I was staying.

This, however, was but the beginning. At every station at which the train stopped on the way north to Johannesburg, there were crowds of sightseers to hoot and jeer and threaten. Many of these were Boer farmers, who had already forgotten the stand I had made on their behalf at home, and for which, also, by the way, I had been stoned and hunted through the streets of towns and cities in both England and Scotland; but these, as a rule, stood looking on and grinning. At one station where the train stopped 15 minutes, and where the mob was specially menacing, I got on to the platform and succeeded in addressing the people. I explained what I had said, and then invited the working men present to say whether they disagreed. For a time no one moved, until a sturdy young blacksmith stepped forward and gripping my hand, said, "Here's one that's going to stand by you; you have spoken the truth," whereat quite a big cheer went up, and one fellow, a blackguard of a journalist who had led the opposition, rushed at me with uplifted stick, but was seized by some of those about him and rushed to the outskirts of the crowd. Next morning the Johannesburg Press reported that I had been stoned out of the station!

But it was at Johannesburg where the storm burst in all its fury. Mr. Connolly, President of the Natal Railwaymen's Union, and a member of the Legislative Chamber, had very courageously accompanied me up from Ladysmith.[2] An Irishman with the heart of a lion, he was in indifferent health, and for some years I have lost trace of him. When we were entering the capital of the goldfields, he was visibly alarmed. He had had some experience of Johannesburg, and knew what its cosmopolitan crowd could do. The station, the approach leading thereto, and the bridge over the railway was one black mass of seething, howling demons. As the train drew up, young Crawford, one of the deported nine,[3] saw me, and signalled to a number of constables, who formed a cordon round the doorway, whilst a number of them surrounded me and led me by a by-path up from the station to where a cab was waiting. The crowd, which was waiting for my exit by the main doorway, was for a minute or two outwitted, but as the cab, guarded by the police, passed over the bridge, someone awoke to what was taking place, and with a shout the mob started in pursuit. Showers of stones smashed the windows, and both the driver and the policeman came in for some nasty cuts. But the horses were good, and we soon out-distanced the pursuers and reached the hotel in safety, and there a cordon of police kept the mischief-makers at bay.

Document 2
Letter from the Cape Labour Party[4] to James Ramsay MacDonald[5], 12 August 1908

>119/121 Strand St.
>Cape Town,
>Aug. 12th. 1908.

James Ramsay Macdonald Esq., M.P.
House of Parliament,
London.

Dear Sir,

We were surprised & disappointed that nothing seems to have been done in the matter of our appeal before your Parliament rose. You evidently do not recognise the awful position the workers here are being placed in. There seems to be a conspiracy of silence on the part of the press & telegraphic agency, but occasionally the newspapers do admit toned accounts of what is going on. I am sending you newspapers from time to time which should confirm what I am telling you. We are not appealing for charity or monetary assistance; but to the brotherly feeling that should exist between the different sections of the Labour Party in the Empire. What a hollow mockery this claim is beginning to appear in the Colonies, when to us it appears that the interests of the savage Zulus, the comfort of the Chinese criminals in the compound, & the convenience of the Indian coolies, seem to be nearer the heart of the English Labour Party than the continued oppression, physical ruin, & death by starvation of hundreds of their white brethren of the same flesh & blood in a British Colony.[6] Must we appeal to you in vain & turn for help to the press of the Empire for that protection & succour we are entitled to while the British flag flies over us? We are appealing to the various Parliaments of the Empire & the Labour Parties in them for some protest, remonstrance, or even enquiry that will strengthen our hands & hearten us in this matter.

>I am Yours faithfully,
>[G. O. Bruce]

Document 3
Letter from F. A. W. Lucas[7] to James Ramsay MacDonald, 15 October 1915

Hillside
Vestry Rd
Walthamstow
15.10.15.

Dear Macdonald,

I find that the situation in South Africa is slightly different in regard to the expulsion from the Party of certain members from what I told you yesterday afternoon.

At a Special Conference of the S. A. Labour Party held in Johannesburg on August 22nd it was decided to adopt Mr. Creswell's "see it through" policy in regard to the war.[8] Ever since the beginning of the war the Party had been working on a basis adopted last December by the Annual Conference of the Party, namely, that each member should be free to follow the dictates of his own reason and conscience. At that Annual Conference the Executive Committee of the Party, consisting of fifteen members, was elected, eleven holding anti-war views. The "see it through policy" has resulted in those eleven resigning in a body. They consisted of some of the most prominent and respected members of the party and included W. H. Andrews[9], the Chairman, a vice-chairman, the treasurer and the secretary.

Andrews, who is a member of the A. S. E., was one of the founders of the S.A.L.P. He has never wavered in his efforts for the workers. This man, who refused to support the newly adopted war policy, was with other workers threatened with expulsion from the party if he stood for Parliament without pledging himself to support that policy. He had prior to the Conference of August 22nd signed the party pledge to abide by the decisions of the parliamentary caucus in matters affecting the aims and objects of the party. After the decision of that conference he asked for the return of his pledge. Instead of being returned to him it was dramatically torn up by the Chairman at the meeting.

The members of the Conference who were opposed to the war, together with their supporting branches, formed the International Socialist League of the S.A.L.P.[10] Andrews and one or two others decided that it was necessary to give the electorate who held anti-war views an opportunity of recording those views even at the risk of expulsion from the party which would follow naturally from their standing in opposition to official candidates of the party. Andrews with the support of the Georgetown branch of the S.A.L.P. is standing for his old constituency Georgetown and Clark for Langlaagte which he represents in the Provincial Council. To anticipate expulsion from the party for supporting Andrews + Clark the League has definitely seceded from the party, the secession being followed by a formal vote of expulsion by the S.A.L.P. Administrative Council.

Mr. Creswell is the prime mover in obtaining the adoption of the "see it through" policy. Of his own personal integrity there cannot be the slightest doubt but the same cannot be said of many of his supporters who have climbed into office over the unpopularity of the views of those who were forced to resign.

The position now is that Andrews, all the prominent Labour members of the

Provincial Council, and nearly all the most active and self sacrificing members of the party have been expelled from the body they helped to create while there places have in most cases been filled by "new chums" who after the success at the Provincial Council elections joined the party.

I shall not be sailing before the 23rd. If there is anything you would care to ask me about I shall be glad to come and see you.

Yours sincerely
F. A. W. Lucas

Document 4
"The Great Native Strike",[11] *The International,* 27 February 1920

Since our last issue the Rand has witnessed the unprecedented spectacle of a strike of 40,000 mine natives. Owing to the compound and indenture system, the general public have seen very little of the strike, as the natives, herded in their compound quarters, are not allowed abroad. Practically the only source of information is "The Star," which is notoriously the Chamber of Mines paper. For a week it has given lists of mines whose natives refuse to work. The lists are not the same every day. To-day the E.R.P.M. natives are out, to-morrow they return and other mines are affected, keeping the average total about 40,000. During the week double this number of native workers must have refused work. Police and military have poured on to the Reef, but there has been very little for them to do, as the native workers have learnt the lesson of absolute passivity to perfection. There have been charges made by the Native Congress of wholesale sjamboking, which of course are denied. There are scant means of verifying these charges at present.

On some mines white workers have taken on the labouring work, and have kept on partial operations. The ethic of solidarity is woefully weak in regard to the native workers. There has been no single clear call from any trade union leader. The only lead given has been by the I.S.L., whose leaflet, "Don't Scab," has been distributed at crucial points, and republished in full on the cable page of Tuesday's "Star" as a heinous example of "Socialist poison," for which publicity we give thanks![12]

The demands of the natives have been vague. The strike is undoubtedly an instinctive mass revolt against their whole status and pig level of existence. The Native Congress has had very little to with the movement, other than to hold a watching brief. The strike is in no man's control. Organisation within the compounds there is, of course, but of necessity there can be very little definite organisation as between mines owing to police surveillance.

There are few incidents to record, owing to the peaceful nature of the strike and the "cordon sanitaire" of police ringed round it.

Needless to say, we view the movement as a splendid example of the power of industrial solidarity, of the power of large industry to smash up tribal psychology. The advice given to the natives by us in our first message to them two years ago was:

> There is only one way of deliverance for you Bantu workers. Unite as workers, unite! Forget the things that divide you. Let there be no longer

any talk of Basuto, Zulu, or Shangaan. You are all labourers! Let labour be your common bond.

The native mine workers have followed this advice to the letter. To-day there are no tribal divisions among industrial natives. Only the chiefs seek to perpetuate these, their old prorogatives. The stern demands of mass industry in South Africa, as in all parts of the world, are moulding the Bantu workers into the image of the world proletariat. The faction fights which used to be so common – and though put down by the police, yet put down good-humouredly as rather too much of a good thing – are rapidly disappearing. The present strike is our witness to it.

The native workers have found a soul to strive for. They have awakened to a new earth. It is potentially theirs from this day out. The immense complications facing capitalist industry are aggravated by this unlooked-for trouble in the production of gold. The natives must be given substantial concessions, otherwise we shall see intermittent strikes on a large scale without end. The native is the very apotheosis of the figure visualised by Marx with nothing to lose but his chains. A day off now and then is for him, IN THE MASS, just as easy as a day at work. Industry can only run by conceding all he wants eventually.

The duties of white workers in the matter we deal with in another article.

Document 5
"Trade Union Notes", *The Bolshevik*, March 1920 (Extract)

The action of the Executive of the Mine Workers' Union in calling upon the miners to scab upon the striking native workers is the limit of treachery to the working class. It is craft unionism in excelsis. The recent struggle along the reef was not a racial struggle but a proletarian one; not a conflict of black versus white but of capitalist versus wage-workers: If the white mine workers had come in line and supported the natives, the proletarian character of the revolt would have been beyond dispute. As it is their action in scabbing is driving the native to look upon his fight as between black wage-workers on the one hand and white workers and capitalists on the other. Were the white workers to adopt the principle of solidarity of labour irrespective of colour or race the spectre of racial warfare would be banished from the land. If we do not open our unions to them now, when "The Day" arrives we shall find the natives fighting for the boss out here as they have already done in France, and Mesopotamia. We need their assistance to win our industrial fights now; we shall need them when we are establishing the workers councils; we shall need them to assist in building up the workers commonwealth. Within a sane social system sufficient of the necessarys of life can be produced to enable all in South Africa, whether white or black, to lead a decent and comfortable existence. Let the workers on the Rand celebrate the forthcoming May Day as they have never done before; not with their feet on the native worker but standing shoulder to shoulder with him in their industrial organizations.

Document 6
M. Lopes,[13] "Socialism and the Labour Party", *The Bolshevik*, April 1920

In a recent issue of our esteemed contemporary, the *International*, appeared a statement to the effect that the International League is not out to fight the Labour Party but to supersede it. This statement is surprising, and may even be construed as being a first attempt to look with a more favourable eye upon the Labour Party which has attained the fleshpots of a certain share of political power. The statement, from a Socialist standpoint, is absurd. Socialism, we know, will supersede Capitalism. Does the *International* consider that also a good reason why we should not fight Capitalism?

The *International* also suggested that Socialist propaganda can be more safely conducted under the protection of a large Labour Party in Parliament. In this connection it overlooks the suppression of the Spartacists by the Ebert Government of Kaiser-Socialists in Germany, the attacks upon the Bolsheviks by the followers of Kerensky, and the prosecution of Revolutionary organisations in England by a Government in which Labour leaders held office. Does the *International* believe Cresswell, Sampson, etc., to be less docile followers of social patriotism than George Barnes or Arthur Henderson?[14] Does it believe that a party representing mainly the white aristocratic Trade Unions and the middle-class to be more favourable to its propaganda amongst the natives than General Smuts or any other Capitalist politician? If not, where does the increased safety for Socialist propaganda come in? We deny that the Labour Party is out for Socialism, or that it is a Workers' organisation at all. It is a Party representing the upper layers of the white workers and the middle class. It represents those aristocratic unions – of the North especially – that, with their feet on the natives, shriek of exploitation; shopkeepers foam at the mouth with anger against the large combines that are cutting down their profits; and the middle class are feeling the pinch of the steady increase in the cost of living. These sections are not out to overthrow Capitalism; rather do they desire to get the most they can out of the present system. Therefore they are out for rent tribunals, Anti-Profiteering Acts, etc., which, they confidently expect, will bring them the relief they desire. At the majority of the Labour meetings Socialism was never mentioned; when it was, it was always accompanied by a pious insistence upon the necessity of constitutional action. These sections, which form the driving force of the Labour movement, do not desire to organise the lower unskilled sections of the white workers or the native and coloured workers, as they fear this would lessen the privileges they enjoy, and also act as an obstacle to the masters granting the skilled workers increased wages. The insistence of the Labour Party upon the British Imperial connection would seem to imply that the party perceives some advantages to be gained from this connection which the Irish, Indian and Egyptian nations have not yet perceived. Its attitude during the great war was for "democracy" and the "fourteen points" of a half-witted President reveals how little it can be trusted in this connection. To sum up - the Labour Party is not out to overthrow capital in the interests of the toiling masses, both white and black, but to obtain concessions for the middle-class and the white Trades Unions of skilled workers. It is not a proletarian organisation, in spite of the fact that many of the workers voted for it. By its attitude to the forcible overthrow of Capitalism, to the organisation of all the workers in One Big Union, to the late war, it betrays the middle class origin of its principles and tastes.

The devil is no more afraid of holy water than is the Labour Party of mentioning

Soviet Russia. The reason is plain: the great tactical lessons of the Russian Revolution are in contradiction to the principles of the Labour Party. The necessity for revolutionary mass action and the dictatorship of the workers through Soviets are being now assimilated by all genuine proletarian organisations throughout the world. By its repudiation of these lessons, the Labour Party definitely places itself "on the other side of the barricade." As the final struggle approaches in all lands, the capitalists will seek to protect their privileges under the cloak of Labour or pseudo- Socialist Governments. These Governments mislead the workers by adopting the slogans of Revolutionary Socialism, and thus endeavour to prevent the rising of the organised workers. They can be appropriately called "Capitalist shock absorbers."

Ever at the beck and call of the exploiters, they appear during a crisis as Revolutionary leaders, establish Labour or so-called Socialist Governments, and endeavour to pacify the workers. Once the danger is over, the Socialist or Labour mask is dropped, and the Capitalist can then proceed to crush the Revolutionary sections of the working class. Thus acted the followers of Kerensky in Russia, and the Ebert "Socialist" Government in Germany. Have we any reason to believe that Henderson in England and Cresswell in South Africa would act otherwise in a Revolutionary crisis? None whatever.

For these reasons, therefore, following the example of the Communist Parties in all lands, we are out to attack the Labour Party and to expose the Social patriots and Labour fakirs that have gathered beneath its banner.

We freely acknowledge that there are many sincere and class-conscious workers in the Labour Party. Their presence in the party only reflects discredit upon their knowledge of scientific Socialism, and their inability to realise the insincerity and hollowness of their parties' catchwords. Their sincerity and devotion to the workers' cause we must admire. The Labour Party, however, we shall fight with all the vigour at our command as being a reactionary organisation, and a pillar of Capitalism. We are confident by our clear insistence on the necessity for the Social Revolution, the Proletarian Dictatorship, and the Republic of Soviets, we shall, as the class-conflict grows more intense and the misery of the workers deepens, rally to our banner all the class-conscious and Revolutionary elements in the Labour Party.

Document 7
"'White South Africa.' Two Voices." *The International*, 27 January 1922

History does not proceed with the logical march of a proposition of Euclid. Wars and disputes never arise over clear-cut issues. A confused situation arises, wheels revolve within wheels, a hundred wires are pulled in a hundred different directions. Then, as the result of conscious "philosophising" by some, and recognition by others of some isolated outstanding feature, there often emerges a popular slogan which, with the aid of more or less interested propaganda, secures acceptance as epitomising the real matter at stake.

"White South Africa," or "the maintenance of the colour bar," has thus been accepted by the white workers as the prime "motif" in this strike, just as "making the world free for democracy" was accepted by the masses in the late capitalist war – only now, years after, to be found out as a piece of humbug. Meanwhile, recognising that "white South Africa" supplies the steam and the ginger in this strike, even to the point of a "revolutionary situation," let us see whether the trouble is really just ethnographical, or whether we cannot find here too the thread that runs through all conflicts in modern society, the thread of the inexorable class struggle necessitated by a capitalist system of production.

As a matter of fact, "white South Africa" (or "Vote White," as per Kentridge's recent election handbills) is a double-edged cry. A recent leaflet issued by Mr. Hendrikz as Secretary of the Mine Workers' Union quoted an article from "Ons Vaderland" by one General Pienaar – whoever he may be, he can scarcely be a member of the working class – referring to the age-long "struggle to build up South Africa as a white man's country and to uphold that supreme principle, THE PRESERVATION OF LAND AND PEOPLE." The Chamber of Mines, says the General, wants to wipe out the dividing line between black and white, involving equal rights for kaffirs, or the black taking his place alongside the white: first on the industrial field, to be followed by the vote and by intermarriage, the native, in receipt of higher pay for doing white man's work, taking such a position in society that many a white girl, impoverished by the lifting of the colour bar, will marry a coloured man. "Agriculture, he proceeds, will suffer from the diminished demand for produce in proportion to the replacement of white by coloured, and" – here comes the rub – "KAFFIR LABOUR ON THE FARMS WILL BECOME UNPAYABLY EXPENSIVE." Finally, he indignantly repudiates the suggestion that the Miners' Union, 85 per cent. Afrikander, has socialistic leanings: and Mr. Hendrikz adds a note that his Union is "specially organised to resist native trouble."

This, then, is what "White South Africa" means in the mouth of its farmer champion (and many of them are preaching this stuff daily from strike platforms). It means the land for the landlords, CHEAP AND SERVILE BLACK LABOUR to work it, and jobs on the mines as an outlet for the disinherited bywoner.

Is this "White South Africa," or is it not much more the BLACK SOUTH AFRICA? Is it not just the capitalist ideal, except that industrial capitalism sees no reason why it should philanthropically provide outlets for the *bywoner*? Is not the General's repudiation of "Socialism" therefore perfectly in place?

Afrikander workers, beware of being sidetracked, as you easily may be owing to your country upbringing, into fighting the battle of a Junker section which shot down the workers in 1913-14, and which can have no interest in the workers' cause, as workers, to-day either.

There is not and never was a white South Africa, and when you shout for it, you are dangerously near shouting for just the black labour country capitalism has made of South Africa. Capitalism, whose first principle all over the world is cheap labour; capitalism, whose profits can be made only at the workers' expense, is responsible for the black man doing the bulk of the work in this country. It is no use "damning the nigger" for that. Bob Waterston, who in 1917 fought Andrews at Benoni with appeals much a la Pienaar, now sees this much at any rate, that "the workers have no quarrel with the natives, their quarrel is entirely with the men who wish to place the natives in white men's positions AT STARVATION WAGES." Natives at starvation wages, that is the thing to attack: that is what ruins the white standard. Well, then, if you want

"White South Africa," your campaign, so far from being on Pienaar lines, must be rather in the direction of encouraging native labour to become "unpayably expensive." Nor again, even though you eschew the Pienaar philosophy, will it avail to talk to and about "the workers" as though they consisted solely of white men, and ignore the rest. The C.I.D. (whose masters dread a black workers' strike above all) will let you run on to your heart's content on those lines; but they are ludicrously untrue, as the Witbank "supervisors" now admit. Parson Mullineux said the other day that if the status quo were eliminated the kaffir within five years would be fighting for higher pay. Of course he will, and whether the status quo is eliminated or not. He will do it because he is a worker under capitalism, and good luck to him!

The white workers are under a very real and proper fear of competition from this cheap labour: in fact, except for the few skilled trades and the protection of the colour bar, they cannot compete with it under capitalism, and in fighting for the colour bar they are at best fighting only a rearguard action. "The people who do the work of a country eventually inherit it."

But if so, then the enemy is the class and system that gives the palm to labour cheapness. Modern capitalism cannot raise wages. It is sick, and cannot pull itself together except by yet further cheapening labour, by yet further reliance on the cheapest labour. Then away with it! This strike, like every other labour movement, has body or meaning or effect only to the extent that it helps to destroy the capitalist system. The deliberate attempt to overthrow the whole rule and government of the capitalist class thus becomes, not a matter for "idealists" or "extremists," but the immediate present-day practical goal of every step taken by organised labour. And if to that end, as a workaday case of "labour solidarity," you decided to secure the support of the mass of the "real workers," well, what could be more proper in a workers' attack on capitalist exploitation?

Fellow-worker, ask yourself, am I really for the whites as whites – landlords, magnates, profiteers, parasites, exploiters and all – or am I not rather for the workers as workers – white brown, yellow, black and all – and against the capitalists as capitalists – THE ONLY REAL BLACK MEN?

It is not in "the spirit of the *Voortrekkers* who conquered Dingaan," as Mr. Pohl would say, that you will achieve a white South Africa. It is in the spirit of the humble but very determined industrial proletariat of Russia, who overthrew the master class and made work, for the common good, the one condition of "status." There is no remedy for the situation, there is no future for the white workers, under capitalism. Communism alone can make South Africa a white man's country, in the sense that Communism alone can secure to every workers – whatever his colour – the full product of his labour. Only when that is secured will a white man be safe: only then can you begin to talk of a "white South Africa."

Document 8
S. P. Bunting,[15] *The "Colonial" Labour Front*, 23 October 1922

"The policy of the Communist International on national and colonial questions must be chiefly to bring about a union of the proletarian and working masses of all nations and countries for a joint revolutionary struggle leading to the overthrow of capitalism".

In these words the thesis of the Second Congress lays down the goal towards which any special methods applicable in particular circumstances, such as support of national liberation movements, peasant movements etc., are intended to lead up.[16] As clause 11 says, such support (especially on the part of the workers in the Home or imperialist countries) should be given "for the exclusive purpose of uniting the various units of the future proletarian parties there". Clause 12: "The victory over capitalism cannot be fully achieved and carried to its ultimate goal unless the proletariat and the toiling masses of all nations of the world rally of their own accord in a close and concordant union".

The supplementary theses say the same. "The masses of non-European subjected countries are inseparably connected with the proletarian movement in Europe, as a consequence of the centralisation of world capitalism" (No. 1). "The mission of the C.I. is to organise the working class of the whole world" (No. 5). "The Communist parties of the different imperialist countries must work in conjunction with the proletarian parties of the colonies" (No. 8).

Not much progress has yet been made in "Colonial countries" with this "United Front" of world labour. The European workers and the workers of subject races or dependent countries are not yet cooperating at all closely. To the delight of the capitalists, they are strangers, even antagonists to each other. Between the workers and the Home or Imperialist countries and those of India or China, for example, there is as yet no real labour union.

In the Pacific the North American and Australian workers are concerned less to cooperate with the Chinese and Japanese workers than to exclude them from their countries as dangerous competitors. In South Africa there is a great gulf fixed between the white and the black workers who jostle together in the country, and local barricades are thrown up entrenching the whites against black competition - and even vice versa. In the United States the negro workers are oppressed and lynched by the whites. Everywhere workers of European race are ready as often as not to take up arms against non-European workers as such. In South Africa, again, we had the strange spectacle this year of white miners on strike instructing their black fellow workers to remain at work, i.e., to scab!

And yet the whites and the non-white workers, when comprised in one country or Empire, may be called not merely fellow workers but fellow countrymen; we may fairly say, for instance, that the workers of the British Empire, "British workmen" in fact, are mostly brown or black men – "natives". Why then the antagonism? The common reply is "colour prejudice". That is certainly potent enough; and the Thesis says "The struggle against deep-rooted petty bourgeois national prejudices, manifesting themselves in various forms such as race hatred, national antagonism and anti-semitism" – we might add "nigrophobia" etc. – "must be brought to the foreground". But actual race prejudice plays a less conspicuous part where, as in Europe or Australia, the opposing races are not in direct contact with each other; thus in Europe colour prejudice is quite weak. The truth is that the prejudice itself is largely based on economic grounds; it is the result of competition in the labour market, and is most acute where such competition is most keenly felt.

This problem of "cheap labour" of subject or dependent coloured race is the one common feature of "colonial questions", though, of course, it arises also in connection with countries that are not "colonies" such as China and Japan. How can the better paid workers of European race be expected to unite with the cheaper labourers who take the bread out of their mouths? And on the other hand how can the cheap labourers cooperate with the better paid worker who habitually becomes their masters' accomplice in "keeping them in their place", closing various avenues of employment to them and even objecting to give them "equal pay for equal work"? How can the Japanese, African or Indian worker be expected to support a movement of men associated with a "White Australia" policy, a "colour bar", an embargo on Lascar sailors, or an anti-Asiatic immigration law? Not but what these things may be justified, but the coloured workers are not likely to see the point of them readily. Why, even in Soviet Russia today, in concerns involving no exploitation for profit, the employee at say 20–30 millions a month can see no justice in others getting 200–300 millions and "riding" as they say "on our necks". Nor does cooperation eventuate even where the competition is not consciously realised. The European workers, for instance, do not yet fully realise how they are injured by colonial labour competition; but they do not any the more for that combine with colonial labour. British congresses may occasionally wave distant greetings to the workers of India; but they still acquiesce in their grinding exploitation; in effect, they ignore the coloured labourers of the world as fellow workers.

How are these obstacles to be overcome? The Supplementary Thesis No. 7 says: "The C.I. and the parties affected must struggle to develop class consciousness in the working masses of the colonies"; and the importance of this is evidenced by the capitalists' profound dread of working class agitation among "natives". But even such agitation or organisation does not of itself produce the World United Labour Front, the "joint struggle", the cooperation and "union of the working masses of all countries" notwithstanding cuumaltive disparities of race, colour, language, pay, grade, standard of living and civilisation, such as is required by the C.I. Rather it seems that some atmosphere of cooperation is necessary before propaganda among the subject or dependent races can flourish; at any rate the two things are interdependent. In S. Africa and the U.S.A., at any rate, the majority of the white workers at present show violent hostility to the very idea of communist propaganda among the blacks, making such propaganda almost impossible for want of the white workers' approval; so much so that Communists in South Africa sometimes feel constrained to say: "Let us leave the natives alone, let them develop on their own lines"; whereas that can only mean "leave them to the sole influence of the capitalists, who will develop them on their own capitalist lines". We cannot leave the coloured workers alone. Men who are good enough to exploit are good enough to organise; especially in view of the enormous proportion of the world's profit that is made from the exploitation of this cheap coloured labour, and therefore the enormous potential anti-capitalist power of such labour – and under Communism this numerical proportion will be at least maintained: the great majority of the workers under communism will also be "natives". But again, even if the white workers should ask for the cooperation of the yellows or blacks, in some industrial dispute for instance, the latter will not unnaturally suspect that they are simply to be made use of and then left in the lurch again as usual after the whites have got what they wanted out of them. And yet the mutual advantage of industrial cooperation is obvious, for instance, between the workers of Europe and those of the Colonial countries (witness the French colonial scabs at Havre), still more perhaps between European and non-European workers in one country, as in the U.S.A. and South Africa.

The Communist Parties in the various countries, with the C.I. as the guiding hand, must therefore pay special attention to bridging this weakening estrangement, exactly as the estrangement in the U.S.A. between "100% American" workers and the cheap immigrant workers from South or Eastern Europe, or between skilled and unskilled workers anywhere, must be bridged. Solidarity and comradeship must be established for common effort against the common enemy. But now we hear the cry: "What, would you make the natives equal to the whites?" – for even that, and not merely making the white equal to the native, is objected to. Well, although questions of "social" equality may be dismissed as petty bourgeois, reactionary and irrelevant, because real equality can only be achieved after, not before, the revolution, yet there can be no doubt that in-as-much as inequality is a bar to cooperation, an attempt must be made before, not after, the revolution to mitigate it so far as necessary to facilitate cooperation, – and by levelling up rather than levelling down; which means that higher paid workers must support every demand of the cheaper workers for better pay. But, says the cheap coloured labourer, I too must live, whereas if I stipulate for nothing less than the white man's wage, I shall not get a job; to which the white worker retorts, if you come into my job (or my country) on a competitive basis, you can always bring my wages down and actually undercut me and take my job away – you are actually doing it all the time – and I too must live. Such obstacles, though mutually inconsistent, are not easy to surmount. But it is impossible to achieve a United Front by ignoring them and leaving each section to concentrate on entrenching itself against the other, with all-white trade unions on the one hand, and all-black trade unions (languishing for want of European support, as in South Africa) on the other. Admitting that it is not possible under capitalism to level up all wages, and that even if it were, the revolution cannot wait for such world wide equality, yet neither is it possible under capitalism to maintain the present glaring wage inequality and prevent the higher from being pulled down by the lower. The Communist movement is less concerned to seek measures designed to make capitalism tolerable to one or another section of workers than to marshal all possible forces for attack on the ruling class.

With this sole object before us, we should patiently and persistently promote conferences between the conflicting elements all over the world with a view to mutual recognition, popularisation of propaganda and organisation among the coloured workers, and in particular, some approach to a modus vivendi purely in order to facilitate a joint plan of campaign and a wholehearted and militant cooperation in the fight. The modus vivendi will be based probably on the principle of equal pay (at European rates) for equal work – not a Communist principle, but we are dealing with a fighting front under capitalism. Absolute "fairness" will be impossible even on this basis, but at least the ice can be broken. And if concessions are to be given, they should, as the Thesis says, be given rather to the underdog, so as to remove his distrust; e.g., sympathetic strikes should be called first in support of the coloured rather than the white workers' demands. And again, "proletarian internationalisation demands the subordination of the interests of the proletarian struggle in one country" (e.g., Australia, and, we might add, "in one section of the workers" e.g., the white workers of South Africa) "to the interests of that struggle on an international scale". Of course it is only when accompanied by a revolutionary outlook that any such modus vivendi can succeed. The point is not equality but solidarity.

A start is being made in the right direction with the Pacific Labour Congress next year. Similar foregatherings should be developed both on a small local scale and, say, within the British, French and Dutch Empires (Home and Colonial workers) respectively, and finally on a world scale. Negro Congresses and Oriental congresses as such no doubt serve a useful purpose, but more useful still for the object now in view is the confronting of these elements with the workers of the imperialist races, the yellow, brown and black with the whites, the common labourers with the "aristocrats of labour" who, often the more servile and ignorant of the two from a proletarian point of view, have the most to learn and unlearn at such mixed conferences.

In cases like South, West and East Africa, or the Pacific taken as one unit, or the United States, where a real national liberation movement of the coloured races is hardly practical politics and a peasant movement with any hope of success hardly exists among the coloured peoples, the only revolutionary movement of the subject races is the movement of their workers organised as workers. At least that movement must be stressed as an additional weapon, and not necessarily one to be postponed in order of time, for the Labour movement nothing comes first, all arms must be brought into action at once. And as the Supplementary Thesis says, "we must in any case struggle against control by bourgeois democratic national movements over the mass action of poor and ignorant peasants and workers for their liberation from all sorts of exploitation."

"Only a Soviet regime can give the nations real equality". National liberation movements, only stepping stones at best, and relevant only because in the countries to be liberated there are workers being exploited, are often destined, even if successful, to prove disappointing, besides failing to attract, if not alienating, the sympathy of the workers of other countries. It is as workers that whites and natives find their point of contact as well as of repulsion. The proletarian movement is, or eventually becomes, the strongest revolutionary weapon in every country; it is the One "Feste Burg", now and hereafter, of the oppressed and exploited of the whole world.

Document 9
Letter from W. H. Andrews to Tom Mann,[17] 26 December 1922

THE COMMUNIST PARTY

Central Executive Office.
Trades Hall
Johannesburg.
26-12-22

Dear Comrade Tom

Your letter from Port Elizabeth and report of the meeting from E. P. Herald just to hand also acknowledgement of amount paid you. There is no doubt that your tour has done a vast amount of good we feel the benefit in our organisation. We had touched rock bottom before you came and now a more buoyant spirit is in the air. The boys are recovering. Big propaganda meetings are held weekly outside the town hall and in other parts and our paper is selling more freely finances improving and we intend to resume weekly publication early in the new year. We have taken a nice new printing office nearer the centre of town with two year lease and option to purchase at £16 00. We shall be better away from the vicinity of Marshall Square. Bill [*Rostion?*] is delighted to be getting into a place where all the work can be done in one room. I am sorry to hear that Cape town has failed to arrange an extension of the tour and surprised to hear that the Australian tour is in some doubt. I was under the impression that it was practically settled. However you may yet get it fixed up.

The commutation of sentences is I think a tribute to the agitation started by the Communist Party and the fact that no more bodies of men executed will be allowed burial outside gaol shows that the big funeral demonstrations are effective.

The Durban Town Hall protest meeting was a surprise also and the red army proposition and its reception although of course only temporary enthusiasm shows the growth of an idea. The papers here are attacking Bunting and the Mail I think it was in a leader urged that he should not be allowed to land owing to his policy of educating + organising the native workers they are on the war path all right. + so are we so that's all right. With best wishes for the new Year and thanks + kindest regards from your friend + comrade

W H Andrews.

Document 10
Industrial and Commercial Workers' Union of Africa,[18]
Flyer announcing Third Annual Conference, 17 January 1923

Industrial & Commercial Workers' Union of Africa.

I. C. U.

— OUR —

Third Annual Conference

OPENS IN

THE MINOR HALL, CITY HALL

ON

WEDNESDAY, January 17, 1923, at 10 a.m. sharp.

ANNIVERSARY COMMEMORATION

MASS MEETING

Will be held on

THE GRAND PARADE

ON

Wednesday, January 17th, 1923, at 8 p.m. sharp.

Do you know what this is going to be? Five years ago you knew nothing of a "Labour

Conference" being held by African workers. On this evening you will see for yourselves Delegates sent by various centres to a Labour Conference. What a remarkable change! How did it come about? Come and see. Come and hear for yourself,

COME ONE AND ALL.

Printed by A. HOLDER, 39, Church Street, and published by the I.C.U. Head Office, 50 Bree Street, Cape Town, where further information can be had.

Document 11
Industrial and Commercial Workers' Union of Africa, *Annual Conference Agenda*, St Phillips School, Chapel Street, District 6, Cape Town, 18 January 1923

1. Minimum or Standard rate of wages for all the African Workers throughout South. Conditions of the Railways workers also to be considered.
2. International Labour Conference under the League of Nations.
3. Compensation to the dependents of the Port Elizabeth Victims in Native Disturbance, October 23rd, 1920.
4. Wages Board as contemplated to be re-introduced in Parliament.
5. Acquiring a Printing Plant and Press for the Organisation.
6. Acquiring a Building for the Organisation at the Head Office.
7. "One Big Union" movement for the African workers, embracing skilled and unskilled, throughout South Africa.
8. Propaganda Fund for One Big Union movement.
9. Labour Bureau in all industrial centres controlled by the Organisation.
10. Consideration of Schools in arrears not provided for the African children.
11. Erection of a Memorial to the Victims of the Port Elizabeth tragedy October 23rd, 1920.
12. Anniversary Commemmoration.
13. Policy of the "I.C.U." in reference to Politics.
14. Consideration of Agricultural Labourers.
15. Review discussion on Sanitorium for the Natives Workers on the Mine
16. Revision of the Constitution and to decide as to Languages in which the Constitution to be printed into.
17. Revision of the Capitation Fee.
18. Report on the work of the General Executive Council, including General Secretary's report for year 1922.
19. Organiser-in-Chief's yearly report.
20. The Acting President-General's report on his tour.
21. Revision of the administrative work of the Organisation.
22. Uniform Badges.
23. Organisation of the Female workers according to Constitution.
24. Impeachment of the Organiser-in-Chief.

Document 12
Letter from T. W. Thibedi[19] to E. R. Roux[20], 27 January 1927

27 January 1927

Mr E R Roux
53 Lensfield Road
Cambridge
England

Dear Comrade

Your letter of the 5th January has been received last night unexpectently. Although when you left South Africa in promised to write us soon when you get we were all surprised that you didnt, still we are pleased to see that you still think of our study class here at 11 Main St, Johannesburg. When we saw that you do not write to us we native students thought that the Capitalists steamer you took and the education they are giving you has changed you from when we (natives) know you to be. Comrade I am writing this being 8.30am and it must be posted before 9am. otherwise shall have to remain until Thursday next week. So allow me to tell you about our Natives Comrades here in South Africa.

Kadalie, Champion, Thomas Mbeki, James Dippa, Theo B Linjiza, De Nor, B.C.R. Mazingi, H.D. Tzamsashe + Co have left the revolutionary camp and moved to the Law + Order camp.[21] There is no freedom of speech in the I.C.U. at all more especially who are known to be the revolutionary camp.

When you write to Lionel, Regina Malemela Ronald as you say you will please encourage Petrosi Malemela + Ronald Kwenyama to attend meetings of the Party. More especially Group Meeting Y.C.L. Meetings on Wednesday night at M'4 Trades Hall and encourage them all to attend open air meetings. I am asked although dismissed by Kadalie Champion + Co for refusing to leave the revolutionary camp + for having given the report you know in Cornelia Mine on the 23 July 1926 to speak in Pretoria on the 30/1/27 by the I.C.U. branch there. I am leaving on Saturday morning coming back on Monday morning but Kadalie Champion and Co does not know that I have been invited by that branch.

What does our C.P. there do in order to stop its soldiers from going to kill the innocent Chinese?[22]

Will you please get me in touch with J. P. Campbell and H. Palliotte both of the C.P.[23] I wish to correspond with them. Are you coming back to South Africa next year?

With best regards from students at 11 Main St, Johannesburg.

Yours for a speedy revolution
T. W. Thibedi
c/o Communist Party
P.O. Box 4179
Johannesburg

Document 13
Letter from John Gomas[24] to C. F. Glass[25], 31 May 1927

24 Parkin Street
Capetown
31st May, 1927.

Mr. C. F. Glass
JOHANNESBURG.

Dear Comrade

As I have promised you when you were in Cape Town that I will communicate with you with regard to the Tailors' Union, I did not do so earlier because I was waiting for some definite decisions that were to arise from the negotiations between the employers and the employees of the Tailoring Industry locally. This broke down. They could not come to any understanding. The bosses were only prepared to pay an average wage per week of £2.10. Our bargainers accepted this at first, but our members at a General Meeting turned it furiously down. Thus the deadlock.

We are now waiting on the Wage Board to lay down a system of wages and conditions. At a General Meeting held on 27th May it was decided to recommend to the Wage Board to do away with "fixed rates" and institute a "time basis". That a beginner will start with 17/6 per week up to £6 a journeyman. Women to receive the same wages as men.

This no doubt you will see, must necessitate a complete reorganisation of the present chaotic state of the Tailoring Industry. What I would like to know, how you had it settled in Joh'burg before the lapse of your agreement and what is the conditions of your new agreement, if that is settled? Have you done away with piece work?

The question of amalgamation I had not yet had the chance to raise. We are very young yet as an organisation and our superiors of the Federation of Trades gives us very little opportunity to meddle with such wider questions. I may say, we are not leading ourself yet. Our Chairman is Mr Riddal of the S.A.T.U.; Stuart, Secretary; and Lindie, E.C. member of the Federation, Treasurer. I have broached the more influential members on it and they certainly favour the idea. But I shall press the question at the next available opportunity. And I think the time is becoming more opportune now in view of the conversations between the Executives of the T.U.C. and the C.F.L.U. and consequently a referendum of their affiliated unions will be taken "on the proposal to set up a joint committee to explore the possibilities of bringing about complete co-operation". This is fortunate.[26] But we will have to press from the bottom against self-aggrandisement, which is the cause of the present aloofness.

When are you falling back into the "fold". I don't think you have made yourself ineligible for membership of the Party, as far as I know?

Thanking you in anticipation,
Yours fraternally
(Sgd.) JOHN GOMAS

P.S. Our union have changed from sections into one "Garment Workers' Union".

Document 14
Letter from C. F. Glass to John Gomas, 7 June 1927

7th June 1927

Mr John Gomas
24 Parkin Street
CAPE TOWN.

Dear Comrade Gomas,

Many thanks for your letter dated 31st, ultimo, giving information concerning the position of the tailoring industry in the Cape Peninsula.

Concerning the proposal of your Union to abolish piecework, I heartily concur in the same. At all times piecework is an unsatisfactory system, as it tends towards intensified sweat. Piecework rates are, also, never stable. So soon as an employer finds an employee earning more than he would earn on the time system he promptly reduces the piecework rate. This has been my experience. In the Transvaal, several attempts have been made to secure the abolition of piecework, but without success. After a long study of the question I have come to the conclusion that the bespoke tailoring industry in South Africa has not come under the modernising influence of capitalism. It still retains most of the characteristics of the handicraft system known to the middle ages, particularly in respect of the relation between employer and employee, which is largely a personal one and seems to correspond to the social types of guildmaster and journeyman.

Hence it seems to me that the piecework and sub-contracting system will persist for many years to come, for it is impossible to impose modern capitalist conditions on an industry which is but a relic of medieval times. When the Industry grows larger it will automatically adjust itself to present-day conditions. But it would be idle to attempt to impose modern methods on an effete system. Only large-scale production can accomplish any radical change, and it appears that that is a long way off as far as the tailoring industry is concerned in this country.

Regarding the question of amalgamation, I note that you will take the earliest opportunity of getting it discussed by the Union. There are far too many organisations for such a small industry, and they are all more or less ineffective. A national Union could, however, accomplish a power of good.

I hope you will keep in touch with me regularly as co-operation between the different centres is essential if progress is to be made. I am in regular communication with the Tailor's Unions in Durban, East London and Port Elizabeth and am keeping the idea of a national union constantly before them.

With kind regards to all comrades – remember me to Pick, Wolton, Harrison and Walt.

I remain,
Yours fraternally,
(Sgd.) C. F. Glass
GENERAL SECRETARY.

Document 15
E. R. Roux, *Black and White Trade Unionism in South Africa*, 28 July 1928[27]

Until recent years there was no native trade unionism in South Africa. The first trade unions in the country were white unions of skilled workers. Most of their members were immigrants from Britain and some of the unions, like the Amalgamated Engineering Union, were simply South African branches of organisations which had their headquarters in Britain. The membership of the white unions was and still is very largely English-speaking. During and since the war there has been an increase in the number of Dutch-speaking (Afrikaans) workers in the unions, as a result of the drift into the towns of large numbers of landless whites from the country districts. The Afrikaner, however, has been slow in taking up trade unionism and even in unions in which the rank and file is preponderatingly Dutch, such as the White miners' union, the majority of organisers, officials and active members are British. However, in the younger generation of White trade union leaders there is an increasing number of Afrikaners.

A few of the White unions admit native and coloured members, but only in the Cape Province. Some national unions, such as the Typographical Union, have a few non-Europeans in their Cape branches but no coloured members are allowed in the Transvaal and Orange Free State branches of the same Union. A similar position exists in the Building Workers' Industrial Union. In general even in the Cape the number of non-Europeans in "White" unions is very small; often a mere handful. Exceptions are the Cape furniture workers union, which has a majority of coloured members and some branches of the building workers.

In the Transvaal the only White union which had non-European members is the Furniture Workers Union. (Secretary Comrade Kalk of the Central Executive of C.P.)[28] This contains about 25 persons of coloured members. Natives (aboriginals) however, are not admitted, though there are a number employed in the trade.

Some of the White Unions are affiliated to the South African Trade Union Congress, with headquarters at Johannesburg; some are affiliated to the Cape Federation; the majority are unaffiliated. A working agreement exists between the Cape Federation and the TUC. The total number of White trade unionists in the country is about 80 000. Of these the TUC claims not more than 20 000.

NATIVE TRADE UNIONISM. The native organisation, the Industrial and Commercial Workers' Union, (I.C.U.) only possesses some of the characteristics of a trade union. In reality it is a loose political organisation with an individual membership organised in territorial branches. Most of its slogans are political ones, though it has also demanded all-round increases in wages for native workers. It has so far failed to departmentalise itself and to organise particular categories of workers. The result has been its failure as a trade union, though (before the complete corruption of its leadership) it rallied large masses of native workers and peasants in a general protest against unbearable economic, social and political oppression.

Up to the end of 1926, the Communist Party had considerable influence in the executive of the I.C.U. (indeed it claims the original parentage of the I.C.U.) This influence was used to try to secure the carrying out of a more militant policy and especially the development of real trade union activity.

By 1926 it was becoming obvious that unless the I.C.U. justified its existence on the industrial field, stagnation would set in. It was no use talking about strikes and promising higher wages if nothing was done to put this policy into practice. The I.C.U. had conducted no strikes for years.

X) It has only conducted 3 or 4 strikes in its whole nine years of existence and the only one of any magnitude was the dock strike of 1919.

It was becomind evident that Kadalie, the leader of the union, was not prepared to carry out the militant policy for which it has been organised.

Kadalie, whose supreme authority in the I.C.U. had previously not been challenged, found his position threatened by the presence of Communists on his executive. With the growing discontent of the members, as it became evident that Kadalie's promises of higher wages would not be fulfilled, it became necessary that something should be done. It was done! November 1926. Four Communists on the executive were expelled and Kadalie openly began to preach "sane trade unionism" and the renunciation of the strike weapon.

To-day the I.C.U. LEADERSHIP is thoroughly corrupt. The organisation is suffering from serious internal breakdown and its membership and prestige are declining, while the Natal section, the most important numerically and financially has succeeded from the main body.

The Communist party has given up its attempt to persuade the I.C.U. to reorganise itself on a trade union basis. Instead the C.P. itself has set about the organisation of native trade unions. Already considerable successes have been achieved in this direction. The following unions are now in existence on the Witwatersrand (membership in June 1928 in brackets):

Native Laundry Workers' Union (600); Clothing Workers' Union (323); Bakery Workers' Union (120); Native Transport Workers' Union (75); Mattress and Furniture Workers' Union (60).

These unions are united in the Federation of Native Trade Unions.[29] It must be understood that these organisations are still in a very young and growing stage. Already a number of strikes have been conducted.

The most important of these from one point of view was the strike in tailoring workshops at Germiston, near Johannesburg, in May 1928. The strike was called by the Witwatersrand Tailors' Association (a white union) as a result of the dismissal of three tailoresses who had taken an active part in organising the union. The native clothing workers, through their organisation approached the White workers with an offer to come out in their support. This offer was accepted and the 120 native workers concerned came out on strike. The number of White strikers involved was 400. The strike was a complete success. As far as we know this is the first occasion in the history of the labour movement in South Africa on which White and Black trade unionists have co-operated in an industrial dispute.

A strike conducted by the clothing workers Union in Johannesburg did not have as fortunate a result. The native clothing workers in a certain factory went on strike as a result of the victimisation of their leader. The native workers in other factories came out in support. Altogether over 200 workers were involved, but in the tailoring industry the majority of workers are whites. The Witwatersrand Tailors Association refused to call out its members in support in spite of the fact that their organisation had been assisted by the C.W.U. in the Germiston dispute.[30]

The police intervened and arrested many of the strikers under the powers given by the Urban Areas Act "for being away from work without permission." Of these 73 were sentenced to £1 find or ten days imprisonment. Five others were prosecuted under the Riotous Assemblies Act and sentenced to fines of from £5 to £7.10/- with the alternative of imprisonment from a month to six weeks. The union was forced to declare the strike off after the men had been out for two weeks. In spite of the defeat the union has increased in strength after the return to work an indication of the growing class consciousness of the native workers. Successful strikes were conducted last month (June) by the Native Laundry Workers' Union in two laundries in Johannesburg.

The Communist party is being inundated with requests to form trade unions from the native workers in numerous industries. At the present moment the Party is scarcely able to comply with these requests owing to the shortage of capable organisers both black and white.

The effect of the new tactic upon the I.C.U. is seen in the fact that that organisation offered its assistance to the Clothing Workers during their strike and Kadalie addressed a meeting of the strikers in the Communist Hall at Johannesburg! Kadalie who repudiated the strike weapon!

OUR ATTITUDE TOWARDS THE I.C.U. The C.P. attitude towards the I.C.U. is briefly as follows: the I.C.U.'s claim to be an "all-in" trade union of native workers is not justified by the facts, since the I.C.U. has consistently failed to do real trade union work among the natives. By forming industrial unions among the natives, we are not "poaching" on the I.C.U.; for the I.C.U. has never attempted to organise these workers. A few of the natives who have come into the new unions may be individual members of the I.C.U.; but that fact has no organisational significance for us; we regard the I.C.U. as a reformist political organisation with a social-democratic structure. Of course we are prepared to make a united front with the I.C.U. leadership to the extent that it is prepared to champion the cause of the native workers. For instance it would have been a wrong tactic to prevent Kadalie speaking to the native C.W.U. strikers after the I.C.U. had offered its support. Of course the opportunity presented itself to reprimand Kadalie from the same platform for his former acts of treachery and to explain to the strikers that a leader who is a friend to-day and an enemy to-morrow is of little value. Whether this was done or not we do not know. This meeting occurred after the delegation left South Africa. In any case it is difficult to lay down a formula for such situations.

As far as the rank and file of the I.C.U. is concerned we should try to win them over to the C.P. in the same way that the German C.P. tries to win over workers from the Social Democrats. Rank and file members of the I.C.U. should *not* be regarded as trade unionists: they are nothing of the kind. The C.P.S.A. should perhaps visualise the possible complete disbanding of the I.C.U. and in any case work for the exposure of its reactionary leadership. This can be and has been done under the general tactic and challenges of the united front. Native political organisations in S. Africa are in such a state of flux that any obsession with regard to the permanence of such bodies as the I.C.U. will only result in serious mistakes being made. We should not help the I.C.U. to crystalise into a solid reformist organisation. Its present state of decay and disintegration is favourable to the further growth of the Communist Party.

IN THE WHITE UNIONS. In spite of the fact that we have only a small number of unionists in the C.P. a large proportion of our trade unionist members hold leading positions in their organisations and are on the General Council of the T.U.C. Our Party is thus able to pull a certain weight as a minority in the T.U.C. It must be understood however that there is no corresponding militant pro-native minority among the rank and file of white trade unionists. When the T.U.C. executive gives public support to the struggle of the native workers this is not due to pressure from the rank and file. On the contrary, the leaders often prove more radical than the trade union membership. Those white trade union leaders who are against the affiliation of the I.C.U. to the T.U.C. but who favour some form of co-operation between black and white workers often excuse themselves by saying that the rank and file will desert the unions if the leaders pursue a pro-native policy. There is a large amount of truth in this. It is often possible to get the T.U.C. executive to pass resolutions (e.g., the resolution endorsing the wage demands of native workers in Bloemfontein in 1925 and the protest against the ban on Kadalie in 1926) which would never stand a chance in the branch meetings of the vast majority of affiliated unions.

It is necessary to understand this difference between the leadership and the rank and file in order to understand the reaction of the T.U.C. leaders to the I.C.U.'s application for affiliation. At the end of last year the I.C.U. applied for affiliation to the T.U.C. on the basis of 100,000 members. The T.U.C. at that time had established in conjunction with the Cape Federation a joint body known as the S.A. Trade Union Co-ordinating Committee. The question of I.C.U. affiliation was considered by this body which issued a memorandum on the subject. The memorandum was a very carefully worded and more or less non-committal document. It pointed out that some recognition would have to be given to the growing political and industrial organisation of the native workers. At the same time it declared that the affiliation of the I.C.U. on the basis of 100,000 members would enable the I.C.U. on a card vote to out-weigh the combined votes of all the white unions "if a division occurred on racial lines", which eventually was thought to be very probable. It was pointed out that the I.C.U. would probably not in any case be able to pay £5,000 yearly in dues, which would be the sum necessary if affiliation took place on the basis of 100,000 members. (This statement subsequently called forth the most violent retorts on the part of the I.C.U. leaders who resented this slur upon their honesty and claimed that their organisation was in an extraordinarily sound position and quite capable of paying the sum required. The fact that four months later the I.C.U. was in the midst of an internal crisis in which the officials were accusing each other of mishandling the funds of the organisation, perhaps shows that this righteous indignation was only a cloak to cover up a very unsound state of affairs within.)

The memorandum suggested that the affiliation of the I.C.U. on the basis of 5,000 members might be possible. In general it favoured joint discussions between the T.U.C. and native workers organisations rather than affiliation at the present stage.

At a meeting of joint executives of the T.U.C. in January 1928 the memorandum of the Co-ordinating Committee was considered. The meeting finally by a large majority endorsed the memorandum, i.e., it was in favour of joint discussions with the I.C.U. but was against affiliation. The Communists voted for full affiliation and the extreme right wing voted against any form of co-operation with the I.C.U.

The I.C.U. in reply refused to accept the offer of joint meetings and declared that as it represented the native workers who were the majority of workers in the country it had the right to dominate any trade union federation in which it happened to be in a majority. The Johannesburg "Star" the organ of the mine owners, came out with headlines "Native workers turned down by T.U.C." etc., though it was obvious that the T.U.C. had made what was really a forward step in making an offer for joint discussions and that the most reactionary and race-prejudiced section of white trade unionists had been defeated.

The decision of the I.C.U. not to accept the offer of the T.U.C. may be considered as a defeat of the forces favouring united front of black and white workers. It has played into the hands of the racialists in both camps.

(24/10/28)
Since Ballinger came the I.C.U. has accepted the T.U.C. offer for joint meetings and the first of these has been held.

Document 16
Letter from Clements Kadalie to E. R. Roux, 10 October 1928

INDUSTRIAL and COMMERCIAL
Workers Union of Africa
(I.C.U.)
NATIONAL COUNCIL

14 MARKET STREET,
JOHANNESBURG.
SOUTH AFRICA.
10th October, 1928.

E. R. Roux,
53, Lensfield Road,
Cambridge.

Dear Roux,

Dr. Norman Leys, of Bailsford, was good enough to send me your original letter you wrote to him with regard to myself and the I.C.U.

Your letter is libelous as well as deceitful when you speak very high of your Party in this country. With your Party, you are not making any success as you are made to understand by your remnants here. On the contrary, the I.C.U. is making remarkable progress under the leadership of Comrade Ballinger, its Adviser.[31] We are establishing Minimum Wages in various parts of the country; meeting Farmers' Organisation. Bear in mind, not a "Good Boy" Union is doing this kind of work, but the original I.C.U.. We are fighting the Pass Laws too; I was arrested after a big speech I made at Pretoria in denounciation of the system, but I won in Courts. Your Party does nothing in this direction, except making usual fruitless noise.

Now let me come to the true object of this letter. Your letter is libelous. I am consulting my Attorneys about it. You say "KADALIE IS AS MUCH A ROGUE AS ANY OF THE OTHERS." You have to prove this. You say also that the finances of the I.C.U. were bad long before and you did not like to expose us then. If that is correct, any sensible person will agree with me that your

–Party–

is rotten to the core since it conived a crime. Of the finances of the I.C.U. your Party only got its information from La Guma, Khaile and Gomas. None of them can say anything ill against me in that connection. But your Party deciced the I.C.U. and you were hopeless and deceitful as Bunting is. I now refer to the way your manager turned both myself and Tyamzashe, our Sub-editor from your premises and threw copy of the Workers Herald in the Street. You are deceitful, because your Party got a lot of moneys from the I.C.U. through your printing press and also propaganda meetings.

Now let me tell you in plain language. Whether I do get pay or not, I shall never join the Communist Party, either in this counrty or in Europe. I studied International politics last year during my so-journ in Europe. I found out the worth of your party in Europe with the exception of Russia, wher I did not go. Perhaps you think that if the I.C.U. were to kick me out to-day I shall join your Party. That is a grave mistake on your party and your click, if you think so. I believe in Socialism and not in Communism with its violence methods.

You are afraid to get I.C.U. literature, because it will prove to you conclusively of its progress under the new regime. I learned a lot last year in Europe and upon my return to this country, I was doing everything to improve the I.C.U. but unfortunately some of my colleagues hampered my work. At last Comrade Ballinger came and he is doing splendid work for African Trade Unionism than the Communist Part has done for many years. The Chamber of Mines or the Joint Councils have nothing to do with the I.C.U. You speak of Mr Howard Pim or Mr Rheinaldt Jones[32], but you should remember that those who were pioneers of Socialism or Communism, held from well-to-do families. For example Karl Marx, Robert Owen, etc. Messrs Howard Pim, Rheinaldt Jones, etc., are helping the I.C.U. in its fight against the Pass Laws, while your Party is silent.

Truly yours,

Clements Kadalie
General Secretary.

Document 17
Letter from E. R. Roux to W. G. Ballinger, 19 March 1929

53 Lensfield rd.
Cambridge
19 March 1929

Dear Ballinger,

Thanks very much for your letter and the report on Kadalie' resignation.

I do not think you have seriously altered the main conclusions of my article. Of course we all believe we are more virtuous than other people. In this matter of the I.C.U. and the Communists I think any unbiassed observer would admit that the balance of virtue lies with the C.P. Kadalie's expulsion of the Communists is on a par with his other acts of treachery and opportunism. You have catalogued many of Kadalie's sins. Are you prepared to add this to the list? Now that Kadalie is out of the way, are you willing to agree to the re-admission of the Communists to the I.C.U.? Your answer to this question will decide whether we are justified in continuing to regard you as a right-winger or not.

The points on which the C.P. insists are: real trade union organisation; strike action not to be ruled out; and freedom of all workers to join the unions (i.e., the lifting of the ban on the Communists). If Howard Pim and Professor Brookes[33] are prepared to assist on this basis, we shall welcome whatever help they can give. But to allow Pim and company to obtain control of the Native trade union movement would be disastrous even from an I.L.P. point of view.

If, as you say, only a miracle can save the I.C.U., perhaps it would be worth while not waiting for the miracle. The Native Trade Union Federation is still young and comparatively weak but it has been established on sound lines and as far as I can judge at this distance is developing in a healthy manner. Why not start here? There is no nasty mess to be cleaned up first, as in the case of the I.C.U. I admit the tremendous difficulties attached to building a Native trade union and I know you have been having an awful time trying to put the I.C.U. house in order. My own idea is to start with a less ambitious programme, building up one trade union at a time and seeing that it functions as a trade union. This is what has happened in the case of the Laundry workers, Native tailors and other unions attached to the SANTUF. There is a tremendous lot of work to be done and very few people to do it. Personally I am prepared to work with anyone who is prepared to work with me on the lines set forth above and I think you will find that the CP itself will adopt a similar attitude. I should like to know more about your offer to the Native Federation. Not knowing any of the details I cannot express an opinion.

If you can convince me that you are not a right-winger according to my definition, I am prepared to write to the "Labour Monthly" withdrawing my statement to that effect.[34]

I hope to return to Africa some time this year. As for the road I visualise, I shall be very interested if not too happy, to travel along it.

Yours sincerely
E. R. Roux.

Document 18
Letter from S. P. Bunting to the South African Federation of Native Trade Unions, 20 September 1930

COPY.

41a Fox Street,
JOHANNESBURG.
September 20th 1930.

The S.A.F.N.T.U.
27a Ferreira Street,
JOHANNESBURG.

Dear Comrades,

Three requests from you or your Secretary were before the last meeting of the Party Executive, one for the use of a table and two chairs belonging to the Party, one for financial assistance for the sending of delegates to the All-in Trade Union Conference at Cape Town, and one for the use of the Party Hall for a social for the same purpose.

The Executive unanimously agreed that the hall be granted but that at the same time I should state that the Party cannot ignore the serious fact that the Federation has seen fit behind the Party's back to appoint as its General Secretary a member expelled from the Party on a serious charge and that until the intolerable situation thus created has been liquidated it is very difficult for the Party, ardently as it desires to assist the Trade Unions, to deal normally with them or the Federation. For this reason no reply can be given to the request for funds and no permission for the removal of the furniture. As a matter of fact the furniture has been removed without permission and the Executive requests its return accordingly.

It is earnestly hoped that your Federation instead of continually adopting an attitude of defiance or hostility to the Party will take the necessary steps to restore that harmonious cooperation between the Party and the Federation which is the essence of its existence. In this connection I may refer you to the concluding paragraph of the Executive's letter of a couple months back to your present Secretary reading as follows:

> 30th June 1930.
> Let us add that your potential abilities in the movement are still recognised no less than your shortcomings and that once it becomes clear that they would once again as heretofore be wholeheartedly and honestly devoted to the single purpose of loyally working for, in and under the Party, the Executive for its part would gladly take up the question of your reinstatement especially as the labourers are still far too few for the harvest.

On the subject of the hall the Executive in its turn has to remind you and the individual unions concerned that in spite of many requests in the past neither the Federation nor any of the Unions has ever contributed anything towards the rent of the hall although it is from the rank and file bodies that funds should be forthcoming. The Party Executive has no source of funds apart from them. The Executive therefore asks for financial support from the Trade Unions to the amount of 10/- per month per union and I trust that you will give the matter your serious and immediate attention.

The active cooperation of the Unions is asked for the campaign now being organized by a Joint Committee including representatives of the Unions, the Independent I.C.U. a section of the A.N.C. etc., for resistance to the Pass Laws. A Conference on the campaign will be held at the Inchcape Hall on Sunday, October 26th, next and it is hoped that all the Unions will send representatives and will attend in force. Coupled with this is a leaflet campaign on the Mines to familiarise the Mineworkers with the idea of trade unionism and the formation of a great Mineworkers' Union, and your assistance is also asked the task of getting these leaflets distributed in the Mine compounds and wherever else Mineworkers can be reached. They will be ready for distribution in a few days time.

Yours fraternally,
S. P. BUNTING,
ACTING SECRETARY.

Document 19
Communist Party of South Africa, Memo on S.A.F.N.T.U. (1930)

COPY.

"*S.A.F.N.T.U.:* Three requests from this body (which had reopened its office at Ferreira Street Johannesburg) were before the Executive. One was contained in a note from T.W. Thibedi to the Secretary asking for the use of a table and two chairs belonging to the Party, to which the Secretary had replied that he would bring the matter before this meeting. It appeared however that in the meantime Thibedi had taken the table and chairs without waiting for permission. A motion that the Federation be allowed this furniture received three votes for and three votes against, and the Chairman gave his casting vote against.

The next was contained in a letter from T.W. Thibedi as General Secretary of the S.A.F.N.T.U. asking the Party to raise funds for the purpose of sending delegates to the All-in Trade Union Conference at Cape Town. On a motion to reply merely that the Party could not raise funds even for its own needs voting was again equal, and the Chairman, being taunted with wanting to vote in a way to please a particular member of the Committee, declined this time to vote.

The third request was put forward verbally by Com. Nzula[35], asking for the use of the Party Hall for a social to raise funds for the same purpose. Hitherto even during the present controversy the Federation had taken the hall without asking leave, still more without paying or offering any rent, and it appeared clear that all these requests were put forward in order to make propaganda against the Party among the Trade Unions in the event of their being refused. It was agreed that the hall be granted but in conveying this decision to state that the Party cannot ignore the serious fact that the Federation had appointed as its General Secretary a member expelled from the party on a serious charge and that until the intolerable situation thus created had been liquidated it was very difficult for the Party, ardently as it desired to assist the Trade Unions, to deal normally with them or the Federation, adding that for this reason no reply could be given to the request for funds and no permission for the removal of the furniture, which must be returned in view of the circumstances of the removal. The voting in favour of this formula was unanimous, the previous voting having been as follows: Coms. Sepeng, Sipobe and Nzula against Coms. Soreson, and R and S. P. Bunting."

Document 20
Letter from S. P. Bunting to the Secretary, Communist Party of South Africa, 22 September 1930

THE COMMUNIST PARTY OF SOUTH AFRICA

P.O. Box 4197,
JOHANNESBURG.
September 22nd 1930.

The Secretary, C.P.
P.O. Box 1176,
CAPE TOWN.

Dear Comrade,

In reply to a letter from Com. Roux of the 18th inst., regarding a telegram signed Thibedi the Executive has hitherto not been able to give any directive because it was itself divided. At our last Executive Committee meeting, however, unanimity was bought at the expense of a grant of the hall (which costs the Party nothing except that the Trade Unions have never contributed a penny towards rent) the Thibedites thereupon consenting to the inclusion of the 'formula' remarks about the intolerable situation etc., referred to in the Minutes (unconfirmed) of which I enclose an extract, not of course for publication. On the request for financial assistance the same formula had been put forward as an amendment to a mere reply that we had no money (which was all the reply the Thibedites were willing to give) but it could not be carried for the reasons stated in the Minutes. I also enclose copy of my consequential letter to the Federation.

Thibedi has a certain following among the old Trade Union members, and as you will see the Party is somewhat in the position of a person being blackmailed, as, if on account of Thibedi it runs counter to the Federation, it is denounced as an enemy of the workers.

You ask whether the Thibedi telegram was official? Well, on the 14th instant some nineteen people met in our hall who called themselves the Federation and elected Thibedi General Secretary of the Federation.

As regards the olive branch held out in the Party's letter to Thibedi of 30th June last (written in reply to a request for reinstatement, and never replied to by him), his defiance of the Party since, amounting to very serious mischiefmaking, has been such as to convince me for one that whether or not he was justifiably expelled he deserves to remain outside now. Possibly or probably however the affair will be "liquidated" by an undertaking from him to be a good boy henceforward – the value of which must remain a matter of opinion meanwhile.

As regards the importance of the S.A.F.N.T.U. being represented on October 4 in the present circumstances this must likewise remain a matter of opinion as the Executive has not been able to declare officially on the subject. I for one might say better drop out this time, as the position is tainted and representation amounts to an insolent repudiation of elementary discipline; but others would retort that in this way the party is showing its hostility to the native trade union movement. In circumstances like these I can hardly travel outside my minuted instructions; even this letter travels outside them.

As regards letters from Richfield to Nzula I do not feel able to do more than ask

Com. Nzula at the next Executive to produce them. I do not know what they are about. Nzula tells me Thibedi has the letters; so I don't expect to see them.

Thibedi came to me for a donation to delegates expenses: I refused.

G.K. Solundurana, Box 75 Brakpan says he paid 5/ annual sub to Umsebenzi & never got the paper. Please put him on the list. He paid the money to Nzula, but must be credited with it.., say from 1 April.

Yours fraternally
S. P. Bunting
Actg Sec

Document 21
Letter from S. P. Bunting to E. R. Roux, 27 October 1930

42 & 43, Asher's Buildings,
Corner Fox & Joubert Streets.
Johannesburg.
October 27th 1930.

E. R. Roux,
P.O. Box 1176,
CAPE TOWN.

Dear Roux,

I posted you yesterday copies of the resolutions passed at the Anti-Pass Conference with three paragraphs of general report at the foot. At the end of the first of these three paragraphs after the word 'districts' make a semi-colon and add "also delegates (European and Coloured) from the South African Trades & Labour Council and the Furniture and Garment Worker's Unions who gave short addresses of greeting to the Conference".

In your letter of the 17th instant you wrote about Solly's article. We did not know anything about this article but he seems indignant that you did not publish it. I offered to telegraph to you for the article so that we could discuss it in the Executive but he prefers to write to you asking you to publish it after all. We have no idea of what it contains but from the proceedings of his Industrial Committee of which he has probably sent your Industrial Committee a copy of the Minutes, I gather that he has assimilated the Moscow pontifical style of pointing out "errors" and scolding for them and seeing no good in the Conference. I ventured a criticism of his Minutes accordingly at the last Executive but he says he has read the Minutes of the Conference and is more of the same opinion than ever.[36]

Our Inchcape Hall Conference was an interesting exposure of the orthodox leaders and also a revelation of grit on the part of I think most of those on the floor, but after all even if there were 600 people present what a flea bite that is out of [*remainder missing*].

NOTES

1 James Keir Hardie (1856–1915) was a Scottish miner who became a trade unionist and journalist and, from 1892 to 1895 and 1900 to 1915, a Member of Parliament. From 1893 he was associated with the Independent Labour Party in Britain, which opposed the British military campaign against the Boers during the Anglo-Boer War of 1899 to 1902. This extract is taken from Hughes (n.d.: 131-2).
2 J. Connolly edited the National Union of Railway and Harbour Servants newspaper and was Labour M.P. for Ladysmith in the Natal Parliament.
3 Archie Crawford (1883-1924) is described by the Simonses (1983:141) as "labour's most notable maverick until Smuts had him deported in 1914". Born in Scotland and a fitter by trade, Crawford came to South Africa as a soldier during the Anglo-Boer War, where he became a trade union activist and a Labour councillor. He published the *Voice of Labour* between 1908 and 1912. The 1914 general strike was catalysed by the government's decision to retrench railway workers in the National Union of Railway and Harbour Servants on Christmas Eve 1913. Martial law was imposed from January to March 1914. Crawford was one of the nine strike leaders abducted from jail by the government and deported to Britain without trial on 30 January. In addition to Crawford, the "deported nine" included: J. T. Bain, H. J. Poutsma, R. B. Waterston, G. Mason, D. McKerrill, W. Livingstone, A. Watson and W. H. Morgan. They were repatriated later that year. Crawford subsequently built up the SAIF, which maintained a white labour policy, and became Secretary of the SAIF in 1922. Hardie's reference to the "deported nine" indicates that this account of his 1907 visit was written well after that date.
4 The SALP was formed in 1910 out of a merger of several groups. It combined an advocacy of white labour policies with a socialist objective. Although modelled on the British Labour Party, trade unions did not form an organic element within the SALP structure. Its electoral popularity peaked in 1920 and thereafter declined. It formed the Pact electoral alliance with the NP in 1924 and from 1943 to 1958 formed electoral pacts with the UP. In 1958 it lost all its Parliamentary seats.
5 James Ramsay MacDonald (1866-1937) was born in Scotland and became a member of the British Independent Labour Party from 1894. He was the first General Secretary of the Labour Representation Committee (later the Labour Party). A prolific writer on socialist questions and a critic of Britain's involvement in World War One, he was a Labour M.P. from 1906 to 1918 and 1922 to 1931. He was Labour Prime Minister from January to October 1924 and June 1929 to August 1931. From August 1931 to 1935 he led a National Government opposed to Labour.
6 In 1906 Natal successfully suppressed what would be the last Zulu military uprising, led by Chief Bambatha. The importation of indentured Indian labour to work on Natal sugar plantations commenced in 1860 and ended in 1911, with the last contract worked out by 1916. Chinese workers were imported on three-year contracts to perform unskilled labour in South Africa's gold mines from 1904 to 1907. By 1910 the last contract had expired and all workers repatriated. The Chinese labour controversy was a major issue in British politics up to and during the 1906 election. Opposition was both humanitarian and racist.
7 Frank A. W. Lucas, an advocate, sided with the SALP's anti-war faction but did not join the ISL. He became Chair of the Wage Board following the Pact Government's Wage Act of 1925.
8 Colonel Frederic H. P. Creswell was a staunch advocate of white labour. He led the struggle against the importation of Chinese workers and was arrested for his role in the 1914 strike. As leader of the SALP, following his return from a campaign in South West Africa in June 1915, he promoted the "See It Through" policy, calling for intensified backing for the war (see Bunting 1981:5-10). At the SALP conference in August 1915, Creswell's pro-war resolution carried, precipitating the formation of the ISL, first as a faction of the SALP, and later as an independent body. Creswell later became Minister of Labour in the Pact Government and promoted the "civilised labour policies" which protected white labour.
9 William H. Andrews (1870-1950) emigrated to South Africa from England in 1893 and organised for the Amalgamated Society of Engineers (later Amalgamated Engineering Union). In 1902 he helped form the first TLC. In 1909 he became the first Chair of the SALP and was elected as M.P. in 1912. During World War One he led the anti-war faction in the SALP and chaired the ISL upon its secession from the SALP in September 1915. With the formation of the CPSA, Andrews became its Secretary and editor of *The International* and in November 1922 was elected to the ECCI. He resigned as CPSA Secretary and became inactive in Party affairs following its December 1924 resolution not to apply for affiliation to the SALP. He was Secretary of the SATUC and later the SATLC from 1925 to 1932. He was formally expelled from the CPSA in September 1931 but reinstated in 1938 and was Chairman of its Central Committee in the 1940s. For his biography see Cope (1944) and Hirson (1993c) for a critical review.
10 For documents of the ISL see Bunting (1981:11-56).
11 In February 1920 black mineworkers struck against falling real wages and the job colour bar. The all-white SAMWU called on its members to scab and defend the colour bar. After the strike's defeat, the state initiated a two-pronged strategy of control and reform. The Native Areas Bill was enacted. The Joint

Councils movement was aimed at the black *petite bourgeoisie*. Mining companies began to discuss plans for modifying the job colour bar for semi-skilled blacks as a means to defuse the frustrations of this potential working-class leadership stratum. In 1921 the Native Recruiting Corporation launched *Umteteli waBantu (Mouthpiece of the Bantu)* with Chamber of Mines backing. It opposed a colour bar in industry.

12 "Don't Scab" was reprinted in *The International*, 27 February 1920.

13 Manuel Lopes, co-founder of the Industrial Socialist League and later Secretary of CPSA, was expelled from the Party for his opposition to the Native Republic thesis. He later supported the SALP-NP Pact electoral alliance and joined the NP in July 1937.

14 Friedrich Ebert was a leading German Social Democratic. His prominence symbolised the victory of cautious bureaucrats over the radical left in the making of the Weimar Republic of 1919 to 1933. Kerensky headed the Russian Government between the first and second revolutions in 1917. Labour politicians held office in Britain from May 1915 until November 1918 as partners in the Coalition Government of Asquith and Lloyd George. They had to deal with the challenge of radical shop stewards organisations and endorsed Government responses which could on occasions be repressive. George Barnes was General Secretary of the Amalgamated Society of Engineers before World War One and a Labour M.P. from 1906 to 1918. He served in the war-time coalition, remained with Lloyd George after 1918 and broke with the Labour Party. In contrast, Arthur Henderson, a trade unionist and originally a Liberal, first became a Labour M.P. in 1903 and became Party General Secretary in 1912. He was the senior Labour figure in the war-time coalitions from May 1915 to August 1917. He quarrelled with Lloyd George over the proposal for a peace conference in Stockholm, left the Government and modernised the Labour Party organisation. He held high office in the Labour Governments of 1924 and 1929 to 1931. The left viewed him as a conservative bureaucrat; his supporters saw him as the epitome of Labour's identity.

15 Sidney Percival Bunting (1873-1936) was born in England and came to fight in the Anglo-Boer War. Influenced by non-conformist ideas, he joined the SALP in 1910 but withdrew in opposition to its pro-war policy. He helped found the ISL and the CPSA and edited *The International*. After his return from the Comintern's Fourth Congress, he replaced Andrews as CPSA Secretary and became Chair in 1924. He moved the Party away from its white labour orientation towards the organisation of black workers. Initially opposed to the Native Republic thesis, in 1928 he wrote *Imperialism and South Africa* as a theoretical foundation for the thesis and organised in Transkei under the slogan. He was expelled from the Party in 1931 along with Andrews and other leading activists. In 1933 he wrote *An African Prospect, and Appeal to Young Africa, East, West, Central South*. See Roux's biography (1993).

16 Between the Comintern's formation in 1919 and its Second Congress in July 1920, international events provoked a reconsideration of the policy on "the national and colonial question". As socialist movements in advanced countries waned, the prospects of an international working-class revolution looked increasingly remote. Within the USSR, the national question had become more acute. The Second Congress was attended by more representatives from colonial regions than the year before. Thus at the Second Congress the main questions concerned the evaluation of national liberation movements as part of the world debate centred around Lenin and M. N. Roy from India. Lenin argued that the Comintern should enter into temporary alliances with bourgeois democratic movements in the colonies. Roy emphasised the distinction between bourgeois democratic movements and the mass actions of peasants and workers. A compromise position was reached in which Lenin conceded that bourgeois democratic movements could be either reformist or revolutionary and modified his earlier idea of support for bourgeois democratic movements to support for national revolutionary movements.

17 Tom Mann (1856-1941) was an English trade unionist, a member of the Amalgamated Society of Engineers who was active in the mobilisations of unskilled workers at the end of the 1880s. He was General Secretary of the British ILP in the mid-1890s and spent several years working in the socialist movement in Australia. He returned to Britain in 1910 as an advocate of syndicalism and was prominent in the pre-war labour unrest. He subsequently joined the British Communist Party and served increasingly as an elder statesman. He made three visits to South Africa: in 1910, 1914 and 1922. The purpose of his last trip was to help revive the labour movement after the crushing of the Rand Revolt and to help campaign for the communication of sentences imposed on its leaders.

18 The ICU was formed as a union of Cape Town dockworkers in 1919 under the leadership of Clements Kadalie. In the mid-1920s its focus shifted from urban trade union protests to rural struggles against proletarianisation. Tom Mann was invited to attend the ICU's 1923 conference; for his impressions see Mann (1923).

19 T. W. Thibedi, described by Roux (1993:116) as "... a genius at getting people together, whether workers in a particular industry, women, location residents, or whatever was needed at the moment", was a veteran socialist from the days of the ISL and IWA, and had worked closely with Bunting. He organised the CPSA night school in the 1920s, the SAFNETU from 1929 to 1931 and the AMWU fifth annual

conference in January 1927, along with Gana Makabeni and E. J. Khaile. Expelled from the CPSA in 1930, he formed the Communist League of Africa in 1932 and produced one issue of *Maraphanga*. Thibedi visited the Cornelia coal mines as an ICU shop steward and published an article describing workers' conditions (see Documents 40-44).

20 E. R. Roux (1903-66), a botanist by profession, was one of the first South African-born white Communists. He helped establish the YCL as a student and, with Willie Kalk, pushed it to recruit blacks. He joined the CPSA in 1923 and was profoundly influenced by Bunting. He was elected Vice-Chair in December 1924. Along with Bunting, he fought for greater interaction with black workers. He attended the Sixth Comintern Congress in 1928 and became a supporter of the Native Republic thesis despite initial opposition. In the 1930s he became increasingly marginalised within the Party and left in 1936. In 1944 he wrote a biography of Bunting, and in 1948, *Time Longer than Rope*, the first major and still indispensable study of the liberation struggle. He pioneered Easy English, a technique for teaching English as a second language. From 1957 to 1963 he was a member of the Liberal Party, and he was banned in 1964. For his autobiography, see Roux (1972).

21 Clements Kadalie (c. 1896-1951) of Nyasaland founded the ICU in Cape Town and was its national Secretary from 1921 to 1929, when he resigned under criticism as it disintegrated. During the 1920s he repeatedly tried to secure recognition for the ICU as a trade union, and in 1927 attended an International Labour Office conference. Despite his initial support of William Ballinger as an ICU advisor, he soon broke from him. In March 1929 he formed the "Independent ICU" but was unable to revive the ICU on a national scale. In the 1930s he participated in political affairs as a member of the ANC. He wrote his autobiography around 1946. A. W. G. Champion joined the ICU in 1925 but was later suspended and in 1928 formed the ICU *yase* Natal. Thomas Mbeki (c. 1900-'40s) was one of the first Africans recruited to the YCL and became a leading organiser for the ICU in the Transvaal. Following Kadalie's expulsions of Communists from the ICU executive, Mbeki opted to stay with the ICU. Hirson (1993a:60) notes that he may have been a police informer. Henry Daniel Tyamzashe (b. 1880) became provincial secretary for the ICU in the Transvaal and later worked with Kadalie in the Independent ICU.

22 In early 1927 Western mass intervention in China seemed a possibility. See Deutscher (1959:316-38) for the positions of the Soviet and Chinese Communists Parties.

23 H. Palliotte is no doubt Harry Pollitt, for many years General Secretary of the British Communist Party. A boilermaker by trade, Pollitt was widely admired outside the Party and seen as its authentic working-class face. J. R. Campbell was a leading member of the British Communist Party.

24 John Gomas (1901-79) joined the ANC, ISL and ICU in 1919. By 1923 he was a full-time ICU organiser, and in 1925 he joined the CPSA. His political development shows several turning points. By the 1940s he was alienated from the CPSA's orientation to white labour and white parliamentary politics and was increasingly in agreement with Trotskyists, while attacking them for their practical inactivity. In the late 1940s Gomas was removed from the CPSA hierarchy but despite his declining role in the Party, he endorsed its electoral candidates and remained a member until it disbanded in 1950. For his biography see Musson (1989).

25 Cecil Frank Glass was a founding member of the CPSA who believed in white labour's revolutionary potential. In February 1925 Glass withdrew from the CPSA Central Executive and resigned from his position as Party Treasurer as a result of its resolution in December 1924 not to apply for affiliation to the SALP. On 9 May 1925 he resigned from the Party on the grounds that its policy had antagonised white workers and led to the Party's isolation. Glass later contacted the International Left Opposition. In 1930/31 he left South Africa and became involved in Troskyist politics in China. In 1941 he left China for the United States, where he joined the Socialist Workers' Party and was a member of its National Committee from 1944 to 1963. See Glass (1930) and Hirson (1988 and 1993c).

26 The CFLU was formed in 1913 to block encroachment by Transvaal-based organisations. For a time, the CFLU was affiliated to the RILU. Its constitution incorporated a commitment for equal treatment of workers regardless of colour or race. In fact, the organisation was hostile towards the ICU on the grounds that it was a political or racial rather than trade union organisation. The SATUC was a product of the attempt by the Pact Government, and particularly Creswell, to enlist the unions' support. A conference held in Johannesburg in March 1925 formed a federation initially called the South African Association of Employees' Organisations. The agenda of the Right was deflected by the fact that delegates chose W. H. Andrews as General Secretary. The constitution of the new organisation admitted unions with coloured and Indian members, and at the second conference in April 1926, it was renamed the SATUC. It subsequently became the SATLC.

27 This document was no doubt written while Roux was at the Sixth Comintern Congress in Moscow (see Part Two). The last sentence was added later.

28 Willie Kalk (1902-89), one of the first South African-born white Communists, was a cabinet maker who

joined the YCL and supported the CPSA's turn to black labour in 1924. He maintained his Party membership through the political convolutions of the 1930s, presenting the "Party line" at Bunting's funeral. He served on the national executive of the SATLC, represented the Leather Workers' Union at the SATLC-convened United Front Conference in October 1936 and remained secretary of that union until 1953 when he was forced to resign under the Suppression of Communism Act.

29 Roux is referring to the South African Federation of Non-European Trade Unions which began in 1928 on the Witwatersrand and brought together five organisations. The SAFNETU was a victim of state repression, economic depression and factional fighting within the CPSA. The first two constraints made organisation extremely difficult; Communist squabbles resulted in the expulsion of key SAFNETU activists.

30 See Documents 13 and 14.

31 William G. Ballinger (1894-1974) came to South Africa in 1928 as an advisor to the ICU but was unable to prevent its disintegration into hostile factions. In 1930/31 he represented the ICU at the Non-European Conferences. He was a member of the Joint Council movement, and from 1948 to 1960 he was a Natives' Representative in Senate for the Transvaal and Orange Free State. He helped found the Liberal Party but later lost sympathy with it.

32 James Howard Pim (1862-1934) emigrated from Ireland in 1890 and became a leading South African accountant. In 1903 Lord Milner appointed him to the Johannesburg town council, and a few years later he was elected deputy mayor of Johannesburg. His practice was hurt when the Chamber of Mines withdrew their audits in 1906 because of his opposition to the importation of Chinese labour. In 1910 he abandoned politics for municipal affairs and community welfare and helped establish the Joint Council movement and the SAIRR. J. D. Rheinallt Jones (1884-1953) emigrated to South Africa from Wales in 1905 and became a leading figure in the Joint Council movement and the SAIRR. From 1937 to 1942 he was a Natives' Representative in Senate for the Transvaal and Orange Free State.

33 Edgar Harry Brookes, a distinguished academic and principal of Adams College from 1933 to 1945, was active in the Joint Council movement and from 1937 served fifteen years as a Natives' Representative in Senate. He joined the Liberal Party in March 1962 after many of its leaders had been detained and became its National Chairman. In the 1970s he became critical of the Liberal Party from the standpoint of traditional liberal individualism.

34 *Labour Monthly*, published in London, was a journal founded and edited by R. Palme Dutt, a leading theoretician of the British Communist Party.

35 Albert Nzula was a teacher who joined the CPSA in August 1928 after hearing Wolton speak at an outdoor rally. He was elected Assistant Secretary at the CPSA's seventh conference in 1928/29 and became Secretary of LAR. Later he attended the Lenin School and wrote for *The Negro Worker*. He died in Moscow in 1933 in controversial circumstances. In the early 1930s he argued for the primacy of the agrarian question in South Africa, articulating a two-stage model of change which followed that outlined by the Comintern at its Sixth Congress (Nzula et al. 1979).

36 Bunting is referring to E. S. "Solly" Sachs (1901–76). Born in Lithuania and described by his brother, Bernard Sachs (1959:44-59) as a "Talmudist and rebel", a political pragmatist who was "the perfect apparatus man" and an admirer of Stalin's political realism. Solly Sachs was expelled from the CPSA in September 1931. His life's work was the predominantly Afrikaner and female Garment Workers' Union, to which he was elected Secretary in November 1928, and the subject of his book, *Rebels' Daughters* (1957). He was forced to resign in 1952 under the Suppression of Communism Act and later went into exile in Britain.

Part Two

Communists and the national struggle: The Native Republic Thesis

> ***EDITOR'S NOTE***
> *Here we see the first serious attempt by South African Communists to relate the issues of national liberation and socialism. The controversy is situated not just within the context of South Africa but also within the broader international Communist debates about colonialism. The complexities of the South African situation are evident in the divisive impact of this new position upon the Party leadership.*

Document 22
Letter from Douglas Wolton[1] to E. R. Roux, 8 May 1928

THE COMMUNIST PARTY.
CENTRAL EXECUTIVE OFFICE,
41A, FOX STREET,
JOHANNESBURG.
8.5.28.

E. R. Roux
53 Lensfield Road,
Cambridge
England.

Dear Comrade,

I have received three letters from you recently. I haven't the dates handy, but was not able to reply earlier as the question of the World Congress was not settled. So far as our information now goes, we understand that it will take place in July.[2]

You have been appointed as co-delegate and Bunting as delegate from the Party here. Further details will be supplied later as soon as we have drawn up our final decisions.

The "task", has caused considerable difficulty here and there is a small minority in favour of the new programme, altho' I am of the opinion that Bunting will return to S.A. with a somewhat different outlook. There has been prepared a majority and a minority report. I will send you a draft of the minority report and Bunting will probably send a copy of the majority report. One is in support of the new task and the other puts a case against it, altho' it is not necessarily a final conclusion.[3]

The situation out here is changing with great rapidity and since the beginning of the year important developments have taken place. No doubt you are more or less conversant with the outstanding events which you would no doubt get from the Capitalist Press and also from the Worker which I believe is still coming to you. You will no doubt know that Ballinger, Secretary of Motherwell Trades Council is expected out here shortly as adviser to the I.C.U. If he has not already left you will probably try to see him.

Andrews leaves on Thursday as delegate to GENEVA. after refusing to be nominated for our World Congress.

I will advise you further in regard to Congress matters.

Fraternally yours,
D. Wolton
Secretary.

Document 23[4]
S. P. Bunting, Statement presented at the
Sixth Comintern Congress, 23 July 1928

[... .] Africa as a whole is a continent with 120 million inhabitants and I cannot say much about most of it, but I want to speak on the proletarian character of the subject races of South Africa; and here we also say that Comrade Bukharin's speech and in fact the Communist International literature in general, treats those races to a certain extent in somewhat Cinderella-like fashion. We know the theoretical importance given to the colonial movement, and I will not speak of that at the moment; but as regards the proletarian value of the African workers I agree with Comrade Ford that to neglect the value of the Negro proletariat is a very great mistake.[5] The fighting strength after all of the colonial masses, for any objective, consists very largely in their working class, particularly in a country like ours where a native movement, proletarian or nationalist for that matter, has no chance for the present of being an armed movement, it must depend on its industrial weapons, on strikes and on political struggles and little more for the present. It is in the field of industrial strikes that the greatest militance is shown and the greatest power exercised in South Africa as in India too, I think.

Of course, the bulk of the Negro population of Africa, even of South Africa, is not proletarian; just as the peasants are [*more numerous than the proletariat in most countries, e.g. in*] the U.S.A. But in Africa, at any rate, far more of them are exploited than just those who would be strictly called working class. In West Africa, peasants nominally independent, are exploited in respect of their rubber. In South Africa again, our large "peasantry" is continuously drawn upon to supply workers for the mines and other large industries or for the farms. Those workers are peasantry part of the time and workers part of the time so that the working class is really very widespread, and it is also by far the STRONGEST section of the native population when it comes to action.

Now if, as is said, as we have always been told, imperialism battens on colonies, has more power than ever before because it has the colonies as a mainstay to supply the super-profits, as fields for investment, as places of refuge for capital which cannot find sufficient profit in the home country, then it must follow that equally important is the labour which provides this profit. As a matter of fact, of course, both in our colony and others, there are capitalist enterprises of great importance. In our country the gold industry is a very first class capitalist development. It is vitally necessary to capitalism, and not least in time of war. It is not a case of "backward industry" in any way. It is highly developed. And iron and steel industry is also about to be launched and other big enterprises of all kinds show that ours is not just a medieval, feudal, peasant country. The power of labour therefore, is of very great importance. I do not know if we ought to say that the colonial section of the labour movement in general is the most important, but I think we can say that it is a most important weapon for the overthrow of capitalist rule. Moreover, colonial labour is responsible for a great deal of the unemployment in the "home" countries of the capitalists. All sorts of causes are assigned, but one cause is that industries have been moved from the home countries to colonial countries, and that is one of the reasons why unemployment increases in the home country. At any rate, this backward labour, or if you like, this "uncivilised" labour as it is called in our country, may play as important a part in the attack on capitalism as the highly civilised labour, of e.g., the United States.

Of course, the native labour movement in South Africa is only an infant movement; but it is a good, healthy, lusty infant, very responsive to our propaganda and is growing fast. Our native workers are true-to-type proletarians, as worthy of being called workers as anybody in the world. In spite of their peasant connections as already mentioned, and in spite of the special disabilities placed upon them as a subject race, nevertheless, I say these are as real proletarians as your typical European proletarians, as any in the world, they are as nakedly exploited, down to the bone; the relationship of master and servant, employer and employed, exploiter and exploited is as clear and classical as it could be. The first native strike in Johannesburg was a strike of "sanitary bucket boys", i.e., engaged in the most degraded "kaffirs' work". In a native school which we are carrying on in Johannesburg, we use the Communist Manifesto as a text book, reading it with workers who are actually workers in the factories, mines, workshops, stores, etc. We read the well known characterisations of capitalism and the proletariat in the Communist Manifesto, and the pupils always agree, after arguing and stuying about what they have read, how completely and correctly every single characterisation applies to themselves: "we recognise", they say, "how we have become workers, how we have been driven off the land, onto the industrial markets, how we are deprived of family life, of property, of culture, etc." exactly as in the history of the European countries. And they have this advantage over the European workers, that they are not sophisticated with petty bourgeois or imperialist ideas (except religion, and even that is not native to them); which all helps greatly in the work of making them revolutionary. And in fact the trade unions which we have formed are applying to the Red International of Labour Union to be admitted to that organisation. It is true that the ICU which hitherto has been a strong union of natives in South Africa, is affiliated to Amsterdam; but the Communist Party, finding this body of no use owing to its reformist leadership, has found it necessary to form fresh trade unions which have already been baptised in the fire of strikes, and which are ready to apply to the Red International for affiliation.[6]

I should like in all modesty to point out that the Communist International gives insufficient attention to this aspect of the colonial masses. I was reading the draft programme of the Communist International, where it says that there are two main revolutionary forces: the "proletariat" in the countries at home, and the "masses" in the colonies. I beg to protest against this bald distinction. Our workers are not ONLY mere "masses", they are as truly proletarians as any in the world. The draft programme assigns to the colonies the one task of revolting against imperialism. All good and well. I may say that such nationalist revolt as we have had so far in South Africa has not been on the part of the black workers, but on the part of the Dutch Nationalists. The Dutch Nationalists have had their fling, and have made peace with Britain, and have agreed on a formula which gives them nominal independence: there is not much more to be expected from them. By all means let a nationalist movement carry on. But we can do more as a working class movement in South Africa. It is not good medical science to have one particular pill which you apply for all illnesses. Is it good politics to say that the function of every colony, irrespective of circumstances, is the same everywhere, and that its ONE AND ONLY task is to revolt against imperialism? What of the colonial proletariat, why is it that they are thus dismissed? There is no reference in the draft programme or in Comrade Bukharin's speech to the colonial proletariat, as such, to the class power of those colonial workers: as a class they are relegated to inactivity.

I was speaking to a comrade of the English Party, and advancing the view I am now advancing, and he said "How can you talk like that? Look at the number of years of experience of capitalism and organisation behind the British working class, which you have not got." Agreed. But we are exploited down to the bone under the capitalist system and we have got the fight and determination to resist; what more do you want? We did not have to wait for capitalism to develop; it has been thrust upon us "fully armed", fully developed.

Is not that distinction between European "proletariat" and colonial "masses" exactly the way our "aristocracy of labour" treats the black workers? The "prejudice" of the white workers is not that he wants to kill the black worker, but that he looks upon him not as a fellow-worker but as native "masses". The Communist Party has declared and proved that he is a working man as well like anyone else, and I want to bring that experience to the notice of the Communist International. If you will regard them also as workers, as proletarians, you will take a different view of the situation. We must abolish this subtle form of colour prejudice, or "colour bar". Uncouth, backward, illiterate, degraded, even barbaric you may call them if you like; they cannot read or write, most of them; but they work, they produce profit, and they organise and will fight. They are the great majority, they have the future in their hands, and they are going to rule not only in the colonial countries, but in the world. We are going to see not 2 or 3% of non-European representatives in this Congress, but 80 or 90% representing the real strength of the entire colonial working class.

I might say that the Red International of Labour Unions seems to adopt a more matter of fact view of the colonial working masses than the Communist International. It takes account of the facts and it invites the workers to join its ranks, as workers, in trade unions.

The Communist International is a chain, and the strength of a chain is the strength of its weakest link. Little parties like ours are links in the chain. We are not strengthened, but belittled in the way I have just mentioned. If our parties are weak, then they should be strengthened. Better communication is required. It will perhaps surprise you to know that until about six months ago we have not had a letter (except for circulars) from the Communist International for five or six years. That is a thing which has to be attended to immediately. At any rate, we ask to be considered a little more as representing equally masses of workers, and not treated with, shall I say, a sort of step-motherly or scholastic contempt as representing mere shameless "masses". When I came here an official of the Communist International said "We are going to attack you". That is rather a poor sort of reception to give to representatives elected by the vote of the Party, in which there is a huge preponderance of natives. It is rather a poor reception to give to their representatives before anything has been discussed – to say, "we are going to attack you". We came here to take counsel together as to how we could strengthen each other. Certainly in our own party, whatever the differences between us, we do not treat each other like that.

We also want better communications, between the different sections of the CI. I could illustrate this in the case of several strikes. We had a shipping strike three or four years ago in South Africa, which affected also Australia, and to a certain extent Britain, and in which our Party took the leading part.[7] We had practically no communication not only with the Communist International on the subject, but even with the British Party. The communication which requires to be perfected is quite as essential between party and party as it is between one party and the ECCI. I entirely endorse Comrade Murphy's[8] remarks that the business of the CI Congress is not just for each Party to come here, as to a sort of father confessor, without reference to other parties; we are here above all to try and link up parties to each other. We parties *are* the Communist International, and as Comrade Murphy said, it is we parties between us who have to build up the leading forces in the world revolution. But there has been very little facility for that so far. A great deal more has got to be done.

Another thing with regard to Africa is that a very thorough study of African conditions is required. Out of that huge continent, the South Africa Party is the only one represented here. At the last congress I was at, there were representatives from Egypt and I believe there have been in the meantime representatives from West Africa. There is an enormous field of study in Africa. Conditions in South Africa are quite different from any other part of that continent. South Africa is owing to its climate, what is called a "white man's country" where whites can and do live not merely as planters and officials, but as a whole nation of all classes, established there for centuries of Dutch and English composition. There are also differences elsewhere, e.g., differences between two capitalist methods of administration – the English aloofness of the official who comes and goes for his term of office and has nothing in common with the people of the country; and the French method, which is rather to fraternise or assimilate. Also the differences between the "eastern" and the "western" methods of administration: the one drawing the natives off the land, the other maintaining them on it. Such differences want a great deal more study than has so far been placed before the CI. I hope, when the next Congress is called, there will be representatives of every part of Africa, from North and South, East and West, who – far better than we, – can put the needs of the whole of the population of Africa. There is a great amount of ignorance. The other day here I was asked of our natives – "are they Dutch?". There was recently in the Inprecorr, one of the most astounding articles on South Africa which could only be called a fairy tale. It was full of the most crass misstatements about the conditions there. Such things tend to discredit our official organ, if it can be called such. The answer might be "Why don't you send correct articles instead?" We have done so in the past, but we have too few people for much of this work, we are very busy, our proletariat even possessing all the qualities I have given to it, is mostly not literate; and we must be forgiven. Nevertheless study and knowledge is required.

Again, in the attention which is given to the colonial masses we should not forget the achievements of the white working class in South Africa, for they have conducted big strikes of a quite revolutionary nature and I think are capable of carrying them out again. Both sides can contribute very powerfully to the weakening of British imperialism.

We in South Africa are at present a vulnerable link in the Communist chain. If we are properly strengthened and developed, and if we are treated as we think we deserve to be, we hope to become a strong link in the chain and thus be able to take advantage of the fact that countries like ours are also vulnerable spots in the imperialist chain. We could do a great deal in the weakening and breaking of one of those links of capitalism just as the Russian link is shown broken on the globe in the famous picture on the cover of the old "Communist International".

Document 24
E. R. Roux, *Thesis on South Africa*, presented at the Sixth Comintern Congress, 28 July 1928

The E.C.C.I. Resolution on South Africa contains the following passage: "The Party should put forward as its immediate political slogan in the fight against British domination *an independent Native South African Republic, as a stage towards a Workers and Peasants Republic, with full safeguards and equal rights for all minorities.*"

The resolution of the E.C.C.I. suggests that the independent native republic will not be founded on the proletarian dictatorship. It will be merely a stage towards a Workers and Peasants' Republic. During this transitional stage what form will the government take? If it is an independent, democratic, bourgeois native republic it presupposes the existence of a native bourgeoisie. If *all* the natives are workers or semi proletarian peasants, the distinction between a native republic and a native workers and peasants' republic is meaningless.

Now if South Africa were like India or Egypt this confusion of terms would not arise; for in the typical colonial country the programme of the Communist International envisages two stages in the revolution: (1) the national revolution led by the native bourgeoisie and embracing all sections of the population, leading to a weakening of imperialism as a result of the separation of the colony from the "mother" country and (2) the proletarian revolution, in which the native bourgeoisie in turn is overthrown by the workers and peasants. A number of variations in this main theme are admitted, depending on the relative strength of the native bourgeoisie and petty bourgeoisie, the degree of development of the proletariat, the composition of the peasantry, etc.; It is recognised that certain upper sections of the native bourgeoisie may go over to the imperialists at any early stage in the national revolution, and it will rest with the masses of the petty bourgeoisie, the workers and peasants to carry through the national revolution under the slogan of a Native Republic or "national independence".

In the case of very backward colonies like Southern Nigeria where the native bourgeoisie is extremely weak or non-existent, the supposition is made that this class will inevitably develop and the stage of a bourgeois native nationalist republic prove unavoidable. The possibility of the *complete telescoping* of the bourgeois nationalist revolution and the development of the proletarian revolution in the *absence* of a native bourgeoisie is not admitted in the thesis of the C.I.

This problem has never been fully discussed. This is due largely to the fact that conditions in tropical and southern Africa have hitherto hardly received any attention from the E.C.C.I. The more rapid development of anti-imperialist revolt in Asia has resulted in the neglect of African questions.

In Africa the conditions for the development of a native bourgeoisie are not as favourable as in India, China, Egypt, Turkey, etc. In tropical Africa monopolist capital comes into contact with people living under tribal conditions. Primitive tribal communism on the one hand, highly monopolist syndicates on the other! There is little chance for a class of native middlemen to develop under these conditions. Native industry is only allowed at the pleasure of the white rulers. The chances of the accumulation of capital in native hands are very limited.

1. *In West Africa* white settlement is impracticable; the natives are allowed to keep their land and are encouraged to produce crops for sale to the white trading syndicates. The natives are exploited commercially and also by taxation. Nevertheless a class of native landlords begins to develop and a small but increasing number of formerly independent producers are robbed of their land and reduced to the condition of propertyless wage earners or poor tenants. The white imperialists also introduce railways and other improvements (often using for this purpose forced, unpaid native labour). Mineral wealth where it exists is exploited. The imperialists find it necessary to train a class of skilled native artisans – train drivers, masons, etc. They also require trained natives for lower posts in the civil service – postmen, clerks, etc. A certain amount of education is therefore given to natives, e.g., the university recently established on the Gold Coast. These factors favour the development of a class of native land-owners, petty-bourgeoisie intelligentsia, aristocracy of labour, etc. in West Africa. But the complete domination of the entire trade of the country by the big imperialist trusts and the fact that the rulers have *complete control from the beginning* over a technically backward and illiterate people necessarily renders the growth of a native nationalist movement a very slow process. The imperialists are in a position scientifically to control the social development of the country in their own interests. So conscious are they of their power that they are already beginning to employ anthropologists to study local tribal customs, in order that imperialist rule may make full use of tribal rites and superstitions! An example of this was seen in Ashanti, where a powerful and warlike native tribe was pacified by the mock obeisance of British representatives before the tribal fetish – a golden stool. In this work the imperialists are receiving valuable assistance from the missionaries who are now adapting their christianity to "suit the psychological needs of the African peoples".

Nevertheless conditions for the native masses remain much better in West Africa than in the rest of British Africa (with the exception of the colonies like Uganda and Basutoland (where the "West African policy" prevails). The chances of a native bourgeoisie and nationalist intelligentsia developing are similarly greater in British West Africa than in Kenya, Rhodesia or the South African Union.

2. *In Kenya* the presence of highlands makes it possible for Europeans to settle in appreciable numbers. The best land is alienated to whites, the natives crowded into reserves, a tax is imposed in order to compel natives to work for the white farmers, native agriculture is prevented as far as possible, the "pass" system is introduced. These are the distinguishing features of the "East African" policy. Here, conditions for the development of a native bourgeoisie and intelligentsia are less favourable than in West Africa, though much more favourable than in South Africa. A greater number of whites are employed in the Government service and as skilled workers but their number is limited and there is a chance for natives to get work in various skilled and semi-skilled occupations. In the coastal regions where non-Europeans are allowed to acquire land there is an opportunity for native and Arab landlordism to develop. The immigrant Indian population (which outnumbers the whites by three to one) consists very largely of traders, and also contains certain professional elements.

3. *South Africa* possesses all the evil features of the Kenya land system and also certain additional features of its own which render the development of a native bourgeoisie and intelligentsia almost impossible. South Africa has a large and well established white population including a large number of unemployed and poor whites.

Except in the Cape Province natives are barred from skilled work. The white aristocracy of labour reserves to itself all posts except those of unskilled workers. The colour-bar, which is industrial, educational, social and political, renders the development of a native intelligentsia impossible under existing conditions.

We see then in Africa (1) a rapid and intense development of the organs of imperialist exploitation, resulting in the break-up of tribal society and the reduction of the main mass of natives to the condition of proletarians or peasant proletarians* and leading to a rapid accentuation of the class struggle in which the native population comes into direct conflict with the white landowners and industrialists, and (2) the development of this conflict in the *absence* of a literate, politically conscious section of the natives.

To these two facts are due the spasmodic and top-heavy but extremely revolutionary nature of the native labour movement. The potentiality of a mass movement exists in every region where large numbers of natives are employed, but in the absence of any sort of leaders nothing appears on the surface.

Where leaders appear the revolutionary movement flares up suddenly, only to die down again when the leaders go to a new district or fail "to deliver the goods".

In Kenya there is no native labour movement strictly speaking. There are only the Kavirondo Taxpayers and the Kikuyu Association, native peasant organisations, owing their existence very largely to the assistance of two or three white negrophiles. However, in 1922, under the leadership of Harry Thuku, a series of demonstrations against the "kopani" (pass system) took place. In Nairobi in March 1922, a demonstration was dispersed by the military, a number of natives being killed and wounded. Harry Thuku was banished to the desert, where he still is. With his removal the revolutionary movement collapsed.9

In South Africa the presence of white communists has made possible the growth of a predominantly native Communist Party. It is not an exaggeration to say that the native labour movement owes its existence very largely to the efforts of white communists. Even Kadalie, the leader of the I.C.U. learnt his first lessons in socialism from the white comrades of the Capetown Branch of the C.P.

The structure and policy of the I.C.U. too illustrates the top-heavy nature of native political movements. This organisation which claims to have attained the amazing membership of 120,000 at the peak of its growth, was largely the outcome of the energy and ability of a single native leader. It is significant too that Kadalie himself is not a native of South Africa, but comes from British Nyasaland where he received a mission school education.

It is conceivable therefore that the Communist Party of South Africa if it succeeds in training the necessary number of capable native organisers will grow into a mass party in a very short time and will even be able to lead the native movement of the African continent as a whole. There is no particular reason why the Party should first set about the building of a nationalist movement. The absence of a native bourgeoisie and the intensification of the class struggle in tropical and Southern Africa makes the organisation of a proletarian mass party a possibility of the immediate future, provided only the trained organisers are forthcoming. There is no need to go through the laborious and (from the point of view of the revolution) dangerous process of building up a native bourgeois nationalist movement the leadership of which must be displaced before the proletarian revolution can be achieved.

In South Africa where valuable lessons (of international solidarity, of trade union organisations, of the technique of civilisation) can be learnt from contact with white workers it would be criminal to allow the movement to develop along purely racial lines. Here where the white workers have already had many bitter conflicts with the imperialist bourgeoisie (1913, 1914, 1922) and where a white trade union movement exists, the slogan of an *Independent Workers and Peasants Republic with equal rights for all toilers* is the obvious immediate and practicable slogan. The slogan of a "Black Republic" presupposes the *presence* of a native bourgeoisie and the *absence* of a large class of white proletarians capable of becoming the allies of the natives in their struggle. For the other African colonies, apart from South Africa, and for native states like Basutoland, the slogan of complete national autonomy and freedom to join or secede from an African Federation would be quite appropriate. But here too, as the establishment of native Soviets will become practicable immediately the imperialists are defeated, the slogan of a Workers and Peasants Soviet Government can be combined with the demand for national independence. Unless it is so combined the slogan of a Republic will be quite useless, for the African is an exploited proletarian not a petty bourgeois shopkeeper.

* I use this word for those natives who are recruited under the indenture system for work on the mines, farms, etc. and who return to their families in the tribal areas periodically. The 300,000 native miners, the most important section of the S. African working class are peasant-proletarians of this sort.

Document 25
E. R. Roux, *The New Slogan and the Revolutionary Movement among White Workers in South Africa*, presented at the Sixth Comintern Congress, 30 July 1928

When we talk about "colour prejudice" as a factor in the South African situation we are accused of a departure from Marxism. We are told that it is necessary to point always to the economic basis of colour prejudice in the economic exploitation of the natives. This we have endeavoured to do. Nevertheless, there is a certain residue of colour prejudice which it is very difficult to explain away, – and it certainly cannot be ignored. The international Socialist movement among white workers often seems genuine enough apart from the "native question". The ease with which white South Africa succeeds in ignoring the natives as human beings is reflected also in the white labour movement. The following brief account of the revolutionary history of the white labour movement in South Africa is given in order to show that this movement cannot be ignored as a factor in the struggle against imperialism.

In 1913 a strike of white miners on the Witwatersrand exhibited the typical features of a workers' strike. A mass demonstration of strikers was dispersed by mounted police armed with pickhandles. Following this the strikers attacked and burnt the building of the "Star", the leading newspaper of the mine-owners. They also burnt the Johannesburg station. The government employed a British dragoon regiment to "clear the streets": about 30 workers were killed and hundreds wounded. Six months later, in January 1914, another strike broke out. The Government arrested the miners' leaders and deported them to England. These events stirred the labour movement throughout the world. In London the deportees were welcomed by the largest workers' demonstration that ever had been seen in Britain either before or since.

In 1922 occurred the historical "Red Revolt" or "Rand Uprising". The main facts about his episode should already be known to all. This strike of white miners once more exhibited features of a genuine working class revolt. There were mass demonstrations of strikers, and clashes with the police and military. Workers defence organisations or "commandos" were formed. The strike culminated in a partial general strike and an armed uprising. Police stations were captured and barricades erected in the streets. Detachments of troops were ambushed in some areas. A white working class suburb in Johannesburg, which had fallen completely into the hands of the strikers, was bombed by Government aeroplanes; and as this failed to dislodge the workers' forces, it was bombarded by artillery.

The revolt was brutally suppressed and a number of summary executions were carried out by the military. Thousands of workers were flung into gaol and general white terror prevailed. During this period the Labour Party leaders shamelessly deserted the workers. It was left to the Communist Party to organise a strike prisoners' release committee and to conduct a campaign against the impending executions. Rising mass pressure eventually compelled the government to stay its hand, but not before four of the strikers had been hanged. How long, Hull and Jewis went to their death on the gallows with the words of the "Red Flag" on their lips is known to all.[10]

In order to demonstrate that white workers in South Africa may show considerable solidarity with proletarian movements abroad, I wish to draw attention to the aid given by the white workers to the British coalminers. When the General Strike broke out in Britain there was much enthusiasm in Johannesburg.[11] A large public meeting called by the T.U.C. passed resolutions of support for the British workers and large sums of money were donated. During the coal lockout the white unions continued to forward money to Britain. A single street collection in Johannesburg for the British miners' wives and children produced over £300. The local committee that organised this collection consisted of representatives of the SALP, the CP and the white trade unions. Most of the collectors were members of the "Women's Auxiliary" of the Labour Party and they displayed great enthusiasm. If workers throughout the world had supported the British miners financially to the extent that the white workers in Johannesburg did, the result of the lockout might have been very different.

Now these same white workers who have given these examples of anti-capitalist activity and international solidarity (and I submit that their revolutionary achievements and this revolutionary tradition cannot lightly be set on one side) – these workers exhibit racial feeling against the natives. The South African Communist Party believes that it is possible to play upon this revolutionary tradition in many ways in order to secure unity between white and native workers. Our tactic in approaching the white workers has been to appeal to them AS WORKERS, to refer to their struggle against the capitalist class, to stress the need for unity with the native workers in the class struggle, to appeal to them as trade unionists not to scab on their native fellow workers, and so on and so forth according to the particular demands of the situation.

It is because we have become so accustomed to this particular line of approach to the class struggle in South Africa, because the unity of black and white workers is so necessary there, that the slogan of the ECCI comes as such a shock to us. It means a reversal of the whole of our previous policy. The various strikes and uprisings of the white workers have been conducted under the slogan of a "white South Africa", i.e., for the maintenance of a European standard of living for white workers, and a struggle against the efforts of employers to reduce white wages nearer to the native level. Against this slogan our Party raises the cry: "Not a White South Africa, but Africa for the workers, black and white." The resolution of the ECCI now means that we must inscribe upon our banner "Not a White South Africa, but a Black South Africa". This is mere perversity, not dialectical materialism.

Document 26
S. P. Bunting, Statement on the Kuusinen Thesis[12], presented at the Sixth Comintern Congress, 20 August 1928

Comrades, I should like to have spoken on colonial or at least on South African matters in general but in the limited time must confine myself to a controversial matter seriously affecting our South African Party.

There is a proposal in the Negro Sub-Commission, presided over by Comrade Bennet[13], that the Party should put forward as its immediate political slogan "an independent native South African Republic based on the workers' and peasants' organisation, with full safeguards and equal rights for all national minorities"; also that the country and land be returned to the black population; a native national revolutionary movement to be developed by the Party in support.

This formulation is opposed by the majority in our Party, mainly for practical reasons, which are very strong. But we may first consider the more theoretical basis of the formula. This is stated in a draft resolution submitted to the Sub-Commission as follows:

"The national question in South Africa, which is based upon the agrarian question, lies at the foundation of the revolution in South Africa."

Unfortunately we Party members in South Africa are so much occupied with practical work, which we have to do in our spare time only, that we have no time for study, so that we are only amateurs when it comes to theorising. But according to our experience, it seems possible to harp too exclusively on the national chord in colonial matters. In an earlier debate on the ECCI resolution, I ventured the opinion, in effect, that it might not be so universally true that the chief function of a colonial people was to engage in a national struggle (predominantly agrarian in character) against foreign imperialism and for independence; and that in South Africa, at any rate, the class struggle of the proletariat (chiefly native) appeared more capable of accomplishing the task – in effect, that the class struggle there is more revolutionary and effective than the national or racial struggle for the same ends.

It is often said that the colonial thesis of the II Congress is authority to the contrary, but I do not find anything to that effect in the thesis. It says, of course, that we should "support the revolutionary movement among the subject nations and in the colonies" – "the FORM OF SUPPORT TO BE DETERMINED BY A STUDY OF EXISTING CONDITIONS". And it does also say:

> There are to be found in the dependent countries two distinct movements, one is the bourgeois democratic nationalist movement, with a programme of political independence under the bourgeois order, and the other is the mass action of the poor and ignorant peasants and workers for their liberation from all forms of exploitation. The former endeavours to control the latter ... but the CI and the Parties affected must struggle against such control and help to develop CLASS consciousness in the working masses of the colonies. For the overthrow of foreign capitalism, which is the first step towards revolution in the colonies, the cooperation of the bourgeois nationalist revolutionary elements is useful. But the first and most necessary task is the formation of Communist Parties which will organise the peasants and workers and lead them to the revolution and to the establishment of Soviet Republics ... .

That is so even when there is a bourgeois democratic nationalist movement in existence, and bourgeois nationalist revolutionary elements to cooperate with. Until recently, nearly all subsequent Communist theory on colonial revolution that I have seen has been based on the assumption that such a movement and such elements are in existence in every colony; the present draft colonial thesis is one of the first to deal on a separate basis with colonies, like most African Colonies, where they are not.

In general, in the case of all national and colonial movements, the II Congress thesis says:

> The CI must establish relations with those revolutionary forces that are working for the overthrow of imperialism in the countries subjected politically and economically. THESE TWO FORCES MUST BE COORDINATED if the final success of the world revolution is to be guaranteed.

And again:

> The policy of the CI on national and colonial questions must be chiefly to bring about a UNION OF THE PROLETARIAN AND WORKING MASSES of all nations and countries for a JOINT REVOLUTIONARY STRUGGLE leading to the overthrow of capitalism without which national inequality and oppression cannot be abolished.

> Real national freedom and unity can be achieved by the proletariat only ... by the overthrow of the bourgeoisie.

> The real essence of the demand for equality is based on the demand for the abolition of classes.

> The colonial and subject countries have been taught by bitter experience that there can be no salvation for them outside of a union with the revolutionary proletariat (which includes presumably the revolutionary proletariat of the imperialist race in the colony itself).

And in African colonies (including South Africa) there is as a rule no native bourgeoisie, and consequently no question of the "Two distinct movements" referred to in the II Congress Thesis; there is only the question of "organising the peasants and workers and leading them to the revolution and to the establishment of Soviets." Put in another way, the class struggle is practically coincident and simultaneous with the national struggle. The object is the same in each case – the removal of all oppression (including all special oppression applying to members of the subject race as such) and the gaining of liberation and power for workers and peasants; the parties are substantially the same, and the weapons and methods of the struggle also. Hence there is no very great point or virtue, even where there is no exploited European class present (as there is in South Africa) in emphasising the national aspect of the struggle as MORE FUNDAMENTAL than the class aspect; rather the reverse is the case. The two struggles would be the same even if the oppressing class were of the same nationality except that there is an additional element of revolt when the oppressor is a "foreign devil". As the draft colonial thesis of this Congress says of such colonies: "The tasks of the class struggle of the workers and other toiling masses COINCIDE in the main with the tasks of the national anti-imperialist liberation struggle."

Now a further complication arises in South Africa from the presence of a WHITE exploited working and peasant class as well as a black one – a minority of one in six perhaps, but still one that cannot be ignored and on which (as in the trade unions) the CP has a good deal of foothold. This minority too rises against the bourgeoisie and imperialists, sometimes in a very spirited and revolutionary way, more so indeed than any modern native national movement hitherto, although it has no RACIAL oppression to fight against. As in the case of the natives, its militant character appears chiefly on its proletarian rather than on its agrarian side.

The South African native masses, in their turn, are being rapidly proletarianised and organised as a working class. The native agrarian masses as such have not yet shown serious signs of revolt: indeed, as the Draft Colonial Thesis of the Congress says: "In these countries the question of the agrarian revolution does not by far constitute the axis of the colonial revolution." At any rate a live agrarian movement has still to be organised in South Africa.

What is the result of these peculiar factors? It is that both black and white exploited are fighting against the same masters. They both fight chiefly (at present) as proletarians, and the natives have the extra stimulus of fighting against masters who to them are a foreign oppressor race, whereas the whites have this in a lesser degree only (i.e., as "South Africans" or "Dutch" against "British", oversea or "cosmopolitan" financiers). The white workers, enjoying privileges and higher wages, are, however, disinclined at present to regard the black workers as comrades in the fight.

What is the duty of the CP in these circumstances? Must it not be the same as ever, or more than ever, according to the II Congress thesis? "These two forces", – the workers of imperialist race and those of subject race, or the "home" movement and the colonial movement – "must be coordinated" for a "joint revolutionary struggle": "uniting the various units of the future proletarian parties", and also overcoming the distrust of the subject races for the workers of the imperialist races.

The draft colonial thesis of this Congress in reference to South Africa and other colonies puts it thus: (Paragraph 12)

> The most important task here consists in the joining of the forces of the revolutionary movement of the white workers with the class movement of the colonial workers, and the creation of a revolutionary united front with that part of the native national movement which really conducts a revolutionary liberation struggle against imperialism.

But this task is no longer so easy. It is no longer a mere case of the national and the class movements coinciding as it were automatically. Here the white exploited are of the very race which the native exploited are, as nationalists, fighting against. It is almost inevitable therefore that the nationalist movement of the natives will clash with their class movement. Similarly the white exploited, finding their race being attacked AS SUCH by a native nationalist movement, are predisposed by their superior economic and political position to side with the masters nationally and forget their class struggle. Special tactics and manoeuvres have to be adopted to prevent this and to harmonise the national and the class movements in this special case, devoted principally to neutralising and correcting white labour chauvinism (or, occasionally, native "chauvinism"). And if there is danger of a clash the question how far it is advisable to play on the national chord, whether the advantages exceed the disadvantages, whether the same result or better can be attained with less risk, becomes important.

Not only have we no native bourgeoisie or bourgeois national movement, but we have in South Africa no really nationalist movement at all of the kind contemplated in the draft resolution of the Negro Sub-Commission; certainly no movement for a native republic as such has been observable. The African National Congress, which the resolution wants us to boost up, is a moribund body, it has had its day. In any case its demands were not nationalist demands proper, but such as the following, reflecting the poverty stricken conditions of the native masses: removal of all special race oppression and discrimination, land and more land, equality with whites, equal votes, equal education, equal justice, equal treatment, rights and opportunities everywhere. It is inclined to ignore the weapon of the native proletarian movement as such, and has usually sought redress for grievances by sending deputations to the King of England, which of course have resulted in nothing. Thus, the existing "nationalist" movement for equality, etc. only demands the same things as the Communist movement (proletarian and agrarian) does, with the extra stimulus supplied by national or race patriotism but from observation of facts we believe the class stimulus is a greater stimulus even to the native masses, it has actually stimulated greater sacrifices and devotion already, and it has the advantage of gaining, instead of perhaps forfeiting, the alliance of the white workers. The CP is itself the actual or potential leader of the native national movement; it makes all the national demands that the national body makes, and of course much more, and it can "control" nationalism with a view to developing its maximum fighting strength. It can and will respond to the entire struggle of all the oppressed of South Africa, natives in particular.

Some reference to the actual work of our Party seems necessary to explain the foregoing. Incidentally, not much interest seems to be taken in this by the drafters of the resolution, any success seems only grudgingly acknowledged, we had to get an appreciative paragraph specially inserted in the draft: concentration of interest on a nationalist movement seems to involve a lack of interest in the day to day struggles against race oppression itself. (It is the same in the draft CI programme, and we have asked for a clause to be inserted in that, laying down that CPs must struggle in the colonies against race or colour discrimination and for absolute equality).

What have we done so far? Our work among the native masses, our chief activity, conducted so far mainly as a working class movement (although an agrarian movement will be developed as fast as we can get contact especially with the distant and not easily accessible native reserves) is limited only by our ability to cope with it. We have 1,750 members of whom 1,600 are natives, as against 200 a year ago, and we are adding to that and also rapidly organising militant native trade unions which have learnt to conduct strikes. We are also combatting and slowly overcoming white labour chauvinism. which we find yields when confronted with organised masses of native fellow workers face to face. We have put through joint strikes of white and black which were victorious, also an amalgamation of white and black unions into one, an unprecedented thing in South Africa. As for the native nationalist movement, though it is somewhat dead and alive, we pay it a good deal of attention and whenever we see any life in it we apply United Front tactics as per the draft colonial thesis. Thus, after years of preparatory effort, we have recently begun to reap substantial success which will continue provided we can find the man power to garner the harvest. Native workers and some peasants are pouring into the Party in preference to joining the purely native bodies, whether national or industrial, which have let them down and fallen into the hands of the bourgeoisie. They fully appreciate the "vulgar Marxist" slogan of "Workers of the World Unite", of joint action by black and white labour against the common enemy: and at the same time they see that the CP sincerely and unreservedly espouses their national cause as an oppressed race. (Recently, in the wilds of Basutoland, we found a well-thumbed copy of Bukharin's ABC of Communism, brought there by an old pupil of ours and now widely read among the members of the "Plebeian Party" of Basutoland, which seeks affiliation with the CP).[14]

Such are the surrounding circumstances in which a native republic slogan would be launched, and we consider it would, not in theory perhaps, but certainly in practice, arouse white workers' opposition as unfair to the minority, and would thereby not only emphasise the contradiction between national and class movements, but put the whole native movement at a great disadvantage unnecessarily and without compensating advantage. It would not avail, when such suspicions are aroused, to put them off the smooth, "empty liberal phrases", to the effect that "national minorities will be safeguarded", especially when no definition is given of these safeguards – for that matter no definition is given of the precise meaning of "native republic" itself. But expressions like "South Africa is a black country", "the return of the country and land back to the black population", "South Africa belongs to the native population", etc., though correct as general statements, do invite criticism by the white working and peasant minority who will have to fight with the black workers and peasants if the bourgeoisie is to be overthrown. They certainly seem to indicate a black race *dictatorship*; they either are an exaggeration or they are calculated to be generally understood as one – and for the purpose of overcoming white labour misgiving that comes to the same thing. If the white working class feels, from the apparent exclusiveness of the phrase "native republic", that the intention is to ride roughshod over it, it will not avail to say: "it is all right, it does not mean that". They will retort rightly or wrongly: "Under a native government built on a nationalist or racial foundation and thus biassed against whites even though proletarians, any 'safeguards' of the white workers and peasants would go to the winds at the first clash. Who will have the power to stop it?" The example of the Ukraine etc. is quoted. But the racial gulf between black and white in South Africa has no parallel there, and besides, the influence and power of the Soviet Union to stand by and see fair play makes all the difference; there was a case of a former empire now turned into a proletarian state, voluntarily liberating its subject nations and having the power to see such liberation through on such lines as a proletarian state would naturally approve. And as regards disposal of the land, the draft resolution does not even speak of safeguards. As the slogan will certainly be interpreted by the exploited whites, as it has indeed been interpreted by ourselves (so much so that its defenders have defended just that interpretation of it) it means that the exploited whites are to become in their turn a subject race, that the native republic in spirit if not in letter will exclude all whites, and that the land without exception will belong to the natives – not as a matter of the verbal drafting of a resolution but as a matter of fact. The slogan will have to be redrafted on less nationalist lines if it is to avoid giving that impression.

Of course, no one denies that *the immense majority must and will exercise its power as such*, from which it follows that a minority of the exploited is also entitled to its proportionate voice and share in power and land. The "native republic" is defended, indeed, as a mere expression of *majority rule*, but it obviously goes beyond that, and the little difference makes all the difference when it comes to combating white chauvinism: it handicaps propaganda to that effect.

It may be asked, why are we so concerned about the fate of a comparative handful of whites. It is certainly strange that we of the CPSA, who are accustomed at home to work almost exclusively among and for the native masses, and who are always attacking white chauvinism, should find ourselves obliged here in Moscow to take up unwonted cudgels for the white minority. But the reason is not any special love for the aristocrats of labour, or any chauvinist preference for the whites, as is superficially and malignantly suggested in the draft resolution, but first the need for labour solidarity and second a true valuation of the forces at our disposal. Our infant native movement, any revolutionary native movement, lives and moves in a perpetual state bordering on illegality; on the slightest pretext it can be suppressed either by prosecution or legislation or by massacre or pogrom. We are therefore always looking for allies, or rather for shields and protections behind which to carry on; and even the *bare neutrality*, much more the occasional support of the white trade unions, etc. is of incalculable value to us. It undoubtedly helps us to avoid being driven underground, which in a country like South Africa, where we are all well known, where there are no crowded masses to hide behind or among, would make our work almost impossible, and besides, in a political agitation for liberation of the mass of the people, publicity is a very valuable weapon. We have always instinctively felt this need of white labour support, but it is only then threatened by this slogan with the loss of it, that we realise how very useful it is to us, and how impossible it is to agree with the defenders of the slogan who say "To hell with white labour support, damn the white workers." It is easy to sit here and, on limited experience of our local atmosphere, to lay down a policy and say "It will be all right, you don't understand, this slogan will not alienate, it will attract the white workers". We who would have to go back and preach it, we who have had all these years to drive a composite team, to work in both camps, black and white, who have learned the art of doing it on uncompromising Marxian lines by long and hard experience of the enormous difficulties arising out of this very race question, the crucial question of South African labour – on a matter like this we must be heard with respect. We say that the white workers are unquestionably going to be alienated by the present slogan and that instead of support from white labour we are thus quite likely going to get its hostility and Fascist alliance with the bourgeoisie. This in turn will also encourage the government to prosecute and the courts to convict everyone who preaches the slogan – we have had many successful legal contests on native propaganda, but the law has now been so tightened that we probably cannot get away with this slogan as a slogan; and thus our movement may be not just "driven underground" but closed down. Indeed a further sequel may be violent race hostilities, a bloody struggle for mutual extermination or subjection between whites and blacks as races, and what is worse, between the white exploited and the black exploited, a struggle in which the class struggle is completely obscured and forgotten, and in which the unarmed side courts defeat – and all for the sake of a formula which will, as far as we can judge, not increase our work or our success in the present weak stage of our Party – it may be different when we are much stronger.

Our present policy is endorsed by good authority. The amendment of the CPSU to the ECCI thesis of Comrade Bukharin for instance says:

> 53. The Congress observes a growth of Communist influence in South Africa. The Congress imposes the obligation upon all Communists to take up as their central tasks the organisation of the toiling Negro masses, the strengthening of Negro trade unions and the fight against white chauvinism. The fight against foreign imperialism in all forms, the advocacy of complete and absolute equality, strenuous struggle against all exceptional laws against Negroes, determined support for the fight against driving the peasants from the land, to organise them for the struggle for the agrarian revolution, while at the same time strengthening the Communist groups and parties – such must be the fundamental tasks of the Communists in these countries."

There is nothing here about a "Native Republic".

The draft programme, English edition p. 563(1) ad fin lays down that

> in colonies and semi-colonies where the working class plays a more or less important part and where the bourgeoisie has already crossed over to the camp of the avowed counter-revolution, or is crossing over because of the development of the mass proletarian and peasant movements (and, as we proposed to add, in colonies, e.g., in Africa, where no native bourgeoisie exists, but where the main mass of natives is being proletarianised) the C.P. must steer a course for the hegemony of the proletariat and for the dictatorship of the proletariat and peasantry which will ultimately grow into the dictatorship of the working class. In such countries, the C.P. must concentrate its efforts mainly upon creating broad mass proletarian organisations (trade unions) and revolutionary peasant unions, and upon drawing up demands and slogans directly affecting the working class. It must propagate the idea of the independence of the proletariat as a class which on principle is hostile to the bourgeoisie, a hostility which is not removed by the possibility of temporary agreements with it. It must imbue the masses with and develop among them the idea of the hegemony of the working class; advance and at the proper moment apply the slogan of Soviets of Workers' and Peasants' Deputies.

Here, too, there is nothing about a native republic.

It is worth while also to quote the views of Comrade Lozovsky in the "Negro Worker" of 15th July, page 5, which recall the language of the 2nd Congress:–

> The Negro workers must understand that the racial question will be solved together with the social question. Real equality and fraternity of workers of all colonies will be forged in the joint struggle against capitalism.

> The Negro workers of the U.S.A., Africa, etc., will achieve equality with the white workers only through the organised struggle against the whole system of capitalist oppression.

After long consideration and having heard all that is said for the draft resolution, and in view of the special complications conditioning Communist progress in South Africa, we are at present, while standing for proletarian equality and for majority rights and all that that implies, against the CREATION of any special nationalitic slogan at all for South Africa, except of course the liberation of the native people from all race oppression and discrimination, and separation from the British Empire.

Document 27
Letter from E. R. Roux to Douglas Wolton, 5 September 1928

> *British Association for the Advancement of Science*
>
> *RECEPTION ROOM*
> *UNIVERSITY OF GLASGOW*
> *5 September, 1928*

General Secretary
C.P.S.A.

Dear Douglas,

I am at present attending the science congress here, having just returned from the continent.

When I left Moscow the question of the new slogan had not yet been finally disposed of though the Negro Commission (in which the matter was discussed at some length though not as fully as I should have liked) had already delivered its judgement. You will probably have heard of the result of our final appeal by the time this reaches you. I hope to see S.P.B. on his return to England and get acquainted with the final position.

However, as a result of the discussions in Moscow I have come to a number of conclusions with regard to the slogan and with regard to Party policy in general, and I think my views might interest the C.E. C.P.S.A. Hence this letter.

In the first place I think the discussion has shown that it is time the C.P.S.A. put its theoretical house in order. We have been content too long to jog along with a minimum of theory. Our reaction to the new slogan showed that we were not up to date in Leninist theory, and I think this is as true of those who supported as of those who opposed the new slogan.

In my opinion we have got to distinguish clearly between the natives as a subject race and the natives as members of the S. African working class. We have got to put forward definite race demands on behalf of the natives, demands which we must fight for in the face of opposition from all sections of whites, even the white workers.

Our trade union work, important as it is, is only a part of our activities. Our slogan on the trade union field is *"workers unite, irrespective of colour"*. But as a general political slogan appealing to the native masses, this is inadequate. I do not say it should not be used as a general political slogan: *it should be used more than ever*. But it is necessary to have an additional slogan or slogans which take account of the position of the natives as a subject race. It is equally necessary to say *"natives unite; unite as black men to free yourselves from slavery."* The demands of the democratic revolution in Africa (the franchise, abolition of passes, equal land laws, free education, abolition of the indenture system and forced labour, right to ride on the trams, walk on the pavement, use the public libraries, enter the city halls, etc. etc.) are demands of the natives *as natives*. They are demands for things which the white workers already have. On the political field these demands culminate historically in a single final slogan – *national independence*, i.e. complete freedom and independence for the native race, complete political power to the natives. As the natives are not a scattered racial minority like the Jews but a compact majority inhabiting a single country, national independence means quite literally a *native republic*. This is the logic of the position and this we must accept.

But before formulating the slogan for complete national emancipation of the Bantu in its final platform form, it is necessary to take two things into consideration. These are (1) the question of the rôle of the white workers in the revolution in S. Africa, and (2) the question of expediency. These two points are very closely linked together.

It is obvious that the white workers, as the only skilled section of the proletariat, cannot in any way be ignored. There is an increasing tendency with some comrades – in their more exasperated moments when the actual requirements of the situation have been forgotten for the moment – to say "let the white workers go hang". We must remember that we should be patient revolutionists and not lose our heads in this matter. To the extent that the white workers are interested in fighting the boss to that extent they can and must be harnessed to the revolution. We entirely disagree of course with the view formerly held by Danchin (I hope he has long since discarded it) that the white workers are the *main* revolutionary element in S. Africa.

As far as revolutionary expediency is concerned it is obvious that this may easily degenerate into opportunism. Our chief difficulty in Moscow was to convince the comrades that there were genuine tactical reasons against adopting the "Black Republic" slogan and that our objections were not founded on opportunist deviations. In the present weak condition of the native movement every foothold in the white trade unions, every little bit of white support must be utilised to the fullest extent, in order to maintain the legality of the native movement, to prevent pogroms and the danger of lynchings, and to secure the rapid development of a cadre of native Communists. I think it is fairly plain that we cannot afford to go underground at the present time.

The *object of the slogan* of course *is not to please the white workers but to rally the whole of the native masses behind the C.P.* This is our main job; everything else is secondary. At the same time there is no reason why we should *unnecessarily antagonise* the white workers. Such unnecessary antagonising would have disastrous results not only for the inter-racial labour movement but also for the native nationalist movement as such. The slogan should therefore be formulated in such a way as to make the maximum appeal to the racial consciousness of the oppressed Bantu and at the same time provide a weapon for continuing the fight in the trade union movement on the basis of working class unity irrespective of colour.

The amendment which I suggested to the Negro Commission in my opinion meets these requirements as far as it is possible to do so. It was *"an independent workers' and peasants' S. African Republic, with equal rights for all toilers irrespective of colour, AS A BASIS FOR A NATIVE MAJORITY GOVERNMENT"*. Supplemented by immediate demands for an equal franchise throughout the Union, the admission of natives to Parliament, and the abolition of all helot relations, this will be a revolutionary rallying slogan guaranteeing to the C.P. the leadership of the racial struggle of the natives. At the same time it will enable us to argue our case in the white trade unions. If we say a "Black Republic" and then qualify this by saying that there will be autonomy for whites, we cannot but expect to be howled down in the white trade unions; we shall not even be allowed to state our case. At the mention of "Black Republic" the bricks will begin to fly and our subsequent qualifications will be relegated to the post-mortem examination. It is much more sensible to approach the white workers in these terms: "You are workers, trade unionists; you are exploited and shot down by the boss; unite to overthrow capitalism; unite with your native fellow workers; demand full equality for *all* workers; the native workers are the majority; YOU must therefore be prepared to *grant* THEM *their* MAJORITY RIGHTS." This will also probably be howled down in many cases, but at least it provides a tactical approach to the subject.

Unfortunately Comrade Petrovsky and the members of the Negro Commission did not trouble to reply to these arguments. They said that the C.P.S.A. had committed Social-Democratic sins of the gravest nature and had to be severely reprimanded. They therefore would allow of no modification in the slogan whatever. They would not ever allow a slight editorial change in the wording, because they said any such slight change would be interpreted as a partial victory for the S. African delegation.

I think this is quite a wrong way of approaching the subject.

I have some further remarks to make with regard to certain practical questions, particularly with regard to Com. Harrison's candidature and the forthcoming elections, but I will keep them for a further letter.[15]

Kind regards to all comrades,

Yours fraternally,
E. R. Roux

Document 28
Letter from E. R. Roux to the Central Executive, Communist Party of South Africa, 25 September 1928

53 Lensfield road,
Cambridge
25 September 1928

CECPSA

Dear Comrades,

Comrade Bunting has suggested that I should write down my views on general Party tactics for the immediate future. When one is 6,000 miles away and not liable at any moment to be biffed by an enraged Dutchman or arrested under the Native Administration Act for inciting to a "feeling of hostility" one's ideas about Party tactics and policy on the colour question may be more doctrinaire than practicable. Comrade Bunting has hinted at some such explanation of my own partial conversion to the new slogan (to the extent of accepting it in the abstract while suggesting tactical modifications in its concrete form), as contrasted with his own unbending opposition.

Whether there is anything in this geographical explanation, and also whether my changing views while in Moscow may in part have been due to the sort of political intimidation to which we were subjected – an intimidation to which com. Bunting is relatively impervious but to which I may have been more susceptible – or whether on the other hand my views are to be taken as due to a more or less independent re-examination of the facts as I now see them, I must leave it for you to decide.

In any case I have long been of the opinion that there are many aspects of Party work in which a more nationalistic attitude should be adopted. For instance before I left home I was already beginning to think that it was rather academic to refer to the natives always as "native workers" instead of just as "natives".

When addressing members of the Labour Party or white trade unionists, of course one wants to draw attention to the fact that the natives are fellow workers and one naturally gets into the habit of referring to the working class and then saying, "You must understand that when we say 'workers' we include the non-Europeans." Now this is very good policy as far as the approach to the white workers is concerned: it has already yielded important results, not the least of which is the recent liaison of the laundry unions. But to say as com. Bunting does that this "pure Marxist" approach all along the line is by itself quite sufficient, is to ignore the other aspect of the native movement – the nationalist aspect.

Before proceeding further it will be necessary for me to say something on the character of these two sides of the native movement. I referred to them in a previous letter but I did not elaborate the point.

The national struggle of the natives comes first in order because, as the C.I. has pointed out, S. Africa is a country in which exploitation is predominantly of colonial type. This national struggle is a political struggle against the S.A. state as at present organised. It is to-day very largely illegal, as is seen clearly in the Native Administration Act, which enables the Government to put in prison anyone who draws attention in public to the fact that the natives *as black men* are exploited and oppressed by the Europeans *as whites*. To point to the exploitation of the workers by the capitalists seems to me to create a feeling of hostility between Capital and Labour; and to point to the oppression of the natives by the colour bar leads equally, as I think any reasonable person will admit, to a feeling of hostility to the whites. It is a mere subterfuge to say that it is only in his capacity of capitalist that we attack the white man and that we do not attack the whites as such. The reply is that when we rally the natives to rebel against racial discrimination we do attack all whites who support or practice racial discrimination harmful to the natives (i.e., the vast majority of white South African); and the fact that there are "100,000 poor whites" is in my opinion quite beside the point. I know someone is likely to protest here and say "Ha! so you do want to ignore the poor whites". I reply that I do not wish to ignore the poor whites, or any other section of the whites for that matter, but I do not see how the existence of class differences among the whites alters the fact of the racial oppression of the natives.

The other aspect of the native movement is the industrial one. This movement is more or less legal at the moment and likely to remain so for a longer or shorter time. In view of the growing extreme shortage of native labour an appreciable rise in native wages will almost certainly take place in the near future, if only to bring money wages to the pre-war level of real wages. The Bloemfontein Award is an indication of the trend of events. In fact we are rapidly approaching the position throughout southern and eastern Africa where capitalists will be prepared to offer substantial increases in wages in order to attract labour. Those who doubt this are advised to study labour conditions in the Congo, Kenya, and Southern Rhodesia as well as in the Union itself. In all these territories the demand for labour exceeds the supply to an increasing extent every day. There is thus every possibility of even a reformist trade union movement, such as the I.C.U. aims at becoming, securing real benefits for some of its members. On the basis of the prestige and position thus gained, leaders of the Kadalie type will then proceed to stifle any further revolutionary advance of the native workers. This is why it is so important that the Red unions now growing up should supersede the reformist organisation. Immediate rises in wages if secured by militant action will encourage the native workers to make further efforts and to combine political demands with industrial ones. If on the other hand they merely result from Kadalie or Ballinger negotiating with the employers, without any real organisation of the workers and without strike action, they will merely make the workers content for the time being and the chance of developing a mass movement will be lost.

Some comrades believe that the industrial movement of the native urban workers will provide the main lever whereby the racial emancipation of the natives will be achieved. They thus give it precedence both in theory and practice over the national agrarian movement. It is true that up to the present some of our most "striking" successes have been on this field. Here we are assisted by the fact that many sections of white workers have an economic interest in the growth of native trade unionism. We may take it that the pro-native element in the white unions will continue to grow. This is largely our achievement; we did the pioneer work. Now we have the pleasure of hearing Moore and Hicks advocating racial co-operation and no doubt it will become quite fashionable in time.

In view of these urban successes some tend to forget the other side of the picture as exemplified by Potchefstroom and Paardekop. The country movement is very largely the nationalist movement. It will have its trade union side no doubt (the whole question of an agricultural labourers union is extremely important), but it will remain predominately political.

The comrades in Moscow suggested that there was some connexion between our refusal to accept the new slogan and our alleged indifference on the agrarian question. While we denied the indifference we had to admit that we knew very little about agrarian conditions. The C.P.S.A. derives what theory it has almost exclusively from its urban (largely trade union) experience. The theory of "pure Marxism" and the slogan "workers of all races unite" have seemed good enough, and we have worked out an empirical method of approaching normally race-prejudiced white workers, with more or less success so far, in the face of enormous difficulties; and I think the Party can be justly proud of its work. But it does not follow that slogans useful in trade union work are sufficient by *themselves* in the broader political struggle which the Party will soon have to face. I say "broader" advisedly, because I do not believe the development of native trade unions will provide the only lever for the racial emancipation of the Bantu.

The direct political struggle (mass demonstrations for the defence of the Cape franchise and its extension, the consolidation of the Communist Party, the development of all the race demands of the natives, particularly the struggle for land) will come to the front; and though trade unionism will form an integral part of the whole, it may possibly only be a smaller part. Under these conditions the slogan of inter-racial working class and trade union unity will be an important slogan tending to keep the whites split on class lines and to keep to the front the native trade union movement as an important factor in the struggle. But the slogans that will rally the main mass of rural and urban natives behind the Party will be "racial equality", "natives in parliament", "land for natives", etc., that is to say nationalistic slogans, the slogans of the democratic revolution in South Africa, the slogans which culminate eventually in the demand for a native republic.

It may be that the demand for a native republic may at the moment be a little premature, but that the demand will come eventually there is not the slightest doubt. This being so (and as com. Kuusinen pointed out) it is up to the Party to be the first to put forward the new slogan. We do not want anyone to steal our fire. At the same time, in view of the very precarious circumstances under which the Party operates to-day, we must put forward the slogan in such a way as to obtain the maximum response from the natives, while at the same time retaining and strengthening our influence in the white unions. I know this is easier said than done. In the first place it will be necessary to explain carefully to our own members the meaning and object of the slogan.

I am afraid I have not quite finished all I have to say, but I think this is sufficient for a single instalment.

With Communist greetings,

Yours fraternally,
E. R. Roux

Document 29
Letter from S. P. Bunting to E. R. Roux, 5 December 1928[16]

Box 1915 [–]
5 Dec 1928

Dear Roux,

I don't suppose you will hear much party news from anyone else, though Kalk & Danchin no doubt gave you their story to date. When we got here we found the party split sideways and endways with quarrels, intrigues, backbiting etc to incredible lengths. The difference over the slogan had led to general bad blood. Woltons and La Guma[17] versus all the rest, but some of the rest also versus Thibedi; the branches also bewildered at this excess of partisanship at head office, and the Trade Unions quite paralysed especially by disagreements between La Guma & Thibedi. As far as I can judge, everybody concerned is to blame, and not least the Woltons for announcing, in the middle of all the trouble, that they are retiring to England at the end of the year. This they did about 10 days ago. We left them last June, despite differences of opinions, on the best of intimate terms, but in our absence they have worked up a case against us to make you shudder and try as we will to ignore it it has destroyed all the real confidence between us. What letters have been sent to Moscow all these months from them and La Guma we can only guess; we see now that our very unpleasant experiences there were the result of a violent secret preparation in the shape of reports which as you know Bennett & Co never showed us, but the contents of which we can imagine from the contents of another missive to Moscow which it seems was read, before despatch by Baker & Thibedi, cutting us & others to pieces – so that we feel we have been unwittingly dealing all this time with some very deep customers. Well, it is all very depressing, and will take a lot of liquidating, but there is meanwhile a smaller staff than ever to do the work. To replace Wolton La Guma is spoken of, but he has just come into a small fortune near Capetown, and possibly will not [*leaved*] anyhow. When he was here (he had just returned to C.T. when we landed) he was on bad terms with several, so one can't be sure he would be a success as secretary. The Woltons are very keen, after they leave, to have non Europeans at the Head office. Well, Silwana is also [*–aitable*], though none of us know quite enough about him to feel sure whether he is up to it. Another complication is that Harrison is only half hearted about his Cape Flats campaign, and in fact is going to England too this month end. If Wolton had stayed, I should love to have jumped into the breach, though where subsistence is to come from I don't know; but as it is I may have to take Wolton's place in one form or another. Anyway, I have given up the idea of restarting legal practice for a good many months to come, and am quitting the office at the end of this month. We also don't know what to do with the children, the prospect of continued [*rations?*] during the holidays is terrible; and if I go to the Cape, what to do with the rest of the family, & the home, is also a problem.

On the boat I wrote a pamphlet on Imperialism & S Africa of which I sent Rathbone a copy last week. It was the best formulation I could think of for the "slogan". We landed in S Africa to find a regular hurricane fire of alarmist newspaper scares about Moscow & S African natives, but we were not searched at Capetown. We were [*pestered?*] for [–] about "Mrs. Rebecca Bunting's opposition to the slogan", and to clear the air I wrote a letter on that subject to the Star of Nov 17, which you may have seen. [- - - - -, - - -] reported in the Star & Mail of Nov 19 which you may also have seen. We were threatened or warned of arrest, but although we have made a number of speeches since, always dogged by crowds of detectives (eg at Evaton, a new branch) nothing has happened beyond Chinese crackers thrown at an indoor meeting at the Trades Hall last Sunday, by a woman in tow with Stewart, the man we spotted at the Capetown Conference 3 years ago, and now openly connected with the C.I.D. Stewart who is boasting of having got [*Weinstock*] & [*Kentridge*] in trouble over a lottery, is now giving out that Bunting will be the next – he [–] ⅓ of the [–]. Since Nov 19, the Press has been carefully silent about us, evidently on instructions.

We advertised a meeting specially for white Trade Unionists, but I don't think any came, the hall was full of miscellaneous whites. Tinker is hot against us. I gather this is the attitude of such trade Unionists as bestir themselves to take any interest at all. *Andrews says he certainly is not going to have anything to do with a Black Republic. Tramwaymen, indicating me, shout to each other "kill him."* Of course, none of this is new, but the white working class can only be won by very patient propaganda of imperialism, and even then they prefer to be apathetic. The SATUC has turned down an invitation to the Anti-Imperialist League, I could see that Andrews was against accepting, though the ostensible reason I believe was lack of funds – as if they'd forgotten that Colraine's expenses were paid!

White bourgeois are generally hostile. but more ready I think to admit that what we say is true, though they want to cling to Empire, not Black Republic. Benson the lawyer said "All of us would be with you if you were not a Communist & and in tow with Moscow."A parson said "That's the stuff we ought to be preaching at St Mary's". And Marks of Market St said "I agree with every word" – i.e. of my speech of Nov 18. Well, if we can even split the white bourgeoisie a little, even though the Trade Unionists hold aloof and the bar loafers are hostile & the Dutch murderous, it is something.

As for the natives, Wolton has reeled off the 100-word slogan at them several times, but I couldn't see that it caught on like that. He has presented it too much as a new incantation fresh from Moscow, but it hasn't appealed like that. We shall see whether there is anything in it, as a "trumpet call", later on. Becky went to Potchefstroom to a woman's meeting, with Molly & Coloured Mrs. Bhola, a new chum from the Af. Nat Congress, & when Molly spouted the magic formula, a member of the branch said "Nothing new in that, it is what we Communists have been always hammering at, and we must go on hammering".

Despite Moscow's malignant obstinacy, I notice both the Woltons and I have presented the slogan as a matter of "majority", in the sense of your amendment: equality, liberty etc; these are the simpler cries that tell. Even so, the ICU has been inclined to repudiate the Black Republic, and the ANC has been silent. Many of our black members & trade unionists are against it, & I have to champion it, (with rather bad grace I confess, for though it is challenging – to whites – it doesn't seem to me inspired or inspiring as regards blacks). try saying: "Well, the wording is a bit harsh, but after all, we have always told the natives they have got to rule;" and I think they will settle down as the October drought gives place to rain. [- -] asked a question. "Won't your black republic fall under Imperialist influence?" The answer is, that this language about "stages" represents sociological rather than chronological sequences (though I think it was dictated by the analogy of a bourgeois democratic native revolution in China, but of course I couldn't say that) as really no black republic in SA could be achieved without overthrowing capitalist rule. And in fact I think the "stage" part of that formula *is* verbiage. My idea is to carry on as best we can with the slogan and see how it goes, emphasising about the "minorities" so as to escape the N. Au Act, but to concentrate rather on agitation and indignation as heretofore. and, at the Cape election, to concentrate mainly on the Cape vote and the 101 degradations/disabilities etc. There is something not quite intelligible to the crowd about "Independent Black Republic" – they [–] ask "look, if that doesn't mean driving the whites into the sea, what does it mean?," and they don't want something that involves a lot of explanation –

Gumede, I heard at Capetown, has been engaged by the SAP to canvass for them in the elections, but says he can also support the C.P.! At Cape Flats the Creswellite is A Z Berman, the Independent, D Haggar, & the SAP I don't know– SAP will be our most formidable opponent.

I am hoping that perhaps the Woltons will get out of their huff and decide to remain after all, though they have sold their furniture & given up their (half share of a) house. If they will stay, I should like the party to second me to fight Cape Flats, though how to meet the expense, I have no idea. [–] promised support before we went to Europe, but now I think he will refuse it on the ground that he doesn't like a Black Republic. I have still to try and [–] up a [*fund for - purpose*] for the party is £100 in debt.

I am sending this letter by hand, and perhaps you will be able to send some sort of reply also by hand in a month or two's time. By the middle of this year you will be coming yourself.

We have made no progress regarding students, but may do so shortly. *The Woltons have so far declined to give reasons for their departure, but the chief one seems to be that the office holders in the party should all be black. But why therefore desert the party & this country?*

The trade unions are suffering for want of a Secretary-Organiser: the right [–] can't be found. I lost the addresses you & Rath gave me.

[–]
S P Bunting

Pass this letter on to Col. C[–] & CI – or rather, send them the substance of it – if possible.

Document 30
Letter from S. P. Bunting to E. R. Roux, 9 January 1929

I presume you had a letter [from] CG, who might be [-] for a reply instead of the procedure below, do which you like, I shall [-].

42 & 43, ASHER'S BUILDINGS,
Corner Fox & Joubert Streets,
Johannesburg.
9 1 29

Dear Roux,

I have only time to say that we got over our crises at our Conference (a very fine one, splendid country delegates). We agreed on interpreting the slogan as meaning much the same as a (predominantly & characteristically native) Workers & Peasants republic, and not meaning a black dictatorship; and though some wanted to move amendments or references back I felt bound, while allowing full discussion for the sake of arriving at an understanding, to disallow these as contrary to the Comintern statutes, enjoining unreserved acceptance. After the $4\frac{1}{2}$ days Conference was over we got a cable from Inkpen (for ECCI) requesting its postponement till March (to allow an emissary to come out & convince us, [*I've*] gather from Danchin), but cabled back that it was all over, slogan adopted, and that we were now trying to finance elections. Wolton came out with his attack on the party, very poisonous & diseased, but in reply he was induced to stop till after the elections, & his charges were not taken seriously. He is to fight Cape Flats & I Tembuland. the head office will have to be in suspense, but we have got a native assistant secretary Nzula whose trustworthiness will still have to be proved, I fear, as his record is not quite irreproachable: but we'll see. Weinbren & Thibedi are still irreconcilable to the slogan, especially W, who is leading the native T.U.'s against it – an awkward position which however must I think burn itself out. (I also think the slogan defective, but we can get along with it, and *may* make a hit, will see.) Will you please pay that money you collected for me (which you appear not to have remitted) into my account at Westminster Bank Ltd, Bloomsbury ([–]) Branch 126 High Holborn WC1, within a week of receiving this, as by next mail I am closing that account before departing for the wilds – a real adventure it will be, & Govt may shut us up there, the law prohibiting meetings there is in force now, & may be stiffened!

[–]
S P Bunting

Document 31
Letter from E. R. Roux to Victor Danchin[18], 6 March 1929

Copy

Camb
6 March 1929

Dear Victor,

I must apologise for the delay in answering your letters, for which thanks very much. I take it that the second book was confiscated by the authorities, as I sent them in a single package. I hope you will not create the impression of being "ultra left" as a result. Perhaps you could make some inquiries at your end. The two books certainly left here safely.

I hope you have now seen No 596 of the SA Worker and also SPB pamphlet "Imperialism and S Africa". I think the CI will find the final programme fairly satisfactory in its immediate demands but I can see breakers ahead as far as Bunting's 60 page effort is concerned. However, we are gradually settling down to the "new line" and getting rid of the "pure Marxist" outlook. SPB moves very slowly but very surely. He is already taking up Hertzog's "kaffir state" cry and saying that that is what the CP stands for: a correct attitude I think. He still thinks of and emphasises the "telescoping" of the bourgeois-democratic and proletarian revolutionary movements in S Africa. I think he exaggerates the amount of telescoping that will take place.

As far as my own views are concerned, I find they are still in a state of flux, though gradually settling down to the orthodox CI view. A point on which I still differ from that view is the extent of the antagonism between the "small" Afrikander imperialism and the "large" British imperialism. The imperialists are still backing the natives to a certain extent against white S.A. – a point which the CI does not realise fully. This is why I still tend to emphasise the NATIVE republic (e.g., demands for racial equality and admittance to parliament, etc.) rather than the *independent* (of the British Empire) native republic.

We shall probably be able to draw important conclusions from the results of the Tembaland campaign. Whatever theory exists at present, if the CPSA continues to approach nearer to the native masses and particularly to the agrarian masses as it IS doing, it must eventually (with the assistance of the CI) work out a decent theoretical picture. I think you will admit that the "picture" hitherto has been rather too sketchy.

Thibedi is an ass about changing the slogan. It would be rather amusing if he could meet Stalin!

I suppose you have heard about Kadalie's resignation, from the article in Worker's Life (1/3/29).

Kind regards to yourself and Willie.

Yours fraternally,
E R Roux

Document 32
League of African Rights[19], Petition, 1929

A League of African Rights

Petition with a million signatures

Members of the African National Congress, I.C.U. Communist Party and other bodies espousing native interests filled the Workers' Hall, Market Street, yesterday afternoon at a mass meeting called to launch an organisation under the above title the object of which was stated to be:

> to mobilise and organise, by mass demonstrations, petitions and otherwise, a nation-wide struggle for the attainment of the following demands:
>
> (a) No tampering with the Cape non-European vote
>
> (b) Extension of the vote to non-Europeans throughout the Union on the same terms as Europeans in the Northern provinces
>
> (c) Universal free education for native and coloured children equally with white
>
> (d) Abolition of Pass laws throughout the Union
>
> (e) Full rights of free speech and public meeting irrespective of race.

In particular, it was decided to circulate a petition embodying the above demands throughout South Africa with the aim of obtaining, before the Native Bills are reintroduced, at least a million signatures of protest against the Bills. This it was stated could be achieved by cooperation between, and use of the machinery of, all the existing native and coloured organisations throughout the country, although the greater number of signatures would probably be obtained from persone hitherto outside any organisation. After discussion on procedure a constitution was adopted in principle providing for affiliation of such organisations, as well as for individual membership at a subscription of 1/ a year, subscribers to receive a red and green badge with the motto "Mayebuye".

An Executive was appointed and the following were provisionally chosen as office holders pending a national Conference to be held on December 15 next, to be followed on December 16 (Dingaan's Day) by simultaneous demonstrations all over the Union in support of the demands;

President: J. T. Gumede
Vice-President: A. Modiagotla
Chairman: S. P. Bunting
Vice-Chairman: N. B. Tantsi
Treasurers: the Chairman and C. Baker
Secretaries: A. Nzula and E. R. Roux, 41a Fox St, Johannesburg.

Document 33
League of African Rights, Announcement of Meeting, 25 August 1929

Workers' Hall

14 Market St.

A MASS MEETING

WILL BE HELD AT THE ABOVE HALL THIS

Sunday, August 25th, 1929

At 3 p.m.

TO CONSIDER THE FORMATION OF A

"LEAGUE OF NATIVE RIGHTS."

TO DEMAND (BY NATION WIDE DEMONSTRATIONS, A "MILLION SIGNATURE" PETITION & OTHERWISE) THE FOLLOWING:

1. No tampering with the Cape Vote.
2. Extension of native franchise to other Provinces.
3. Universal free education for non-Europeans.
4. Abolition of Pass Laws.

ROLL UP! ROLL UP!

THE CASE IS URGENT!

NOTES

1 Douglas Wolton was an Englishman who joined the Cape Town Party branch in 1925 and married activist Molly Zelikowitz from Lithuania. They were the chief proponents of the Comintern's "New Line" in 1930. See Part Three, n. 9.
2 The Sixth Comintern Congress marked a decisive shift in Comintern policy. In previous congresses consolidating the proletarian revolution and building socialism in the USSR had been subordinate to the proletarian struggles waged in the advanced countries. At the Sixth Congress, the theory of socialism in one country became official doctrine. In this view the USSR became the leading force in the world revolution and construction of socialism in the USSR became the first goal of the international proletariat. All local and particular struggles, including class struggles and anti-imperialist national liberation struggles in other parts of the world were important but subordinated. Hence, the Comintern's attempt to apply the Native Republic thesis to the divergent conditions in the U.S. South and South Africa and the efforts to deny South Africa's distinctiveness.
3 The ECCI's draft resolution on South Africa reached the CPSA in 1927 and was discussed by its Central Executive (CEC) on 15 March 1928. This split, with James La Guma and Douglas and Molly Wolton in support, and Victor Danchin, E. S. Sachs, Bennie Weinbren, Gana Makabeni and T. W. Thibedi, opposed. On 3 May the CEC split 4 to 4 on whether to send Bunting or Wolton to represent the CPSA at the Sixth Comintern Congress. At a CEC meeting on 10 May Bunting and Wolton presented their respective views on the draft resolution. Bunting's position was supported, 8 to 2. The CEC decided to send both majority and minority reports to the Sixth Comintern Congress, and Bunting was elected as delegate, 6 to 3, to be accompanied by Rebecca Bunting and E. R. Roux, then studying at Cambridge (Roux 1993:7-10).
4 Documents 23 to 26 are taken from the stenographic transcriptions made at the Sixth Comintern Congress. For background to the debates on the Native Republic thesis and the proceedings of the Sixth Comintern Congress see Roux (1993:118-39) and *Searchlight South Africa* (1989), 1, 3, July, 67-83.

5   Nikolai Bukharin represented the CPSU in the ECCI and was leader of the Comintern from 1926 until April 1929 when he was unseated. An architect of the "socialism in one country" doctrine, he was subsequently expelled from the Politburo of the CPSU in November 1929 and branded as leader of the Right Opposition. In 1938 he was a star defendant in one of Stalin's show trials and was subsequently executed. Comrade Ford was an African-American delegate.
6   The Red International of Labour Unions was a trade union federation linked to the Comintern. "Amsterdam" refers to the home of the non-Communist International Federation of Trade Unions.
7   Bunting is no doubt referring to the 1925 seaman's strike in Britain, South Africa and Australasia (Hirson and Vivian 1992).
8   Bunting was probably referring to J. T. Murphy, a leading member of the British Communist Party who had risen to prominence as a member of the war-time radical shop stewards' movement.
9   Harry Thuku, a clerk in the Kenyan colonial administration, was a founder of the Young Kikuyu Association in 1921. Although tribally-based and initially concerned with protesting low wages and poor working conditions, the Young Kikuyu Association is seen as marking the origin of Kenyan nationalism in its aim of uniting the various peoples of Kenya as one nation. Thuku became the first president of the Kenya Africa Union in 1946.
10 Following the Rand Revolt, Parliament passed the Indemnity Act of 1922 which allowed the Attorney-General to waive the right of individuals to trial by jury. Eighteen individuals were charged with high treason and sentenced to death; four were hanged. S. A. "Taffy" Long, H. K. Hull and D. Lewis were executed on 17 November 1922. As they went to the gallows, Long allegedly told Hull and Lewis: "Come boys, we will show them how Britishers die", and they died singing "The Red Flag" (Walker and Weinbren 1961:157).
11 The nine-day British General Strike of May 1926 took place in support of locked-out miners who were resisting wage cuts. It was notable for the solidarity of the rank and file and the capitulation of trade union leaders. The miners' lock-out lasted until November, ending in defeat.
12 Bunting's statement on the Kuusinen Theses is discussed in Roux (1993:126-8). Otto Kuusinen became more influential in the Comintern leadership after Bukharin's elimination.
13 Comrade Bennet (or Petrovsky) was Secretary of the Comintern's Anglo-American Secretariat, whose scope included sub-Saharan Africa and which was mandated to make the final decisions on the South African question.
14 Bukharin's *ABC of Communism* was a standard Communist text of the 1920s. The "Plebeian Party" refers to the *Lekhotla la Bafo* (League of the Poor or, more literally, "Council of Commoners") of Basutoland (now Lesotho). This was formed by two brothers, Josiel and Maphutseng Lefela. It had regular contact with Communists such as Albert Nzula, S. P. Bunting, Jacob Tjelele, J. B. Marks and Edwin Mofutsanyana.
15 W. H. Harrison came to South Africa as a military artificer during the Anglo-Boer war. A member of the ILP in the early 1900s, he moved later to the ISL and was a founding member of the CPSA. He wrote of his experiences on the left in *Memoirs of a Socialist in South Africa* (1948). In the 1920s the Cape was the only province where blacks still had a vote even though only whites could contest seats, and blacks formed half the electorate in only two constituencies, Cape Flats and Tembuland in Transkei. Although Harrison was initially suggested as a Communist candidate for the Cape Flats in the 1929 Parliamentary elections, Douglas Wolton later contested the seat. Bunting campaigned for election in Tembuland.
16 Documents 29 and 30 are utilised extensively by Roux (1993:131-5).
17 James La Guma (1894-1961), leading ICU activist, joined the CPSA in 1925. In 1927 he attended the League Against Imperialism conference in Brussels and visited Moscow with J. T. Gumede. He was twice expelled and readmitted to the CPSA. He helped found the NLL and later joined the army. Gumede was president-general of the ANC and a prominent political figure in Natal for several decades. He helped form the Natal Native Congress in 1900/01 and later edited *Ilanga lase Natal*. Gumede was a founding member of the SANNC (from 1923, the ANC). Disillusioned with the outcome of the SANNC's deputation to England and Versailles in 1919, he moved to the left. In 1927 he attended the League Against Imperialism conference with La Guma and visited Moscow, and he later became president of the LAR. After a conservative backlash within the ANC, he was replaced as president by Pixley ka Izaka Seme.
18 Victor Danchin was a CPSA member who opposed the Native Republic thesis and later had some dealings with Thibedi and other Left Oppositionists. See Document 43.
19 During Bunting's electoral campaign in Tembuland he founded the League of Native Rights which formed the basis for the LAR launched by the CPSA in Johannesburg. On the Tembuland campaign see Roux (1993:135-42). Van der Post (1934:309-34) describes a fictional campaign by a socialist trade union organiser in Bambuland (Tembuland) which government provocateurs turned into a riot.

Part Three

The Comintern and the New Line

EDITOR'S NOTE
The first thorough evidence of tightening Comintern control over national Communist parties came with the imposition of the New Line, sometimes called Class Against Class. Within each Party, those supportive of the New Line were elevated; firm critics were relegated to the sidelines or expelled. The South African case was inevitably complicated by the recent adoption of the Native Republic thesis. The new Class Against Class policy, with its insistence on the construction of independent revolutionary class-based organisation, necessarily meant an amendment to the Party's position on the national question.

Document 34[1]
Letter from the Executive Bureau, Communist Party of South Africa, to the Executive Committee, Comintern

To the E.C.C.I.

Dear Comrades,

We have received the following cable dated Berlin 22 October. Our reply by cable was sent on 25 October 1929 as follows. "Petition (is a) form of mass protest; involves local organisations; no danger (of) fusion (or) reformist leadership. Suggestions December noted."

We enclose copies of the constitution, petition form and circular letter of the League of African Rights. In taking the initiative in the formation of the League, we have been acting on the decision of the Sixth Congress (and also the suggestion of Comrade Paul[2] when he was here in June) to try to unite "existing embryonic national organisations among the natives; such as the African National Congress". "The Party, while retaining its full independence, should participate in these organisations, should seek to broaden and extend their activity." [See "The South African Question in the "Communist International" – English Edition, 15 December, 1928.]

As you will see from the circular letter, we do not aim at making the League a mere organisation of leaders, but desire to develop it on the basis of affiliation of local organisations, formation of local groups, etc. There is no danger of the Party fusing with reformist organisations or losing its identity or its leadership of the mass struggle. So far the bulk of the native leaders have held aloof from the League. Kadalie is opposing it, ostensibly on the ground that his organisation has already put forward demands similar to those of the League, but really because he fears the League will still further undermine his own declining influence. Gumede has joined the League in his individual capacity. His organisation as such has held aloof though in some districts members of the African National Congress and of both ICU's are assisting the League. Modiagotla of the Ballinger I.C.U. has joined, but other leaders of this organisations including Ballinger are opposed to joining.[3] The participation of native leaders and the affiliation of national organisations has been sought and would be welcome if it were forthcoming; but primarily we are appealing to the native masses over the heads of their leaders to unite in opposition to the Hertzog bills.[4] It must be remembered that existing native organisations are weak and have a very small membership, the main mass of natives throughout the country being completely unattached politically. To sweep into political activity the vast mass of unorganised natives is the main task of the League.

In an attempt to give some substance to the work of the league other than mere haphazard propaganda meetings, and in order to get many hundred of thousands of natives to participate personally in the struggle for national freedom, we have started a "Petition of African Rights." Like the "Great Charter" of the XIX Century in England[5], the petition embodies certain elementary, popular demands of the democratic revolution. Together with the slogan "Mayibuye!" ("Return to us our country!") it forms a programme of immediate demands on which we hope to unite the whole of the African people. This petition (for which we hope to obtain hundred of thousands of signatures) cannot be described as a mere reformist gesture. In fact the reformists have already taken fright at the petition and are boycotting it accordingly. They desire that a few "good-boy" natives leaders should request the Government to modify its native policy. The mass character of the petition, penetrating as we hope it will to every corner of the country and expressing the aspirations of millions of Africans, is such as the missionaries and other bourgeois reformists cannot countenance though they cannot openly oppose its demands without discrediting themselves in the eyes of the masses.

The petition is couched in the form of a demand. Like an election campaign or referendum (c.f. recent campaigns initiated by the German C.P. against the return of the Kaiser's property and the building of cruisers) it can be used to spread revolutionary propaganda among the broad masses who would not be reached otherwise. The collection of signatures goes hand in hand with the holding of meetings, mass demonstrations and the campaign for a nation-wide protest and street processions on Dingaan's Day. We hope also to make the presentation of the petition to Parliament an occasion for mass demonstrations in Capetown accompanied by a demand for the bearers of the petition to be heard at the bar of the house.

We are already meeting with evidence that the signing of the petition is not a "safe" reformist gesture but an act demanding a certain amount of courage and will on the part of those who sign. During Comrade Bunting's recent election campaign in Tembuland there were many sympathetic natives who failed to vote from fear. "If we vote Communist we shall be killed," they said. Similarly some are *afraid to sign* the petition lest they be *subsequently punished* by the Government for this *act of defiance*. We have had great difficulty in persuading them that the Government is unlikely to prosecute individual signatories.

In view of these facts we cannot agree that the petition should be dropped as reformist in character. We hope that our reasons will convince you of this.

Another and more permanent use for the League is as an auxiliary organisation to spread the influence of the Communist Party among the native peasantry and toilers in the small towns and country districts. We are not anxious to enrol directly in the Communist Party those politically immature elements, who nevertheless display at times considerable enthusiasm for the national cause and are anxious to join an organisation. It has already been agreed, in discussions with the C.I. and in conversations between ourselves and Comrade Paul and between Comrade Roux and the Colonial Department of the British C.P., that suitable national organisations, peasant organisations, etc., should be set up to cater for these elements. It is of course understood that these organisations should come under the general political leadership of the

Communist Party while retaining their organisational independence and mass character. The League is such an organisation. It is also a step towards the unification on federal lines of all existing national organisations and leaders still capable of waging a fight against imperialism. Conditions are very complicated and difficult here and the C.P.S.A. must be allowed to experiment in finding out the best methods of awakening, organising and uniting the different sections of the African people.

We are also concerned with a probable approaching period of illegality. The Minister of Justice and the Minister of Native Affairs have announced their intention of revising the Native Administration Act of 1927 which was intended to stop revolutionary propaganda among natives, but which proved unsatisfactory for that purpose. (You probably know how convictions of Communists under the "hostility clause" have recently been squashed by the Supreme Court.) Now that the Government has learnt by its mistakes of the past, and particularly now that it has a complete majority and is assured of the co-operation of the S.A.P. opposition (see recent speech of Smuts advocating that the Native Administration Act should be "tightened up") we may expect drastic legislation against native agitators and particularly against the Communist Party. Pirow, Minister of Justice, has stated that he intends to introduce legislation enabling the government to deport those who agitate among natives, "particularly Europeans not born in this country."[6]

The organisation of the League of African Rights is thus in one sense a preparation for approaching illegality of the C.P. It is less likely to be proscribed than the C.P. itself, but this is not so important as the fact that as a result of the formation of the League we are broadening our influence and making contacts among natives all over the country thus improving our chances of resistance should the Government attempt to drive us underground.

We agree with your suggestions regarding slogans for the Party and the demanding of payment for Dingaan's Day.[7] As for a stoppage on Saturday 14 December we do not think we are strong enough to bring this off. The Federation itself is very weak largely as a result of internal divisions over a long period, and the big industries, even in Johannesburg are unorganised. However, in co-operation the Federation we shall act if sufficient support is forthcoming.

We shall report more fully later on the progress of the campaign and the results of the Dingaan's Day demonstrations.

Yours fraternally,
E.B. C.P.S.A. Secretary

Document 35
Letter from John Gomas to the Executive Bureau, Communist Party of South Africa, 29 October 1930

Communist Party of South Africa

Cape Town Branch
Box 1176, Cape Town
29 October 1930

The Executive Bureau
Communist Party (S.A.)

Dear Comrades,

We understand that a move is on foot to remove Comrade S. P. Bunting from the Executive Bureau as a result of differences of opinion between him and other members. Judging from the information so far received, all our sympathies are with Comrade Bunting. We do not wish to pass judgement, however until we have a full report before us. We therefore request you to furnish us with an official statement of the differences which we are given to understand exist between Comrade Bunting and the E.B.

We have also written to Comrade Bunting, asking him to supply us with his version of the case.

The following telegram was sent to Comrade Bunting this morning: "Dont resign branch unanimously sympathetic letter following inform executive".

Yours fraternally,
JOHN GOMAS
pp. E.R.R
Secretary

Document 36
Letter from E. R. Roux to the Executive Bureau, Communist Party of South Africa, 18 November 1930

Box 1176
Cape Town
18 November 1930

The Executive Bureau
Communist Party of South Africa

Dear Comrades,

I was very pleased to learn of Comrade Douglas' return and hope that it will mean an extension of Party activity particularly in the country districts. We have reached a stage now where, thanks to the paper, the Party has become widely known in the country districts. What is wanted now is consolidation and the building up of branches in the areas where the paper now circulates. We have recently obtained agents for "Umsebenzi" in a large number of new areas, including Kingwilliamstown, Bell (Eastern Province), Naauwpoort, De Aar, Pearston (Cape), Port St. Johns (Transkei), Zuurbrak (Cape), Wynberg and Dysseldorp (Cape). Durban is now taking 20 dozen as is also Oudtshoorn. Pretoria is taking 12 dozen. Our free numbers sent to Native voters in Kingwilliamstown and Queenstown districts are beginning to bear fruit. We now have two agents in the Kingwilliamstown area but only one in Queenstown. However I expect we shall meet with further responses.

We have sent out an appeal to a number of subscribers for a monthly guarantee to maintain the weekly publication of the paper. This will probably bring in enough to keep us going until the end of the year at any rate. I propose (if you are not unwilling) to close down the publication of the paper between December 19 and January 9, thus providing me with a fortnight's holiday. I shall be able to attend the Party Conference on Boxing Day, though I do not yet know where I shall get the train fare. Perhaps the E.B. could help me with this.

The Cape Town Branch is making preparations to send a delegation of about four members and is organising a social to raise the necessary funds.

With regard to Dingaan's Day celebrations in Johannesburg, the Cape Branch (in reply to your query) asks me to say that they think you should go ahead with the burning of passes if you get a demonstration approaching in size that of last year. If only a mere handful turn up of course you will have to do something less spectacular. We think however that the publicity given to the demonstration by the Anti-Pass Conference and by the capitalist press plus whatever we can do between now and the sixteenth by way of meetings, leaflets, organisation of Anti-Pass Committees etc., should guarantee a crowd at least equal to last year's. I think we should defy any ban Pirow may place on our meetings on Dingaan's Day, particularly in large centres like Johannesburg, Bloemfontein, Pretoria, Durban and Cape Town.

With regard to a possible transfer of the paper from Cape Town to Johannesburg, I sent you a couple of weeks ago a statement of the various difficulties that will have to be overcome before this will be possible. It depends partly on the amount of money at the disposal of the E.B. for the upkeep of the paper and whether we desire to continue to run it as a weekly. It is of course highly undesirable that the paper should be a one-man-show as at present. We must remember however that it is many years since the Party organ ceased to appear weekly (1925 I think it was). Since we became a weekly once more our circulation has increased considerably and is still rapidly rising. I think therefore that the present arrangements should not be terminated until we are definitely certain that we can continue to maintain a weekly paper in johannesburg. However we can discuss these matters in greater detail at the Conference.

I understand that the E.B. now has two resolutions (political and organisational) from the ECCI. Are these suitable for publication in "Umsebenzi"? If so, please let me have copies as soon as possible.

Comrade Bunting informs me that he and I are condemned by the ECCI for racial chauvinism. I should like to know definitely what the charge is and in what details I have offended against Comintern policy. I admit having made certain slips, e.g. my opposition to the new slogan in 1928 and a certain article in Umsebenzi last May in which I adopted a rather unMarxist attitude towards the Pirow dictatorship. The latter

I think is a small matter: since May I have tried to keep the policy of the paper as near to that of the Comintern as possible and I think I have not made any serious mistakes since then. With regard to my previous opposition to the slogan, I have long since retracted. I think I understand the significance of the slogan as well as any comrade in the Party. I have persistently preached it on the public platform, and, what is more, I have tried to give comrades in the Party some idea of the theoretical basis of Comintern policy with regard to the national question and modern imperialism.

If I am now accused of racial chauvinism by the ECCI it can only be because they have received incorrect reports of the situation in South Africa. I sincerely appeal to comrades Dougie and Solly to write to the ECCI explaining the position. I would point out that the latter comrade a year ago when I was in Johannesburg was still very hazy about the slogan. Very few of us have a really good understanding of the theoretical basis of Party policy and I do not see why I (who have offended less than many) should be picked out. With regard to Comrade Bunting, any charge of racial chauvinism directed against him is obviously ridiculous and the sooner the whole party protests against such a travesty of the truth the better.

I should like to have a letter from Douglas as soon as possible.

Yours fraternally,
[E. R. Roux]

Document 37[8]
Letter from S. P. Bunting to E. R. Roux, 29 November 1930

42 & 43 Asher's Buildings,
Corner Fox & Joubert Streets.
Johannesburg.
November 29th 1930.

E. R. Roux,
P.O. Box 1176,
CAPE TOWN.

Dear Roux,

Wolton is leaving tonight for Cape Town to introduce the "new line" to the Cape Town branch.[9] At the Johannesburg branch meeting last night at which I was absent owning to stomach trouble (my first absence this year) he held forth something on the lines of the enclosed. It reminds me of the Conference of two years ago when he made a violent attack on me, and the rank and file said that they did not want to listen to all this quarreling. I cannot help thinking that under cover of theses, C.I. resolutions, etc., there is a long standing personal antipathy or jealousy – just as Thibedi (who has now been expelled again from the Federation by his recent backers, prospects having been offered them from a different quarter) used the cry of "white domination" to cover peculation.

I hate fighting for position and have not yet decided whether I ought to do it or not. I am afraid this campaign is again militating against the Pass Campaign, in which neither Wolton (the "Comintern Representative", and with all the dictatorial airs of one) nor Sachs is taking or intends to take any public part. My letter to the Executive has been ignored and scarcely anybody has read it, although I think it is the truth.

Yours fraternally,
S. P. Bunting

Document 38
"How to Build a Revolutionary Mass Party in South Africa: A letter from the Executive Committee of the Communist International,", Umsebenzi, 12 December 1930[10]

To the Communist Party of South Africa.

Dear Comrades,

Recent events in South Africa show that tnis country, which has the formal right of a British Dominion, but which in reality is a semi-colony, has entered a period of deep crisis, which finds expression in:
(a) the crisis in a number of branches of industry and a sharpening of the general agrarian crisis;
(b) the attack of the bourgeois ruling classes on the native working masses and on the lower paid section of the white workers;
(c) in the upsurge of the class struggle and the struggle for national liberation.

The maturing world economic crisis has affected with special force the whole of the Negro part of Africa, where already mass revolts have broken out in recent months in French Congo, Nigeria, Kenya, Gambia, the Lower Sudan and Rhodesia.

Growing Economic Crisis
1. The growing disparity between the growth of South African industry and the limited internal market owing to the extremely low standard of living of the broad masses of the native population, the inability of the technically backward South African industry successfully to emerge on the world market, the penetration of foreign capital, especially of British capital, into the country in spite of the protective policy of the nationalist government, and, finally, the fall in prices on the world market of a number of the principal products of South Africa (wool, grain, sugar, fruit, diamonds, etc., which comprise 50% of the exports of the country), all this has brought about a crisis in a number of branches of industry (diamond, clothing, etc,).

The continuous increase in the native population in an already frightfully congested territory, in which they live, the so- called reserves, the simultaneous worsening of the conditions of the mass of the native land workers in the European districts, and the continuous decline in prices for agricultural products while the price of land is greatly inflated, are the causes of the growth and sharpening of the agrarian crisis.

Hertzog's Repressive Land Policy
This situation has induced the parasitic land-owning class, assisted by the colonial

government, to accelerate the process of transformation of the present feudal-like system of land utilisation represented by the squatters' system – labour tenantry and share-cropping, into large-scale intensive farming employing actual serf labour. The amendments to the Land Act of 1913, contained in the proposed Native Bills, will, if passed, result in the native peasantry being reduced from the position of a semi-serf to a position worse than slavery; the share croppers and labour tenants will be converted into "servants", obliged to work 180 days a year for the right to live on the land. This would enable the landowners to develop large-scale intensive farming.

Poor Whites
Simultaneously, with the worsening of the situation of the native masses, the poor white farmers, and especially "bywoners" are being expropriated and compelled to migrate to the cities to swel the growing ranks of the unemployed, who are competing with the miserably paid native workers, and this sharpens the "poor white problem."

Fierce Attack on Native Toilers
2. The European ruling class, represented by the Hertzog Government, which depends on the nationalist party (the slave-owner Party of the Boer farmers) and by the South African Party, which represents the interests of British imperialism, – primarily the industrialists and particularly mining industrialists, in its efforts to find a way out of the impasse into which the economy of the country has landed, has commenced a fierce attack on the native toilers and the poorer sections of the white workers. The attack finds its expression in the efforts to force down the standard of living of the workers in general and in the introduction of a whole series of legislative measures directed against the revolutionary movement of the native toilers. The conflict between the two parties of the European ruling class over the "Native Bills" which became more acute during the recent election campaign, is merely a conflict between slave-owners, who are disputing as to the methods of attaining their common end, i.e., to transfer the burden of the crisis to the shoulders of the Native toilers, who are already inhumanly exploited, and to crush the rising revolutionary movement.

S.A.P. Smoke Screen
The present role of the South African Party, aided by the Native reformists and under the cloak of hypocritical liberal phrases is to furnish a smoke-screen for the policy of the Hertzog Government, which takes part in all repressive measures against the Natives. The raid on the Native quarter of Durban was carried out by a bloc of all the bourgeois parties, including the "Labour" Party.

3. The Native masses, groaning under the yoke of ever-increasing oppression and the danger of their already unbearable conditions becoming worse, are in their struggle passing to a counter-offensive against the European slave-owners. This is seen in the increase in the number of strikes, which rapidly assume a political character, the riots in Durban and Robertson, which were accompanied by desperate clashes with the police, the boycott movement, the revolts in Northern Transvaal, the mass demonstrations of the unemployed in Johannesburg, the demonstrations in connection with the Riotous Assemblies Act, in open violation of slave laws, like the pass laws, refusal to pay taxes, etc.

These processes now taking place within the labour and nationalist movements have already strengthened the Communist Party and the revolutionary trade unions.

Communist Party Weaknesses

4. The Party's work has resulted in certain achievements: partial successes in the recent election campaign; the increase in agitation among the Native masses, the large number of Native workers recruited for the Party, etc., all of which proves that the Party has become a real political force in the country, which in turn has called forth increased persecutions on the part of the bourgeoisie.

Nevertheless, the ideological and political influence of the Communist Party is by no means keeping pace with the growing mass discontent. The influence and activity of the latter is still confined to a narrow sphere chiefly around Johannesburg. The Communist Party has not yet begun seriously to tackle the question of establishing contacts with the basic masses of Native workers. It still has little or no contact with the workers in the mines. The contacts of the Party with the basic masses of Native workers are so weak that it is practically isolated from the spontaneous movement of the masses, and it drags at the tail of that movement.

The Party leaders are committing serious mistakes of a Right opportunist character. The reason for this is the fact that the Party leaders have not yet carried out the 1928 resolution of the C.I., which demands that the Party take the initiative in and lead the struggle of the Natives against the foreign yoke under the slogan of an Independent Native Republic.

An Independent Native Republic means, primarily, the return of the land to the landless population and those with little land, which is impossible without revolutionary liberation from British imperialism and the organisation of a revolutionary workers' and peasants' government on the basis of Soviets. The correctness of this slogan has been doubly confirmed by the desperate attacks of the South African ruling classes against it, by the opposition of former members of the Party known for their chauvinism and opportunism, e.g. Andrews, and especially by the development of the Native national movement. The principal feature of the Right opportunist mistakes committed by the Party is the failure to understand the decisive importance of the hegemony of the proletariat and the complete independence of the vanguard of the revolutionary proletariat, the Communist Party, in the nationalist revolutionary movement and the failure to understand the significance of the dictatorship of the proletariat in the social revolution.

(To be continued)

"How To Build a Revolutionary Mass Party in South Africa: A letter from the Executive Committee of the Communist International", *Umsebenzi*, 19 December 1930

(continued from last week)

5. In a country like South Africa, where the overwhelming majority of the population consists of peasants, the revolution, in its first stages, can be only a bourgeois democratic revolution, carried out by the peasants and workers under the leadership of the latter.

But the nationalist revolutionary movement in South Africa can be victorious and bring about an Independent Native Republic only under the leadership of the working class. There is no other class in South Africa capable of uniting the diffused, scattered and unorganised masses of Natives who are already rising for the agrarian revolution and for the revolutionary struggle for national liberation. The Native bourgeoisie exists only in an embryonic form. The intellectuals (Native teachers, Native parsons) are mostly in the service of the European ruling class. The only class capable of uniting the national revolutionary fighting front is the Native proletariat, supported by the most exploited masses of the white proletariat. Without leadership from the proletariat, the nationalist revolutionary movement which is overwhelmingly a peasant movement, is inevitably doomed to defeat, as is every peasant war.

But the proletariat cannot restrict its task only to the nationalist revolution. The latter is a task which does not exceed the boundaries of a bourgeois-democratic revolution, and history provides examples when historical tasks like these were carried out by the bourgeoisie. The agrarian revolution and liberation from the imperialist yoke, which are the main content of the South African nationalist revolutionary movement, have no further aim than the reform of bourgeois society. The proletariat, however, can emancipate itself and the toiling masses from exploitation only under socialist society. For this reason, the proletariat will not stop at an Independent Native Republic; it will go further, and transform this republic into a Socialist Republic.

This ultimate aim must not be lost sight of for a moment. To forget this will inevitably lead to the proletariat becoming absorbed in a petty-bourgeois nationalist movement; the leadership will then pass into the hands of petty-bourgeois politicians and adventurists like Kadalie, and this will inevitably lead to the defeat of the movement. Communists must always bear in mind the example of the Mexican revolution, in which the Mexican proletariat failed to win the hegemony.[11] Only by being organised as a separate and independent force, with its own aims and carrying on its independent policy, will the proletariat succeed in winning the leadership of the nationalist revolutionary movement.

This independence of the proletariat can be guaranteed only by its vanguard being organised into an independent class revolutionary Party, having for its aim the complete carrying through of the nationalist revolutionary struggle, and, as the subsequent stage, the socialist revolution. The South African Communist Party must be such a Party.

6. Failure to understand the bourgeois-democratic and the socialist tasks of the South African proletariat is reflected in the fact that both the leaders and the members of the Party have not yet understood the significance of the slogan of Independent Native Republic. The white members of the Party, who have not yet cast off the remnants of white chauvinism, do not understand the nationalist tasks of the revolution, and try to reduce the whole of the struggle of the South African proletariat to a purely proletarian class struggle, while the Native members, who are still influenced by petty-bourgeois-peasant nationalism, on the contrary do not understand the tasks of the proletarian class struggle, and try to reduce the struggle to a nationalist- revolutionary movement. The whites do not understand the necessity for the hegemony of the proletariat in a nationalist revolution. The Natives do not understand the necessity for the dictatorship of the proletariat in the social revolution.

This lack of understanding leads, in practice, to a position where both sections of the Party, in different ways, commit the same mistake with regard to the growing nationalist revolutionary movement. The whites simply deny the nationalist revolutiouary tasks of the proletariat and in this way deny the hegemony of the proletariat in this movement. The Natives, by restricting the tasks of the proletariat solely to nationalist revolutionary tasks, in practice would cause the proletariat to become absorbed in the broad petty-bourgeois movement, and in this way destroy its hegemony in this movement.

7. In practice, this fundamental mistake (failure to understand the hegemony of the proletariat in the nationalist revolution and its dictatorship in the social revolution, and in connection with this, failure to understand the importance of an independent Communist Party with an independent policy) has given rise to a number of other mistakes.

The policy carried by the Party leaders in the League of African Rights is an example of how the Communist Party abandons its independent role. The League bears the character of a political party with a reformist programme. By allowing this League to serve as a substitute for our Party, our Party not only abandons its independent role, but the Communist programme of the Party is eclipsed by the reformist programme of the League.

The League's programme shows to what extent the Party is lagging behind the Native movement. At a time when the Natives are proving their revolutionary determination to struggle by openly violating the slave laws – refusing to pay taxes, – the Party, through the agency of the League, puts forward an extremely mild reformist programme, well within the framework of South African legality, a programme from which the slogan of an Independent Native Republic is completely absent. While Native reformist organisations like the National Congress advance radical slogans in order to catch the masses (for instance, the Cape National Congress put forward the slogan "Africa for the Africans" and advocates an extension of the boycott, etc.) our Party, during the Durban raids, issued a manifesto in which it urges the Native toilers to "keep cool keep your heads, do not be rushed or bluffed into false moves even by your leaders".

After organising the League the Party handed it over to the reformists, like Gumede and others, and joined the League itself as a Communist Party, thus surrendering the right to criticise the reformists. In this way the Party accepts full responsibility before the Native masses for the waverings of the reformists, including the low treachery of the vice-chairperson of the league, Modiakgotla, who, speaking in the name of the League at the recent conference of non-European clergy in Bloemfontein, openly supported the Native Bills on the ground that they were beneficial to the Natives. Thus we have an actual union of the Communists with the national reformists in the League, which makes the Native masses believe that not only the League, but the C.P. itself does not differ from the nationalist reformist organisations. One of the fundamental conditions for the independence of the Party is that it openly ceases its affiliation with the League because of its failure to put up a real fight for the rights of the Natives.

8. In close connection with the failure to understand the significance ef the hegemony of the proletariat in the bourgeois- democratic revolution, are the reformist methods of struggle adopted by the Party in fighting against the Native Bills and the preparation for the demonstration on Dingaans Day. It is quite evident that the struggle against the Native Bill is transforming itself into a struggle against the entire system of imperialist oppression. Therefore, special attention must be paid to this struggle.

Increasing numbers of Natives are being drawn into this struggle. The Party hould have tried to develop this spontaneous movement of the masses into one for the refusal to observe laws and for the boycott. It should have elevated this struggle to a higher plane. The Party should have organised demonstrations of protest among the Native and white workers, organised committees of action, declared strikes in factories and ought to have turned December 16th into a review of the revolutionary forces which are ready to struggle against the existing political order, against the slave-owning government, against its parliament, against the constitution, for an Independent Native Republic and for the defence of the Soviet Union. Instead of this revolutionary mobilisation of the masses, the Party gathered signatures to a petition to the South African slave-owning imperialist parliament. Instead of coming out boldly at the head of the nationalist revolutionary movement and leading the masses, which is the only way of guaranteeing the hegemony of the proletariat in this movement, the Porty attempted in the manner of the reformists to turn the masses from the revolutionary road.
(To be continued)

Document 39
Statement by S. P. Bunting, October 1931

Private, for circulation among members *of the Communist Party only.*

P. O. BOX 1915,
JOHANNESBURG.
October, 1931.

DEAR COMRADES OF THE COMMUNIST PARTY,

No doubt you have heard of the recent expulsions, and perhaps you have wondered what is the reason for them. Speaking of my own case only, I believe the great majority of the comrades, and the African comrades in particular, will say they know of no reason why I should be put out of the party.[12]

The trouble does not emanate from the membership, however, but from the "new leadership" installed at (or rather before) last conference, which really means Com. Wolton, for the rest of the leading personnel remained much the same as before. Some of you may remember how bitterly, and as I think, falsely Com. Wolton attacked me at our 1928/9 conference, and how that conference did not want to hear anything of such quarrels. Since Com. Wolton's return from Europe last year, however, the attack has been greatly intensified, until it has become almost a "frame up." What have I not been charged with during the past few months? "Chauvinism," "opportunism," "right wing deviation," "being against Trade Unionism," "against the Pass Campaign," etc., etc., to all of which I plead, and I believe your verdict should be, *not guilty*! Similarly with the charges published in "Umsebenzi" of 4th September last about "sabotage work" or "fractional activities" in connection with T. W. Thibedi, the African Club, etc. – rather thin charges, I think you will agree, even if true, but actually *quite false*, as the members of my group and all others who know the facts (except a mere handful attached to Head Office who have reasons for not knowing them) will testify.

In short, my expellers *cannot clearly state any of their reasons except by grossly and knowingly distorting the truth.* Or they say I do not follow the "party line". The only party line I know is that published in our party programme, Conference Resolutions, etc., in accord with the Communist International, and this I follow. No other "line", even if authoritative, has been given out, except this lying "anti-Bunting" line, to the propaganda of which much valuable time and man power has been sacrificed, with the result that much real party work *has been scamped or most inefficiently conducted*, and *party membership and general agitational activity* have shrivelled almost to a skeleton (and then they blame me for all that too!)

Well, without engaging in anything like an opposition or a split, I am obliged, in applying to the next Party Conference for reinstatement, to ask you all for your support. That does not mean that I hanker after "leadership"; let the best man lead, whoever he is. For a year already I have worked hard as a rank-and-filer, especially on the founding of a miners' union, and should have been content so to continue. I only want this "ban," *passed by a small dictatorship without giving any notice (much less a hearing)* either to me or to you, to be removed, so that I may resume doing my bit in the great war for African emancipation – free this time, I hope, from the persistent misrepresentation, boycott and persecution, especially behind my back, to which I have been subjected for over a year past.

It will not be so easy for you to do what I ask. The present leadership will possibly do its utmost (and controlling the party machine it can do much) to prevent you from securing free expression of your will, through your own freely-chosen delegates, at the conference. It may say "this appeal of Bunting's is fractional" or "opposition to the leadership cannot be tolerated" or "Bolshevism does not believe in hearing both sides", or it may try to shelve the matter altogether. But *if there is something wrong* with a party or its bureaucracy, if there is some danger or poison or disease at work, *must you just hold your tongues and say "Ja baas"*? No, you cannot be deprived of your right to put matters in order at a party conference, and for that purpose to ascertain and discuss all the facts beforehand. If, therefore, you think that in the interest of the party and the African masses I should be reinstated, I beg you not to be indifferent or inactive, not to be bluffed or intimidated, but to assert yourselves by insisting on the conference being held and the matter properly placed on the agenda, and by sending delegates definitely instructed to cancel the expulsion resolution.

Yours ever fraternally,
S. P. BUNTING.

NOTES
1. The original document was hand-written and included a number of editorial changes which the version reproduced here incorporates.
2. In the original, Merker is crossed out and replaced by Paul.
3. Conan Doyle Modiagotla was an activist in the ICU and ANC and Vice-President of the short-lived LAR. He was elected to the ANC National Executive Committee and became a supporter of A. B. Xuma.
4. The Hertzog Bills, for which Prime Minister J. B. M. Hertzog had campaigned for ten years, included the Representation of Natives Bill and the Native Land and Trust Bill. The Representation of Natives Bill curtailed the Cape franchise and proposed to incorporate Africans through indirect representation under a Natives' Representative Council with solely advisory status on so-called Native issues. The Native Land and Trust Bill reasserted the restrictions on black landholding rights to scheduled areas. The Bills were passed by Parliament in 1936.

5   The 1840s Chartist movement in Britain advocated a six-point democratic programme. Their campaign culminated in a mass petition as part of a mobilisation in 1848. Although the campaign was effectively defeated by the British state, its radical democratic legacies were significant for both British Liberalism and the labour and socialist movements.
6   The Native Administration Act was passed by the Pact Government in 1927 when Tielman Roos was Minister of Justice and was used to prosecute those protesting the unjust treatment of blacks. Its Clause 29, the "hostility clause" was aimed at anyone allegedly seeking to create hostility between blacks and whites. Oswald Pirow became Minister of Justice following the 1929 NP electoral victory.
7   Dingaan's Day commemorates the anniversary of the Battle of Blood River on 16 December 1838, when Zulu chief Dingane and 100 000 Zulu warriors were defeated by *Voortrekkers* on the banks of the Ncome River in Natal. The defeat precipitated a civil war in the Zulu kingdom. While descendants of the *Voortrekkers* have celebrated 16 December as a day of victory, within the liberation movement it became known as Heroes' Day: MK was launched on 16 December 1961.
8   Document 37 is used by Roux (1993:148-9).
9   In South Africa the introduction of the New Line was largely the work of Douglas and Molly Wolton and of Lazar Bach, an emissary from Moscow who probably arrived in South Africa in late 1930. The Woltons went to England in December 1928 (Document 29). In July 1930 they attended the Fifth Congress of the RILU in Moscow, and they helped the ECCI draft two directives on South Africa regarding the "right-wing danger". On Douglas Wolton's return in November 1930, he began pushing the New Line and convinced Roux, then editor of *Umsebenzi*, to transfer the paper from Cape Town to Johannesburg. Following the Party's ninth annual conference in December, a new Central Committee of nineteen blacks and four whites was elected. These latter included Wolton as General Secretary, and Roux, E. S. "Solly" Sachs and C. Baker; Bunting and Sam Malkinson of Bloemfontein, who had trained a number of African comrades, were excluded. A series of expulsions followed: in September 1931 the Party expelled Bunting, W. H. Andrews, E. S. Sachs, C. B. Tyler, B. Weinbren and F. Klenerman. The Woltons left South Africa for England in late 1933. This left Bach relatively marginalised. Although factional fighting continued and, under Bach's leadership, the CPSA expelled Moses Kotane, Josiah Ngedlane and E. R. Roux in September 1935, Bach was subsequently recalled to Moscow following the Comintern's policy shift at its Seventh Congress in August 1935 and died in a Siberian labour camp in 1941. Moses Kotane (1905–78) joined the ANC in 1928 and the CPSA in 1929. In 1931 he attended the Lenin School in Moscow. In the mid-1930s he helped steer the CPSA away from the New Line. He was CPSA General Secretary from 1939 until his death. For his biography see Bunting (1975).
10 This letter, published in a series of instalments in *Umsebenzi*, is based on the *Praesidium of the ECCI to the Communist Party of South Africa*, dated 7 May 1930 (Simons 1983:438-40). It indicates a shift in thinking about the Native Republic thesis. Here, the achievement of an Independent Native Republic is seen as possible only through the leadership of the black working class, supported by the most exploited section of white workers. Thus, it argues, the CPSA's programme should be based on joint activity of black and white workers.
11 The Mexican Revolution began in 1910 and was directed against an oligarchic regime. The revolution enjoyed the sympathetic support of radicals such as John Reed; its outcome had no socialist content.
12 On Bunting's expulsion see Roux (1993: 156-64).

Part Four

The origins and development of Trotskyism in South Africa

EDITOR'S NOTE

The impact of changes within the international Communist movement was not restricted to the CPSA. As with their counterparts in several other countries, dissident members of the CPSA left and aligned themselves with the emerging Left Opposition associated with the exiled Leon Trotsky. This section demonstrates the complex reasons which brought individuals to the Left Opposition. Some placed their emphasis on the Comintern's authoritarianism; others objected to the strategic implications of the Native Republic thesis. The organisational legacies in South Africa bore similarities with their counterparts elsewhere, with serious attempts to theorise problems of socialist strategy undermined by continuing organisational squabbles and splits. The historical explanation of this phenomenon remains complex. Clearly, it had an international dimension which must be juxtaposed to specific South African causes. Inevitably, in small organisations personal differences played a significant part, but there remains a broader question of the space available for new revolutionary initiatives in the 1930s. One of the legacies of the Bolshevik Revolution has been the near equation in most societies of revolutionary socialist politics with official Communist Parties. Once this became fixed, the development of alternative revolutionary organisations became difficult.

Document 40
Letter from T. W. Thibedi to the
Communist League of America[1], 26 April 1932

April 26, 1932.

Secretary
Communist League of America
84 East 10th Street
New York

Dear Comrade:–

In our last meeting held on the 22 of April, 1932 at 9 Fuller Street, Bertrams, Johannesburg, all the undermentioned negro comrades decided to apply for membership to your league. Regarding you appeal for your literature agents it was agreed that we request you to send us 8 dozen copies of the Militant per week which we hope to sell and return you the money. We are particularly anxious to introduce the Militant amongst the African workers and for handling the same a committee consisting of 12 of us has already been selected. Send us 2 dozen copies of your constitution, send us, say 12 copies of advertising bills with attractive cartoons if you consider necessary with every issue of the Militant. Send us from time to time propaganda leaflets for free distribution if you have any.

The first copy of the Militant that came to our notice is Volume V, whole No. 97 dated January 2, 1932, in which we find on page three an article entitled "Stalin and the Chinese Revolution" but we were disappointed for not having been able to obtain a previous copy of the Militant, the issue which we believe contains the first part of that article, so will you by the next mail send us 2 copies which we desire to keep on our files.²

Comrades, do not be worried in seeing all these applicants being negroes and think that we are purposely refusing to unite with European comrades, no we are not. It is only about 2 months ago that we have been considering joining your League. Although it is difficult for a negro comrade to organize a European worker, we hope that later on white militant follow our lead. The color question makes organizing difficult. Negro workers are generally considered inferior even on such matters as revolutionary organizations, and as usual European workers are considered superior. We have been calling ourselves "Communist Party of Africa".

The undermentioned negro comrades pledge themselves to see that your instructions in connection with the revolutionary movement for a complete overthrow of capitalism and the establishment of communism in Africa are carried out. Please address all communications and literature to the secretary. We are:–

George Malefo, chairman, T.W. Thibedi, secretary, Simon Molefi, Treasurer, Scott H Seroke, Jim Makapane, James Mokwane, Alfred Mokkatle, Cyrus M. Letlojane, B. Dau Madiseng, Stephen Mokkethea, Johannes Maskigo, Alphies Maliba, George Makua, Thomas Moekitsi, France Mopu, Rapalana J. Tjekele, Timothy Pongosi, J. Chusi, Lucas Malop, Johannes Chileane, Samuel Mohlati, Sam Khuduga, etc.³

I am,

Yours for a speedy revolution,
T. W. Thibedi, Sec'y
Communist Party of Africa
P O Box 4143
Johannesburg, So. Africa

Document 41
Letter from the Communist League of America to T. W. Thibedi, 30 May 1932

THE MILITANT

May 30, 1932.

T. W. Thibedi
P. O. Box 4143
Johannesburg, So. Africa.

Dear Comrade:–

We sincerely welcome the announcement of your decision contained in your letter of April 26th. This is the very first information which we have had about your group and naturally we are not yet well acquainted. We are therefore desirous of obtaining some information from you in order to be able to learn about your group and to reciprocate by likewise informing you about our position as fully as we are able.

Is your group newly constituted or has it been functioning for some time under its present name or under any other name? If you can, will you give us in brief outline information about the history, and development about your group. That we would appreciate very much and it would help facilitate our mutual acquaintance, understanding and possible harmony. If you can in this information also include a description of the kind and character of activities in which you have been engaged, adding also information about what influence, following and contact you may have.

Second:– Has your group formulated a program or platform on its views? If you have such, will you kindly let us have a copy or give us the information of its main contents.

Third:– Have you any relations with the official Communist Party of Africa, the section which is affiliated to the Communist International, or does your party constitute that section? Are you or have you been affiliated to the Communist International? Would you kindly clarify us on this point?

Lastly:– We assume that you know that the Communist International under the present Stalinist leadership has adopted a policy of self-determination for Negroes. We do not presume to express an opinion on what this policy would mean in So. Africa or apply to actual existing conditions there. But we do know that this policy will have some specific implication when applied to the actual existing conditions in the United States and we know are now considering a final formulation of our attitudes to this question as it presents itself here in the United States. Will you give us your views on the question?

As you have read some copies of the Militant we assume that you are fully informed that the Communist League of America (Opposition) represents the views of the Left Opposition. We do not know how well you are familiar with the history and development of the Left Opposition. That you will be able to learn from a continued reading of the Militant and from our literature. Being a faction of the Communist movement, representing the views of the Communist International under the leadership of Lenin and Trotsky and concretely formulated in the first four Congresses, today, the Left Opposition considers its main objectives to be the struggle to influence the official Communist Parties sufficiently to return to these views of the Communist International. In that struggle we come into an irreconcilable conflict with the present Stalinist bureaucracy and the policies it represents. Our League is made up, as are all the sections of the Left Opposition, in the main of members expelled from the official Communist Parties. But we recruit to our ranks all Communist workers we find having sympathy and in agreement with our Left Opposition platform.

Since we are only one section of the International Left Opposition, we will later have some substantial proposals to make to you in regard to affiliation. Should we find that after a little mutual communication and clarification that we are in agreement, that you accept the Left Opposition platform, which we hope to already be the case, then we expect our proposal to you to be to affiliate directly to the Left Opposition as the Left Opposition in South Africa, affiliated to the International Left Opposition, and not directly to the Communist League of America.

Any subsequent and practical proposals to be worked out in this connection we can take up later if and when we find that we are in agreement. We will therefore submit a copy of your letter to the International Secretariat of the Left Opposition which is located in Berlin and we will attach a copy of this reply to your communication and similarly send the same material to Comrade Trotsky.

Meanwhile, however, we would appreciate if you would consider us the connecting link for this discussion and any proposals which you many have to make and which the International Secretariat will have to make until such time when this question is settled to mutual satisfaction. Naturally, we would also appreciate if you would keep in constant touch with us about your views.

We have already entered you on our mailing list to receive the Militant. Of this issue we have sent you only 50 copies, but we shall increase the future issues to 100 as you request. We will also send you along some advertising material which we have for the Militant. We do not possess much in this respect, neither do we at the present have any leaflets for mass distribution. But we have published considerable literature, a full description of which you will find in the Militant. Our books and pamphlets can already today be obtained by Vanguard Booksellers, 51a Van Brandes Street, Johannesburg, So. Africa.[4] We will send you a complete set (one of each) of all our literature, expecting that you will be able to remit for it and should you desire to handle it direct, we shall be very glad to furnish it to you. We will send you bills and statements regularly, as, being a proletarian organization, poor in the financial sense, we would appreciate prompt remittances. We also sent you a few copies of the special Militant issue which you request and should you desire it, we shall try to gather a complete file of the Militant from the first issue published and send it to you, even though some of the numbers are very scarce.

We repeat, we sincerely welcome the fact that such a group exists in So. Africa and agree with you that no distinction is made in our ranks of Negro and white revolutionary workers, as no such distinction is made in any Communist revolutionary organization. We welcome the fact that such a group exists in So. Africa, holding the views which we have expressed, which we consider essential in the task of the proletarian revolution. With revolutionary greetings, we remain,

For the Communist League of America,
Arne Swabeck

Document 42
Leon Trotsky, "Closer to the Proletarians of the 'Colored' Races!", *The Militant*, 2 July 1932[5]

Prinkipo, June 13, 1932

To the International Secretariat:
Copy to the National Committee of the American League:

I have received a copy of the letter of an organization of Negro comrades from Johannesburg, dated April 26. This letter, it seems to me, has a tremendous symptomatic significance. The Left Opposition (Bolshevik-Leninists) can and should become the banner for the most oppressed sections of the world proletariat, consequently, in the first place, for the Negro workers. Upon what do I base such an assumption?

The Left Opposition represents at present the most consistent and the most revolutionary current in the world. Its sharply critical relations to all and every form of bureaucratic conceit in the labor movement makes it possible for it to pay particular attention to the voice of the most oppressed sections of the working class and toilers in general.

The Left Opposition has to suffer the blows not only of all the bourgeois governments of the world, but also of the Stalinist apparatus. This fact, which, in spite of all the slanders, enters gradually into the consciousness of the masses, will have to attract towards the Left Opposition the sympathies of the most oppressed sections of the international working class more and more. From this point of view, the letter to us from the South African comrades appears to be not at all accidental, but deeply symptomatic. In their letter, bearing 24 signatures[6] (it further follows: "and others") the South African comrades expressed particular interest in the questions of the Chinese Revolution. This interest should be recognized as fully grounded. Precisely the working masses of the oppressed peoples who have to carry on the struggle for the elementary national rights and for human dignity, stand the greatest risk to suffer from the confused teachings of the Stalinist bureaucracy on the subject of the "democratic dictatorship." Under this false banner, the policy in the style of the Kuo Min Tang, that is, the complete deception and the unpunished crushing of the toiling masses by their own "national" bourgeoisie, may still do the greatest harm to the cause of liberating the toilers.[7] The program of the permanent revolution based on the incontestable historic experience of a number of countries may and should assume the leading significance for the liberation movement of the Negro proletariat.

If the Johannesburg comrades did not as yet have the possibility to acquaint themselves closer with the views of the Left Opposition on all the most important questions, it cannot be an obstacle in getting together with them as closely as possible even today and to help them fraternally to come into the orbit of our program and our tactics.

When ten intellectuals of Paris, Berlin or New York who have been in various organizations, address themselves to us with a request to be taken into our midst I would give the following advice: Put them through a number of tests on all the questions of program; wet them under the rain, dry them in the sun, and then after a new careful examination accept one or two.

The matter changes basically when ten workers connected with the masses come to us. The difference in our relation to the petty bourgeois and to the proletarian groups does not require any explanation. But if the proletarian group works in a district where there are workers of various races, and in spite of this, it consists only of workers of a privileged nationality, I am inclined to regard them with suspicion: are we not dealing with the workers' aristocracy?[8] Isn't the group poisoned by slave holding prejudices active or passive?

It is quite a different matter when we are approached by a group of Negro workers. Here I am ready to consider beforehand that we are achieving agreement with them, even though this is not yet obvious; because of their whole position they do not and cannot strive to degrade anybody, oppress anybody, or deprive anybody of his rights. They do not seek privileges and cannot rise to the top except on the road of the international revolution.

We can and we should find a way to the consciousness of the Negro workers, of the Chinese workers, of the Hindoo workers, all these oppressed colored races of the human ocean to whom belongs the decisive word in the development of humanity.

L. TROTSKY.

Document 43
Letter from T. W. Thibedi to Leon Trotsky, 10 August 1932

10th August 1932.

Leon Trotsky
Prinkipo Islands,
Constantinople,
Turkey.

Dear Comrade Trotsky,

I hope that by the time you receave this letter from me you shall have seen a letter I send to the Communist League of America Opposition. Quite a lot has happened in the communist party of south Africa, private meetings are still continueing, expelled Stalinist and those who are still in the Party are forming a common front in killing the Communist League of Africa (Left Opposition) instead of specialising in fighting against the true enemy of the oppressed people of Africa viz Capitalists they waist time in fighting the most revolutionary (the left oppositin) in trying to bluff the left oppositions they tell us that Trotsky is an outcast and that the left opposition only exists in America and no where else and yet if one reads the Militant regularly would soon see through the tactics of the Stalinists worshipers in the Communist Party of South Africa. They tell us that the left Oppositionists are lazy individuals who only sit down in their office critizing the leadership of the Communist International, that the left opposition is going to help the capitalists when the next war against U.S.S.R. is made by the Capitalists. They conisder the Militant a very dangerous paper to be read by the negro workers of Africa in particular. But all those negro workers that has been reading the Militant do not want to part with the same, I hope that by next year we shall be able to start the paper to be written in the languages spoken by the South African negros, by this I mean a paper for spreading the views of the left opposition in south africa. We need a lot of articles on the conditions in South Africa to appear in the Militant. We are busy organising the negro trade unions and we are already considering of forming "Artuo" (Africa Red Trade Unions Oppositions) and for the Communist League of Africa (left opposition) we have already taken an office at 9 Berea Street, City and Suburban, Johannesburg, from where these trade unions are being organised, we received feww pamphlets from comrade T. Stamm of the communist league of Amerika these we keep in our office for those comrades who cannot afford to by to read at our office we need plenty more literature of the left opposition because the Stalinists bureaucrats has for some years been hiding such a literature to be known by the African Negro workers, I must thamk Comrade Victor Danchin who helped to get some of the left opposition translated for me from the Russian left opposition literature, because to day I can a lot in seeing some negro workers to understand the unpardonable mistakes which are purposely being committed by the Stalinists bereacrats who governi the Communists Party of South Africa.

Perhaps this shall interest the members of the left opposition to hear, there is a great selfishness that is being done by the Stalinists in South Africa, viz students from negro comrades who have proved themselves to be absolutely loyal to the instructions fromm boss Stalin are now being for their education to moscow but all those who have tryed to ague are being expelled from the C.P.S.A. and are being left out not to be given a chance to go and learn but the left opposition in South Africa is quite alive to these manuvering of the Stalinist when these students retturn shall fifht bitterly against the left opposition of south Africa again these creatures refuse us to buy and read the official organ of the E.C.C.I. I think that they are afraid we shall compare it with the Militant.

I joined the revolutionary movement in 1916, and since that time I have been on its E.C. and for many years the only negro comrade. from 1928 I organised the following trade Unions, Laundry Workers Union, Clothing Workers Union, Furniture Workers, Metal Workers, Meat and Cold Storage Workers, Domestic Servants, Dairy workers, Canvas and Rope Workers, Transpoort Workers, Chemical Workers, International Working Women Mechanic and Motor Drivers Union, Etc etc. I also formed the following branches of the Communist Party of South Africa. Pretoria, Potchefstroom, Evaton Vereeniging, Paardekop Bloemfontein, and at Ndabeni Location (Cape Town). We formed the Federation of Trade Unions in October 1928 but to day there is no longer any single trade union under the control of the party almost all the branches are now dead are purposely left to die by the Stalin bereacrats governing the Communist Party of south Africa, and yet if people oversea reads the official organ Umsebenzi would think that these bereacrats are doing a splendid job for the revolutionary movement in South Africa. If Joseph Stalin did not know that he was being told lies about the condition in South Africa left him hear it from the Militanyt he should also try to fined out why the Negroes are living the Party apart from those who are expelled. They are turning the Official paper of the Party into a lieng organ for no one would believe being in south Africa news in the Umsebenzi. Since the beginning of these year a lon prayer has been drawn up by Comrade S. P. Bunting signed by Comrade Gana Makabenim Simon Mafisa, Willie T. Twayi, and B. Dau Madiseng all negro comrades some do not know the contents of that prayer to Boss Stalin requesting him to be merciful and reinstate them into the Communist Party Of South Africa, I personally was refused admitance the day when that prayer was finally read to be send these immediately created suspicion because I should have been left to hear what it was for I am also an expelled member of the party. So far no reply has been received to that prayer, the drawer of these long prayer is not prepared to join the left Opposition and yet those who signed have no objection in joining the left opp[osition].

We received a letter from comrade Vitte of the International Secreatariate of the Left Opposition but he did not give his address so we can't reply to him direct[9], Please tell him that I do not read German or French but read English, Dutch, Zulu, Sesotu, Chiswina, Shangaan, TsiVenda, Xosa and various other negro languages.

Hoping to hear from you,

Yours for the Overthrow of Capitalism in Africa
T. W. Thibedi
P. O. Box 4143,
Johannesburg,
Communist League of Africa Left Op[position]

Document 44
Letter from Leon Trotsky to T. W. Thibedi, 4 September 1932

Prinkipo, September 4, 1932

Dear Comrade Thibedi:–

Thank you for your communication which I am transmitting to Comrade Witte.

It would be a very great step forward if we could establish an organ in the negro language. I suppose that the material hindrances would be great in this time of deep crisis. Are many negro comrades unemployed in Johannesburg and in South Africa in general?

The Stalinists state that the Left Opposition is almost non-existent. The information is not correct. It is true that we are only at the beginning of our great educational and organizational war, but our progress in the last year is very satisfactory in many of the European countries, and we can hope that the comrades who work in the double persecution of the bourgeois state and the Stalinist bureaucracy will become steeled into good revolutionaries. Discipline is necessary but discipline alone is sufficient for a capitalist army, not for a revolutionary party. We are far from exaggerating our forces. The revolutionary movement must remain very honest in the estimation of its own power: it is the only way to win the confidence of the workers.

Have you among your comrades, workers and students, and what is the proportion of the one to the other?

Have you any connections with negroes in America? I hope that the hour is near when the great awakening of the exploited negro masses will give rise to good Marxists and theoreticians from among their ranks.

My Communist greetings and best wishes for the success of your work,

Leon Trotsky

Document 45
Letter from the International Secretariat of the International Left Opposition to Cape Town comrades, 23 October 1932

Berlin 23/10/32

Cape Town, South-Africa–

Dear comrades,

We received your letter from 22/9. Have you already established the connexion with the Communist League of Africa? If not it is desirable to do it immediately. Do you dispose of our literature, pamphlets, documents, periodicals, etc? Wich language do the comrades speak? It is necessary to know in wich language we shall send you literature and correspond with you.

Please write for wich reasons the comrades were expelled out from the Party.

As to the conditions of membership into the Left Opposition, we must say, that, exact prescriptions and conditions are not worked out. But, on the other hand, the Left Opposition is based on the four first congresses of the Komintern (3d Communist International). It is necessary to take our position on the questions of the anglo-russian comittee, and of the chinese revolution; to the same manner, on this following questions: fraction or Party, and: characteristic of the Russian State. Therefore, the Left Opposition rejects in an unmistakable manner the idea of a fourth International and a new Communist Party. The Left Opposition is a fraction of the third International only.

As concerns these questions the American League has published sufficient material wich must be communicated to the members.

Some editions of the Permanente Revolution will be send regularly in the future.

With best communist greetings,
I. S.

Document 46
Letter from the International Secretariat of the International Left Opposition to Johannesburg comrades, 23 October 1932

Berlin 23/10/32

Johannesburg, South-Africa–

Dear comrades,

We are glad to receive your letter of the 4/10 and are expecting your informational letter for publication. The great importance the Left Opposition takes on the question of communist negro workers, also appears in the letter of Trotski relative on the question. How many comrades are members of your League? Probably, the Communist Party (official) has much more members than your League. Is it not so? Please write us the proportion of membership and the number of members of your League. The american comrades write that the number is about 2000. Is it not the case?

Do you know the platform-documents of the Left Opposition (chinese Revolution, anglo-russian committee, russian question, our position to the 3d International, etc)?

The possibilities of financial support are extremely restricted. Our sections are composed of workers, who are to a great extend, unemployed. Our periodicals are struggling with great difficulties and often their economical life is really endangered. Notwithstanding we will undertake all possibilities for your financial support.

Have you the intention of publishing a journal or, at least, a multiplicated bulletin? Is it not possible to correspond with you on the german, french or russian language? Who is Victor Danchin? We only know, that he ordered some russian literature of the Left Opposition.

Hoping to take with you the most active connections,

we are with fraternal greetings,
I. S.

Document 47
"International Communist League Formed in South Africa", *International Bulletin of the International Communist League*, New Series, 2, September 1934

(We have received the following letter from our newly constituted Communist League of South Africa. – Ed.)

Dear Comrades:

The Bolshevist Leninist League of Johannesburg, which held its first meeting as a formally constituted group in April 1934, has instructed me to get into touch with the *Militant*, with a view to affiliating our group to the Fourth International.[10] Since it is as readers of the *Militant* that most of us were drawn together, we turn naturally to you for assistance in building up a South African section of the Fourth International. Our group consists at present of twelve members, five of whom are Africans, the rest Europeans.

You will probably be interested to learn what became of the previous group which communicated with you. It finally collapsed through lack of experience, of political leadership and of perspectives. Our comrades made an attempt to revive the group. At first this was not successful but we did establish a training class for African workers, it has continued for more than a year and is now part of our present activities.

It is with circumspection that we now approach you; there is, of course, no guarantee that our group will not suffer the same ignominious collapse as its predecessor. We can only hope to demonstrate our sincerity and theoretical soundness by our future activities.

Our activities up to the present have been restricted to hammering out a program at League meetings held once a week, besides such training classes, weekly lectures, study circles, fraction work – in trade unions and other workers organizations – as our severely limited material and human resources permit. We are also tackling the task of organized African workers, a task which the C.P.S.A., with its bureaucratic regime and Comintern leadership has not only failed to inaugurate, but has rendered even more difficult. We have begun with the native bakery and laundry workers.

We also hope to publish a monthly duplicated bulletin in the very near future and are preparing a declaration of our program and principles for publication in the first issue. We hope to increase our membership considerably upon the appearance of this bulletin.

We have written to the Lenin Club, Cape Town, and have received formal acknowledgment of receipt of our letters and the promise of a detailed reply at a later date, but up to the present no discussion has taken place between us.

During the recent period our trade union committee has held a series of factory gate meetings at the laundries which employ on the Rand about a thousand native workers. As a result of these meetings, a general meeting at which nearly all the laundries were represented, was held in June, and a new African union formed, the last union having disintegrated after the expulsion of its crooked secretary. The secretary and organizer of the new union are excellent militants. At this general meeting the Stalinists were decisively rejected by the workers. Our efforts are now bent towards ensuing a correct policy for the laundry workers union by building up the Bolshevik-Leninist fraction within the union. We have also tackled the task of reorganizing the native bakery workers. Leaflets are being issued and contacts made. We fear that the bakers' union, however, will present immensely greater difficulties than the laundry workers union and it is not unlikely that we may fail in this task owing to the many adverse factors.

We enclose a copy of our draft constitution to be formally adopted upon affiliation to the Fourth International; and a copy of a letter to the Political Bureau of the C.P.S.A. submitted in April 1934 and followed by the immediate expulsions from the party of Comrades ... for open "Trotskyist" activities.[11] These expelled comrades are now members of the League.

With revolutionary greetings,

Document 48
Lenin Club, *Draft Thesis: The Native Question* (Majority) (1934)[12]

The basis of the economic structure of South Africa is the Native population. This is not only because it is numerically the predominant section, but because the Native is the direct producer in agriculture and the mines, and also, though to a lesser degree, in industry generally. Almost all the productive labour on the farms is performed by the agricultural Native labourer. There are about 1 1/2 million Natives forming the land proletariat in South Africa. The productive part played by European labour in agriculture is comparatively insignificant. In the gold, coal, and other mines, as well as on the alluvial diggings, the Native plays by far the greatest part in productive labour. In September, 1932, the ratio of Native labourers employed on the Rand mines compared with Europeans, artisans and labourers was 9.3 to 1, on coal mines 16.8 to 1 and on the alluvial diamond diggings 4.5 to 1. In this primary industry of mining about half a million Native workers are employed.

In other industrial enterprises, as well as in commerce and transport, the Native worker is playing an increasingly important part. With the growing rationalisation of industry, the practice of substituting unskilled for skilled labour is continually extending, and this process must lead to an ever greater prominence of the Native worker, both numerically and as a producer.

The main characteristic of the South African economic system, as it is to-day, is the exceptionally low level of the wages of the unskilled and semi-skilled workers. There are very few countries in the world where Capitalism is able to extract such tremendous profits out of the meanest type of exploitation. In England the average rate of the skilled to the unskilled wage is 15 to 11; in Germany the rate is even more favourable to the unskilled worker. Over the whole range of South African industry the rate of the skilled to the unskilled wage is 6 to 1. On the Witwatersrand, taking all types of employment, the rate is 7 to 1. But taking the mining industry only, the rate averages 10 to 1, in spite of the hard and dangerous nature of the toil involved. In the Railways and Harbours Service the week's wage of a Native labourer is 15/1, just equal to the day's pay of a checker or a guard, but less than the day's pay of an artisan. In the building industry the average wage of a Native labourer is 3/6 per day, or £1 per week, while the skilled wage runs from 2/- to 3/- per hour for a 44-hour week.

Because of this intense exploitation of the black workers, the exploitation of the white workers is comparatively much less vigorous. In this way Capitalism strives, as always, to divide the workers, and, with higher wages, bribes the European workers to side with the employers in the event of the black workers venturing to give expression to their discontent.

This was the policy in the past. There are already indications of a change at hand.

The great crisis which deepens and widens the gulf between the productive capacity of world industry and the consuming capacity of world markets is tending to lower the rate of profits. Capitalism, which is interested only in profits, will naturally try to recover these profits by lowering the wage bill. This will be accomplished by severe cuts in the wages of the skilled worker, since the unskilled wage cannot be cut down any lower than it is. Indirectly, the wage bill will be further lowered by more complete rationalisation of industry. The introduction of machines which do not require skilled attention, will inevitably lead to the displacement of skilled workers in favour of unskilled and semi-skilled, and to a general lowering of the skilled wage. The capitalist will compel the white worker to accept the low wages at present paid to the Native, or else will replace the white worker by a Native.

In face of this, the present remedy is for the whole working class in South Africa, and every section of it, to strive for a raising of the unskilled wage, and so narrow the gap between skilled and unskilled, and to organise the Natives, recognising them as fellow-workers, with a right to the same pay as the white man gets for the same work. Only thus will the workers be able to resist the future onslaught of Capitalism on their standard of living.

The first task of a revolutionary workers' party must therefore be to bring class-consciousness to every member of the working-class. The party must show him that his real interests are in direct opposition to those of the capitalists and imperialists. It must show him the bitter results of a policy framed and followed by a collaboration of classes. And at the same time it must show him clearly the way out of his misery.

What is the way out for the European worker? Is it to accept the crumbs from the super-profits of the capitalists, crumbs which are sweated out of his Native fellow-worker, the crumbs which he will inevitably lose tomorrow? Or is it to fight for the emancipation of the whole working-class to fight for the Revolution, to fight for the abolition of all oppression and exploitation, to fight for a Soviet South Africa?

But this is only a part of the Native Question. As South Africa is still predominantly an agrarian country, the bulk of the population is to be found on the land engaged in agriculture. Therefore the far greater part of the Native question is the Agrarian Problem. With the exception of a million urbanised Natives (in the Urban Locations) the Natives are all peasant in character, notwithstanding the fact that from time to time they work in industry, mines, and commerce, that is, when they are forced into the towns. But the special characteristic of this peasantry is that it is a landless peasantry. The constant Native farm labourer (500,000), the variable seasonal farm labourer (600,000 to 700,000), the so-called "squatters" (500,000), these three groups, living on land owned by whites, constitute about one-third of the Native population, and live in virtual serfdom. The other part of the Native population is living in "their own territories", administered partly on a tribal, and partly on an individual ownership basis.

To gain an understanding of the distribution of land in South Africa and the acuteness of the Agrarian Problem it is necessary to study the following figures:–

Density of White population in rural districts is 1.44 per sq. mile.
Density of Native population in Reserves and Territories is 57.99 per sq. mile.
98,674,600 morgen of land are in the hands of the White Population.
9,959,000 morgen of land are in the hands of the Native Population.

Thus, accepting the conservative figures of the Official Year Book, No. 14 (pub 1934) which gives 1,889,500 Whites to 5,681,100 Bantu, we see that there is 51 morgen of land for every White person and only 1.75 morgen of land for every Native.

The distribution of the land and size of the farms in the hands of the European population is as follows:–

3,687 farms under	5 morgen occupy	8,700 morgen
8,210 " from	5 to 20 " "	83,900 "
8,976 " "	21 " 100 " "	513,000 "
30,334 " "	101 " 500 " "	9,098,000 "
19,535 " "	501 " 1000 " "	14,443,000 "
13,252 " "	1001 " 2000 " "	19,049,000 "
4,474 " "	2001 " 3000 " "	11,223,000 "
3,571 " "	3001 " 5000 " "	13,861,000 "
2,078 " "	5001 " 10000 " "	14,443,000 "
832 " "	over 10000 " "	13,952,000 "

Now, if we subtract the 20,873 poor farmers who own only 605,600 morgen, and the 30,334 middle-farmers who own 9,098,000 morgen, that is, almost as much as the whole native population, we find that *32,787 farmers own 33,492,000 morgen, which is 32 per cent, and 10,955 farmers own 53,479,000 morgen, which is more than 50 per cent of all the occupied land of South Africa*. These figures speak for themselves. They make clear that the only solution of the Native Problem is the Agrarian Revolution.

Before elaborating our programme for the solution of the Native Question, which means to estimate the development of the revolution in South Africa, its forms, its forces and reserves, its obstacles, and so on, we should first examine the solutions offered by the other working-class parties of South Africa.

It is not necessary to spend much time on the programme of the party of reformism and class-collaboration, the South African Labour Party. If the parties of the Second International are covered with the glory of betrayals, with the laurels of treason, the S.A.L.P. surpasses them by its reactionary role in the Labour movement. If the parties of the Second International try to cover themselves with revolutionary slogans and Marxist phraseology, the S.A.L.P. makes no attempt to hide its pure slave-owners' and slave-drivers' programme, a programme of complete segregation of black and white, a programme of reprisals and discriminations. If the rule of Britain in India was never so brutal, the prisons never so full, the misery never so great, as when the British Labour Party was in power, so the Native Policy of the government of South Africa was never so ruthless and oppressive as when the S.A.L.P. participated in the "Pact" Government. It was this Government that passed the infamous Colour Bar Act and the Amended Masters and Servants Act.[13] These white chauvinists, hard-headed bureaucrats, and corrupt politicians deny to the Natives their rights to land, to work, to education. They speak of a "White South Africa", "South Africa for Europeans", "the Black Menace", etc. they even "ignore the Natives" to the extent of omitting them from "the population of South Afric". These "socialists" are the greatest enemies of the Native workers and therefore we must recognise them as the greatest enemies of the Revolution. By sowing their venomous white chauvinism in the ranks of the white workers they split the working-class on racial lines, prevent the workers from attaining class-consciousness, prevent unity, and thus preserve the rule of Capitalism and Imperialism.

Quite different is the programme and aim of the Communist Party of South Africa. They strive for a revolutionary change, for the liberation of the whole working-class, and for the full emancipation of the Natives. This is undoubtedly their aim. But good intentions are not enough. Good intentions lead only to failure if the strategy and tactics of the revolutionary party do not correspond to the actual situation, if they are not in harmony with reality. The entire programme of the C.P.S.A. is based on an incorrect estimation of the revolution and of the correlation of the forces in South Africa. Their whole strategy of the revolution is wrong.

If the white chauvinist policy of the S.A.L.P. flows from the assumption that South Africa is a "White man's country", the main and central slogan of the C.P.S.A., the slogan of "Native Republics" flows from the equally false assumption that South Africa is exclusively a "black man's country". This antithesis, which entirely ignores the white population, is equally harmful, because it is bound to antagonise one section of the working- class against another. Instead of uniting the workers it again splits them on racial grounds. To ignore the fact that unlike India and China, the white population of South Africa does not consist of a temporary officialdom, but is an integral part of the population, means to be blind to reality.

In the red tape style of a bureaucracy, the Comintern from afar and above has forced upon the C.P.S.A. a strategy cut to the patterns for India and China, without having learned anything from the blunders and mistakes of the Chinese Revolution. Just as in China the Comintern suppressed the class struggle and agrarian revolution and supported the national-liberation (anti- imperialist) movement, so in South Africa they are basing their strategy on the national-revolutionary struggle instead of on the class struggle. The calling for "Native Republics" involves subordinating the class struggle to the national struggle. As "Umsebenzi" says, "The Bantu Republic" will be a "democratic people's government". The revolution will be "an anti-imperialist revolution, a democratic revolution, a people's revolution, an agrarian revolution, giving to the African people real national freedom".

In short, it means that the revolution will be a national, bourgeois, democratic revolution. But they forget to consider who is going to accomplish the revolution, who will lead it, under the hegemony of which class it will be brought about. They forget that we are living in the age of Imperialism, in an epoch of decaying Capitalism, when the bourgeoisie is no longer a revolutionary force, and when a revolution, to be successful, must be led by the working-class. But by stressing national liberation and ignoring the white workers, the C.P.S.A. excludes the possibility of a *united* revolutionary working-class, and only such can lead the revolution. Never in history has the peasantry by itself succeeded in a revolution. The peasantry can make insurrections, but they cannot accomplish a revolution. The Native Republics (*as a step towards* the Workers' and Peasants' Republic) means a bourgeois republic (*not* a Workers' and Peasants' Republic), even though it implies the overthrow of the rule of British Imperialism. Here again is apparent the red tape style.

If it is possible for India and China, at least in the theory of the Comintern, to throw off the yoke of Imperialism by a united front of all classes, including the national bourgeoisie, and still retain the old social order, then why not in South Africa? They forget that there is no Native bourgeoisie in South Africa, and that there is no Native bourgeois democratic national movement of any importance in existence. They forget that all the forces of Capitalism, British and Dutch, farmer and industrialist, nationalist and imperialist, republican and monarchist, Malan and Stallard, *ALL* will join hands in the counter-revolutionary struggle against any anti-imperialist struggle on the part of the Native workers and peasants.[14] It should be obvious that here in South Africa a fight against Imperialism is conceivable only as a fight against Capitalism. Our Revolution will not be a national but a social revolution.

To sum up, the programme of the C.P.S.A. is full of mistakes, blunders, and contradictions, and the most harmful of them is the slogan of "Native Republics".

Since Lenin died, revolutionary Marxism-Leninism, has given way, in the Comintern, to opportunism and scholasticism. The old theory of "the democratic dictatorship of workers and peasants", which was thrown into the dustbin by Lenin in April, 1917, was pulled out again. The Marxist theory of the permanence of the Revolution was exchanged for the theory of "Socialism in one country". In conformity with this theory all countries were divided into four categories, according to their ripeness and ability to build socialism independently. A schematic theory of preliminary stages of the revolution was invented, from which not one state can escape, of which not one stage can be skipped. National bourgeois revolution, bourgeoisie democratic revolution, democratic dictatorship of workers and peasants, workers' and peasants' government, Soviet Revolution, then Socialist or Proletarian Revolution with the Dictatorship of the Proletariat, – all this scholastic scheme of categories, periods, and stages, which has led only to defeats, must be condemned. Even if the first tasks which the Revolution has to solve are problems which ought to have been solved by a bourgeois revolution, problems such as national unification, liberation from Imperialism, the agrarian difficulty, etc., nevertheless, there can be now no question of a bourgeoisie participating in or supporting a revolution. In every revolution, if it is to succeed, the working-class alone must be the leader. *The October Revolution, although it had to solve all the above-mentioned problems, was not a bourgeois democratic revolution but a proletarian revolution.* We need not, therefore, apply to our Revolution this scholastic and schematic theory of categories and preliminary stages – "as a step towards it".

WHAT IS OUR PROGRAMME?

There is no other way of solving the Native Question than through a revolutionary change of our social-economic structure. Only hopelessly muddle-headed Fabians, and Liberals of all brands belonging to the bourgeois camp, can speak of a solution of the Native Question by reforms, through education, or democracy. With decay of Capitalism, democracy and reforms are speedily passing away. In the face of the approaching fascisation, we have to fight for those few democratic rights which are still left and which are in danger of being taken away. *The emancipation of the working-class and the liberation of the oppressed races are closely bound together and can be achieved only by throwing off the yoke and chains of Capitalism and Imperialism.*

As in South Africa today, so in Czarist Russia the majority of the population (57%), the oppressed nationalities and races, groaned under the yoke of Czarism and Capitalism, and only the October Revolution, the Social Revolution, brought their full liberation and emancipation together with that of all the toiling masses of Russia. Until the other parts of the world follow the Russian example, oppression and exploitation, misery, starvation, and unemployment will be the lot of the majority in African and America, in China and India. It is time to realise that the so-called national liberation movements of the African National Congress here, of the Swaraj in India, of the Wafd in Egypt, and of the Kuomintang in China, are futile, that they can lead to nothing except the betrayal of the workers, and that only the workers can lead the real struggle against Capitalism and Imperialism.[15] This message must be brought to the Native masses. Their way to liberation and freedom lies in the Social Revolution, in a South African "October".

The Native Problem is mainly the Agrarian Problem. In a country predominantly agricultural, where 95% of the population is rural, the axis of the revolution revolves round the agrarian problem. The more so, since the Native population of South Africa, 87% of which still lives on the land, is deprived of the land, and is *entirely* debarred from acquiring land even if it had the means to purchase. Crowded into the Reserves which cannot give him the barest subsistence for himself and his family, and yet burdened with heavy taxes, poll tax, hut tax, quitrent, squatter's tax, he is forced to find work in the mines or on the farms. There, under the infamous pass system, the Masters and Servants Act, and the Native Service Contract Act, he is reduced to conditions of serfdom. The majority of Native farm workers are serfs, if not actual slaves. In a country where 3,300,000 people own less than 10 million morgen of land while 43,000 people hold 87 million morgen, it is impossible to talk of agrarian "reforms". Only the Revolution can solve this agrarian question, which is the axis, the alpha and omega of the revolution. The pauperisation of the Natives, the pauperisation of the small white farmers, the Native Problem and the Poor White Problem, not only hamper but bar the way for the development of the country. There is no future for South Africa, there is no place for industrial development and growth, until the internal need is studied and supplied, the level of internal consumption raised, the whole internal market systematically developed. Stagnation and decay, poor whiteism and the degradation of the standard of living to the uncivilised level, that is the lot of the toiling masses if the present system of the oppression and subjection of the largest part of the population continues to prevail. It must be made clear to the workers and intelligentsia of South Africa that the Native Problem, the Agrarian Problem is *their* problem, that the liberation of the Native is *their* liberation.

It is true that the Native suffers also from racial oppression and therefore the national question also forms a part of the Native Problem. But while we by no means deny and neglect the national question, we must not put it in the forefront of our strategy and tactics as the C.P.S.A. does. The national struggle must not obscure the class struggle. We must not pander to the cravings of petty-bourgeois Native Nationalists. We must not compete with the African National Congress in Nationalist slogans in order to win the Native masses. We must keep our strategical line clear of the swamp of petty-bourgeois Nationalism. National liberation in Russia did not precede the October Revolution. National liberation was a result of the proletarian revolution. A man needs first of all bread, and then liberty. The Native needs first of all land, and then national emancipation. The national question is not the fundamental problem of our revolution; the agrarian question is and will remain the basic task. Our main slogans must be "Land to the Natives" and "Every man has the right to as much land as he can work". The unconditional active support of the peasantry will thus be assured to the proletarian revolution. *By popularising among the workers the needs of the peasantry, and vice versa, the Bolsheviks succeeded in their revolution.* So also can our revolution succeed.

By uniting and defending in combined effort the common aims and interests of the workers and peasants, black and white, the revolutionary movement can bring about the overthrow of Capitalism and the establishment of a Soviet South Africa.

THE RESOURCES OF THE REVOLUTION

At the present time the revolutionary forces are very small indeed. The working-class is divided into black and white. The level of political education and class-consciousness is very low. The Trade Unions, which embrace only the more skilled workers in the towns (and actually, for the most part, only the white workers) are naturally weak. Their leadership and apparatus are in the hands of a reactionary, white-chauvinist bureaucracy. Their policy is that of the white labour aristocracy, which accepts the crumbs from the Capitalist and Imperialist exploitation and thus indirectly shares in the brutal oppression and exploitation of the unskilled and unorganised workers. The Native agricultural workers and the Native peasantry, enslaved, downtrodden, backward, are only *potentially* a great revolutionary reservoir, which so far has not been permeated, has to a great extent not even been touched, by revolutionary propaganda, revolutionary ideas, revolutionary outlook. The more educated Natives are easy victims to the religious influence of the missionaries or the petty-bourgeois National Congress. A very hard and difficult task confronts the revolutionary party. Hard, steady, systematic spade work is necessary. A gigantic task of educating white and black, of spreading propaganda near and far, of organising the unorganised in town and country, of giving a revolutionary lead to the Trade Unions, of guiding and winning the confidence of the workers and peasants. Whoever is not afraid of this tremendous task must come to the new revolutionary party – for this is the only way out.

Revolutions are not "made". For a revolution certain objective and subjective conditions are necessary. The discontent of the oppressed is not enough. Tsarism ruled against the wishes of the whole population, and so does Britain in India. But when the four necessary conditions are present, that is,

WHEN the disintegration of the ruling class sets in;
WHEN the oppressed will no longer tolerate the old system but demand a change;
WHEN the ruling class can no longer rule in the old way;
WHEN there is a strong, independent, revolutionary party present to use the revolutionary situation so as to give a lead to the leading class in the revolution, that is, to the workers, and to direct the revolutionary will of the people into the proper channels;
THEN we have a revolution.

The greatest misfortune that can befall the working-class of South Africa is if the fourth necessary condition, the Revolutionary Party, is not ready when the revolutionary situation arrives. Our task is to prevent this disaster. The capitalists are striving towards the fusion of their reactionary forces. *We* must strive for the unity and mobilisation of the revolutionary forces, combining all workers, black and white, into one single Trade Union Organisation. We must fight relentlessly any prejudiced, chauvinistic feelings against the oppressed that may exist among the workers. We must fight unceasingly for the removal of all repressive legislation against the Natives and all other workers. But while we fight for these partial demands, we must always hold fast our sure conviction that all this can be achieved in the revolutionary struggle, and that our main fight lies in the preparation and mobilisation of all possible forces for the future Revolution.

Document 49
Lenin Club, *Draft Thesis: Introduction* (Minority) (1934)[16]

[....] The Native problem is the most important to us, not only because the Natives comprised more than four-fifths of the whole population, not as in the Thesis of the Majority Group, even because they form almost the entire producing element in agriculture and mining, and are steadily increasing their value in all town industry. That applies to every exploited section of the population in every country.

What is characteristic and peculiar about the Native problem is that it crosses, reflects and expresses all the problems, conflicts, antagonism and contradictions of the socio-economic structure of South Africa, nourishing and casting its shadow over every social problem.

Herein is the peculiarity of the development of Capitalism in South Africa, that one side, on the side of the ruling class we find the most modern and perfected system of oppression and exploitation, the highest form of concentrated monopoly-capitalism, and on the other side we find the Native – the overwhelming majority of the exploited, whose stage of development is the lowest imaginable.

Living for the most part on the land, the Native is not only pre-capitalistic but even pre-feudal in his backwardness. Living, as they do, still in the stage of very primitive tribes under chiefs, it is ridiculous to pose the Native problem as the Agrarian Problem. [....]

The Native "Problem" as such
What is the economic background for all the anti-native legislation and taxation which encircles the native and oppresses him?
1. To maintain his low standard of living. By no means must he lose his charm as cheap labour, for his exploiters. Therefore he is enclosed in the hopelessly insufficient Native territories and locations.
2. Reducing the Natives to such conditions that they are forced to go in search of work, to sell his labour power.

These two points are of great importance and must always be kept in mind. Only by a complete understanding of the combination of these two points can we explain and understand why the Natives cannot be classified as peasants in the modern sense.

The peasantry of Europe and part of Asia was developed under feudal relations, into which social body penetrated the new bourgeois productive relations.

By undermining the old feudal system and dissolving it, the bourgeois brought to the surface of modern society the so-called Agrarian Movement with its variety of problems in the different countries of Europe and Asia.

That a peasantry in this sense does not exist in South Africa can hardly be questioned, and there is no possibility for its creation under the conditions of Imperialism.

The Native territories do not form a developing internal market in South Africa. Their main function in the economy of the country in general and of the mining industry in particular is to serve as a reliable reservoir of extremely cheap labour. All political force is used in order to ensure the smooth functioning of this system. [....]

We thus find the Natives, without having passed through all the known historical phases, being flung out of his primitive tribal life against the most perfected of imperialisms, i.e., the last stage of Capitalism.

From the most simple of economic formations, he is transformed into the modern proletarian, occupied in the most highly concentrated of industries. Here we have before our eyes the very curious social phenomena of a people stepping over different historical stages of development.

From this we see that the interests of all the natives, not only those already proletarianised in the town – but also the potential proletarians in the native reserves – that their interests clash directly with that of British Imperialism, that is, with that of the Mine Magnates and their agents, who stand on top of the social ladder in South Africa. It is these gentlemen who see to it that the whole of the class structure of the exploiting class in South Africa is maintained no matter which of the bourgeois parties are in power.

Next to these on the ladder comes the national bourgeois of town and country, who turning their faces away from the Imperialists nevertheless lean their back-sides on them, in order the more severely to exploit and mercilessly suck the life-blood of the natives.

From this short analysis it is quite clear that the Native problem is not the Agrarian problem at all, but the problem of Imperialism and Capitalism. Only when we approach the problem from this point of view can we conclude that the Labour Party talk of segregation – the Communist Party talk of a Native Republic is Utopian as an idea reactionary as a movement – and counter-revolutionary in effect. [....]

Is the Native Movement the Agrarian Movement?

The mere fact that Natives suffer from a shortage of land or that they have no land at all does not make the Native Problem the Agrarian problem any more than it makes the problem of the poor towns population the Agrarian problem. [....]

The sharp point of the Native problem is directed, not against the remnants of feudalism, but against the Capitalist-Imperialist productive relationships in South Africa which has transformed the native during the last fifty years into the most exploited, actual or potential proletariat in the world, keeping him in reserves (territories) just as the millions of unemployed in the whole Capitalist world, form a reserve army. It is quite true, that subjectively the natives, especially those who still live in the territories, due to their primitiveness are still far from having a proletarian psychology and ideology – this is surely a fact which we must take into consideration. But, objectively, and this is what is of the first importance, such is his position, his class function in the Imperialist-Capitalist Society of South Africa. [....]

This increases manifold the function of the revolutionary proletarian party as the education of this peculiar working class in South Africa – a class which consists of such a rich variety of material and colour; a class whose internal contrasts are as great as for instance the gap between the skilled English tradesman with his hundred years of Trade Union tradition and experience and the natives who still live in the Kraal.

The greatest, hardest and most important task of the revolutionary movement in South Africa is the bringing together of these heterogeneous elements and to mould them ideologically into one integral, indivisible class not only in relation to the other classes, but also in relation to themselves. From this follows the tremendously important role of the white section of the working class (although it is numerically the smaller section) – the development of trade unionism, co-operation and proletarian education for the whole working-class of South Africa.

Now it is quite clear, that the revolutionary party must put forward such slogans as will serve the purpose of uniting the two sections – black and white – of the South African proletariat. Its slogans must demonstrate the mutual interests and the unconditional necessity of their unity, for the solving of their historical class task – to destroy the existing exploiting class society and the establishment of Socialism.

Only if we approach the native problem from this angle, will the reactionary harmful and dangerous nature of the slogans of a "Native Republic" become clear, a slogan which instead of uniting, splits and alienates the two sections, and in this way serve the cause of the white rulers in their desire to keep the native in his place, to keep him in his backwardness, and not to allow him to reach the road to the historical necessary unification and moulding of the very peculiar working-class in South Africa.

We must have our own revolutionary perspectives, based on the general situation, on the structure and relations of the classes; the contradictions of Imperialism in South Africa; the Native Problem; the poor-white problem; the exceptional insecurity of the white workers; the ruination of the farmers and the lower middle classes by the tremendous concentration of finance and monopoly capital; the crushing of the coloured workers between the black and white proletariat. All these are tremendous potential revolutionary forces, which will give the presence of a revolutionary party with a correct leadership, put the South African proletariat in the vanguard of the world revolutionary movement. [....] There is, we must admit, an intensified antagonism between the various sections of the ruling classes. Is it possible that South Africa is an exception in this case? No! In South Africa a semi-colonial country of British Imperialism, that contradiction is very sharly expressed in the contradictory interests of Imperialism which maintains its grip on the whole country, crushing and squeezing all its classes, farmers, industrialists, petty bourgeois, not even to mention the workers and peasants. Is the antagonism between Imperialism and National Bourgeois expressed in the political life of the country? Of course! We can say that the whole political history of the country for the last forty years is the history of that contradiction.

Due to the exceptional backwardness of the working-class in general and of the natives in particular, their struggle did not up to now find a very strong echo in the political life, excluding several small exceptions (Johannesburg 1922 strike and a few isolated, spontaneous outbreaks of natives). But, on the other hand, the National Bourgeois expressed politically their interests first through the S.A.P. but later the Imperialists succeeded in buying over the leadership of that party, but she could not abolish the class contradictions between Imperialism and the National Bourgeois. This forms the expression in the Nationalist Party under the leadership of Hertzog. Now we stand again before such a situation where Imperialism succeeded in buying over the leadership of that National Party, and a great part of the apparatus and the National Bourgeois create over again their party under the leadership of Malan.

Need we be indifferent to this struggle? Certainly not! Because that contradiction hastens the process of the disintegration of the ruling class. What must be the attitude of the workers and its political party to this struggle? In order to answer this question, it is necessary first to answer another question: Who is the main enemy of all the oppressed and exploited in South Africa? Is it Imperialism or the National Bourgeois, etc? If we want to be Marxists Leninists, we must answer clearly and precisely, that British Imperialism is the main enemy. From this it follows that in the struggle between Imperialism and the National Bourgeois, (the farmer-landlords, industrialists) is a smaller exploiter, a smaller blood sucker, than the foreign financier. (Chamber of Mines, etc.?) No! On the contrary, the exploited masses fell their hatred and rage to the direct blood-suckers who are the local bourgeois rather than to the foreign banker who exploits and sucks them through agents in thousands, invisible and semi-visible forms. We know quite well that the non-Europeans in this country mostly supported up to now the parties of British Imperialism against the National parties. It is no secret for us that British Imperialism understood how to play and utilise the racial hatreds and posed itself before the Natives and coloured people as their protector. But our task is emphatically to tear off the mask of these "good friends", the Imperialists, and to expose them before the masses in their true nakedness. As long as Imperialism rules South Africa the whole system leans on it. The whole structure of oppression and exploitation. As long as the Imperialist will be the boss, there is no hope for improvement and therefore we have to support the National Bourgeois in so far as they still struggle and are forced to fight against Imperialism. It is true that her fight against Imperialism is only the fight of two robbers over the division of the spoils. But as long as the robbed are not yet capable of fighting for themselves against both robbers together they must logically support the smaller robber against the stronger one, to intensify with it the fight amongst the robbers themselves, and to extend and develop that fight because with it up to a certain stage will struggle be raised to a higher stage, and shaking the foundations of the existing Social structure of the country, bring it to the essential and unavoidable point on the road of the revolutionary development, until the process of the disintegration and rottenness of the ruling classes will get fully ripe so that they shall no longer be able to rule in the old manner. Does it follow from this that we need to unite with the National Bourgeois, that we need to go into their party, to fuse with them? No! A thousand times no! We must build up our revolutionary party, to maintain with all emphasis its independence and integrity. But we must, as Marx expressed himself in relation to the struggle of the Bourgeoisie against the feudal lords in the 19th century, march separately and strike together, strike them who at the moment are the main enemy, as Lenin patiently and unceasingly hammered in the heads of the communist parties in relation to the colonial and semi-colonial countries. This was included in the programme of the Comintern at the 2nd Congress, to support the colonial bourgeois against Imperialism! "Conclude with them temporary agreements for definite and concrete tasks." [....]

Document 50
Lenin Club, *Draft Thesis: The Trade Union Question* (No division on this question) (1934)

[....] The position of the Trade Unions in South Africa reflects the backwardness of the South African worker. All the Unions are under the control of reformist leaders. Furthermore, the Unions are stultified and pacified by a blanket of industrial legislation which aims at settling disputes by mutual agreement instead of by direct action. Most of the Unions, and this is the most important point to keep in mind, are the close preserves of the white aristocracy of Labour. Natives are debarred or discouraged from entering these Unions and are in the majority of cases completely unorganised and helpless against the continual attacks on their meagre standard of living.

The majority of Trade Unions in the Cape are affiliated to the Cape Federation of Labour Unions, while those in the northern Provinces, as well as a few in the Cape, are affiliated to the Trades and Labour Council.[17] The Cape Unions follow a more liberal policy in connection with non-Europeans, and in the majority of Unions in the Cape it is permissable for Natives to join. Unfortunately, this cannot be said of the Transvaal, Free State, or Natal.

On the other hand, the Cape Federation of Labour Unions is, in general, one of the most reactionary bodies that ever existed in the ranks of the working-class. In no way does it advance beyond the American Federation of Labour, for even the reformist, yellow Trade Union International (the Amsterdam International) is for the Cape, as for the American Federation, too revolutionary.

When we examine the Trade Union policy of the two existing Workers' Parties, the South African Labour Party and the Communist Party, we see the same erroneous and harmful attitude as towards the Native problem in general, that of the S.A.L.P. being chauvinist and that of the C.P. being separatist and sectarian. The policy of the S.A.L.P., a policy of white Trade Unionism, barring the way for Natives in the existing Trade Unions, is not only most detrimental to the interests of the whole working class of South Africa, which includes both white and black workers, but is even against the interests of the white workers organised in the white Trade Unions. [....]

While we must emphasize the fact that some good work was done in the Trade Unions by the CP for a number of years prior to 1928, and this should be remembered and appreciated, we must also say frankly that with its entry upon a new "ultra-left" road, the road of adventurism, its policy of the "Third Period", the "Native Republics", the "Red Trade Unions", and more especially its Trade Union policy, has been since 1928 most harmful and disastrous. Its views on Trade Unionism found expression in the slogans, "Out of the Trade Unions", "For New Revolutionary Trade Unions", a policy contrary to the interests of the working class. It is a policy of despair, of pessimism, and corresponds with the general loss of faith in the masses by the Communist Parties, the Comintern, and the Profintern. [....] This policy of detaching the best elements from the masses means isolating these revolutionary workers on the one side, and abandoning the great bulk of the workers to the full influence of the Trade Union bureaucracy on the other side. It is not difficult to see how harmful to the interests of the working class such a policy is.

What Shall Be the Attitude of the New Party to the Trade Unions?
The new Revolutionary Party will be able to defeat the existing Trade Union bureaucracy and wrest from them the leadership, only when it has learned how to win the confidence of the masses. This cannot be achieved by detaching the most class-conscious element from the masses, but by participating in the daily struggle of the masses, in their daily needs and hopes. [....]

1. The economic struggle should follow the slogans of increase in wages, improvement of labour conditions, and the defence of the fundamental rights and interests of the workers.
2. We must be clear on this point that this cannot be achieved by class collaboration, which is the policy of opportunism and bureaucracy. While not entirely rejecting

collective bargaining, we must point out to the workers the relatively slight value of this, and keep in mind the fact that the capitalists always violate the collective contracts whenever it is to their advantage. Therefore, the fundamental policy of the Trade Unions must be direct action.

3. The problem of unemployment must engage our close attention. The capitalists are continually trying to split the workers; they pit those who are still employed against their unemployed comrades. But unemployment menaces every worker and therefore the struggle must be directed against its causes. For this is a matter of life and death and we must rally both the employed and the unemployed, skilled and unskilled in the Unions into one united, solid, fighting body.

4. For the same sound reason, the unity of the workers, we must above all fight for the abolition of the "Colour Bar". We must point out to the workers the deadly danger of division, which is in the interests of the capitalists only, and the pressing need of unity of black and white in the Trade Unions. We must fight for equality of labour and conditions and equal pay for equal work independent of race or sex.

5. We stand for a united Trade Union movement of all workers irrespective of race, colour, creed or sex. It is the duty of every member of ours in the Trade Unions to agitate for the removal of the Colour Bar where such exists. But, *until such time as this can be achieved*, we must organise into separate bodies all those who are actually debarred from joining the existing Trade Unions. Under no circumstances, however, do we regard such purely Native Trade Unions as opposition Trade Unions or as a goal in themselves. They are only a step towards the amalgamation of all the Trade Unions, black and white, into one central organisation of Trade Unions of all the workers of South Africa.

6. But while conducting or participating in the fight for the improvement of the conditions of labour, for raising the standard of living of the workers, and so on, we should always bear in mind that it is impossible to solve all these problems within the frame of the capitalist system. While gradually forcing concessions from the ruling classes, compelling them to enact social legislation, we shall ever and again point out to the workers that only the overthrow of Capitalism and the establishment of the dictatorship of the proletariat can solve the social question.

Document 51
Leon Trotsky, *Remarks on the Draft Theses of the Workers' Party of South Africa*, 20 April 1935[18]

The theses are written without doubt on the basis of a serious study of both the economic and political conditions of South Africa as well as of the literature of Marxism and Leninism, particularly that of the Bolshevik-Leninists. A serious scientific approach to all questions is one of the most important conditions for the success of a revolutionary organisation. The example of our South African friends again confirms the fact that in the present epoch only the Bolshevik-Leninists, i.e., the consistent proletarian revolutionaries, take a serious attitude to theory, analyse the realities, and are learning themselves before they teach others. The Stalinist bureaucracy has long ago substituted a combination of ignorance and impudence for Marxism.

In the following lines I wish to make certain remarks with regard to the draft theses which will serve as a programme for the Workers Party of South Africa. Under no circumstances do I bring forward these remarks in opposition to the text of the theses. I am too insufficiently acquainted with the conditions in South Africa to pretend to a full conclusive opinion on a series of practical questions. Only in certain places I am obliged to express my disagreement with certain aspects of the draft theses. But here also, insofar as I can judge from afar, we have *no differences in principles* with the authors of the theses. It is rather a matter of certain polemical *exaggerations* arising from the struggle with the pernicious national policy of Stalinism. But it is in the interest of the cause not to smooth over even slight inaccuracies in presentation but, on the contrary, to expose them for open deliberations in order to arrive at the most clear and blameless text. Such is the aim of the following lines dictated by the desire to give some assistance to our South African Bolshevik-Leninists in this great and responsible work to which they have set themselves.

The South African possessions of Great Britain form a Dominion only from the point of view of the white minority. From the point of view of the black majority South Africa is a Slave Colony.

No social upheaval (in the first instance, an agrarian revolution) is thinkable with the retention of British Imperialism in the South African Dominion. The overthrow of British Imperialism in South Africa is just as indispensable for the triumph of Socialism in South Africa as it is for Great Britain itself.

If, as it is possible to assume, the revolution will start first in Great Britain, the less support the British bourgeoisie will find in the Colonies and Dominions, including so important a possession as South Africa, the quicker will be their defeat at home. The struggle for the expulsion of British Imperialism, its tools and agents, thus enters as an indispensable part of the programme of the South African proletarian party.

The overthrow of the hegemony of British Imperialism in South Africa can come about as the result of a military defeat of Great Britain and the disintegration of the Empire; in this case the South African whites can still for a certain period, hardly a considerable one, retain their domination over the blacks. Another possibility, which in practice could be connected with the first, is a revolution in Great Britain and her possessions. Three-quarters of the population of South Africa (almost six million of almost eight million) is composed of non-Europeans. A victorious revolution is unthinkable without the awakening of the Native masses; in its turn it will give them what they are so lacking today, confidence in their strength, a heightened personal consciousness, a cultural growth. Under these conditions the South African Republic will emerge first of all as a "black" Republic; this does not exclude, of course, either full equality for whites or brotherly relations between the two races (which depends mainly upon the conduct of the whites). But it is entirely obvious that the predominant majority of the population, liberated from slavish dependence, will put a certain imprint on the State.

Insofar as a victorious revolution will radically change not only the relation between the classes, but also between the races, and will assure to the blacks that place in the State which corresponds to their numbers, insofar will the *Social* Revolution in South Africa also have a *national* character. We have not the slightest reason to close our eyes to this side of the question or to diminish its significance. On the contrary the proletarian party should in words and in deeds openly and boldly take the solution of the national (racial) problem in its hands.

Nevertheless the proletarian party can and must solve the national problem by *its own* methods.

The historical weapon of national liberation can be only the *Class Struggle*. The Comintern, beginning from 1924, transformed the programme of national liberation of colonial people into an empty democratic abstraction which is elevated above the reality of the class relations. In the struggle against national oppression different classes liberate themselves (temporarily!) from material interests and become simple "anti-imperialist" forces. In order that these spiritual "forces" bravely fulfill the task assigned to them by the Comintern, they are promised, as a reward, a spiritual "national-democratic" state (with the unavoidable reference to Lenin's formula, "democratic dictatorship of the proletariat and peasantry").[19]

The thesis points out that in 1917 Lenin openly and once and for all discarded the slogan of "democratic dictatorship of the proletariat and peasantry" as if it were a necessary condition for the solution of the agrarian question. This is entirely correct. But to avoid misunderstanding it should be added (a) Lenin always spoke of a revolutionary *bourgeois* democratic dictatorship and not about a spiritual "peoples" State, (b) in the struggle for a *bourgeois* democratic dictatorship he offered not a bloc of all "anti-tsarist forces" but carried out an independent class policy of the proletariat. An "anti-tsarist" bloc was the idea of the Russian Social-Revolutionaries and the Left Cadets i.e., the parties of the petty and middle bourgeoisie. Against these parties the Bolsheviks always waged an irreconcilable struggle.

When the thesis says that the slogan of a "Black Republic" is *equally* harmful for the revolutionary cause as is the slogan of a "South Africa for the whites", then we cannot agree with the form of this statement: whereas in the latter there is the case of supporting complete oppression, in the former, there is the case of taking the first steps towards liberation. We must accept with all decisiveness and without any reservations the complete and unconditional right of the blacks to independence. Only on the basis of a mutual struggle against the domination of the white exploiters can be cultivated and strengthened the solidarity of the black and white toilers. It is possible that the blacks will *after victory* find it unnecessary to form a separate black State in South Africa; certainly we will not *force them* to establish a separate State; but let them make this admission freely, on the basis of their own experience, and not forced by the sjambok of the white oppressors. The proletarian revolutionaries must never forget the fight of the oppressed nationalities to self-determination, including a full separation, and of the duty of the proletariat of the oppressing nation to defend this right with arms in hand when necessary!

The thesis quite correctly underlines the fact that the solution of the national question in Russia was brought about by the October Revolution. National democratic movements by themselves were powerless to cope with the national oppression of Tsarism. Only because of the fact that the movement of the oppressed nationalities, as well as the agrarian movement of the peasantry gave the proletariat the possibility of seizing power and establishing its dictatorship, the national question as well as the agrarian found a bold and decisive solution. But the very conjunction of the national movements with the struggle of the proletariat for power was made politically possible only thanks to the fact that the Bolsheviks during the whole of their history carried on an irreconcilable struggle with the Great Russian oppressors, supporting always and without reservations the right of the oppressed nationalities to self-determination including separation from Russia.

The policy of Lenin in regard to the oppressed nations did not, however, have anything in common with the policy of the epigones. The Bolshevik Party defended the right of the oppressed nations to self-determination, *with methods of proletarian class struggle*, entirely rejecting the charlatan "anti-imperialist" blocs with the numerous petty-bourgeois "national" parties of Tsarist Russia (P.P.S., the party of Pilsudski in Tsarist Poland, Dashnaki in Armenia, the Ukrainian nationalist, the Jewish Zionists, etc., etc.).[20] The Bolsheviks have always mercilessly unmasked these parties, as well as the Russian Social-Revolutionaries, their vacillations and adventurism, but especially their ideological lie of being above the class struggle. Lenin did not stop his intransigent criticism even when circumstances forced upon him this or that episodic, strictly practical agreement with them. There could be no question of any permanent alliance with them under the banner of "anti-Tsarism". Only thanks to its *irreconcilable* class policy was Bolshevism able to succeed in the time of the Revolution to throw aside the Mensheviks, the Social-Revolutionaries, the national petty-bourgeois parties, and gather around the proletariat the masses of the peasantry and the oppressed nationalities.

"We must not", says the thesis, "compete with the African National Congress in Nationalist slogans in order to win the Native masses". The idea is in itself correct, but it requires concrete amplification. Being insufficiently acquainted with the activities of the National Congress, I can only on the basis of analogies outline our policy concerning it, stating beforehand my readiness to supplement my recommendations with all the necessary modifications.

1. The Bolshevik-Leninists put themselves in defence of the Congress as it is in all cases when it is being attacked by the white oppressors and their chauvinistic agents in the ranks of the workers' organisations.
2. The Bolshevik-Leninists place the progressive over, against the reactionary tendencies in the programme of the Congress.
3. The Bolshevik-Leninists unmask before the Native masses the inability of the Congress to achieve the realisation of even its own demands, because of its superficial, conciliatory policy, and develop in contradistinction to the Congress a programme of Class Revolutionary Struggle.
4. Separate, episodic agreements with the Congress, if they are forced by circumstances, are permissible only within the framework of strictly defined practical tasks, with the retention of full and complete independence of our own organisation and freedom of political criticism.

The thesis brings out as the main political slogan not a "national democratic State", but a South African "October". The thesis proves, and proves convincingly,
a) that the national and agrarian questions in South Africa coincide in their bases;
b) that both these questions can be solved only in a revolutionary way;
c) that the revolutionary solution of these questions leads inevitably to the Dictatorship of the Proletariat which guides the Native peasant masses;
d) that the Dictatorship of the Proletariat will open an era of a Soviet regime and Soviet regime and Socialist construction.

This conclusion is the corner-stone of the whole structure of the programme. Here we are in complete agreement.

But the masses must be brought to this general "strategic" formula through the medium of a series of tactical slogans. It is possible to work out these slogans, at every given stage, only on the basis of an analysis of the concrete circumstances of the life and struggle of the proletariat and peasantry and the whole internal and international situation. Without going deeply into this matter, I would like briefly to deal with the mutual relations of the national and agrarian slogans.

The thesis several times underlines that the agrarian and not the national demands must be put in the first place. This is a very important question which deserves serious attention. To push aside or to weaken the national slogans with the object of not antagonising the white chauvinists in the ranks of the working class would be, of course, criminal opportunism, which is absolutely alien to the authors and supporters of the thesis: this flows quite clearly from the text of the thesis, which is permeated with the spirit of revolutionary internationalism. The thesis admirably says of those "socialists" who are fighting for the privileges of the whites that "we must recognise them as the greatest enemies of the Revolution". Thus we must seek for another explanation, which is briefly indicated in the very text: the backward Native peasant masses directly feel the agrarian oppression much more than they do the national oppression. It is quite possible: the majority of the Natives are peasants: the bulk of the land is in the hands of a white minority. The Russian peasants during their struggle for land had for long put their faith in the Tsar and stubbornly refused to draw political conclusions. From the revolutionary intelligentsia's traditional slogan, "Land and Liberty", the peasant for a long time accepted only the first part. It required decades of agrarian unrest and the influence and action of the town workers to enable the peasantry to connect both slogans.

The poor enslaved Bantu hardly entertains more hope in the British King or in MacDonald. But his extreme political backwardness is also expressed in his lack of national self-consciousness. At the same time he feels very sharply the land and fiscal bondage. Given these conditions, propaganda can and must first of all flow from the slogans of the Agrarian Revolution, in order that, step by step, on the basis of the experiences of the struggle, the peasantry may be brought to the necessary *political and national* conclusions. If these hypothetical considerations are correct, then we are not concerned here with the programme itself, but rather with the ways and means of carrying this programme to the consciousness of the Native masses.

Considering the small numbers of the revolutionary cadres and the extreme diffusion of the peasantry, it will be possible to influence the peasantry, at least in the immediate future, mainly if not exclusively, *through the medium of the advanced workers*. Therefore it is of the utmost importance to train the advanced workers in the spirit of a clear understanding of the significance of the Agrarian Revolution for the historical fate of South Africa.

The proletariat of the country consists of backward black pariahs and a privileged arrogant caste of whites. In this lies the greatest difficulty of the whole situation. As the thesis correctly states, the economic convulsions of rotting Capitalism must strongly shake the old barriers and facilitate the work of revolutionary coalescence. In any case, the worst crime on the part of the revolutionaries would be to give the smallest concessions to the privileges and prejudices of the whites. Whoever gives his little finger to the devil of chauvinism is lost. The revolutionary Party must put before every white worker the following alternative: either with British Imperialism and with the white bourgeoisie of South Africa, or, with the black workers and peasants against the white feudalists and slave-owners and their agents in the ranks of the working class itself.

The overthrow of the British domination over the black population of South Africa will not, of course, mean an economic and cultural break with the previous mother-country, if the latter will liberate itself from the oppression of its imperialist plunders. A Soviet England will be able to exercise a political economic and cultural influence on South Africa through the medium of those whites who in deed, in actual struggle, will have bound up their fate with that of the present colonial slaves. This influence will be based, not on domination, but on proletarian mutual co-operation.

But more important in all probability will be the influence which a Soviet South African will exercise over the whole black continent. To help the negroes to catch up to the white race, in order to ascend hand in hand with them to new cultural heights, this will be one of the grand and noble tasks of a victorious Socialism.

In conclusion, I want to say a few words on the question of a legal and illegal organisation (Concerning the Constitution of the Party).

The Thesis correctly underlines the inseparable connection between organisation, programme, and tactics of a Party. An organisation must assure the execution of *all* revolutionary tasks, supplementing the legal apparatus with an illegal one. Nobody, of course, is proposing to create an illegal apparatus for such functions as in the given conditions can be executed by legal organs. But in conditions of an approaching political crisis there must be created special illegal nuclei of the party apparatus, which will develop as need arises. A certain part, and by the way a very important part, of the work cannot under any circumstances be carried out openly, that is, before the eyes of the class enemies.

Nevertheless, for the given period, the most important form of the illegal or semi-legal work of revolutionaries is the work in mass organisations, particularly in the trade unions. The leaders of the trade unions are the unofficial police of Capitalism; they conduct a merciless struggle against revolutionaries. We must have the ability to work in mass organisations, not falling under the blows of the reactionary apparatus. This is a very important, for the given period most important, part of the illegal work. A revolutionary group in a trade union which has learned in practice all the necessary rules of conspiracy, will be able to transform its work to an illegal status, when circumstances require this.

Document 52
International Secretariat of the International Communist League (B-L), Minutes of meeting, 23 April 1935 (Extract)

South Africa. The comrades of the Cape Town Lenin Club have asked us to intervene immediately in the discussions now taking place. The majority of the Bolshevik Leninists of South Africa (there are groups in three cities) are in the process of founding a party upon theses which the minority of the Lenin Club condemns (particularly the one on the constitution of the new party), the latter do not think they can participate in the unified organization.

The IS reaffirms its first communication. While rejoicing about the unification, the IS is not of the opinion, in view of the very weak membership of South Africa and in view of the insufficiently mature conditions of the elaboration of the fundamental principles, that the present moment is propitious for sonstituting itself as a party.

But whatever the differences may be, the IS advises the comrades of the minority to preserve the unity of our ranks in South Africa, not to split over differences on the proposals of a party which is yet to be created, and to seek a solution of the conflicts in the ranks of the organization itself. The theses on the constitution of the party, as well as the criticism on the part of the minority will be seriously studied by the IS.

As regards the fundamental questions of S.A., the IS holds it necessary to pose before our comrades a number of problems of great importance, not broached by them. In this connection there are two clashing viewpoints in the ranks of the IS relating to the question of races and nationalities. One, summed up in the slogan: "Africa for the Negroes," "Independent Negro Republics," is the opinion that in view of the fact that the proletariat and the small peasants are all Negroes and that all whites in SA are direct or indirect exploiters (the enormous differences between the pay of the whites and colored workers) the movement of social and national liberation will inevitably be the struggle of the colored against the whites and that the task of revolutionists must be to support this movement, even if it takes on nationalist forms, which would be a hundred times less dangerous than white nationalism (Imperialism). The implacable struggle against English imperialism and for separation from England must be our slogan.

The other viewpoint proceeds from the fact that the white population of SA in contradistinction of colonial countires like India and China, comprises an integral part of the population, a minority it is true; and that there exists a white proletariat, a workers aristocracy, the important part of which is privileged and degenerate, but nevertheless threatened by capital. Hence salvation for SA is in the proletarian resolution of united revolutionary proleatariat both black and white, on the basis of the agrarian revolution.

We must stick to the undiluted Marxist idea of the class struggle (the exploited and the oppressed against the exploiters and the oppressors). And oppose ourselves to all mationalist tendencies, black or white. As for the races, we must agitate for equality.

Document 53
"Remarks of Comrade Dubois"[21], Internal Bulletin of the International Communist League (B-L), no. 2, May 1935

The efforts of our South African comrades do not sufficiently stress the *essential* point of the question: that in the first place, it is a matter of *attacking British imperialism*; all other questions are subordinate, their correct solution stemming from the outcome of the question which we have just called the fundamental one. That means that the entire strategy, as well as the choice of tactics which are useful and effective in South Africa, revolves around the essential question: how to weaken the domination of British imperialism in South Africa? The slogan, "Land to the Natives," for example, entirely correct in itself, remains completely inadequate because it is not based on any other *political* slogan except one of *pure, abstract propaganda*, summed up in the slogan of a "South African October." Although useful in providing a perspective, this slogan remains empty in the present circumstances. For the rest, the comparison made by our comrades between the Russian October and that of – in the future, naturally – South Africa, reveals the hollowness of their understanding. We will not push the matter of their simplistic interpretation of October: that the workers listen to the grievances of the peasants, and the peasants, those of the workers ("and vice versa"), after which a union takes place and the revolution is won; but what the thesis says on national liberation in Russia ("after the proletarien revolution") to justify their haughty disdain for the slogan, "Africa – Black Republic", shows that the question, hardly having been posed, is seen from an angle at the same time too narrow and – apparently – too wide. For, if "October" remains the goal to attain everywhere and in all circumstances, the repetition of that slogan can hardly be said to mobilise the masses. Here, in Africa, it is a matter of setting the natives against the oppression of *whites*, who are the British imperialists. This is why the potential of an *effective* slogan has to be closely studied with the greatest care. The absence of a black bourgeoisie, at least of any significance, noted in their theses, demonstrates that *seemingly* "nationalist" slogans are not harmful if they mobilise the masses. One is opposed to the purely statistical explanations found in these theses. It is true that the statistics state that the part of white workers imported into Africa by imperialism is important. But it is not a question of galvanising this present state nor of a schematic equalisation of white workers with workers of color: for white workers are, unfortunately, in South Africa (as elsewhere) first of all to represent the oppressors, the imperialists who use them, so to speak, in the front line by granting them privileges which the black workers do not enjoy. This is why the still-born schema of our comrades' thesis does not address the question which is the central one from the strategic as well as tactical point of view. One might ask, for example: what to do with and for white workers? But when the thesis so often repeats the expression "development of class consciousness", unfortunately, it is always directed at blacks. The tactical question which we have just posed depends, on the contrary, entirely on the development of class consciousness *amongst white workers*, and the outward sign of this development is the adoption of the slogan: down with *British* imperialism (not an *abstract*, general imperialism). That is to say, down with the privileges of the white race, natives to the fore, and the right of total separation from the British empire. The same is true for the agrarian revolution. One cannot imagine an agrarian revolution outside of a *political* framework. The agrarian revolution both poses and resolves, at the same time, what is called the national question of this country. This is why the two questions are inseparable. The thesis, instead of indicating the connection, neglects it, separating the two sides of the *same* question quasi-independently of one another. This is why this thesis remains weak, not providing any tactical guidelines and offering only inadequate and abstract propaganda.

Document 54[22]
Letter from the International Secretariat of the International Communist League (B-L) to the Communist League of South Africa and the Workers' Party of South Africa, 24 July 1935[23]

24 July 1935

W.G.

your letters (from the Communist League, 27 and 31 [V], and the Workers' Party of South Africa (14 and 29.V.1935) have been discussed at length by the Intern. Secretariat and it was decided to once again convey to BOTH groups our opinion in a comradely manner.

We all place great significance on the development of the South African group. The approaching war will shake the English Empire to its very foundations; consequently, the movement in the British colonies and dominions will be decisive for the fate of imperialism and the domination of the bourgeoisie in general, and for the development in England and in all of Europe. At the opportune time, a revolutionary movement in South Africa CAN substantially determine the expansion of colonial liberation movements in Africa; the early stages of the Italian war of plundering against Abyssinia reveal embryonically what GREAT revolutionary possibilities also exist on the "dark continent".[24] It is clear, therefore, that we are not of the opinion that your work within the "stabilised" South African capitalism is futile; this capitalism is PRESENTLY in fact "stable". No one can predict, however, how long it can continue in the midst of the instability of revolutionary upheaval; and there are signs that a reversal could occur VERY QUICKLY.

It therefore goes without saying, that we desire for you (and us) the rapid and thorough overcoming of your present internal difficulties in order to pave the way for positive revolutionary work and for the preparation of the situation discussed above. The liveliness of your discussions, the quantity of documents you have produced, demonstrate to us that a sensible way must be found. This is because any possible positive tendencies of your heated discussions will very soon be transformed into negative ones, if you let a POLITICAL debate over your differences turn into personal accusations and suspicions, and incite yourselves at the same time into an atmosphere of a hopeless conflict which makes any co-operation impossible.

The decisive point is that YOUR POLITICAL DIFFERENCES CAN UNDER NO CIRCUMSTANCES JUSTIFY A SPLIT IN YOUR ORGANISATION. Many of the questions raised remain open to an INTERNATIONAL discussion. The article by Comrade L. D. paves the way for an instant agreement concerning the immediate practical tasks. WE THEREFORE URGE YOU TO GIVE ALL "GROUPS" AND ALL COMRADES WHO HAVE SOMETHING TO SAY ABOUT THIS THE POSSIBILITY TO AVAIL THEMSELVES OF WRITTEN AND ORAL PRESENTATIONS OF THEIR VIEWS.

Now to your organisational situation. ALL of us in the International Secretariat were AGAINST the founding of the Workers Party, which for political and organisational reasons we considered to have been PREMATURE. A Communist League seemed to us at the present stage more practical and appropriate for the real situation. For that reason we do not, however, intend to either publicly rebuke you or to demand that you reverse the step taken, since that would not be of any help to your work. However, the illusion should not arise, that just because a group of revolutionaries gives itself the name "party", it thereby creates a REAL party, let alone a REVOLUTIONARY and COMMUNIST one. In all countries we have been very careful about the founding of PARTIES. Consider the example of the AMERICAN comrades, who only after long, systematic preparation (in a situation in which the LOW LEVEL of stability of the Capitalist Regime was demonstrated to the American workers through tremendous mass actions which led to the awakening of class consciousness), and AFTER the fusion with the pilot group they declared themselves a PARTY.

THEREFORE WE CATEGORICALLY REJECT THE COMPLETELY UNFOUNDED CONTENTION THAT THE "CONSTITUTION" OF THE WORKERS PARTY IS ALREADY SUCH A SOLID STATUTE, THAT THOSE COMRADES WHO ARE IN OPPOSITION TO IT, WHO ALSO COME FROM A SMALL AND OBJECTIVELY STILL COMPLETELY UNINFLUENTIAL GROUP, COULD ONLY BE ACCEPTED TO THIS "PARTY" AS SINGLE INDIVIDUALS, AS THOUGH IT WERE A REAL PARTY, GENERALLY ACKNOWLEDGED, SUPPORTED, TESTED BY THE PROLETARIAT AND IN ITSELF CONSISTENT. Only such a party could demand that the acceptance of decisions made by them should be a PRECONDITION for membership of the party. But when they first split (with reference to the Schiboleth of a NAME – since more of a PARTY is unfortunately not there –), then make decisions AMONG THEMSELVES, call themselves "party" and AFTERWARDS demand submission to party decisions by the same comrades from whom they split, then it is not justified by anything and CANNOT UNDER ANY CIRCUMSTANCES be considered sensible. On the contrary, we take this organisational EVASION of a political discussion to be a SERIOUS POLITICAL MISTAKE, which one must correct immediately, since it will otherwise compromise and destroy all your work.

The foundations must FIRST BE LAID for a PARTY in South Africa that can be taken seriously. To that end, serious THEORETICAL work is necessary, serious ORGANISATIONAL EFFORTS and achievements, serious WORK AMONG THE MASSES, ESPECIALLY AMONG THE COLOUREDS, IN THE UNIONS, by taking advantage of any existing legality, and by violating the hypocritical "legality" which will persecute work among blacks as "illegal". You must welcome into this great enterprise EACH comrade, EACH GROUP that stands on the platform of the 4th International, and MOST CERTAINLY you must welcome THOSE comrades with whom you worked together yesterday. To take up shelter behind such expressions as "majority" and "minority" is all the more wrong, since in any LIVING organisation that takes a SERIOUS position vis-à-vis all questions, this majority-minority relationship can always change. WE URGE YOU THEREFORE WITH ALL EARNESTNESS, NOT TO MAKE A FETISH OUT OF THE WORDS "PARTY" OR "MAJORITY".

Thus we propose the following measures:
1. Fusion of both groups WITHOUT THE EXCLUSION OF ANY COMRADE. Election of a JOINT ACTION COMMITTEE proportionate to the existing forces or, even better, composed on the basis of a COMMON AGREEMENT to ensure that the MOST CAPABLE comrades of BOTH trends are elected.

2. Creation of an INTERNAL discussion bulletin (mimeographed); discussion of all controversial questions and JOINT EDITING.
3. Discussion material for our INTERNATIONAL press, e.g., for the "Militant".
4. Expansion of the "Spark" into a PROPAGANDISTIC-POLITICAL ORGAN, which must devote A FEW PAGES ESPECIALLY TO NEGROES AND PEASANTS, if possible in BANTU LANGUAGE.
5. Preparation for a party conference after a few months of joint work; preparation of AN ACTION PROGRAMME, preparation for the implementation of the proposals made in our last letter.

We are convinced, that working through our suggestions will lead you out of the cul-de-sac in which you presently find yourselves. EVERYTHING depends on you alone. Even the premature proclamation of the Workers Party need not be an obstacle to a favourable development, since what is important is the CONTENTS of the work, and even a small group of genuine revolutionaries can quickly rise to play a GREAT role in a country like South Africa.

With com. greetings on behalf of the International Secretariat of the ICL
DUBOIS.

Document 55
Letter from the International Secretariat of the International Communist League (B-L) to the Workers' Party of South Africa and the Communist League of South Africa, 12 October 1935[25]

Geneva, 12th October 1935

To the WORKERS PARTY and
to the COMMUNIST LEAGUE, of South Africa

Dear Comrades,

we have read with great interest and great attention the documents and letters you have sent us. In particular, we have devoted attention to the efforts that both groups have paid to the *Negro question*. It seems to us that as a result of the given circumstances in Africa, a considerable part of the issues of conflict that have even led to a split between the two groups, has to be shifted into the background in light of the current significance which Africa has received during the last few weeks. We therefore advise both groups once again and with all seriousness, to *pay attention to what both have in common* in place of the dividing differences, and to *jointly tackle the current task*.

These current issues are characterised by the complications in the Abyssinian-Italian conflict, due to the position taken by the British. The greatest, strongest and most brutal of imperialistic colonial oppressors has adopted the role of the champion of freedom of a hitherto virtually independent black African people and country, and the English *working class* follows these imperialistic troubadours of *peace* in that they, following the social-patriotic enthusiasm of their largest organisations – Trade Unions and Labour Party –, loudly declare themselves prepared, without fuss and in the name of peace to fight a *war* against the disturber of the peace, Italy.

To fail to point out in this situation in *Africa*, that it is a question of miserable imperialistic talk, when English labour organisations, instead of calling upon *their* colonial people not only to support Abyssinia, but also to set as their own goal the struggle for independence from the English (as well as from the white imperialist robbers and slave traders), means to be co-responsible *through the stupefaction of the working class for the preparation of the next imperialist war.* That Stalinists are in full agreement with this position, they will try to hide with nice words, but their actions in the League of Nations as well as their eloquent silence over the Italo-Abyssinian conflict during the 7th Congress are apparent enough.[26]

This imposes upon the genuine communist groups everywhere, but in particular in Africa, the obligation to muster all their forces in order to raise their voices in a clear, unambiguous and unanimous manner in order to make organisational progress, so as to *clearly explain to the natives that in addition to the white oppressors there also exist white revolutionaries, who proclaim the right of every people to severe their ties to the imperialists, and emphasise in Africa, that the white oppressor has no business in Africa.*

We urge you, dear comrades, not only to maintain your contact with us, but *also with each other*, i.e., to speedily and seriously re-establish contact among both divided groups, for the benefit of the whole movement.

With communist greeting,
on behalf of the I. S. DUBOIS.

Document 56
Extract of a letter of 24 October 1935 from the COMMUNIST LEAGUE OF SOUTH AFRICA, *Press Service of the International Secretariat, International Communist League (B-L)*, 15 November 1935

The Italian–Abyssinian dispute continues to be the chief concern of the working class movement and our consistently Marxist stand on this question which is in full accord with the position taken up by the other sections of the Fourth Internationalists, have drawn to our banner a great number of workers, mostly coloured and Native. We in South Africa have an important role to play because, as a British Dominion this country will be greatly affected by the role taken by the British Imperialism in the dispute. The imperialist press are endeavouring to make out that British Imperialism is playing the role of defender of the small nations, and our first duty is to counteract that propaganda and expose the predatory policy of British Imperialism.

The war has aroused intense feeling among the coloured and Native workers and there is a great danger that they will be mislead by the combined propaganda of the Stalinists, the Churches, the S.A. Labour party and the Imperialist press into supporting the war aims of Great Britain. All these organizations support "sanctions" and place their faith in the League of Nations. We have put forward the slogan "BOYCOTT FASCIST ITALY" and it is meeting with some success among the working class.

While our increased activities have drawn to our banner a number of workers, it has also attracted the unwelcome attention of the reactionaries. The comrades which had been arrested in connection with a meeting in the Native Location were each fined ten shillings. Our last two open air meetings broke all records. Last week, over a thousand workers listened to our views on the Italian–Abyssinian war, and this week nearly two thousand workers were present. Both these meetings were noteworthy, because there was an organised attempt on the part of the Grey Shirts – an Anti-semitic organization with Fascist tendencies – to break up our meeting.[27] This is the first time such a thing has occured in Cape Town. ...

With warmest proletarian greetings,
For the Fourth International
(signature).

Document 57
Letter from the Communist League of South Africa to the Workers' Party of South Africa, 13 January 1936

The Communist League of South Africa,
35, Waterkant Street,
CAPE TOWN.
13th January, 1936

General Secretary,
Workers' Party of South Africa,
P.O. Box 1940,
CAPE TOWN.

Dear Comrade,

Your letter of the 10th December has received the careful consideration of a business meeting of the Communist League.

All comrades expressed great satisfaction at the friendly tone and the evident agreement on the desirability of unity as expressed in your letter.

We agree to your suggestion that a special bulletin be attached to our respective organs, in which the problems affecting the revolution in South Africa can be discussed. We feel, however, the need that immediate steps be taken to bring this proposal into reality, and propose that you elect a sub-committee to act in collaboration with a sub-committee elected by the above mentioned meeting, to arrange the production and editing of the Bulletin, also to continue the discussions begun through this correspondence. We feel that otherwise there is a grave danger of prolonged negotiations before anything is really done.

We fail to understand your reasons for rejecting our "United Front" proposals. Our attitude towards the Italo–Abyssinian War is that of all the Fourth International Groups and of the Left Opposition, i.e. opposition to League Sanctions, for a Workers' Boycott and Workers' Sanctions. We are confident that you cannot differ from that attitude.

As regards our attitude to the Native Bills, whilst you will find it outlined in the January issue of the "Workers' Voice," we can hardly credit your statement that you do not know our attitude to these Bills. Surely you cannot seriously doubt our strenuous opposition to Bills which threaten to further degrade the native masses.

Apart from the above considerations, we feel that only by and through "United Front" actions can theory be tested, and if necessary, corrected. It is precisely because we are confident that the unity of our organisations must come, that we stress the importance of presenting a "United Fourth International Front," on questions which are to-day rousing the masses of Africa to action on a scale unprecedented in modern times.

The members of the Sub-committee appointed to meet you, are: Comrades Davison, Gool, Averbuch, and H. M. van Gelderen.

We hope that you will agree to this proposed co-ordinatery committee.

FOR THE FOURTH INTERNATIONAL,
p.p. H. M. van Gelderen[28],
GENERAL SECRETARY
F.D.

Document 58
Letter from the Communist League of South Africa to the Workers' Party of South Africa, 18 February 1936

The Communist League of South Africa,
35, Waterkant Street,
CAPE TOWN.
18th February, 1936.

The Secretary,
Workers' Party of S.A.,
P.O. Box 1940,
CAPE TOWN.

Dear Comrade,

We are extremely disappointed that we have so far had no reply to our letter of 17th January, 1936, relating to our proposals for Unity and a united fron against the Native Bills and the Italo–Abyssinian War.

As you are aware, we have several times approached you on this subject as we feel sure that the Fourth International Movement would be enormously strengthened in this country if we combined our efforts. There can be no doubt that the original split in our ranks has produced certain beneficial results, for, dialectically, a conflict of opinion is essential if a correct policy and programme is to be achieved. But, to-day, unity and combined efforts are again indicated.

We appreciate the fact that complete unity on all points may not yet be possible. A great deal of preliminary work and discussion is still necessary. Nevertheless, since we do agree on certain principles, we feel that these principles should form a basis for the dicussion of our differences. Moreover, much valuable time is being lost. The crisis is rapidly approaching, and should not find us divided.

There may, of course, be some reason, of which we are unaware, why you have not yet replied to our last letter, but in view of the urgency of the position, we must ask you to advise us immediately, one way or another, as to your intentions. In any case, a bare acknowledgement of our proposals is at least indicated.

As you are aware from our last letter, we have suggested the concrete proposal that 4 of our comrades should meet a delegation consisting of an equal number of comrades from the Workers' Party. The names of these comrades from the Communist League were also mentioned. We feel sure that this provides a good basis which may eventually bring about the desired unity.

In accordance with your previous suggestion we are publishing in the next number of the "Workers' Voice" our analysis of the economic position of the native in this country, but, as our respective papers are only published monthly, it will necessitate the passage of several months before all our differences have been thoroughly discussed.

We shall appreciate an early reply, as up to now we have been left somewhat "up in the air", and that naturally handicaps us in the formulation of our future plans.

Yours, FOR THE FOURTH INTERNATIONAL!
p.p. THE COMMUNIST LEAGUE OF SOUTH AFRICA,
G. H. Gool[29]
CHAIRMAN.

Document 59
Letter from the Workers' Party of South Africa to N. J. Barclay, 21 February 1936

141 Longmarket Street,
CAPE TOWN/.
21st February, 1936.

N. J. Barclay

Dear Comrade,

Comrades Grant[30] and Frost are in a better position than myself to inform you about the development of our movement in Johannesburg. I will confine myself to Cape Town.

We will take as a starting point the Lenin Club which was formed in 1933 by four or five Jewish-speaking members, two of which had been expelled from the Communist Party (Stalinists) as right-wingers. The L.C. grew slowly (almost exclusively Jewish-speaking) until the end of 1933 and the beginning of 1934 when the Left Wing of the Independent Labour Party joined. (The I.L.P. blew up before achieving an organ or even a constitution.) As a result of its growth the Lenin Club became English-speaking, the Jewish members taking a less and less active part in its work which consisted of holding regular lectures (twice a week) and issuing occassional leaflets. The Lenin Club stood for the International Left Opposition and propaged its views but in the opinion of some of the comrades it was Left Opposition before it had been communist (with a small "c"). Although united on the international problems, the Club rapidly developed two points of view on all the South African questions. As a step towards forming a Party, it was decided to elaborate theses on the South African questions. The Theses Sub-Committee split and submitted minority and majority theses to a series of general meetings of the Club where the theses were accepted after discussion by a majority of the members. The accepted Theses, the Majority Theses, have been sent to you together with the Minority Theses.

On the basis of the Theses accepted by the majority of the Lenin Club the Communist League was formed but, and this is very important, after discussion with the Johannesburg group, the Communist League decided to change its name to Workers Party. (Reason: in most Bantu languages there is no separate word for League as opposed to Party which led to endless confusion between us and the Communist Party (Stalinists).) The Communist League became the Workers Party but the Lenin Club minority whose theses had been rejected picked up the discarded name of Communist League.

The position now was that there were two political organisations, the Workers Party which issued and issues the "Spark" and the Communist League both inside the Lenin Club. It was decided to ask the International Secretariat to decide between the two groups on the basis of their theses but the I.S. counselled peace, peace, peace, and detailed Dubois to comment on the Theses of the W.P. The ignorance of Dubois was equalled only by his cocksureness but L. T. wrote a "Remark" (a copy was sent to you) which is now the Magna Charta of our Party. The arrival of L. T.'s "Remarks" had no effect upon the Communist League and in June 1935 the split was widened by the withdrawal of the Workers Party from the Lenin Club.

The position to-day is this. The Lenin Club-Communist League carries on and issues "The Workers' Voice". The Workers Party has formed the Spartacus Club here and in Johannesburg, in Alexandra, and in Benoni, and issues "The Spark". Negoitations are are present being carried on between the W.P. and the C.L. but whether or not a basis for unity will be found I cannot say at this date.

The opinion of the W/.P. is that the C.L. is not communist in so far as South African questions are concerned but actually takes up a left-socialdemocratic position, i.e., opportunism, on all South African problems. I leave to you the task of comparing our "Spark" with the "Workers' Voice", and of studying the various theses.

Document 60
Letter from the Workers' Party of South Africa to the Communist League of South Africa, 3 March 1936

The Workers Party of South Africa
P.O. Box 1940
Cape Town.
3rd March, 1936.

The Communist League of South Africa,
Cape Town.

Dear Comrades,

We have two letters from you, dated respectively Jan. 13 and Feb. 18, on the subject of unity and a united front for our two organisations, and we are sorry that the pressure of exceptional anxieties and urgent duties has prevented an earlier reply.

We regret further that the demands of our normal imperative duties oblige us now to say that *at present* we do not see our way to expending time and energy on the proposed negotiations for union and the proposed special Bulletin for full discussion of the issues that led to our separation last year. We are wholly convinced that such negotiations and discussion are a necessary preliminary to union, but at present the Workers Party has not its full man-power available for the considerable amount of extra work involved, without neglecting to some extent fundamentally important work already undertaken.

On this last point we owe you an explanation of the changed circumstances which in our opinion require that *for the time being* the Workers Party shall not assume any additional new obligations, but shall concentrate on its main existing duties, viz., systematically planned and intensive instruction and training of enquirers and new comrades besidea the lectures and discussions provided for the benefit of all; the maintenance of "The Spark" in full vigour and with such developments as may be found practicable; and recurrent endeavour to rouse, enlighten, and direct mass feeling in the way so successfully begun at our October Celebrations last year, and promising increasingly valuable results.

Our present diminished man-power is due to the temporary loss of certain valuable comrades removed far from this neighbourhood, and to decreased activity on the part of others who have reached a very exacting stage in their professional studies, and similar unavoidable matters affecting the livelihood of the comrade and his dependants. This will right itself in time, if we concentrate on the positive task of building up a strong militant group.

You may perhaps say that all this would not necessarily hinder the formation of a united front. But that suggestion at once brings up the old disabling difficulty – or shall we say, impossibility? – of speaking from one platform, of composing a common manifesto, when minds are not agreed. In your letter to us of 13th Jan. you talk of "questions which are to-day rousing the masses of Africa to action on a scale unprecedented in modern times". To us that appears a ludicrous exaggeration, far removed from the realities with which we are faced. Again, in your leaflet, "Fiht the Native Bills", you say, "we must prepare for a General Strike". But to our thinking it is irrational and irresponsible to urge the workers to prepare for a General Strike in a country where the necessary objective and subjective conditions simply do not exist. We have noted, moreover, with keen regret the similarly inflated, sensational, adventurist tone of the Communist League's communications to the Militant" and to "La Verité", giving what is in our opinion a false and misleading view of the African situation.

Please do not think that these comments are offensively meant. We merely want to remind you that less than a year ago you and we were in the painful process of finding out that we could not work fruitfully together while our minds and methods were widely divergent. It is, however, just barely possible that, in spite of the very short time that has since elapsed, negotiations and discussions might find a way of overcoming the paralysing effects of divergency, and it is therefore with some reluctance that the Workers Party has definitely decided that *at the present time* it cannot justifiably release comrades from their essential constructive work in order to enable them to enter upon what would certainly prove a long and arduous task, and not improbably a sterile one.

Meanwhile, if our two groups labour earnestly in the fundamental task of building up fully equipped militant workers in the revolutionary Marxist tradition as preserved and interpreted in the 4th International, we shall be most certainly drawn nearer together, i.e., towards union.

With Communist greetings,

Document 61
Minutes of the meeting of the Workers' Party of South Africa, Johannesburg Branch, held at 90 President Street, Johannesburg, 25 March (1936) at 8.30 p.m.

Present: Freislich, Kahn, Phashe, Gosani, Pompey, Sapire, Lee[31] (sec)

Com Phashe was elected chairman.

The minutes of the previous meeting were read and confirmed.

A letter replying to C. B. J. Dladla was read.

Com Freislich reported that 14 had attended the last lecture at the Spartacus Club. The order of the next two lectures was changed to 1) sapire, 2) Gosani.

Com Phashe reported that on Saturday night among native miners he had spoken on trade unionism.

Com Gosani reported that in his weeks organising tour he had visited in turn Benoni Location, West Springs, Daggasfontein, Nigel, Lago Collieries, Welgedachte, Klipfontein and Simmer and Jack. He had made contacts and secured promises from individuals in these districts to act as local correspondents for the bulletin. After discussion it was decided to bring up again at future meetings the question of making regular and systematic tours in accordance with a general plan of campaign.

Com Phashe reported that he had visited Heidelberg. No meeting had been held by Dladla.

There were reports on the progress in classes, literature sales, and library.

Com Lee reported that articles had been submitted in English and Sesotho for publication in the bulletin.

Com Kahn reported that to date a total of £25.1.3 had been collected towards the Press Fund.

There was a general discussion of practical matters arising in connection with future party activities.

The meeting concluded at 10 p.m.

Chairman:
Secretary:

Document 62
Minutes of the meeting of the Workers' Party of South Africa, Johannesburg Branch, held at 90 President Street, Johannesburg, 3 April 1936 at 8.20 p.m.

Present: Comrades Phashe, Gosani, Sapire, Freislich, Kahn, Lee, (secretary)

Com Sapire was elected Chairman.

The minutes of the previous meeting were read and confirmed.

The Treasurer, Com Sapire, reported 4/6 in hand.

Com Freislich reported that the attendance at the Spartacus Club was improving again. Com Gosani would lecture next Wednesday evening on "Bantu Woman's Place In Politics." It was decided that Dunbar be invited to lecture on "War", also Findlay, Danchen, B. Sachs (on "Trotsky, man, thinker, revolutionary") Ballinger (on "The Future of the Native Worker") F. A. W. Lucas, De Moore.[32]

Com Gosani reported that the rains during last week had interfered with activities in the townships. Com Phashe reported a similar postponement of miners' meetings.

Com Kahn reported receipt of current "Spark" and pamphlets from U.S.A.

Com Gosani reported that a reading Room was being organised in the Club. Com Sapire offered to supply regularly, the Star; Com Kahn, the Mail; Com Gosani, Umteteli; Com Phashe, Bantu World; Com Pompey, Umsebenzi and Umvekeli; Com Freislich, K.C.A.; The Party would donate the New Militant, New International and the Spark.

It was decided to carry on the library without subscriptions or deposits but on the basis of 6d. per month.

Com Lee reported on Classes and Bulletin. Com Phashe reported that he was writing a question and answers series. Com Lee was instructed to convene a meeting of the E.B.

General: Com Gosani reported that he was working out a plan of campaign.

The meeting concluded at 9.5 p.m.

Chairman:
Secretary:

Document 63
Letter from Workers' Party of South Africa to the International Secretariat of the International Communist League (B-L), 11 April 1936

THE WORKERS PARTY OF SOUTH AFRICA

P.O. Box 1940
Cape Town
South Africa
11.4.1936

I.S., L.C.I. (B.-L.)

Dear Comrade Adolphe,

A comrade of our Club here, the Spartacus Club, has been working in secrecy to bring out the first Afrikaans (i.e., South African Dutch) translation of "The Communist Manifesto". The translation is now complete in manuscript, and is being typed by comrades in readiness for the printers.

Only one thing is lacking to crown the work, and that is a little Introduction from the hand of our great leader. Will Comrade Trotsky honour this small offering to the revolutionary movement by sealing it with his approval and recommendation? We shall indeed be grateful, if he can find time to do this for our remote and backward country.[33]

South Africans, with the exception of a handful of scholars, do not read the Dutch of the Netherlands, and revolutionary literature is not yet to be found in the Afrikaans language, which is the language of more than half the white population and of a large proportion of the people of mixed descent, so that this effort will open up a whole new field of propaganda for Marxism and the Fourth International.

We earnestly hope that you will understand our eagerness for the fulfilment of this task, and we ask you to be so kind as to forward without delay our respectful petition to Comrade Trotsky. Now that the translation is complete, the matter of the printing becomes urgent, lest our secret should leak out before the booklets are ready for circulation.

Fraternal greetings,
C. R. Goodlatte, W.P.S.A. Cape Town
Paul Koston[34]

Document 64
Letter from the Workers' Party of South Africa to the International Secretariat of the International Communist League (B-L), 1 July 1936

WORKERS PARTY OF SOUTH AFRICA.
P.O. Box 2639,
Johannesburg,

1st July 1936.

To the I.S.
L.C.I. (B.L.)

Dear Comrade Adolphe[35],

In answer to your enquiries in your letter of 10th May 1936 I am giving you some particulars.

The Workers Party consists of two small branches at Cape Town and at Johannesburg. As a distance of one thousand miles separates us each branch is practically self contained and there is no national leadership in the sense of a single committee controlling both. The functions of the General Secretary are confined to external relations (with the I.S., etc) rather than to the internal relationships within the party. Our unity is based theoretically on the common acceptance of the principles contained in the theses written by Comrade Burlak and organisationally upon the fraternal exchange of minutes of meetings, correspondence and a common support for the "Spark," which continues to be produced in Cape Town under the control of an editorial committee of Cape Town comrades.

The Communist League exists only in Cape Town and the Johannesburg branch of the Workers Party has followed the policy of leaving all decisions and negotiations between the two sections to the discretion of the Cape Town comrades. We have taken sides against the Communist League only on the basis of their published theoretical divergences from the principles espoused by the Workers Party.

Discussions within the Workers Party have centred in the Native Bills introduced into Parliament by the present United Party Government which consists of an alliance of the wealthy Boer landowners with British Imperialism. In the matter of the Native Bills a difference has arisen between the attitude taken by the Cape Town branch as published in the "Spark" and the attitude of the Johannesburg branch as expressed in the enclosed article which has been submitted to the Spark as a discussion article. There has been some friction between the branches on the matter of the divergent points of view but this I think has been due more to misunderstanding than to actual differences. These misunderstandings will probably be liquidated by means of further discussion.

At the time of writing there is being held in Bloemfontein an All African Convention to which all political organisations that have non-European members are sending non-European representatives. Three representatives of our party are attending. There is a movement afoot to transform this Convention into a permanent national organisation "representing the interests of the native people". In the growth of this movement there are distinct possibilities for a revolutionary wing, provided that the development of our party keeps pace with the upswing in the broad masses. The Communist Party has already committed itself to a people's front policy of collaboration with the native reformists. Thus it is upon our grouping that the task falls of providing the core of the left wing in name as well as in actuality.

Our efforts have been bent mainly on the task of surrounding oursevles with the beginnings of a proletarian party. With agonising slowness we have added to our circles one by one and this has meant direct personal propaganda. Where in other countries a kind of clearing has been effected by the liberal bourgeoisie, by reformists, by Stalinists, we are in this country faced to a large extent by virgin jungle. It is not difficult to reach those who have already had some grounding in political theory, but these make up altogether only a tiny handful – among natives only a few intellectuals have the necessary grasp of the language to be reached by our written propaganda and these few are subjected to an ideological bombardment from the churches, the Chamber of Mines, the bourgeois nigrophiles and the African nationalists, not to mention the privilges which Imperialism is enabled by its incredible super profits to dole out to submissive native leaders. ("good boys.")

Our activities up to now in Johannesburg have consisted in establishing a popular central workers club, the Spartacus Club, with a fair sized hall, with social and educational activities in addition to daily lunch hour propaganda lectures and classes and with lectures every evening. Branch circles have been set up in Pretoria, (40 miles distant), Nigel (40 Miles), and Orlando, (the largest native workers district in the vicinity of Johannesburg). These circles are as yet unstable. Attempts at trade union organisation and the formation of workers' councils (vigilance committees for redress of local grievances) in the native townships have so far met with little success. Similar activities are carried on by the Cape Town comrades.

We hope to issue a printed paper in native languages in the coming months. The publication of a popular agitational paper in the native languages and the carrying out of a planned organising tour in the surrounding districts will enable us to emerge as a party; up to now we have had merely a pre-natal existence.

The main task that confronts the proletarian party once revolutinary cadres are established, is the organising of the totally unorganised native miners who number 300,000 on the Rand alone. The native miners union, given revolutionary leadership is the battering ram that will smash down British Imperialism in South Africa: in our present isolation it is almost too audacious even to dream of initiating this colossal task. The native miners are recruited from the "reserves" and their periods in the mines are ten months episodes – nightmares – in a "normal" existence on the insufficient scraps of land where their families are located. They are almost out of reach of propaganda not only through ideological difficulties, (language, illiteracy, political inexperience and backwardness) but also through physical difficulties – they are virtually imprisoned in the "compounds" under police guard most of the time they are above ground.[36]

On the other hand, the intense concentration of numbers ensures the rapid spread of militant revolutionary doctrines once they are introduced. The experience of past movements, (the African National Congress, the I.C.U.) has demonstrated that a revolutionary platform propagated by a determined band of agitators finds enthusiastic support among the miners. Both the A.N.C. and the I.C.U., after an initial revolutionary flowering, degenerated into reformism and consequently decayed as rapidly as they rose. There are the first signs now of a revolutionary upsurge among the native workers (isolated spontaneous strikes, an increased confidence due to the trade revival and the diminishing of unemployment,) and so the toally discredited A.N.C. and I.C.U. leaders are leaping forward to seize the reins. Hence the necessity for the formation of a revolutionary wing in the All African Convention in which this political awakening is first manifesting itself. These are the immediate perspectives of our Party.

As to languages we can understand French and German but not Russion; naturally we prefer English to all the other languages.

I hope in future reports to fill out the rather sketchy outlines of this preliminary letter.

Yours fraternally,
General Secretary.

Document 65
Minutes of the meeting of the Workers' Party of South Africa, Johannesburg Branch held at 90 President Street, Johannesburg, Friday, 24 July 1936 at 8 p.m.

Present: Kahn, Sapire, Phashe, Pompey, Dladla, Moloenyane, Lee (Secretary)

Com Dladla was elected chairman.

Com Dladla proposed seconded by Com Phashe that Com Philip Moloenyane, 69 Good Street, Sophiatown be accepted as a member of the W.P.S.A. This was unanimously agreed.

The minutes of the previous meeting were read and confirmed.

A letter from Com Goodlatte dated 14/7/36 together with the minutes of the W.P.S.A. C.T. Branch dated 13/7/36 were read. A letter from Com Goodlatte dated 18/7/36 with enclosed cutting was read; and further a letter from Arne Swabeck to Com Kahn with reference to the New Militant and New International.

Com Kahn reported on the Spartacus Club in the absence of the Secretary, Com Freislich. The next lecture would be by Com Freislich followed by a lecture by P. Masekela on "The Other Side of the Picture."

Com Pompey reported that a meeting would be held at Newclare next Sunday to discuss the formation of trade unions. Himself and Com Dladla after attending this meeting in the morning would attend the Spartacus Club meeting at Orlando in the afternoon.

Com Kahn reported that a meeting of the African Laundry Workers Union would be held next Sunday morning. Coms Phashe and Moloenyane were instructed to attend this meeting. Com Pompey was instructed to interview Mngade.

Com Kahn reported that the Stalinists had now come out openly in favour of a colour bar in the Commercial Employees Union and were trying to use the colour issue to force her out of the Committee. It was decided to continue agitating for a non colour bar union even at the expense of being excluded from the committee.

Com Phashe was instructed to interview certain native commercial employees.

It was decided to make the attempt to issue the first number of our bulletin on September 1st 1936. All articles should be submitted by Friday next.

Com Dladla reported that a small group discussed in the Spartacus Club the agitation for equal franchise rights for Africans. Those present formed a committee to meet on

Saturday week.

Under general Com Phashe proposed lecturing at a future date on unity. Enquiries concerning absentees from the present meeting showed that Coms Freislich, Makhudu, Nxahe and Maseko[37] were unable to attend through having to work at night.

It was decided to allot a small amount from the party funds each week to pay subscriptions on certain papers for the reading table in the club.

The meeting concluded at 9.45 p.m.

Chairman:
Secretary:

Document 66
Letter from the Workers' Party of South Africa, Johannesburg, to the Cape Town branch, 21 February 1937

WORKERS' PARTY OF SOUTH AFRICA
90 PRESIDENT STREET,   P.O. BOX 2639,
JOHANNESBURG   JOHANNESBURG
21st February 1937

Secretary,
W,P.S.A.,
C.T. Branch,
Cape Town.

Dear Comrade,

We have been busy organising the African Metal Trades Union and as you will see from the letter they have sent you, battles lie ahead of us. In leading the first strike of 1937 the "counter revolutionary" Troskyites are flinging the lie in the faces of the wretched Stalinists.[38] I will keep the Cape Town Branch in constant touch with developments. Please make the fullest use of our resources, the Spark, Spartacus Club, etc in giving pulbicity to, and gaining support for the strike of the African metal workers. Miners are joining our union and a victory in this strike will give to the Troskyites the leadership in the rising strike wave which shows signs of inundating South Africa.

Yours fraternally,
R. Lee
Secretary.

Document 67
Letter from the African Metal Trades Union, Johannesburg, to the Workers' Party of South Africa, 21 February 1937

AFRICAN METAL TRADES UNION
P.O. Box 2639. JOHANNESBURG
90 President Street, Johannesburg.

21st February 1937

Secretary,
Workers' Party of South Africa,
Cape Town Branch,
Cape Town.

Dear Comrade,

I have been instructed by the Committee of the above Union to urge you to support us in the bitter struggle that now confronts us. Messrs, Scaw Works, (Steel Ceilings & Aluminium Works, Ltd.,), one of the largest employers in the metal trades have contemptuously rejected our demands for the recognition of our Union and the amelioration of our conditions, and they force us to take strike action against them to protect our elementary rights. We ask you, therefore, Comrades, to stand by us in our struggle, to give us every aid, moral and financial that you can. Unless the employers agree to arrive at an agreement with us within the next 48 hours a strike is inevitable. A secret ballot has already been taken which has shown that our members are unanimously decided to adopt the only weapon calculated to gain concessions from the bosses, namely the strike weapon. We appeal to you therefore to hold yourselves in readiness to organise aid for us in the districts where you are situated.

Yours fraternally,
R. Lee
Secretary.

Document 68
Letter from the Workers' Party of South Africa, Johannesburg, to the Cape Town branch, 26 February 1937

WORKERS' PARTY OF SOUTH AFRICA
90 PRESIDENT STREET,   P.O. Box 2639,
JOHANNESBURG   JOHANNESBURG
26th February 1937

Secretary,
W.P.S.A.
C.T.

Dear Comrade,

I write to keep you informed of the progress of the strike now occurring at Scaw Works. After months of secret preparations, our demands were presented and the developments took place with great rapidity, because we dared not give the bosses time to lay up a stock of their products upon which to keep going.

Our demands presented last Friday, were rejected on Saturday. Overtures made on Monday by the Labour Department on our suggestion were ineffectual, and on the same evening the decision to strike was taken and carried out the following morning by 100% of our members, who drew out half the non-union men with them leaving ten scabs behind.

We sought on Wednesday to open negotiations with the bosses through a deputation sent by the S.A. Trades and Labour Council, but with no success. The bosses declared themselves to be "supremely indifferent." On Thursday they thawed out sufficiently to approach some of the workers individually and now finally they have started to arrest the men they need most on trumped up charges of violence;: one was arrested yesterday and promised by the detective in charge withdrawal of charges and his job back at higher pay if he would scab. He refused. The others have just placed themselves in the hands of the Native Affairs Department. We await news of their arrest.

Up to now we have only placed persuasive pickets in the neighbourhood of the factory and at the Pass Office. The backwardness of African workers causes them to scab unintentionally and some are even being forced physically to continue to scab. The factory however is managing to limp along, thanks to the treachery of the European "trade union members" who are training and supervising the scabs, and the "European youths" who are actually themselves replacing strikers. We must agitate energetically against this, I have appealed to the S.A. Trades & Labour Council and the Unions concerned and as you might expect the bureaucrats shake their heads sadly, and offer us financial aid to appease their consciences (or whatever vestigial remains still persist of this faculty in these casehardened swine). If the strike fails it will be due to this stab in the back dealt us by "fellow workers."

We need every penny that can be raised to keep the men and their families housed and fed and for legal defence. Success in raising money will render us independent of the European Unions and enable us openly to label them as Pinkertons. The lesson must be drawn by the European workers and it is for us to hammer on this question till it gets home. Here is an opportunity to bring it forward and you will I am sure not be slow to bring every pressure at your disposal to bear on organisations and individuals around you.

News has just come that 8 more men have been arrested, bringing the total to 10. I suppose I am next in order, though I cannot imagine any charge they can possibly fake up against me.

Money and agitation against European scabbing – it's up to you, Comrades.

Yours for the Fourth International,
R. Lee

Document 69
Letter from the Workers' Party of South Africa, Johannesburg, to the Cape Town branch, 22 March 1937

WORKERS' PARTY OF SOUTH AFRICA
90 PRESIDENT STREET,   P.O. BOX 2639,
JOHANNESBURG   JOHANNESBURG
22nd March 1937

Secretary,
W.P.S.A.
C.T. Branch.

Dear Comrade,

The strike of the African Metal Workers Union has been defeated with considerable loss to the Union in so far as we receive an initial setback. The strike was originally undertaken by the workers on these terms: either we will force up wages or else we will seek other jobs. Some of the workers refused to apply for their jobs back again. Others went back only upon my urgent persuasion to try and rebuild the union in this factory. Others have taken jobs elsewhere after being turned away by Scaw works. This tends to disintegrate the union although most of them continue to pay subs and remain true to the principle of workers' unity. The remainder are still without jobs since the word "Scaw works" on their passes brands them as militants and subjects them to victimisation.

Please keep on collecting as we have to face the problem of finding rent money for them at the end of the month. Our comrades here have thrown in their last pennies and exhausted their credit, £105 having been subscribed by local party members. Not one penny was received from the European unions or the Stalinist organisations.

The reasons for the defeat were:
1) The sectional nature of the strike.
2) Scabbing of Europeans.
3) Natives scabbing through the general inexperience of African workers.

I will write to draw the lessons of the defeat later.

Two strikers are now to be charged with violence or threatening under the Riotous Assemblies Act. They are each on £10 bail. We have briefed Hansen for twenty guineas and the case starts on 26th March 1937.

The Stalinists did their damndest to sabotage the strike by refusing to publish a notice of it when it broke out, by spreading false rumours during the first few days that the strike was defeated, thus sabotaging collections and finally by publishing a notice in Umsebenzi that the strike was defeatd before the Union officially acknowledged defeat, thus trying to destroy our last remaining chances. Far from protesting against the European workers who supervised scabs they actually defend them.

With the present business boom in Johannesburg the workers have reacted to the fading of the unemployment spectre by a wave of militancy. The bold action of the Scaw workers would have been impossible two years ago with jobs so scarce, but today we may expect similar action on a wider scale in many branches of industry.

Your donations of £10.0.0 and £1.2.6 were deeply appreciated by the strikers particularly in contrast to the silence of other organisations.

Did you receive acknowledgement from the I.S. for money sent for Com Trotsky's case?

Yours fraternally,
R. Lee,
Secretary

Document 70
Letter from the Workers' Party of South Africa, Johannesburg, to the Cape Town branch, 26 August 1937

33 Strathearn Mansions,
cr. Wanderers & Bree Streets,
Johannesburg.
26th August 1937.

The Workers Party of S. A.,
P.O. Box 1940,
Cape Town.

Dear Comrades,

I enclose herewith 15/–. being the September affiliation fee to the I.S.

In my last letter to Comrade Goodlatte, I stated that I would in due course send a more lengthy report as to the activities here. As you are aware Comrades Lee, Kahn, Freislich and Heaton recently left for Europe and needless to say, this has weakened our ranks considerably. Outside of myself and three comrades from Holland, who are not very well aquainted with the English language, the rest of the comrades are all natives who remain rather backward theoretically. No doubt Comrade Lee reported in full the details of the strike and its defeat, and this has naturally had the effect of weakening the Metal Workers' Union. Same is, however, being rebuilt and I have every hope that in the near future it will be considerably strengthened. We received very little financial support from outside sources and the tremendous expense involved by the strike resulted in our having to give up our relatively spacious premises at 90 President Street, and we have had to move in to a small room in Fox Street. In addition, we were compelled to cease publication of our organ "Umlilo Mollo".

Our position has now become worse owing to ill-health overtaking me, and this has disabled me from active participation for nearly six weeks. As a matter of fact I am at present under Doctor's instructions to avoid both theoretical and practical work of any nature. However, I am still optimistic as to the possibilities of rebuilding and re organising the Workers' Party here and I have retained contact, although of a rather loose nature, with most of the members of the Party. You can, however, understand that a Party without an efficient and active secretary inevitably tends to lose its revolutionary nature.

In a more general way, however, the growth of the Fascist movement here in Johannesburg, has resulted in numerous anti-Fascist organisations springing up like mushrooms, one of which is of a particularly militant nature since it has been formed for the express purpose of combatting Fascists by the use of force. I am watching this organisation carefully.

I shall be pleased to receive periodic reports in connection with the activities of your Branch.

In addition if you will forward me a dozen copies of the "Spark" monthly, I do not think I shall have any difficulty in disposing of them here, particularly among the University students who are beginning to take an active interest in the movement.

With revolutionary Greetings,
M. SAPIRE,
Secretary, W.P.S.A.
(Johannesburg Branch.)

Document 71
Spartacus Club October Revolution Celebrations,[39]
Oddfellows Hall, 70 Loop Street, Cape Town, 6 November 1937

PROGRAMME

1. Chairman's Address   2. Speech   3. Auction
Interval   Refreshments

"THE SPARK"
A Play in 3 Acts (12 Scenes) and Songs
Songs: "The Spark"
"7th November" (in Xhosa)
"The Earth is Good"

ACT I.
Scene 1.   At a Dutch farm, Transvaal, 1913, just after the Native Land Act has been passed, which drove thousands of Natives off European-owned farms where they had lived as squatters.
    Characters: The Farmer's Wife, Anna, a young Native girl, Stephan, the Farmer, Jan, an old Native, Ann's Father.

Scene 2.   The same day, later, in Jan's hut. The Father and Mother submit to staying on at the farm as servants, but the two young people, Lukosi and Anna, make up their minds to go to town. The rest of the play shows what happens to them.

	Characters: Jan, Jan's wife, Anna, Lukosi, the Son.
	Songs: "Kudala Sizula"
	"Isn't it hard to be a Black Man?"
Scene 3.	In town, some weeks later. Lukosi meets his cousin, Ntombela, who is a teacher. Though he is educated, he has just as much to learn and as far to develop as Lukosi and Anna, before the three of them work with a common purpose at the end of the play. A policeman catches Lukosi, the cousin escapes.
Scene 4.	In jail. Lukosi is thrown in by policeman.
	Songs: "Simple Black Man".
	"Tax Song" (off stage)

ACT II.
Scene 1.	A year or so later. Court Room. Anna is being tried for leading a crowd of women to burn their passes.
	Characters: Anna, Prosecutor, Judge.
	Song: "The Spark" (1st Verse)
Scene 2.	At the Mission School, we see how Ntombela is developing.
	Characters: Nkomo, a middle-aged Native, his Wife, Ntombela, Tsolo, and other students, Dr. Msomi, head of the school.
Scene 3.	In town, a church entrance.
	Characters: A white man, Lukosi, Police sergeant.
Scene 4.	In a mine.
	Characters: Lukosi, Nkomo, Roji, White Boss.
	Song: "Dig for Gold"

ACT III.
Scene 1.	Port Elizabeth, 1920. Ntombela in a miserable room. Since he left the mission school he has been to the mines and now he takes any work he can get in Port Elizabeth. So far, his experience has made him despair. But the appearance of Lukosi puts new life into him. Lukosi, whom experience has not crushed, has got into touch with a white organiser of workers. He persuades Ntombela to join him. Anna is in Pot Elizabeth too, and Nkomo.
	Song: "Tom, Tom, the Worker's Son".
Scene 2.	Mass meeting of dock-workers.
	Characters: Lukosi, Ntombela, Anna, Nkomo, Dr. Msomi, Tsolo, Nkomo's wife and a crowd of others, Bill Martin, white organi
	Songs: "O You Workers All Together Stand".
	"The False Leader".
Scene 3.	Anna and Ntombela meet in the street. News of Lukosi's arrest.
Scene 4.	Committee meeting to arrange for a mass meeting to protest against the arrest of Lukosi and demand his release. Anna's mother has arrived tin town.
	Characters: Bill Martin, Anna, Nkomo, Ntombela.

Scene 5. A room overlooking the square where a crowd of 3000 workers gathered to protest against Lukosi's arrest. Mounted police and others faced the crowd, who were not disorderly. A crowd of white men also gathered. It is not known who fired the first shot, for the order was not given. Three policemen were unhorsed, and the retreating crowd fired upon, causing many casualties. Anna is killed. From their window, the two women, Lukosi's mother and Nkomo's wife, watch the scene in the square. They do not leave the safety of the room which Anna has found for them.

    Songs: "Lament"
             "The International".

xxxxxxxxxxxxxxxxxxxxxxxxxxx

[....]

ATTEND THE LECTURES AT THE
SPARTACUS CLUB
99 Hatfield Street
CAPE TOWN
EVERY SATURDAY AT 8 P.M.

xxxxxxxxxxxxxxxxxxxxxxxxxxx

Document 72
Letter from R. T. R. Molefe to London comrades, 21 February 1938

Johannesburg.
21.2.38.

Dear Comrades,

I am writing to you about the things which is said about com RL [*Ralph Lee*], which is absolutely lies.

Towards the beginning of January last year, we workers of Steel Ceilings and Aluminium Works Ltd. formed our "African Metal Trade Union" which so far appointed com RL to be our secretary. Now as our fellow workers were so hasty we were bound to come out on strike. Com RL advised us several times that the best way is to organise more workers as many as possible from other metal works, we found that to be a hard task that will take years, while we were suffering on account of low wages.

We – the committee instructed our secretary com RL to write our letter of demands to the manager of Scaw works.

1. Increase of 25% in wages
2. Two weeks paid holidays a year
3. A week notice in dismissal etc.

All were rejected.

We all signed for strike and on the 23rd. February 1937 we gave "one hour" notice to the bosses, and we left the premises patiently at 8.15 am. We marched through the town to the hall, and counting the group found that about four workers missing. We put our pickets we found that three left in the promises one is arrested. Comrade RL tried with means to trace which police station our member in, but all in vain, until he was released on £10 bail after a week before the magistrate.

Through the strike I was with com RL to see the Trade Labour Council, who took no steps to our requests.

I – with four others go to Scaw works to fetch our parcels others were given and I was handcuffed and driven to the police station. Coms RL and Sapire came to bail me out. The seargeant refused. The following morning I was released, as there was no charge laid on me. Two days later arested six of our strikers but also acquitted in the same way. Afterwards arrested one man said to be pulling out workers on the day of stike, com RL and com Sapire took him out also £10 bail.

Now two of they appeared in court, one was found guilty. £2.10.0 fine, which was paid by com RL and com Sapire "One not guilty".

During the strike we had enough food cooked by our cooks in the AMI union hall. Each get an sufficient pay every saturday.

We have collected in January and February of about £16 before the strike starts. The money that did not carry us even a week. All friends both white and black races tried to give us money for food, more especially white comrades collected big amount of money for strikers including our treasurer comrade Sapire, and coms Heaton, Frieslich, Kahn etc. ...

Before the end of March the strike continued most of our workers returned back to Scaw works and others got other jobs in different places here in town.

During the strike com RL and comrade Sapire worked their duties satisfactorily. Our secretary RL shall never be forgotten in our minds. Even today our members wished him back.

Com RL left for England in June, while the strike was three months over.

Now comrades only lies you have been told there.

Your comrade, R. T. R. Molefe.
Member of the Committee African Metal Trades Union.

Here is some of the comrades who were on strike last and are quite astonished that comrade RL is in trouble over there. They sign their names that you should not accept such lies there is no such a thing here com RL left us in peace. They wished him back again.
1. Mr. Cecil.   2. Carrington.   3. Mr. Isaac.   4. Readwell.   5. Chubb.
6. Harney.   7. Simoney.   8. J, Matchaya.   9. Eleijah Dani.
10. Comrade Saucepan.

Document 73
Letter from *The Spark* to M. S. Njisane, Flagstaff, 15 September 1938

THE SPARK
Organ of the Workers Party of South Africa
P.O. Box 1940,
CAPE TOWN.
15th September, 1938.

M. S. Njisane,
Nkozo Location,
FLAGSTAFF, C.P.

Dear Comrade,

Please excuse our long delay in replying to the questions you raised in your letter.

You will remember that there has been a great deal of talk in Government circles about the delimitation of livestock in the Reserves. Year in year out the Magistrates and the Bhunga have been harping on this question and each year with greater intensity than before.[40] During the last session of the Native Representative Council, and also of the Bhunga, this question was raised, and the Chief Magistrate of the Transkei gave a warning that if the Natives did not cut down the number of their cattle, the Government would do it for them. Judging from your letter, the threat is being fulfilled.

The pretext for this delimitation crusade is that the Territories are overstocked, and this results in soil erosion. This is quite true, but it is equally true that the Territories are overpopulated. Is the Government going to suggest the delimitation of Natives in the Territories? The problem of overstocking is the problem of overpopulation, and this in turn is the problem of insufficiency of land. Thi is the crux of the matter, and any "solution" that does not touch this fundamental problem – the land problem – is sheer hypocrisy and can solve nothing.

There are about a million Natives in the Transkei and they have about 800,000 morgen of land between them. Every Native in the Transkei has to be a small peasant. He must have a piece of land to plough in order to provide food of a sort for his family, yet "in 1928–1929, 11,000 married hut owners had no arable plots".

Giving evidence before the Native Economic Commission, Mr. S. Butler, then Head of Tsolo School of Agriculture, stated that the number of oxen that the Natives in the Transkei had was far below their needs, and to make up the deficiency the Natives were forced to use calves and cows for ploughing purposes. The staple diet of Natives in the Transkei is mealies and milk. Mr. Butler showed that the cows in the Transkei did not produce sufficient milk for all the people in the Transkei.

This last may be attributed to the fact that the Natives keep scrub cattle which do not produce much milk, but the Government has made very very weak attempts to help the Natives stock better cattle. The Government is not prepared to finance the scheme and the bulk of the people, who of course have no money, will never have these Friesland cows. Only the well-to-do can afford these expensive cows, and the Government takes every opportunity of showing these cattle to tourists as an example of what the Government is doing for the Natives.

All this goes to show that the problem is not overstocking but insufficiency of land.

But before we go into this question of land, there is another question: what is the Government doing to ensure reasonable prices for the cattle the people are being forced to sell? And the answer is: nothing. There used to be a meat market in East London where people could sell their cattle direct to butchers, but this does not exist anymore so far as I know. But this did not even begin to solve the problem for the bulk of the Transkei Natives, because to make the thing pay, one had to sell at the same time a large number of cattle. It would be absolutely ridiculous to rail three or four cattle to be sold in East London. What little you would make would be swallowed by the transportation.

The Government will do nothing to ensure reasonable prices for the cattle which they will force the people to sell. The cattle dealers, who already make large profits, will make still larger ones.

Now seeing that the problem boils down to more land for the Natives, why does the Government not give us more land? And this brings us to another question: is the Government really worried about the misery of the Bantu in the Erserves? Whether they have scrub cattle or no cattle at all? What is the aim of the Government with respect to the Natives in the Reserves?

The Reserves are for the Government nothing but a reservoir of cheap Native labour for the mines and for the farms, and the misery in the Reserves is fostered towards this end. Do you think that if the Natives had sufficient land and sleek fat catttle they would go to the mines and to the farms to look for work? Of course not, and that is why the Government will not give Natives sufficient land to plough and to graze their cattle on. But this was not enough, and so additional pressure in the form of Poll-Tax had to be put on the Native to force him out of the Reserves to work for the mines and the farms at any price. This is the whole story in a few words. "Starve the Native out of the Reserves, so that he is forced to go to the mines and farms to look for work and take any wage that is offered him."

But some will say that the Bhunga is doing something for the Natives. Do you think that if the Bhunga meant to do anything for the Natives there would be Native demonstrators going without jobs when the territories need them so badly? Do you think that the abundance of water in the Transkei would be allowed to go waste instead of having it conserved for irrigation purposes? No, the Bhunga is not meant to help us, it is only an institution of parasitic bureaucrats for which we pay dearly, as you know, and which is used to suck us dry "in the name of the Native people of the Transkei".

There can be no solution of this problem, no answer to your questions so long as we live under a system based on the exploitation of man by man. Only under Socialism, in a system that will be concerned with serving the needs of the people and not with making profits, can we hope for a solution of the land problem: a society in which there will be a scientific distribution and use of land, a society whose motto will be, "From each according to his ability; to each according to his needs".

yours for Socialism,

Document 74
Letter from the Workers' Party of South Africa, Johannesburg, to Cape Town comrades,
2 November 1938

W.P.S.A.– Johannesburg.

P.O. Box 2639,
Johannesburg.
2/11/38.

Dear Comrades,

As promised I am furnishing herewith brief details of our activity. Our membership has increased to 11, 9 European and 2 Bantu. We have had two further applications for membership which have to be considered.

Our primary work at this stage is in the trade union field and our collective activity is directed to the formation of trade unions among the Bantu workers. Our experience with the African Metal Trades Union reveals that this will not be done in the style of Gordon, who being himself a bureaucrat, has been unable to avoid a bureaucracy growing up in the Laundry Workers Union. It does not appear to us that Gordon exercises any control over this bureaucracy any longer.

We have up to now been unable to rally the former members of the A.M.T.U. When this Union was first formed the workers earned 18/– a week. We demanded 22/6d. Now they are getting £1.4.–. This is no doubt partly accountable. Through the agency of one of our comrades a European building worker belonging to the B.W.I.U, we have made contact with a number of african building workers and have turned our attention in this direction. We are now holding regular meetings outlining our program and policy, and although progress is slow our comrade is putting his back into it and expects to bring in many workers with whom he comes in daily contact.

Three of our European comrades are members of the Furniture Workers Union, probably the most militant of the European Unions in Johannesburg. One of them exercises a certain amount of influence in this Union as is demonstrated by the fact that the workers recently elected him as a delegate to the Industrial Council. This comrade considers this to be a victory for our line as he points out that he has consistently fought for Unity of the European & African F.W.-U'S. Many years of experience in this Union have enabled our comrade to couple with sound theoretical knowledge, methods of approach and explanation easily comprehensible by the workers.

With fraternal greetings to you all,
M. Sapire.
Secretary.

P.S. To comrade Koston – Don't forget 3 October N.I's.

Document 75
A. Mon (M. N. Averbach), "The Historical basis for the Programme of the Fourth International Organisation of South Africa", *Workers' Voice*, 1, 1, July 1944

The programme of the Fourth International Organisation of South Africa is built chiefly upon the necessary struggle arising out of the imperialist exploitation and oppression of the toilers of South Africa. The peculiarities of South African development, structures and relationships arise out of the ways in which imperialism exploits the resources and peoples of this country.

"Combined Development" – Industrialisation

The proper imperialist exploitation of South Africa by modern imperialism dates from the discovery and exploiting of diamonds and, soon afterwards, of gold. Before this time the imperialism of the Dutch and British in South Africa was not of the kind defined by Lenin in "Imperialism", being associated more with commercial than industrial capital. From 1652 to 1805 the Dutch used the Cape as a military outpost and refuelling station and not as a market for exported commodities, a source of cheap labour, raw materials and a field for capital investment – characteristics of modern imperialist colonial exploitation. It was much the same with the British rule over the Cape Colony. The type of life was slow, patriarchal in parts; subsistence farming covered most agriculture. Slavery and not wage-labour was the dominant form of exploitation up to about 1835, and thereafter semi-serf forms of labour-service prevailed until wage-labour became the fundamental form. Small-scale industry and subsistence farming existed instead of capitalist production. It was only with the opening of the diamond and gold mines that the real modern imperialist exploitation of South Africa began in earnest. It was from this time that the class struggle of the workers against the capitalists began to take shape and grow. Before this time there had been minor slave revolts and artisans' strikes, especially in the Western Cape; there were wars of exterminations and expropriation against the Bantu, and warfare between the Boers and the British. But there was no chance for the class struggle between the major contending social forces of a capitalist society to develop and flourish until the conditions for this were established by the opening up of the diamond and gold mines by imperialism.

British imperialism set about the exploitation of these mines. Capital was exported to this country; machinery was brought in, factories erected, railways and harbours developed; commerce stimulated, financial houses reared. British commodities poured into South Africa. South African diamonds, gold and some agricultural products went to Britain. Cheap labour in South Africa was utilised, and an elaborate system of reserves, compounds and colour bars constructed to maintain and extend the cheap labour supply. In coming to this country, imperialism set out from British soil, from the classical country of industrial capitalist development during the nineteenth century. Industrialisation developed the modern form of imperialism in the mother country. On the other hand, imperialism brought industrialisation to South Africa. Industrialisation flowed from the imperialist conquest of the country. At the same time imperialism strengthened itself through industrialisation, so that to-day, with the strongest economic structure in Africa, South African capitalism turns its face towards the exploitation of many regions in Africa itself.

Precisely because imperialism introduced industrialisation into the crawling backwardness of South Africa, because imperialism had the task of producing the COMBINED DEVELOPMENT of South Africa with more developed countries, imperialism produced tremendous UNEVENNESS OF DEVELOPMENT. In tending to level up the economy as a whole with overseas countries, imperialism intensified, extended and enormously developed unevenness within the economy and social structure of the country. It adapted backwardness to its purposes, hurled some sectors of the country (e.g., the cities) forward, while throwing back others (e.g., villages and farms). COMBINED AND UNEVEN DEVELOPMENT WENT HAND IN HAND.

"Uneven Development": – Imperialism's South African Creations

Imperialism, in conquering South Africa, destroyed many pre-capitalist forms of existence, especially the tribal life of the Bantu peoples. Imperialism adapted some of the old forms of life to its own requirements. Imperialism, finally, built up on the ruins it destroyed and the basis of adapted forms, new forms of exploitation and oppression. Imperialism built up in South Africa the system of RESERVES, the COMPOUND system, the COLOUR BAR; and step by step deprived the non-Europeans of what little rights they had before the advent of modern imperialism into South Africa. Imperialism CREATED, really, the unique system of race- oppression which holds the majority of the toilers by the throat; and has built up the colour bar, segregation and race-discrimination system as an essential component in the whole mechanism of exploitation in South Africa.

The wars against the Bantu tribalists steadily drove the Bantu peoples off their long-held land, herding the African people into areas which were ruthlessly diminished until today the Africans, 70 per cent. of the population, occupy (without owning) a mere 10 per cent. of the land area. By means of these anti-Bantu wars, by means of expropriation, non-Europeans suffered ever-growing political oppression. The "socialist" movement did not bring to the toilers of South Africa what it had brought to the toilers of Europe and England. This is because the "socialist" movement here was a "middle-class" movement, and not a proletarian movement. The "class" struggle of the white workers was not a real class struggle, but only a struggle of a tiny section for exclusive rights. The "class" struggle was not a real labour struggle, because the non-Europeans did not yet take part in it, and were often fought against by white labour.

It was not only the Labour Party which based itself in its "socialism" upon the "middle-class" white labour aristocracy. The socialist movement in South Africa, leading up to the formation of the Communist Party, though in words it followed the October Bolshevik revolution, in its composition was mainly a white organisation, and in its policy was more concerned with the white unions and political struggles. Communist Party leaders like Bill Andrews based themselves heavily upon the interests of the white labour aristocracy; their talk about equality with the black workers often served the ends not of the black workers, but of the skilled whites (e.g., when Andrews raised the slogan, "Equal pay for equal work", it really served the skilled white workers, for a white employer would obviously take a white worker at the same pay to do a certain job than to take a non-European worker to do the same work at the high wage of the skilled white worker. This slogan, as used by Andrews, meant protecting the skilled white workers against the performance of skilled work by lowly-paid Bantu workers. He and others in the Communist Party, even in those days, did not raise the slogan of equal pay as a slogan of the black workers). Even negrophiles in the Communist Party like S. P. Bunting, to take the best example, approached the Bantu and the non-European generally with the attitude of the missionary (in spite of their vigorous opposition to liberalism they adopted a zealous patronising approach to the black workers, going towards them from the whites, trying to bring them to the whites, and not basing themselves upon the Bantu workers as the firmament of the movement, as the centre of gravity of the struggle, towards which the white workers have to travel if labour unity is to be achieved). In one way or another, in degrees ranging from Andrews to Bunting, the Communist Party itself never really based itself upon the non-Europeans, but from the standpoint of the "enlightened" white "socialists". At no time have non-European party members played a prominent, influential role inside the Communist Party, nor has this party concerned itself with the development of a socialist movement resting on the class struggles *springing* fundamentally from the non-European workers and *drawing in* the white workers. The orientation was ever tinged with a patronising negrophilism and militant liberalism.

The Hereditary, Urbanised, Non-European Proletariat and Intelligentsia
It was no accident that the "socialism" of both the Labour and the Communist Parties should have been either in opposition to or apathetic towards (Andrews) or negrophilistic (Bunting) towards the non-European. For the non-European movement itself was very tardy in developing. The artificial stifling of the proletarianisation of the Bantu played a heavy part in this slow growth. The movements that there were among the Bantu (I.C.U., etc.), Indian (Gandhi march, etc.) and Coloured people (post-war strikes, A.P.O. petitions) were either slight or else directionless though spontaneous (e.g., large strikes on Reef after the last war), or else nipped in the bud due to feebly equipped leadership and the semi-peasant nature of the city Bantus joined in many of these struggles.

But during the last 25 years since the end of the last war, there has been a considerable urbanisation of the Coloured and Indian toilers, and the development of a large, stable, settled, politically energetic city proletariat, especially in the Western Cape. At the same time, there has been a growth of a settled Bantu city proletariat, although not in large numbers, and although the degree of illiteracy and political backwardness is still heavy, especially in the case of the Bantu city proletariat, in comparison with the Coloured city worker. During the last quarter-century, in spite of the dullness and sluggishness and illiteracy and backwardness chiefly among the African workers, there has been a large urbanisation of non- Europeans, a large industrialisation and proletarianisation of these urbanised masses, and the development of a small but growing advanced stratum among the non-European workers, militant, class-conscious and embracing the doctrines of socialism more and more.

Parallel with this development has gone a relatively tremendous growth of a non-European militant intelligentsia, especially in the Western Cape. From the non-European teachers and students come sturdy revolutionary elements who come into a genuine socialist movement, forging a programme for this movement, going to the advanced element among the non-European workers to build a revolutionary, socialist programme and party. The development, especially since the end of the last war, of a politically advanced group of industrial non-European workers, and of a radical group of teacher and student intellectuals, formed the material ground for the growth of a socialist movement expressing, *through its composition and its roots*, the interests and needs of the largest, heaviest, most important bulk of the workers – the non-European workers; and basing its socialism, in applying it to South African conditions, upon the most urgent needs of the vast majority of the workers; orientating itself from this bed-rock foundation, attempting to realise labour-unity not through missionary approaches to or work amongst the Africans by well-meaning whites, but through the building up of a powerful movement of unskilled chiefly *non-European* workers, a movement which would draw *behind it* and *with it* not only the seven millions on the farms and in the tribal reserves, but also the poor white workers and even the skilled whites, under the most fiery conditions of revolutionary upsurge and convulsions. This party, which alone has really fashioned a programme genuinely based on the principle of the class struggle in South Africa, building its transitional programme upon the nature of this class struggle – *especially its anti-imperialist character* – this party is the Fourth International in South Africa. This organisation, struggling to assert itself as the real expression of the aspirations of the masses of toilers in South Africa, has arisen in a milieu inside South Africa in which it can fruitfully raise high its banner of revolutionary struggle, a struggle which will draw behind the urban proletarians the seven millions from the farms and reserve villages; a struggle of the oppressed toilers, with the city workers at the head. A struggle and a programme at complete variance with the "white socialism" of the Labour Party and the approaches of the Communist Party throughout its various somersaults in this country.

Our Transitional Programme: The Anti-Imperialist Struggle
The peculiar conditions created by imperialism in industrialising South Africa has created the need for a programme clearly expressing the struggle against imperialism. The anti-imperialist fight is the major, central, and internationally most significant, fight in South Africa. The struggle for democratic rights, the national-liberatory struggle, the struggle for land and for "bread", cannot be separate struggles, cut off from one another by one screen or another. The struggle for democracy, to use the broad term, includes the anti-imperialist fight (for national liberation, independence, self-determination, a republic). The fight against imperialism, wrote Trotsky in 1938, is a part of the fight for democracy in backward and colonial countries. The fight for land, for "bread", and for political rights, forms part of a general fight, a fight soluble only through social revolution. These struggles integrate into the common onslaught against imperialism and landlordism.

The fault of many organisations in the past has been that they dealt only with one aspect, one sector of the general integral struggle against capitalist-imperialist rule and exploitation, instead of unifying these struggles on the basis of a common class struggle, with the spearhead of this struggle directed against imperialism. The economic struggle, the agrarian struggle, the struggle for political rights, the struggle for national liberation from imperialism, are interlocked. To emphasise one of these at the expense of the others is to give the movement a lop-sided, narrowed-down character, to emasculate it, to enable it to draw behind it only certain limited strata of the population. The I.C.U. and non-European trade union bureaucrats who keep "politics" out of their unions (i.e., proletarian politics) laid the emphasis on the wage-struggle, to the relative exclusion of the political, agrarian and national-liberatory struggles. The I.C.U., although it performed a historic mission in rallying many thousands of Africans to a keen struggle for economic rights and, to a lesser extent, political rights, did not seriously take up the land question, and neglected the fight against imperialism for national liberation. This, in addition to misleadership, brought about its downfall.

The Emphasisers of the Agrarian Struggle

The agrarian struggle – the fight for the expropriation and the division of the land taken away from the expropriated land-companies and rich farmers – is intimately an *anti-imperialist* fight.

The Reserve-land forms the recruiting field for capitalist- imperialist exploiters, and the fight for the mechanisation of the backward reserve areas hits at the pit of the imperialist reservoir of labour.

The land owned by big land-companies is tied up financially with imperialist banking houses, and the fight for the division of this land is directed against imperialism.

The farming lands themselves are owned, in many instances, by large Chamber of Mines houses – cattle farms, citrus farms, maize farms – and the struggle for the expropriation of the land-owners comes up against the strongest bastion of imperialism in the Union – the Chamber of Mines. Since large numbers of those toiling on the farms are not semi-serfs, half-bound peasants, but wage-labourers (1,000,000 strong), the agrarian struggle is linked up with the proletarian struggle against wage-labour exploitation. The peasant-tribal movement is tied to the proletarian movement through the farm-proletarians (and the peasants temporarily in the cities). The farm-workers' struggle requires the building of agricultural labourers' trade unions, a process already starting in the Western Cape on a small but important scale. The agrarian struggle is bound up with the *trade union struggle*.

The land-shortage and land-hunger assumes, to a large extent, black-white relationships, for those chronically in want of land are mostly the Bantu, the oppressed black ruralists. The unequal division of the land is, with the exception of the poor whites, a racial division. There are laws prohibiting the purchase or occupation of land by non-Europeans, laws which come on top of the host of anti-non-European legislation withholding the land from the vast masses of the oppressed, through labour-reservoirs, poll taxes, rural money-lenders who blood-suck the Bantu reserve- dwellers, reserve traders who place millions of Bantu toilers into debt and in permanent debt-bondage and all the other measures designed to keep the non-European landless and divorced from means of production. The agrarian struggle, therefore, cannot be separated from the struggle against *race- discrimination*, which binds together the host of other ways of rural exploitation, directing these mostly against the African, Coloured and Indian ruralist – peasant and farm-proletarian alike (e.g., the tot-system, which mediævally oppresses over 100,000 Coloured farm-workers in the Cape Province).

The agrarian struggle cannot in any way be regarded as distinct from, separated from and more important than any of the other components of the anti-imperialist struggle. The struggle against capitalist-imperialism in South Africa requires not the emphasis of the agrarian struggle, nor the elevation of this struggle to the heights of being the "alpha and omega" of the whole struggle (i.e., the whole struggle itself). The struggle against capitalist-imperialism requires the co-ordination of the struggle on the economic plane, the struggle for agrarian reform and development (summarised in the slogan: "Land"), the struggle for full democratic rights, and the struggle for the complete national liberation of the colonial masses from the obnoxious yoke of British rule and imperialist subjugation (summarised in the slogans: "National independence and self-determination" and "For a Republic of Workers and Peasants").

The Emphasisers of the Political Struggle
Organisations like the A.P.O., the African National Congress and the Indian Congress of South Africa, claiming to represent the Coloured, African and Indian communities respectively, failed not merely because they adopted cringing, reformist, begging methods of conciliation towards the ruliing classes.[41] They failed also because of a lopsided emphasis on the winning of political rights only (the vote) and of certain rights of benefit mainly to the petty bourgeois non-Europeans (trading rights, land-holding rights, right of investment). Although other "points" appeared on the programmes (on the social colour bar, land, the right of workers to organise, etc.), these were sidelines, and are not seriously carried forward except, in some cases, as eye-dust to blind workers into following the Abdurahmans, Xumas, Jabavus, etc.[42] Such organisations almost totally neglected the struggle for "bread", land, and against imperialism. The All-African Convention, formally the most ideal type of organisation to build a strong national-liberatory movement (provided individual membership is free to develop as the mainstay of the organisation, instead of a federation of officials, bureaucrats, doctors and principals), has soft-pedalled the anti-imperialist struggle, and placed no political objective, *no type of government*, as a goal for the movement. The leadership of such organisations soft-pedalled issues of trade unionism, issues of expropriation and division of land held by the rich, and the fight for independence from imperialism. If organisations like the A.P.O., the Indian organisations, the African Democratic Party[43], the All African Convention are to flourish and rally the people around a militant programme, then they have to develop an all- round and not a lopsided (purely political or mainly political) programme, and have to form some kind of federation (without in the least impeding the formation of the *main basis* through *individual membership*) to work out and act upon such a programme.

While organisations like the Non-European United Front and the National Liberation League in words spoke against imperialism and stood for full democratic rights, these organisations never came forward with a bold, clear programme dealing with the economic (trade union) and the land struggles. Nor did they stress that the struggle was an anti-imperialist struggle. This programmatic shortcoming in the N.E.U.F. and N.L.L. which, together with the false policy pursued by the Stalinists and the failure to draw in the African masses (except to a small extent on the Rand), brought about the collapse and dismal failure of these formerly promising bodies.

An Integrated Programme
Hitherto no political party has come forward with a programme *based* upon the need to struggle against capitalist-*imperialist* exploitation and rule in South Africa, with the exception of the Fourth International. No other organisation has come forward with a programme resting on this anti-imperialist basis, which integrates the various sectors of the struggle – the trade union sector, the agrarian sector, the struggle for equality (away with race-discrimination and for full democratic rights), and the struggle for national independence and self-determination under a Republic of Workers and Peasants. This four-point programme, expressing the most burning desires, needs and strivings of the workers, peasants, tribalists and the poor and oppressed in general, is the transitional programme which will organise the masses of oppressed peoples behind

the city proletariat, and the city working class behind the revolutionary programme and party of the Fourth International in South Africa. The programme of "bread", land, democratic rights, national independence and self-determination will come more and more to the fore as the struggle of the workers develops, especially the struggle of the non-European toilers. On the other hand, this programme, borne aloft by a mass anti-imperialist organisation (analogous to the Indian Congress of India, with some important distinctions, will tremendously accelerate and deepen the process of unifying the various sections of the non-Europeans, the workers and peasants and the workers of all colours.

The task of the revolutionary party in South Africa is to guide and participate in the organisations fighting on any front against the capitalists – whether these capitalists be the Chamber of Mines, the industrialists or the rich farmers. In doing this, the revolutionaries have constantly to endeavour to foster the movement to unite all the workers.

The First Step
The first step in this unification is the bringing together of the non-European workers – African, Coloured and Indian. This is made possible by the double oppression of the non-European toilers: firstly as workers exploited, and secondly as peoples oppressed because of their colour. The common colour oppression which weighs down on the three sections of the 8 1/2 million non-Europeans forms the common factor making it possible to unify these sections as the broad mass basis for the anti-imperialist struggle for land, "bread", democratic rights and independence. All kinds of divide and rule politics dividing the non-European toilers have to be ruthlessly attacked – religious denominationalism, tribal divisions, sexual differentiations in pay, treatment and tribal customs. In common action, the unity of the commonly exploited and oppressed non-Europeans, the 80 per cent. of the nation, has to be forged. This is the first step, and the most weighty to be taken in the development of the unity of the working class in South Africa. The unification of the non-European toilers must inevitably have its centres in the cities and towns. From these centres of economic, social and political life, the unity movement will spread out to the country, the reserves, whither it will be brought by waging struggles of farm-workers against the farmers; of peasants against moneylenders, traders, recruiters, government institutions and agents, and farmers exploiting peasants as semi-serfs; of tribalists against chiefs, magistrates, recruiters, the poll tax, soil erosion, starvation, disease and all the miseries attendant upon the reserve system. In this way, by carrying the struggle into the countryside, and bearing the programme to the backward, illiterate rural masses in the shape of live struggles, the difficult process of unifying the peasantry behind the city proletariat must take place. *The unifying of the peasantry and proletariat has to go hand in hand with the unifying of the workers of different colours.* The realisation of the two processes are interdependent, although one may at a given moment shoot ahead of the other, depending upon the combination of complex circumstances which composes South African history.

The Second Step
But the unity of the non-European workers, in town and country, can bring the revolutionary movement against imperialism only to a certain point. The non-European proletariat, in the lead of the non-European petty bourgeoisie and tribalists, etc., cannot take power unless it draws to its side the mass of white unskilled and even skilled

workers, and the bulk of the white soldiers. *Black and white labour have to be united if the struggle for socialism is to succeed in this country.* Although the whites constitute a mere 20 per cent. of the total population, yet the whites constitute a full 50 per cent. of the city population. And it is in the cities that the decisive struggle will be waged. Secondly, the white workers, unskilled and skilled, constitute a fair proportion of the urban, mining, and industrial and transport working class, and occupy very important positions in the economy. This is even more true of the armed forces, which, if not neutralised or won over, will make a successful struggle the most difficult process, if not utterly impossible. The white workers, especially the majority, the unskilled workers, have to be won over to the non-Europeans and the great anti-imperialist struggle.

This cannot be done by wooing the whites. It cannot be done by appealing sentimentally to abstract principles of labour unity. It can and will take place as the result of certain developments in the economic structure of the country and because of the development of a powerful movement against imperialism and for full democratic rights, resting essentially upon the non-European toilers. The white workers will not come over automatically to the non-European workers if their wages are cut into, if they are thrown out of work, if they see their wages reduced by the mine- magnates and industrialists to cut into the costs of production. The mere economic process itself will undoubtedly reduce the standard of living, and the rates of pay of thousands of white workers in times of economic crises, slumps, unemployment, inflation, etc.

But this economic process of levelling the white workers down to the wretched plane of the non-European workers (and "poor whites") will not *by itself* bring into being labour unity. In fact, it can do the very opposite, as indeed it has in the past. It can throw the menaced white workers into the camp of the fascists, as it has done in the case of the Ossewabrandwag. In this case, as in other respects, the South African white workers behave as did the desperate, unstable, insecure labour-fearing, capitalist-aspiring middle classes of Italy and Germany when these middle classes, in town and country, built up the social base of the fascist party. Both skilled and unskilled workers have gone over to the fascist movement in this country in the past. They will do so again in times of economic crises, wage-cuts, inflation, etc., unless there is a force which can bring them over to the working class leading the anti-imperialist camp, instead of letting them drift or rush into the fascist camp.

The economic process of levelling up does not bring the white worker automatically over to the side of the non-European toilers, but merely brings the white workers to a crossroad, a forking of the ways. At this point the political, and not the economic factor, comes into full play. Either the fascist force draws the white workers into the maelstrom of destruction, or else the powerful anti-imperialist movement, the movement for full democratic rights waged by the mass of non-European toilers, will draw over the white workers into the struggle. If there is not such a strong movement, chiefly of non-Europeans (though naturally not exclusively so), then the white workers will unquestionably fall prey to their own deep colour prejudices and anti-working class feelings, as has formerly happened, and form the social bulwark of the fascist movement in this country. The white workers cannot possibly play a neutral role in the revolutionary struggles. They will, by the logic of things, fight either by the side of the reaction, or else come over to the non-European camp fighting for liberation and socialism. It is because of this, because the white workers will be a dangerous foe, a bastion supporting imperialism itself, fascism in South Africa, if they are not won to the revolutionary movement, that it is so vital and indispensible that the white workers join hands with the movement of the non-European workers. This unification of white and black labour will take place if the non-European movement is powerful, and if this movement wages a struggle which is in the interests of all the workers, white included.

The white workers must be drawn to a movement fighting to raise the standard of life of the non-European workers, for the higher this standard the less the drop which the white workers can plunge down. The struggle for "bread" is the struggle of all the workers. It must draw in the white workers. The fight against the colour bar, which is tied up with the phenomenon of poor whitism, will be accepted by the growing strata of the white workers themselves as in their interests. Against this, colour prejudice and race-hatred will fight dourly, but the levelling process and the fact that there will be no way out other than the revolutionary fight against imperialism, plus the ardour of the workers' party, will combat the traditions and conservatism of centuries. The struggle for land is a fight in the interests, in the long run, of the impoverished white peasants, although many of the bywoner type will fight stubbornly against the revolutionary movement for a long while. Finally, the anti-imperialist struggle itself, the fight for a Workers' and Peasants' Republic, in spite of fierce colour prejudice, dragging conservatism, will eventually tend to draw in many workers, especially Afrikaner workers who already profess to be anti-imperialist. The programme of the national liberatory movement will, with difficulties, draw the white workers in their majority, and also the bulk of white soldiers, into the army of the proletariat and peasants fighting for power.

"The Road to Democracy Passes Through the Socialist Revolution"
The movement of unifying the workers of all colours and the workers of town and country is a difficult, arduous one. But the very difficulties will steel the participants. This struggle will, in many shapes, organise the masses for the socialist revolution. And the socialist revolution alone will solve the transitional democratic programme. The socialist revolution alone will solve the democratic tasks, although many democratic concessions may be wrung from the ruling class in the course of the struggle for power. This struggle will inevitably place the proletariat in power as the ruling class. The proletariat will rule as the leader of the oppressed nation, chiefly the peasantry. A Workers' and Peasants' Republic (independent of foreign imperialist rule) will be the government of the country. This government will set up about solving the problems fought for in the stormy period organising the revolution; it will set about the socialisation of important sectors of the economy, and introduce the socialist order into South Africa. The government will help to spread the revolution, will draw aid from other revolutions, will defend the country from invasion, and will play its historical role in the process of the world revolution. In this role the party of the Fourth International alone can and will lead, as also in the long struggle for power itself. And, in playing this great leading part, the Fourth International bases itself on an understanding of the imperialist exploitation of South Africa.

NOTES

1. The Communist League of America (Opposition) was one of the first formal Trotskyist organisations in the United States. Its organ, *The Militant* began publication on 15 November 1928. Its first National Conference took place in Chicago from 17 to 19 May 1929. The number of adherents was reported as about 100. The total number reported in 1931 was 156. Its leading figure was James P. Cannon.
2. Stalin's policy towards China in 1925 to 1927 was a key element in his growing dispute with Trotsky. In the mid-1920s Trotsky believed, contrary to Stalin, that the revolutionary prospects in China were not limited in the short term to a triumph for the national bourgeoisie. In the 1930s, he believed that the Japanese invasion of China would accelerate the coming of revolution. Nevertheless, his supporters in China remained very few in number. The Trotskyist position is thought by some critics to have placed too much emphasis on the role of the Chinese working class in the making of the revolution and too little on the role of the peasantry.
3. Most of the signatories are unknown. Alpheus Maliba was a migrant worker-activist who joined the CPSA in 1936 and from 1939 to 1950 served on the Party's Johannesburg District Committee. In 1939 he founded the Zoutpansberg Cultural Association (later the Zoutpansberg *Balemi* (Ploughmen's) Association) in the Northern Transvaal, and he wrote several political pamphlets based on his experiences organising against state intervention in the rural areas (Bunting 1981:138-47). Rapalana J. Tjekele may have been Jacob Tjelele, elected to the CPSA's Central Executive in 1927; B. Dau Madiseng was a supporter of Bunting (see Document 43).
4. Vanguard Booksellers was owned by Fanny Klenerman who took over Frank Glass' bookstore when he left South Africa and reopened it under the name of Vanguard on 17 April 1931. It became a radical intellectual centre and was for many years the only supplier of left-wing literature in South Africa, stocking *The New Masses*, Left Book Club publications and the Modern Library series. Its employees included, among others, anti-apartheid activist Helen Joseph and Bloke Modisane, author of *Blame Me on History*.
5. Another translation is in Trotsky (1973:111-12).
6. In fact, Thibedi's letter of 26 April lists 22 names.
7. The Kuomintang was the political organisation associated firstly with Sun Yat Sen and then with Chiang Kai-shek. Between 1925 and April 1927 Soviet policy sought to strengthen the alliance between the Kuomintang and the Chinese Communist Party. The underlying postulate in terms of Marxist theory was that the Kuomintang would make a bourgeois nationalist revolution and that they should be supported in this venture by Communists. Pragmatic concerns of Soviet foreign policy were also a factor. The alliance went so far as to involve the admission of the Kuomintang as an honorary member of the Comintern in 1926. The policy failed disastrously in April 1927 when the leadership of the Kuomintang launched a counter-revolutionary attack on the Left in Shanghai. This followed a successful workers' rising in the city which had removed a traditional administration. Chiang Kai-shek's response was to order a massacre in which tens of thousands of Communists and their supporters were killed. Within the context of Soviet politics Trotsky had been critical of the strategy of Communist accommodation with the Kuomintang.
8. The expression "workers' aristocracy" is a variant on the concept of labour aristocracy frequently employed by historians and activists. Although often associated with a Marxist position, its employment has been much wider. It has often been used to indicate a stratum of relatively privileged workers whose strength may be dependent on an effective claim of skill which gives them a scarcity in the labour market. Or, it may indicate a privileged stratum based on ethnicity which can itself be linked to claims of skill. Alternatively, the concept has been employed by writers such as Lenin to emphasise the role of bureaucracy within labour movements where the privilege is based upon organisation of resources and access to existing power-holders. Frequently, the concept has been employed to explain stability and reformism and has often therefore been associated with those of a radical persuasion. For a classic historian's presentation of the concept see Hobsbawm (1968:272-315 and 1984:214-72).
9. Comrade Vitte is actually Comrade Witte.
10. Ralph Lee and Murray Gow Purdy were the main personalities in the BLL. Lee was apparently part of the Lithuanian Jewish community around Johannesburg. He reputedly joined the CPSA around the time of the 1922 Rand Revolt and was expelled sometime later for unknown reasons. He helped form the Johannesburg WPSA but after an unsuccessful strike at SCAW Works left for England in 1937. He returned in 1940 and in 1944 established the WIL from remnants of the SWL. In the late 1940s he emigrated to Britain and became involved in Trotskyist politics there. Purdy was briefly Secretary of the African Laundry Workers' Union before leaving South Africa in the late 1930s. He finally settled in India where he formed a succession of tiny Trotskyist groups (Hunter 1993; Ervin 1988/89).
11. This refers to Max Basch and J. Saperstein, who were expelled from the CPSA for criticising the factional politics behind Lazar Bach's purges. Basch went to Europe in late 1934; Saperstein went to Spain during its Civil War.

12 The majority's draft thesis on the native question was written by Yudel Burlak, a Polish exile who came to South Africa in 1930. He played a major role in formulating the WPSA's draft theses and continued to exert a powerful but behind-the-scenes intellectual pull over younger WPSA members through the 1950s. This document is reprinted, along with the draft thesis on the trade union question, the majority tendency's thesis, concerning the constitution of the party, the minority and majority theses on the war question, and other WPSA correspondence and ephemera in *Revolutionary History* (1993) 4, 4, Spring. Copies of all the draft theses are at the Mayibuye Archives, University of the Western Cape and at the Borthwick Institute, University of York.

13 The colour bar is a policy of job reservation in which whites were given the most skilled, highest-paid jobs while unskilled and low-paid jobs went to blacks. The Colour Bar Act refers to the Mines and Works Amendment Act (1926) which protected white workers from competition by issuing skilled labour certificates to whites and coloureds only. However, most of the laws underpinning the colour bar were in place before this, including the Mines and Works Act (1911); the Status Quo Agreement between the Chamber of Mines and white mining unions (1916); and the Apprenticeship Act (1922). The 1904 Master and Servants Ordinance defined black labour tenants on farms as servants rather than contractual wage labourers, thus reducing their legal protection against landlords. The Masters and Servants Act similarly made most strikes by Africans illegal and subjected the participants to imprisonment.

14 Daniel Francois Malan, politician and theologian, became an M.P. for the NP in 1918, joined the Pact Government in 1924, and with the formation of the Fusion Government in 1934, formed the Purified National Party, which became the opposition. Following the 1948 electoral victory of a reunited NP, Malan became Prime Minister. Frederick Stallard was the principal figure behind the 1922 "Stallard Report" by a Transvaal Local Government Commission which argued for strict restrictions and controls on African movements into towns. This report influenced Prime Minister Smuts to push through the Native (Urban Areas) Act of 1923, which extended segregation to towns.

15 The Swaraj Party was formed in January 1923 as a more collaborationist faction within the Congress Movement in India. It considered that participation in legislative councils could produce benefits. Its members were prepared to take the oath of allegiance. The Party had some impact in the mid-1920s but lost ground in the elections of 1926. From 1929 its remaining adherents boycotted in accordance with Congress policy. The Wafd was the dominant Egyptian nationalist movement formed at the end of World War One and opposed both to the British and to the traditional indigenous elite.

16 This minority draft thesis was probably written by Moshe Noah Averbach who frequently used the pseudonym A. Mon. Averbach emigrated from Europe to Palestine and then to South Africa, where he owned a grocery shop in District Six, Cape Town. He joined the CPSA and the Gezerd (*Gezelshaft far Erd*), a predominantly Jewish, Yiddish-speaking CPSA organisation meaning "Go Back to the Land", which supported the settlement of Russian Jews in Birobidjan, in eastern Soviet Union. He and the core of the Lenin Club were expelled from the Gezerd, following the 1932 visit of Comintern representative Gina Medem. He returned to Palestine after World War Two.

17 The SATLC was the result of a conference held in Cape Town in October 1930. This decided to establish an organisation open to all genuine trade unions and concerned with the interests of all organised workers. The SATLC was effectively the successor of the SATUC.

18 Trotsky's 1935 letter was written in response to the draft theses of the Lenin Club's majority tendency, which became the WPSA. It was published in *Workers' Voice: Theoretical Supplement*, November 1944 and reprinted in Trotsky (1974:248-55). On the FIOSA's assessment see A. Mon (1945), where the WPSA is incorrectly called the minority tendency.

19 In 1905 Lenin believed that the tasks of the bourgeois revolution in Russia would be fulfilled by "the democratic dictatorship of the proletariat and peasantry". In 1917 he revised this view, believing that the bourgeois revolution could be transcended in Russian conditions, provided that socialist revolutionary movements would come to power in advanced capitalist societies.

20 The PPS was the Polish Socialist Party. Pilsudski was the military leader responsible for the counter-attack which defeated the Red Army at the gates of Warsaw in 1920. In May 1926 he staged a coup and established an autocratic system in Poland which he dominated until his death nine years later.

21 Ruth Fischer (1895-1961) or "Dubois" was a founder of the Austrian Communist Party and leader of the left wing of the German Communist Party, along with Arkady Maslow, in the 1920s. The original document is in French. A slightly different English translation, probably by Clare Goodlatte and circulated amongst South African Trotskyists in the 1930s, is reprinted in *Revolutionary History*, 4, 4, Spring 1993, 114-19. Dubois' comments evidently rankled some South African Trotskyists. See Document 59 and Hunter (1993:68).

22 Documents 54 and 55 are translated from the German.

23 Following the division in the Lenin Club, the majority faction established itself as the WPSA and

published *The Spark* from March 1935 to June 1939. The minority became the CLSA and produced *Workers' Voice* in 1935/36. This grouplet collapsed during the war but the tendency was revived in the early 1940s as the FIOSA, whose organ was also called *Workers' Voice*.

24 Italy's invasion of Abyssinia in October 1935, following the failure of League of Nations and international diplomatic efforts, sparked massive protests in South Africa. From June through August 1935 dockworkers in Durban and Cape Town refused to load goods on Italian ships. Socialist groups reaped huge propaganda gains from their support for and coverage of the Abyssinian struggle. Sales of *Umsebenzi* shot up to 7 000 a week; *Umvikeli-Thebe/The African Defender* sold out at 10 000 an issue. But Italian troops entered Addis Ababa in mid-1936, and by the year's end resistance had fallen apart. Once news of the defeat reached South Africa, popular interest in the Abyssinian struggle waned.

25 The date of this document is significant. At this time, the Baldwin Government in Britain claimed to support League of Nations sanctions against Italy, and a month later it won a decisive victory in a general election. Once this had been obtained the Government's position shifted rapidly and Foreign Secretary Hoare entered into a deal with the French leader Pierre Laval (the Hoare-Laval Pact) which undermined the credibility of League opposition. The document was written a few days after the British Labour Party had debated Abyssinia at its annual conference. The result of the debate was a thorough victory for the advocates of League of Nations sanctions, an outcome symbolised by the contribution of the trade union leader, Ernest Bevin. This involved the defeat both of pacifists and of a left which characterised the League of Nations as an alliance of capitalist states.

26 The international campaign to support Abyssinia used two types of sanctions against Italy: workers' sanctions, where workers withdrew their own labour to hinder Italy's war efforts, and League of Nations-endorsed economic sanctions designed to prevent Italy from receiving specified war-related goods. League of Nations sanctions depended upon the support of member nations and were ultimately unsuccessful in curtailing Italy's war capacity because some major powers, notably the U.S., refused to endorse them. According to C. L. R. James (1937:387-9), then a Trotskyist, the Comintern came out for League of Nations sanctions, and it sidelined the issue of worker sanctions at its Seventh Congress in August 1935, even before internal Abyssinian resistance had fallen. *Umsebenzi* supported dockworker protests in September 1936 despite the Comintern's shift, although the CPSA's League Against Fascism and War later joined the call for League of Nations sanctions against Italy (Bunting 1981:123-5).

27 The Greyshirts was an organisation founded in 1933 by Louis Weichardt to promote Nazi ideas in South Africa. It was strongly anti-Semitic. Its limited support did not reflect accurately the impact of such sentiments.

28 Charles and Herman van Gelderen, twin brothers, were active in Cape Town left politics and members of the Lenin Club in the 1930s. Charles left South Africa in the late 1930s and became involved in Trotskyist politics in Britain; Herman was in the CLSA and was a delegate at the 1939 NEUF conference in Cape Town.

29 Goolam H. Gool (1905-1962) was a British-trained physician who joined the Lenin Club and initially supported the CLSA faction but later moved to the WPSA. He formed the NEF in 1937 and was briefly President of the NLL. He was a founding member and on the Executive of the AAC and the Anti-CAD and Vice-Chair of the NEUM but became profoundly disillusioned with NEUM politics in the 1950s.

30 Ted Grant left for Europe in late 1934. He later became a leader of the Militant Tendency which worked inside the British Labour Party until its proscription in the mid-1980s. Prior to proscription, the Militant Tendency acquired significant influence in some local Labour Party organisations, most notably in Liverpool, where for a period it played a major role on the City Council.

31 Very little is known about the members of the Johannesburg WPSA. D. Gosani was a trade unionist and organiser for the JCATU. In the 1940s he was Secretary of the CNETU but resigned in 1945 over accusations of inactivity. It is noteworthy that most of the youthful white members left South Africa in the late 1930s. Ralph Lee, Millie Kahn, Richard Freislich and Heaton Lee left for Britain in 1937 and became involved in British Trotskyism. Millie Kahn was married to Ralph Lee; subsequently, she married Jock Haston, a British Trotskyist.

32 Andrew Dunbar (1879-1964), a blacksmith by trade and veteran socialist, who maintained that national oppression could be reduced to class exploitation. He led the 1909 Natal railway strike and the January 1911 Rand tramwaymen strike which resulted in the formation of an IWW branch. He was over the years a member of the IWW, the SALP, a founding member of the ISL who later formed the Industrial Socialist League, and the CPSA. Bunting described him as an "industrial Cincinnatus at his forge", and in 1928 he wrote under that pen-name in *Forward*. Communist advocate George Findlay, author of *Miscegenation*, defended black workers in a strike led by the ICU. Bernard Sachs, a writer, was the brother of trade unionist Solly Sachs. His autobiography, *Multitude of Dreams*, deals in part with his experiences on the South African Left.

33 The WPSA published the Afrikaans translation of *The Communist Manifesto* in 1937, commemorating the ninetieth anniversary of its writing, with a preface by Trotsky. A copy of the pamphlet is in the CPSA Collection, Hoover Institution Archives, Stanford University. There is no information as to how many pamphlets were actually produced or distributed. Trotsky's preface, "Ninety Years of the Communist Manifesto", is translated and published (except the last paragraph) in Deutscher (1964:285-95).
34 Clare R. Goodlatte (1866-1942) was a nun in the Anglican Community of the Resurrection in Grahamstown and principal of the teachers training college until her retirement at age 55. She moved to Cape Town, became increasingly radical, joined the ILP, the Lenin Club and then the WPSA, where she was Secretary and editor of *The Spark*. She resigned in 1939 due to ill health. Paul Koston ran Modern Books in Cape Town before emigrating to Britain. The minutes of the Cape Town WPSA for 18 May 1936 indicate nine members, including Isaac Bangani Tabata and Janub "Jane" Gool, who were organising in Langa. Tabata (1909-90) was born near Queenstown in the Cape and educated at Lovedale and Fort Hare. In 1931 he left university and moved to Cape Town, where he worked as a truck driver, joined the Lorry Drivers' Union and became a member of its executive. He also joined the Cape African Voters' Association. In 1933 he began attending meetings of the Lenin Club with Goolam Gool and joined the WPSA. In the early 1940s he was one of a group of radicals who took over the leadership of the AAC, arguing for a boycott of all racial structures proposed by the government. As an organiser for the AAC he made yearly trips to Transkei in the late 1940s and early '50s. He was banned in 1956. In 1961 he established and became president of APDUSA. Tabata was married to Jane Gool, sister of Goolam Gool, and an activist in the Anti-CAD, AAC and NEUM. They left South Africa in 1963 and lived in Zambia and then Zimbabwe. Tabata's writings include Th*e Rehabilitation Scheme: "A New Fraud"* (1946), *The All-African Convention: The awakening of a people, Boycott as a Weapon of Struggle* (1952), and *Education for Barbarism*.
35 Comrade Adolphe was the pseudonym of Rudolphe Klement (1910-1938), Trotsky's secretary, who was kidnapped and murdered in July 1938 by the GPU, in the midst of preparations for the foundation of the Fourth International.
36 The Johannesburg WPSA sold *The Spark* on the mines, and its ephemeral organ, *Umlilo Mollo*, contained a number of letters from mineworkers and metal workers. Fanny Klenerman noted in her memoirs that a few miners came to some of the WPSA's public meetings.
37 Comrade Maseko may have been Isaiah MacDonald Maseko, one-time CPSA member, chair of the Orlando ANC during the Defiance Campaign and elected to the ANC National Executive Committee in December 1952. He was expelled from the ANC for allegedly organising a left-wing faction known as *Bafebagiya*. He was placed under house arrest in 1962 and moved to Swaziland. He served as President of the Swaziland National Union of South Africa and Deputy-President of the Swaziland Progressive Party.
38 On the AMTU see Hunter (1993:75-7). Lee's role in the AMTU strike was reported in the *South African Worker*, 18 March 1937.
39 Roux (1964:312) notes that the plays produced by the Spartacus Club "... merited a wider public, [*but*] never achieved publicity, being performed only before small and rather select audiences in Cape Town".
40 The *Bhunga* refers to the United Transkeian Territories General Council, an African mock parliament controlled by white officials.
41 Founded in 1902, the African Political Organisation – later renamed African People's Organisation – sought to extend the legal and political rights held by coloureds in the Cape Colony to those in the northern colonies. Led by the medical doctor, Dr Abdullah Abdurahman (1872-1940), who was president from 1905 until his death, the APO was a significant political force until the mid-1920s, when it became more of a mutual benefit, burial and building society, and an object of scorn to the generation of coloured radicals entering politics in the 1930s. The ANC, formed in 1912 as the SANNC and, in its first decades, representing the interests of African educated elites and chiefs, sought to influence the South African government through deputations and petitions. By the early 1930s, it was largely defunct, but a concerted and ultimately successful effort to revive it and broaden its social base began in the late 1930s. The SAIC was formed in 1920 to fight anti-Indian legislation and remained dominated by an Indian merchant class until 1945/46 when Communists and radicals captured the leadership of the NIC and TIC.
42 John Tengo Jabavu (1859-1921) was a teacher and editor of the influential Xhosa Eastern Cape weekly, *Imvo Zabantsundu (Black Opinion)*, which expressed the aspirations of the emergent black *petite bourgeoisie*. Alfred Bitini Xuma (c. 1893-1962) was a medical doctor and the first black person to get a Ph.D. from the London School of Tropical Medicine and Hygiene. In 1935 he became Vice-President of the AAC, and in 1939, President General of the ANC, which he reorganised and rebuilt in the 1940s. In 1949 he was unseated by the more radical ANC Youth League.
43 Believing in the need for a dynamic counterpart to the ANC, the ADP was launched on 26 September

1943 by, among others, Paul Mosaka, Self Mampuru and Dan Koza. Former Communist Hyman Basner addressed its inaugural meeting, criticising the ANC-CPSA alliance. The ADP had a social democratic programme and aimed to unite people across colour lines. It had some influence in Alexandra and Orlando and lasted about five years. For its Manifesto see Karis and Carter (1973:391-5).

The International Socialist League, a breakaway from the South African Labour Party founded in 1915, was a precursor to the Communist Party of South Africa.

Black workers in the African National Congress's 1919 anti-pass campaign in Johannesburg – surrounded by mounted police.

The Bolshevik Leninist League, formed in 1934, organised a number of trade unions around Johannesburg. Murray Gow Purdy, a Trotskyist who later went to India, is sitting front row center.

In 1928 the Communist Party of South Africa adopted the Native Republic slogan, later called Black Republic, under the influence of the Communist International.

The Communist Party of South Africa's Johannesburg District Committee, around 1946. The portraits are of Moses Kotane, General Secretary (left) and W. H. Andrews, National Chairperson (right). Seated at the podium (left to right) are Patsy Gilbert, Bram Fischer, Joe Slovo and Rusty Bernstein. Below are Gana Makabeni (second from left), David Gosani, Mr and Mrs Peter Raboroko and Arthur Damane.

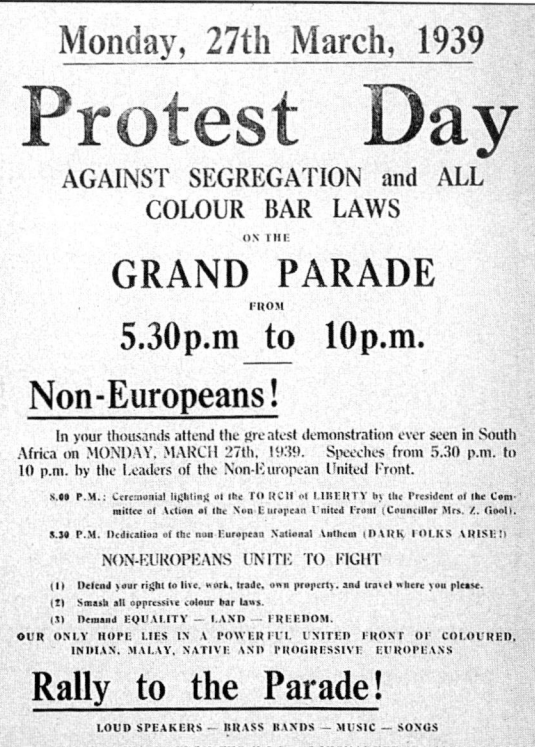

In the late 1930s the Non-European United Front organised mass protests against discrimination.

In 1945, Dr G. H. Gool (left) was a leading figure in the Anti-Coloured Affairs Department and the Non-European Unity Movement. Mrs Z. Gool (centre) was a prominent member of the Cape Town City Council. Reverend Z. R. Mahabane (right) was Vice-President of the All African Convention.

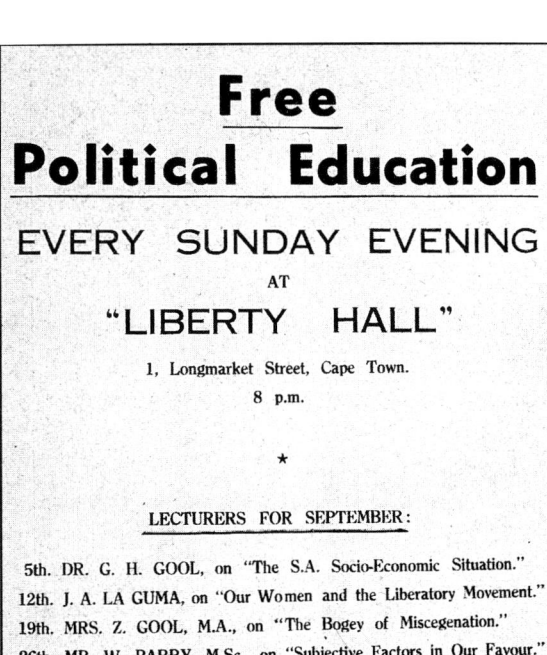

In 1937 the National Liberation League of South Africa advertised weekly lectures in its monthly journal *The Liberator*.

Part Five

Building political alliances: Workers' unity and black united fronts

EDITOR'S NOTE

From the mid-1930s the shape of South African socialist politics was affected radically by both international and local developments. The defeat and destruction of the Left in Germany followed by the takeover of the Right in Austria produced a gradual shift by the Comintern away from the New Line. In 1935 the Seventh Comintern Congress unveiled the People's Front policy. This argued that the crucial challenge was fascism and that Communists should form broad progressive alliances with Social Democrats and with progressive Liberals. The model examples were the Popular Front government elected in France in 1936 and the Republican administration formed shortly before the start of the Spanish Civil War. But for South Africa, the relevance of that strategy was ambiguous, since for most of the population there was no bourgeois democracy to defend. South Africa's specific conditions heavily impacted the politics of the Left as the Hertzog Government adopted a strategy to remove all remaining African voters from the common electoral roll. Here, then, was a classic example of South African Communists having to apply a strategy derived from an analysis of European conditions to a radically different environment. Trotskyists viewed the People's Front strategy with scepticism. They felt that working class interests, particularly those of black workers, would become submerged in cross-class politics that were unacceptable on socialist grounds and which had limited relevance in the South African context. One significant point of dissension between Communists and Trotskyists came over the legal reforms initiated by the Hertzog Administration. These curtailed the African franchise, restricting African voting rights to the election of a limited number of Europeans as Native Representatives. Initially socialists united in rejecting such a racist solution but Communists, pursuing the logic of the People's Front policy, resolved to use the available machinery to recruit support. In contrast, Trotskyists remained committed to a boycott strategy. Here, refracted through the divisions within the international socialist movement we see one of the classic dilemmas in the politics of national liberation.

Document 76
Communist Party of South Africa,
What is the Native Independent Republic? (1934)

The Communist Party of South Africa had already a few years ago put forward the slogan of a "Native Independent Republic" as the immediate aim for which the workers and peasants of South Africa should fight. This slogan, which quite correctly reflects the fundamental interests of the Native toiling population, is the banner around which the workers and peasants should unite for a joint struggle for a better life. But for this purpose it is necessary that the slogan should become clear to every toiler in South Africa, that every toiler should understand what the Communists are calling upon him to fight for, what the Independent Native Republic would give him. For it is known that whilst the Communist Party is the leader and organiser of all the workers and toilers, irrespective of colour, there are in the ranks of the masses certain organisations who pretend to champion their cause. These organisations, the African National Congress, the Industrial Commercial Union, not only do not put forward such a slogan but even fight against this slogan put forward by the Communist Party. The African National Congress and its leaders of the type of Seme, Dube[1] and others tell the toiling Natives of South Africa to be patient and submit to the highhanded treatment of the European capitalists, the farmers and the Colonial Government, to submissively bear all their privations and misfortunes, so that the European oppressors will condescend to notice their humility and will cease to oppress the Natives, will cease to get rich at their expense and "Universal peace will reign between the whites and Natives and happiness for all".

Is this really so? Will the imperialists (the Anglo-Boer landlords, manufacturers, mineowners and the Colonial Government) voluntarily give up the oppression of the Native population and the imperialist exploitation of the white workers and poor whites or not? That is the crux of the problem. And in order to understand it, it is necessary to attentively see how the imperialists are oppressing the Native workers and peasants, to find out what the Native toiling population is suffering from. Not everyone as yet knows *the reason* why he is suffering, starving and becoming more and more impoverished and *how* to rid himself of all this.

Let us begin with the peasants, as they compose the overwhelming majority of the Native population. It is generally known that the peasant cannot conduct his peasant household without land. But land is just what the Native peasants have not got. Ninety-two percent of the entire land that is most suitable for agriculture, has been seized by the Anglo-Boer imperialists. The European population which is only 25% of the entire population of the Union of South Africa, more than half of whom live in the towns and have no connections with agriculture whatever, own 92% of the land and the Native population composing 75% of the population, the majority of whom are engaged in agriculture, own only 8% of the land. But at one time the Native population were the complete masters of *all* the land. The Anglo-Boer aggressors have taken the land from the Native population by force, with arms in their hands, have organised big farms and branches on this land and now sell tens of tons of butter and wool from which they derive huge profits. (There are also poor farmers among them but we shall speak about them later) Then what is there left to do for the Native pesants who have been deprived of the land? Part of them went to the reserves and locations kindly left to them by the imperialists on the Crown and missionary lands, and the other part, the smaller part, were compelled to go upon the European farms.

Until 1913, they lived on the European farms or as squatters renting the land from farmers for money, for a share in their crops or as worker tenants, working on the fields of the farms for the land that they got or, finally, as plain workers. But the promulgation of the Native Land Act by the Colonial government in 1913, prohibited the Native peasants from renting land from the white farmers for money or for a share in their crops. These peasants either had to leave the farms (but where could they go) or remain upon the farm as labour tenants who, according to this law, had to work on the farms not less than 90 days a year and now, according to the Native Service Contract Act of 1933, the labour tenants have to work not less than 180 days a year on the farms. Thus a considerable part of the Native tenants were converted into ordinary serfs working half the year for the land owner. [....]

This already suffices to show how difficult it is for the labour tenants to live and how harshly they are oppressed by the white land owners. But the labour tenants cannot get away from the land owners as they have no land of their own and besides, are usually always in debt to the landowner and for that reason the latter does not let them go if he can use them. If the labour tenant is no longer necessary to the land owner, the latter simply drives him off the land.

The position of the Native peasants in the Native reserves is no better. The chief trouble from which the Native peasantry on the reserves suffer is the terrible lack of land as a result of which they cannot feed themselves (in Transvaal, e.g. there is from one to two acres of pastures for each head of cattle, while, according to the opinion of experts, a minimum of six acres is required), and the other part has no allotments whatever. [....]

But on these absolutely inadequate allotments of land, the peasants also have no rights whatever. In the reserves where there is communal use of the land, the land is at the disposal of the tribal chief and the use of the land is enmeshed with a thick network of old tribal customs and imperialist limitations. The fate of the peasant is in the hands of the tribal chief. In order to get land the peasant must pay the chief a special tax, work for him, seek his indulgence. All the peasant has to do is to loose the good graces of the chief and the latter proclaims that he is unreliable and with the aid of the colonial police he is driven out of the reserve, and his allotment of land is taken away from him. The peasant has no right to sell, mortgage or hand over his allotment for inheritance to his son, nor has he the right to rent it without the permission of the tribal chief and the European officials. Besides, the constant subdivision of the land does not give him any guarantee that tomorrow he will still be able to have use of the allotment upon which today he puts in his labour. [....]

The imperialists, however, are not content with having robbed the Native peasantry of the land.

For the oppression of the Native population, the Colonial Government maintains a lrage staff of officials, police and an army. And in order to maintain this apparatus for the oppression of the Native population, in order to pay the high salaries of the officials and also in order to force the Native peasants to go and work for miserable wages, the Colonial Government has imposed high taxes on the Native peasants and the Native workers and these taxes are constantly being increased notwithstanding the "respectful re‚uest" of the African National Congress to decrease the taxes. [....]

Deprived of land, pressed down by taxes, exploited by the merchants and money-lenders, the Native peasantry on the reserves have no means for the technical improvement of the farms. The technical methods on the peasant farms is still most primitive and simple. [....] The increase in the shortage of land, the stagnation of methods of technique, the reduction of pastures, the decline in the crops and the collection of wool, the impoverishment of the peasantry – these are the tendencies of development of the Native peasants holding in the reserves.

The lack of land, the seizure of the land by the Anglo-Boer land owners (in addition to high taxes etc.) – these are the main troubles from which the Native peasants suffer. Then, where is the way out? Is it possible to hope that the Anglo-Boer land owners and farmers will voluntarily return at least part of the land to the Natives? It is clear to everyone that this is not so. The white big farmers and land owners will never voluntarily give back a single acre of their land to the Natives, even if it were not needed by them and was not being used (and there is a great deal of such land). It must be understood that it is necessary for the imperialists to have a landless Native peasantry, not only to assure the white farmers of land but also in order to compel the landless peasantry to work on these farms, factories and mines, as a peasant who has enough land (and of course implements of labour) will not go to work for others. Perhaps the Hertzog-Smuts Colonial Government will make the farmers return at least part of the land to the Natives as the peasants in the African National Congress try to believe. [....] The Colonial Government does not want to return to the Natives even the land which is not yet divided among the European farmers and is at the direct disposal of the government, the so-called Crown lands. It prefers to collect rent from the Native peasants who live on these lands. No, the Colonial Government will not make the farmers return the land to the Native peasants.

Perhaps the Native peasantry can purchase their land from the white imperialists who stole it from them, as some "friends" of the Native peasantry advise? But, first of all, the purchase of land is severely restricted, almost prohibited, and secondly, even with the maximum amount of savings on his food, with the maximum reduction of his expenditures, the Native peasant who is extremely poor, could not collect enough money to buy back even a tenth of the land if he were permitted to do so.

It should be clear to all that the peasant will not get the land and will not be able to get out of his poverty as long as the Anglo-Boer imperialists rule in South Africa. Only by driving the imperialists (the land owners and miner owners) out of the country and making the Native people of South Africa independent will the peasants get back their land.

Let us now proceed to the Native workers. Besides farms the imperialists in South Africa have several thousand factories, mills and a big mining industry. Here, just as on the farms, they need Native labour. Everyone knows that the European mine owners in South Africa get bigger profits than in any other country in the world. Why is that so? Where do these profits come from? This is only because the imperialists do not pay the Natives what they ought to get for their labour, because the wages of the Native workers are much lower than those of the white workers in the capitalist countries of Europe, not to mention the wages of the privileged part of the European workers in the Union of South Africa. It is only the labour of the Natives and nothing else that is the source of the big profits received by the European capitalists in the Union of South Africa. The Anglo-Boer imperialists have done, and continue to do, everything to compel the Natives to work for them for a miserable pay.

Very often we hear and read in the papers complaints of the mine owners and the European farmers that there is a shortage of Native labour power. However, even the most superficial acquaintance with South Africa will show that they are complaining not of the shortage of labour power as such, but of the shortage of *Free, cheap labour* power. While depriving the Native peasantry of all means of subsistence converting the majority of them into paupers, imperialism does not permit them to become proletarians in the capacity of free workers who sell their labour power on the labour market. In order to compel The Native peasant to work for miserable wages on the neighbouring white farm, the imperialists have chained him to his place by means of the pass system, have deprived him of the opportunity of freely looking for work and in that way have made him work on the neighbouring farms for a few pence. Not having the possibility to feed his family and to pay the taxes, being enmeshed in debts to the European merchants and moneylenders, the Native peasant would willingly go to work for wages. Immediately he steps out of the boundaries of his reserve, he is arrested by the first policeman whom he meets. For, together with the innumerable quantity of his passes, he cannot show a receipt that he has paid his taxes. While wishing to go to work he is compelled to sit in the reserve until the agent of some recruiting company arrives and recruits him to work in the mines or on the European farms and plantations. Only by signing a contract, not as a free worker but as a serf, deprived of all opportunities of choosin his work, he, together with the others, can leave the reserve and go to work on any conditions proposed to him.

But even those peasants who have paid their taxes and who freely go to work in the town, having a tax receipt in their pockets, are deprived of the opportunity of freely selling their own labour power. The pass system does not permit a worker to remain without work in any place for more than six, or at best, twelve days, and the same pass system does not permit him to move about freely from one place to another. Arriving in the town the peasant is compelled to hire himself out to the first employer he comes to and at any condition or he has to return back to the reserve and wait until he is contracted. Otherwise he will unavoidably be arrested by the police, put into prison and from there will be sent to work for the farmer as a prisoner. In either case the peasant cannot freely sell his labour power. He is a serf to imperialism both as a peasant and as a worker.

The Natives, who are becoming proletarianised, the Native proletariat, not having an allotment of land and not running their own farm, (and there is already a considerable number of them in the towns in South Africa) are also not free workers. On the labour market, the Native worker first of all encounters the so-called colour barrier. In 1927 a special law was enacted – the Colour Bar Act – officially prohibiting the Natives to do skilled and semi-skilled work in the mining industry (this was also done before by the white employers, but it was not obligatory for them). The law applies only to the mining industry, but in the manufacturing industries the position of the Native workers is no better.

The policy of civilised labour which is now being carried out in the secondary industries means that the Native workers will be entirely excluded from doing even semi-skilled work. In 1922, a law was passed about apprenticeship according to which minors, who become apprentices, have to pay a definite training fee, but as the Native minors have no opportunity of getting this fee, and the majority of them are absolutely illiterate, this means that Native apprenticeship is virtually prohibited. The Natives have [been] deprived by legislative measures of the opportunity to acquire skill. They have been prohibited from doing skilled work and are thus forced to do heavy unskilled work and after that it is stated that the Natives are in general not capable of doing skilled work, that his lot is "Kaffir work".

This heavy "Kiffir work" is not paid as ordinary unskilled labour but like some sort of special work, as work done by some inferior being. A skilled European miner in South Africa gets ten times higher wages than an unskilled Native miner and often he gets considerably more even in cases where he does the same work as is done by the Natives. This disparity between the skilled work of the Europeans and the unskilled work of the Natives cannot by any means be justified by the different standard of living of the skilled and unskilled worker and there isn't a single country in the world where there is such a group disparity between the two.

In 1930 the Ballinger, the Industrial-Commercial Union, appealed to the Transvaal Chamber of Commerce and Industry with a proposal to call a wide conference of the Chamber with representatives of the Natives and a number of European organisations to establish a minimum wage for Native workers. The Chamber refused to consider the question of Native wages altogether and cynically stated: "No, there is no serious reason for raising the wages of the Natives. If this were done they would have an opportunity to earn the same money as they do now in a shorter period of time and as a result the influx of unskilled labour power would be cut down and this would be of no material advantage to anyone." In this way the imperialists acknowledge with cynical frankness that low wages are a powerful means in their hands for compelling the Natives to leave their villages and go and work for wages more often and for a longer period of time.

This the situation of the Native workers. Land-robbery of the Native peasantry which causes a big influx into the towns, the pass system, the colour bar, etc., the restrictions imposed upon the Native, the miserable wages, the absence of any defence of the Native workers by the colonial government – these are the main troubles which afflict the Natives as workers. Is is possible to hope that the imperialists will sometimes or other abandon this exploitation of the Native workers, remove all the restrictions from Native labour, and raise the wages for the Native workers? Of course not. They will never satisfy their greedy appetites for cheap Native labour and will not make the situation of the workers any easier. It is naive to think that any European capitalist will voluntarily agree to reduce his profits and raise the wages of his Native workers. Perhaps they can be compelled to pay higher wages to improve the conditions of labour, etc? If the workers form strong trade unions and in solid ranks will conduct a systematic struggle against the employers through the united front, they can, of course, force them to give some concessions to the workers. But these will be such concessions which cannot under any circumstances substantially change the situation of the Native workers, and secondly, these will be temporary concessions which the employers will take back again as soon as the workers slacken their pressure upon them. In the European capitalist countries the working class has strong and old trade unions, a great deal of experience in the struggle against the employers, and still the employers, with the assistance of their capitalist governments, systematically worsen the conditions of the workers, reduce their wages, etc. In addition to this, it should not be forgotten that there is a great deal of difference between the European capitalist countries and the colonies which the Union of South Africa is for the Native toilers.

No it cannot be expected that the imperialists will make any improvement in the situation of the workers. Only a harsh joint struggle, on the basis of the united front, can the workers achieve some temporary concessions and only if the imperialists will be driven out of the country will they attain a radical improvement of their position.

In order to still more strongly consolidate their rule in South Africa, to secure for themselves the possibility of exploiting the Native toiling population, depriving them of all possibility of defending themselves, the imperialists deprived the Native population of all political rights.

Composing the overwhelming majority of the population, being the original Native population in the country, paying heavy taxes to maintain the apparatus for their own suppression, they are entirely removed from political life, not to mention participation in the government of the country, and are brutally suppressed every time they make an attempt to defend their human rights. The imperialists have converted the Native toilers into their slaves. In the Transvaal and in the Orange Free State the entire Native population is deprived of the vote. In the Natal province there is a decisive law according to which a Native has the right to vote if he has been living in his province for 12 years, has been removed from the effect of the Native laws for seven years, has a certain amount of immovable property, can present the recommendation of three Europeans regarding his reliability. At the present time there is one (!) Native voter in Natal. In the Cape Province a Native has the right to vote if he owns real estate valued at £275 sterling or receives wages of not less than £50 a year and has a definite level of education (for the European there is no qualification whatever except age). In the Cape Province there are approximately 15,000 Native and Coloured voters. But what does that give them? They have no right to elect their representatives from amongst the Native and Coloured people to Parliament. [....] The Native population is only given the right to have very limited self-government. In the Transkeis there is the Bunga, the members of which are selected by the government and the tribal chiefs from among the Natives who have sold themselves to imperialism. But even in this especially selected Native self-governing body, a European magistrate presides and all its decisions are subject to confirmation by the European authorities. In the Native locations in the towns there are the Native Advisory Boards which are allegedly elected by the Natives, but in actual practice the majority of the members are appointed by the European superintendent, and he himself is the chairman. Many Natives are even deprived of the right to participate in the elections to these Boards. All these attenuated Natives self-governing bodies are simply auxiliary institutions for the better suppression of the Native population and they are given the appearance of self-government in order to deceive the Native population. [....]

The Native inhabitant of South Africa is oppressed and exploited not only as a peasant and as a worker, but also simply as a human being. The imperialists do not consider him to be a human being. In their eyes he is some sort of inferior being who only deserves to be oppressed and despised. He is not permitted to live together with the Europeans in the European towns, not permitted to travel with them in the trams, to use common restaurants, libraries or sit together in the theatre, etc. He has to live in the filthy slums of the Native locations. He has to carry on him about a dozen different passes, has to get permission for every step that he makes and he has to pay for it, (while the Europeans do not have to carry passes). He can be arrested in the street by any policeman who might take it into his head to do so. He has no right to be seen on the streets of the town after 10 o'clock in the evening. [....]

It should now be clear to every worker and every peasant that their interests and the interests of the imperialists are diametrically opposed. The British imperialists are becoming daily richer at the expense of the oppression, poverty and the immeasurable sufferings of the Native peoples and this is why they will never do anything to improve the situation of these Native peoples.

In order to do away with this shameful slavery of the Native peoples of South Africa, to liberate the working class and the peasantry from their abominable conditions of poverty, it is above all necessary to drive the Anglo-Boer slave drivers out of South Africa and set up the power of the working class and the peasantry, the Independent Native Republic. Only people of the type of Dr Seme, the president of the African National Congress, can advocate collaboration of the Native population with the imperialists and eulogise General Hertzog as a "statesman who is laying the foundations for the great cathedral of justice, peace and good will with regard to all the peoples of our country, regardless of race and colour of the skin." The African National Congress by calling upon the masses of the Natives to be submissive sow illusions among them regarding the possibility of improving their difficult situation under the rule of imperialism. However, during the past 100 years the situation of the toilers has not improved one single bit, but, on the contrary, it is getting worse day by day and will continue to get worse in the future. Only the driving out of the imperialists and the national liberation of the country will give the Native peoples freedom and an opportunity to immediately and radically change their position. But it is impossible to drive out the imperialists without waging mass armed struggle against them, without an anti-imperialist revolution. So, *the Native Independent Republic* for which the Communists call upon the toilers to struggle, *first and foremost means the anti-imperialist revolution, i.e., the driving out of the imperialists and the national liberation of the country.*

[....] we now have to understand *what improvements* the Independent Native Republic will bring to the workers and peasants *immediately* after sustaining a victory over imperialism. The enemies of the toiling people are striving to assure the Native peasants that immediately after the imperialists are driven out the Communists will take away all the property of the peasants. This is a lie and a deception! The Communists *will never take away the property of the Native and the poor white peasants*, on the contrary, an independent Native Republic means that the land which has been taken from them by the white landoners will be returned to them and all the conditions will be created for the development of peasant economy. The Communists, of course, do not conceal the fact that the *ultimate* aim of their struggle is to build a socialist society where there will be no private property of the means of production, where there will therefore be no exploitation of man by man, but the Communists will never permit any violence to be used against the small and middle peasants. the construction of the socialist society will begin only when the peasants, in the conditions of a Native independent republic, will themselves become convinced that a really prosperous and happy life is possible only in a socialist society, when, together with the workers in the towns, *under the leadership* of the Communist Party, they will themselves take the matter in hand. Then we will have the stage of the socialist revolution. But the revolution against the imperialists, *the anti-imperialist revolution* in its first stage, when the majority of the toiling population is not yet aware of the necessity of building a socialist society, will be *not a socialist* but a bourgeois-democratic revolution, as it is usually called. Not the immediate building of socialism *but the liberation of the country from the imperialist yoke* – this is the essence and the task of the anti-imperialist revolution. Hence the fundamental and all-determining task of the revolution for an independent Native republic will be the defence of the national independence of the country, the suppression of the resistance of the European and Native bourgeoisie remaining in the country, clearing Native society from the old customs and the raising of the material and cultural well-being of the toilers. [....]

These fundamental measures of the Native Republic will be the following:

1. All the land will be confiscated and divided among the Natives, the coloured and the Indian peasants and the European poor farmers and bywoners who have no land. The system of distribution will be laid down in accordance with the desires of the peasants themselves. The land owned by the Natives and also the land of the small farmers which is not used as a means of enslaving the labour-tenants and farm labourers will not be confiscated. The peasants will have the full right to dispose of their allotments according to their own discretion. The local government organs will only see to it that a great deal of land is not concentrated into one man's hands.

2. The mining industry, the railways, ports and banks will be nationalised and become the property of the Republic. This will be absolutely necessary as, unless it is done, it will be impossible to achieve any independence. In the towns only the large manufacturing industries and those that are of importance in the life of the country, and the factories belonging to the run-away imperialists will be confiscated. The remaining enterprises will be left in the hands of their former owners – the white, Native, Indian and other capitalists – if they agree to work under the control of the revolutionary government and obey the new laws of the Republic. The small enterprises of the run-away imperialists will be given by the government of the Republic as concessions to the Native capitalists. Taking into its hands the chief branches of industry and transport, the revolutionary government will utilise the profits that it derives from them, which are now being sent to London or wasted by the employers on the spot, for the further development of the national economy in South Africa, for assistance to the peasantry, for improving the material situation of the working class.
3. For the defence of the Republic from imperialist intervention, and for suppressing the resistance of the class enemies within the republic, the revolutionary government will form its workers' and peasants' army and will arm all the toiling people.
4. The pass laws and all other anti-Native laws enacted by the imperialists and the entire system of social discrimination will be abolished.
5. The present system of taxation will be abolished and a unified progressive income tax (the greater the income the more will the person have to pay in the form of taxes) which places the main burden upon the bourgeoisie, will be introduced for the needs of the revolutionary government.
6. Measures will be taken to immediately and radically improve the situation of the working class. The revolutionary government will do away with the colour bar, will introduce legislation for the 8 hour working day, and social insurance, will raise wages, improve the conditions of labour and the housing conditions, will abolish the compound system, etc., etc. The recruting of workers will immediately be prohibited. Workers organised in trade unions will have every opportunity of introducing everything necessary through the revolutionary government for the improvement of their situation and for the protection of their rights by various acts and decrees.
7. Immediate measures will be taken to assist the peasantry – such as irrigation, the struggle against soil erosion and pests, cheap credit, guaranteeing the possibility of cheap purchase of agricultural implements, machinery and artificial fertilisers, the opportunity to freely dispose of their own produce and sell it to their best advantage. Freedom of trade and freedom of occupation will be granted.
8. Special attention will be devoted to popular education. Free and all embracing education in the Native languages and in the languages of all nationalities inhabiting South Africa, will be introduced. The doors of the middle and higher schools will be thrown wide open for all the toilers.[2]
9. Special care will be taken of the women, primarily of the women workers, such as providing them with paid leave during pregnancy, material assistance for the birth of the infant, the organisation of children's nurseries and kindergartens, the prohibition of difficult and harmful work for women, etc., etc. [....]

Native society is not homogeneous in its composition. It is divided into different social groups and classes having different interests. In it we have the tribal chiefs, the Native bourgeoisie, the peasantry, and finally, the workers in the towns who have cut all their ties with the land – the proletarians. It can be asked whether all these classes in the Native society will participate in the anti-imperialist revolution, and, the main thing, which of them will play the chief role as organiser and leader of the masses in this revolution? Let us analyse this.

Can the tribal chiefs be the organisers and leaders of the national liberation struggle? [....]

The chiefs are not only exploiters themselves, but they also help the imperialists to exploit and suppress the Native people. A considerable part of them are now direct allies and agents of imperialism. Imperialism has maintained the tribal organisation of the Natives and the power of the chiefs, adapting it to the interests of the exploitation of the country and of the oppression of the Natives. [....]

The majority of the present chiefs have been appointed by the colonial government from among people who are entirely loyal to imperialism, who serve it faithfully and truly. The chief collects the taxes and the rent, helps to recruit workers, drives the Natives to work on the so-called public works, spies upon the members of his tribe and denounces to the police all those who in one way or another show their discontent with imperialist rule. By making use of his authority and the old traditions of submission to him, he keeps back the Native from any struggle against imperialist robbery and arbitrary actions. Imperialism could not maintain itself without relying upon the tribal chiefs, without active assistance from them and the very chiefs themselves could not exploit their people in such a way if imperialism were not behind them. The overthrow of the imperialist rule, clearing the way for the free development of peasant economy, at the same time means an end to the exploitation of the peasantry by the tribal chiefs. This means that the tribal chiefs, as a rule, are not interested in driving out the imperialists. If some of them now come out against some measure of the existing imperialist order then it is only because the imperialists are grabbing the lion's share of the spoils obtained from robbing the Native peasants and leave little for the chiefs. If they sometimes also come out against different imperialist anti-Native laws, concealing themselves in this with the name of the people, then it is only in order to get greater opportunities to enrich themselves at the expense of their tribes. In the anti-imperialist revolution the majority of the chiefs will be on the side of the imperialists and will help them to strengthen their rule just as they do now. It is not outside the realm of possibility that some of the small chiefs who have little land, for instance, will go together with the rising people against imperialism, but as they themselves are interested in the exploitation of the Native toilers they will never go together with them up to the final victory of the toilers against all forms of exploitation and oppression. *The tribal chiefs cannot be the organisers and the leaders of the anti-imperialist revolution.* [....]

Let us proceed. Can the Native bourgeoisie be the organisers and leader of the anti-imperialist revolution? Some "friends" of the people are endeavouring to assert that there is no native bourgeoisie in South Africa. This is absolutely incorrect. It is true that the Native bourgeoisie is still weak in its development, that it is predominantly a small bourgeoisie judging by the size of its business, but its existence cannot in any way be denied on these grounds. there is a large number of Native business men who are gradually getting rich at the expense of the toiling Native population. When such a Native business man has four houses (for instance, in the locations in Marabastab in

Pretoria and other places), rents them to the Natives, and receives £14 to £18 a month in rent, then does he do that for pleasure or in order to assist the Native workers? Of course not. He does this because it brings him profit, because it gives him an opportunity to enrich himself *at the expense of the Native inhabitants in the locations*. He is an exploiter, he is a bourgeois. [....] And the higher traders, the moneylenders, the owners of small shops with hired labour? All these constitute the Native bourgeoisie who exploit the Native population in the towns. [....]

The business of this Native bourgeoisie is considerably restricted by imperialist rule and their development and enrichment is retarded. The prohibition of Native trading in the villages and European towns, high taxes upon the Native merchants, restricting their freedom to move about, etc., create extraordinary difficulties for the development of the Native bourgeoisie. For this reason there is a definite contradiction between the Native bourgeoisie and the Anglo-Boer imperialists and that is why the Native bourgeoisie sometimes comes out against the anti-Native laws which restrict their activity. The Native bourgeoisie would like to get unrestricted rights to trade everywhere, the right to move about the country freely, would like to get rid of the taxes imposed upon them, would like to limit the competition of the European merchants, etc.

The anti-imperialist revilution which will establish the independence of the country from imperialism and abolish all these restrictions thus accord with the interests of the Native bourgeoisie also.

Hence the Native bourgeoisie should support the anti-imperialist revolution and help the working class and the peasantry to throw off the yoke of imperialist oppression. But we do not see this in South Africa, just as we do not see this in other colonial countries like India, Indo-China, Egypt, etc. The Native bourgeoisie is afraid that the workers and peasants, when taking power into their hands after driving out the imperialists, will bridle their exploiting aspirations and set up definite boundaries to its development. That is why the Native bourgeoisie vaccilates in the revolutionary struggle against imperialism and prefers the peaceful way of coming to terms with the imperialists, to get from them the necessary privileges and gradually do away with the restrictions that are now in force. And imperialism, being in need of the support of the Native bourgeoisie, makes some concessions to them: every year more and more territory is being opened up for Native trade and the Native bourgeoisie have been exempted from passes, etc. [....] But as has already been indicated, there are certain contradictions between the Native bourgeoisie and imperialism. That is why the bourgeoisie very often comes out against anti-Native laws, which retard its development and doing this they conceal themselves behind the interests of all the people, but as soon as the people rise to a determined struggle against these anti-Native laws, the bourgeoisie immediately calls them to order, to obedience and betrays them. That this is so is confirmed by the activity of the Industrial-Commercial Union, an organisation that absolutely reflects the interests of the Native bourgeoisie. During the first years of its existence it put forward the slogan of "political and industrial emancipation of South Africa" and called upon the masses to struggle. But as soon as the Native toiling masses rose to the struggle, the ICU began openly to voilate the imperialist laws, to organise strikes, demonstrations, etc., the ICU hastened to expel the communists from its ranks and to assure the government of its loyalty to imperialism. Since that time the ICU has never again put forward the slogan of political emancipation of South Africa. In 1930 when the broad masses of the toilers entered into open struggle against the imperialist regulations (uprisings in Worcester, Byana, Die Transvaal, the boycott of the beer halls in Durban, the railway strike in East London, the burning of passes) the leaders of ICU kadalie, Champoin quite openly betrayed them and helped the imperialists to brutally settle accounts with them. The year 1930 should never be forgotten! All this shows that when the toilers rise to a determined struggle against imperialism, the Native bourgeoisie will not be with them, but with the imperialists which does not exclude the fact that some section of the smaller bourgeoisie will fight shoulder to shoulder with the toilers in the battle for national independence and freedom, but by no means can they be relied upon as a consistent force.

Neither the tribal chiefs nor the Native bourgeoisie can be the organisers and leaders of the anti-imperialist revolution. The Native proletariat together withe white workers who had come over to the side of the revolution, can and must take the task upon themselves. In South Africa there was not and there is not any other class except the proletariat which would raise the banner of the anti-imperialist revolution. But the proletariat alone, withou the alliance with the majority of the Native toiling population, the peasantry, cannot achieve victory and at the same time the peasantry alone, withou the alliance with the working class cannot drive out the imperialists and secure land. Only by uniting their forces of the working class and the peasantry can victory be achieved. But the leading role in this alliance must belong to the proletariat. The experience of all countries and all revolutions teach us that the peasantry can achieve victory only in an alliance with the workers of the towns and only under their leadership. The town workers work in large bodies for one employer, one capitalist and hence they are already accustomed to joint organised axtion in holding meetings, strikes, demonstrations, etc. Working under a definite regime in the factories, they are more disciplined, already have experience in organisation. The workers in the town are more cultured and more developed politically; they are better able to see who is a friend and who is the enemy of the toilers. The town workers have their party – the Communist Party – which defends the interests not only of the workers but of all toilers. In South Africa there are already considerable cadres of a Native proletariat who have already gone through a lot of schooling in the class and anti-imperialist struggle forming their class organisations – the Communist Party and the trade unions.

So tht we see that the alliance of the workers in the towns with the peasants is the basic force which is capable of bringing about independence of South Africa. But being the basic force they must call all those to their banner of struggle who are groaning under the yoke of the Angl--Boer imperialist regime, all those to whom the interest of the national liberation of the country is dear, all those who want to get rid of the chameful slavery.

In the suburban Native locations there are Native handicraftsmen who are not exploiters, who suffer from various imperialist restrictions and limitations, who together with the other toilers are subjected to social discrimination. Their material situation is not better and sometimes even worse than that of the Native workers. They have nothing to expect from imperialism. Exhausting toil, want and privation is their lot in the conditions of imperialist rule. Only the anti-imperialist revolution, the Independent Native Republic will open the path to them for a real human life.

In the villages and especially in the towns there are large numbers of Native intellectuals, especially teachers. Imperialist rule has deprived them of all opportunities to develop intellectually, opportunities for a cultural life. It has closed the doors of the highest schools to them, has subjugated them to the control of the European missionaries, paid them not only less than the European but even less than the Indian teachers and their pay is hardly more than that of the Native workers. The extremely poor development of Native education and the complete lack of cultural work among the Native population restricts the sphere for the employment of the labour of the Native intellectuals to an extraordinary degree and that is why, despite all the restrictions regarding middle and higher education, there is now such a number of Native unemployed intellectuals. A Native cannot become an egineer, a technician as all the industries have been grabbed by the European capitalists who do not want to employ Native engineers to work for them. As a teacher in a bad, overcrowded school, under the supervision of a missionary preaching the religion of his master, as a government employee suppressing the Native population – this where the Native intellectual can apply his knowledge and all that for a miserable salary in the conditions of social discrimination, derision and mockery.

The Native intellectual, just like the worker, the peasant and the handicraftsman, cannot expect anything from imperialism. Only the establishment of a Native Independent Republic will create the conditions for the full flourishing of national culture, will open for the Native intellectual the path to all-round scientific, pedagogical and cultural work and will place him in conditions such as he cannot even dream of under the rule of the imperialists. The Native intellectuals should give their efforts to the cause of liberating the country and together with the working class and the peasantry, fight for the Independent Native Republic.

Thus the leader and organiser of the anti-imperialist revolution will be the town worker, the proletariat. But fot this purpose the proletariat must constitute itself an independent revolutionary force, strengthen the class organisation – the Communist Party and the revolutionary trade unions – and by its devoted and unselfish participation in the common struggle of the toilers, it should secure for itself the recognition of this independent significance and of its leading role. [....]

Let us now analyse the following question: What sort of a government will there be in the Independent Native Republic and how will it be organised? It appears to be clear that if the workers and peasants in an open struggle against the imperialists drive them out of the country and set up an Independent Republic, then they already take power into their hands and organise the workers' and peasants' government. But there are people who assert that the slogan of an "Independent Native Republic" and the slogan of a "workers' and peasants' republic" are not similar, that the first slogan is broader than the second. [....] The question of the similarity or dissimilarity will be decided by the class struggle, by the co-relation of class forces within Native society in the period of the anti-imperialist revolution. This is the question as to whether the workers and peasants, with the Communist Party at their head, will succeed in sezing power after the overthrow of the rule of the imperialists or whether Kadli, Guemedi, Seme and Co., the agents of the Native bourgeoisie and chiefs will seize power. For us this should be absolutely clear that after the imperialists have been driven out, the Native bourgeoisie will attempt to seize power and to utilise the victory of the toiler over imperialism for *their own class aims, against* the toilers.

Here there is a great danger for the toilers, inasmuch as even the masses of the workers have not yet an entirely clear idea of the fact that their interests are entirely opposite to the interests of the Native bourgeoisie. The latter being but slightly developed, they do not as yet stand sufficiently clearly from among the masses of the Native population, and are not yet sufficiently clearly contrasted to the Native population and the working class in particular. On the contrary, making use of the hatred of the toilers towards Anglo-Boer imperialism, they sow illusions regarding the community of interests of the entire Native population and speak of the unity of a classless Bantu Nation. These contradictions will become revealed sufficiently clearly immediately the imperialists are driven out, when the Native bourgeoisie will get greater possibilities for its development and when it will no longer be able to conceal its class interests with talk of a united national front against imperialist oppression. If after the imperialists are driven out, the power will be seized by the Native bourgeoisie, and in that case it would undoubtedly enter into an alliance with the white bourgeoisie remaining in the country, it will utilise this power to again enslave the toilers.

The working class cannot allow the power to get into the hands of the bourgeoisie. [....] The power in the Independent Native Republic must belong to the workers and peasants' government. But it would also be a gross mistake to think that this workers' and peasants' government will be the dictatorship of the proletariat. The dictatorship of the proletariat is the utilisation of the power by the proletariat for the construction of socialism, and in South Africa, as has already been pointed out, the first stage of the anti-imperialist revolution there absolutely is not and cannot be the task of immediately constructing socialism. The policy of the workers and peasants' government will be determined not by the interests of the immediate construction of socialism but by the interests of the immediate interests of free development of peasant economy, by the interest of improving the material conditions of the working class. The workers' and peasants' government will be a government of two classes – the proletariat and the peasantry under the leadership of the Party of the working class – the Communist Party. The government organised by them will, firstly be a revolutionary government, arising in the process of the revolution and continuing the revolutionary struggle against imperialism and the old order. Secondly, this will be a democratic government elected by the workers and peasants themselves.

The Native bourgeoisie can be allowed to take part in the elections of the government and the local organs of power if they will not conduct a counter-revolutionary struggle, but the main force will still be the working class and the peasantry under the leadership of the Communist Party. This will be a workers' and peasants' government. While being democratic for the workers and peasants, this government will be a revolutionary dictatorship against the white bourgeoisie remaining in the country and against the resisting tribal chiefs and the Native bourgeoisie, inasmuch as it will have to suppress their resistance. Such a government is called a revolutionary democratic dictatorship of the proletariat and the peasantry.

The question as to the form in which the power of the working class and the peasantry will be organised will be decided by the victorious people but the experience of the USSR and Soviet China shows that the best form of power for the triumphant workers' and peasants' is The Soviets of Workers' and Peasants' deputies. [....]

In conclusion we shall once more dwell upon one important question: What will the white toilers who will form a national minority receive from the establishment of a Native Independent Republic? The Anglo-Boer imperialists and their agents try to inflame the hatred of the white toilers against the National Liberation movement of the native workers and peasants. They spread monstrous statements that the Independent Native

Republic is directed against the whites as a whole. Trying to keep the white workers back from unity with the native toilers, they let loose such slogans as "South Africa for whites", "White superiority" over the natives, and so on. [....]

All the demagogy of the "civilised labour policy" cannot hide the fact that tens of thousands of white workers who replace the Natives, work 10–12 hours a day for the pay of 2 shillings. It is an indisputable fact that in the so-called "White South Africa" the poverty of the white workers and toilers is increasing. The number of poor whites – toilers who are deprived of means of subsistance by the very white Anglo-Boer bosses, is about 300,000. The ruination of the poor white farmers is growing daily. Thousands of them are forced to leave the land and to wander about in search of work. The standard of living and the conditions of the white bywoners, tenant farmers and small sub-farmers, is not much better than those of the Natives.

Thus, when we analyse the position we see that for the vast majority of the white workers and toilers the "white superiority" is nothing but a bluff, by means of which the imperialists try to fool them. We see that the system of the Anglo-Boer exploitation in South Africa which rests upon the national enslavement of native people, is directed also against the interests and conditions of life of the white workers.

The white worker must therefore understand that he has nothing in common with the imperialists, that his place is in the united struggle together with the native masses for an Independent Native Republic. The rule of the imperialists has brought the white workers and poor farmers to the impass in which they find themselves now. On the contrary, the overthrow of this rule, the national liberation of the native toilers, will bring them big material advantages as they themselves will be liberated from the imperialist exploitation of the big landowners, the banks, the wholesale firms and from the yoke of debts and taxation.

An Independent Native Republic would first of all mean not a lowering of their standard of living but a rise in the standard of living of the Native workers and the lower paid white workers up to their level, and, secondly, it would open the way to a general rise in the material and cultural well-being of all the toilers such as has never before been seen by the white workers. An independent republic would mean not a curtailment of their political rights, but, on the contrary, giving them political rights, the very broadest worker-peasant democracy, democracy put at the service of the working class and the peasantry, democracy which would make them, together with the Native toilers, the real masters of the country. The white workers of the Union of South Africa can liberate themselves from hired capitalist slavery only through the Independent Native Republic.

The small white farmers have nothing to lose from the anti-imperialist revolution. Their land will not be confiscated. The revolution is above all directed against the landowners who utilise the land to enslave the Native peasantry. The republic would bring the small white farmers as well as the white workers full political rights, complete freedom. The revolutionary government will give them the necessary assistance just as to the Native peasants. The poor whites will get land without having to purchase it, will have an opportunity to return to the land and conduct their own farms. The Independent Native Republic will be the republic not only for the Native population but a republic for all the toilers regardless of the colour of their skin.

This is what the Independent Native Republic for which the Communist Party of South Africa calls upon you to struggle, means. The Independent Native Republic is the path to national liberation from imperialist oppression, the path to clearing the country of the Anglo-Boer oppressors, the return of the land to its real owners – the Native peasantry. It is the path to the liberation of the working class from imperialist exploitaion, the path to a better life, the path to the fraternal union of the European and Native toilers. [....]

If the Native workers and peasants will submissively bear the derision and bad treatment of the white masters and support the empty resolution of the African National Congress or the Industrial Commercial Union, then they will not ACHIEVE their independent republic for a long time. But if the workers and peasants will offer collective and organised resistance to every manifestation of imperialist oppression, then the final victory over imperialism will come soon. Hence the workers in the factories, and in the mines, the worker-tenants and the agricultural labourers on the farms and plantations, the peasants in the reserves now have to jointly discuss the causes of their miserable situation, draw up their demands to the employers, to the Colonial Government, and attain their fulfilment by a collective organised struggle. Hence it is necessary right away to form and strengthen organisations which would conduct the daily struggle for these so-called partial demands, revolutionary trade unions for the workers, a league of worker-tenants for the peasants on the European farms, committees of action in the reserves, etc. Organisation and solidarity constitute the force which we can oppose to the pact of imperialists. Hence all those who desire the struggle for the independence of the country – the Native and European workers, the Native peasants and the poor whites, the Native intellectuals and the Native city poor should join the existing revolutionary organisations, form new ones and in the daily struggle against the imperialist rule strengthen the ani-imperialist front, the front of the fighters for an independent South Africa, for an Independent Native Republic.

Document 77
M. K., "Fascism in South Africa", *Umsebenzi*, 13 January, 1934

In this article I want to discuss the possible aspects and development of fascism in this country. It is generally taken for granted (and this assumption is strengthened by the statement of Mr. Pirow about "life and death struggle between black and white," etc.) that since the whites are in the minority in South Africa, it would not pay to ferment anti-semitic feelings and that therefore, fascism in this country will only be anti-Native.

If this is the case then fascism would be very simple and would not need any change in the administrative methods, because, so far as we Natives are concerned, we have always been and are treated in a fascist manner. One needs only to look at the laws and the treatment of the Native people in this country to be convinced that it needs only to carry out in full all the anti-Native laws and you have fascism pure and simple.

But fascism is not so simple as this. Fascism is a political form of government – open bourgeois dictatorship. The bourgeoisie do not rejoice in passing over from the "democratic" parliamentary phase to open dictatorship – fascism. The bourgeoisie would only be too pleased if it was still possible to perpetuate the parliamentary democratic phase, but this is no longer possible – the conditions have radically changed.

The problem is deeper than some people think. What is at fault is the material basis of the present society. The economic system of present society has failed. The economic crisis which now enters its fifth year, is a demonstration of this fact. The productive forces are in conflict with the productive relations – the social character of production and the individual appropriation of the products. The development of technique has outstripped the productive relations. More things are produced than can be exchanged at a profit.

Now, producing for profit is the basis of the present "civilization" – production and exchange. Because the prices of world commodities do not realise this profit, stocks have accumulated and are rotting in the warehouses, while the majority of the people are badly in need. This is just the crux of the matter. The system is decaying and has prospects of further decay. Any seasonal revival in trade can only be temporary. Capitalism cannot give work to vast armies of unemployed, cannot solve the problem of unemployment and cannot develop the productive forces further.

Having now established that the contradictions of the "civilisation" or economic system are insoluble except by the overthrow of the whole system, I will proceed to discuss the two forms of fascism in South Africa. Fascism is a form of self-defence and attack on the part of the bourgeoisie against the revolutionary proletariat, in South Africa, against the revolutionary national emancipatory movement and struggles of the toiling Native and Coloured masses.

This is quite evident and needs no emphasis.

But by suppressing the national liberation movement of the Native people one does not liquidate the poor white problem nor does one solve the problem by constant sensational talks about "rising tide of Colour" and "Black versus White". The poor whites want land and the Natives have no land, and are earning three to five shilling a month as farm labourers. The white unemployed want work and the politicians tell them that the Natives are doing the work which should be done by whites.

It is important that we examine this work. The work of the Natives in towns is the unskilled common and often the dirty work – "Kaffir work." There are very few Natives doing skilled work (e.g., pressers in the garment and laundry industries). These are there because they have proved to be quite efficient and very cheap. Cheap labour, by the way, is the basis of our national economy!

To shatter this foundation of our national economy is tantamount to a revolution in our national life and culture. From what is stated above this is an impossibility. It should be borne in mind that South Africa is a bi-cultural country – mining and poor farming. Because of inefficiency the farmers are gradually losing their farms. Their farms are passing into the hands of big finance.

The passing of farms into the hands of big finance, means that the erstwhile self-sufficing farmers are falling at the same rate into the camp of the poor whites. Subsequently the cry for land increases and the smart politician refers the ruined farmers to the Jews, saying that the Jews are the mortgage holders, pawnbrokers, money lenders and therefore have taken away their land.

Industrially South Africa is undeveloped. The only key industry (mining) is based on cheap labour and the Chamber of Mines and the State will see to it that nobody interferes with this industry, the only one of its kind in this country.

In the secondary industry the gentiles play a less important role. This is a fact which no one can dispute and I have seen in some papers that "75 per cent of the trade is in the hands of the Jews." Even the Labour Party manifesto speaks about the commerce of the country being "in the hands of strangers."

With the further decline of the profits, that is, when the price of commodities does not cover the cost of production, and when the vast army of the unemployed, ruined petty bourgeoisie and thousands of white youth who leave the universities and high schools every year, demand employment you cannot tell this class of people to go and do the "kaffir job" with impunity. You can tell that to the poor white.

These people do not go to school to eventually come and sweep the streets. Their ambitions are to be commercial and public men. Then men will "suddenly discover" that the Jews are dominating the public institutions (commerce, politics and professional life). Propaganda to remove the Jews from these positions may flare up in the whole country.

Thus the position can be summed up as follows:

a) Fascism as reactionary movement of the capitalist class, the open dictatorship of the bourgeoisie against the working class, in South Africa, will primarily be against the national liberation struggle of the oppressed and exploited Native toiling masses.
b) That to be a popular or mass movement fascism will have to find the scapegoat for the failures of the capitalist system. And
c) That this scapegoat cannot be the Natives, since economically the Natives possess nothing. The white workers, the university and college students do not desire to become street cleaners and road diggers. They want decent jobs and decent wages. The expropriated farmers and the poor whites want land. The cry therefore will be raised against the Jews as "bankers, mortgage holders, money lenders, pawnbrokers, traders, doctors, lawyers, manufacturers, politicians and dominating the cultural institutions."

Document 78
"What is the Communist Party? A South African Native Republic, Lesson 3: The Native Republic 1", *Umsebenzi*, 24 February 1934

We have explained in an earlier lesson that the Communist Party is fighting for communism. But we cannot go straight to communism, because many things that are needed for communism have not yet come about. Even in the Soviet Union, where the working class has been ruling since 1917, they have not yet got communism, though they are marching steadily towards it. In order to build communism we must: firstly, make a REVOLUTION and throw out the capitalists from their place as rulers; secondly, set up a government of the workers together with the poor peasantry; thirdly, build up a socialist industry, that is to say the workers' government must take charge of the factories, mines, etc., and the workers must learn how to manage these things themselves; fourthly, collectivise the small peasant farms, by getting the peasants to come together and work their land together instead of each man by himself; fifthly, do away with all the capitalist and exploiting classes, by taking away their land and capital and making them work like everybody else; and sixthly, educate all people as communists to work in a communistic way for the good of all.

In South Africa the first step in the revolution is the fight for democratic rights (which is what the workers already have in the capitalist "home" countries, and what the white workers already have in South Africa.) The first step also means the fight for the independence of South Africa from British Imperialism and for the return of the land to the Native people (mayibuye).

By DEMOCRATIC RIGHTS we mean freedom of movement (that means the end of the pass and curfew laws); freedom to organise as workers (that means the end of the Master and Servant Laws and other such laws); freedom to become skilled workers and to enter all trades and professions (that means the smashing of the Colour Bar Law); the right of all people to own land (that means the end of the Native Land Act); free primary education and the right of all Non-Europeans to enter the high school and the universities; the right of the oppressed Native people to rule themselves, to be independent, to set up their own free Native government in this country. As the Native people are the majority, this means an INDEPENDENT SOUTH AFRICAN NATIVE REPUBLIC. Such a Native Republic, being a democratic republic, would give freedom and right of independence to all the smaller oppressed nations in South Africa, to the Coloured People; the Indians, etc., if they should want it. It would give the white workers and poor farmers full rights as citizens in South Africa but would do away with the ruling power of the white imperialists.

Document 79
"What is the Communist Party? Lesson 4: What will be Done in the Bantu Republic?", Umsebenzi, 17 March 1934

In our last lesson we spoke of the Bantu or Native Republic of South Africa, for which the African workers and peasants will fight under the leadership of the Communist Party. We must now answer two questions. Firstly, what will be done in the Bantu Republic, what will it give to the workers and peasants, how will it help the Bantu? Secondly, how will the Bantu Republic be brought about? In this lesson we shall answer the first of these questions.

The Bantu republic will do away with the racial oppression of the Bantu. It will make South Africa an independent country, not ruled over by the English or any other imperialists. It will mean that the black majority will have MAJORITY RIGHTS in their own country. It will mean "Mayibuye", the return of the land to the Bantu people, from whom it has been stolen by the imperialists. The Bantu Republic will use the land, the mines, the riches of South Africa for the good of all the workers and toiling people in South Africa, both black and white. It will fight against the imperialist oppressors and will not allow them any longer to rob the people of this country.

When people are oppressed because they belong to a certain nationality, they do not only ask for equal rights, but also the right to rule themselves: because they thank that this is the only way to make sure that they will not be oppressed. And so the Bantu are asking and will ask more and more for the right to rule themselves, to have their own government of black people. (The Dutch Afrikaners also said in the past that they were oppressed by the English and they wanted an Afrikaner Government.) The Bantu know that while they are ruled over by another race they will never be sure that they will not suffer because of the colour of their skins. Therefore the Communist Party fights for the right of the Bantu to rule themselves; therefore it fights for an independent Bantu republic.

In this republic for the first time the Bantu will be able to enjoy real freedom as a nation in South Africa. They will be able to come and go freely without passes. They will not be kept out anywhere on account of their colour, neither from the schools and universities, nor from the trams and trains, nor from the cafes and bioscopes and towns halls, nor from the libraries and museums and zoos. There will be no law to stop the Bantu becoming skilled workers and engineers, lawyers, doctors, magistrates and judges, professors and directors of business and industry. Of course at first there will be very few black men and women about to do the most highly skilled work, because the Bantu under imperialism have not been allowed to enter the schools and universities and become skilled workers like the whites. But this will only be at the beginning. Very soon thousands of Bantu will take advantage of the schools and factories which will be open to them under the Bantu Republic, and they will begin to push their way up and to show what they can do. All this will be possible only when there is a Bantu Government and not before.

In industry the Bantu Republic will also bring big changes in the life of the black, coloured and Indian workers. For the first time they will have the right to organise into trade unions, and once they have this right they will be able to improve their wages and conditions a great deal. The land workers will no longer suffer under the sjambok of the farmer; the Contract Law, the Master and Servant Law, will be gone. People will no longer be forced by poll tax and land hunger and starvation to go and work down the mines. The standard of living of the Non-European workers will increase. The Bantu Proletariat will grow stronger. The differences between white and black workers will grow less. A united proletariat fighting for socialism will come into being.

The life of the peasants will also change very much. The land will be taken away from the rich land-owners and imperialists and every Bantu peasant and his family will be able to have as much land as they can use. The Land Act of 1913, which does not allow Bantu to own land except in reserves, will be gone. Everyone who wants land will be able to get it, and so no one will have to starve. The people's government will help the peasants in many ways, with ploughs and tractors and oxen and seed and with irrigation works. The whole nation will unite to fight the drought and the locusts, and these pests will no longer cause misery and death to thousands.

Document 80
"The Communist Party Points the Way to Freedom: ANC Leaders have no Programme of Struggle", *Umsebenzi*, 7 April 1934

(CONTRIBUTED)

The leaders of the African National Congress lose no opportunity of attacking the Communist Party. They try to make out that they are the only real defenders of the toiling masses of South Africa. Unfortunately many people still believe them. But it is time for the workers and peasants of South Africa to know the truth about the self-styled leaders of the A.N.C. The organisation and its leaders must be judged not by their words but by their actions. But even the public declarations of the Congress leaders are sufficient to condemn them.

Let us consider a number of political issues of the last year or so, and let us see what part was played by the Congress leaders and the Communist Party respectively in connection with these important matters.

THE NATIVE SERVICE CONTRACT ACT

In 1933 a law of slave labour contracts was passed by the slave-drivers' parliament, legalising the slave conditions of African peasants on European farms.

The Communist Party immediately called upon the peasants to resist the enforcement of this abominable law. In the "Umsebenzi" of 22 July, 1933, the Party stated: "This barbarous act aims at transforming about two million Native peasant leaseholders into virtual slaves of the landowners and plantation owners. On the other hand, as a result of this law, hundreds of thousands of squatters will be driven off their land into the starving reserves or into the ranks of the town unemployed, and will be deprived of the slightest means of subsistence. The landlord, who will now get 180 days free labour from every 'labour tenant' will not require so many squatters, so that thousands will be evicted and forced to seek a home elsewhere.

"The task of the Communist Party is to mobilise the masses on the farms, in the reserves and in the towns for mass united front demonstrations against the Native Service Contract Act. In the first place we must organise mass resistance on the basis of mass refusal to sign the contracts and mass struggle against the ejection of peasants from their land."

This was the answer of the Communist Party which did not only call upon the masses to fight, but began in actual practice to organise the struggle against the new slave law. Propaganda against the Contract Law was developed among the Native peasantry in different parts of the country. In Natal, as a result of distributing a leaflet calling upon peasants to refuse to sign themselves into slavery, Comrade Ngcwangu, a member of the Communist Party, was sentenced to a year's imprisonment.

On the other hand what did the A.N.C. do – this organisation which claims to represent the interests of the African people?

The Special Conference of the A.N.C. in January, 1933, passed the following resolution: "This special conference of the A.N.C. voices a resolute protest against the measures which are being carried out by the Union Government in an attempt to solve the problem which has such serious consequences, the problem of regulating racial inter-relations between white and black in South Africa, to define the political fates without the interested race participating in it, and in open violation of the principles of consultation laid down in the Act of 1920."

The A.N.C. apparently did not worry about the fact that the Contract Act aimed at turning the peasants into serfs of the white landlords. All it worried about was the way in which the law was introduced. They objected because they were not "consulted" about it. They objected because they were not given the opportunity of participating in the working out of anti-Native laws.

"We used to be recognised as a connecting link between the government and our people," said Professor Jabavu. The desire to be a Government-appointed "leader" of the Bantu people, one who is "consulted" by the Government and who in return carries out the policy of the Government, appears to be the chief concern of the "esteemed" Professor Jabavu.

In practice the A.N.C. has done absolutely nothing to prevent the introduction and operation of the Contract Law. They have even gone so far as to call upon the people to support the Coalition Government, the Government which will administer the law. Speaking at the A.N.C. conference in April 1933, the President, Dr. Seme, said: "With fright and alarm I should like to say a few words about the new Coalition Government. It is true that the attention of the whole country is directed towards the new Cabinet, which represents the best political heads that can be found in the country. And this is really a very rare combination of the most powerful and most capable people. Through the medium of our Congress we should like to express our hopes and our faith in the members of the Government whose names have earned in our country, as well as in the whole world, the highest reputation."

And like sheer mockery sounds the praising hymn to the serf owner – General Hertzog: "Let the name of General Hertzog go down in history as the name of a statesman who laid the foundation of a great temple of justice, peace and goodwill for all peoples of our country, irrespective of their race or colour." (Seme).

The question arises, how can a person who links the boots of this bloody imperialist robber so shamelessly be a leader of an oppressed people against imperialism?

Document 81
D. I., "What the 'A.C.C.' Means", *Umsebenzi*, 26 January 1935

For the last couple of years the African National Congress has been carrying on a wide campaign for the creation of a "National Fund," the so-called "Isivivane" or "Isithabathaba" and has repeatedly appealed to the Native toiling population to bring their last pennies to this fund, and Mr. Plaatje recommends those who have no money to subscribe with cattle.

In making this appeal the Congress promises "to give the Africans a higher economic status" through the organisation of Congress Stores, a banking corporation, a building society, automobile clubs, garages and so on. Mr. Plaatje assures us that "All this will create avenues of employment which will continue to increase as the business increases." This scheme failed as was to be expected and Dr Seme now comes forward with the new project for the organisation of "African Congress Clubs."

The "A.C.C." according to Seme's plan should be a private company with limited liability. It should not be however, an ordinary joint-stock company as "the idea of making the Africans take shares as in European concerns is still unsuitable for the African masses today." The shareholders, who are the managers of all the affairs of the "A.C.C." will be the special Trustees of the African National Congress, appointed by its Executive. All money necessary for the "A.C.C." will be drawn from the National Fund – the Isithabathaba.

The "A.C.C." undertakes to open consumers' stores and ware-houses, Native eating houses, slaughter houses and other commercial undertakings. Seme promises in this way to give the Natives cheap goods, work for the unemployed, etc. In return for this Seme calls on the Native toilers 1) to pay contribution to the National Fund, 2) to buy goods only in the stores of the "A.C.C." thirdly – to eat one day a week only food of Native production. At first sight it seems that Seme acts exclusively in the interest of the toiling masses and that therefore the latter are duty bound to support this undertaking by every means in their power. But after careful examination of this plan it appears that Seme has in view not the interest of toilers but the interest of the Native bourgeoisie.

The Native businessmen not being provided with sufficient capital are not in a position to compete with the European companies and traders. Especially now in a time of crisis and depression, when competition is becoming extremely sharp, the Native bourgeoisie feels its helplessness in this struggle. And Seme appeals to the toilers to collect their last pennies and save the Native traders and other businessmen from the effects of the crisis. As a matter of fact what does "A.C.C." mean? The toilers who bring their money to the National Fund are nevertheless deprived of all possibilities of influencing the affairs of the "A.C.C." At the head of the "A.C.C." will stand the group of trustees chosen from the Native businessmen, and such businessmen will also manage the organised stores and other commercial undertakings. At the expense of the toilers this company of Native bourgeoisie will be organised, which will exploit the Native consumers in just the same way as the European traders do. Besides, suppose that by mismanagement on the part of the "A.C.C.", the whole thing comes to smash, who will be the real losers? Of course the toiling masses who gave the funds but were not allowed a voice in the management.

We are not against the organisation of the toiling Natives as consumers. No at all. On the contrary we shall give them every assistance in this direction. But it must not be a company on the lines of the "A.C.C.", but consumers' cooperative societies, organised by the masses themselves and by the people elected by the masses and under their daily control.

For instance, the residents of the Langa location organised such a cooperative, themselves fix definite shares, which will form the basis of the original capital of the cooperatives elect the management board and take active part in the daily work of this cooperative. Such a cooperative, directly connected with the masses and working under their daily control can really give some relief to the toilers. And to such a cause we shall be pleased to render every assistance. The creation of the National Fund and the organisation of the "A.C.C." is nothing more than an attempt to shift the burden of the crisis from the Native bourgeoisie onto the shoulders of the toiling Natives.

Document 82
"Is There a Native Bourgeoisie?" *Umsebenzi*, 2 February 1935

To the Editor of "Umsebenzi"

In your issue of last week, "D. I." says that the "African Congress Clubs" movement is nothing more than an attempt to shift the burden of the crisis from the Native bourgeoisie on to the shoulders of the toiling Natives. He also tells us that the "Native bourgeoisie" is suffering heavily from the crisis. I was sorry to hear this and wonder how the Native "Bourgeoisie" are managing now that they have to give up their Rolls Royces and content themselves with Fords. I am also grieved to think of the money they have lost speculating in gold mining shares and how they have accumulated heavy overdrafts at the banks. It must be difficult for them to keep up their expensive flats and mansions now that rents have risen!

To be serious Comrade Editor, is it not rather far-fetched to talk about a Native bourgeoisie in South Africa to-day? It would be more correct, I think to describe Seme's "A.C.C." as an attempt to CREATE a Native bourgeoisie at the expense of the toiling masses. But when "D. I." talks of a Native bourgeoisie as if it were already in existence, we all begin to ask "Where is this Native bourgeoisie";

CONSTANT READER

(For the benefit of some of our readers who might like to know the meaning of the word "bourgeoisie" we would explain that it refers to the capitalist class, or exploiters who live by employing workers in factories and other businesses. There are a number of Native business men who make a profit by exploiting the labour of their fellow Africans. Examples of this class are the Native eating house proprietors, of whom we know about half a dozen in Johannesburg, some of them employing as many as four or five workers. There is no doubt that these people are living on profit made at the expense of the workers, but whether they are sufficiently numerous or powerful to be referred to as a class, the NATIVE BOURGEOISIE is a matter for discussion and we welcome the opinions of readers on this point. – Editor)

Document 83
"Native Bourgeoisie as a Class", *Umsebenzi*, 16 February 1935

To the Editor of "Umsebenzi"

In your issue of 2 February, there appeared an article under the heading, "Is there a Native Bourgeoisie in South Africa?"

I maintain that this article is a naive and sarcastic criticism of an article which appeared on January 26, entitled "What the A.C.C. Means." The latter article deals in length with the role of African National Congress, which is the institution of the Native bourgeoisie, whose existence is at present being disputed. Further the article very clearly explains how the oppressed Native bourgeoisie feels the pinch of the crisis and thus makes all attempts to shift this burden on to the shoulders of the exploited workers and peasants.

This is very clearly reflected in Dr Seme's scheme of African Congress Clubs. To consolidate this exploiting scheme, Dr Seme, on behalf of the Native bourgeoisie, appeals to the workers and peasants to contribute very liberally towards the so-called National Fund. This fund as well as the proposed stores will be under control of persons selected by the A.N.C. And who will be selected? The businessmen and traders, of course, who to-day constitute the membership of the A.N.C. This definitely indicates the class interest of Dr Seme's scheme. Now what class does he represent? He undoubtedly represents the Native bourgeoisie, who exist as a definite class, practically and ideologically, and form the social basis of national reformism in South Africa.

Where can we find this parasite class, known as the Native Bourgeoisie? On the Reef we have the Native businessman and trader in every location from Nigel to Randfontein. We have this type in each and every location in the Union and also in some of the large towns.

What and how does this class exploit? This parasitic class exploits wage-labour and secures high profits during the course of the distribution of commodities. The fact that the exploiting possibilities of the Native bourgeoisie are very much restricted by the oppression and strong competition of Anglo-Boer capital cannot be denied. But this does not mean that there is no Native bourgeoisie in South Africa. The Native bourgeoisie referred to have not all the same capacity for exploitation, nor have they all the same amount of capital. Thus we have to differentiate between the Native bourgeoisie and the Native petty bourgeoisie. To present a vivid picture of the Native petty bourgeoisie in South Africa I should have to make an elaborate class differentiation of the Native peasantry. This I hope to do at a later stage.

Many comrades will ask, "Why is there so much ado about the Native bourgeoisie?" The answer is that in order to be able to determine the moving forces of the South African revolution one must have a clear understanding of the different classes within Native society. Such an understanding will enable us to distinguish between the revolutionary forces, the counter-revolutionary forces – and the fellow-travellers.

J. B. Marks.[3]

Document 84
A. Z., "Is There a Class of Native Capitalists in South Africa?"
Umsebenzi, April 13, 1935

It is quite obvious to anyone who looks on this question from the class point of view, from the point of view of the working class and the toiling masses, that there are Native bourgeoisie in South Africa and could not help being. This is an inevitable law for all countries, and South Africa is no exception. In stating this, I foresee that there will be shouts from opponents that I am using general phrases, abstract theories, and that these theories do not apply to the exceptional special conditions of South Africa. This is the old and long-since refuted theory of Bunting on South African exceptionalism! Would it not be better for our opponents to throw this theory aside and look attentively around themselves to try to understand what the bourgeoisie are in general. Their chief mistake (and is it only a mistake?) is that they do not admit the existence of any capitalists except industrial capitalists, the owners of factories who engage workers and openly and brutally exploit them, sweating them to coin money for themselves. They define the bourgeoisie as exploiters living by the exploitation of the workers in the factories. This is true about the industrial bourgeoisie, but not true when we want to define the bourgeoisie in general. The question of the existence of a class of Native capitalists is replaced by the question of the existence of class of Native industrial capitalists. In South Africa, it is true, there are no industrial (Native? – Ed.) bourgeoisie. Imperialism has monopolised the entire economy of the country and does not make it possible for Native industry to develop. But even here there are some first shoots. It cannot be denied that there are small furniture factories and other workshops in South Africa belonging to Natives and employing as many as 10 or even more workers. Do they do this for pleasure, or just for the sake of giving jobs to Native workers?

Of course they do not. They engage workers so as to make a profit. The source of their profit is the exploitation of the workers. Like the European capitalists, they appropriate part of the value of the product of the workers, which is what we call exploitation. You will not deny that there are building contractors in South Africa who also exploit the workers. These, of course, are not yet industrial bourgeoisie, but they are first beginnings. And we are not discussing the industrial capitalists, but capitalists, Native exploiters in general. We will speak about them.

Capitalists are people living on an income obtained without labour, and on profit obtained from the exploitation of other people, irrespective of the form in which this exploitation takes place (this does not include the tribal chiefs, who are also exploiters, but they exploit in forms belonging to pre-capitalist society). They are primarily commercial bourgeoisie – traders shopkeepers, etc. You probably know that there are very many Native traders in South Africa (their association even passed a resolution against revolutionary activity in the locations – Umteteli Nov. 19, 1932). The Native economic commission pointed out in its report for 1930–32 that in the Witwatersrand locations there are over 5,000 Native traders, in Bloemfontein 250, in Alexandra Township there are 45, etc. Many of them employ 2 or 3 helpers, others do business without hired labour. Why do they carry on trade? Is it so that they can give cheap goods to the Native consumers? Of course it is not. They are in business because it gives them a profit, because they can sell goods dearer than they buy them. The source of their profit is therefore the pocket of the buyer, primarily the workers and the toiling people in general. Gradually but surely they get rich at the expense of the Native workers and toiling people as customers. Are they not exploiters? Of course there are also Native "traders" (small peddlers, etc,) who are only in business to try to feed their families. They are traders against their will. Among them are many people who would rather work but who cannot find work and are forced to take up small trading. We must not class such "traders" as bourgeoisie. You will not deny that there are Native owners of eating houses who employ 3 or 4 workers. And who are they? Are they not exploiters?

And how is it that you do not see the commercial house ownership in the locations? Everybody knows that there are Natives who build 2,3 or even 5 houses and let them out to Natives for rent. Do they put their money into houses for the sake of giving homes to Natives? Ask the people who live in these houses and they will tell you how much the house costs the landlord and how much rent he gets for it. We cannot say that every toiler is a capitalist if he has built a small house and takes lodgers in one of the rooms, but likewise we have not the right to consider as one of the toilers a Native who has 5 houses and an income of £16 a month, (Read "Race Relations," No. 6, 1934) There are also Native sub-renters. They rent 2 or 3 houses from white people and then let out rooms to the Natives, getting 2 or 3 times as much as they pay themselves. You will find such sub-renters among the Native officials.

Money-lenders must also be classed among the Native bourgeoisie. In most cases they are the same traders, house-owners, etc., who lend out money for interest. On December 16, 1933, the "Star" stated that a Native, Jim Lang, in Dunedin, lent £418 to an Indian merchant. If you consider that the "normal" interests on a money-lender's loan in South Africa amounts to150 per cent per annum and sometimes over 400 per cent, it will be clear to you what a wide field for exploitation is here. Finally, on January 13, 1934, "Umteteli" stated that there is a Native, Richard Baloyi, in Alexandra Township who has 5 omnibuses. The owners of small factories and workshops, the traders, the house-owners, the sub-renters of houses, the money-lenders, etc., – these are an army of Native businessmen living at the expense of the toiling population and receiving profits from the pockets of the Native workers and toilers in general.

It is true that these are still small capitalists as far as the size of their business is concerned, and they cannot be considered as being in the same category as the European capitalists. But does this make them cease to be exploiters? What if they are small capitalists who have not yet Rolls Royce motor cars, rich offices and bank accounts. Just the same, they live at the expense of the toiling Native population, although they are sometimes harassed by the imperialist government. You, our opponents, do not want to understand that these small capitalists have attached themselves to the workers and all the toilers and are sucking from them the last drops of blood left by the imperialist blood-suckers. It is true that the Native bourgeoisie suffer from the imperialist order, but does this make them cease to be exploiters of the toiling Native population?

You will now say, yes, that is true. There are Native exploiters, but there is not yet a Native bourgeoisie as a class. But is this the important thing? It is not a question of whether there is a class or not a class, but of the fact that these Native capitalists are exploiting the Native workers, the toiling people in the most varied forms. Stop these academical arguments about whether there is a Native capitalist or not, and explain to the workers that Native society is not united, as Seme and Co. depict it, that it has classes, that it has capitalists who exploit the workers and whose interests do not coincide with the interests of the toilers, and who therefore occupy a special position in the anti-imperialist movement. Instead of helping the workers to get a clear idea of the relationship of class forces, you are helping the national reformists to deceive the workers and all the toilers by your talk about the "United Bantu Nation." Even Seme, the representative of the interests of the tribal Chiefs, who resist the development of Native capitalism, is now forced to raise the question of defending the interests of the Native bourgeoisie, of helping the development of Native capitalism. This is precisely what he has in view in his "A.C.C. Programme."

We must get an absolutely clear notion of one question, that the denial of the existence of the Native bourgeoisie logically leads to the denial of a struggle against national reformism, to the denial of the struggle for the hegemony of the proletariat in the anti-imperialist revolution. We will deal with this in detail in the next article.

Document 85
E. R. Roux, "The Native Exploiters: A reply to 'A. Z.'", *Umsebenzi*, 20 April 1935

I am glad that A. Z.'s article, "Is there a class of Native capitalists in South Africa," has been published, as it gives one an opportunity of re-opening the discussion on this question, a discussion which in my opinion, should never have been closed, and should not be closed now until complete clarity is reached. One of the reasons for the low political level of comrades in this country is that discussions on important questions have been considered "taboo" in the columns of our paper. Even to day I doubt whether the average rank and filer in the party has a clear picture of the Native Republic. This is due to our failure to use the columns of our paper, as they can and should be used, to achieve clarity on all important questions.

With regard to the present controversy, I want to say definitely that there is no doubt that there are numerous bourgeois elements among the Native people. I do not take the line of Comrade Coka[4], who fails to see so much as a trace of a Native bourgeoisie. These Native bourgeois elements exploit their fellow Africans by ordinary methods of capitalistic exploitation. At the same time they provide the economic basis of petty-bourgeois Native national reformism in South Africa. No one in our Party to my knowledge has ever talked about a "United Bantu Nation," and A. Z.'s polemic on this point is simply the setting up of ninepins in order to knock them down again.

The points at issue are: whether the Native bourgeois elements constitute a Native bourgeois class or only a petty bourgeoisie; whether the Native bourgeois elements may be considered to have gone over to the imperialist camp, or whether they are still lined up against imperialism. On the answer to these questions depends the whole attitude of the Party towards the Native bourgeoisie.

In their anxiety to prove that there are exploiting elements among the Bantu, comrades like A Z indulge in all sorts of exaggeration. Seme's "A.C.C." and Isitabataba become a means of "saving the Native bourgeoisie from the effects of the crisis," whereas they are no more than another "get rich quick" scheme on the part of the Congress leaders. It is true these same Congress leaders are petty bourgeoisie or people of a petty bourgeois turn of mind, who are trying to climb up on the backs of their fellow Africans. But to consider them as an organised Native capitalist class is ridiculous. Actually Seme's "A.C.C." scheme never became anything more than so much hot air. The very disunity and ineffectiveness of the various sections of the Congress and I.C.U. and the complete failure of the A.C.C. scheme are proof of the fact that "there exists no Native bourgeois class in South Africa but only individual bourgeois elements." – Thesis of the Sixth Congress of the Communist International on South Africa.

It is hardly necessary to emphasise the effect of the present policy of Anglo-Boer imperialism upon the Native petty-bourgeoisie. Such measures as the Urban Areas Act, Wage Act, Native Service Act, etc., etc. have as their object the almost complete extermination of all those classes of Natives who are not ether wage workers for white bosses in the mines and factories or labour tenants on the farms. In a future article I should like to deal in detail with the effect of this legislation on the Native artizans and petty-bourgeoisie. It is quite clear that these "fellow travellers" will travel a very long way with the workers and peasants in the struggle against imperialism.

Document 86
E. T. Mofutsanyana[5], "The Native Exploiters in South Africa", *Umsebenzi*, 27 April 1935

There is a hopeless confusion in the ranks of the opposition in our party on every question at issue, whether it be on the question of an independent Native Republic, or that of the Native exploiters in South Africa.

Comrade E. R. Roux accuses his supporter, Comrade Coka, of failing to see "so much as a trace of a Native bourgeoisie." But he, himself, sees not further than "Native bourgeois elements." Comrade A. Z.'s article, which gave Comrade Roux "an opportunity of re-opening the discussion on this question" definitely points out that capitalists are those people who are living on an income obtained without labour, and on profit gained from the exploitation of our people, irrespective of the form in which this exploitation takes place. This no Marxist can deny. But Comrade Roux has not yet defined what kind of a person is an element of exploitation, or, to use his own words, a "Native bourgeois element."

To Comrade Roux clarity can only be reached by using the columns of the organ of our party, by allowing all the confused elements in the party to speculate on these questions. To him, in this way the "average rank and filer" in the party will arrive at a complete clarity.

I definitely say that this is absolutely wrong. If Comrade Roux will say that an independent Native republic is a stage towards a workers' and peasants' government, and I say that it is a workers' and peasants' government, what will the average rank and filer who Comrade Roux speaks of, understand?

I say there are Native exploiters, he says there are only elements of exploitation in South Africa. Why not discuss such questions in any form he likes within the party until we come to an understanding? I maintain that speaking of clarity of the average members of the party, when the leading party members are not in agreement on this question, is nonsense. It is only when the leading members of the party arrive at an understanding that we should not only go to the rank and file members of our party and explain to them, but Umsebenzi will give them a line, and not two opinions, to confuse them.

Comrade A. Z., in his article, gave us concrete figures of the exploiting Natives in South Africa.

Recently a company has been formed and registered in Pretoria under section 76 of Act No. 46 of 1926, and this company has a capital of £9,000 (Nine thousand pounds) divided into 36,000 shares of 5/- each. Who are on the "Board of Directors?" They are: Chief Archibald Velile Sandile, Chief Silimela Makinana, Dr W. B. Rubusana[6] and others. Here we are given the names of prominent people only. The object of this company, we are told, is to carry on the business of financiers and traders among the Bantu races, and it proposes to lend money on security.

Is it for profit that this company has come into being, or is it merely to help the Bantu people? No, it is for profit. I am in complete conformity with comrade A. Z. that a denial of the exploiters in South Africa is a denial of a fight against national reformism in this country.

May I in conclusion ask Comrade Roux how much capital one has to have in order to be an exploiter? How many workers has one to exploit and in what form? When do the petty bourgeoisie qualify to be the bourgeoisie? How many exploiters make a class? The industrial bourgeoisie we have not got.

Document 87
"Lessons of the All-Bantu Convention", *The Spark*, 2, 2, February 1936

The All-Bantu Convention which was held on 16th–18th December at the Batho Location, Bloemfontein, was such a farce, with features so disgraceful and so distasteful, that we would prefer not to write about it at all. When an event which should be of first-class importance turns out to be not only a failure but a farce, it is usual to think that the less said about it, the better. But it is not so in this case; and, however much we dislike the task of criticising it, we feel that it is our plain duty to undertake this unpleasant job. Not because we believe that Conferences, Conventions, Congresses, can bring a solution of our ills. Just the opposite. We believe only in the class struggle, in the revolutionary struggle of the masses, and not in resolutions and speeches of so-called rational leaders. There is nothing more dangerous for the revolutionary struggle than illusions. Illusions of every kind must be destroyed. Unfortunately, even in the revolutionary camp there are many, far too many illusions. [....]

But the revolutionary Marxist [...] must patiently follow the historic process and search for ways and means to influence and accelerate it. For this reason we cannot satisfy ourselves with the mere fact that the All-Bantu Conference was just another failure and disappointment in addition to the many previous failures and disappointments. To those who may not have realised the fact for themselves, we must show that it was indeed a failure; then we must analyse the various reports of the proceedings and discover why it was a failure, and who is responsible for this failure; we must decide further whether the failure was unavoidable; and having done all this, we shall be in a position to draw lessons from this Convention for guidance in future action and tactics.

First of all, in fairness to the delegates, we must note that the gathering at Bloemfontein was not conducted as a convention in the sense in which that word is commonly used, and the delegates cannot be blamed for the farce that followed. They were not presented with any agenda; the "election" of officials, committees, and sub-committees took place before the main bulk of the delegates arrived; the resolutions were forced down their throats. Professor Jabavu, in the chair, adopted steam-rolling tactics, and played off upon the delegates the unscrupulous trick of not allowing any addition or alteration to the resolutions. When the Convention dared to put through a resolution of its own, the Executive Committee brushed it aside, re-drafted it. Thus the blame for the failure must be attributed not to the Convention, but to the small clique of Jabavu and Co. It was a one-man show. Jabavu in the most dictatorial manner ran the Convention just as he wanted it. No wonder that he is the only one who is satisfied with the results. Even those two paid tools of the ruling classes, "Umteteli" and "The Bantu World"[7], who for months have devoted all their leading articles to the Bills and the coming Convention, have now after a single short summary closed their mouths and taken refuge in silence. As if by magic they switched over to miscellaneous matters, such as, "Behaviour of the Bantu", "Good Manners", "Good Wishes for 1936", and so on, but not a word about the Bills and future action. Are they ashamed of the results of the Convention? Or have they received fresh instructions? We do not know. We may presume that some sense of shame is at work. All the "Umteteli" could say after the Convention was that the Bills "shall not become law *in their present form*". A little alteration here and there would meet the case and "Umteteli" would be happy! "The

Bantu World" is happy already in the mere fact that "in spite of the extravagant (?) language used by some of the delegates, the Convention was not permeated by a revolutionary spirit, but by a spirit of friendliness ..." If the expression of Jabavu's face during the Convention is taken as a criterion of the Convention spirit, then it was indeed a spirit of "friendliness". For Jabavu was continually shouting with laughter and grimacing like a jackanapes. Even now, the Professor is still happy, so happy that the proceedings of the Convention have evaporated from his usually brilliant memory. Only two weeks after, he stated in Kokstad that "all the resolutions were passed without a single dissentient in the General Convention" ("Cape Argus": 7.1.35). This is simply a lie. Every delegate, every reporter can tell him that even the main resolution on the franchise was *passed by a majority only and amid cries of* "No! No!" This, however, by the way. It is harmless.

But far different is his activity on the Convention. When we ask the question, who was responsible for the failure, for the farce, there can be only one answer, clear and unhesitating: Jabavu. *He* is reponsible; *he* is to blame. His clique, Xuma, Dube, Godlo, Ka Seme, etc., are only secondary figures. We may hope that the Bantu intelligentsia and the Bantu masses, who are as yet blindly following their idol, will learn from this Convention what we have known all along, namely, that Jabavu is a tool of the oppressors, consciously betraying the cause of Bantu freedom. As we dealt extensively with Jabavu in No. 7 of "The Spark", it would be superfluous to waste more paper on his speeches during the Convention. They are beneath any serious criticism.

In the October issue of "The Spark" our anxiety concerning the outcome of the Convention was expressed as follows:

> Those who know the past history of the African National Congress will understand our anxiety. The proposal is that the All-Bantu Convention be called under the auspices of the African National Congress by the President of that body, Dr. Ka Seme. If the All-Bantu Convention is to consist of Paramount Chiefs, Chiefs, Bishops and other Ministers, headmen and "some other" leaders, and if the Convention is to be under the leadership and influence of Dr. Ka Seme, Professor Jabavu, and similar leaders, then we may say that the Convention is doomed. We shall see yet another document drawn up, *respectfully and humbly begging the government to show greatness of heart* in consistence with *the high Christian principles,* etc., etc., ad nauseam. Then the "Umteteli" can continue to warn its readers against the dangerous agitators on the Rand and Jabavu can reiterate his fear of the Bantu becoming communistic. The Bills will be passed.

The Convention procedure and resolutions have fully confirmed our predictions. Its results, if we are to judge from the resolutions, were even worse than might have been expected.

There was no determination at all *to fight* for the rights of the Bantu, even for those remnants of rights of which it is now proposed to rob them.

There was not even a definite *condemnation* of the Bills *in toto*, as might have been expected after the ferment of the past six months and the repeated expression of Bantu public opinion, supplementing the adverse Resolutions sent up to Government from the five Regional Conferences.

There was not even a clear pronouncement of rejection, a pronouncement that the Bantu will never accept this insult and injury. No. Instead of this, instead of demanding their rights, the Convention passed a resolution on the Natives Representation Bill which amounts to an admission of defeat beforehand. It limits itself to "opposing", it pins its faith in the Senate, in the Governor-General as Paramount Chief, in the British Parliament and the British King, and as a last resort in an appeal to the Almighty.

The same old, worn out illusions in spite of all. It is tragically sad to read that an All-Bantu Convention, representing, or pretending to represent six million Bantu, i.e., three-fourths of the population, *had nothing to offer but an appeal to observe Sunday, Jan. 19, as a day of humiliation and prayer.*

And how typical of Jabavu is the following passage from the Resolution:

> The denial to the African people of participation in the government of the country, of which they are an integral part, on the basis of common citizenship, is not only immoral and unjust, but will inflame passions and fertilize the soil on which propagandists will sow the seeds of discontent and unrest.

The Convention (or, to be more exact, Jabavu?) is here not so much concerned with the political status of the Bantu, which will resemble that of the slaves of ancient Greece and Rome if they continue to listen obediently to Jabavu and Co., but is above all else afraid of propagandists. The Professor and Co., have been using this "high diplomacy" for the last fifteen years. In the same sentence they fire off a threat to the Govenrment that its measures will rouse agitation, and a warning to the oppressed to beware of those criminals, the agitators. But the threat is not seriously meant. The Govenrment and the ruling classes may laugh at it, and Jabavu, their servant, may laugh with them. It is the old, familiar language everywhere of the servants of Capitalism: of the Jabavus, Brookeses, Ballingers, The slaves must be obedient; the slaves must not listen to the agitators and propagandists, lest they lose their chains and go free. Capitalism and its servants must prevent this at all costs. [....]

Then something extraordinary happened. The Convention passed a resolution all by itself, without the leaders. But school-children must not dare to do such a thing without the schoolmaster and all the teachers! And so the blunder was quickly wiped out. Dr. Xuma, as Chairman of the Executive and Vice-Chairman of the Convention, came out with a statement to the press which sums up and concludes in the most bewildering, in the most astounding manner, the whole pitiful farce. It is hardly believable, yet it is a fact. The Doctor, who is a tool of the Professor, announced that the Executive Committee had definitely brushed aside the findings and resolution adopted by the Convention and had substituted for it another resolution of its own. "In a statement handed to the 'Friend' Dr. Xuma dissociated himself and the Executive Committee from the general protest against General Hertzog's black manifesto and the attitude of the Union Government towards the Natives". ("Cape Times": 20.12.35.)

It is too much for Jabavu, Xuma and Co. to *protest* against Gen. Hertzog's policy and against the oppression and repression of the Bantu. They prefer to substitute for it another resolution in which we read: "*And we now pray as his Majesty's loyal subjects who have been patient 'like asses' and loyal,* despite all these disabilities, that His Majesty's Government *should consider* the redress of their grievances and alleviate the black man's lot." (Our emphasis. – Ed.) Having read this, what can we do but wash our hands in disgust? What can be said of such a scandalous attitude? What comment can be made on such cynical mockery of the rights and findings of a Convention? What words can sufficiently condemn this servile crawling on the belly? Pah!

The Conference was a failure in yet another aspect. For years we have heard appeals for "National" unity among the Bantu. For years we have heard that the curse of the Bantu, the cause of all their troubles, is their internal strife, their inability to form a United Front on account of tribalism and traditional feuds. But the painful thing is that every Bantu "leader" is so continually exploiting for his own personal ends the cry for unity, is so incessantly declaiming "Union is strength", that nobody any longer takes them seriously. We are for once in agreement with the "Bantu World", when it says on the subject of corrupt leaders: "The majority of our educated men will not do anything for the race unless there is a profit to be derived from it."

The Convention also revealed this ugly feature. Remembering this, it is easy to understand the sudden outburst from the Rev. J. L. Dube, one of the "leaders", and a member of the clique. Evidently the "leaders" have fallen out among themselves. The Rev. J. L. Dube represented Natal, being the *President of the African National Congress of Natal*, which claims to put the "National" cause above everything else. Moreover, this same Rev. Dube not long ago issued a booklet entitled "The Enemy of the Black Man is Himself", in which he clearly shows that, so long as the Bantu are divided, and so long as they fight among themselves for leadership, there can be no progress and no hope for the liberation of the Bantu people. Now, not during the Convention, but just after it has ended, when his action would be more effective and more harmful, Mr. Dube comes out openly with an attack on the Convention, an attack on the Cape vote, and other matters. And of course the Imperialist press hastened to give prominence to his statement in capital letters: "Bitterly Disappointed by Convention Resolutions, Says Rev. Dube". What was the cause of his attack? Was it that even the meek resolutions and Jabavu's steam-roller tactics in stifling opposition did not satisfy the "serious and moderate thinkers present" whom Mr. Dube claims to represent and protect? "The language irritated them and the Conference failed to achieve the object for which they thought it was called." Was this the cause of the Reverend's outburst? Or was it that he had not been appointed Vice-Chairman, or to some other coveted position? Or was it another personal quarrel? We do not know. But at any rate it was calculated to do harm to the Convention, to lower its prestige in the eyes of the ruling classes. It has shown that the hope of those "National" circles, that the Convention would at least bring the Bantu nearer together and produce a United Front of North and South against enslavement and oppression, has not materialised. The rift is as wide as ever, because the leaders are as corrupt and stupid as ever.

If you read carefully the Convention Resolutions and compare them with Pamphlet No. 1, "Criticism of the Native Bills", by Jabavu, you will see that they are in substance, if not in words, identical. And we need not repeat now what we said in October. The question now is whether this failure was unavoidable. What was needed in order to bring about a different result?

In order to change the course of the Convention, in order to ensure the adoption of a different attitude, a firm stand, a firm NO to oppression, a firm demand for equal rights, a firm demand for land, *their l*and, a firm demand for equal taxation, a firm refusal to accept discrimination on the ground of colour of the skin; in order to adopt such an attitude instead of that of inferiority ("junior partners", according to Jabavu), the Convention would have had to brush aside the whole clique of the leaders – Jabavu, Ka Seme, Xuma, Dube, Godlo, and the rest, and to bring in those who are not paid Government officials, those who are not afraid for their jobs, those who have not been corrupted by the bourgeoisie, those who are ready to fight for the freedom, liberation, rights, and welfare of the Bantu, those who are able to lead the fight. The question, whether such a leadership was present there or not, is irrelevant. The fact is that it did not come to the fore. The fact is that in the whole Convention there was none to come forward openly, to expose the traitor's part played by the clique, to show the Bantu where these leaders with their treacherous method of submission have brought the Bantu, there was none to show them a new way, *there was none to give them a lead.* The Convention was a failure, inasmuch as there was not even a small revolutionary wing present at it (a few of the C.P. delegates were more busy with drinking than with the Convention), and there was as yet no sign that such a wing is going to develop. In these circumstances the failure was unavoidable.

Nevertheless, there is no cause for despair. For, after all, the question of rights and land will not be settled by Conventions, Conferences, Parliaments. The question of freedom and of land for the Bantu can be settled in one way only – the way of Revolution. Only ignoramuses or supporters of Imperialism can look for effectual concessions, liberal reforms. It must be borne in mind that Imperialism-Capitalism is not going *to give* equal rights to the Bantu, no matter the Union Parliament consist of 150 Hertzogs or of 150 Sir-James-Rose-Inneses.[8] The Bantu can only get his rights, his national freedom, by Revolution, by overthrowing Imperialism-Capitalism, by *taking* what belongs to him. Moreover, it must be realised that no matter whether the scheduled released areas are already occupied by Natives or not, no matter whether the total of additional land freed for them is 3 1/2 million or 7 1/2 million morgen, no matter whether Parliament will or will not provide the Trust with sufficient money for the appropriation of this land, Imperialism-Capitalism is not going *to give* the Bantu sufficient land to live on. For it needs his cheap slave-labour on the farms and mines and in industry in order to make its profits.

But the Bantu is not going to remain a slave for ever, he is not going to suffocate for lack of land in the Reserves, he is not going to be forever driven from the towns to the Reserves and from the Reserves to the farms and mines. The Bantu is not going to perish. He will take the land, he will take his rights. He must revolt and he will revolt. No Jabavus, no Ka Semes can keep him chained for ever to the slavery wagon by pretending to help him with a better kind of yoke, or to ease his chains a bit. He will find out their tricks, he will learn by experience that they, the pretended leaders, who are dragging him away from the revolutionary camp, are his enemies; and he will deal with them accordingly. This All-Bantu Convention by its failure is bound to make him think and learn in this direction. This and the subsequent events will open his eyes and will free him from illusions. This is the main thing. Then we shall see Conventions wholly different from this of Bloemfontein, which was not a Convention but a Farce.

Yet we cannot look passively on at the historical process. We cannot leave the Bantu to learn by experience, waiting till he then comes to us. We must go to him, we must show him the way to the revolutionary camp, we must guide him, and make it easier for him to part with his old illusions and to smash his old idols.

Document 88
"No Compromise", *Umsebenzi*, 29 February 1936

Hertzogs' New Bill

The All African Convention has issued a statement explaining why they must not compromise. They see the new plan of separate register for Native voters as an "atrophied form of the Cape Native franchise." They stand for full political equality of black and white as citizens of the Union. They say that they are convinced that the fundamental principle of full political equality, till now entrenched in the Cape Native franchise, will be wilfully and unjustly violated "by the passing of such a measure." They maintain that "the policy of common citizenship is the only one that would ensure harmony between the races."

The Convention has correctly interpreted the Bill, even the amended Bill, as an attack upon the principle of equal citizenship for black and white in the Union of South Africa.

It is not to the point to argue, as many do, that the principle of full equal citizenship never has been upheld in the Union; that the Cape Native franchise is useless; that as the Natives in the other Provinces have no vote therefore the Natives in the Cape should lose their vote. All these arguments are put forward to confuse the issue and to mislead the people. It is true that the Natives of the Transvaal, Free State and Natal have never been allowed to vote. But that is not a good reason why the Natives should surrender their rights of citizenship in the Cape Province! The remedy would be to give the vote to all the Natives in the Union, on an equal basis with the whites! It is not true that the vote of the Cape Natives has done them no good in that Province. On the contrary it is the fact that the Natives are better off in the Cape Province than anywhere else in the Union. For example they do not have to carry passes!

FIGHT THE NEW BILL

The position is that the first Bill and the new Bill in its altered form are equally unacceptable to the Bantu citizens of the Union. Both are an attack on the fundamental principle of full citizenship in the Union for both black and white. A special register for Native voters is of no use to Natives. What we demand is inclusion of all Natives in the Union on the ordinary voters' roll on an equal basis with the whites.

Now that agitation and resentment have accomplished so much in having made the Prime Minister change the Bill a little, we must continue the fight still more strongly. We must agitate for full voting rights, equal to those of the white man. We must not rest till we have made the Cape Native franchise safe! And we must fight on till we have won the vote for all the Natives throughout the Union. When we have won all these demands there is another thing to fight for: the right to elect Natives to sit in the House of Assembly. Only when this is won can we say that the Natives have real citizenship in the Union of South Africa.

EFFECT OF NEW BILL

Speaking on the new form of the Native Representation Bill which was introduced by Hertzog on Wednesday, Mr Rheinallt Jones of the Institute of Race Relations said: "Whether the Natives get three representatives or thirty in the House it does not matter. The issue is that the Natives consider that their political standing can only be protected by a common citizenship expressed through a common franchise. A separate roll would mean dividing the country into two or more racial groups. It would crystallise racial divisions into racial antagonism."

This is very clearly put. Let us add a comment. It is clear that the interests of the white and black man in this country are so entangled and linked together that they cannot possibly be separated. What hurts the white also hurts the black and what hurts the black is also, sooner or later, dangerous to the white. The workers of both races are oppressed by the capitalist rulers of this country. To pretend that their interests are somehow different, so that they must be placed on separate voters' roll and have separate representatives, is a dangerously unsound plan. Those who have conceived this plan have done so in the belief that they can succeed in persuading the black workers of this country that their interests are different from those of the white workers. When they manage to do this they think that they will be able to oppress both sections much more easily than if the two sections see clearly that they are united in a common struggle against oppression in all forms. The whole scheme is a vicious device of the capitalist rulers of this country. They hope to deceive the workers. But in this they have not succeeded. From all over the country resolutions of protest are pouring in. The first effect of this storm of opposition has been to force Hertzog to modify somewhat and to present in a disguised form the main item of the Bill the destruction of the Cape Native franchise.

Document 89
"People's Front and the Cry for Unity in South Africa", *The Spark*, 2, 4, April 1936

The drive for Unity in the working class and for the establishment of a broad "People's Front" to stop fascism and war, proclaimed by the Seventh Congress of the Communist International as a panacea for all ills in all countries, was bound eventually to reach South Africa. Together with all the other Stalinist parties, the Communist Party of South Africa, i.e., the few officials left from the former Party, received this important communication. And as they have to carry out the instructions, no matter whether they are or are not suitable or even possible, they tried to do their best, just as they had done before with the separate "Red" Trade Unions, or with the "Native Republics" as a step towards a Workers' and Peasants' Republic.

A "braod" League against fascism and war was duly formed – on paper, of course; and, when the Italo–Abyssinian War broke out, a subsidiary organisation of this League sprang up with a fine-sounding name: "Hands off Abyssinia Committee", and with the usual principles of the broad People's Front, that is to say, without principles. Anybody and everybody was welcome, from the Fabians to the Young Men's Christian Association, and from the University Women's Association to the Society for the Prevention of Cruelty to Animals. And as might be expected, the most prominent place was given to the Churches. It is true that some of the Churches did not make use of this golden opportunity to show their ardent desire for peace. Especially conspicuous was the absence of the Roman Catholic representative, though we had been told by the Stalinists that the hostility of the Catholic masses towards war is astounding, and to-day more than ever. We presume that all the Churches and denominations (are they not all for peace?) were invited. In spite, however, of this *broad mass (!) basis*, and good advertising, the People's Front did not prove a success. It may be argued that here as everywhere else it accomplished its task, viz., to bring pressure to bear upon the Government to fulfil its obligation to the League of Nations and apply sanctions. As a matter of fact, the Hands off Abyssinia Committee did send a wire to the Prime Minister to this effect. But, since the Prime Minister stated that without their reminder the Union of South Africa had already voluntarily subscribed to all the League sanctions (including the payment of £150,000 to Italy, the annual shipping subsidy, paid with the approval of the League of Nations), there was nothing left for the Hands off Abyssinia Committee to do than to die peacefully with a clear conscience, feeling that it had done everything possible for Abyssinia and against Mussolini.

But the People's Front idea has not died. It may seem that as a good article to have in stock, it soon found imitations in all corners, set up by every would-be leader. The cry for Unity was always a strong card in the S.A. Labour movement, and was used by every Labour politican and demagogue. But it had grown stale. Here was something new. And during the last two months the so-called Labour Press has been full of appeals for United Fronts and broad People's Fronts against fascism and war. But it does not take long to discover that they are the same old trash that is repeated every week in the official organ of Stalinism, "The Inprecor". And it does not take long to discover that the leaders are the same old and young bureaucrats and demagogues, who used the Labour movement as a source of income and now look upon it as a hunting ground for fatter jobs; they are the same unscrupulous officials who will go over to any party that promises a better job. Fusion nowadays is so popular with the bureaucracies of the Second and the Third International everywhere, why not Fusion in South Africa? And People's Fronts are so popular with those bureaucracies everywhere, why not in South Africa? It is true that the fusion of two corpses, such as the Stalinist Communist Party and the Labour Party, will produce nothing but a bigger stink. But why worry? The main thing is the job.

That old demagogue, E. Sacks, in a "statesmanlike" review of the whole situation, makes a fiery appeal for (i) a United Front of workers and poor farmers, and (ii) for a People's Front against fascism and war, and (iii) for a United Trade Union movement ("Forward", 14.2.36). As a way out he makes the following suggestions: "Given the necessary leadership, energy, courage, and determination, a mighty United front of mine workers, railway workers, workers in the secondary industries, civil servants, shop and office workers, the landless and those struggling with a bit of land, the intellectuals and lower middle class people, and *all people who value the hard-earned democratic rights*, can be built up, both on the industrial and political." (Our emphasis. Ed.) Then, after calling upon the leaders of the Labour Party and the rest, to remember the solemn duty resting upon them, he concludes with the question: Who will take the lead?"

First of all, like every statesman in this country, he speaks *only* of the white population, the white miners, the poor white landless, etc. And then this Trade Union leader, who calls himself a Marxist, who was once a member of the C.P., proposes a United front of all the people of South Africa. If in the first part of his proposition the big capitalists and mine-owners are not included, they may still come into this mighty United front, according to the second part. All people who value the democratic rights may come in! And who but the Grey Shirts do *not* value the democratic rights? Even General Smuts, even Abe Bailey value the democratic rights.[9]

But "friend" Sacks is not very original, because two or three months before his appeal, there was a similar appeal made in the United States by the leader of the American Communist Party, who went even further: "The new anti-fascist mass party of toilers should also strive to include sections of the sprouting fascist or partly fascist organisations and tendencies, such as Company Unions, American Legion Posts, and groups of the Coughlin and Huey Long movements"[10], etc. (The Communist, Oct. 1935.)

The appeal was, of course, promptly accepted by Henderson, Secretary of the Labour Party, who agrees that "something must be done for the good of the people", and is prepared to take the lead!

He admits that he cannot promise a Utopia, but you must consider the advantage of having "one political organisation entitled to speak on behalf of the workers". And of course this organisation will be the South African Labour Party with its programme of complete segregation of black and white!

"In taking this step, the Labour Party wish it to be clearly understood that there is no question of fraternising or pacts with any other political party".

In other words, the Stalinists shall hand in an application for affiliation in the Labour Party, as they have already done in Great Britain? Otherwise, no People's Front, no lead for the workers? Poor South Africa! It will have to remain without a People's Front, in spite of the fraternisation of Weinberg with Burnside. For, after all, the exclusion of the Bantu and Coloured could be done once (at the inaugural meeting of the League against Fascism in Cape Town), but a second time it might be too much even for the well-drilled Stalinist corps.

The Labour Party is dead. Even the most prominent members of the Labour Party themselves have admitted that the Party is dead. If Mr. Sacks wants to resurrect the Labour Party, having in mind some leadership, or – who knows? – a seat in Parliament for himself; if the C.P. wants to resurrect the Labour Party in order to carry out the instructions of the Comintern, for the sake of building a United front or a "broad" People's front, the working class in South Africa has no interest whatever in the resurrection of the S.A. Labour Party. Let the sleeping dogs lie; let the dying dogs die. A party which has produced only traitors to the working-class cause, a party which has always been a place of refuge for adventurers and job-hunters, a party which has lately become infected with vermin, infected with fascism, to such a degree that the few old die-hard supporters have had to leave it, a party which was always, even at its best, based on racialism, on patriotism, on white chauvinism, a party which supported the bourgeoisie against the workers, neglecting working-class interests for the sake of the small aristocracy of Labour, a party which put on its banner: "Keep the Kafir in his place", has itself no place in the Labour movement to-day. Not only on the question of war, but even on the question of fascism, there can be no talk of United fronts with the so-called Labour Party, for how can a party, which supports all anti-native (fascist) legislation, fight against fascism? And how can a party which is not a working-class party do the work of a true Labour Party?

There is no need to argue that the Communist Party is dead. The thing is obvious. Everyone knows it. The few leaders left are fighting each other, and that makes a noise. But children learn at school that it is the empty barrel that makes the noise, not the barrel that is full of wine. The C.P. is pretending in order to be kept going – not by its membership; it has almost no members – but by the few intellectual lawyers and doctors, who have no need of theory, Marxism, criticism, class struggle. They are satisfied with the prestige of the Soviet Union, and flattered by the friendship or the services of the Stalinist bureaucracy. When they can go to Moscow for a trip – and they can afford to go – and are received there in princely fashion, they lose their head completely and are happy serving without asking questions. People's fronts are the real place for these loose adherents. It gives them a chance to call themselves revolutionaries, feeling sure that the Revolution will not come in their time. "Let Socialism be built in the Soviet Union and we will be satisfied with this shining example and conversion by means of it". Yet they mean well. It is not their fault that they are not Marxists. There is so little time for reading and study!

United Fronts! This term is too much and too often abused and misunderstood. A united front is not a remedy, a cure for everything under any circumstances. For in the last instance a United front is only a part of revolutionary tactics *in a revolutionary situation*. With the exception of a united front for specific, strictly defined issues, it serves no purpose to establish United fronts where no revolutionary situation exists. Yet another condition is necessary for a United front, namely, the presence of parties which have a big following, which have the masses of the workers behind them. But besides the fact that there is as yet no revolutionary situation in South Africa, where are the parties which can claim to have the masses of the workers behind them? The Communist Party? the Labour Party? the Farmers and Workers Party? It is therefore ridiculous to indulge in talk about marching separately and striking together, as many of our demagogic revolutionaries in all quarters are doing, including even some who claim to be followers of the Fourth International.

So, then, it is idle to *talk* of United fronts, for we have no parties to form them. We have only shadows and corpses. Even more foolish is it to talk of People's fronts, to fight the battles against fascism and war, battles which only the working class *can* fight out. None will do it for us; we ourselves must do it. But for this a new Party is necessary. Not based on chauvinism like the Labour Party; not based on the orders and ukases of a bureaucracy which is concerned only with building Socialism in one country; not based on fantastic dreams and appeals to morality and justice like the Lucas group. Not these, but a party based on the science of Revolutionary Marxism, on the teachings of Marx, Engels, Lenin and Trostky, a Party which representes the true interests of the *whole* working class, with a clear revolutionary programme, corresponding to the real national and international situation. Only such a Party will be able to fight the decisive battle against fascism and war, which means in the last instance the battle for the Social Revolution.

Document 90
"Hertzog's Native Bill Passed: Only 11 Oppose Reactionary Measure", *Umsebenzi*, 11 April 1936

HOFMEYR SURPRISES US
General Hertzog's Bill, disenfranchising the Cape Africans, was carried at its third reading by a joint sitting of both houses of Parliament last Monday night. The voting was: 169 for, 11 against.

Among those voted for the Bill were the three members of the "Labour" Party. We record their names that posterity may know what SOCIALISM meant in South Africa in 1936:– Walter B. Madeley, Brurnside and van der Berg.[11]

The following voted against the Bill: J. H. Hofmeyr, Colonel C. F. Stallard, J. S. Marwick, C. W, A. Coulter, J. G. Derbyshire, J. Chalmers, A. J. McCallum, R. S. du Toit, R. M. Christopher, Senator F. S. Malan and M. Alexander.

Mr J. H. Hofmeyr's action comes as a very pleasant surprise to us. We had thought he had already gone too far on the road of demagogy and compromise to speak and vote as he did. It was said in some quarters that he has committed political suicide. It was believed by many that he has at least as good a chance as Mr Pirow of becoming the future premier of South Africa. Now that chance is gone. But we hope Hofmeyr will stick to his guns.

Comrade MASIU Holds Up the Bill

On Tuesday an interesting incident happened. A Cape African who is on the voters roll has applied for an interdict by the Supreme Court declaring the Act illegal.

A sensation was caused in the lobby of Parliament when the Sheriff attempted to serve notice of the application upon Mr Speaker. The Sheriff was refused admission to the House, and he then tied the notice to the members' entrance nearest to Mr Speaker's chambers.

The aplication has been set down to be heard on Friday, April 17, and pending the determination of this matter it is unlikely that any further steps will be taken towards having the Bill certified and made law.

Masiu's action is a sequel to the point raised at the joint sitting yesterday afternoon by Mr C, W. A. Coulter when he argued that Parliament has no power to take off the common register the name of any Native appearing on it.

The procedure adopted by Masiu follows that used in the famous case of Trewothem versus the Attorney-General of New South Wales, in which an attempt was made by Mr Lang, then Prime Minister of New South Wales to override the provisions provided for the amendment of the State constitution which were declared invalid in law.

In this affidavit filed before the Supreme Court of the Cape Province Masiu says: "it is essential for the vindication of the rights of the applicant that the hearing of this application should occur before certification of the Bill by Governor-Geoeral." The applicant goes on to state "I am specially and particularly interested in the matters dealt with by the said Bill. In particular Section six thereof prescribes that the Minister of Native Affairs, or some other Minister acting in his stead, shall cause the register (hereinafter referred to as the Cape Native Voters' Roll) to be compiled which .. in particular shall include my name, and upon the lists of person qualified to vote at the elections of members of the House of Assembly, shall be removed therefrom."

ALL EYES TO THE NATIONAL CONVENTION

All eyes are now turned on the African National Convention which meets in Bloemfontein in June to consider how to carry forward the fight for democratic rights for black men in South Africa. They will have to decide whether to follow the policy of abstention (that is to have nothing to do with the working of the new Act) or on the other hand to use the new All-Union Bhunga as a propagandist platform from which to demand the extension of the franchise and the vote for all South Africans (black and white) on the same basis.

The Communist Party must give a lead to the toiling masses of South Africa on this all-important question.

Document 91
John Gomas, "The Native Representation Bill is Passed: What Must be Done Now?" *Umsebenzi*, 25 April 1936

Despite the vast majority of Natives and many other freedom-loving people of South Africa being strongly opposed to the Native Representation Bill of General Hertzog, the joint session of Parliament and the Senate had the brazenness to pass the Bill. It is correct to say that this Parliament and Senate do not represent the interests of the greater section of the South African population – the Native people – but only that of the small group of capitalist and landlord exploiters. The fact is clearly demonstrated that we have a dictatorship established over all the toilers of South Africa, and particularly over the Native people by this minority whose sole object is to exploit the toilers for profit – for Big Business.

Had this government been a democratic state, i.e., carrying out the wishes of the majority of the people of South Africa, then the uncompromising objections against the Native Bills at the All African National Convention and the protests all over South Africa should have been taken into consideration and the Bills dropped. But no, fairplay and rule by the majority is a thing that these capitalists plunderers of human rights can ill afford, for that would spill the domination of their system of robbery.

This government of imperialist robbers are not satisfied that they have robbed the Native people entirely of their land, subjected to a state of beastial misery, cruel exploitation and treated worse than the disease affected foreigners in our own home land. The passing of the Hertzog bill has for its object to deprive the Native people of the Cape of the last vestige of the elementary democratic right – the vote – thus to further stifle progress and "keep the nigger in his place".

If our reformist friends, who prate so much about adopting constitutional methods to gain our rights are at all serious, then it is high time that they took this lesson seriously to heart. It must be only too obvious to any sensible person that the white rulers are determined not to render any betterment in the conditions of the Native people but is studiously planning to increase this exploitation and oppression, as instanced by the oppressive legislation and restrictive measures passed against the Native people from time to time.

Why is it that the white rulers treat the Native people with the utmost contempt? It is because the Native people do not put up a sufficiently *powerful mass organised struggle* for better conditions of living and for all elementary human rights of freedom.

The Communist Party have always for many years stated that the *Unity of Action* of the whole Native population and its organisations is the main and decisive condition which will make our struggle for freedom victorious. Ten years ago, when the Native Bills of Hertzog were presented to the country the Communist Party proposed that united action with the African National Congress and the I.C.U. should be established for the fight against these Native Bills and for the immediate demands of the Native people. The proposals of the C.P. was not only turned down by the leaders of the A.N.C. and I.C.U. but they energetically opposed the C.P. in its efforts to bring about unity of action in demand for the most essential needs of the Native people. It cannot be denied that this attitude of the A.N.C. and I.C.U. leaders have strengthened the hand of the oppressors. However, we say to these people there is still time to repent and make amends to their countrymen. We therefore greet most heartily the uncompromising stand of many of these leaders against the Native Bills at the Bloemfontein All African National Convention.

The Native Representation Bill which, as is boasted, is the better part of General Hertzog's life work, is to tie down the Native people further into perpetual slavery. This Bill is passed, and the other Bills undoubtedly will be an easy-going matter through Parliament. Whilst it can be said that these reactionary and despotic have aroused the bitter resentment and indignation of the whole Native, non-European and white democratic minded population against the government of oppressors, it must be honestly admitted that the "peaceful", "uncompromising" form of opposition to the Bills as decided by the Convention was hopelessly ineffective, and left the Government stone cold.

There is no doubt that the government was aware that the mind of the Native people was agitated to a point of revolting indignation against the Government. But the Government was promptly reassured by the "academic" form of "uncompromising" opposition and the *defeatist* attitude taken up by the leadership of the Convention. Professor Jabavu said: "we cannot fight the Government for we do not possess guns". This assertion, coming from the leader of the Convention, simply damped the spirit of militancy and expectancy for action that was prevalent at the Convention from the begining. It was apparent, too that every attempt was made to curb and keep in check the virile individuals who made proposals that the convention should decide for militant action in the form of protest demonstrations, passive resistance, to organise a general strike, to refuse to pay taxes, etc.

This was curtly turned down from the stage and all the meek and mild and defeatist "leaders" were given every opportunity to discourage the delegates of the Convention, finally these leaders succeeded in passing lengthy pious resolutions as an attempt to "educate" the "misguided" government and calling for a "day of prayer and humiliation" on the 19th January, the only effect this had on the government was the satisfactory assurance that the indignant masses of Native people were well under control of chickenhearted "leaders."

FOR A PROGRAMME OF ACTION
Now what must be done? Undoubtedly the significance of the Convention is of enormous historical importance to the Native people's struggle for freedom. New intensive preparations must be made to make the 28th June meeting of the Convention (at Bloemfontein) a mighty force which must decide to work out a programme of organisation and action of an all in National Liberation Movement with the general slogan "Equality, Land and Freedom."

All delegates must come to the Convention with constructive proposals to work out a programme which should contain the most immediate and essential needs of the Native people. In brief, it should contain demands for the complete abolition of all discriminating and oppressive laws against the African people in all spheres of life; for an equal redistribution of the land; for complete equality with the white citizens; and to participate equally in the governing, administrative, productive, commercial, judicial and educational institutions of this country. Such a programme which will challenge in every respect the whole system of exploitation, oppression and discrimination must meet with the whole-hearted support of all the Native and coloured people.

FOR AN ALL NATIONAL LIBERATION MOVEMENT

What form of organisation must this Convention hammer out? At present the Convention is not established on a membership nor even on a basis of organisations affiliated to the Convention. The millions of Native people are unorganised and none of the existing organisations can claim that it is the leader of the people in their needs and aspirations. Therefore an entirely new organisation must be built up by the people, existing under the democratic control of the people, an organisation that is connected closely with the people and is at the same time able to unite and co-ordinate the actions of the existing organisations. This organisation must be based on individual membership as well as providing for other organisations of the non-European people to affiliate to it, such as Trade Unions, churches etc.

As the Trade Union form of organisation for workers is their most powerful weapon and since the Native workers are the largest and lowest paid section of the working class in S. Africa, this new national mass organisation must give every assistance to forming Trade Unions of Native workers, which must be affiliated to the National Liberation Movement. It is also necessary that this organisation provide for the establishment of a united front with those sections of the white population which are also exploited by the capitalists and landlords. Such unity with the OPPRESSED PART of the white population would add additional strength to our movement for national emancipation and create a fuller guarantee of victory.

As to what this national liberation or anti-imperialist organisation should be named is not important. What is vitally important is that the programme should outline clearly the demands in the struggle for national liberation, to determine effective methods of struggles in the past showed clearly that the Union Government did not take note of our demands and resolutions, and that only a proprety militant organised mass movement can force the Government to fulfill our demands.

It now becomes our BOUNDEN DUTY to minimise all minor differences, to establish co-operation between organisations and individual leaders to work energe [-----] tion to have represented at the 28th June Convention the most politically advanced, brave, energetic and patriotic leaders pledged to the cause of our liberation; to arouse the masses of African people to the necessity of supporting and to become active in this mass liberation movement; to form local committees in towns, villages, locations and kraals to carry out these tasks successfully.

The Communist Party is ready to support wholeheartedly the united front of the people against hunger and slavery. The Communist Party will devote all its energy and will put forward its forces for the preparation of this 28th June Convention so as to assure its success as a broad, fully-representative people's Convention. All hands to the cause of freedom!

Document 92
"Communist Party of South Africa Plenum Held from 5th to 8th April 1936", *Umsebenzi*, 16 May 1936

RESOLUTIONS
1. That this Plenum of Activists decides that immediate steps be taken to give every assistance in the formation of an Anti-Imperialist and national Liberation movement on the lines of the Programme of the National Liberation League of Cape Town, and if necessary, in conjunction with the latter, and under the slogan of "Equality, Land and Freedom".
2. That every attempt should be made to arouse the non-European people, particularly the Native people, to the significance of the June meeting of the All National Convention in the struggle against the worsening of the political, economic and social conditions of the Native and non-European people.
3. That every effort be made by the Party to bring the Convention onto a permanent organisational basis on the lines of the Programme of the National Liberation League as started in Cape Town.
4. That while this Convention or National Liberation Movement will have for its object the organisation of the non-European people for the struggle against national oppression, for every privilege denied, for land and freedom, to also undertake seriously the task of organising, industrially to struggle for a higher standard of living and better working conditions; to undertake the tasks to organise Native peasantry into peasant unions; to carry on the struggle against heavy taxation, for the cancellation of debts for land.
5. That the Party give special attention to the June All National Convention by sending out organisers to tour the country, to give to this Convention special prominence in "Umsebenzi" and through leaflets and pamphlets for wide distribution throughout the Union.
6. That no opportunity should be missed to enlist the sympathy and support of the white toilers to strive to bring about the organisational unity between non-European and white toilers in the struggle for national and class emancipation.
7. That this Plenum decides to assist in the formation of a Farmer-Labour Party, which will have for its object to organise politically the working class, affiliated through their Trade Unions and other workers' organisations; also the political organisation of the intellectuals, poor farmers and the struggling petty bourgeoisie.
8. That under the present situation of division and lack of unity in the ranks of the black and white toilers, the Party must be a means to bring about unity of struggle in the ranks of white toilers, in particular against the capitalist offensive, against fascism and war and for the repeal of all repressive law, such as the Riotous Assemblies Act, etc.
9. To take up the struggle for better economic conditions, for the extension of democratic political rights for all people, including all civil servants on the same basis as other white citizens.
10. That the policy of the United Front Party should be democratic enough to stand for extension of equal rights for the non-European people, in particular for the repeal of such anti-democratic laws as the Pass Laws, Masters' and Servants' Act, Colour

Bar Act, etc.
11. For extensive taxation against the rich capitalists and landlords.
12. That the policy of this broad united democratic front be established on the basis of political parliamentary and extra-parliamentary action.
13. That through this United Front Party the CPS, in directing its influence and activities, will bring about more unity of struggle and organisation between black and white toilers.

Document 93
S. B., "Unite Against Reaction and Oppression: United Front Against National Oppression and Fascism", *Umsebenzi*, 23 May 1936

We have dealt last week with the effects and possibilities of the united front in European countries and now we must analyse the methods and chances of a united front here.

The position in South Africa is very much complicated by the racial question. On the one hand a very strong anti-Native prejudice on the part of the whites, on the other hand the Natives are so much oppressed racially that this racial oppression is bound to obscure to them the class issue.

We must go out from the following two starting theses. First of all when dividing the anti-fascist united front tactics into countries threatened by fascism and those already under fascism South Africa, strange to say, belongs to the two categories simultaneously. As far as the Native people go, we have a fascist or, something very similar, an Imperialist dictatorship all the time. They have no democratic rights and are kept in subjection by physical terror. On the other hand as far as the white population goes, South Africa is still one of the most democratic countries, but is being threatened by a developing fascism, these threats coming mainly from the growing fascist tendencies of the ruling parties as evidenced by their legislation (Industrial Conciliation Act, Riotous Assembly Act, Special Service Battalion, etc,).

Secondly it must be remembered that there are two kinds of united fronts, a "workers united front" and the "peoples united front."

The first is there to pursue the class struggle along the road to socialism, the second, a much wider one and embracing wide strata of the bourgeois intellectuals and liberal bourgeoisie generally has the objective of defending the democratic rights of the people against fascist aggression.

Let us first deal with the workers united front. In the course of its natural development capitalism must strive to level up the standards of life of various sections of the workers. This is a Marxist axiom. In this country there was always a very deep gulf between white and native workers, a gulf which created obstacles to the unity of the working class much more serious than mere race prejudice – obstacles of an economic nature. The pauperisation of the white agricultural population and the consequent creation of a vast army of white unskilled labour gave the capitalists of this country a chance to bring down the wages of large masses of whites almost to the Native level. On the other hand the development of secondary industries has created a large number of factories in which mixed labour is employed. These two factors must tend to break down the racial prejudices in the workers ranks and to open the eyes of the workers to the fact that they can achieve nothing wihout unity of white and black in the industrial field.

Signs are not wanting that this development is proceeding apace. Let us quote chapter and verse. After the strike of 1922 the miners union executive passed a resolution about the desirability of the Native mine workers being organised. Then came the big movement of the unemployed in which whites and natives participated together, then the furniture workers and leather workers union with their large number of coloured members, then the garment workers union which actually went so far as to organise a native branch to their union. Finally this year for the first time the May Day Committee in Johannesburg admitted a joint demonstration, and a native speaker, an official of a trade union, spoke from the platform and was accorded an attentive hearing and applause by the white workers audience. We have quoted but a few of the examples showing how capitalism in this country as elsewhere is digging its own grave by bringing the two sections of the workers together.

The task of the workers united front must be further to develop these small beginnings, to teach the workers the necessity of class unity irrespective of race, to build up native unions or wherever possible, native branches of white unions is to lead the natives in supporting any struggle of the white workers and to demonstrate to the white workers how impossible it is for them to be victorious even on smaller issues without the co-operation of the natives. The final objective of these activities must be a 100 per cent organisation of the workers, which could open the vista not only of a bettering of conditions for the working class but of an actual conquest of power leading to socialist society.

In the rural areas the landless White peasantry must be rallied to the slogan of confiscating the big landowners estate and it must be pointed out to them carefully but persistently that this can only be achieved with the help of the Native peasantry in a republic free from imperialist rule and governed by the toiling population, (people acquainted with rural conditions know that the gulf between the White and Native agricultural proletariat is negligible and that very often cordial relations exist between the two, especially in the Cape.

For the effective working of such a united Workers front in the political field a Workers and Peasants Party must be created without delay with the agrarian revolution inscribed on its banner.

As to the "peoples front," it is evident that the difficulties of having such a front of Whites and Natives together are at present insurmountable because there is no economic base for the rapproachement of the White bourgeois elements that go to make up such a wider front with the Natives for the moment. Besides the Natives who are already subject to impirialist dictatorship fascist in character cannot be called upon to DEFEND democratic rights which they have not got. Furthermore, they could not even adopt the tactics recommended by Comrade Dimttrov to workers in fascist countries, namely, entering the fascist organisation, since these are closed to them.[12] It is therefore evident that apart from help by the revolutionary conscious section of the Blacks whenever such help is required or useful, this part of the Natives in the peoples front must say the least be limited for the time being to Whites,

But as in other countries so in this the people's front is unavoidably leading to a strengthening of the Workers Front and to its ultimate victory. The Workers Front, the Workers organisations and Parties are the moving force of the wider people's front and when the time will be for a general working class offensive. The task of the Communist Party and all other organisations genuinely pursuing a proletarian policy should be to prepare the Workers united front and to nurse it to such strength that it should be able to take over and to continue where the peoples front task stops.

Document 94
"The United Front in South Africa: A Reply to S. B.",
South African Worker, 13 June 1936

Editor, Umsebenzi,

Perhaps you will be so kind as to allow me to reply to the article in "Umsebenzi" of May 23rd, signed "S. B.". However, no one will doubt the sincerity of S. B. He definitely shows his desire to assist in creating unity in the movement, and correctly says that a common level is being developed by modern capitalism which is leading to united action between the Natives and the whites. But while he is correct in this, he then proceeds to destroy his promise by raising a number of fundamental questions and drawing conclusions harmful to what he desires to achieve.

He also correctly points out: "As far as the Natives are concerned we have a fascist or something very similar, an imperialist dictatorship all the time." But then he proceeds to divide their struggle from that of the white workers because: "as far as the white population goes, South Africa is a most democratic country." Even this latter statement may be challenged, and it is fundamentally wrong to politically separate the Natives and plays right into the hands of the segregationalists both white and Native. This is just what the imperialists want and constantly propagate.

After wrongfully driving this wedge into the united front movement that must develop around our common struggle, we are told there are not only two fronts based on degrees of oppression of Natives and whites but these fronts are based on political objectives – a "workers front" and a "peoples front". The first is "to pursue the class struggle on the road to socialism" and the second "to defend the democratic rights of the people against fascist aggression". So presumably we have an offensive fight for socialism and a defensive one for preserving democratic rights. Herein is embodied definite segregation of the Natives in a general united struggle for S. B. says: "the Natives already subject to imperialist dictatorship, fascist in character cannot be called upon to defend rights they have not got."

Fellow Workers, I must confess not being a member of the C.P. of S.A., I am terribly disappointed to find such articles in a Communist paper. But this is not all. We are told at present the difficulties "are insurmountable because there is no economic basis for the reapproachment of the white bourgeoisie that go to make up the wider front with the Natives". Thus he sounds the "last call" over the bodies of all who are endeavouring to build a united front over as wide a field as it is possible. This is an entire underestimation of the role that can be played right now by a fairly wide strata of the middle-class who are in danger of being dragged down to lower levels and are, given the right approach, ready to join the workers front, which must include the Natives, and that will rapidly become a peoples' front in the face of the danger of fascism and war.

And where does this line lead to. Even the intelligent middle class will ask S. B.: "Where is the line to be drawn? Are we to set other artificial barriers and drive another wedge between the poor whites, who are rapidly being driven down to lower levels, and, in some cases to the level of the Natives, and those lucky enough to find employment on a higher economic level?" This is the logic of S. B.'s line. No, this is not the way to develop unity. These academic abstraction can only assist the enemy. We must start to build unity from the basis of one all in and gigantic United Front Movement. It must be broad enough to include all those who are prepared to fight against fascism and war as well as for the economic and political demands of all workers irrespective of race, colour or religion. It is to the advantage of both the white and Native people to confront Anglo-Boer imperialists with one powerful front built upon the economic and political interests of all.

Is there no identity of interests between the whites fighting to preserve their democratic rights and the Natives who must and will struggle against national oppression and for their democratic rights? Of course there is. The one is supplementary to the other. A fight for Native rights is a struggle to defend what the white people have got in the face of the attacks of the growing fascist danger. The demands for the repeal of all anti-working class legislation must go side by side win the repeal of all laws oppressing the Natives. And is there not such a thing as immediate economic necessity giving way to political expediency? Yes there is. We have to choose between becoming united in a joint struggle for a higher standard of living and against war and fascism or being hung separately, and this includes the small shop-keepers etc.

But our friend does not end here. He will now have "created immediately" a "Workers and Peasants Party". This is "for effective working of a united workers front in the political field" to carry through the "agrarian revolution". Therefore we are to have another split, and allot another abstract slogan to further confuse the movement. We want no more parties. What we want now is unity of the existing ones. We must, as Dimitrov has said, set ourselves the perspective of building one party in South Africa which will lead the revolutionary struggle. This can be done only by developing the widest united front so that in practice and daily struggle we shall lay the foundation for such a Party.

Even such an organisation as the African National Convention existing does not mean two fronts. This movement exists to mobilise the widest number of Natives and to specialise on their particular problems, and much the same as a trade union specialises while working in the general interests of the whole of the working class. It is but one sector of one closely knit united front. This united front can take care of all the demands. It will be built upon the needs of the rural as well as the urban areas. It will demand land and work for the people, while developing the struggle against war and fascism. And it will do so with the full weight of an all-in united front that can and will become the only real challenge to British imperialism and their lackeys in the United and Dominion parties.

Let us have done with these abstract theorisings that lead to splits and make confusion worse confounded. Look in front of us and see what the workers and poor farmers are asking for. See what are the needs of the Natives. Find all allies in the wider sections of the population. Take these demands, create a programme, and connect them with the main political questions oppressing the people and the fight for peace and against fascism. Then we can go forward on a common front, delivering blows to the enemy on every sector and finally we shall win political power and go forward on the road to socialism.

Geo. Robertson, Johannesburg.

(The correspondence on this subject is now closed. – Ed.)

Document 95
"Welcome The All-African National Convention! African National Convention Must Mark Beginning of National Liberation Movement", *South African Worker*, 27 June 1936

The African National Convention must receive the whole hearted welcome of all people both Native and European. Herein lies the beginnings of National Liberation. It is the answer to the further encroachment upon the oppressed African people, expressed in the anti-native laws passed during the recent session. It must mark the beginning of a permanent movement for liberation from all oppressive laws and administrative acts and from perpetual violence practiced against the Native.

There Must Be No Division!
Compounds, pass laws and acts of Parliament limiting Native movements, the imposition of poverty and illiteracy slums in the filthiest of surroundings, eating at delicate children's lungs, driving Natives to early graves – ALL MUST GO. The African Convention at Bloemfontein can give the answer. There must be no divisions.

Chiefs or headmen, Native representatives or others who receive remuneration from the Government must refuse to become politically isolated from Native interests. They will become richer, intellectually and materially, by serving the people from whom, they sprang. They cannot be free while the mass of the Natives are oppressed. To free the Native means to let loose wider opportunities for all. Intellectual and professional people can advance only with expanding liberaties.

WE WANT BREAD, WORK LAND AND FREEDOM'
DEMAND "BREAD AND WORK, LAND AND FREEDOM!"
These can be got by organising. To unite the Native people in a struggle for economic uplift and political rights must be the aim of the convention. don't underestimate Native desires and aspirations. The government of imperialists act as if they were non-existent. Let the Convention be otherwise.

Natives Must Have the Right to Organise
Demand the right to form Native Trade Unions of Native Workers in all industry, and unity with the white workers where possible. Form peasant organisations in the rural areas. Create your own political councils in the Reserves, locations and compounds. From these send militant and loyal Natives to the Native Representative Councils etc.

limited as they are. Make the limited hybrid councils a political issue in every place where Natives congregate.

United Action Will Strengthen The Cause of The People
Expose those who are responsible. To elect representatives to them by no means implies acceptance. They are there. Use their limited possibilities. They give you the right to recommend. See all your recommendations are aimed to liberate the Native people. Political activity around the issues of the work and bread, land and freedom will embarrass the imperialists, and advance the Natives interests. This activity will educate, strengthen and develop the people and enable them to drive on the National liberation movement. Connect your movement with the Workers and Peoples United Front to fight against War and Fascism.

Document 96
"C. B. I. Joins Workers' Party",
Umlilo Mollo/The Flame, 1, 1, September 1936

The following letter was sent by Comrade Dladla to the C.P. which thereupon discovered that he was "a police spy."[13]

To the Political Bureau,
Communist Party of South Africa,
Johannesburg.

Dear Comrades,

The Seventh Congress of the Comintern adopted a line of a united front action of the workers and the formation of a People's Front against Fascism and War. This might be described as a right wing policy and comrades in Johannesburg might have expected that the leadership within the Communist Party in carrying out this line would have been entrusted to those comrades who have consistently advocated this line for the past years; but it was found that Comrade Roux and other right wingers still remained the Opposition and the leadership has remained in the hands of those who yesterday advocated the very left policy of the so-colled Third Period. From this it is clear that the Comintern does not wish its present right wing policy to be carried out under the leadership of party members who genuinely believe in this policy and have always advocated it. On the contrary all that it requires from the leaders of the C.P. is that they shall immediately obey orders from Moscow and take up positions left and right according to the dictates of the ruling bureaucracy in Moscow. This attitude places a premium on rank opportunism of the basest sort and selects for leaders of the C.P. those elements like Joffe and his company of flunkeys and adventurers who are prepared to alter their principles – that is if they have any at all – to remain in the leadership.

The recent economic demands of the C.P. published in "Umsebenzi" namely, 5/- per day for the native and 10/- per day for the white workers for certain equal work in certain defined skilled trades, shows a retreat from the principle of equal pay for equal work back to white chauvinism and this chauvinism has always been displayed by the majority of white comrades in the C.P.. This attitude, i.e., attitude of the party, is an opportunistic attempt to reconcile with the chauvinistic elements of the white working class.

The slogan of the Independent Native Republic is in my opinion stupid, incorrect, misleading and confusing and consequently unfit for a revolutionary Bolshevik-Leninist Party let alone "Identical with a Workers' and Peasants' Government." To say that we have a native bourgeoisie in South Africa is muddleheadedness and madness. Moscow has ruled that there does exist such a class; but Moscow and Stalin and Dimitrov are thousands of miles away and therefore we cannot just be told anything by them about South Africa.

Joffe[14] and Co. are mere time servers and faithful lackeys of their Moscow paymasters. A party dominated by such unprincipled, corrupt and untrustworthy braggarts can never assume the leadership of the revolutionary workers in the serious struggles that lie ahead of us. On the other hand it is impossible to remain within the party as a supporter of Eddie Roux's opposition which has capitulated in the most cowardly manner to the ruling bureaucrats. If Roux and his chicken-hearted supporters have failed to draw the correct conclusions from the recent turn in the party, namely that the C.P.S.A. is nothing but a degenerate appendage of corrupt Moscow bureaucracy headed by Stalin, this need not deter genuine revolutionary elements from realising that the correct course must be to break with the decayed Third International and to build anew a revolutionary International which shall embrace the best elements of the Second and Third Internationals.

Yours for the revolution,
C. B. I. Dladla

Document 97
"Advisory Board Elections: Communist Party calls on Location Residents to support All-African Convention for Better Conditions", *South African Worker*, 26 September 1936

Advisory Boards and Native Bills

The Communist Party of South Africa calls upon All Native residents of locations to realize the importance of the coming elections for members of the Advisory Boards.

The nominations for members of the Advisory Board must be made in writing at public meetings called by the location Superintendent in the month of December. Elections must be held within fourteen days after that meeting.

All registered occupiers of locations are eligible:–
1. To nominate members.
2. To be nominated as a member.
3. To vote for the election of members.

A registered occupier is one whose rent has been paid up to date, therefore it is necessary to pay rent up to date in order to vote.

Our first task is to see that the Elections are legally carried out. (Study the location regulations which must be posted up at the Superintendent's office.)

Our second and most important task is to see that the best fighters for our rights are nominated and elected as members of the Advisory Board.

This is very important for Every Resident:
BECAUSE: The members of the Advisory Boards should be our leaders in the struggle for:–
BETTER HOUSING.
LOWER RENTS.
ABOLITION OF THE LODGER'S FEES.
CHEAPER SANITARY AND WATER RATES.
BETTER SANITARY SERVICE.
BETTER WATER SUPPLIES.
CLEANER LOCATIONS.
FREEDOM OF MOVEMENT FOR YOURSELVES, YOUR FAMILIES AND YOUR VISITORS (ABOLITION OF THE CURFEW.)
FREE EDUCATION FOR YOUR CHILDREN.
A CHEAP MILK SUPPLY FOR YOUR CHILDREN.
MATERNITY HOMES FOR THE MOTHERS.
HOSPITAL AND MEDICAL SERVICES FOR THE SICK.
CHEAP AND EFFICIENT TRANSPORT.
THE RIGHT TO BREW BEER FOR PERSONAL CONSUMPTION.
BETTER SOCIAL SERVICES AND BETTER SOCIAL CONDITIONS FOR ALL.

The Advisory Board members have the ears of the Superintendent, the Municipality and the Native Affairs Department.

If the Municipality and the government does not listen to the Advisory members when they put forward your just demands, the Advisory members must call meetings of residents, lead deputations and demonstrations and compel the rulers to fulfill these demands. The Advisory Board members must be REAL LEADERS AND FIGHTERS FOR YOUR DEMANDS.

Elect the best men; men who have proved themselves; men you can trust. Don't elect "Good Boys" of the Government and the Superintendent. Don't elect leaders and men who advise you to remain quiet under real grievances.

Advisory Boards Vote under New Bills
The coming elections are also very important because they are the first elections since the NATIVE BILLS have been passed.

The Advisory Boards have the right to nominate and elect the Senators and the members of the NATIVE REPRESENTATIONAL COUNCIL Under the Representation of Natives Act, 1936.

The Residents of locations must see that the members of the Advisory Boards will nominate and elect Senators and members of the Representational Council.

Approved of by the All-African Convention
Although through its Provincial Branches the Native Bills were passed by the Government to destroy the Cape Native Franchise and to mislead the Native masses by empty and powerless organs of representation yet these Native Bills have opened a great

avenue for Protest and Propaganda against all reactionary and detrimental legislation and for demands of social and economic freedom of the Native masses.

We must make use of these opportunities.

We can only make use of them by electing senators and members of the Native Representational Council who will fearlessly and sincerely fight for the demands laid down by the Communist Party and All Convention. These demands are:–
a) Land for the NATIVE PEASANTS.
b) STATE RELIEF In time of famine.
c) ABOLITION OF police brutality and pick-up vans.
d) AID to the Native farm population to ease the burden of debts, etc.
e) THE RIGHT OF ALL NATIVE WORKERS to organise in the Trade Unions.
f) ABOLITION of all oppressive legislation, etc.
g) The repeal of the act disfranchising the Cape Natives and the extension of full democratic rights to all Natives with the right of domicile.

We can only achieve the demands by organisation active struggle in the reserves, locations, factories, mines and places of employment. The members of the Native Representational Council must lay them before Government and resist all detrimental legislation.

We must choose reliable men who receive the endorsement of the African Convention.

Choose members of the Advisory Boards who will loyally and actively co-operate with the African Convention and will vote for the men chosen by the African Convention responsible for their actions to the All African Convention.

Document 98
"The All African Convention",
Umlilo Mollo/The Flame, 1, 2, October 1936

At the beginning of October 1936 the all African Convention held its conference of the Transvaal section, and once again as in the July and December conferences the fatal weakness of the convention was displayed: it has no programme. The leaders "blow off steam" as Professor Jabavu cheerfully puts it, once again; the African people are once again urged to "unite." But when it is asked: "to unite in order to do what?" there is no answer forthcoming.

Our delegate, Comrade C. B. I. Dladla pointed out to the Conference that the attempt on the part of the Cape native voters to keep their names on the common role by appealing to the imperialist courts was doomed to inevitable failure; to advocate a struggle by "peaceful" and "constitutional" methods was to take a path that could only lead to ultimate disillusion and despair on the part of the African masses. He urged a boycott of the Representation Council, and in its place a genuine and serious representation of Africans through delegates elected on the basis of popular mass voting.

If Africans once cherished the hope that the day would come when the Cape Native Franchise would be extended to all Africans in the Union, that hope is now dead. Far from increasing the influence of the African vote in the Union parliament; that vote has been cut down, hedged around, rendered worthless. The door has been slammed in the face of African aspirations to ultimate political equality with Europeans in the Union, slammed and bolted and barred.

In the face of this fact, the political task of the all African Convention becomes imperative: it must set up a separate independent Parliament, a council of delegates elected on the basis of universal adult suffrage. A campaign must be inaugurated to bring to the consciousness os the masses of voteless, rightless Africans the necessity for a constituent Assembly to express their needs, their national unity, their revolt against their present slave status.

A manifesto must be issued, a new Voters' Roll compiled containing the names of all applicants who possess the necessary qualifications to vote, the same qualifications that Europeans must possess to have their names entered on the present Voters' Roll of the Union Parliament. On the basis of the new voters' Roll, parties can be invited to nominate their candidates for electoral districts, polling booths can be set up, and an election carried out, if possible on the same day as the General Elections for the Union Parliament in 1937.

The Union Parliament is a mock parliament, since it represents only a small fraction of the population of this country. A rightless majority is being taxed and legislated for by the representatives of a minority. It is the task of the African people to transform this mockery into a real Parliament by the creation of a body of their fellow citizens properly elected by ballot and given mandates to speak on behalf of the masses of the people.

These were the ideas, this was the plan of action set forth by comrade Dladla in his speech to the conference, and he urged the delegates present to give definite instructions to its Executive Committee to make a start with a political campaign to compile the Voters' Roll.

But the "leaders" were panic-stricken at the idea that leadership implied more than merely collecting fees and passing pious resolutions. They flinched at the suggestion that they would be required to leave the safe paths of court action, to stop "blowing off steam" and to utilise that steam in the locomotive of a practical, positive programme that would draw the masses our of apathy, despair and slavery into the path of militant struggle for their rights.

The Stalinists (so-called "Communists") rushed to the aid of the "leaders," and ridiculed this programme, the first serious call to the Convention to take action, as the "Mock Parliament." They defended the "leaders" against the criticism that had been justly levelled against them of failing to produce any programme whatsoever and so leading the Convention to inevitable collapse. Thanks to this timely aid from the co-called "Communists" the leading group was able to shelve Comrade Dladla's resolution. Now it can settle down once more to its quiet slumbers and its pleasant dreams of defeating Imperialism in the Law Courts of Imperialism.

But the most militant section of delegates, deeply impressed with the proposal of commencing the struggle for equal rights for all races by a campaign for representation, deeply disappointed by the failure of the Convention to point a path, have formed a National Committee to go in more detail into the proposal. In the formation of this Left Wing we see new hopes for the All African Convention, new hopes for the exploited and oppressed African masses.

Document 99
Edwin T. Mofutsanyana, "All-African Convention: Masses Must Support It", *South African Worker*, 9 January 1937

The All-African Convention came into being as an answer by the Native People to the Government's unjust Native Bills. It was born from the resentment and disgust which were felt by all Africans at the manner in which they they were treated by their white "guardians" in this country.

Representatives from all over met in Bloemfontein in a militant spirit determined to create a united front against the slave morality and mentality of these Bills, determined to voice their disapproval and to create a fighting organization to win freedom for the Native people in their own homeland.

The All-African Convention met with the blessing and goodwill of a united people. They expected great things of their Convention.

So far the All-African Convention has not fulfilled any of the expectations of the masses who support it.

It is true that the tide of feeling which mounted against the Government has receded after the excitement of the passing of the Native Bills. It is true that not sufficient time has passed for Convention to achieve its full organisational strength.

It is true that there are a great many factors which excuse the comparative inactivity of the Convention since its inception.

But already a great weakness is apparent in the composition of the All-African Convention, and a weakness which will prove fatal to the Convention if it is not quickly remedied. The All-African Convention is not sufficiently representative of the Native masses. Its leaders do not address themselves to and confide in and consult the people who gave them their prestige and their power.

Without the active support of the masses the All-African Convention will go the way of the I.C.U. and African Congress, empty shells making a noise without substance.

The coming elections for the Senators, Members of Parliament and Members of the Representational Council are now exercising the minds of the masses. The excitement of an election campaign is gathering force and gives the Convention a chance to bring the masses into action.

The elections must not be the subject of political intrigues amongst the leaders. They must not be cut and dried affairs in which the personal choice of the leaders is forced upon the All-African Convention.

It is necessary for the Convention to formulate its election platform and plan of campaign. The Convention's platform must be based on the grievances and demands of the Native people. In the forefront is the demand for land and the demand for liberty. Bread for the African People, and freedom of movement and rights of organisation are the first essentials.

The plan of campaign of the All-African Convention must give a lead to the Native people how to achieve these demands. It must clearly point out that the election of Senators and Native Representatives will not help the Native people. Only mass demands and demonstrations, mass organisation and a militant spirit will shake the Government out of its stupid, selfish, reactionary attitude towards the Natives.

The record of British and Boer Imperialism is too black and consistent for the Native people to hope to achieve anything by appeals to fair play, justice, etc.

Only the organised, determined might of a united people will win bread and freedom for the African masses.

The candidates, therefore, must be chosen not as worthy, respectable citizens who will persuade and win over Hertzog and Co., and do wonders in Parliament, the Senate and the Native Representational Council. The candidates must be chosen as militant fighters for the rights of the Native people; not men who will have tea with Hertzog and use soft words in the Council, but men who will work in the reserves, in the locations, amongst the African masses.

Whoever is acceptable to Smuts and Hertzog is not acceptable to the masses or the African Convention. The only men acceptable are proven fighters and men who will speak with the weight of the organised might and threat of the Native masses.

The life of the All-African Convention depends on the mass work it will do, and the quality of the candidates it chooses for the coming elections. If it nominates opportunists and collaborates with the government it will lose the interest and support of the masses. If it nominates militant candidates who believe in mass action, who will organise and lead the masses, it will grow from strength to strength as the rightful leading organisation of the native, as the organisation which will be in the forefront of the inevitable coming fight for bread and liberty for the African masses.

Document 100
"15th Anniversary of 1922 Rand Strike: Communist Party Calls Mass Demonstration to Commemorate", *South African Worker*, 27 February 1937

The traditions of the labour movement in South Africa young as it is are traditions that we can be proud of and that we should not allow to slip into a dim memory of the past, but to commemorate in a fitting manner from time to time. In particular does this apply to the Great Strike of 1922 on the Rand, commonly known as the Rand Revolt, when the workers of the Rand supported the miners against the Chamber of Mines and the Government for which they were brutally shot down by the aeroplanes, machine guns, artillery and rifle fire of the Government troops instructed by that arch-enemy of the workers, General Smuts.

Many names come to our mind when we recall this epic event in South African working class history. Hull, Lewis and Long who went to the gallows singing the "Red Flag", hurling defiance at the executioners and striking fear into the hearts of the capitalist class; Fisher and Spendiff, gallant defenders of Fordsburg. The Hanekom brothers, Smith and Dowse, the former mere boys, shot down without even a trial at the Rosettenville Kopjes, and the hundreds of working class martyrs that gave up their lives in the struggle for freedom from exploitation. We must not let these names fade into oblivion; we must keep them alive, not only with annual commemorations, but must follow the militant spirit of struggle that pervaded the actions of the gallant Rand miners and workers of 1913, 1914 and 1922.

This in itself is not enough. We must learn from the defeats that our comrades suffered and reason out why they suffered these defeats. With the militant spirit of our heroic martyrs, and by correcting their mistakes, we will march forward to victory, that will be ours, however much the capitalist class may rave and shout and murder and kill.

UNITED DEMONSTRATION

The Communist Party of South Africa calls for a MASS DEMONSTRATION ON SUNDAY EVENING, MARCH 14, at 8p.m. on the City Hall Steps, Johannesburg, to commemorate the 15th ANNIVERSARY OF THE GREAT RAND STRIKE OF 1922. Every miner, every worker, every lover of freedom and liberty must be present at this demonstration. The Communist Party has written to the S.A. Trades & Labour Council, the S.A. Labour Party, the People's Front, the S.A. Mine Workers Union to make this demonstration a United JOINT DEMONSTRATION and show the solidarity of the working class in South Africa.

We are sure it is in this spirit that our brave comrades, had they been alive, would have liked us to commemorate the struggle of the Rand workers.

KEEP THE DATE OPEN

Sunday Evening, at 8 o'clock, March 14, City Hall Steps, Johannesburg.

Document 101
Letter from Workers' Party of South Africa to G. H. Gool, 4 March 1937

To Dr. G. H. Gool,
1 Stilton Rd,
Wynberg.

4.iii.1937

Dear Comrade,

We talked of the matters affecting the Liberation League at our meeting yesterday, + I summarise the main points:

We must distinguish between members of the Party and members of the Club, the former being under stricter obligations than the latter. As a Party, we boycott the Natives' Represent^x Act completely. And we who are members of the Party do not bind ourselves to any action taken by the Liberation League. We are in no way allied to the said League.

But we leave you a clear field in the League, hoping that you will work within it for the Fourth International. We shall not write for the League organ, and if a comrade who is one of our members takes part in a Liberation League election League, or the like, it will be to put forward the *Party* point of view, not the League point of view. But we do not bind you to observe strictly the Party principles. This was unanimously agreed.

We think a leaflet for this time of nomination [-] election would be useful, and are arranging for the preparation of one in Xhosa + one in English. These will, of course, set forth our own standpoint.

Document 102
Workers' Party of South Africa, *Liberation League* (c. March 1937)

Liberation League

Comrade Dr. Gool was permitted by the Spartacus Club to accept the Presidency of the African Liberation League. Last week he brought me three points that have arisen. (1). The Liberation League is, I understand, prepared to boycott altogether the Natives Repr. Council elections, but is keen on taking part in the election of the 3 members to the House of Assembly. It wants to support D. B. Molteno's candidature, which has the support of the C.P.[15] I told Comrade Dr. Gool that we boycott the *whole* Act concerning Native Repres^x, because *every* part of it involves the segregation of the Native voters. But we would like a definite ruling on this point, and I promised to put it before you.

And, secondly, he wants the League to have a weekly paper, a printed paper, and asks if we will undertake to contribute two or three, or several, articles to each issue, very simple, + only the A.BC of the revolutionary line. I didn't see how we c^d unless we can find more comrades to write.

Thirdly, Comrade G. G. wants from the Party or the Sp. Club speakers for the Liberation league platform when the election meetings are being held for Molteno's candidature. The point, however, falls away, if we boycott the elections altogether, and I pointed this out to Comrade Gool.

Document 103
Programme of the National Liberation League of S.A. as Revised and Adopted at First Congress, Cape Town, March 1937

PREAMBLE

Contrary to the generally accepted idea the Emancipation of Slaves in 1834 did not bring freedom to the non-European peoples of South Africa. It merely substitued the present day wage-slavery with its scientific methods of intensified exploitation for the chattel slavery of those by-gone days.[16]

Taking stock of the non-Europeans position in the body politic one hundred years after, it is obvious that "emancipation" had only made possible the imposition upon the non-European peoples of South Africa of a form of servitude a hundred times more subtle, deadly and dangerous than their ancestors of pre-emancipation days experienced.

Formerly the slave owner had an interest in keeping his "property" in workable and consequently profitable condition. To-day the "free" labourer is paid a miserable pittance in exchange for his labour and whether this suffices for the maintenance of himself and his dependents in ordinary comfort and decency is no concern of anybody, much less the master. One hundred years after his "emancipation" the slave possesses only the "freedom" to starve.

When in 1834 the shackles of chattel slavery were struck from his limbs, he stepped forward upon the path toward his rightful heritage – freedom in the land of his birth. To-day he faces only disillusionment; poverty and discrimination is his lot. The stifling atmosphere of the pre-emancipation days still pervades his environment.

The modern slave finds that his oppressor does not intend to permit him to rise to equality with his white fellow-workers. Laws bar his access to the machine. Colour prejudice and poverty strangle his aspirations to culture. His women-folk are subjected to economic exploitation by day and sex exploitation by night; his children herded in slums, prematurely aged, a prey to the germs of disease.

Pass Laws make it impossible to travel freely. Statutes give the right to the white land-owner to flog his black servant without recourse to the law courts. Taxed without representation in the governing and administrative bodies of the country; denied recognition of the right to organise into Trade Unions; systematically being deprived of the franchise and other rights previously held in the Cape; and a total denial of ordinary citizenship rights in the other Provinces; as well as an intolerable burden of oppression and exploitation which is daily being added to; is the lot of the non-European.

Without land, bread and equality of opportunity, there can be no freedom. After a century, the non-Europeans must still fight for that freedom which should rightly have been his since 1834.

THE WHITE WORKER

Neither did the fusion of Anglo-Boer imperialism typified in the Act of Union, 1910 bring freedom to the white people formerly oppressed by British Imperialism.

British Imperialism holds down the white people of South Africa, denying them their national freedom and hampering their movement for liberation with the assistance of misleaders such as Smuts, Hertzog, Malan.

The white worker, natural ally of the non-European peoples in their struggle for freedom from imperialism is corrupted and mislead by certain Trade Union leaders who pledge the support of the white working class to the imperialist regime with the assitance of a system of bribes in the shape of occupations reserved for Europeans only. (Colour Bar in Industry. The Civilized Labour Policy.)

Ample investigation into and ocular proof of the ever lowering standard of the white working class demonstrates the impossibility of more than a favoured few reaping any material advantage from the operation of this policy. The vast majority of the white workers have no prospect of national freedom or future, except the increasing burden of militarism and the horrible sacrifices of war on behalf of imperialism.

Just as the fate of the non-European peoples is inextricably bound to that of the white working class, the white workers cannot strike off the fetters of wage slavery from their necks unless they assist in striking the shackles from the limbs of the non-Europeans.

Neither the white workers nor the non-Eurpean masses can achieve real froedom unless they achieve complete solidarity in their fight against their common enemy, the white capitalist-imperialist.

THE NATIONAL LIBERATION LEAGUE OF SOUTH AFRICA therefor calls upon the non-European peoples and especially the non-European workers to discard and overcome their prejudice against the white workers. To realise that even if some of them have been corrupted by the flesh pots of capitalism-imperialism and their own misleaders to uphold the supremacy over and persecution of the non-European peoples, they still remain as a class the inevitable ally of the non-European masses.

At the same time THE NATIONAL LIBERATION LEAGUE OF SOUTH AFRICA calls upon the white workers to cut themselves loose decisively from the policy of their ruling class toward the non-European peoples, to disavow once and for all the attitude of white superiority which has proven to be only a chain which binds them to the imperialist regime.

Unless white labour wishes to be dragged down to the oppressed and degraded position of the non-European toilers, unless it wishes to have heaped upon itself the thousand and one persecutions which plague labour with a black skin, unless it wishes to remain in perpetual wage bondage and misery, let white labour extend its arm of alliance and solidarity on every issue which faces it as well as the non-European peoples.

As a preliminary to the sucessful struggle for national liberation of the oppressed peoples of South Africa, it is imperative that the understanding be firmly established that no one section can be free while the other section – the vast majority – namely the non-Europeans remain enslaved.

The struggle for national liberation therefor prescribes a unity of all elements opposed to imperialism, having in mind always that the interests and aspirations of the great majority, the non-Europeans take precedence.

Both white and black anti-imperialists stand therefor squarely before the alternative, either a determined fight for freedom, or submission to further enslavement, degradation and poverty.

Resolutely facing the issue, THE NATIONAL LIBERATION LEAGUE OF SOUTH AFRICA comes forward with a programme for the liberation of the oppressed peoples.

DECLARATION

The National Liberation League of South Africa identifies itself with the convictions and aspirations of the South African peoples, more especially the non-Europeans, and determines to develop and realise those convictions and aspirations.

It declares in direct opposition to all assertions concerning an alleged "civilizing" mission of the imperialist nations.

In opposition to all assertions concerning the alleged superiority of certain races and peoples.

It declares that no natural or social superiority or subordination exists within the human race and that any such superiority or subordination is inadmissible.

AND WHEREAS THE NATIONAL LIBERATION LEAGUE OF SOUTH AFRICA is of opinion that the continued domination of the South African peoples, especially the non-Europeans is no longer tolerable, it is no longer desirable to limit themselves to passive acquiesence under the increasing burden of discriminating and oppressive laws. A determined struggle must be carried on against such, along with the awakening forces of the oppressed peoples of the world.

WE THEREFOR HEREBY ANNOUNCE THE FOUNDATION OF THIS LEAGUE TO ALL OPPRESSED PEOPLES AND TO ALL THE OPPRESSED CLASSES IN THE IMPERIALIST COUNTRIES.

We appeal to all those who do not profit from the oppression of other peoples, to all those who hate modern slavery and are longing for their own freedom and the freedom of their fellow-men and women, to affiliate or co-operate with our organisation and support it as far as it lies in their power.

We are confident above all that we will receive the support of the advanced working class in all countries who, like ourselves, have "nothing to lose but their chains".

We maintain that the national liberation of the peoples of South Africa, providing as it will for the development and upliftment of the non-European masses, will not diminish the achievements of civilization nor limit the possibilities of material and cultural developements, as is frequently asserted by reactionary demagoguoes. On the contrary, with this freedom cultural developement will experience a revival on a scale never before witnessed.

In this sense the struggle of the oppressed peoples for their freedom is like the struggle of the advanced worker, a struggle for a freer and fuller life for toiling humanity.

Everyone attached to the movement for national liberation shall adopt the watchwords and fight

FOR NATIONAL LIBERATION
DOWN WITH THE "COLOUR BAR"
DOWN WITH IMPERIALISM IN SOUTH AFRICA.

And we are sure that in waging a common and militant struggle for equal rights and against persecution of the non-European peoples, our united strength shall grow from day to day until it welds us into a force, powerful enough, conscious enough, determined enough to bring to full fruition the ultimate aims expressed in this programme.

LONG LIVE THE NATIONAL LIBERATORY MOVEMENT OF THE OPPRESSED PEOPLES OF SOUTH AFRICA!

SPEED THE WORLD MOVEMENT OF THE COLONIAL AND OPPRESSED PEOPLES AGAINST IMPERIALISM!

OBJECTS OF THE LEAGUE.

TO UNITE AND ORGANISE ALL INDIVIDUALS, ORGANISATIONS AND OTHER BODIES IN AGREEMENT WITH THE PROGRAMME OF THE LEAGUE TO STRUGGLE FOR COMPLETE SOCIAL, POLITICAL AND ECONOMIC EQUALITY FOR NON-EUROPEANS WITH EUROPEANS IN SOUTH AFRICA.

a) Equal adult suffrage for non-Europeans on the same basis and qualifications as Europeans.
b) Direct representation in Parliament by such candidates as shall be freely elected on the aforementioned basis without discrimination as regards colour, having in mind that under existing conditions such Parliamentary candidates only shall be approved and supported who are members of the League and have demonstrated by past activities to be in agreement with the objects set forth in this Programme.
c) For the right of non-Europeans to hold office in any or all governmental, administrative, juridical and educational institutions of the country.
d) For the aboliton of all existing taxation which discriminates between European and non-European (Poll Tax. Hut Tax.)
e) For the complete abolition of all Pass Laws affecting the non-European peoples of South Africa.
f) Against the whole social system of segregation in which the non-European, especially the Bantu are set apart from the rest of the population as a despised and outlawed people.
g) For the right of non-Europeans to purchase or hire landed property or reside in any or all parts, districts or municipal wards throughout the Union of South Africa.

h) For the repeal of all laws prohibiting intermarriage which legalise the fiction of race inferiority.
i) For the right of non-Europeans to bear arms on an equal basis with Europeans.
j) For the right of non-European athletes to take part in all national and international sporting events on an equal footing with Europeans.
k) For the boycott of and mass protests against educational, theatrical, business concerns, publications, etc, that in any way whatever degrade or discriminate against the non-European.
l) Against all ideas of superiority of one race over another whether by European, Bantu, Coloured or Asiatic.
m) For the abolition of the "tot" system.
n) For free compulsory education of non-European children and abolition of all forms of discrimination in schools.
o) Adequate facilities for education in industrial, agricultural and technical pursuits for non-Europeans.
p) For the legal enforcement of pro rata employment of non-Europeans to Europeans in industry, skilled trades and other occupations with equal pay for equal work.
q) For the legal recognition of Trade Union organisation of the Bantu.
r) For national unemployment insurance and no discrimination on the grounds of colour in unemployment, old age or other forms of relief.
s) For the right of free speech, Press and assembly.
t) To establish Branches of the League throughout South Africa.
u) To establish a Press to propagate the aims and objects of the League.
v) To establish unity with all other oppressed peoples throughout the world with a view to conducting a joint struggle against imperialist oppression.
w) For complete independence of South Africa from imperialist domination.
x)

METHODS OF STRUGGLE
The struggle for national liberation shall be carried on by means of:–
a) Meetings, Resolutions, Petitions,
b) Public mass demonstrations and or boycott.
c) Testing the legality wherever necessary of discriminating Statutes, Ordinances and Regulations.
d) Election of approved candidates to the governmental and other public institutions of the country.
e) Enquiries and investigations into the grievances of the people and the exposure of such by lecture, publication and distribution of literature dealing with the same.
f) Demonstrative candidature to Parliament.
g) The strike weapon whenever expedient or necessary.
h) Passive resistance movements of the peoples.
i) All such further methods as may be deemed necessary.

CONSTITUTION OF THE LEAGUE
THE NATIONAL LIBERATION LEAGUE OF SOUTH AFRICA shall consist of and be constituted as follows:–
a) Branches of its local and district members.
b) Organisations or bodies affiliated to it.

c) All social, political, educational, cultural, economic, sport, or Church bodies, etc; formed for such purposes as are allied to the Objects of the League, subscribe to its Programme or are not in conflict therewith; and are prepared to co-operate in carrying out its Programme.

GOVERNMENT OF THE LEAGUE
The Government of the League shall be vested in the Annual Congress composed of:–
Members of the General Council
a) The accredited delegates of Branches of the League.
b) The accredited delegates of Organisations and Trade Unions affiliated to the League.
c) The representatives of Churches supporting the League.
d) The representatives of tribes, clans, territories, protectorates, etc, supporting the League.
e) The hereditary Kings, Chiefs, Princes, etc, of the Bantu peoples who subscribe to the Programme and support the League.

NOTWITHSTANDING THE PROVISIONS OF THE FOREGOING SECTION, HAVING REGARD TO THE SOUTH AFRICAN SITUATION AND ITS COMPLEXITIES, IT SHALL BE LAW THAT THE LEADERSHIP OF THE LEAGUE SHALL ON ALL GOVERNING BODIES BE PREDOMINANTLY NON-EUROPEAN.

ANNUAL CONGRESS
a) There shall be an Annual Congress of the League held at such time and place as the General Council shall decide.
b) Each Branch delegation shall not exceed four members including its Chairman and Secretary.
c) The delegations shall be elected for their knowledge of the situation affecting the non-European peoples particularly and be conversant with the provisions of the Programme of the League.

REPRESENTATION OF AFFILIATED ORGANISATIONS
The representation for affiliated organisations shall be two delegates for any number of members up to (500) five hundred. No delegation shall exceed four members.

AFFILIATION FEES
Affiliated Organisations shall pay an affiliation fee of (£1.1.0.) one guinea per annum for any number of members up to (500) five hundred, and (10/6) ten shillings and sixpence for every additional three hundred and fifty members.

Delegates of affiliated organisations shall possess the same rights and privileges of voting and discussion as delegates of Branches of the League.

THE GENERAL COUNCIL
The General Council shall be elected by and be the decisive governing body between the Annual Congresses.

The General Councill shall be representative of all such bodies as are affiliated to the League including the Branch representatives of its own Organisation.

Officers of the League shall be ex-officio members of the General Council.

POWERS OF THE GENERAL COUNCIL
a) To make decisions upon and to carry out, manage or conduct all movements or affairs of the League including the full control of its Branches and members.
b) To appoint, suspend, expel, prosecute or take legal action against any officer of the League and its Branches.
c) To give or withold approval of any Rule already existing or hereafter passed by any Branch should it be deemed necessary.
d) To demand or cause to be made an audit of the books and accounts of the League or any of its Branches and for the purpose to demand delivery of and take possession of all books, accounts, documents or other writings from any officer of the League or Branch thereof.
e) To revoke, set aside, approve or rescind and Resolution, act, matter or anything carried out or executed by any Branch of the League if necessary.
f) The General Council shall have power to appoint or dissolve subcommittee's to deal with matters affecting the League and its activities. Such sub-committee's shall make recommendations to the General Council but shall not have legislative or binding authority.
g) The decisions of the General Council shall be binding upon all Officers, members and Branches of the League during the periods between Congress of the League at which such decisions shall be subject to review and rescind.
h) The General Council shall meet prior to each Congress and at such other times as the political sitauton or matters affecting the League shall demand.
i) The quorum at meetings of the General Council shall be seven members including either or both the President and General Secretary.

OFFICERS OF THE LEAGUE
a) The Officers of the League shall consist of a President, senior Vice-President, Junior Vice-President, Treasurer, General Secretary and three Trustee's.
b) No person shall be elligible to hold office or position unless he or she is a bona-fide member of the League.
c) All officers shall be eligible for re-election providing no charge of misconduct can be proved against them during the period interveing Congresses.
d) It shall be the duty of all Officers to make themselves conversant with the Programme of the League and to further the provisions of same.

OFFICERS AND THEIR DUTIES
a) PRESIDENT
   The President shall be elected at each Congress and shall hold office for one year. He or she shall deliver a Presidential Address at each Congress subsequent to it having been approved by the General Council.
b) *VICE-PRESIDENTS*
   The Senior or Junior Vice-Presidents shall act in the absence of the President in order of seniority.
c) *TREASURER*
   The Treasurer shall check all accounts at Head Office in accordance with the system of administration and the requirements of the General Council.
d) Three Trustee's shall be elected by each Annual Congress. All properties of the league shall be held by them in trust for the League.

e) *GENERAL SECRETARY*
   The duties of the General Secretary shall be to propagate the Programme and policy of the Organisation. To convene and address meetings with a view to protect and further the interests, aims and objects of the League. He or she shall supervise the administration of the Head Office of the League and its existing Branches, and shall be empowered to act in questions of enforcing discipline upon members of the League. His decisions shall be submitted for approval or otherwise by the General Council of the League.
f) The General Secretary shall deliver a Report to each Congress of the league.
g) The salary of the General Secretary shall be determined by the General Council.
h) In the event of the General Secretary desiring to relinguish his position he shall give three months notice to the General Council of his intention to do so, and a like period of notice shall be given by the General Council to the General Secretary should they desire to dispense with his services.
i) Not withstanding the foregoing provision, in case of gross misconduct or violation of the Programme or policy of the League by the General Secretary a specially summoned meeting of the General Council shall decide the issue in the best interests of the League. [....]

AGREEMENTS

Any Agreement, political or otherwise made between the League and any other body, institution, or authority shall be valid only after it has been approved of by a majority vote of the General Council. Such approval shall be further subject to the Annual Congress of the League. [....]

BRANCH ADMINISTRATION REGULATIONS

a) To control the affairs of a Branch of the League, eleven persons shall be elected by the members of such Branch. From these further election shall determine the Offices of Chairman, Vice-Chairman, Treasurer, Secretary and Trustee's of the Branch.
b) Only bona-fide members of the League shall be eligible for these and shall hold office for a period of twelve months, after which a fresh election shall be held.
c) All Branch officials shall be eligible for re-election providing no charge of misconduct can be proved against them during the intervening period.
d) A Branch Executive Committee may make rules for the efficient management of their Branches, but such rules shall not be inconsistent with the rules herein laid down, and shall be subject to the approval of the General Council of the League.
e) Any Branch Executive Committee may remove one of their number at a Special meeting called for that purpose and may appoint another in his or her place with the approval of the majority of the members of such Branch. A report of such substitution shall be sent to the Head Office of the League.
f) Branch Secretaries shall keep a correct record of all financial transactions and other proceedings of their respective Branches and shall carry out as part of their duties such other reasonable demands as their respective Committees shall impose.
g) All monies of the Branch shall be banked within forty-eight hours after receipt of same.
h) A quarterly financial statement of each Branch shall be forwarded to the Head Office of the League, such statements to be signed by the Chairman, Secretary an

Treasurer certifying same to be a true and correct statement or pointing out any discrepancy and explaining such as may appear therein.

i) Office requisities, books, stationary, etc for the administration of a Branch must be obtained from the Head Office of the League on a Requisition signed by the Chariman Secretary of the Branch. Such requisites shall remain the property of the League and books and accounts shall be at all times open to inspection of a member of the Branch Executive, only credentialed member of the General Council or any Officer of the League.

j) Branches shall remit monthly to the Head Office of the League a Capitation Fee of one penny per member of the Branch.

k) The Chairman, Secretary and Trustees and Treasurer shall be held jointly responsible for all properties of the Leagues Branches controlled by them.

l) Decisions of a Branch regarding a matter or issue of public or national import shall first be submitted to the General Council of the League for approval before being acted upon.

j) All business ventures shall be transacted in the name of the National Liberation League of South Africa and a report of such transaction be submitted to the General Council. of the League.

k) The relations of the Branches and the League toward other bodies of a progressive nature shall be of a fraternal character.

STANDING ORDERS AT CONGRESS
a) Examination of Credentials.
b) Business to be proceeded with according to Agenda.
c) Speakers shall stand up when addressing the Chair.
d) No speaker shall be allowed to speak more than once on any subject, nor longer than ten minutes unless with the consent of the Congress.
e) The period of time for debate shall be at the discretion of the Congress.
f) In question of voting, the Chairman shall have a deliberative vote only. In the event of a tie in votes the question shall lapse.
g) Voting for election of officials shall be by ballot. In other questions it shall be left to the discretion of the Congress.
h) A motion once carried shall not be debated again unless a motion to that effect be carried by a two-thirds majority of those present.
i) No absent member shall be nominated for office unless his or her consent in writing has been previously obtained and produced at Congress.
j) A delegate shall be allowed to withdraw any motion or amendment by consent of the Congress only.
k) Any delegate refusing to obey the Chairmans ruling shall upon a vote being taken, withdraw from the Congress and the Congress shall have the right to suspend such delegate for any period it may deem fit.
l) The election of Officers of the League shall be the last item on the Agenda.

DOWN WITH IMPERIALISM IN SOUTH AFRICA.
DOWN WITH THE "COLOUR BAR".
FOR EQUALITY, LAND AND FREEDOM!

Document 104
"Boycott the Elections!" *The Spark*, 3, 4, April 1937

For months past, "the Bantu press" has been working very busily. This so-called "Bantu press" is, of course, simply the press agency of the ruling classes to spread their propaganda among the Bantu people, and has therefore been making a big effort on behalf of the coming elections to be held in June under the Natives Representation Act of 1936. [....]

For more than two years these leaders and their press were shouting at the top of their voices: "UNITY! Let us unite! Let us sink our differences in face of the enemy's attack!" Today they are all at each other's throats, though between whiles they pause in their senseless strife to pick up again and wave aloft their worn and torn banner of Unity! Two years ago they were vying with each other in order to fight the Government's enslaving Native Bills. Today they are fighting each other for the honour of betraying their people by making a success of these same enslaving Bills. The ruling classes may congratulate themselves on a success so easily achieved. They threw a cheap dummy as a bait and achieved marvellous results.

No longer do the leaders talk of "picking up the gauntlet", or of "rather dying in prison than enslave our children and posterity". Today the talk is: "Whom shall we elect?" "Let us elect wisely!" "Let common sense play its part in the elections!" On all sides these and similar slogans are heard. Today there is not a single voice (except our own) which is exposing the falsehood and telling the Bantu the truth. The election talk goes on as though it were a question of electing Bantu members to the House of Assembly, to the Senate, and to a Native Representative Council that would be truly representative of Native opinion. But there is nothing genuine about these elections; they are a fraud and a sham.

It may be that many of the Bantu will be taken in by the worked-up excitement of the leaders, who are continuing in their old treacherous policy. It is probable that the leaders will once more succeed in dragging the Bantu people along this road that will cheat all their hopes. But we will never be a party to this, even though today we have to swim against the stream.

It is necessary at this point to go over all the old ground again. It is not necessary to prove again here what everybody now knows, what the ruling classes, indeed, never tried to conceal or deny during the passage of the Bills through Parliament and during the jubilant clebrations in the Free State of the victory that had been won over the black race. That victory eliminated the Bantu people from the political arena, provided for their political and territorial segregation, confirmed their political and economic enslavement. A year ago the African Convention agreed that these slavery Bills must be rejected by the Bantu. A year ago unity of the Bantu was in sight, a unity based on the common struggle for rights and freedom. Only on this basis of common action, only by removing the wedge between North and South, the wedge cleverly driven in and pressed home by the ruling classes, only so could unity be achieved.

Now, after the passing of the two Bills, when the privileges of the Bantu in the Cape, privileges in connection with property rights, right of occupation, freedom from pass laws, were already taken away or were going ultimately to be taken away, nothing any longer stood in the way of at last achieving unity in Bantudom. What was left of former rights in the Cape was only a mocking appearance, worthless and humiliating. In such circumstances, it did not require much political wisdom to see the correct line of action, namely to throw back to the oppressors this appearance of a right, as the price to be paid for Bantu unity by the Bantu people, united in a common struggle for full rights and liberty. This was the only way, and we explained at the time why there must be a rejection of the Bills and a complete boycott of them. As this is a fundamental point, we reprint from The Spark" of November, 1936, the following passage (see pages 6, 7: "The Wrong Policy of the All-African Convention"):

> The ruling classes introduced the Native Bills in order to enslave the Bantu completely, to deprive him of his few reamining rights, and to shut fast the door for his economic, political and social emancipation. In order to fight against these sinister intentions of the slaveholders, the All-African Convention was formed by the Bantu people. The Convention did not succeed in wrecking the Bills, and could not do so in Parliament, since it had no voice there. Yet this did not mean that the Bills can become laws simply by Parliament's acceptance of them. *As long as the people whom these Bills concern refuse to accept them, they remain a dead letter*, no matter whether they are called Bills or Acts. It is up to the Bantu people to make them laws or to leave them dead scraps of paper. This was quite clearly realised by the ruling classes. Pirow, when he made his appeal to the so-called Opposition, stressed this point most decisively, He, and with him the whole press of the ruling classes, were under no illusion in this matter; they knew quite well that Parliament's passing of the Bills was not enough to transform them into law. Thus the declaration in the "Cape Times" of 8th April, 1936, after Pirow's appeal: "It will be easy to go among the natives denouncing the Bill as wicked, illiberal and repressive, and working them into a mood of sullen resentment. *By doing so, the Bill will be wrecked as completely as if it had been defeated on the third reading*". (Our emphasis. Ed. Spark). [....]

Today the Bantu leaders, ignoring what has happened during these last two years, are desperately clinging to the appearances and shadows of rights, are fighting for them, to the great amusement of the oppressors. But are not the Bantu to have three segregated, communal representatives in the House of Assembly? Not even that! Black and coloured, slaves and serfs, may not have even observers of their own race sitting in a Parliament of the "white man's country"! But three members of the ruling race, of the "divinely chosen race", and most certainly belonging to its ruling class, may be elected to "represent" the Cape blacks. Over 2 million Bantu in the Cape will be able to boast that they are "represented" in the House of Assembly by three members of the ruling race, three dummies, figures for show. Perhaps not everybody knows that the 6 1/2 million Bantu in the Union have always had 4 representatives in the Senate – dummies again, for they have never said or done anything of the least importance – and under the new Bill provision is made for the election of four senators by the Bantu. But everyone knows very well that the Senate itself is a dummy!

And yet the Bantu leaders are fighting today over the 3 dummies to be elected by the Cape and the other 4 to be elected by the Union. It is painful to see that, for many of these "leaders", the question, "Whom shall we elect?" is merely the question, "Who will give us the bigger bribe?" It is more painful to see that almost all of these leaders are thinking only of their own personal interests, and do not care two pence about the interests of their exploited and downtrodden fellow-Bantu.

It is natural in the animal world to find the pain and agony of the weaker creatures closely linked to the fierce joy of the stronger beasts, anticipating their prey and lusting for its blood. And that holds good in capitalist society. It was to be expected that, as soon as they smelt blood, all the beasts of prey would hurry to the scene.

£700 a year, in addition to other privileges, and this for five years, with hardly any work and no very irksome obligations, is quite an alluring prospect for unscrupulous men. All that is required as a qualification for the job is the ability to cheat the unsophisticated Bantu, the ability to bribe leaders and chiefs with money or promises. Those who make it their profession to mislead the Bantu, who make it their profession to be the "friends" and "champions" of the Bantu, were naturally on the spot at once. All these professional "friends" have appeared in the election field: Rheinallt Jones, Ballinger, Professor Brookes, Sir Clarkson Tredgold, Advocate Stuart, Advocate Molteno, Advocate Buchanan, and the rest of the team. [....]

But what about the Natives Representative Council? It has been argued that this Council, though it is in itself without any power, authority, or effective function, may still be of some use to the Bantu people as a means of propaganda, as a platform where Bantu may voice the grievances of their people, and thereby expose the reactionary measures, the anti-Native measures of the ruling classes. But this is a false and illusory idea, based on two childish assumptions. Firstly, it is assumed that the ruling classes would permit the Council to become the Central Propaganda Organisation for the Bantu people. And, secondly, it is assumed that the Council will have a majority of members who are prepared to carry on a struggle against the Government. But only people who are deliberately misleading the masses, or who have never troubled themselves to study the Act, can make these foolish assumptions.

The Council will consist of 22 members. Of these, 10 will be Government officials: the Secretary for Native Affairs (who will act as Chariman of the Council), and five other Europeans (Chief Native Commissioners), sitting as members with a consultative vote, and four Bantu appointed by the Government, which means that these four will also be Government officials. Only 12 out of the 22 will be "elected" – if, indeed, the word can properly be used for a system of elections which recalls the most cynical schemes of Machiavelli.

For even these 12 will not be elected by direct universal vote, or as many people seem to think, by all Bantu taxpayers. The great majority of Bantu taxpayers will have no part at all in the elections, because in tribal areas the Chief will nominate and elect for all his subjects; and in urban locations the Native Advisory Board will act for the whole location.

The Chiefs, the Local District Councils, and the Advisory Boards constitute the *units* in the Electoral Colleges. But there still remains a small number of taxpayers who do not fall under any of these bodies. These form another unit, the Electoral Committee, which consists of not less than three, or more than five members for each district. As each of these units will represent the total of its taxpayers, and as the urban Natives still mainly pay their tax in their home district so that their vote is included in that of the home district, and as no unit with less than 2,000 votes behind it can make a nomination, it is easy to see that the Chiefs of the tribes are made the dominant factor in these iniquitous "elections".

Out of the 12 elected members of the Council, 3 will be elected by the United Transkeian General Council, 6 by the Chiefs and headmen and other officials, and 3 will be elected by the Advisory Boards. But even in the case of these last-named bodies safeguards were devised to prevent and possibility of a "mistake". Since a unit cannot nominate unless it has a voting strength of not less than 2,000, and since there may be no split in the vote of a unit, a progressive minority will be unable to exercise its vote. We are therefore inclined to think that, out of the 16 Native members of the "Representative" Council, the Government will have 16 most obedient tools.

But, lest some miracle should happen, one more safeguard is provided, in case a member should slip in and prove not to belong to the well-drilled team of "the good boys". Without any legal form or public action, the Minister of Native Affairs can notify him that he has become unfit to be a member of the Council, whereupon his place at once falls vacant.

Paragraphs 26 and 27 of the Act, in dealing with the Meetings and Functions of the Council, complete the gloomy picture of a cheating, autocratic Government and a dummy Council. The two paragraphs make it positively and decisively clear that the Council will deliberate only on what the Minister for Native Affairs will select and allow; that it will meet *where* and *when* the Minister will decide; and that the provision that the proceedings of the Council shall take place in public is made *subject to such limitations as may be prescribed by regulation.*

The Natives Representative Council is a fraud, a deception, an empty, meaningless show. The only substantial thing in it is the annual bribe, over a period of five years, of £120, plus expenses, for each of the 16 "leaders" of the Bantu.

Just as the Bills cannot be both rejected and accepted, so also they cannot be both partly rejected and partly accepted. In some quarters a proposal has been made to reject and boycott the Representative Council, while accepting the fraud of the Cape segregated "franchise". This proposal is both ridiculous and dangerous.

It would be most selfish and unjust on the part of the Cape Bantu to ask the Bantu of the northern provinces to give up the Representative Council, even though it is a mirage without any substance at all, *if* at the same time the Bantu in the Cape were refusing to give up a similar mirage.

The proposal is obviously ridiculous. But it is also dangerous to the growth of Bantu unity. Such a proposal may easily widen the rift between North and South, by increasing ill-feeling and suspicion – the very conditions which the ruling classes are eager to use and exploit to the utmost.

Whether our appeal prove popular or not, we have no hesitation in calling upon the Bantu to reject the Bills and consequently to boycott the elections.

BOYCOTT THE ELECTIONS!
BOYCOTT
THE
ELECTIONS!

Document 105
John Gomas, "Cape Town: Liberation League Activities", *South African Worker*, 17 April 1937

2 000 Protest against Discriminatory Legislation

To protest against the new proposed colour bar legislation a mass meeting was held in the City Hall, Cape Town, on March 22 last. It was organised by the National Liberation League of South Africa and supported by the S.A. Indian Congress, Cape Malay Association, African National Congress, Communist Party, Socialist Party, S.A. Railway and Harbour Workers Union and S.A. Garment Workers Union. Coloured, Native, Indian, Malay and European leaders of these organisations were the speakers, who all emphasised the aim of the new colour bar legislation proposed by the Union Government, which will affect all Non-Europeans alike. The crowded hall of 2,000 people approved the speakers' exposure of the Government's evil intentions "to rob, filch and debar Non-Europeans from their rights."

The Government is passing oppressive and repressive laws against all sections – Natives, Coloured, Indian, Malay and White workers – during this session of parliament. The Marketing Bill provides for setting up of boards for control and pricing of agricultural products, from which the Non-European farmers will be excluded. The Native Laws Amendment Bill, Amendment to the Urban Areas Act, gives power to the Minister of Native Affairs to expel Native people from one town or location to another. It further deprives Native voters in the Cape Province of the right to stay in towns outside the segregated Native locations and to introduce "stop orders" for the deduction of rent from their wages.

The Anti-Mixed Marriages Bill is to prevent Indian and other Asiatics from marrying or co-habiting with Europeans, Coloureds and Malays, and if it does happen, the latter will, like Indians and Natives in Transvaal, be deprived of and forfeit the right to own land and property. So, too, the Asiatic Land Tenure Bill sets out to curb and suppress further the already limited right of Asiatics to own land, property and to trade in the Transvaal.

The Provincial Legislation Powers Extension Bill will give power to the Provincial Councils and Municipalities to discriminate against granting licences and permission to carry on trade and business to Non-Europeans. The meeting unanimously passed the following resolutson:

> This meeting emphatically protests against the proposed anti-colour legislation and expresses its resentment against the principle of subjecting Non-Europeans to special disabilities because of their colour. This meeting demands that the Non-European people be guaranteed complete equality, equal rights to work and education, and full right to vote, organise, serve on juries, and hold public office. This meeting requests the organisations present to lay before the Select Committee of parliament the reason for their rejection of the proposed Bills and pledges itself to do all in its power to resist the passing of the proposed iniquitous anti-colour laws.

The passing of continuous reactionary laws by the ruling class shows the vital need for UNITY OF STRUGGLE – amply demonstrated by the enthusiasm of the 2,000 people present at the meeting – in a mighty anti-imperialist and anti-Fascist movement.

Resolutions of First Congress
The following resolutions were passed at the first Congress of the National Liberation League held at Cape Town on March 28 and 29, 1937.

> This First Congress of the National Liberation League of South Africa, having in mind the efforts of certain leaders of the white working class to further divide the movement of the oppressed people against imperialism by advocating division on racial lines, and in addition the efforts of imperialists to draw away the white worker with such concessions as the "civilised labour policy", and other anti-colour legislation, points out the urgent and dire necessity for the conscious white worker and Socialist leadership to educate their followers upon the impossibility of achieving freedom from imperialism without unity of black and white anti-imperialist forces in South Africa.
>
> We, here assembled pledge ourselves to do all in our power to build the anti-imperialist movement of the non-Europeans with the aim of eventual unity with the white worker for the overthrow of imperialism in South Africa.
>
> Bearing in mind the atrocities committed upon the people of Africa by the imperialist nations, and in particular the sufferings of the non-European people under former German colonial Government, and in view of racial theories propagated by the Hitler Nazi regime, this Congress is in determined opposition to any intention declared or contemplated by the other imperialist powers to return mandated territories or colonies to the German Government. The League does not give preference or condone the rule of the present exploiters and oppressors of the colonial peoples.
>
> It declares unequivocally for the right of the colonial people to determine their own form of government, to rule and develop their respective countries free from imperialist domination.

Document 106
"Notes of the month",
Umvikeli-Thebe/The African Defender[17], 9, June 1937

The Native Law Amendment Act, which has lately gone through Parliament, is one of the worst laws against black persons ever made in South Africa – and South Africa has always had a bad name for bad behaviour to persons who are not white.[18] It is not so much that the new Act puts forward any new idea for keeping the Bantu down. The things it puts forward have been seen in our country for a long time.

But though there have been bad laws there has at all times been something different about them in different parts of the country. There was one sort of law in the Transvaal, another in the Orange "Free" State, another in Natal, and so on. The Cape has generally been free from some of the worst laws against the black man. In addition, even in places like Johannesburg, there were sometimes holes in the laws – places where a black man might by a happy chance get through.

Now all that is changed. There is one system of law throughout the country for all Bantu men and women.

Of special interest is the new law giving power to the authorities to send back to the country-side any Bantu living in towns who are "unnecessary" from the point of view of the white business men and others who make use of black workers. The Act makes it clear that there is to be no place in the towns for any black person who is not working for some white man. The white rulers of this country have no desire to see any Bantu who are not dependent for their living on the whites. The desire of the government is to put a stop to any growth of Bantu business or trade, however small. The Bantu were stopped by the Colour Bar Act (1926) from becoming expert workers. Now an attempt is being made to put a stop to them becoming business men or private traders. They have to be servants of the white man, doing the rough work for little payment – "sons of Ham" in fact!

That, at any rate, is the desire of the government. Are the eight million black and Coloured persons in this country going to put up with this?

We say "eight million" because it is not only the Bantu who are being attacked. The rights of the Coloured and the Indians in addition are being smashed by new colour bar laws. The Marketing Act gives rights to white farmers and traders only. It is a bad blow to the Indian and Native banana and sugar farmers in Natal. A new law is being made to put a stop to chances for Indians in the Transvaal. Indians are at present not able to have property in land in that part of the country. Government has a fear that some of the Indian business men may get married to women who are whites or Malays, in which event it would be possible for the wife to have property in her name.

Another law, which is still under discussion in Parliament, has the purpose of making it a crime for a white girl to do work in an Indian business. Another has the purpose of putting a stop to all "mixed marriages."

We hear that the Cape Provincial Council is thinking of making a law which will put a stop to all who are not white riding in trams and buses together with the white people and to drive the Coloured people out of the towns into special locations. In Johannesburg the authorities have chased out all the Coloured persons who were living among the white people in town.

Unity of all the black people in this country is the ONLY remedy which will help us. We have to organise ourselves and fight for our rights if we desire to be free.

Document 107
"Johannesburg Municipal Elections: Communist Party asks Labour Party for Working Arrangement", *South African Worker*, 12 June 1937

Appeal to Labour Party
The General Secretary.
S.A. Labour Party,
Johannesburg

Dear Comrade

I am directed by our Central Committee to communicate with you in regard to the coming municipal elections next October. For a large number of years the Johannesburg City Council has been ruled by the Ratepayers party, representing the rich landlords and the vested interests. The Ratepayers caucus has carried out a policy in the interests of their financial masters and aimed against the workers and poor people of Johannesburg. The recent inhuman and scandalous eviction of hundreds of people in Bertrams, and the throwing them on the streets without a roof over their heads, is a clear indication of the reactionary policy of the Ratepayers City Council. Even after public indignation was aroused on the question of these evictions the City Council refused to take the blame for this barbaric action and held the evicted tenants responsible. At the very time that this unfortunate event occurred the City Council was spending £20,000 on participation in the coronation ballyhoo.

The tremendous increases in the salaries of heads of municipal departments, such as the Town Clerk, Chief Engineer, which makes their salaries higher than those paid to Cabinet Ministers, whilst at the same time refusing to increase the low wages of European and Native labourers in their employ, reveals the class nature of the Ratepayers caucus, viz., municipal government of the rich against the poor.

The costly arbitration proceedings which the Johannesburg Tram and Bus workers were compelled to take to enforce a decent standard of living shows the anti-working class outlook of the City Council ruled by the Ratepayers. By recently refusing to hire the City Hall to the Friends of the Spanish Republic for a mass protest meeting against the fascist atrocities in Spain, at which Comrades W. B. Madeley, M. P. and A. A. Moore were to be amongst the speakers, the Ratepayers party gives objective support to Franco and his fascists.[19]

These facts are only a few examples of the policy pursued by the Ratepayers caucus. The time has arrived when the Ratepayers party must be kicked out of office, and for the election of a Labour majority in the City Council. This Labour majority can be elected on their pledge to carry out a militant programme in the interests of the workers and the poor people of Johannesburg. My party proposes that for the coming elections a united front be established on the basis of our programme which we submit herewith.

My party also intends to put up candidates at the coming elections and we are sure that we can come to an amicable working arrangement in the best interests of the workers of Johannesburg. I will therefore be pleased if you will consider this letter with the least possible delay.

For the United Front against Fascism and War.

Yours fraternally,
I. WOLFSON[20]
for THE SECRETARIAT.

Communist Party Programme of Action: Make the Rich Pay!
1. Active and adequate slum clearance, without the repetition of the inhuman evictions of poor people at Bertrams.
2. Reduction in tram and bus fares for workers by the following methods:–
a) weekly season tickets at reduced rates.
b) monthly season tickets at reduced rates.
c) reduced fares between 6a.m. and 8:30 a.m. and between 4.30p.m. and 6.30p.m.
3. Increase in wages for all unskilled European and Native workers in municipal employ, commencing wages to be not less than 10/- per day for European workers and 5/- per day for Native workers.

    Adequate and immediate attention to grievances of tram and bus workers.

    All municipal workers to receive at least two weeks annual holiday on full pay (no interference with leave regulations where more than two weeks already granted).
4. Improved Health and Sanitary facilities which shall include:–
a) Extension of waterborne sewerage to all areas including Native Locations.
b) Municipal Health Clinics.
c) Municipal Creches for the children of working mothers.
d) Better inspection of houses, compelling landlords to keep houses in good condition, build bathrooms where these are not provided.
5. Adequate care for aged people, including suitable accommodation and provision of good food at greatly reduced rates.
6. Reduction in rates to people that live in their own houses.
7. Municipal regulations prohibiting rent racketeers from increasing rents in working class areas.
8. Reduction in Light and Water charges in working class areas.
9. Public Hot and Cold Baths in working class areas at reduced fees for the workers.
10. Municipal Bakeries organised to produce good, wholesome bread at greatly reduced prices.

RELIEVE THE BURDENS OF THE WORKERS AND THE POOR PEOPLE!
MAKE THE RICH PAY!

Document 108
"African National Congress to be Revived: Leaders' Co-ordinating Committee's Work", *South African Worker*, 4 September 1937

A meeting of African leaders convened by the Co-ordinating Committee that was recently set up was held on August 25 at the Bantu Men's Social Centre, Johannesburg, under the chairmanship of Rev. Tema.[21]

The secretary, J. B. Marks, in presenting the report of the Co-ordinating Committee, said that the grave situation at home and abroad called for serious consideration on the part of the Africans. The war in Europe and in the East meant the danger of a new world war, which would vitally affect the Africans, while at home oppressive legislation and persecution were making slaves of the Africans in the land of their birth. The need for unity was urgent and the Co-ordinating Committee took stock of the position, considered all existing organisations and decided that it was necessary to revive the African National Congress, which is to be in this country what the Indian National Congress is to the Indian people – a national organisation to speak in the name of the people as a whole. The existing organisations must continue to work in their particular spheres, but the A.N.C. must become the mouthpiece of the African people. If this was agreed to, the Co-ordinating Committee would carry on its work in the name of the A.N.C.

After a discussion, in which a number of A.N.C. leaders participated, it was agreed to revive the African National Congress. After the aims and the objects of the A.N.C. were read out, the constitution was referred to the committee for amendments and additions.

FUTURE WORK

A number of practical decisions were then taken, such as the working out of a plan of meetings under the auspices of the A.N.C. throughout the Transvaal. This was to be done by the committee in conjunction with the A.N.C. Committee, which had planned a series of meetings for the Reef.

It was agreed on the suggestion of Comrades Edwin T. Mofutsanyana and G. Radebe[22] that on September 29, the day of the sitting of the conference of local authorities on the Native Laws Amendment Act, protest meetings be held in every location and resolutions of protest be sent by letter and telegram to the conference. As the meeting was informed that no Native organisations would be allowed representation at the conference, a deputation to be elected by the committee, is to interview the Acting Minister of Native Affairs, General Smuts, on the question of the Act.

Cases were quoted of the operation of the new lew in practice at the present time. The committee was instructed to deal with such cases.

The question of a press and the raising of funds were discussed, the decision being that the committee devise ways and means of obtaining funds for a national press, and that collection lists be issued to collect money for its work.

The meeting agreed that a statement on the decisions of the conference and the future work of the conference be issued.

The conference was marked by a spirit of desire for action and unity. It was repeatedly pointed out that the masses were ready, waiting for a lead, and that it was the task of the leaders to give that lead.

The decisions taken are practicable, and should lead to the rebirth of the African National Congress, as a broad and powerful national movement of the Africans. It is essential that practical work be done, and that no possible attempt of a disrupter or misleader be allowed to interfere with the work.

Document 109
G. H. Gool and J. A. La Guma, "Appeal of the National Liberation League for a National Convention of the Subject Peoples of South Africa", *The Liberator*, September 1937

FELLOW NON-EUROPEANS, Business men, Professionals, Intellectuals, Workers! History confronts the subject peoples of South Africa with a momentous question! Either a determined struggle to weld our divided and unorganised peoples into one united force for the struggle against Imperialism, for political freedom, or to continue as we are, divided and unorganised, facile subjects to the imperialist policy of "Divide and Rule."

It must now be obvious to all that our political line since the granting of the franchise to the non-European of the Cape has been tactically and ideologically incorrect.

Instead of a progressive rise in our political and economic status, the non-European peoples of today, Bantu, Coloured, Indian, find themselves dispossessed of many rights previously held and barred in all directions to further progress and development.

"A White South Africa"
Not satisfied with the present lowly position of the non-European population, the Anglo-Boer imperialists are straining every nerve to drive us still lower. British Imperialism, satisfied with the agreement to hand over the non-European population of South Africa to the unrestricted exploitation and subjection by the Boer Imperialist in exchange for the assurance that the dividends from investment in mine and workshop would be safeguarded and SECESSION be dropped as a policy of the South African Government. This agreement is exemplified in the present FUSION GOVERNMENT.

The determination to make this a "white man's country" has often been expressed by leading members of the reactionary white population. What does this phrase imply? *It means the relegation of all non-white peoples to a position of social, political and economic inferiority.*

How is it to be accomplished?

Politically
The non-European masses must be rendered politically impotent. It must not be possible for them to exercise any influence on the legislature or policy of the Imperialist through their voting strength. And in accord with the favourite tactics of Imperialistic rule in the colonies, it must be carried out sectionally. It is well known how the Bantu were deprived of their vote.

To launch an attack upon all sections of the subject peoples at the same time is not in accord with the tactics of the Imperialists. Having dealt with the Bantu, the next for consideration are the Coloured people. The possibility of the Coloured vote threatening the designs of Imperialist in South Africa has been largely removed by granting the franchise to the white women and the introduction of adult suffrage for Europeans.

In this way the political value of the Coloured vote has been reduced to the worth of the paper it is recorded upon at every election. Whatever other possibility may still exist for influencing the trend of political affairs in South Africa by the Coloured vote will presumably be dealt with in the forthcoming year.

The Protectorates
To further strengthen their hold upon our lives and destinies, to broaden the base for

exploitation of the man power of the subject peoples and the mineral and other wealth of their respective territories, Boer Imperialism negotiates with its partner, the British for the annexation of the Native Protectorates.

Industrially

None can dispute the fact that the cities of the Union of south Africa were raised by predominantly black labour. Non-European artisans, Coloured, Malay, manned the scaffold, Native labourers prepared the material for the proud edifices that to-day grace the cities of the Union.

The brawn of the Bantu made it possible to delve into the bowels of the Transvaal earth. Risking life and limb for the gold that has placed South Africa upon the world map. Indian workers were dragged from home and kin to transform the virgin soil of Natal into flowering plantations of profit for the Imperialist. Profits from the employment of cheap Coloured female labour made possible the establishment of many secondary industries. South African agricultural products compete successfully on the world markets at the expense of a lifetime of misery for the vast majority of the population, with illitierate black peasantry and agricultural worker. All this, in exchange for what?

By the subtle operation of the government's "Civilised Labour Policy" non-European artisans are gradually being ousted from skilled trades. Those still in employment go in daily in fear of the displacement process. Our youth find increasing difficulty in obtaining apprenticeship to the skilled trades. It is easily discernible that the policy is to reserve semi-skilled occupations to Europeans FIRST if not ONLY. This visualises a future for our children as unskilled labourers in industry. Even in the ranks of the unskilled preference is given to European labour, particularly in government employment. By these methods will we be consigned to the menial tasks in the South African society of the future. This devilish scheme to blast our future and that of our children does not end here. There remains still another door to be barred.

Commercially

With the aim of preventing the rise of the non-European in the sphere of commerce Provincial authorities refuse trading licences without even giving reason for so doing. And they are supported in their action by racially prejudiced "white South Africans."

With a government of "white South Africans" in power it required very little intelligence to assess how meagre will be our opportunities in the field of commerce. Particularly when we note the intentions of the Boer Imperialist to dispossess the Indian communities of the North of what has already been acquired by them. These vicious intentions are embodied in the amendment to the Asiatic Land Tenure Act, No. 5, of 1885.

Heavy attacks are being made upon Indian industrialists in the North. Whatever hopes the other non-European communities may have entertained in this respect will suffer considerabe disillusionment after the recent disclosure of the designs of "white South Africa."

Socially

Absurd theories of race inferiority and unfounded assertions of immoral practices are levelled against the non-white population, to justify anti-colour legislation, actually intended to complete the economic and political subjection of the subject peoples.

Cultured non-Europeans from other parts of the world are denied permission to visit our country while Europeans are permitted permanent residence in thousands. Our student youth are refused passports to proceed overseas, to acquire the culture denied to them in the land of their birth.

Not only are the Bantu, the great majority, denied the right to organise into trade unions, but also subjected to the stigma of Pass Laws, irrespective of the standard of culture individually acquired. Another section of the non-white population, the Indian, with a civilisation and culture older than that of the European, are also confined to certain areas, denied the right of free movement in the country, stigmatised on no other grounds than that of race and colour.

Discrimination against the non-white population in every walk of life is the common every-day experience of non-Europeans in South Africa.

Why Is This So?
To understand our task, it is necessary to discard many of our old conceptions of politics. We must clearly understand that Britain came to Africa not with the intention of "civilising" the poor heathen, but primarily to gain control of the gold, mineral and other wealth of the country. For the same reason that Belgium went to the Congo to "civilise" the native races with "red rubber." The same as Germany "civilised" the native races of South West Africa by driving thousands of the Herero tribe into the desert to death by thirst and starvation and almost exterminated the Hottentot peoples. The same as Italian Mussolini is "civilising" the people of Abyssinia with poison gas and machine gun. This is IMPERIALISM. The subjection of one people by another with the object of exploiting such without let or hindrance. We have such a situation in South Africa, and more: WE HAVE AN IMPERIALISM WITHIN AN IMPERIALISM.

In 1901 we saw the Boers conquered by Britain, with the economic and political control passing into the hands of the British. But the conquered Boers were not satisfied with their defeat. They strove on through the years for political power under the leadership of General Hertzog and the Nationalist Party, with SECESSION from the British Empire as the main plank in their Republican platform. Eventually the Boers gained political ascendancy and were returned to govern in 1924.

It was expected that with the accession to power of the Boers the fight for freedom from British Imperialism would take fresh strength. Such was not the case. Instead, the Hertzog Nationalist bargained with the british Imperialists. *And the terms of the bargain were, that Great Britain shall not interfere in the political and economic subjection of the non-European, Hertzog gained the "right to wallop his own nigger," in exchange for the promise to drop the secession issue and thereby constituted themselves loyal and obedient guardians of British profits from investments and ensuring a ready field for economic exploitation.*

Such could be the only solution for a reactionary nationalism, since any struggle for freedom from British Imperialism without the unity of the entire population would be futile. Much as the Boer Nationalist would desire to be free from British Imperialism they have no intention of granting equality to the non-white population, since they are themselves Imperialists. How apt and true are the words of a certain writer, "No people can be free who oppress another."

For reactionary nationalism to maintain itself in power it must have a mass basis; in other words, there must be a section of the population which supports the idea and who derive a benefit from such an arrangement. Obviously the forces of the Imperialist themselves are inadequate to provide such a mass basis. Here is where the forces of white labour are made use of.

With the aid of mythical race superiority theories, "Civilised Labour Policy," reservation of best jobs for whites, etc., the white working class are chained to the Imperialists. Though the return for such allegiance is meagre and inadequate as witness the deterioration of the white toilers into "poor whiteism." And in addition they are compelled to bear the burden of Imperialist wars when called upon.

Thus we have first, British Imperialism exploiting the whites and blacks combined, its representatives in Parliament being the South African Party. Next, the Boer Imperialist, represented in Parliament by the National Party, subjecting the blacks, and Britain, for all its vaunted love of fairplay and justice calmly looking on as long as her economic interests are not threatened.

Our Political Past
Either our past leadership was ignorant of the machinations of Imperialism in the subject colonies, and under the impression that freedom could be gained thus, pledged themselves to the Imperialist Paarty machine (South African Party – Nationalist Party, now fused into United Party) or they have deliberately refrained from exposing these designs and consequently betrayed their trust.

The outcome of either this ignorance or treachery has meant that for decades the subject peoples of South Africa have been following a political line totally opposed to their interests, finding themselves to-day enrircled by a forest of "colour bars" of every description. It may be said in extenuation by the leaders of the past that they chose the lesser of the two evils. How incorrect this choice was is proved by the fact *that both evils have now fused into one and the subject peoples find themselves without a friend in the hour of the need.*

Where Shall We Find a Friend?
Acting on the principle that "A man's best friend is himself" the Organisation hereafter named are convinced that no good can accrue to the oppressed peoples of this country, either black or white, through support of the Imperialists or their political Parties.

Our only hope lies in unifying all those forces that feel the weight of oppression as we do, into a cohesive and determined whole in opposition to Imperialism in South Africa.

That we centre our hopes in the masses of the subject people, as the ONLY force that can bring freedom. We desire to wage an open and straightforward struggle, free from the intrigues, political graft, compromises on vital issues and the thousand and one deceits that have brought us to this miserable and degraded pass.

As the first step into the new era, we call upon all the organised bodies of the subject peoples, political, social, religious and all liberty loving individuals to rally round and support us in this call for a
National Convention
of the subject peoples of South Africa.

At this convention we will strive to lay the foundation of future UNITY of all sections, Bantu, Coloured, Indian, Malay. All those that suffer from the "Colour Bar" in South Africa shall form the united front against oppression. And this front we shall cherish *and weld as the only means to Equality of opportunity for all, irrespective of race, colour or creed.*

We ask you to consider well. Either we continue on the old lines of division, in the meantime every session of Parliament sees more legislation to blast your future and that of your children, or we strive to unite our forces. *Our future welfare and progress depends upon your affirmative decision and support.*

Representatives of the following Cape Organisations support a National Convention of the subject peoples:–

The S.A. Railway & Harbour Workers Union (non-European); The Cape Indian Congress; The Docks & Stevedoring Workers Union; The Cape Malay Association; The African National Congress; The Coloured Peoples Welfare Association; The African Advancement Association; The Communist Paraty (Cape Town Branch); The Laundry Workers, Cleaners and Dyers Union (Cape); The Domestic Employees Union; The Butchers Blockmen & Ordermen's Union.

On behalf and for the General Council, the National Liberation League of South Africa,

G. H. Gool, President, J. A. La Guma, General Secretary.

Document 110
"All-African Convention Forthcoming Conference,"
South African Worker, 13 November 1937

From the 13th to the 16th of December this year there will take place at Bloemfontein another national conference of the All-African Convention. This usual gathering of the oppressed and exploited Africans will meet at a very critical period, when the imperialist offensive against the Natives as a whole has reached tremendous heights. When, on top of the terrifying amount of legislation under which they are groaning, the self-interested government politicians, under the deceitful slogan of "White South Africa," are crying for more suppression and oppression of the Africans.

Under such circumstances the Bloemfontein conference of the All-African Convention *must come out with a definite policy of practical, positive work*, and not concern itself with pious resolutions.

Every right-minded African to-day wants to know whether these conferences are convened merely for the purpose of listening to the "African intelligent oratory" and the passing of resolutions, or whether the time has come that such conferences should definitely decide the methods of struggle *for national emancipation* of the South Africans from slavery.

Unity, in theory, has long been achieved, but no work has been done to mobilise and rally the masses around the All-African Convention. Without the revival of defunct organisations, such unity does not count. It is only when there are organisations affiliated to the All-African Convention that such unity will have a meaning. See to it that the forthcoming conference is representative of the workers and peasants.

Document 111
Letters from Moses Kotane to John Gomas,
14, 17, 18 and 23 December 1937

Bloemfontein
14/12/37

Dear Johnnie,

Just these few lines to inform you that we had a very pleasant journey. In the train we of Capetown seemed to agree rather miraculously. We seemed to be miraculously in agreement on all important issues and the line to be adopted here at the Convention. But Kekana, Nduma, Masius, Mrs. Bola and Prof. Thaele were not in the same train, and they are excluded from this "miraculous agreement" among the Western Province delegation.[23]

We arrived here on Monday morning, the day of the opening of the Convention. Things were not as smoothly as one might expect and it was even a hard job to get the door opened until about an hour late. The secretary was running about for the key. The agenda is atrocious, full of ommissions and badly arranged.

The leaders are scared out of their wits. The Presidential address dealt mainly with the question of the Protectorates and mentioned nothing about the activities of the Executive since the last meeting of the Convention and this item appears no where in the Agenda. The Western Province dele[ga]tion made a stink about this, but they were overruled.

There is very little enthusiasm here. Rumours are current about burying, removals and what not. The Cape Province delegation (especially Mr. Oliphant) seething with anger against the leadership, against Jabavu in particular. However, our "miraculous" agreement soon came to an end. It came to an end because some of us are malicious.

About money for my fare to Johannesburg, I am afraid there is nothing doing. I have seen Mofutsanyana. He is strongly doubtful. So I rely on Capetown in this matter.

I am in hurry. I shall write in detail when I have time.

Yours comradely,
Kotane

Bloemfontein.
Dec. 17, 1937.

Dear Johnny,

The Convention ended on Wednesday, 15th. instant and all the delegates to it are gone save those who are also delegates to the African National Congress.

I am not disappointed with the Convention at all. Be it what it may it has come to stay. It now has eleven affiliated and officially registered organisations, and many more give the impression that they are going to affiliate soon.

"Revolutionaries" may be disappointed but those who have a little knowledge of Africans and African affairs and attitude have ground to be optimistic. I cannot and do not intend giving an official report in writing as I must tender that in person before the D.P.C.

Jabavu is again elected President by 50 votes, against Dr Xuma's 14 votes. Rev.

Mahabane is the Vice President; Msimang, secy.; Dr. Moroka, Treasurer; J. G. Masiu, Recording Secy.[24] You will unmistakably see or notice that the Convention is moving towards the right. However, not too bad. There is, in it, a strong tendency and willingness to organise. No! Do I hear you saying phrasemongering?

I am now going to Thaba Nchu. Some more later.

Moses M. Kotane

Thaba Nchu
O.F.S.
Dec. 18, 1937

Dear Johnnie,

I thank you so much for yours of the 15th instant. By the time you get this letter I guess you will have received my two letters to you. I have seen "Futsi" and has already wired to Johannesburg. Before I left Bloemfontein for here I met him again about the matter. He told me that they, at JHB, have not reply to his urgent wire. He too thinks that there is nothing doing.

The Convention was a moral success though theorists might be holding a different view on this. It put the Congress, with its "Jubilee publicity stunts," in the shade. At its Congress, now in session, it only has 27 delegates, and at that questionable. The whole thing has been a flop since its opening on the 16th. instant and was even worse on the 17th. However, let us not be jealous! Nevertheless, I think they should thank their lucky stars that the Convention was held at all, and at such an opportune moment.

Our train to Thaba Nchu left before their elections yesterday and I am not in a position to tell you who all were elected to the leadership of Congress. The Cape W.P. delegates were engaged in a terrific wrangling and quarrels, and the atmosphere was highly demoralizing to the delegates. The African National Congress is today in its death pangs. This statement of mine does not, however, exclude any possibility of averting the catastrophe. Far from that!

I shall be very much pleased if it were possible to get rid of Dr. Seme. If that were done or was to be done, the disastrous corner might be easily turned without a mishap.

I intend resting a bit here with my in-laws. They seem to be extremely kind. I am not in a position to tell you anything about Thaba Nchu yet, I shall do so later on when I am well acquainted with the surroundings. But one thing is certain and unmistakable: there is no hiding place to answer nature's call!

Yours – Kotane

Thaba Nchu, O.F.S.
Dec. 23rd, 1937

Dear Johnnie,

[....] I think by now you have probably received my short report about the All African Convention. I wrote a short report because it is easy to do so and because I know that I am going to give a report to the D.P.C. on my return. I think too that J. A. L. G. will tell you about everything meanwhile.[25]

As I have no copy with me, I do not know what all I wrote to you. Nevertheless, I shall give you two more points even at the expense of repeating myself. (a) The Convention will meet every 3rd. year. You see, there were three proposals for: five years, three years and two years meeting. The African N. Congress people favoured the five years also did Professor Jabavu. Seeing that and the fact that to meet once in five years is equal to burying the Convention we compromised and fought for the three years proposal and that was adopted. And (b) The Convention has a surplus budget of £113.7.9. It only spent £19.19.3d out of an income of £133.7.0d in 1937!

It also has adopted our [–]sational schemes: Re "District Committees," and to help organising the organised and unorganised non-European workers affiliated to it and to be affiliated to it (the Convention). Of course the wording isn't exactly the same but the idea may be taken as such. The former is embodied in the policy of the A.A.C. and the latter in the Constitution.

Yes, Professor Thaele was there but did not open his mouth. He seemed to have been very much impressed by the whole Convention. He listened attentively and clapped his hands every now and then. I understand that the African National Congress did not officially recognise him at its Conference. As I left while the Congress was still in session I am not in a position to give you an account of what transpired there.

Coto wants me to become his secretary, and strangely enough Oliphant supports him in this. Matseke too "wants" me for the same purpose![26] Matseke has been saying this long ago. I made a lot of friends there, young and old. So the Communist Party had a third star shining in the Convention besides Mofutsanyana and Radebe. Therefore the Capetown D.P.C. did well to send me there, but all thanks and congratulations are due to J.S.G. for his unselfish act.

I had a long talk with Leepile and his chief.[27] They came to Bloemfontein for the Convention but they were a day late! They came a day after the Convention sessions so they attended the Congress one. He looks quite fit and healthy. He wants: "Inpreco," Week-ends Argus, pamphlets, and frequent communications. But all his stuff should not be sent directly to him. We must protect him and therefore adopt an indirect communication – safer method.

His boss is quite a reasonable young fellow who is also quasi-militant in a number of issues. I am sending under separate cover, D.D.T. Jabavu's Presidential address, December 13th, 1937. Here, in Thaba Nchu, I am enjoying myself immensely.

With best regards.
Kotane

Document 112
Note from Claremont branch of the
National Liberation League of South Africa, 26 March 1938

National Liberation League of S.A.

"The Stables",
Belvedere Road
Claremont.
26/3/38.

Claremont.

That this meeting of the Executive of the Claremont Branch moves unanimously that the exclusion of white members occupying any position of importance in the N.L.L. would be against the Principles of the League as laid down in the Programme; which states the officers shall be *PREDOMINANTLY* Non-European.

Chairman: L. J. Allan
Secretary: R. A. Abrahams.

Document 113
National Liberation League of South Africa,
Honesty is the Best Policy (c. 1938)

WHAT LEAD UP TO THE SPLIT?
The composition of and dissatisfaction in the officials of the Non-European United Front.
1. Mr J A La Guma the General Secretary of the N.L.L. at the time was proposed as Secretary of the N.E.U.F. but declined the position
2. The General Council of the N.L.L instructed Dr G H Gool its representative on the Committee of Action of the N.E.U.F to move a joint secretariat be formed consisting of Messrs La Guma, Kontane[28] and Pilsania. This was not done by the representative.

HOW THE SPLIT OCCURRED
1. The annual Conference of the League was attended by 69 delegates from 15 Branches, affiliated bodies and members of the G.C.
2. The credentials of the delegates were examined and found in order my Mr J A La Guma in his capacity as G.S.
3. The Constitution of the League reads "That the LEADERSHIP of the N.L.L. must always be predominantly Non-European."

> Mr La Guma moved on behalf of a section of the Cape Town Branch (Approximately 50 out of 700) the following resolution

> BUT after moving the resolution Mr La Guma stated that "If his resolution was not accepted he was not prepared to carry on"

The resolution was as follows "That whilst Europeans could be members of the organisation they would not be allowed to hold any official position"

4. The motion was lost by an overwhelming majority. Later seven or 8 members walked out including Mr La Guma.
5. The Question is,
Is the Organisation to be the will of the majority of the people or is it going to be run by individuals.

The Nett Results
1. These members who walked out in Conference have been asked to explain their actions to the Governing Body of the League i.e. the General Council. They have refused to do so and have been expelled.
2. These members of the Capetown Branch who have disobeyed instructions of the G.C and who were asked to explain their actions and have refused to do so have been expelled.
3. The National Liberation League of S.A. is growing day by day, stronger and stronger and is more determined than ever to fight for the principles for which it stands.
4. It has now 21 BRANCHES and a membership of at least 4000.
5. The African People are with us and have formed a real fighting Branch at Langa.
6. With our slogan of Unite to Fight we are going forward.

A MEETING OF THE MEMBERS OF THE CAPETOWN BRANCH WILL BE HELD ON 11th THURSDAY EVENING IN THE COSMOPOLITAN HALL PONTAC STREET AT 8 P.M. AGENDA. I Future activities of the Capetown Branch. 2 Election of officials. MEMBERS ONLY.

Issued by Booker Lakey G.S. and L Merley-Turner Asst. Sec N.L.L. on behalf of the General Council.[29]

Document 114
(National Liberation League?), How To Work Among Urban Africans

In this statement an attempt is made to indicate the lines on which our work among Africans in urban areas should take. The statement is confined to work among Africans in urban areas because of the following:–
a) Being in touch with modern forms of organisation and having imbibed new ideas they are the basis and potential leaders of the national liberatory movement of Africans in this country;
b) Methods suggested in it do not suit tribal rural South Africa, and could not therefore be apply there; and
c) As a Party we have no organisational contact or base in the rural areas.

To prevent any misunderstanding regarding the aim and object of the proposed lines of work it is necessary to point out at the outset that: the suggestions are merely intended as aid to the building of a solid and broad independent militant national emancipatory movement among Africans and a leadership for such a movement. In no way should the suggestions be taken as the abandonment of the building of that movement.

Of the seven and a half million non-Europeans in the Union, there are three distict groups; the Coloured, the Indian and the African. The three of them differ in custom, tradition and cultural development. The African, the least developed of the three, is by far the largest. Comprising six and a half millions. It is with this group that we are concerned here.

Because of their backwardness and greatness in number, Africans have come to be looked upon by the ruling class in this country as an economic asset. To the ruling class the Africans' great number means a rich field for exploitation and their backwardness a safeguard against any interruption in this exploitation.

In order to perpetuate their exploitation Africans have been robbed of land, starved of education, paid a miserable wage, heavily taxed; in fact denied every elementary political, economic and social right.

But they must be given a piece of land on which to squat, breed and eke out a meagre existence; hunger and heavy taxation must force them to come out and work on the mines, farms, factories and workshops so that the capitalists may get their profits. Their movements must always be strictly controlled by means of harassing and harsh Pass Laws, and they must not be taught anything or allowed participation in the political life of the country for this would make them dangerous and unexploitable. So "their culture" (backwardness) must be preserved and developed for them.

Because of this policy, one and a half million of the six and a half million Africans in the Union have already left the reserves for the towns. They did not leave their reserves with the intention of altogether breaking away from their tribes. They left them intending merely to go and earn some money to improve their economic positions at home. But things being what they are they never managed to better their conditions. To-day they have become a part and parcel of the South African urban population, though an unaccepted one. This has happened despite the official policy of preventing the development and urbanisation of Africans.

Though oppressed and exploited, Africans have not yet developed efficient organisations and independent leadership. This is due to the fact that the bulk of them have been accustomed the old forms of tribal organisation; that they have not yet altogether shaken off tribal ties and instincts, and that modern methods of organisation and struggle are still new to them. Work among them have been conducted on wrong lines, in that in doing work among them no regard was had of their social background and development.

Those of the Left and the African leaders who have been working among them have ignored this. They merely saw before them a mass of oppressed and exploited people who could be roused against social injustices. So they put before them questions of national importance and spoke to them as they would to an advanced and homogeneous group. Forgetting that as yet one could not rightly speak of an African nation; a political and economic group with a common medium of expression.

This does not, however, suggest that Africans have a peculiar mentality. Given a chance they can quickly adjust themselves to a new environment. But they have not had a chance. Only yesterday they were merely tribesmen whose interests were limited to the narrow bounds of their respective tribes. Notwithstanding that fact those who have now settled in towns are being fast detribalised. Common oppression and the experience of working and living together bring about that hitherto lacking social relationship which produces common interest and a national outlook.

It is in urban areas where a Zulu, a mXhosa, a Mosutho or a Motswana ceases thinking in terms of his tribe and tribal interests, when he starts thinking as an African in common with his fellow workers and residents, that work among them is made easier. But it is important that we must know what to do and how to do it. That is what questions to take up so as to sustain their interest and to get them to act together.

The failure to know what to do and how to do it to be able to maintain the interest of the semi detribalised African masses was one of the chief things responsible for the fall of the Industrial and Commercial Workers' Union of South Africa and the decline of the African National Congress. These once great African organisations lost their influence over the masses because though all agreed with the demands which they put forward: more land, higher wages, better education facilities, abolition of Pass Laws, Poll Tax and the Colour Bar, the actual fight for these was conducted in a general way. With the exception of one or two instances there were no trade unions or other local bodies set up which could have locailsed and concretised these demands. So no practical experience was gained and to a great mass of African the whole thing seemed good but unrealisable.

This brings us to our point. And that is, in every industrial centre of the Union there is a big permanent African population. Johannesburg has over 230,000; Durban 70,000; Pretoria 45,000; Bloemfontein 30,000; Port Elizabeth 28,000; East London 24,000; Pieter-Maritzburg 16,000; Cape Town has only between 15 and 16,000 and Vereeniging about 14,000. The Reef, Johannesburg included, has over 677,000.

Practically all these people earn their livelihood by working for an employer. As wage earners they have similar interests and their grievances are more or less the similar. It is our duty therefore to see to it that they are organised into trade unions so that they can collectively fight for the redress of their grievances and the betterment of their general conditions. Common grievances of African workers are generally: low wages, long working hours, no compensation or if any the scale being ridiculously low, no paid holidays, bad treatment in factories and workshops; and then the Pass and the Colour Bar.

By taking up these points and their other day to day complaints, Africans can be organised into trade unions as has already been done at Johannesburg. At Johannesburg there are a number of African trade unions already in existence. But a majority of them is run inefficiently because of lack of experience and technical backwardness on the part of their leaders. Help given them in this regard by European Party members should be appreciated by these trade union leaders.

The help will be very much appreciated if given in a straightforward manner, without giving the impression of some ulterior political motive. Those who help should really do the helping. They should assist these inexperienced and technically backward African trade unionists to get the necessary experience and overcome their technical backwardness without seeking publicity for assisting. Their main concern should be the building of an independent African trade union leadership. Facts and figures are essential for a well drawn memorandum. The Party has or knows persons capable of compiling facts and figures of production, profit, etc, of any given industry. These persons should be got to help in that connection. But first of all a comradely approach must be made to the trade union leaders and the offer to assist made to them. Let there be no self imposition on them.

Besides being workers, however, these Africans are also residents with social needs to be satisfied. But as segregated beings they are made to live apart from others in areas specially set aside for them outside towns, locations. Here members of of different tribes live cheek by jowl with one another, a factor in detribalising them and developing their national consciousness So, although location policy is bad for political and social reasons, still there is that factor to be said for it. It detribalises and de-individualises the individuals. This is especially so in Municipal locations.

In Municipal locations several thousands of people live together under similar housing and other conditions. More often than not the deficiency in all things which make for comfort, good health and beauty is throughout. So the grievances of Mkize are also those of Mokoena and others. And as the residents are all tenants of one landlord it facilitates united stand and representation. It is an advantage over the system of different landlords, as is usually the case in towns.

But though conditions in locations are favourable for organisation this is still lacking in many locations. This could be remedied if sufficient work were to be done on the lines of: better housing, water, refuse, rent and street politics. This could be done by local bodies such as the residents associations or vigilance associations allied with blockmen wherever they exist. While propaganda and organisation on national lines must not be relaxed, special attention should be paid to these popular local organisations. Experience has shown that these are easily understood by Africans and that they freely and eagerly take part in them. Because they deal with their day to day complaints and demands, and concentrate on local politics.

In this statement by "local politics" is meant questions involving or relating to the following: housing conditions, sanitation, rents and evictions, water supply, lodgers' fees, the permit system, schools, clinics and creshes, lighting and road-lighting and roadmaking, recreation facilities, transport and cheaper fares, police raids and pick-up vans and the right to trade.

Another point which should be remembered is that through these bodies residents are able to control the Advisory Boards by getting elected to these boards men of their own choice.

It would be in the interest of the national liberatory movement were our African Party members to work for the election of good elements to leading positions in the residents' associations and as blockmen. There can be no doubt that with Party influence and guidance these could develop into militatn and independent bodies. And experience gained in their every day struggle against city and town councils would be experience gained for the general fight for national freedom.

Document 115
Hawa H. Ahmed (Halima Gool[30]), *Address Delivered at Inaugural Meeting of the Non-European Women's Suffrage League*[31], Cosmopolitan Hall, Cape Town, 24 August 1938

NON-EUROPEAN SUFFRAGE
Analysis of Population of the Union of South Africa

1938 CENSUS

European population: 2,043,700;	Enfranchised: 924,354.
Non-European population:	Enfranchised:
Bantu 6,744,300	None.
Coloured 785,200	23,392 (Cape) 343 (Natal).
Indian 224,600	1,401 (Cape) 10 (Natal).
7,753,500	(No Non-Europeans enfranchised in Orange Free State or Transvaal.)
	Total Non-European vote – 25,046.

Thus, out of a population of nearly 8,000,000, only 25,046 are directly represented. Whereas since 54 per cent. Europeans are enfranchised, we should have a little over 4,000,000 votes. The Coloured vote would be 400,000. As it is, only one-sixteenth is enfranchised, i.e., out of every sixteen eligible Coloured men and women there is only one voter; and out of every 160 non-Europeans there is only one voter.

COLOURED VOTE

The positions is this: while the Non-European man with his 25,046 votes "enjoyed" the vote, in actual fact it had no effect on the social and economic life of the people as a whole, because a million whites, male and female were enfranchised since –
a) The granting of votes to white women (1930 White Womens Suffrage Act);
b) The granting of votes to white males (1931 White Male Suffrage Act).
The latter Act removed certain wage and other qualifications previously imposed on white males in the Cape and Natal. In the Transvaal and in the Orange Free State the white males always had the vote without the impositions of wage or property qualifications.

The Coloured vote may have had a local effect in the Cape. This vote could, according to Dr. Marais (lecturer in history, University of Cape Town), influence 10 constituencies in the Cape Peninsula. The Coloured leaders accordingly brandished about words like "Balance of Power" during election times, giving the Coloured electorate to understand that their 24,000 votes were *deciding factors* in 10 constituencies – which they are not! This was definitely creating a false impression, as their so-called "Bargaining Power" was really a meaningless phrase.

Unfortunately our past leadership had fallen into this political trap set by the South African Government and specially prepared for them. They seemed to have forgotten that during the South African elections the Coloured man had no alternative – *since he was without direct representation* – but to vote for either the Nationalist or the South African Party in the old days, or to-day to vote for the Nationalist or the United Party. It was a case of six of one and half a dozen of the other. I shall explain later how the policies of the Nationalists and the United Parties coincide eventually; that is why I am using the words "six of one and half a dozen of the other."

COMPOSITION OF GOVERNMENT

The composition of our governmental machinery being such that whatever party came into power, the same machinery would function and would relentlessly pursue its work of passing legislation detrimental to the Non-European as a whole.

The present politico-economic structure of South Africa is so built that it has for its main support the pillars of racialism, exemplified by the colour-bar legislation now on the Statute Book of South Africa. Any weakening of these pillars would mean a weakening of the whole structure; therefore the machinery of the State is there to see that there is no weakening.

The creation of a white mass-basis in the form of a *white electorate*, male and female, was a necessary step on the part of the ruling class to ensure the smooth running of this machinery.

The creation of this white mass buffer was a step on their part to consolidate their position in South Africa, because the ruling class did not fear so much the Coloured, the Bantu or the Indian, but feared the militant Afrikaans-speaking people who formed the major section of the white population of South Africa; and it was with this class that a conciliation had to be effected and a compromise made; but it was a compromise that meant the further ruination and enslavement of the Bantu, the Coloured, and the Indian – because in the enactment of any "anti" legislation they always received the support of the white electorate – English as well as Afrikaans.

GOVERNING MACHINERY

So, our position has always been that of spectators in the game which appeared to be played on behalf of democracy, but was in reality a game on behalf of the white oligarchy.

We were witnessing the two principle white sections in South Africa coming to grips, which appeared almost a death struggle over the almost dead body of the Black man. The whole election was concerned as in past times, with how much more could the Bantu, the Coloured and the Indian be degraded. The United Party was for a little at a time, and that gradually; and as it had the State machinery in its hands, it therefore had the power to act accordingly. The Nationalist Party – the opposition – was for a more quickened tempo of degradation and enslavement. (We know that opposition to governmental procedure means that the bark is much louder than the bite.)

The only difference between them – Nationalists and United Party – is that the Fusionists stood for slow torture and the Malanites did not pretend and were more brazen and brutally frank in their attacks upon the Non-Europeans. So the time factor was the *only difference fundamentally*. The end in view was the same. In reality the two policies coincide, for both parties stand for the present constitution of South Africa, in so far as it means the retention of the colour-bar laws, etc.

MEANING OF THE VOTE

In the so-called democracies of England, France and America, where adult suffrage prevails, the people can elect their own representatives to plead their cause, and make known their grievances – and form their own party organisations.

The three party system existed in England for a number of years, the Conservatives, representing big business and land-owners; the Liberals, representing the middle classes; and the Labour Party, which represented the working class. It has now boiled down to a two party system, the Conservatives or the National Government and the Labour Party.

Through a political evolution which took a considerable number of years, we now have in all European countries the representatives of the monied classes and the representatives of the labouring class opposing one another in the form of political organisations.

CLASSIFYING THE NON-EUROPEAN

To what class does the Non-European belong? We have 224,000 Indians of whom only 10 per cent. own something, the 90 per cent. own only their labour power, i.e., their power to labour. Then we have three-quarters of a million Coloured people, who are mostly working-class people; and almost seven million Bantus, practically all working either in the mines, on the land, or are unskilled workers in the urban areas.

Therefore we must ask ourselves what were the conditions of the working people in England before they had the vote. There was no freedom of speech, assembly, or press for them then. The vote broadly speaking gave them this. Their position when disenfranchised was almost similar to the position of the Non-Europeans of to-day, who have no direct representation in the Parliamentary institutions where their representatives can give utterance to their grievances. So the vote does mean something. In fact it means a good deal in life.

We must not be fooled into the belief, however, that the possession of the vote is everything. It is only the proper exercise of the vote which can do something. It can be used as a means of educating the public, and is always a means of testing the level of political consciousness reached by any people.

WHITE VOTE

The European need only be 21 years of age or over when he or she is entitled to the vote. There is no sex, race, culture, wage or property qualification.[32]

The white women obtained the franchise and other democratic rights here in South Africa with comparative ease. An obliging Parliament lifted their status to a level in some cases even higher and more dignified than that of their sisters in advanced European countries. The reason why a Parliament up to now representative of the white men of this country volutarily elevated the status of women are twofold: in the first place the struggle carried on by the women of Europe and America over the course of the last fifty years has not failed to make an impression on the legislators of South Africa. The fear of an independent feminist movement, and the effect it would create on the minds of the disenfranchised Non-Europeans, impelled the Government to remove serious legislative disabilities around which a popular women's movement may have crystallised. The suffrage movement in South Africa never approached the serious dimensions it did in England, for instance.

The second important reason for the ease by which white women have obtained their present status in South Africa lies in the presence of the vast Native and Coloured population. The "menace" of the Natives swamping the white people in this country can only be met by harnessing every white citizen of South Africa, irrespective of sex or creed. It is for reasons of this "ideal" of white unity that the position of white women has been juridically and socially improved. This essential unity could not be attained if the white women of this country were deprived of, and so struggled for, privileges which she considered her inalienable right. Such a struggle would inevitably splinter the unity of the white people. The bitterness and intensity f the Suffragette struggle at one time threatened the very basis of English society. For this reason the South African women were "granted" certain obvious rights and privileges with the hope, a hope borne out by subsequent events, that this "gift" would act as a fundamental harmonising and unifying influence among the white people of this country.

THE STATE MACHINERY AND POOR WHITEISM

The working of the State machinery is such that it must always give preference to the white population. They have a poor white problem and – also the safeguarding of interests of the big business men who *must* have an unlimited supply of cheap Native labour. The Non-Europeans having no vote cannot force the Government to deal equitably with their demands. The Coloured men's vote is only a sugar-coated pill – it is a sop calculated to fool them into the belief that they are also "enjoying" democracy. The whole State machinery is based on the exploitation of the Non-European workers.

In 1920 the series of agricultural crises came to a head; consequently there was a huge influx of poor whites into the urban areas. Now the farmers and even the "by-woners" are wedded to the soil, and only a major upheaval could uproot the countrymen and cause them to migrate to the town.

The Carnegie Reports on the Poor White problem analyses the whole situation.[33]

The result was that the government was faced with the rehabilatation of a substantial proportion of the poor whites whose influx into the urban areas was caused by the recurrent agricultural crises and other factors. This led (according to the "Year Book," No. 16, page 189):–

". . . to the development of the sentiment favourable to the employment of European labour in occupational spheres hitherto regarded as adapted primarily for Native labour. This sentiment, which took practical shape under pressure of the acute unemployment following the economic depression of 1920, was further by the adoption, *as a part of public policy, of the principle of the widest possible utilization of European labour in the Government services*. A subsequent development in this connection was the formulation of the *Civilised Labour Policy* which was defined in one of the earliest public documents, issued by the Government, formed by General Hertzog in July, 1924. . . ." (Our emphasis.)

The "Year Book" goes on to say: "Since the issue of the circular, the different Governmental departments have systematically endeavoured to give effect to the policy outlined therein; and in (I) *Railways and Harbours Services*, the civilised labour policy has had far reaching effects, a wide field of employment having been opened to European unskilled and semi-skilled labour." (Our emphasis.)

Not only that but "avenues were further opened up in manufacturing industries for the employment of European workers. In several instances industrial councils have already included in their agreements suitable provisions to meet the requirements of *Civilised Labour* (!) in occupations not hitherto available for them." (Page 204, 1934–1935 "Year Book.")

This "Year Book" also gives details of the other avenues of employment opened for Europeans. The permanent measures for the Relief of Unemployment is as follows (Europeans only), page 205, 1934–1935 "Year Book":–

LAND.
    (II)   a. Anti-soil Erosion Schemes.
            b. Eradication of Joint Cactus and Noxious Weeds.
            c. Rural Rehabilatation and Housing Schemes.

IRRIGATION WORKS.
- (III) a. Vaal-Haartz Scheme.
- b. Vaal Dam.
- (III) c. Loskop and Riet Rivier Irrigation Works.
- (IV) Special Service Battalion.
- (V) Pioneer Battalion.

The Coloured Commission Report is a saga of the degradation and suppression of the Coloured people; and a great deal of it is directly attributable to the so-called Civilised Labour.

FALLACY OF THE COLOURED VOTE

I have explained the Civilised Labour Policy at some length to give you an idea of the basis of this "democracy" and the ineffectiveness of the Coloured vote with the special qualifications and restrictions attached to it.

An analysis of the vote shows that over 54 per cent. of Europeans (out of the total population) who are over 21 years of age are registered.

Taking 50 per cent. of the Coloured population as being over 21 years of age (Note: In Europe 54 per cent. are over 21 years of age) then the number of eligible voters on a population basis should be 400,000; but only 23,392 are registered. And taking the Non-Europeans as a whole, then their voting strength should be just a little over 4,000,000.

QUALIFICATIONS OF COLOURED VOTE

Now what are the qualifications which neutralises the Coloured vote? I will again quote from the "Year Book" (the official Government publication):–

1) Education

"Although qualified in every other respect (not mentally disordered, not guilty of murder, etc.) no Non-European person may be registered as a voter unless he is able to sign his name and write his address and occupation; such persons who were registered as Parliamentary voters in any fiscal division of the Cape Province on the 1st January, 1893, are, however, exempt from this provision, provided they can show that they have since continued to reside in such a division.

2) Occupation and Property

"Occupation within the Union or the Mandated Territories of South West Africa (either solely or jointly with other persons) for not less than twelve months next before the day on the registration commenced, and for the last three months of such period within the electoral division for which such person claims to be registered, of a house, warehouse, shop or other building which, either separately or jointly with any land within the electoral division, is of the value of £75. If there is more than one joint occupier, the share of each occupier claiming to vote must be of the value of £75.

3) Salary and Wages

"Real and bonafide receipt for not less than twelve months of salary or wages at the rate of not less than £50 per annum. In order to possess this qualification, it is necessary that he shall have really and bonafide earned such salary or wages within the Union or the Mandated Territory of South West Africa for the space of twelve months next before the day on which the registration commenced and that for the last three months of such period he shall have resided within the electoral division for which he claims to be registered."

NATAL PROVINCE

Every male Native resident in, or possessing the necessary qualification in Natal is disqualified for registration as a voter under the provisions of the Natal Franchise Laws, unless he possesses a certificate from the Governor entitling him to be registrered.

Persons who (not being of European origin) are Natives or descendents in the male line of natives of countries, which had not, prior to the 23rd May, 1896, possessed elective representative institutions founded upon the Parliamentary franchise, are disqualified from being registered as voters unless possessed of certificates of exemption granted by the Governor-General-n-Council.

The qualification for registration of Non-White male persons (other than Natives as voters are: (a) ownership of property; (b) income; (c) residence within the electoral division.

a) Ownership of immovable property of the value of £50 or the renting of such property of the yearly value of £10 within an electoral division in Natal. In the case of joint occupation, the value or the rent of the property if equally divided among the joint occupiers must be sufficient to entitle him to be registered.

b) Income, inclusive of allowances equal to £96 per annum, together with a total residence of three years in the Union. Only persons who do not possess the property or rental qualification may claim this qualification.

c) Residence of three months out of the last seven months in the electoral division, immediately prior to and including the date of the commencement of registration.

TRANSVAAL AND ORANGE FREE STATE

The franchise is confined solely to Europeans or white persons."

My object in explaining the restrictions attached to the Coloured mans' vote and the civilised labour policy is to show that these two instances are the bases on which the anti-colour legislation is founded; and also to show that it is a fallacy that the Coloured man has a vote. *The Coloured man has no vote!*

The third factor that finally crushed the voting power of the Coloured man was the fact that the white women were enfranchised while the Coloured women were not. What little voting power the Coloured men may have had prior to this was rendered ineffective.

The last general election (May, 1938) proved this. The Coloured people voted 80 per cent. solid for the Socialist candidate in Castle (Cape), but he was defeated – by the vote of the white women!

The advanced and educated Coloured women had never felt the stigma of being disenfranchised so much before as they did then, and among the women of the Cape Peninsula there was an awakening of political consciousness.

> *There is one very important factor we must not overlook or forget for one moment: that the struggle for women's enfranchisement is only one part of the whole fight for rights of the Non-Europeans in South Africa, and we cannot separate the two.*

It is my earnest desire to have the Womens Suffrage League broadened into a mass Suffrage movement, linking up the struggle of our disfranchised menfolk with that of the women.

I believe and maintain that we cannot separate the one from the other; the fight for full equality cannot be isolated from *our* fight for political and economic recognition.

There is danger in purely a women's movement; it clouds the real and fundamental issue: the class struggle.

I concede that by initiating a women's movement we bring out the women who had hitherto regarded the duties of attending to the home, children and husband as their sole occupation. To activise and instil political consciousness in the women is a fine aim; and in so far as the women's movement can bring that about, I am with it.

Another point of decisive importance is this: Are we limiting this suffrage movement to fight only for the Coloured people? We must use no stupid and opportunistic phrases such as "driving in the thin edge of the wedge" by vaguely terming our movement "Non-European," and meaning the Coloured people alone.

The National Liberation League claims to be a National body, and fights for the rights of all oppressed Non-Europeans, and even Europeans. We have therefore to adhere firmly to the principles of the League, and make the suffrage struggle a national one.

Perhaps even more important than the vote is the unity and solidarity of the Non-European people. For too long have the ruling minority kept us, the ruled majority, divided and sectionalised. We have been easy prey – we have been amenable to their propaganda of "divide and rule."

INDIAN REPRESENTATION – COMMUNAL OR COMMON ROLL?

Senator S. S. Brisker, at a welcome function, given in honour of the Agent-General for India, Mr. Rama Rau, by the Muslim Institute in Durban on July 9th, 1938, made the following statement, and confirmed it when interviewed by the "Natal Mercury":–

> I do not know what form of representation the Government has to offer you, but when the proposals should come and these will be held out at no distant future, it will be a stepping stone.

On July 12, 1938, the "Natal Mercury" published a message from its Pretoria correspondent stating that the–

> Governmental circles there knew nothing of the proposed Bill to give Indians in South Africa Parliamentary representation. In fact, the Department of the Interior states that the matter had never been considered, and that no legislation of such a nature has been contemplated.

Mr. A. I. Kajee, Secretary of Natal Indian Congress and official spokesman of the Indian trading class and well-to-do element of the community, when interviewed by the "Natal Mercury," said:–

> The ideal plan would be to adopt the Adult Franchise Act of 1932, which gave the vote to all persons over 21. *But I am not prepared to advocate this in view of the opposition it would arouse among Europeans. A compromise which would be acceptable to Indians would be a common electoral roll, but with added qualifications such as educational, property, or other qualifications. This can be so tightened up that any fear on the part of the European of being swamped will be removed. We can keep to a given percentage, too . . . . We are quite prepared to elect Europeans and to trust them to do their best in the interests of all the communities who have made this land their home, and for the good of South Africa.* – ("Indian Opinion." July 15th, page 251.)

This view was further supported by the "Indian Opinion" in an editorial dated July 15th, 1938, in which the following statement appeared: –

> As regards the qualification, Europeans have the Adult Suffrage, i.e., that every person over 21 years of age has the right to vote. Now there is only one point why the Indian may not be put on the same basis as the European, and that is, there is a *large illiterate labouring class that might not be able to exercise the vote in a proper manner* . . . . In that event we would be prepared to go only to this extent that the same qualifications which existed prior to 1932 in the case of Europeans, would now be applied to Indians, namely, the ownership of immovable property worth £50, or payment of annual rental of £10 . . . . Under no circumstances are we prepared to go further than that. (Emphasis ours.)

From the above statements it must be clear that both Kajee and the "Indian Opinion," who claim to represent the *whole* of the Indian community, i.e., the "illiterate labouring class" as well as the "literate" trading class (!), are voicing the opinions of only a small section of the Indian community – that small section that will be eligible for the Franchise!

The "Indian Views," on the other hand, unlike the "Indian Opinion," is not a paper for the working-class Indian; the distinction claimed by the latter paper, which was founded by Mahatma Gandhi being that it is the official mouth-piece of the poor and suffering Indians.[34]

The "Indian Views" is the Liberal mouth-piece of the Indian merchant class, and as such, has no fixed policy. Thus we find, in an editorial on the question of the agitation following Senator Brisker's statement (July 15th, 1938), the following statements: –

> (1) It is indeed fortunate that Mr. A. I. Kajee was down to address the Institute of Race Relations on this very subject, and his address certainly put the present outlook of the articulate section of the community very clearly . . . . (The salient points of the address are pointed out by us.)

Here the "Views" is in agreement with Kajee for a limited Franchise for the Indians.

> (2) Property qualifications are being eliminated in most democratic countries, and it is a backward step to advocate their institution in South Africa. A high property qualification would of necessity mean that only the moneyed members of our people would have the privilege of the vote, and the mass of the poverty stricken community would go unrepresented. We have still to learn that the moneyed members of our people are in any way different from the moneyed members of any other community. They would tend to concentrate on their own interests to the detriment of their less fortunate fellows, and to find a community of interests with their European prototypes.
> (3) The question must not be allowed to remain purely a matter for the consideration of the upper strata of the community. Therein lies danger, and might we even suggest all the elements of failure. With the whole community solidly behind the demand, there exists a considerable prospect of success.
> (4) A great deal of European prejudice will have to be overcome before Mr. Kajee's irreducible minimum is likely to be granted in South Africa, and we owe it to ourselves to at least consider *any alternative* which might be offered or suggested. (Emphasis ours.)

What "alternative" had the "Views" in mind?

Following from the latter statement it is perhaps not surprising that we find on August 26th, 1938, the "Views" editorially advocating *communal representation on the same lines as the Natives have it at present.*

Is this the "alternative" they are prepared to consider?

S.A. SOCIALIST PARTY

Mr. Duncan Burnside, leader of the "Socialist" Party, and erstwhile member of he Labour Party[35] – a party whose proud boast it is that it has for 21 years consistently advocated the only correct policy for the Native people, *the policy of complete segregation*, favours communal representation for the Indians in South Africa. To quote his own words – It was the duty of Indian leaders to consider very carefully any offer of communal representation." – (Indian Views," September 30th, 1938.)

The reason for Mr. Burnside's break from the Labour Party was that he was against the policy of Madeley & Co. – segregation. It appears that he has not changed much since he left the Labour Party. Like the leopard that cannot change its spots, so too, Mr. Burnside cannot get away from the old Labour policy of segregation: for to advocate communal representation is to fall in line with the Imperialist policy of "divide and rule," for communal representation means segregation.

In his address at the Methodist Institute Hall, Durban, on September 21st, 1938, Mr. Burnside made violent attacks on liberalism, for, according to him, "It was not a creed that could cope with modern tendencies. Liberalism as a creed has no policy." And yet he accepts communal representation – *exactly what the Liberals did in* 1936 after the passage of the Native Representation Act. So much for Mr. Burnside's "Socialism." If this is the policy of the South African Socialist Party, then the sooner such a party is boycotted by the non-Europeans the better it would be. We advise Mr. Burnside to return to the Labour fold, where he is sure to meet many more freinds to support his policy of communal representation.

COLOURED LEADERSHIP

That our liberal intellectuals are not able to see through the farcical Representation of the Bantus by the three white liberals as a temporary hindrance in our task of educating the Bantus politically is perhaps not so strange when we consider the case of Doctor A. Abdurahman – the leader of the Cape Coloured people.

At the A.P.O. General Conference, January, 1935, in an exceptionally lengthy address, Dr. Abdurahman analyses the anti-Non-European legislation. To quote his own words –

> I have no doubt that the position of political helotage of Non-Europeans to-day is *solely due to the psychology of the Voortrekkers* who left the Cape Colony in 1836, and returned to our Province in 1910 and then completely revolutionised its political framework. – ("Sun," January 4th, 1935.) (Emphasis ours.)

Our object in quoting him is that at the Conference the worthy "leader of the Coloured people" made a statement which brands him as an enemy of the working classes. "The man on the sand-hills is not worth a vote," was his reply to a question whether the Coloured people should fight for Universal Adult Suffrage. – ("Cape Argus," January 3rd, 1935.)

Our reply is that the "man on the sand-hills" needs the vote more than anyone else – as a weapon to protect his small interests. Without it he has become the prey to economic exploitation.

It has been suggested, and Dr. Abdurahman falls in line with this suggestion, that the "Great Trek" was a protest against the so-called "liberalism" of the British towards the Coloured people. In the first place the Trek was *not a protest*, but the *only means of escape* from the *system* of government introduced by British Imperialism in the Cape. The system of government being based on commodity-economy, and superseding the preceding pastoral-agricultural economy of the Dutch.

Moreover, as Professor MacMillan, the liberal historian, points out in "Bantu, Boer and Briton": Of all the causes of disaffection among the Dutch colonists, slavery was perhaps the least."

Then again – "Boer Republicanism had broken out *before* 1833 (the Act of 1833 freed the slaves) at Swellendam and Graaff Reinet, in the last days of the Dutch East India Company." – ("Bantu, Boer and Briton.")

No analysis was made of the role of British Imperialism in South Africa, and the form of State institution it introduced to keep the various sections, Boer, Bantu, Coloured and Indian divided.

We could not have expected the doctor to come out openly against Imperialism at this stage in his political development; for did not the A.P.O. consistently support the political parties that were, and are, the mouth-pieces of the Chamber of Mines? First it was the South African Party, then the Fusion Party, and even in this age of enlightenment – 1938 – the United Party!

The remedy suggested by the doctor (we will again quote from his address to the Conference) is: –

> I fear there is little hope of any improvement until and unless the iniquitous and blasphemous Colour Bar is removed from the Act of Union, and until the vigorous Constitution of that cruel Civilised Labour Policy is stopped. If that is not done then our *only hope is to appeal to the younger generation of white South Africa.*
>
> There is growing up and trained at the Universities a body of white students – male and female – to whom I am afraid we must look as the saviours of their country. They are receiving the necessary scientific training to view the social facts objectively, and to ponder the problem in the interests of the country as a whole. Many of them are displaying a rationalism and a humanism lacking in the older generartion, whose nationalism is founded upon a narrow racialism. – ("Sun," January 4th, 1935.) (Emphasis ours.) No comments necessary!

BANTU LEADERSHIP

A word should now be said of the official policy of the All African Convention, – the Bantu organisation that formed itself into a permanent body in July, 1936, in regard to the Native Representation Act (1936), an Act that disenfranchised 11,500 Natives in the Cape, and put them on a separate electoral roll.

Although the Bantu leaders condemned the Act, and declared that they were not going to compromise on such a vital issue, they actively participated in the farcical elections of the Senate, the Parliament and the Representation Council. This very act of theirs showed that they *did* compromise on this "vital issue."

The Bantu people were clearly against both the Native Representation Act and Native Law Amendment Act (1937).

Clearly these Acts could not have been made to work without the co-operation of the so-called Bantu leaders. [....]

Knowing full well that the method of election would "not give adequate scope for the representation of various interests and aspirations of he African peoples," the "leaders" of the Convention struggled not for the creation of an organised movement to resist the Slave Laws, but instead struggled for the "honour" of a seat in the Native Representation councils.

Here too we have a clear indication, just as in the case of Kajee and Co., only here the names are different, being Jabavu and Co., filling admirably the role of traitors to the Bantu labouring-classes, and hindering in every possible way the development of political consciousness of the masses. This development, with each new act of betrayal made clear to the oppressed peoples, must by the very nature of things, take place, in spite of a million Kajees, Abdurahmans and Jabavus!

CONCLUSION

We are glad of these statements by the professed "leaders" of the oppressed Non-European peoples. Although many of us had no illusions about these fine gentlemen – their open and blatantly reactionary opinions merely confirm what we had already thought of them – the very fact that they have completely ignored the "illiterate labouring classes" in their demand for the most elementary democratic right – the vote is further proof, if proof be at all necessary, what constituted our past leadership.

I do not think it necessary now to go into the details of the importance of a Non-European United Front. It is by this time clear to all why such a Front should take place, and why all oppressed Non-European races should make common cause in their fight for political, economic and social rights.

In collective action the rulers will see danger, and everything will be done to bring about division and antagonism. They may even enfranchise the Coloured women, or drop the restrictions at present attached to the Coloured mens' vote. That will be a sop calculated to break up the United Front. We know that the Government, when it finds itself in a tight corner and unable to extricate itself, will seek for a compromise.

We must guard against opportunists who will fall for this compromise and thereafter abandon the fight for the rights of the other sections.

Forward Then Towards the Unity and Solidary
of the Oppresed Non-European Peoples!!!

Down With Imperialism in South Africa!

Document 116
Committee of Action of the Non-European United Front, *Non-European United Front*, Cape Town (*1939*)

THE POPULATION of South Africa consists of 2,000,000 Europeans, 6,500,000 Natives, 219,928 Indians, and 750,000 Coloured people.

Since the act of Union, 1910, many Statutes and laws have been passed depriving non-Europeans of certain of their rights of citizenship.

Their right to vote and to be elected to Parliament and other legislative bodies on an equal basis with Europeans has been completely taken away from the Native, while the Coloured people are also deprived of the right to represent themselves directly in Parliament, and enjoy the right to vote, but on a different basis from the European.

The freedom of movement of the Natives is restricted by the Pass Laws and the Urban Areas Act.

The commercial and trading rights of Coloured, Indian and Native are very limited, and are in practice confined to certain areas.

In industry, agriculture and in the mines the bulk of the non-Europeans is limited to unskilled and semi-skilled work earning low wages.

The number of non-Europeans engaged in skilled occupations is diminishing as the result of the operation of various industrial laws (Wage, Industrial, Conciliation and Apprenticeship Acts), the Civilised or White Labour Policy, and racial prejudice generally.

Educationally and socially, the non-Europeans are given facilities and services which are inferior and unsatisfactory as compared with those enjoyed by Europeans.

VARIOUS SEGREGATION PROPOSALS BEFORE THE COUNTRY
Under various acts and ordinances the power to segregate non-Europeans already exists in most parts of the Union. By means of the Native Lands Act, and Native Urban Areas Act, Natives can be compelled to live in special areas or locations.

Legislative machinery also exists in the Transvaal and the Orange Free State whereby Coloured and Indian are prohibited from owning or occupying land, and are being compelled to live in Separate Areas.

Fresh attempts are now being made to take away from every non-European his right to live or trade where he pleases.

1. **THE DRAFT SEGREGATION ORDINANCE (Cape)**
   This Ordinance proposes to give the power to local authorities (Municipalities and Village Boards) to segregate non-Europeans into separate areas from Europeans in the Cape, and to prevent them from using the same halls, public parks, places of amusements, trains and buses as Europeans.
2. In Parliament a Bill will be moved by Mr. A. Friend of the United Party giving all Provincial Councils and Municipalities the right to confine non-Europeans to special residential and trading areas.
3. **THE NATIONALIST PARTY PETITION**
   The Nationalist Party is circulating a petititon throughout the Union for signature by White South Africans only, calling on the Government to pass laws to segregate non-Europeans residentially, to make mixed marriages and miscegenation between

Europeans and non-Europeans a criminal offence, to separate Europeans from non-Europeans in industry, and to take away the vote and other social rights still possessed by the non-Europeans.

4. **STUTTAFORD'S SERVITUDE SCHEME**

The Government (the United Party) through Mr. R. Stuttaford (the Minister of Interior) contemplate introducing a Bill which will result in segregating the non-Europeans.

The Union will be divided up into various areas or districts. If in any district 75 per cent. of the registered property owners vote in favour of segregation, then the Government will register free of charge a servitude (a legal restirction) against the title deeds of every property in that area, to the effect that no non-European may in future occupy, lease, own or inherit property in that area.

DIRECTIVES OF METHODS OF STRUGGLE AGAINST THESE SEGREGATION PROPOSALS:

These various proposals attack valuable rights and privileges of all sections of the non-Europeans, and must therefore be resisted by joint collective and united action.

1. **REGIONAL CONFERENCES**

In every centre a regional conference of all organisations in that district and in the near neighbourhood should be called.

Local Committee's of Action should be formed to conduct a joint campaign not only against the segregation proposals but also against existing colour-bar laws.

2. **MEETINGS AND PROPAGANDA**

Each organisation individually should raise the question with its members and hold meetings of protest and opposition. Joint meetings should also be called by local Committees of Action to explain the dangers of segregation to the people and rouse them to organised participation in the anti-segregation campaign.

Explanatory leaflets, pamphlets and posters should be written, and letters and articles to newspapers circulating in the district.

3. **COUNTER-PETITION AND PETITION DAY**

The Counter-Petititon against Segregation (enclosed) should be circulated for signature by all organisations and local Committees of Action in order to obtain about 250,000 signatures protesting against segregation and demanding the removal of all the repressive colour bar laws affecting Coloured, Malay, Indian and Native.

This petition will be presented to Parliament by the end of May, 1939, as an expression of the people's discontent.

House to house canvassing for signatures on a systematic basis must be organised in every town, village, reserve or country district.

Tables with petitions should be regularly put out in the streets calling for signatures. Petitions should also be kept in shops.

In addition Saturday, 25th day of March, 1939, should be regarded as Petition Day, on this day, in every centre simultaneously, organisations **must** conduct a house to house canvas.

4. **NATIONAL PROTEST DAY**

Monday the 27th of March, 1939, will be NATIONAL DAY OF PROTEST. On this day, meetings and demonstrations of protest must take place simultaneously throughout South Africa, so that a continuous chain of meetings will be held on this day. DAY OF PRAYER: On the preceeding Sunday, that is the 26th of March, 1939, every Church and Minister of Religion should be urged to oppose segregation and racial discrimination.

5. Local deputations should be elected to inform the Member of Parliament, the Member of the Provincial Council, and Municipal Councillors of the opposition of the people and their determination not to accept segregation in any form.

Resolutions passed at meetings should be similarly forwarded.

6. **TOURS**

Tours by prominent speakers will be organised to go through the country and address a planned series of meetings.

7. **FINANCE AND FIGHTING FUND**

A special fighting fund must be built up and properly administered. The sum of £10,000 is aimed at. Funds should be raised by means of donations, collections, voluntary levies, the holding of functions, dances, baazars, raffles, etc. Amounts collected should be forwarded to the Hon. Treasurer, Box 2706, Cape Town.

8. **ANTI-SEGREGATION STAMPS**

Special stamps will be printed and supplied on request. These stamps will be for sale throughout South Africa, the proceeds going to the Fighting Fund. These stamps, suitably designed, should be affixed to all letters, thus drawing constant attention to the campaign against segregation and the colour bars.

9. **PROTEST POSTCARDS**

Printed postcards, with suitable messages of protest, will be sold so that on appropriate occasions these can be posted and delivered simultaneously to individuals or bodies about to deal with Segregation Bills or Ordinances (e.g., to the Municipal Executives Congress at Oudtshoorn on April 16th, 1939, the Cape Provincial Council, or Members of Parliament).

10. **NON-EUROPEANS UNITED FRONT CONFERENCE**

This event will be of the greatest importance. A conference will be held on Saturday, 8th of April, 1939 at 3 p.m. – 6 p.m. and on Sunday 9th and Monday 10th April in the City Hall, Darling Street, Cape Town, at 9.30 a.m. to 1 p.m. and 2.15 p.m. to 6 p.m.

Every bona fide organisation or branch of an organisation, whether Coloured, Indian, Native or European is entitled and invited to send its delegates.

Organisations include: trade unions, sporting clubs, churches, social and economic, political and national and civic bodies, lodges and societies. This conference will be representative of every section of the people and will establish and constitute on a truly nation wide scale the United Front of the people against Segregation, Racial Oppression and the Colour Bar Laws. It will lay down a basis of United Action, and prepare and carry out a campaign of action and struggle for the emancipation of all non-Europeans, Native, Indian and Coloured alike.

It will decide upon further and effective methods of struggle, of organisation, of forms of active and passive resistance, of boycott, and issue a programme of demands on behalf of the oppressed peoples which will be its Charter of Struggle for Freedom and Equality.

An Agenda is being prepared, but every organisation must, in order to achieve the unity of all, arrange for its delegates to attend what will be the most vital conference ever held in the history of our people.

11. **RULES OF CONFERENCE**
a) Each organisation is entitled to send duly accredited delegates to the conference, provided it has a minimum membership of twenty members.

    An organisation whose membership is 20 or more but less than 100 is entitled to **1 (one) delegate**.

    Where the membership is over 100 but less than 150, 2 (two) delegates may be sent.

    Where the membership is over 150 but less than 200, 3 (three) delegates may be sent.

    Where the membership is 200 or more 4 (four) delegates may be sent. No organisation may be represented by more than 4 delegates.
b) Every delegate must hand in credentials, signed by the chairman and secretary, authorising his presence at the conference as an official delegate.

    Each organisation must notify the Committee of Action by not later than Tuesday, April 4th (or earlier if possible) whether they are sending delegates, the name and address of the secretary of the organisation and the number of members.
c) Each organisation is entitled to submit resolutions, motions and proposals to be discussed by the conference.

    All resolutions will be submitted to the Committee of Action for the purpose of inclusion on the agenda.

    Resolutions must be signed by the chairman and secretary and must reach the Committee of Action by not later than Saturday, April 1st.
d) Organisations with less than 20 members, or unorganised communities, may send official observers with no power to speak or vote.
e) There shall be payable a Conference Fee of 2/6 per delegate.
f) While all delegates are expected to provide their own accommodation, the Committee of Action will make every effort to find accommodation in private homes for delegates if sufficient notice is given by the intending delegates.

(Issued by the Committee of Action of the Non-European United Front, 1 Longmarket Street, Cape Town.)

PRESIDENT: Councillor Mrs. Z. Gool, M.A.[36]
VICE-PRESIDENT: Mr. Ahmed Ismail, C.O.
TREASURER: Mr. W. H. Andrews.
SECRETARY: Mr. C. C. Palsania.
ASSIS. SECRETARY: Mr. M. Kotane.
TRUSTEES: Mr. J. A. La Guma; Mr. W. H. October

Document 117
Non-European United Front of South Africa,
Statement of Passive Resistance Movement (1939)

The National Committee of the Non-European United Front of South Africa has considered its attitude to the proposed Passive Resistance Movement in the Transvaal.

While the Non-European United Front will, at all times, give assistance and support to any section of the oppressed people engaged in a struggle against Segregation or Colour Bar Laws, it is of the opinion that it would be premature for a group within the Indian Community to launch a separate and independant campaign against the Government. It is essential that all the oppressed races should combine in joint and simultaneous action, particularly in view of the fact that the Indian community is itself divided on the desirability of initiating passive resistance so soon as the 1st August, 1939. The salvation of the Non-European lies upon the path of a United Front of Indian, African, Coloured, and Malay, against racial discriminations and the inhuman suffering under which all live.

The Government in the past has enacted law after law against the non-European by dividing and keeping apart the various races. The reply of the non-Europeans to the Government should not be a separatist and isolated sectional struggle by only a part of the Indian people. Passive resistance is only one of the methods of struggle and in view of the fact that the South African Indian Congress has convened a Conference for the 31st July and 1st August, 1939 at Durban to decide whether to support passive resistance or not, and in view of the lack of the preparations necessary for waging a successful and effective campaign against the Government, in the interests of Unity and of the people, the United Front expresses the urgent hope that passive resistance will not hastily be embarked upon until mutual consultation and preparation for simultaneous action be taken by the leading Organisations of the non-European people.

Sectional action is the very negation and contradiction of a United Front of African, Indian, Coloured and Malay, who are already strenuously preparing to fight the Government with every means in its power to free all South Africans from the abomination of racialism, segregation and all discriminatory laws.

Moses M. Kotane
Secretary.

Document 118
Johannesburg District Communist Party,
Call to a Non-European United Front!

*CALL TO A NON-EUROPEAN
UNITED FRONT!
TO ALL ASIATICS, COLOURED AND AFRICAN PEOPLE
SEGREGATION THREATENS US*

The Government proposes to drive Asiatic and Coloured people into locations! It proposes to push them into a set of special areas for residence and trade! It intends to allow European Landowners to vote for this removal from one area after another.

Already it allows Licensing Boards to refuse them Trading Licenses. They deceitfully do this ON RACIAL GROUNDS but they are not compelled to state their reasons. The Law invites the Boards to cheat Asiatics in this manner and they do so!

In a few years time there will be no Coloured or Asiatic t r a d e r s unless all non-Europeans stand together and by PASSIVE RESISTANCE refuse to submit to these inroads.

At the same time Africans are being attacked in the FAGAN BILLS which aim at clearing them out of the "Black Spots" – the areas where they hold land individually; and in the "Native Taxation Bill," a scheme is started to force Africans into any employment that Commissioners direct IN ORDER TO TAKE THEIR WAGES FOR TAXES.

WE ARE ALL BEING ATTACKED AT THE SAME TIME
The Asiatics are banding together to offer PASSIVE RESISTANCE to these measures, to refuse to be hounded out, deprived of their living and degraded.

ALONE THEY CANNOT SUCCEED
The Coloured people must join with them in passive resistance – in a refusal to be segregated, residentially and industrially.

At the present time it is possible for some Coloured people to become skilled workers, we must fight to extend these opportunities and not allow all the Coloureds to be pushed down to the level of unskilled workers.

The Asiatics must lend aid to the Coloured people and the Africans. They must give them rent reductions and must give them skilled employment.

THE ASIATIC AND COLOURED PEOPLE WERE CHEATED
When the Africans were being brutally segregated, Asiatics and Coloureds stood aside because they were promised that nothing of the kind would happen to them. The Government made insincere and dishonest statements that Coloureds must be absorbed into the European group, and the rights of Asiatics would be protected.

Now they see that they were being cheated! It was a manoevre to prevent united action by non-Europeans. Hofmeyr lent himself to this by urging them not to form a non-European United Front.

AFRICAN COMRADES
Do not make a mistake. YOU TOO need the strength that a non-European United Front will give you.

CO-OPERATE WITH THE ASIATICS AND COLOUREDS!
JOIN WITH THEM IN PASSIVE RESISTANCE.   FIGHT THE COLOUR BAR.
Wthhold your support from Colour-Bar shops and businesses. Let the Asiatic supporters of the non-European United Front have your support; let them give you openings for skilled employment in exchange. Do not let the Government divide you into hostile groups and then deal with you piecemeal as it likes.

Under the new laws more Commissioners will be appointed who will force you to work on farms and then take the money you earn for taxes

DO NOT SUBMIT TO THIS! Join the non-European United Front and make your refusal effective. Do not wait till they force you with GAOL or FORCED LABOUR.

Let us unite now! We must make it known that as free men we shall choose Gaol every time. They cannot imprison us ALL. We have it in our power to call the Government bluff by UNITED ACTION.

AFRICANS! ASIATICS! COLOUREDS!
RALLY TO YOUR ORGANISATIONS!   CALL YOUR MASS MEETINGS!
GET ALL YOUR GROUPS TO JOIN
THE NON-EUROPEAN UNITED FRONT.

Document 119
Non-European United Front of South Africa, Minutes of Conference held in City Hall, Cape Town, 8 to 10 April 1939

The Conference was formally opened in the City Hall, on Saturday, 8th. April, 1939, at 3.30 p.m. when addresses of welcome were delivered by Councillor Mrs. Z. Gool (President, National Liberation League of S.A.), Mr. Ahmed Ismail (President, Cape Indian Congress), Mr. M. A. Gamiet (President, Cape Malay Association), Mr. M. Kotane, Mr. C. C. Palsania, Mr. J. Gomas, Mr. S. Kahn and the representatives of other organisations.

A reception and Dance in honour of the delegates was held in the evening.

The report of the Credentials Committee was received on Sunday and the Roll was then called, there being 125 delegates present, representing 83 organisations.

Mrs. Z. Gool presided.

REPORT ON SEGREGATION
Reporter Mr. S. Kahn[37]

Mr. Kahn pointed out the difficulty of his task, as he had no clear conception of the Government's segregation proposals, as none had been issued. The Government had not announced what the nature of the Bill would be because it still relied on a huge non-European vote but at the same time wanted to pacify certain whites. He could only get his information from Press reports and statements of the Ministers concerned.

Nationalist Petition

Dealing with this Petition, Mr. Kahn pointed out that here were clearly indicated the demands of the Nationalists – complete segregation. In their Petititon they ask for: (1) Complete Residential Segregation; (2) Making mixed marriages a criminal offence; (3) Political Segregation; (4) The introduction of a separate voters' roll.

Draft Ordinance of Conradie

In September 1937 the Provincial Council passed a resolution proposing to give the Town Councils the right to introduce segregation in transporation and the using of Town Halls. It gave the Administrator certain rights that were almost dictatorial – he had the right to add to or subtract from any Bill sent to him by the Town Councils.

Arbitration. Mr. Friend, a United Party member, introduced a resolution to provide for residential segregation between Coloureds and whites, and that trading areas be set aside for Coloured traders. This was a technical move on the part of the United Party not to lose its support. The Town Councils shelved their question and left it to the Administrator, and the Provincial Council left theirs in favour of Mr. Stuttafords'.

The S.A. Indian Congress had sent deputations in connection with the illegal occupation of the land in the Transvaal which had been proclaimed to be gold areas. The Government appointed the Foetham Commission to investigate the case of the gold area. The Commission, in its finding, recommended that the areas occupied by Coloureds and Indians be set aside for them. Certain Ministers suggested that the Government should leave the whole matter in the melting pot of Segregation.

Servitude Scheme. In his scheme, Mr. Stuttaford proposes that the country set aside for occupation by non-whites be divided up into demarcated areas (outside scheduled Native areas), if the property owners want segregation, all they have to do is to register a 75% vote for it and the government will carry out its segregation scheme. Stuttaford also goes on to show that there is no intention of depriving the Coloureds of any existing rights they have at present. But Coloured people will not be allowed to sell their property to other Coloureds – the buyer must be white. The Minister further pointed out that this scheme would be a vertical colour bar and not a horizontal colour bar, so that Coloureds on the one side and whites on the other side would be able to aspire to the same heights. The same old story of letting the non-whites develop along their own lines.

Since the foundation of the O.F.S. Republic, the law has stated that there shall be no equality between black and white; the Transvaal later adopted this law and has been fighting for it ever since. The Act of Union introduced a law to change Land Tenure Act. The Native Land Act, which was the beginning of the reserve, was introduced in 1913. It was then found that the reserves were inadequate and more land was set aside deemed fit for occupation by Africans. In 1923 the Cape Law was declared invalid and the Government introduced the Urban Areas Act. This Act was amended in 1937. Africans were allowed to live in white areas, but only as servants. In the Free State, the Coloureds were treated on the same basis as the Africans. Once a Bill was passed, it would be the easiest thing for the Government to tighten its hold on the people and oppress them more than ever. He stressed the fact that owners would have the final say if the Servitude Scheme was introduced and the Coloureds of District 6 did not own 75% of the property there. If the Bill was handled by local authorities who, at least, knew something of the conditions of the people and might have a little appreciation of the position, it would be better, but the Government would not even do that.

Mr. Kahn moved the following resolutions on behalf of the Committee of Action:
1. "That this Conference having considered the various Segregation Proposals before the country, including the Government Servitude Scheme as outlined by General Hertzog and Mr. Stuttaford, is uncompromisingly opposed to Segregation in any form and is determined to resist the introduction of Segregation by all the means at its disposal."
2. "This Conference calls for the extension of complete equality and full freedom to all races and their right to own, reside and occupy land where they please and demands the repeal of existing laws under which Africans, Indians and Coloureds are already segregated in reserves and locations."
3. "That Segregation is oppressive, humiliating, undemocratic and a source of racial antagonism and in the interests of both Non-Europeans and Europeans must be strenuously opposed on the grounds that
a) It bars the Non-Europeans from cultural progress and worsens their economic position.
b) It robs them from their civic and political rights and degrades them to a state of slavery.
c) It intensifies the problem of unemployment, slums, low wages, and poverty of European and Non-Europeans.
d) It is obstructing the task of achieving the unity and freedom of all races in South Africa."

Mr. W. Cookson (Chemical Workers' Union) moving the following resolution said that it was regrettableto draw the church into politics, but the attitude of the D.R.C. was not in accordance with the principles of Christianity and brotherhood.
3. e) "That Conference herewith resolves to organise a national wide boycott of the

Dutch Reform Church on account of its Segregation policy and to request other Church Councils to make a statement of their policy."

Mr. B. Lakey (National Liberation League) in opposing the motion said that most of the schools were under the control of the D.R.C. That in 1936 there were 199 schools under their control, employing 269 male and 207 female teachers and there were 17,517 pupils. Should we boycott them, they in turn might boycott us, and in that case the teachers and school children might be the sufferers.

Mr. October (Stevedore Workers Union, C.T.). "We have supported the D.R.C. and the Congregational Church long enough. It is time that we ran our own schools and get support by raising funds from our own poor people to run the schools."

Mr. Buchner (A.P.O., Swellendam) opposed the motion to boycott the D.R.C.

Mr. van Gelderen (4th. International) asked Conference to lay down a minimum programme. Unless something definite was offered to them, Africans would not be attracted. The fate of the Africans yesterday was the fate of the Coloured to-day and the fate of the white worker to-morrow. We must be on the offensive, not the defensive and must fight not only against the present threat but against all reactionary legislation.

Mr. J. B. Marks (United Front, Transvaal) said that in the Transvaal they were still tasting the bitter fruits of segregation. There the Africans had no vote, lived in reserves, carried passes and were a humiliated people. Talks that non-Europeans would develop along their own lines once they were segregated were dangerous illusions. The Malanites were not the main danger, but the Government itself. Conference should make it its duty that Africans were not used as an instrument to safeguard the interests of the Coloured people. He therefore supported the idea of a minimum programme. Conference should oppose the transference of Native Education to the Native Affairs Department.

Mr. Cupido (Porterville Welfare Association) opposed the boycott of the D.R.C. The Mother Church policy, he said, was segregation while the Mission Church was fighting against segregation. The Missions were built by our fathers and ourselves. We should not leave the D.R.C. and lose everything which we have invested in these churches but we should demand Coloured Ministers for Coloured Churches.

Mr. S. Hoho (Cape African Congress) said that Langa was an example of segregation. Africans were governed by whites without any representation. It was backward Africans who said that we were better off segregated. The Coloureds fought side by side with the Africans in 1936, therefore the Africans were in duty bound in the present struggle agaisnt segregation to support the Coloureds.

Mr. J. Mtini (Railway & Harbour Workers Union – Non-European): Segregation began inside the churches. We built the churches but we did not control them – they were controlled by our enemies. We should establish our own National Church, a Church which we could run ourselves.

Mr. Kies[38] (New Era Fellowship)[39] moved as an additional clause to resolution 2. "That this Conference calls for the drafting of a minimum programme and should make clear its minimum demands". He said that it was necessary that people should join the United Front but on the basis of its programme.

Miss Ahmed (Laundry Workers' Union): We should state what methods we were going to use and what our objectives were. The amendment of Mr. Kies supplied scope for that. The Government knew that thousands of near whites were absorbed in European society and were more dangerous than the Europeans, regarding this segregation question.

Moved by the *Hawston Welfare & Building Society*:

5. "We the Coloured citizens of Hawston, and Union Nationals are strongly opposed to the Segregation Draft Ordinance and will vigorously combat against it to rid ourselves of same. We further pledge ourselves supporters of the leaders of each and every organisation which is fighting Segregation in all its forms."
4. "That Separate Residential Areas be rejected" was moved by *Mr. Klaassen* (A.P.O., Waenhuiskrantz branch), who hoped that Conference would support them in what they demanded.

Mr. M. M. Kotane (African National Congress, Western Province) thought the amendment of the New Era Fellowship was a good one, but opposed it as being out of place as the needs of the Africans were covered by other motions. He said that the Africans enjoyed the rights they had before the passing of the Native Laws Amendment Act of 1937. They had something to lose if the Coloured were to be segregated. There were different organisations in the United Front with different points of view and methods of struggle and it was desirable to seek a common ground for concerted action.

Mr. G. R. Baloyi (Transvaal United Front): The Agenda was quite in order. Because the D.R.C. had a few ministers who fought for us, it did not mean that we should praise it. The Non-Europeans should stand on their own feet. They should have their own Church without white men. The four suffering provinces should speak in one voice. If we were united we would stand like a rock and out of fear the Government could support us. Money makes the man, without it, nothing could be done.

Mr. J. J. Kruger (Non-European Vigilance Organisation – De Aar) spoke in Afrikaans to show that the D.R.C. had taught us even their language. Politics began in the Church. We should first instil in others the spirit of fighting for their rights, then we could discuss the question of boycott.

Mr. M. Kruger (N.L.L., Kensington). Instead of helping us, the D.R.C. has introduced Boer Houses. The parents paid for schooling and not the D.R.C. One of their Ministers had said that segregation was a good thing for us. The Ministers were there not in the interests of the people, but to enrich themselves.

Mr. C. J. Thomas (N.L.L., Ryland Estate) said there were all sorts of societies, but not to defend the rights of the Coloured. The United Front was the first Society which came forward to defend the rights of the Coloured people. He would not go to Church until he could be served by his own Coloured Minister. Rev. Forbes was the only Minister who formed a Coloured Church.

Mr. Zilwane (Lange Vigilance Committee): The white churches oppressed non-Europeans and took their money, therefore the non-Europeans should build their own schools and churches, independent of the whites. £40,000,000. has been collected by the Government in the form of poll tax, but how many schools were there for us. We were restricted in our own country and could not move about as we pleased. It was imperative that all non-Europeans should unite against the common enemy. In Langa the people were fenced in and were not allowed to stay in town. They had no vote. We should build up ourselves and take an example from the Indians.

Mr. C. J. Baker (Hawston Welfare & Building Society). The chief thing among our people was disunity. Mr. Gamiet gave an example of how we were disagreed on methods of fighting against segregation or to fight the D.R.C. Why should we pick out one church only. There were other churches which were worse than the D.R.C. The United Front would lose thousands of followers if it boycotted the D.R.C. He suggested that the motion of boycott of the D.R.C. be withdrawn.

Mr. Hoosain (Northern Football Association) said that to build our own organisations we needed money. We should demand money from the Government to develop on our own lines. We should not condemn the Jewish firms but we should condemn the Government.

Mr. L. Stone (N.L.L., Kensington), spoke against the motion calling for a boycott of the D.R.C. The motion of boycott was too drastic and our leadership in the rural areas was not developed at all.

Mr. L. J. Allen (N.L.L., Claremont): We should not only condemn the D.R.C., but all Churches which supported segregation.

Mr. L. M. Turner (General Workers' Union): spoke in favour of the boycott. The policy of the Church was the policy of the ruling class and dominated the workers.

Mr. A. Ismail (Cape Indian Congress): Many Indians were Christians. The United Front was for the people in the towns and on the platteland. The Church declared "there shall be no equality between blacks and white in Church and State". It was the duty of the United Front which was the uncrowned Parliament of the non-Europeans in South Africa, to show the non-Europeans who their enemies were".

Dr. Adams (N.L.L., Tiger Valley). The D.R.C. collected £350,000 to provide for poor whites; the Government collected £20,000 for segregation.

Mr. P. Abrahams[40] (N.L.L., Cape) thought it was not fair to take up a vindictive attitude towards the D.R.C. – all Churches should be discarded. Mr. Kies' amendment was more important. We should respect the religious feelings of the people who to a great extent comprised the United Front. The Anglican and the Roman Catholic Churches were more cunning than the D.R.C.

Mr. M. A. Gamiet (Cape Malay Association): The object of the Conference was to fight against segregation, not to discuss the D.R.C. There was no Christian country where colour prejudice was not found. Colourd people should have their own Coloured Ministers.

Mr. S. Kahn (Cape Hairdressers' Association) replying to the discussion said that the D.R.C. should be boycotted. If we issued an appeal to the people to boycott the D.R.C. it would be supported, and the eyes of the people would be opened to the menace. The demands of the United Front should come under Methods of Struggle. The Non-Europeans were suffering because their education was not up to the standard of the Europeans. When one section of the non-Europeans was oppressed, others would suffer with it.

On the MOTION being put to the vote, Resolutions 1, 2 and 3 were unanimously *carried*. The amendment of Mr. Kies was defeated by 35 to 12 votes.

3 (e) was *referred back* to the National Committee "for their consideration".

4 and 5 were unanimously *carried*.

ECONOMIC and INDUSTRIAL REPORT.

Reporter Mr. J. GOMAS

Mr. Gomas said that the economic and Industrial aspects of segregation were of vital importance to the non-Europeans, who were almost excluded from skilled occupations in the country by law. To-day Africans were merely hewers of wood and drawers of water, and were given no opportunities for development. Unless the Coloureds fought for the maintenance of their position in industry, they would sink to the level of the Africans. Trade Unionists were making a grave mistake by saying that they want no politics in their unions. There were only four coloured apprentices in the electrical trade in the whole country. Coloureds have lost whatever skilled trades they held. Non-Europeans in the Trades and Labour Council and the Cape Federation did not do their duty towards their race. These trade union bodies refused to send Coloured delegate to Geneva to represent the workers. Non-Europeans therefore should put their demands before the Government. Unless this is done, we may drop to a level where we will psychologically accept the idea that we are inferior to the whites.

Private firms should be approached with the idea of opposing the white labour policy, failing which they should be boycotted. Such measures if tactfully carried out, will be very helpful. The Nationalists were conscious and outspoken reactionaries. Dr. Malan reminded White South Africa that the Second Blood River was still to be fought – the segregation question.

Improvements in our economic conditions would mean an improvement in our psychological outlook and would lead to a better understanding of all workers in this country. Organised workers get better wages than unorganised and workers should therefore organise into trade unions.

Mr. Gomas moved the following resolutions:

8. "That in view of the inadequacy and impoverishment of existing native lands, which leads to overcrowding and unemployment in the towns, that Africans be given sufficient additional land to meet their requirements adequately."
9. "That the Master and Servants' Act be repealed and that Non-Europeans be given full rights and equal opportunities to organise in trade unions and to engage in skilled occupations."
11. "That the white (civilised) labour policy be abandoned and that no restrictions, whether legal, administrative or practical be placed in the way of Non-Europeans practising professions or of obtaining employment as civil servants, clerks, typists, railwaymen, etc."
12. "That Africans, Indians and Coloured be granted the right to trade and to obtain licences on an equal basis with Europeans."
13. "That the Wage Board be empowered to determine minimum wages to be paid to all workers, whether agricultural, mining, government and local authorities, such wages to e a minimum of £2.8.0. per week."

Mr. H. W. Cookson (Chemical Workers Union): It was not true to say that the Non-European trade unionists were not pulling their weight. It was the work of the Government to stop the importation of artisans into South Africa when local artisans were available. Trade Unions should organise and fight these issues.

Mr. Everson (General Workers' Union): said that the unskilled workers on relief work were in a very bad position, as they did not know how long they would work.

Mr. Zilwane: The wages of Africans were very low and hardly enough to live on. African miners did the most important work in the country and in return got very low wages. Workers should be paid on their merits.

Mr. Cloete (Namaqua Mission Church): Motion 8 dealing with the needs of the Africans only should be withdrawn, because it gave the impression that we wanted nothing but land.

Mr. Dunjwa (Laundry Workers' Union): We should support any tendency to improve the conditions of the workers. Laundry workers got an average wage of 18/– per week. We should demand a minimum wage of 48/– per week.

Mrs. I. Fortune (N.L.L., Capetown): Boys spent years at College with the intention of being apprenticed to one of the various trades but because of their colour had no chance. Coloureds were ousted from factories by whites. We should unite and fight against this sort of thing.

Mr. J. B. Marks: The African question was the land question. The fight of the African ws the fight against being removed from one area to another and to be given the right to live where he wished.

The President (Mrs. Z. Gool): The Government's promise to release more land for Africans has not been carried out. After the passing of the Native Land and Trust Act, all the Government's promises were forgotten. Land which was bought for occupation by Africans was sold at about twice its value.

Mr. Kruger: The Government might misinterpret motion 8. Africans should enjoy civic privileges on an equal basis with Europeans.

Mr. Allan: We should get as many non-Europeans as possible in skilled trades. We should build ourselves and would get self-respect in every sphere of life.

Mr. B. M. Kies: Moved as an amendment to motion 8:

> That in view of the inadequacy and impoverishment of the land now occupied by the Africans, Coloureds, Indians and white peasantry, resulting in over-crowding and unemployment in the towns, the Government should provide loans for the acquisition and development of the land on the same basis as it provides to the white farmers.

Mr. Cupido: Unskilled labourers get from 15/– to 20/– a month on farms. Skilled workers get from 5/– to 10/– per day. Let us demand a minimum wage for unskilled labourers, but not as much as 48/– per week, which was an unreasonable demand for farm labourers.

Mr. Kotane: We do not take the needs of the people into consideration. We ask for things, which, from a revolutionary point of view may seem correct, but which in fact did not reflect the real needs of the masses. We should demand what our people themselves demanded. The Government had promised to release 7 1/4 million morgen for occupation by Africans in 1936, but up to now nothing has been done.

Mr. Turner: Unless we were able to back up our demands by mass action, it would be useless for us to speak. We should act.

Mr. Buchner: There were Coloured farmers on the platteland who were able to supply our needs. We should boycott white farmers and support coloured farmers. Give us a chance to do business with you.

Mr. du Preez: Some people in the country districts were paid in kind and others a low wage. The 48/– a week demanded by the Conference would not be acceptable to the farmers. Coloured farm labourers who demanded it would be told to go.

Mr. Gomas in replying to discussion, supported Mr. Kotane and opposed Mr. Kies in saying that the European peasants should be included in the motion dealing with the land question. He said that substantial increases should be made in the wages of non-European workers in all spheres of employment. This shold be our main object.

Motions 9, 11 and 12 were unanimously carried. No. 8 was defeated by 26 to 15 votes and the amendment of Mr. Kies was carried. The amendment to motion 13 was unanimously agreed to, the motion now reading:

> 13. "That the Wage Board be empowered to determine minimum

wages to be paid to all workers, whether agricultural, domestic, government and local authorities."

ELECTION OF OFFICIALS

After some discussion it was decided to reduce the number of members on the National Committee from 40 to 30, in order to avoid a lot of absentees at committee meetings.

The following were elected:

President: Mrs. Z. GOOL.

Senior Vice-President:	Mr. R. G. Baloyi.
Junior " "	Mr. H. W. COOKSON.
Secretary:	Mr. M. M. KOTANE.
Assistant Secretary:	Mr. B. LAKEY.
Treasurer:	Mr. W. H. ANDREWS.
Trustees:	Mr. H. W. OCTOBER, Mrs. N. ABDURAHMAN, and Mr. J. GOMAS.

Country Representatives:

Messrs.   J. J. KRUGER (De Aar); J. B. MARKS (Johannesburg);
H. B. DU PREEZ (Mossel Bay); J. CUPIDO (Porterville);
J. W. LA VITA (Kimberley); THOMAS (The Strand);
A. I. BUCHNER (Swellendam); D. R. PIETERSE (De Aar);
C. J. BAKER (Hawston); M. Y. DADOO (Johannesburg);
H. A. NAIDOO (Durban); A. KLAASEN (Waenhuiskrantz);
and C. [*FRINKIE*] (Mossel Bay).

Mr. Buchner said that some country delegates regretted the fact that domestic troubles have been uppermost at this Conference. He asked delegates to put domestic troubles aside and to support the President who has done and was still doing the people a great service. Country people could not demonstrate because of the hostility of the white farmers towards non-Europeans' meetings. Whenever he addressed meetings, the "Asvoel Club" broke them up. Leaders should support each other. His organisation donated £1.1. towards the United Front Fighting Fund.

Mr. Hoho asked the Conference to allow *Mr. S. Oliphant* to deputise for him. This was agreed to.

REPORT ON POLITICAL SITUATION

Reporter Mr. B. Lakey

If all non-Europeans had the vote on the same basis as the Europeans, there would not have been this strife for unity. With the fight for industrial and economic equality, should go the fight against all other discriminatory laws. The non-Europeans should have the right to elect Non-Europeans to represent them in Parliament. Since Union, the policy of the North has prevailed over the liberal policy of the Cape. The introduction of the Women's Enfranchisement Act of 1931 made the vote of the non-Europeans lose its value. The Africans were removed from the Common Voters' Roll and put on a separate voters roll. They were given 4 members in the senate and 3 in the House of Assembly. This meant that 6 1/2 million Africans were representd by 7 men in Parliament as against 190 representing 2 million Europeans.

Mr. Lakey then formally moved the undermentioned motions:

6.   "That the franchise laws be amended so as to grant to all Non-Europeans the right

to vote and to be elected to Parliament and other Legislative bodies on the same basis as Europeans."
7. a) "That all laws which restrict the freedom of movement of African, Indian and Coloured and their right to travel freely within the Union and Overseas be repealed.
b) "That laws restricting the democratic rights of freedom of speech and freedom of assembly be repealed".
c) "That this Conference condemns as dictatorial and autocratic the proposed Hertzog bills which endanger the freedom of the press, the political rights of *teachers* and civil servants, and the right of people to organise."
13. "That this Conference is not satisfied that non-Europeans are treated equally before the law and demands the right of non-Europeans to sit on juries."
14. "That the Poll Tax and other discriminatory taxes be abolished."

Mr. S. Oliphant: Africans who did not carry their tax receipts were refused driving licences and were liable for imprisonment."

Mr. Kies: We should realise that we were asking for votes for both men and women on the same basis as Europeans.

Mr. Ernstzen (New Era Fellowship): Why should people who hardly earn enough have to pay special tax? The object of the Poll Tax was to force the Africans from the land to the Mines and farms, because South Afrian economy was based on cheap "Native" labour. It was feared that if the Poll Tax were abolished Africans would not be forced to go to the mines and farms and thus upset the economic structure of the country.

Mr. J. Mtini: Railway workers wanted the aboliton of the Poll Tax, as it was a heavy burden on the Africans, who were not allowed to go anywhere without the Poll Tax Receipt. The tax was out of proportion to the wage received by Africans, who are excluded from all benefits enjoyed by other workers on the railways. This tax was most unjust because it had to be paid by all Africans of the age of 18 and over, whether they were in employment or not. African workers on the railways could not get medical attention without producing tax receipts.

Mr. S. Kahn: It was impossible to cover all the bad implications of the Poll Tax. The Poll Tax was used to force Africans to do whatever the Government wanted them to do and they suffered at every turn or twist.

Mr. Wilson (De Aar, Non-European Vigilance Organisation): If the rights of the people were curtailed, teachers would suffer more than any other section. Not all teachers were political leaders, but they played a major part in educating the people politically.

Mr. H. Snitcher (Socialist Party): In this country there was one set of laws for non-Europeans and another for the Whites; one law for the rich and another for the poor. The Non-Europeans were afraid to report assaults by the police and evictions by the landlords, because there was no justice in our law courts. Laws were administered properly where possible. Free groups of legal advisors to the United Front should be formed throughout South Africa. There was no legal bar against non-Europeans serving on juries and application should be made by non-Eruopeans to be put on the Juries Roll immediately.

Mr. Thomas: Not only has the vote of the Africans been taken away, but also that of some Coloureds in the backveld.

Mr. Everson: Non-Europeans get no protection from the Government, and we should protest against this and against police brutality and demand justice.

Mr. Fester (Coloured Welfare Assn., Elsie's River): We should demand that Non-European women should have the vote on the same basis as Europeans.

Mrs. Gool: We should demand the right to represent ourselves and have a say in the ruling of our people. We should break all colour bars which have been erected against us. The Non-European Women's Enfranchisment League had only suspended its activities in order to take part in the Anti-Segregation Campaign.

Mr. Allan: The Government was getting Europeans from overseas to come and settle in South Africa in order to outnumber the Non-Europeans and avoid the possibility of the Non-Europeans ever becoming the ruling majority in future.

Mr. Cookson: The Africans paid 2/–. a month for a pass and were liable to imprisonment for failure to produce it when required. This pass system affected trade unions a great deal, as pass bearing Africans were not allowed to form trade unions.

Mr. Stone: It was the task of the teachers to educate the people in the backveld who were still backward politically, but instead, some teachers were teaching the people to abide by the laws of the country.

Mr. Welcome (Bantu Dockworkers' Union): We should not only blame the local Government, but also the Imperial Government which was mainly behind these oppressive laws.

Mr. Baloyi: Africans were treated worse than dogs. In the Transvaal the police did not even bother to establish a charge before arresting Africans. The police simply put African into "Pick-up-Vans" and then asked them to produce tax receipts, passes and specials. When all these were produced, a charge of "drunk and noisy" was preferred against them.

Mr. Kruger: People who had no work were forced to pay taxes. How were they able to do it?

In replying to the discussion, Mr. Lakey said that the Minister for Justice had the right to refuse the holding of meetings. We should fight for the rights we have lost.

Resolutions 6, 7 (a), (b), (c), 18 and 14 were put to the vote and were unanimously *carried*.

It was *agreed* that Mrs. Z. Gool, Messrs. R. G. Baloyi, M. A. Gamiet, A. Ismail and M. M. Kotane be sent to the *A.P.O. Conference*.

REPORT ON SOCIAL CONDITIONS

Reporter Mr. M. M. Kotane: Under the present system of colour bar, when non-European boys and girls left school they found all avenues of employment, especially in the skilled occupations, closed to them. This state of forced idlessness led to crime. Laws were made purposely to stop the progress of the non-European people. The future of the non-Europeans was very dark and unless we fought for the maintenance of our rights, these would be taken away one by one. The education of the non-Europeans suffered because it was not adequately subsidised. All our demands for a subsidy on the per head basis have been ignored. We should demand equal subsidy on the same basis as that for European children. We should strongly oppose the transfer of "Native" Education to the Department of Native Affairs. We should demand equal treatment in social services. The declared policy of "White South Africa" was that there should be no equality in Church and State between white and black. This meant that non-Europeans were to be people of an inferior status politically, socially and otherwise. And this in turn has corrupted the administration of justice in this country. We non-Europeans were required to contribute to the economic well-being of the state, without getting any help when in need. The United Front should fight for equal treatment in all social services.

Mr. B. M. Kies: A White child got £15. per head, Coloured £5, and African child £2. per head in subsidy. Mr. Kies then moved the following resolution:

> 10. "That this Conference condemns and opposes the proposals of the Minister of Labour to place African trade unions under the control of the Native Affairs Department. It calls the amendment of the Industrial Conciliation Act so that the definition of the term 'employee' shall include the African worker".

Mr. S. Kahn: Under the Pensions laws Europeans were to receive £3.10. a month and Coloured £1.15. Detailed examination showed that Coloured pensioners in the country districts were not getting more than 10/–. a month. We should demand that the Coloured should also get £3.10. per month. This should also cover the Africans.

Mr. Foster: The National Bond sent a deputation to the Government about the treatment of Coloured convicts, but nothing came of that deputation. Coloured children were often brought before the Courts and convicted because of lack of proper defence. These children were sent to work on the farms under slave conditions.

Mr. P. Abrahams (N.L.L. Capetown): We should force the Government to remove the obstacles in the way of the non-European children. In the Transvaal, Africans holding standard 6. certificates were allowed to teach. This did not make for sound education. The United Front should see to it that African schools were staffed with qualified teachers. Prisons were schools of crime. For small ofences juveniles were sent to prison and came out hardened criminals. The prisons should try to reform character instead they worsened and degraded character. Non-Europeans went bare-footed and received rotten food.

Mr. van Gelderen: Industrial organisation like the I.C.U. was what was needed. We should fight as wage slaves because the main fight was the class fight. We should use strike as our weapon in getting our grievances redressed. We should force the trade unions to carry out the resolutions passed by the Federation of Trades. If the Africans were properly organised our victory would be certain.

Mr. Cookson: The strike weapon was most effective. Active trade unionists should force the Federation to carry out their resolutions. We should stop buying from Stuttaford and then he would withdraw his Segregation Bill.

Miss Ahmed moved:

> That we demand the right to bear arms and to form a defence unit to fight against police brutality and against Imperialism."

"The Boycott" she said, "cut both ways. It sounded revolutionary, but it was not. We would be supporting Imperialism if we boycotted local commodities. Our struggle was an anti-Imperialist struggle.

Mr. H. Snitcher: The instigators of violence caused racial hatred. We should enlist the support of as many European workers as possible in order to prevent racial strife in this country. The Trades and Labour Council was predominantly white. We should have more black in it. We should encourage the organisation of parallel trade unions where the white workers were not ready to accept non-European workers into their unions. We should try to put our resolutions into action.

Mr. Cupido: In deciding on our methods of struggle, we should bear in mind that politically certain organisations had no say, they were doing social work. In other centres and organisations where non-Europeans found themselves in the minority and whites in the majority, it was sometimes impossible to carry out radical political work.

Mr. Turner: Equality could only be achieved by force. The Government had everything and we had nothing but our labour power. I have organised unskilled workers who had no saving bank and sick fund, but were politically conscious. The tot system should be done away with. Economics and politics were closely interwoven and could not be dealt with separately.

Mr. P. Abrahams. We should try and raise a nation-wide fund. We needed money badly. Country people should fight with the most effective methods at their disposal. They need not endanger themselves unnecessarily. A tour of the country was desirable. Good speakers should go and spread the gospel throughout South Africa.

Mr. Kies: Mr. Snitcher's remarks on constitutional fight were correct. The Government had legal and constitutional methods of stopping us from striking, so our methods as proposed in our resolutions were unconstitutional, as far as the Government was concerned. Our struggle should be a broad minded struggle with the aim of educating our people to the importance of the strike weapon and of fighting imperialism. We should organise all Pass-bearing Africans against carrying passes.

Mr. Richfield. The Butchers would be the first to be attacked. Something should be done to protect any organisation against attack. We should see to it that trade unions join the Non-European United Front.

Mr. J. B. Marks: We should not lose sight of fact that economy of South Africa is based chiefly on Native labour. Our organisational work should include mines, agriculture, railways and harbours. Any action which we might take would be considered unconstitutional by the Government. We should have our own newspapers to carry out our agitational and propaganda work in a fashion that would reflect our aims and struggles. This was purely a non-European affair and whites should remain in the back-ground. We should take care, however, not to antagonise any forces, because that would harm our cause. We should have a conscious leadership at the head of affairs, which would not lay down hard and fast rules.

Mr. A. Ismail: The I.C.U. was a powerful organisation, so much so that the leaders of European labour movement became jealous of its organisational strength. Personally he had no antagonism towards trade unions as such, but European trade union leaders had done more harm to the cause of non-Europeans than the capitalists.

Mr. Gomas: We should increase the membership of our organisations and not merely talk but act. We should demand smaller things while we were organising for complete equality.

Mr. S. Kahn: The United Front was the vanguard of the non-European peoples and its first task was to organise the people and explain to them the meaning of segregation and how it would affect them as a people. We needed financial and moral support of the people to ensure victory in our struggle.

Mr. Kruger: Country and town should stand together and fight hand in hand for freedom.

Mr. Hoosain: We should not fight for King and Country, but against segregation.

Mrs. Gool: We should first organise before we could do anything. The biggest obstacle so far as we were concerned was lack of organisation. People should be urged to join organisations and then link up with the United Front. This should be our first and primary concern. Therefore before we speak of a national strike we should see to it that we were solidly organised. When we do strike we should strike hard and the fighting morale of the people should be raised to a higher political level.

Mr. Cookson: Trade union delegates should be advised to urge their trade unions to join the United Front. Factory meetings should be held to explain the aims and objects of the Non-European United Front. Mr. Cookson then moved:

> 23. "That Conference herewith resolves to organise action of all workers with a view to bringing pressure on the Government to withdraw its segregation and Colour bar laws "

Mr. Kotane: We could not decide on any definite action at the moment. The most important thing at this stage was organisation and our energies should be concentrated in that direction. All resolutions passed by this Conference should be placed before the proper authorities. We should take up the daily needs of the people. These were little things which went a long way.

Mr. Kirby (Die Sione Helpmekaar Genootskap): I wanted to leave this Conference, not as a delegate of a Welfare Association, but as a political man to fight for the rights of our people. Those who were better speakers should go out and explain and help us to organise our people.

Mr. Everson: Coloured areas should be policed by Coloureds.

Mr. Kruger: Some teachers could not impart knowledge; we should demand higher education for our people. Teachers desiring to further their education should be given financial assistance by the State.

Mrs. Abdurahman (N.L.L. Capetown). The pension of a coloured pensioner is withdrawn when child of pensioner reaches the age of 14, as it is assumed that he would be able to support the parent. This was very unjust and hard on the people, as work was not always available and the wages paid to minors too little to support a family. The Non-European United Front should ask that Coloured inspectors should attend to Coloured requirements. This would provide work for Coloured educated youth.

Mr. Fester: We should know the various laws relating to children.

The undermentioned motions were put to a vote and were unanimously carried:
15. "Free and compulsory education for all children up to the age of 16, and the abolition of the present discrimination in educational subsidies paid per head to European, Coloured, Indian and African children be demanded."
16. "That the transfer of African education from the Department of Education to the Native Affairs Department be opposed."
17. That the discrimination existing against Non-Europeans in educational, social, medical and clinical services be done away with and that Non-Europeans be granted equal facilities and equal Old-age Pensions, Blind Pensions, Mothers' Allowances, Workmen's Compensation.
19. "That the Minister of Justice be requested to appoint Coloured Prison Inspectors, also in cases where juveniles appear before a Magistrate undefended, that the Magistrate be informed that the local Welfare Society will watch the proceedings on behalf of such a child."
20. (a) "That the conditions of Non-Europeans in prison be improved and that

Non-European convicts be given similar treatment to that of the Europeans.

(b) "That the system of indenturing Non-European juvenile delinquents to farmers and employers be abolished and that industrial training schools be provided instead."

22. The Conference protests against the shooting by the police of a Coloured schoolboy aged 12 years."

21. "That this Conference strongly protests against the use of armed police with rifles and bayonets on orderly procession after the Segregation protest meeting on the 27th. March, 1939. It views with grave concern the police brutalities against innocent and unoffending citizens and demands a judicial enquiry into the many charges of hooliganism on the part of the police and calls for the immediate disarmament of all police in non-European areas."

23. (referred to on page 12).

24. "That this Conference of the Non-European United Front strongly protests against the brutal attack by the Italians on Albania and places on record condemnation of this unwarranted attack on a peacefully disposed country."

25. "That Conference protests most emphatically against the action of the Govenrment in cancelling the Labour delegation to Geneva merely because one of the two delegates elected is a non-European."

ORGANISATIONAL

26. (a) "That the control, management and government of the Non-European United Front of South Africa, be vested in the *National Committee* consisting of 30 members, 20 of which shall reside within the Western Province. The Headquarters of the National Committee shall be in Cape Town. The National Committee shall be elected by the Conference and shall include a President, Vice-President, Treasurer, Secretary, and Assistant-Secretary, three Trustees (all of whom shall reside within the Western Province).

(b) "That the National Committee be empowered to draft a Constitution for the N.E.U.F. of S.A., a copy of which shall be sent to each affiliated organisation. This constitution shall be of force and effect until the next Conference when the Constitution shall be submitted for adoption, approval and/or alteration as Conference deems fit."

27. (a) "The National Committee shall be a body corporate and have the right and power to own property in its own name, to enjoy perpetual succession, to sue and be sued in its name."

(b) "The National Committee shall have the right to suspend, expel or take other action against any affiliated organisation or official or person and to accept or refuse affiliation, such right to be exercised bona fide and on good ground which must be specified. Any organisation suspended, expelled or refused affiliation shall have the right to appeal to Conference."

METHODS OF STRUGGLE

28. "The methods of struggle to be employed by the Non-European United Front of South Africa shall be all and any means which will assist in the attainment of its main objective, namely the EMANCIPATION of Non-Europeans from oppression, colour-bars and racial discrimination. These methods shall include amongst others, the use of Boycott, active and passive resistance, strike protest and demonstration."

TREASURER'S REPORT
The Treasurer's Report (annexed hereto) was accepted.
The Conference was formally closed by Mrs. Gool late on Monday evening.

(signed) Z. GOOL, President.
(signed) MOSES M. KOTANE, Secretary.

Document 120
Draft Programme of the Communist Party of South Africa
(c. 1940)[41]

[....] **3. The Struggle for National Liberation**
The Communist Party is pledged to work unceasingly and without qualification for the absolute freedom of the Non-European peoples in the political, economic, and cultural spheres of South African life. Socialism cannot tolerate the imposition of the slightest discrimination or restriction upon any section of the workers. The achievement of a socialist republic for South Africa is impossible except by means of the most active and loyal support of the Non-European peoples. The release of the Non-European peoples from their present stage of bondage is the most urgent task that awaits the South African working class and democratic movements.

The divisions between the workers and oppressed peoples originate in the first place in differences of racial type, language, customs, and tradition. In addition the people are divided by discriminating laws and differential privileges. The Communist Party aims at the abolition of such discrimination, and at the extension of social services and rights to the members of all races, equally and without distinction. Only by granting equality of treatment and of opportunity can a solution be found to the race and cultural problems of South Africa, and the people be enabled to develop their abilities to the full in the interest of themselves and the society.

Social and legal discrimination, by perpetuating and strengthening the sense of difference and disunity arising from racial and cultural divisions, serves the interests of the capitalist and the imperialist. By education and propaganda, by unequal distribution of social services, by the grant of special privileges to different sections of the working class, the capitalists are able to prevent unity of workers and oppressed people in their struggle for bread, freedom, and socialism.

The African is bound down by pass laws and the segregation system; he is made to pay discriminating tax; he is not allowed to buy land; he is shut out from the skilled trades, the professions, and government employment; he is denied the right to vote. He does the hardest work, gets the lowest pay, and receives the least education. The Coloured people are given a slightly higher "status"; in the Cape their men have the right to vote if they comply with the electoral qualifications; they may buy land; they receive more education than the African; and they include amongst them a number of skilled workers. The Indians, subject as they are to a wide range of discriminating laws and segregation measures, deprived of the elementary rights of freedom of movement, residence, and occupation in the greater part of South Africa, nevertheless include amongst them a small group of well-to-do traders and business men.

Even between the sections of the Non-European peoples, therefore, differences of legal status and privilege exist in addition to language, cultural and racial differences. But the incessant attacks that are being made upon each and all of them in the name of "segregation", and the growth of understanding of the root causes of their oppressed state, are creating a consciousness that they have interests in common and tasks in common for which unity is required. At the same time they feel that their interests are not share by the main body of European workers.

Europeans, whether rich or poor, capitalist or worker, form a privileged class. They enjoy free and compulsory education; they have the right of admission to all branches of employment; they are provided with social services like unemployment assistance, medical attention, workmen's compensation, old age and blind persons pensions, on a more liberal scale than the Non-Europeans. They may move about freely, buy land, and live where they please. Above all, they possess adult suffrage for men and women, and may vote and stand for Parliament.

The workers of each racial group naturally clings to its privileges and is afraid to share them with others in case its share will be smaller. The less privileged look with resentment upon the superior advantages and treatment accorded to those of a higher "status". The loaf to be divided is too small to satisfy all, and therefore each tries to get enough for himself without thinking of those who starve. But the smallness of the loaf is the direct outcome of the capitalist system, which enables the capitalist class to obtain the greater portion of the wealth produced by the workers of all races. Only under socialism, when there is enough to go round for all who work, when the fear of unemployment and of starvation will have disappeared, will it be possible to eliminate competition and antagonism between the different racial groups. But the workers will understand the need of unity before socialism comes to South Africa.

The basis of disunity is the grant of special privileges to one or other group of workers. The capitalist class of South Africa will not continue indefinitely to pay the cost of such privileges. Already attacks are being made upon the Coloured and Indian people to drive them down to the level of the African. Already one-fifth of the European population has lost most of its economic privileges, and has been forced into the class of "poor whites". Capitalism reduces all workers down to the same low grade. Low wages drive out high wages. The capitalist wants "cheap" labour, and thousands of white workers are to-day earning little more than the Non-Europeans.

The frightful cost of this war, leading to the impoverishment of peoples and the bankruptcy of large sections of the capitalist world, will bring in its train determined attacks upon the standard of living of the working class. The Prime Minister, General Smuts, has uttered the warning on behalf of the ruling class: after the war, he said, "this will be a much poorer world. It will probably be a world of unprecedented impoverishment after the most colossal destruction in history". But the capitalists will want to keep their profits, and will try to do so at the expense of the workers, above all of the highest paid European workers.

The war will merely accelerate a tendency constantly at work under capitalism, to replace highly paid workers by low paid workers. Reorganisation of industries, rationalisation, the introduction of the conveyor belt system in the factories, are the means used to create the "semi-skilled" class of workers, who take the place of the skilled artisan. Under capitalism the bulk of the privileged workers must fight a constant battle to retain their superior economic position, and they cannot succeed unless and until they join hands with the Non-European workers. The lesson of the need of working class unity is being learned by increasing numbers of European workers, for the same reason that it is being learned by the Non-European peoples.

Segregation and the colour bar serve the purpose of blinding the workers to the unity of their interests in the face of attacks from a common enemy, the ruling class. The policy of "industrial" segregation, the professed aim of which is to give the European workers a preference or a monopoly over certain jobs, is regarded as a means of reducing the wages of the European workers and at the same time preventing them from realising that they and the Non-Europeans have the same interests in spite of racial and legal differences. Every step taken to separate the workers in different groups must clearly accentuate the absence of unity between them, and therefore further weaken each section in its attempts to maintain and advance its standard of living.

Freedom from racial and national oppression for all people in South Africa will be found essential to preserve the rights and improve the welfare of the European workers. But freedom is a vital and immediate necessity of the Non-European population. Representing eight million out of the total population of ten million, the Non-Europeans have a right to claim equality of opportunity and treatment for themselves, and their future, and the future of South Africa, depend upon their ability to press for and secure such rights. They, and only they, can throw off their chains. No one else can win freedom for them.

4. The Non-European Liberatory Movement

The Communist Party supports the national liberatory movements of the Non-European peoples against racial and colour discrimination and for equality of political, economic, and cultural rights. Only through the extension and development to more advanced stages of their national movements can the Non-European peoples succeed in abolishing the oppressive restrictions that have been placed upon them; only in the course of their struggle for freedom can the people of South Africa succeed in building a socialist, classless and republican society. All genuine movements towards national liberation are progressive because they develop the people's abilities and widen the scope for the employment of their mental and physical capacities, and because they weaken the basis of imperialism, and, therefore, aid in the task of creating the workers' socialist state.

The Non-European is a citizen and taxpayer, but does not enjoy the rights of citizenship. He is a worker, but is prevented from making full use of his capabilities. Gaols and prisons are filled to overflowing with hundreds of thousands of men and women of colour, who have committed no crime, but have merely broken one of the many oppressive laws – pass, tax, segregation, liquor, master and servant laws – that harass the people. Slums are crowded with Non-Europeans whose only offence is that their wages are low, but who are denied the opportunity to increase their wages by performing skilled work. The Non-European peoples are deprived of the elementary rights and opportunities that even capitalist democracy grants to the people as matter of course.

The Non-Europeans are "backward" and uneducated because the ruling class refuses to provide them with a sufficient number of schools and teachers. The ruling class keeps them ignorant and backward, and then makes their ignorance an excuse for refusing them political rights. The attitude is that of the Nazis, who say that the mass of the people cannot think for themselves, but must blindly follow the commands of a "higher" race or leader. Without the vote, without the right to take part in the government of South Africa, the Non-European cannot fulfill his duty towards himself and his race. Without political rights he cannot remove the barriers of segregation and colour bar that prevent him from receiving education and keep him in poverty. Without the vote he cannot be free.

Each race has its own special problems and difficulties. The African demands more land and the right to buy land without restraint, abolition of the poll tax, and removal of all segregation laws. The Indian demands the right to trade, and to move about freely in the Union. The Coloured, who until recent years, had more rights in the Cape than other Non-Europeans, want these rights maintained and extended. But there are demands that are common to all Non-European peoples. They are united in wanting more education, better health and medical services, adequate old age pensions and unemployment benefits, the right to enter any branch of employment, whether in government service or industry, and the right to vote and stand for elections to parliament, provincial and municipal councils.

There are sectional and common Non-European organisations such as the African National Congress, All-African Convention, National Liberation League, Indian National Congress, and Non-European United Front, that can become mighty weapons in the struggle for these demands and for equal rights for all citizens irrespective of race, colour, or nationality. In these organisations there is a place for all Non-Europeans, who are determined to fight for the removal of all forms of discrimination against their people. In this struggle the Communist Party is ranged without hesitation or qualification on the side of the Non-Europeans.

At the same time the Communist Party fights for absolute unity between the European and Non-European workers. Without such unity it will be impossible to maintain an independent workers' policy and class struggle in the face of the attempts of the ruling class to lower the standards of the workers of all races. The Communist Party therefore stands four-square against the so-called "liberals" and "friends" of the Non-Europeans who advise him to undercut the European worker in order to get his job. The "cheap" labour policy must be abolished, not by bringing down the standards of the European workers, but by raising those of the Non-Europeans. The profits of the capitalists, not the pay envelope of the worker, must be made to bear the cost of granting equal opportunities and rights to all workers.

Unity must not however be bought at the price of the Non-Europeans' subordination and acceptance of the colour bar in industry, social services or government. In these circumstances unity would be false, and would constitute a betrayal of the interests of Non-European and European workers. The Communist Party therefore repudiates the policy of these labour and trade union leaders who stand for the maintenance of the colour bar, and hinder the development of working class solidarity. The policy of these leaders has caused them to become the allies of the ruling class and to betray the interests of all sections of the working class.

The false slogan of "save white civilisation" is echoed parrot-like by the Labour Party and trade union leaders who have ranged themselves on the side of the capitalists. In this way they attempt to deceive the European workers and to cover up their own betrayal of socialism and working class interests. The slogan is false because civilisation is not something that is the property of any one race along. Western civilisation is descended from the cultures of India, China, Egypt and Arabia, as well as of Western Europe. Civilisation is the product of all mankind. It belongs to all men. Civilisation is being destroyed by capitalism, and the working class is entitled and in duty bound to demand the abolition of capitalism before humanity will have been reduced to savagery. Civilisation in South Africa is being threatened by the forces of capitalism; it can be saved only through the unity of the workers in a struggle for socialism, based on racial and national equality.

Racial peace and harmony will be finally achieved only when the establishment of a socialist republic has eliminated the competition between workers for jobs and higher wages. The fear of unemployment and of being replaced by badly paid workers will disappear only when the productive forces of South Africa have been freed from the fetters of the capitalist system. Collectively owned, the mines, factories, and land can be developed to meet all human needs. The liberation of the productive forces will bring with it the liberation of men and women and the raising of all to high levels of material and cultural development. With the removal of backward features from the lives of the peoples of South Africa, the causes of racial prejudice and antagonism will disappear.

[....] **8. Immediate Tasks**
The present period is dominated by the war between British Imperialism and Nazi Germany for power, markets and colonies.

This acute form of capitalist rivalries has been preceded by the growth of Fascist and Nazi States in which working class organisations have been suppressed with brute force, workers' leaders executed, tortured and imprisoned, democratic rights abolished, and the standard of living of the people reduced to starvation level.

Fascist dictatorship, the rule of the political gangster on behalf of the banker and monopoly capitalist, is the organization of capitalism for imperialist war and the re-division of the world. [....]

The Communist Party of South Africa, recognising the dangers that confront the working class under conditions of the imperialist war and the advance of the Fascist armies, calls upon the workers to close their ranks, strengthen their organizations, and resist the attacks of the ruling class.

Realising that the working class must be rendered powerless by division into hostile and competing racial groups, the Communist Party calls for unity of all races based on an unqualified determination to work for the removal of race and colour discrimination.

The democratic elements in the Union's constitution and the rights of the workers cannot be rendered secure from attack until the eight million Non-European peoples have been liberated from oppression and backwardness.

The struggle of the working class is a political struggle for power to influence the state and parliament, and it cannot end in victory unless the Non-European masses join in the struggle.

The Communist Party recognises that the emancipation of the Non-European peoples is essential for the defeat of fascism, the defence of working class rights and standards, and the establishment of socialism.

The immediate tasks of the working class are to unite with Non-European liberatory movements in their demand for the removal of industrial colour bars, residential segregation, discriminating taxation, and racial differentiation in the administration of educational, health and socil services, and in the demand for the extension of the parliamentary, provincial and municipal franchise on an equal basis with Europeans;

To demand the repeal of emergency, industrial conscription and other regulations or laws, such as the Riotous Assemblies Act, Native Administration Act, and Natives (Urban Areas) Act that restrict the right of the workers and oppressed peoples to freedom of speech and political action;

To demand the raising of wages for all workers to civilised standards, satisfactory working conditions and hours on mines, farms and in factories, state unemployment insurance for all workers, and the prevention of profiteering and checks upon the rising cost of living;

In fighting for and gaining these demands the people of South Africa will prepare and strengthen themselves for the ultimate triumph of socialism.

Document 121
A. Mon (M. N. Averbach), "The Colour Bar and the National Struggle for Full Democratic Rights", *Workers' Voice*, 1, 2, November 1944

To some people in the Left movement it may still sound strange that we should put great emphasis on the national unification and organisation of the non-European for the purpose of achieving full democratic rights. There are still some whose memories float back to the dreamy days when "socialists" in South Africa were mainly European and concerned themselves mainly with the Europeans, who think that this national struggle and unification is at variance with the ideas of the class struggle. We, on the other hand, who consider ourselves the best followers of Marx and Engels in this country, attach importance to the anti-imperialist, national liberatory struggle and organisation precisely on account of a proper application of the Marxist principle of the class struggle to the peculiar conditions obtaining in South Africa. People who minimise the importance of the anti-imperialist, mainly non-European, movement and organisation, do not understand the class structure of South African society, and therefore cannot understand the relationship of social forces here. This way of thinking formed the approach of the people who built the Labour Party and the White trade unions. And what do we see as a result of their work? Not only did they not bring us one step nearer to socialism, but, on the contrary, they helped to form the social bulwark for reaction – segregation and the colour bar – in South Africa, the White labour aristocracy in particular.

THE "BLACK REPUBLIC" SLOGAN OF THE STALINISTS
This, likewise, was the approach and attitude of the people who formed and built the Communist Party here. They also approached the South African scene with a purely abstract and mechanical handling of the Marxist principle of the class struggle. Hence their meagre and trivial achievements in the field of the South African class struggle in the quarter of a century of their miserable existence here. The "Black Republic" was their highest achievement, their climax and anti-climax, and at the same time the starting point of their disintegration, until they were partly revived by the victories of the Red

Army and the fact that the Soviet Union came into the camp of the Allies. Nor should it be forgotten that the "Black Republic" theory was not the outcome of an internal theoretical development, but something brought in from outside, imposed from above, by the Stalinist bureaucracy in 1928.

We do not want to create the impression that we consider the slogan a correct one. Far from it! We are not attacking this slogan from the right, as it was by the Communist Party elements here at the time, but from the left. We do not attack it from the point of view of the White labour aristocracy, but from the viewpoint of the non-European toilers. We say it is empty and hollow; it does not create a method of struggle; it does not express the real situation and sentiment of the non-European people as they are.

This slogan of a Black Republic does not express the desire of the non-European masses, awakening to-day to political consciousness. The real desire of the non-Europeans, a desire expressed by the embryonic Unity Movement, is for Full Democratic Rights for All. It is for equality with the Europeans, for the abolition of all discriminatory distinctions between European and non-European, for a State where European and non-European will no longer exist as hostile, race-warring groups, and where race-oppression of one colour by another will be neither contemplated nor practiced. There is no politically expressed desire on the part of the non-European to oppress the European. The growth of the movement for full democratic rights, drawing in more and more Europeans over to the side of the non-Europeans to achieve full democratic rights for all, irrespective of colour, must more and more attenuate anti-White feeling. At the same time, the intensification of oppression of non-European by the European rulers naturally produces an anti-White reaction. But because it is in the interests of the democratic movement to unite the oppressed of all races, it strives always to build up not an anti-White front, but a front against segregation and the other policies of reaction

Not only is it in the interests of the struggle, the movement for full democratic rights to combat anti-White feeling, to unite Black and White toilers, and not to alienate the White workers with threats of "Black Republic" or "non-European rule". More than this. We do not envisage a perspective where one race will rule another race in South Africa. The very coming into being, into power, of a democratic State in South Africa will depend upon the collaboration of the bulk of the non-White and White toilers. Otherwise, it is an impossibility. The nature of the struggle, the unification of the exploited and oppressed of all races and colours, must determine the nature of the State, the government, which will arise out of this struggle. Should the struggle be defeated, and reaction triumph, then race-rule will continue and be worsened. Should the struggle succeed, and it can do so only through the eventual unity of the bulk of the population, non-European and European, then race-rule will be thrown upon the rubbish-heaps of our history. A revolutionary perspective for South Africa precludes race-rule and oppression of one nationality by another.

The "Black Republic" slogan went counter to this perspective. Its effects were purely negative – alienating a potentially White ally from the non-Europeans. If offered nothing positive as is contained in the demand for full democratic rights. The "Black Republic" slogan did not even hint at this simple idea.

SOCIALISM AND DEMOCRACY
Now, the question arises: How will this ideal, which lives in the heart first of every non-European, whether educated or not, and also in the hearts of a large number of

Europeans, be realised? The immediate reaction as a "pure and simple" socialist will be: "Why, socialism is the solution! That is the key to the problem!" Yes, we reply, it is quite correct that socialism will bring full democracy to the people who do not possess it now. We go yet a step further and say that without socialism it is unimaginable that democracy can be materialised and the colour bar abolished. This, in spite of a recent editorial in the "Guardian" that the colour bar is not an essential feature of capitalism in South Africa. Capitalism, wrote the Stalinist editor, may continue to exist nicely and develop without the colour bar – again a lack of understanding of the elemental condition of South Africa' capitalist economic structure. But, and this is the whole crux of the matter: How can socialism be materialised in South Africa? What are the forces which will bring it about?

"WHITE SOCIALISM" IN SOUTH AFRICA

The history of the last 30 years of a White "socialist workers'" movement is sufficient to prove to anyone who wants to see the truth that not only was it not a movement towards socialism, but a movement away from it: that it was a factor towards reaction, a social bulwark for the colour bar and race-oppression. The ruling class, both imperialist and local, always used the White trade unions and Labour Party in order to fortify its colour bar and "civilised labour" policy. The White worker is always in between the broad mass of super-exploited non-European labour, and the White ruling class. There his economic, social and political position is always privileged, and at the same time threatened by the surge of cheap labour. Greater and greater sections of the lower Whites are reduced in the social ladder and transformed into Poor Whites. Therefore, when there is economic prosperity, then their prosperity rests on the super-exploitation of the non-European workers; and when there is a crisis and poverty, the remedy of the ruling class is to increase the misery of the non-European and also widen the gulf between Black and White. And so it was with the White workers in general always in any social crisis in the history of the last 50 years, whether it was to build the colour bar for a White South Africa in the 1922 Rand strike, or whether it was in their flocking to the Greyshirts, O.B. and other fascist bodies.

The White labour aristocracy is part of the social bulwark of imperialism in this country. But imperialism views this aristocracy with an ambivalence of emotions. It uses it as a social base for its policy of segregation, colour bar and race rule against the non-Europeans. Its main slogans, in this regard, are "White civilisation must be maintained", "White Labour Policy", etc. At the same time, and on the other hand, imperialism finds this social bulwark rather expensive. Its high wages, among the highest in the world, make their costs of production uncomfortably high, especially in a time of economic crisis. It would like to reduce this expense of maintaining its bulwark, and at the same time trembles lest is lose this social support. To cut down the burden, to it,of sharing its super-profits with the privileged White workers, it brings in the slogan of "Equal pay for equal work". In this way it strives to replace highly-paid White labour by lowly-paid, un-skilled non-European labour, and thereby to reduce its costs of production. But the way in which it carries out its stratagem is such that the White worker sees the danger not as coming to him from above, from imperialism, so much, as rather from below, from the non-European workers. Feeling rises, as it did in 1922, against the non-European workers, and the divide and rule policy of British imperialism once more triumphs. Imperialism in this country tries to ride two steeds –

the White labour aristocratic stallion, and the non-European beast of burden. For the imperialist rider to be unseated, the steeds must wrench the reins of power out of the hands of the imperialist.

In order that the greatest section of the White workers should turn towards socialism, it is absolutely essential that the greatest bulk of the South African population, the actually producing and exploited ones, the eight million non-Europeans, the 80 per cent. of the whole population, should itself become an active, forward-striving, political movement, an independent force to reckon with. Only then will a real possibility be given to the White worker to help materialise socialism on a sound basis, and so save the White workers from themselves.

It is high time to realise that the main basis, the foundation for any revolutionary change for South Africa, which alone can solve the many complex problems in this country, is the non-European. Either he will perform this change, or there will be no revolution at all in South Africa! Now, when we come to this conclusion, then such a conclusion will determine the character and form of the organisation which is best suited for the struggle here, and which flows from the nature of the elements comprising the movement.

THE BACKWARDNESS OF THE AFRICAN MOVEMENT AND THE ADVANCED TECHNIQUE OF THE RULING CLASS OF SOUTH AFRICA

Before going further, let us stop here a while to consider another question. The question is: How explain the fact that for the last 75 years, so stormy in South African history of the final subjugation of the African, pushing him into reserves, compounds and locations, transforming him into a beast of burden, taking away any vestige of human rights, putting on him all kinds of taxes and passes – that in all this long period we see almost no form of social protest, no uprising, no political, national or cultural movement in which the whole misery, humiliation and oppression of the African should somehow find a form of expression? Why were the few incidents like the Boelhoek affair and the I.C.U. movement so sporadic, local (except the I.C.U.) and so early in their disintegration? Why do we not find a wide agrarian movement with its national ideologies accompanying it, as we find in other countries in similar situations?

The only proper answer to this question is to be found when we analyse the nature of the forces which caused and the methods whereby these forces subjugated completely the non-European in this country. These forces were those of the British imperialists – the most modern, the cleverest and most cunning of all imperialisms which have ever existed. They fell on, and attacked like birds of prey with the most modern and best equipped technique, a primitive and helpless people. They did this in such a way that they succeeded in breaking up and completely disintegrating, pulverising and atomising the whole African economic and social structure, preserving only those forms of tribal life which could be made use of for the benefit of the subjugator. These forms they call "allowing the Native to live his own way of life". But this was not yet enough. No. On the ruins they built such a superstructure of laws, rules, regulations, paragraphs and by-laws that it became impossible for the broken Africans to stabilise themselves on the land permanently as agrarians, as agriculturists, as a peasantry. By the whole taxation and labour-conscription system, the African was forced to go to the mines and farms as cheap labour.

But, once in the mining and industrial centres, the African could not settle there either, and become urbanised and crystallised as a modern city proletariat. No, this would be too dangerous! He may form trade unions and acquire political ideas which may develop him and transform him into a very revolutionary element! And so the imperialists built up in the mining and industrial centres compounds and locations, and the whole infamous system of the colour bar and segregation upon which the whole capitalist system in South Africa rests.

Now, we can see how superficial is the view expressed by the "Guardian" and mentioned above, that after all the colour bar is not an essential feature of capitalism in South Africa. Exactly the opposite. The colour bar is the iron hoop which binds together the whole structure of imperialist-capitalist exploitation and oppression. It does not allow the formation of an African peasantry. Nor does it allow the settling down and crystallisation of an urbanised proletariat. It keeps the African always in permanent flow from reserve to compounds and locations and back again.

And so, up to now, the African did not succeed in stabilising himself in the ordinary class formations of any settled society, which is the basis of any social, political, cultural and national movement. The colour bar makes it possible to keep the reservoir of just atomised, nearly classless, human cheap labour to supply the bottomless mines and farms and industries with labour, the demand for which can never be completely satisfied. This is the position of the African, who numbers about seven million out of about eleven million in general.

THE COLOURED PEOPLE

The position of the Coloured people, numbering nearly one million, is not much better. The Coloured people, living mostly in towns of the Western Cape, really supplied for over two centuries after the White settlement here all the trades and crafts which the young and slow-growing population needed. During the last 50 years the position of the Coloured community has deteriorated tremendously, due to the imperialist industrialisation of South Africa, to building up of the whole net of colour bars to its perfection which have cut off the way of progress along the lines of becoming more integrated in society and its classes. And so they became isolated, segregated, locationised, cut off from nearly all trades, skilled arts and crafts, and forced into the only possible development left open: the unskilled job, slumdom, tuberculosis, and skollydom recruited from the declassed Coloured toilers.

However, contrary to the African, the Coloured people formed a community which in the course of 250 years of assimilation and absorption with the White community, taking over their language and many customs, feel more strongly and are much more sensitive to the dwindling and loss of the little rights they ever possessed. Their reaction against it is much more concentrated, and takes the character of a national and political movement. This movement is all the more mature, especially when compared with that of the African, because the bulk of the Coloureds are permanently urbanised, and hereditary proletarians of the cities and towns of the Cape; and because of the existence of a large Coloured intelligentsia which has sprung from the loins of the Coloured working class.

THE INDIAN COMMUNITY

The position of the Indians is slightly different, because of their comparatively late appearance on the South African scene, with the opening of the sugar industry in Natal, and because of the existence of an Indian capitalist here. Their ties are still strong with their mother country, India (ties fostered by the Indian merchants), under the Indian capitalists, and they keep themselves partly aloof from the general non-European community. But their problems are fundamentally the same, for they are also within the orbit of the colour bar, whose wheels are strangling and crushing them.

This, then, is the lot of the eight million non-Europeans in South African under the colour bar system.

THE WAY OUT OF THE DILEMMA
Now, if it is clear to us already that any radical decisive change cannot come from a movement flowing from a White section only, then we must realise that it must originate, develop and get strong and powerful through being a flood which can engulf the whole of oppressed South Africa including the Whites. This means that it must basically be a non-European movement.

But here the problem arises. We are all accustomed to think, and quite correctly, that any social movement (progressive or reactionary) must be based on definite social classes, on the working class or the peasantry, or the middle classes, or the capitalists, or the aristocracy. And here in the vast sea of the non-Europeans from whom the revolutionary movement must flow we do not find crystallised, settled classes at all, due to the colour bar system here. So what can we do about it? This is not merely an abstract theoretical difficulty. It actually gave a theoretical justification for many an honest but hopelessly confused socialist or communist in the past 50 years here for ideas such as "civilised labour policy", "equal pay for equal work", "separation instead of segregation", and "the colour bar is not essential to capitalism", etc.

We come to the conclusion that we must find the weakest point of our enemy, and then attack him there. The colour bar is the iron hoop of imperialist-capitalism in South Africa, to keep together the structure of South Africa's degrading and oppressing society. Why not take the imperialist's own method and use it for our own advantage – to break these iron hoops, so that the enemy's whole structure will fall to pieces? We shall use his colour bar, by fighting it, as a means to unite all the oppressed, exploited, impoverished and starved masses, first of all the non-Europeans, in one single mighty movement which will erase and smother the whole imperialist-capitalist system.

When we come to scattered, dispersed, detribalised, declassed, disenfranchised masses with the beautiful ideas of a socialist society, they look at it as a dream, an illusion, beautiful but unrealisable. But when we bring the message of a national organisation to fight the colour bar in all its ramifications, in order to achieve full democratic rights, then it is tangible, it is real, it is a means to snap the iron chains which bind every and any section of the non-Europeans from the cradle to the grave. The oppressed must fight in order to live; he must break the colour bar in order to save himself from being strangled by it. To do this he will build this national organisation, and this national organisation will be the means by which he will forge the weapon to transform himself into a mighty political force, something to reckon with.

This is something which has never happened yet in the terrible, long history of non-European suffering in this country. And this force, this weapon of a national organisation, when it will start working, will be effective to such an extent that it will go far beyond its original borders. It has often happened thus in human history. As the biblical story goes: One goes to look after the forlorn asses and finds a Kingdom.

NOTES

1. Pixley ka Izaka Seme (1881–1951), a lawyer by profession, was a principal founder of the ANC and a proponent of the notion of black economic self-help. He proposed the idea of upper and lower houses to represent chiefs and commoners in the ANC, based on the British bicameral system. Under his presidency from 1930 to 1937, the ANC became increasingly conservative and inactive as he promoted the interests of the aspirant African commercial class and sought closer ties with chiefs. Seme was much criticised, even by his supporters and was finally replaced by Z. R. Mahabane in 1937. John Langalibelele Dube (1871-1946) was first president-general of the ANC until 1917 and remained president of the Natal ANC until 1945. He launched the *Ilanga lase Natal* (*Natal Sun*), Natal's first African paper, in 1903. Like Seme, he was an advocate of black self-help, yet their political relationship was marked by personal rivalry. Dube successfully fought the challenges of younger and more radical leaders in Natal, especially A. W. G. Champion of the ICU and J. T. Gumede, who formed an independent ANC in 1926.
2. Note the similarity between this sentence and Clause 8 of the Freedom Charter, "The Doors of Learning and Culture Shall be Opened".
3. John B. Marks (1903-72) joined the CPSA in 1928, studied at the Lenin School in Moscow and became a full-time Party organiser and trade unionist upon his return. He was a member of the Party Politburo from 1930 to 1937 when he was temporarily expelled. In 1946 he was elected to the Party's Johannesburg district committee and, shortly before its dissolution, to its Central Committee. In 1939 he was an organiser of the NEUF, and he helped revive the ANC in the late 1930s, becoming a member of the Transvaal ANC Executive in the early 1940s. He helped form the AMWU in 1941 and was Chair of the CNETU. In 1946 he was elected to the ANC National Executive. He was banned in 1952, left South Africa in 1963 and in 1969 became Chair of the CPSA in exile.
4. Jameson Gilbert Coka (1910-60s), a journalist, attended Adams College and left to join the ICU in 1927. As the ICU waned, he joined the CPSA and wrote for *Umsebenzi*. He was expelled in 1935 for questioning the existence of an African bourgeoisie. He worked briefly on *Ikwezi* and started the short-lived *African Liberator*. In 1946 he was one of the ANC members charged under the Riotous Assemblies Act and war measure 145 with inciting the African Mineworkers' Strike. See Coka (1936).
5. Edwin Thabo Mofutsanyana, born in 1899 in Witsieshoek, joined the CPSA in 1926 and attended the Lenin School in Moscow in the early 1930s. For most of the 1930s he was a member of the CPSA's Politburo and in the 1940s, Chair of its Johannesburg District Committee, member of its Central Committee and editor of its newspaper, *Inkululeko (Freedom)*. He was one of the people charged with inciting the African Mineworkers' Strike of 1946. He ran, unsuccessfully, as a Communist candidate for the NRC in 1937, '42 and '48. He was elected to the AAC's Executive Committee in the late 1930s but put his energies into rebuilding the ANC. After being banned, he moved to Basutoland (Lesotho). He was married to Josie Mpama (or Palmer), for many years the only African woman leader in the CPSA.
6. Reverend Walter Benson Rubusana (1858-1936) was a leading figure in the Congregational Church and became vice-chair of the Congregational Union of South Africa. In 1909 he became first President of the South African Native Convention, in 1910 he was elected to the Cape Provincial Council on a Progressive Party ticket but lost to a white candidate in 1914 after Jabavu ran against him and split the African vote. He was a founding member and a Vice-president of the SANNC and in 1919 helped draft its constitution.
7. These were the two major African language newspapers. *Umteteli wa Bantu* was launched in the aftermath of the 1920 Black Mineworkers' strike (see Part One, n. 11). *Bantu World* was started in 1932 by B. G. Paver and I. J. la Grange and financed by Howard Pim. The journalist R. V. Selope Thema was associated with it.
8. Sir James Rose-Innes (1855-1942) was a Cape politician in the 1880s who established a liberal reputation on the issue of race. He subsequently became eminent in the legal profession and during the Anglo-Boer War supported the annexation of the Dutch Republics. In 1902 he was appointed Chief Justice of the Transvaal. In September 1914 he became Chief Justice of the Union of South Africa, a post which he held until his retirement in February 1927. He then played a leading role in the formation of the non-racial franchise association which sought to replace racial criteria with a "civilisation qualification".
9. Sir Abe Bailey (1864-1940) amassed a fortune as a Rand mining magnate and entered politics as an ardent advocate of British interests.
10. Father Coughlin and Huey Long were right-wing American populists in the early 1930s. Long was Governor of Louisiana and assassinated while in office.
11. Walter B. Madeley (1873-1947) was a white labour leader who joined the Hertzog Pact Cabinet in the 1920s and the Smuts war-time coalition Cabinet in 1939. In 1945 he resigned from the SALP over the issue of franchise rights for Indians. Duncan Burnside briefly left the SALP to form the South African Socialist Party.
12. George Dimitrov was a Bulgarian Communist and chief exponent of the People's Front strategy unveiled at the Seventh Congress of the Comintern in 1935.

13 The Johannesburg WPSA produced three issues of *Umlilo Mollo/The Flame* in 1936. C. B. I. Dladla became an organiser for the Johannesburg WPSA after his expulsion from the CPSA, was a delegate to the AAC and was later in the NEUM. In 1937 he met with African-American social scientist Ralph Bunche on his visit to South Africa (see Bunche Collection, box 65).
14 Louis Joffe and his brother Dr Max Joffe were members of the CPSA. Louis, the Party's financial secretary and a staunch supporter of the Comintern, was a close ally of Douglas Wolton and Lazar Bach before their departures. The Joffe brothers were part of a very small number of leftists, which included trade unionists Max Gordon and Arnold Latti in Port Elizabeth, who were interned without trial by the government during World War Two.
15 Donald B. Molteno was a Native Representative for the Cape Western region in the late 1930s and '40s. A founder of the Liberal Party in 1953, he later joined the Progressive Party, an offshoot of the United Party which supported a qualified but non-racial franchise, and which pulled away some Liberal support.
16 The early agrarian and pastoral Cape economy under Dutch colonial control was dependent on slave labour, which was imported from the seventeenth through the nineteenth centuries, mostly from Asia but also from Mozambique and Madagascar. Following Britain's occupation of the Cape in the early nineteenth century, it initiated a number of legal reforms. The importation of slaves was banned in 1807, and slavery was abolished in 1834, although slaves had to serve a four-year unpaid apprenticeship until their complete emancipation in 1838. At that time there were 36 000 slaves in the Cape Colony. Despite the abolition of slavery, Cape colonial social structure was not radically altered as most freed slaves lacked land or other resources and many continued to work on white-owned farms in servile conditions.
17 *Umvikeli-Thebe/The African Defender* was produced by *Ikaka labaSebenzi* (Labour Defence), a branch of the Communist organisation, International Red Aid, which arranged defence for arrested Africans. It began during Italy's invasion of Abyssinia but sales collapsed once it became clear that the Abyssinians were losing.
18 The Native Laws Amendment Act of 1937 imposed severe restrictions on African freedom of movement to towns, limiting the size of the African urban population to the minimum necessary for the needs of employers and placing Africans under the constant threat of being removed from towns to rural areas.
19 Archie A. Moore was President of the SATLC. He participated in united front activities with the CPSA in the late 1930s but in 1941 he refused to give any support to Communists interned in government camps during World War Two.
20 Issy Wolfson (1906–80) was a South African-born white Communist who organised and led the textile workers' and tailors' unions. He joined the CPSA in 1934, becoming prominent after the departure o Lazar Bach. Following the Party's appeals to white labour in 1936/37, he supported its proposal o differential minimum wages for blacks and whites and introduced a motion to this effect to the SATLC of which he was a member of the National Executive. He was banned under the Suppression of Communism Act in 1952.
21 Reverend S. S. Tema was a Dutch Reformed Minister who in 1937 was chair of the Transvaal committee responsible for rebuilding the ANC after it had begun almost defunct under Seme's leadership. Following the ANC's adoption of the Programme of Action in 1949, Tema distanced himself from the Congress leadership and aligned himself with Selope Thema's National-minded Bloc. He was a founder of the Interdenominational African Ministers' Federation and became its president in 1961.
22 Gaur Radebe (1906–83) was a political activist, linked initially with the CPSA and ANC. In 1941 he was involved in the formation of the AMWU. He was expelled from the CPSA in 1942 and supported the launch of the ADP the following year. He was a leader in the Alexandra bus boycotts of 1943/44. In 1951 he helped form the National-minded Bloc, then became an Africanist and joined the PAC, which he represented in exile in Tanzania and Zambia.
23 "Professor" James M. Thaele (1888-1948), a leader of the Western Cape ANC in the 1920s and '30s, studied at Lovedale College, then obtained a B.A. and a Bachelor's in theology from Lincoln University in the United States, where he was influenced by the ideas of Marcus Garvey. He and his brother Kennan subsequently organised an ANC branch in Cape Town. Under the leadership of the Thaeles and two Communists, Elliot Tonjeni and Bransby Ndobe, the Western Cape ANC became a powerful force amongst farmworkers in the late 1920s. In 1930 Thaele became involved in power struggles with Tonjeni and Bransby, who formed an Independent ANC, having already broken with the CPSA in 1929. Thaele retained control of the Cape-Town based ANC but became politically marginalised in the 1930s as a result of the government's crackdown on Western Cape activists. Mrs M. N. Bhola, an associate of "Professor" Thaele's, organised the women's section of the Western Cape ANC in the late 1920s. She was the first woman prosecuted under the 1927 Native Administration Act. In the 1930s she was involved with the AAC.
24 Reverend Zaccheus Richard Mahabane (1881-1970) was a long proponent of black political unity. From

1924 to 1927 and 1937 to 1940 he was President-General of the ANC, and he was a leading figure at the series of Non-European conferences that met between 1927 and '34. From 1937 to 1954, he was Vice-President of the AAC and, from 1943 to 1956, President of the NEUM. He actively sought a rapprochement between the AAC and ANC. He was pressured to resign from the NEUM in 1956 over his opposition to their boycott of Bantu Education school boards. From the late 1940s, he was a leader in the Interdenominational African Ministers' Federation. Henry Selby Msimang (1886-1982) was an ANC activist and AAC Secretary at its formation. In 1953 he broke with the ANC and helped establish the Liberal Party, in which he played a leading role until banned in 1965. Dr James S. Moroka (1891-1985), a physician trained at the University of Edinburgh, was an early leader of the AAC. He then served on the NRC from 1942 to 1950, arguing the need to expose the institution's bankruptcy by working in it. Paradoxically, in 1949 he was elected as ANC President-General on the pro-boycott platform of the ANC Youth League, even though he was still in the NRC and not at the time an ANC member. In 1952 he lost his bid for re-election to Albert Lutuli.

25 J.A.L.G. is no doubt Jimmy La Guma.
26 S. Peter Matseke (1878-1941) was a member of the ANC national executive in the 1920s and in 1933 became president of the Transvaal ANC. He helped found the AMWU in 1941.
27 This is probably L. L. Leepile, born in Bechuanaland (Botswana), a Communist and secretary of the Party's Cape Town branch in the 1930s. In the context of South Africa's attempt to wrest control of Bechuanaland, Swaziland and Basutoland from Britain in the early 1930s, Leepile and Lazar Bach put forward a minority interpretation of the Native Republic thesis which argued for a federation of independent Native Republics of the Sotho, Tswana, Swazi, Zulu and Xhosa peoples.
28 Kontane should be Kotane.
29 Booker Lakey was General Secretary of the NLL and Assistant Secretary of the NEUF. Lance Morley-Turner, Assistant Secretary of the NLL, fought in World War Two and was one of the spirits behind the formation in 1941 of the Springbok Legion, an organisation which aimed to provide a fair deal for soldiers and ex-soldiers, promote racial harmony and defend democracy.
30 Hawa H. Ahmed was the pseudonym of Halima Gool (d. 1993), active in Cape Town radical politics in the 1930s and '40s and married to Goolam Gool. She was secretary of the NLL and the Anti-CAD and organised a Laundry Workers' Union which she represented at the 1939 NEUF conference. Her notebooks contain one lecture on "The Evolution of Society: The Epoch of Barbarism", and another on the "History of Women", which examines the basis of matriarchy in the ancient world through a consideration of the writings of Engels, Darwin, Briffault and Lafargue. In 1941 she addressed the Durban-based Liberal Study Group, attended by NIC radicals, on the status of women; the following year the group formed a Women's Class, possibly inspired by Gool's talk.
31 The whites-only Women's Enfranchisement Act of 1930 had the practical effect of diluting the black vote in the Cape and, consequently, had a radicalising impact on black politics there. Cissie Gool, for instance, tried to bring black women into the liberation movement through the establishment of the Non-European Women's Suffrage League in August 1938. By then, Africans had already been removed from the common voters' roll in the Cape. Thus, the Non-European Women's Suffrage League proved to be an ephemeral organisation: the issue appealed to the small stratum of Coloured women who would have qualified for the franchise were it not for their sex.
32 This claim was not universally applicable in Europe. Apart from cases of one-party rule the franchise was restricted elsewhere. Women did not have the vote in France and Switzerland. In Britain a small minority secured additional votes through business or educational qualifications.
33 The Carnegie Commission (1929-32) was established to investigate the "poor white problem" on the initiative of the Dutch Reformed Churches. It produced a five-volume report and found that ninety per cent of whites classified as very poor were Afrikaners. The report influenced the Hertzog Government in its decision to form a Department of Social Welfare in 1934.
34 Mohandas Gandhi lived in South Africa from 1893 to 1914. His use of *satyagraha* established a distinctly Indian tradition of protest in South Africa, laying the basis for the development of a common Indian ethnic identity which crossed class lines. Tactically similar to passive resistance but premised on non-violence, *satyagraha* is defined as a soul force in which opponents are defeated through one's own suffering. In 1906 Gandhi launched a campaign against the registration of Indians in the Transvaal but failed to retain Indian merchant support when the government linked registration to the renewal of trading licenses in 1908, and the movement collapsed. He revived *satyagraha* as a method of protest by agitating amongst Indian coal workers at Newcastle, whose 1913 strike over the treatment of passive resisters in the Transvaal catalysed a general strike throughout Natal and the repeal of several discriminatory laws. *Satyagraha's* association with the strike influenced the subsequent decision of Indian Communists and radicals to employ passive resistance in the late 1930s and '40s, and its influence on anti-colonial politics

in India bolstered the ethnic ties between South African Indians and India.
35 Duncan Burnside, the Labour M.P. for Umbilo, founded the South African Socialist Party in early 1937, following the SALP's refusal, at its annual conference, to join the People's Front and its reaffirmation of segregation. The CPSA criticised the initiative on the grounds that the real choice was either to join them or to try to reform the SALP from within. Cissie Gool was briefly a member, and Harry Snitcher represented it at the 1939 NEUF conference.
36 Mrs Zainunnissa "Cissie" Gool (1900-63) was the charismatic daughter of Abdul Abdurahman, sister-in-law of Goolam Gool and a prominent Cape Town political leader. In the early 1930s she unsuccessfully challenged her father's leadership of the staid APO; then, with Jimmy LaGuma and Johnny Gomas founded the NLL in December 1935, serving as its first President. She was a founder and first President of the NEUF, a member of the short-lived SASP and served on the CPSA's Political Bureau. From 1938 to the 1950s she represented District Six on the Cape Town City Council and for many years was the only woman on the Council. She was restricted under the Suppression of Communism Act. See Everett (1978).
37 Sam Kahn, a lawyer by profession, joined the CPSA in 1930 and became a member of its Central Executive in 1938. He organised several trade unions, was active in the NLL, served on the Cape Town City Council from 1943 to 1952 and from 1949 to 1952 represented Africans of the Cape Western district in Parliament before his expulsion for being a Communist. He was banned in the mid-1950s and left South Africa in 1960.
38 Benjamin M. Kies (1917-79) was a prominent Cape Town-based black intellectual, active in the NEF and a leader in the TLSA, Anti-CAD movement and NEUM. In 1937 he was one of a group of young radicals who ousted the old-guard APO-supporting leadership of the TLSA, moving the organisation in a more radical direction. For many years a teacher, in 1956 he was banned from teaching because of his political views and subsequently became an advocate. He edited the TLSA organ, *The Educational Journal*, as well as *The Torch*. His ideas on the origins of segregation and his thesis of "teachers as a vanguard" who could disseminate political ideas amongst the oppressed were extremely influential within NEUM circles. In the late 1950s he and Hosea Jaffe led an Anti-CAD faction within the NEUM which argued that many AAC leaders were moving towards bourgeois African nationalism. His writings include: *The Background of Segregation* (1943) and *The Contribution of the Non-European Peoples to World Civilisation* (1953).
39 The New Era Fellowship was a radical discussion and debating society which was formed by Goolam Gool in 1937 and which ran until the late 1960s. It met at the Stakesby Lewis Hostel and in the Fidelity Hall on the edge of District Six in Cape Town. It provided a forum for young black students at the University of Cape Town who were isolated from the university's all-white intellectual life, inviting UCT lecturers and foreign visitors to speak, and it also drew in blacks from outside the university as well as political activists. The NEF initiated the campaign against the Government's proposed Coloured Advisory Council and its attack on the Coloured franchise, launching the Anti-CAD on 28 February 1943. The NEF established other local fellowships in the South Peninsula, the Southern Suburbs, the Northern areas, Langa and Paarl.
40 The novelist Peter Abrahams, in the 1930s a struggling writer, gave an eyewitness account of left-wing politics in Cape Town in *Tell Freedom* (1954).
41 This draft represents the position of the CPSA between the outbreak of World War Two in September 1939 and the German invasion of the Soviet Union in June 1941.

Part Six

World war and the suppression of socialism

EDITOR'S NOTE
South Africa's controversial entry into World War Two initially produced hostile responses from both Communists and Trotskyists. The CPSA seems to have experienced little of the internal debate that characterised some European Communist Parties that had previously been strong advocates of military resistance to fascism. The position of the CPSA changed dramatically in June 1941 when the Nazi armies invaded the Soviet Union. From then on the CPSA was committed to the war as a progressive crusade, and it sought to extend its influence amongst an expanding industrial working class. This meant that the Party had to walk a tightrope between support for the war and a credible articulation of workplace grievances. In contrast, and despite the notable achievements of trade unionists associated with the Trotskyist tendency, such as Max Gordon and Dan Koza, Trotskyist organisations remained small. They failed to expand their influence despite the CPSA's strategic problems from mid-1941. The Allied victory over fascism found most Communist parties in a relatively strong position, and some of that optimism is present in the early post-war statements of the CPSA. Yet whereas most of the victorious Allies following the defeat of fascism elected moderately progressive governments, in South Africa this was emphatically not the case. The international victory against fascism was followed by increased domestic repression and, in 1948, by the election of a government containing some individuals who had been overt Nazi sympathisers. Once again, the distinctiveness of the South Africa experience overlay the wider international developments and in this harsher climate the divided socialist movement faced a new strategic problem – survival.

Document 122
"Manifesto Against Imperialist War", *Socialist Action*[1], August 1939

UNITE AGAINST EXPLOITATION, OPPRESSION, WAR AND FASCISM! FORWARD THROUGH THE CLASS STRUGGLE TO INTERNATIONAL SOCIALISM AND FREEDOM!

Workers of South Africa!
World war may break out at any moment. General Hertzog refuses to say what the Union Government's attitude to war will be. But you have a right to know – it is your blood which will be shed in the near future.

You are confronted with the horrors of a new IMPERIALIST WORLD WAR. It is a monstrous lie that the war will take place between "democratic-peaceful" and "Fascist-warlike" nations, because the "Democracies" are already allied with many dictatorships and when war breaks out the first result will be the destruction of the democratic rights already largely undermined in the "peaceful" countries.

The Anglo-French imperialists, who mercilessly beat down the fighters for independence in South Africa, India, Jamaica, Syria, Tunisia, Algeria, Palestine and elsewhere, recognise nothing but their "independent right" to exploit millions of slaves, black, brown and white, throughout the world.

The capitalist world is mortally wounded. In its agony it exhales the poisons of Fascism and war, which threatens to subject the workers and farmers everywhere once more to a new and horrible servitude. In the midst of abundance, with a productive apparatus which could, well organised and directed, satisfy all the requirements of humanity, capitalism dooms millions of men to unemployment, miserable doles or starvation. It is utterly incapable of assuring the well-being of the masses and equally incapable of assuring peace. Less than a generation has passed since the last "war to end war" and we are already on the threshold of a new world war, infinitely more horrible than the last one.

Once more the exploited are called upon to destroy each other for their respective imperialist masters. Once more fields will be transformed into blood soaked trenches and cities into devastated tomgs – so that the imperialists may preserve their profits and their colonies or acquire new ones.

A Bandit War!
All the ruling classes of the capitalist countries are bandits. Their war, whatever the pretentions and hypocritical slogans, will be a war between bandits. It will not be a workers' war, but on the contrary, the workers, the exploited in general, will be its victims. All imperialists are aggressors, and it does not matter who fires the first shot.

The Nazis boast of having solved the unemployment problem, but they merely poured the wealth of the German nation into armaments. The Nazis are starving their population into submission, they smashed all Trade Unions, and all workers are at the mercy of their employers.

England, France and the United States of America, called "Democracies" although they have enslaved the greater part of the world in their empires, are following Hitler's footsteps. These capitalist "democracies" are trying to "solve" their unemployment problems, the eternal capitalist riddle, by absorbing millions of unemployed workers in the armament industries and by sending the rest to the fronts to be killed. This is the Capitalists' idea – Fascist or Democratic – of "solving" the world's troubles, their contribution to peace.

South African Workers!
Your salvation does not lie in war. Imperialist wars settle nothing. You – South African Workers – must realise this. The Imperialist bosses are again going to fight for the division between themselves of the colonial countries, the factories, the mines and the land – the results of your sweated labour.

No Defence of Imperialism and Capitalism!
Do not defend this system, which is rotten through and through. Do not defend your exploiters. Do not sacrifice your lives for a system that will bring Fascism, War and Ruin to you at home.

Remember that International Finance backed Hitler, Mussolini and the Mikado, Franco and the Kuomintang in China, and the financiers will, when they find it necessary to maintain their profits, plunge you into the inferno of war.

Neutrality
The Nationalist Party calls for neutrality – but this is a sham – the powers in the Malanite Party are in complete sympathy with the aims of German imperialism. Already the Malanites are imitating the Nazi system of race hatred and persecution.

Afrikaner Workers! The Malanites have duped you. They represent the rich farmers, the lawyers, the predikants – but they **do not represent you,** the landless farmer and the town worker. The choice before you is not Hitler Nazism or British Imperialistic rule. Deal with your own boss class first, unite with the oppressed of all races to overthrow imperalism. Let no one tell you that you will play into the hands of the foreign invader by doing so. Remember the fate of the Spanish working class who were told to resist the "foreign invaders" first and to advance their social and economic claims afterwards.

British imperialist rule means 500,000 Poor Whites – increasing poverty – will you defend such a system?

Coloured Workers! British Imperialism means race persecution, segregation, no jobs for you, slums for your children. You fought for the Imperialists last time and what was your reward? More anti-colour legislation!

Bantu Workers! The imperialists robbed you of your land. Will you fight again to defend locations and compounds, pass laws, Poll and Hut Taxes? You are persecuted and hounded in the land that was once yours – let no man tell you that German fascist rule can possibly be worse.

Labour Leaders – Imperialist Lackeys!

In South Africa to-day no working class party exists which will put forward the needs of all workers irrespective of race, colour or creed. The Labour and Communist Parties have gone over into the Imperialist camp even before the war has started. They shout "Hands off Africa" to Hitler, but not to Chamberlain, Daladier & Co., the greatest exploiters of colonial peoples.[2] They to-day are the best recruiting agents for these Imperialisms.

It is obvious that – on the eve of the coming war – the Attlees and Greenwoods in England, the Popular Frontists like Cripps and Pollitt, the Madeleys and Burnsides of South Africa, men like Thorez in France and Browder in America, and the leaders of the Socialist and Communist Internationals are all solidly backing their Capitalist Govenrments.[3] The Labour leaders of to-day are mere Imperialist lackeys.

The Fourth International

In all this welter of confusion that exists in the ranks of the working class, the Fourth International alone stands irreconcilably opposed to imperialist war. It calls upon you workers of South Africa to organise solidly within its ranks for the struggle against our imperialist oppressors.

WORKERS OF SOUTH AFRICA!

Unite for the freedom of colonial peoples and against the tyranny of imperialist rule.

Unite in the only just war – the war against the oppressors, the exploiters, against their perfidious agents in the working class.

Fight against capitalist rule for the liberation of all oppressed regardless of race, colour or creed.

Build the Fourth International.

Fourth International Club, Capetown.
Socialist Workers' League, Johannesburg.

Document 123[4]
Statement of Dr Y. M. Dadoo[5], Secretary, Non-European United Front (Transvaal), before the Court, 6 September 1940

In submitting the following points for the consideration of the Court, I feel that this matter is not one that concerns me alone. It is one that concerns all the Non-European people, and this case is one that might set a precedent for similar actions against other Non-European people. In view of the fact that I am a public figure among the Non-European people, and one to whom many of them look for guidance, I feel that it is my duty to submit a statement to the Court.

One of the mass Non-European organisations, namely, the Non-European United Front of the Transvaal, of which I am the Secretary, works for the complete economic and political emancipation of all the Non-European peoples. When it was confronted with this question of the war, it had, in accordance with its avowed policy and principles, to give an honest and truthful lead to its people; and therefore the question was very seriously considered by its Council, and after proper deliberations it decided to issue a leaflet reflecting the true and accurate picture of the position and status of the Non-European people as a whole, and giving them a guidance on the necessity for certain definite conditions being fulfilled by the Government of this country before the Non-European people could be expected to participate in the war efforts of the Government. I was, in my capacity as Secretary of this body, accordingly instructed by my Council to carry this decision into effect, and I did so willingly and wholeheartedly.

In view of the oppression and tremendous disabilities of my Non-European people, I submit that if the Council had taken any other course than the one it did take, it would have consciously and deliberately and against all canons of justice betrayed the very principle for which it stood, and it would also have, to its and its people's utter shame and degradation, lined itself up with reactionary and opportunist organisations. I am, indeed, proud to say that the Non-European United Front had the courage of its convictions to stand up, and give the right guidance to its people, although it had to do so at a most trying and difficult time.

It is my contention that the contents of the leaflet which forms "Annexure 2" of the Charge-Sheet, sets out the true position of the Non-European people, and that the Non-European United Front had given, which it was entitled to do, the right and correct guidance to its people, and therefore I desire to point out to the Court at this juncture by means of proof and examples that the leaflet in question was not mala-fides, or issued with any intention to mislead or defraud the public or a section of the public. Furthermore, I contend that "incitement" could be calculated to be caused, or a "feeling of hostility" to be engendered only when attmepts or appeals are made on malicious grounds and with the utilization of all known methods of falsehood to warp the reason and rouse the base instincts of man to gain certain ulterior motive or motives by setting one section of the public against another section.

The appeal of the Non-European United Front, as contained in the leaflet, is based on facts and directed in a perfectly legitimate and righteous fashion to the conscience and the instincts of reason and justice inherent in the mind of man not to allow the further perpetuation of injustice and oppression, but to work for their removal.

PASS LAWS AND POLL TAX. – The Pass System has inflicted an unbearable burden on the African people. An African has to carry a number of passes, including (a) Native Service Contract Pass, (b) Permit to travel from one area to another to seek work, (c) Special Pass required to be on the streets after 9 p.m., (d) Poll Tax Receipt.

If he has three passes on his person and one in his room, he is arrested and convicted for breaking the law.

Natives paid in taxes, 1938, (all males over 18)	£2,310,747
Number of Non-Europeans prosecuted, 1938	700,000
Out of the above number, the number convicted was	588,329

Approximately 66% of those convicted were sent to prison for paltry and, at times, inadvertent breaches of such iniquitous laws like Pass Laws, Municipal Bye-Regulations, Location Regulations, Municipal Bye-Laws, etc. Such an intolerable state of affairs and indiscriminate convictions have tended to create a band of criminals out of a simple, hard-working and honest race of men. Little wonder then that, from time to time, eminent authorities like Dr. Krause and even some of the leading newspapers like the "Star" and the "Daily Mail" have openly called for the abolition of the Pass Laws and Poll Tax.

SEGREGATION. – Africans must live in locations and they are prohibited from owning property or from conducting business in European areas. Coloureds and Indians are prohibited from living in many reas, and are, in effect, segregated. Ownership of land and property is denied to Indians in the Transvaal and restricted for the Coloured people. The Asiatics (Transvaal Land and Trading) Act of 1939 has prohibited the issue of new licences and tremendous difficulties are put in the way of transfers of trade from one name to another, or from one place to another.

WHITE LABOUR POLICY. – This bug-bear is used to play up to the prejudices of the European people. Thousands of Africans and Coloureds have been displaced from work by Europeans. But instead of Europeans benefitting from such a policy, their standards are dragged down because it is the usual practice for employers to dismiss the Africans at one door and re-engage them at another door to force down wages of both Non-Europeans and Europeans. This policy is definitely aggravating the Poor White Problem.

LOW WAGES. – This is an undeniable fact. The average annual wage of 343,380 African workers employed on the Gold Mines was £40 in 1939; whereas in that year the average wage of 39,974 Europeans on the Mines was £400.

ON FARMS: – The cash wages per annum average from £6 to £12.

UNSKILLED LABOUR. – 26/6 per week in Capetown; 17/11 per week in Durban; 19/7 per week on the Witwatersrand; 11/- per week in the Sugar Mills.

Thousands of Africans in Engineering and Building Industry earn just over a pound per week on which an African is expected to bring up himself and family. The African workers have managed to obtain a slight increase in their wages in those industries or factories wherein they have been organised into trade unions.

The Indian labourers in the Sugar industry are receiving very low wages. They receive 45/- per month. The Fact Finding Commission on the Coloured Question has reported on the poverty of the Coloured people due to low wages and unemployment.

The low wages have reduced the purchasing power of the vast majority of the South African population, particularly the non-European people, to such a low level that the local manufacturers are finding home markets too small for the development of local industries; and therefore the Chamber of Industries and dozens of press editorials from time to time are demanding that there should be a rise in African wages.

POVERTY, HIGH RENTS AND UNEMPLOYMENT. – Poverty is rife among non-Europeans, especially Africans. Rents paid by non-Europeans are very high. For example, the rents in Sophiatown and Vrededorp are as high as £1 5s. per room per month. The housing conditions are appalling. Most of the streets in non-European areas, e.g., Sophiatown, Newclare, Alexandra Township and other locations are not streets at all, but veritable mud-tracks. Sanitary services are negligible. Overcrowding is an undoubted fact. There is no unemployment relief. Unemployed are liable to be forcibly transferred to areas where labour shortage occurs. No accurate statistics are kept which could give one some idea of the appalling misery of the Non-European people. The Unemployment Benefit Act operates in certain scheduled industries such as Mining and Motor, but the Africans are deliberately excluded though they are the lowest paid and the first to lose their jobs.

COLOUR BAR LAWS. – These are too numerous to quote in full. Suffice it to say, one sees the revolting sign: "Europeans Only." Trams, Lifts, Hospitals, Trains, Places of Amusement, Libraries, Universities, Skilled Jobs, Parks, Halls – in fact, all the essential requirements of the community are reserved exclusively for the Europeans, whilst in some directions wholly inadequate facilities are provided for Non-Europeans. Yet the use of all these has only been made possible thanks to the labour of the Non-European people. They are not permitted to use the things which they have helped to build.

EDUCATION. – Total expenditure on education in 1938	£9,819,804
of which on African education	£827,058
on Coloureds and Asiatics	£812,325
which means, in other words, that the amount spent on	
European per head of population was	£4 16 0
whereas African was	0 2 9
Coloured and Asiatic was	0 18 2

DEMOCRATIC RIGHTS. – Most legislation on the Statute Book is repressive class legislation in the interests of the governing wealthy class. And most of this repressive legislation is still more oppressive in its effect on Non-Europeans. The laws in question are too numerous to quote in full but the following list will serve to give us some idea: Pass Laws, Tax Laws, Segregation Laws, Native Urban Areas Act, Apprenticeship Act, Colour Bar Act (Mining Industries), Industrial Conciliation Act, Unemployment Benefit Act, Wage Act, Anti-Asiatic Acts like Law 3 of 1885, Gold Law of 1908, Transvaal Land Tenure Act of 1932, Land and Trading Act of 1939, the Riotous Assemblies Act. This brief resume of the intolerable conditions under which the non-European people have to live in this country conclusively proves that these conditions are deliberately created and fostered by the Government and European capitalists, in order to reduce the mass labour power of the Non-European people into a commodity which could be used and utilised at will to increasse the wealth, luxury and happiness of a small, well-to-do section of the European community. The Non-Europeans are used as one would use an orange – the labour to be mercilessly squeezed out and the skin and pips to be thrown aside.

CONCLUSION. – In conclusion, I maintain before this Court that during the last World War of 1914–1918 the Non-Europeans played their part and thousands made the supreme sacrifice. But, after the war, the promises for a better life were not fulfilled; on the contrary, the oppression has become worse. The profiteers and big industrialists waxed fat and the position is the same to-day. In the Gold Mines, 1938, paid in Dividends £15,573,904 or 35%, and Estimate for 1940 £20,000,000.

The "state of war" was declared by the Union Government, after a very small majority decision of Parliament, but the part, on which, I desire to lay particular stress is this: that at no stage during the time that this momentous decision was being taken were the Non-European peoples, who constitute over 80% of the citizens of the Union, directly consulted or allowed the opportunity to declare their considered opinion on a vital question of life and death, that of whether this country should go to war, or not.

I submit that on a question of such vast magnitude and severity, it was the supreme duty of the Government to directly consult every section of the citizens of the State. Despite this act of deliberate omission, the Union Government, in the prosecution of its war efforts, made an intensive and extensive drive to obtain the active services of the Non-European people. The war and peace aims were at no stage clearly defined by the Government, but appeals were issued that it was a War for Democracy, Freedom and Independence of Nations, Countries and Peoples. These appeals were not clearly understood by the vast majority of the Non-European people, since, they were not allowed by the State to enjoy the fruits of Democracy, Freedom and Independence, and therefore it fell on the shoulders of their mass organisations and leadership to explain to them the true position in relation to the war and then, after a full explanation, to give them a correct and proper guidance on the matter.

The workers are called upon to bear the greatest part of the brunt in this war; they have to go to the Front and lay down their lives; they have to speed up in Industries and Factories, but their wages are not raised, their lives not bettered.

The present war is an imperialist war, and therefore an unjust war. It is not a war to free the people, but to maintain and extend imperialist domination. Even at this critical juncture, the Union Government would not even consider the request to postpone the sitting of the Asiatic Penetration Commission for the duration of the war, thus showing, that it is not one whit concerned about affording any relief to the Non-European people. Under these conditions, I submit to the Court, how could any representative body of Non-European Public Opinion, or I, as one of the leaders, be expected to acquiesce in the war efforts, if we are to remain truthful and loyal to our people.

This war could only be transformed into a just war for the preservation of Democracy and the defeat of Fascism when full and unfettered democratic rights are extended to the Non-European people of this country and when the oppressed peoples of India and the Colonial and semi-colonial countries are granted their freedom and independence. If these conditions and rights are given them, only then, could we believe that this is a war for the preservation of Democracy and the institution of a new Social Order; and, there would be no sacrifice too great and no risk too hazardous for us, the Non-Europeans, to offer for the defence of this New Social Order.

In view of these facts, I plead not guilty to both the charges alleged against me. Whatever the decision of the Court be, for us there is no cause so sacred, and no cause so noble, as the cause for which the Non-European United Front is fighting, and shall go on fighting, surmounting every obstacle, suffering every consequence, till justice is vindicated and freedom won.

Document 124
Letter from Max Gordon[6] to Fanny Klenerman[7], 21 December 1940

> M. Gordon,
> Internee No. 12/40.
> Anti-Nazi Camp,
> Ganspan No. 2,
> P. O. Andalusia,
> via Border.
> 21/12/40.

Dear Fanny,

I received your letter dated 14th. and the box of books and the parcel were received with appreciation. It appears that till 24th. instant parcels will be accepted by the Railways. We have not yet been allowed newspapers and on receipt of your letter we immediately approached the Commandant who promised to enquire but stated he could do nothing until he received his orders. A list of the names of internees whose wives are not well off and require assistance will be forwarded to you as well as those who would like arrangements to be made to facilitate their wives visiting them. Regarding the list of goods you have a fairly complete list but please do not send us tea and coffee as we are issued with an ample ration. Money may be sent to our Chairman Mr. E. May Snr., who will distribute any donations that may be sent in. Thanks very much for the £1.

I had an interview with the Chief Control Officer yesterday and for the first time learnt the reasons for my internment. They are as follows.

a) That I organised native trade unions for the purpose of exploiting them by pocketing the subscriptions, and being secretary as well.
b) That I have been constantly agitating amongst the Africans so as to bring about ill rest and hostility between them and their employers and that during 1936 I organised a very big strike in the laundry trade which caused a lot of trouble.
c) That I am a Communist and used the Trade Unions as a channel for proganda and spreading my views.
d) That I attempted to incite hostility between black and white by organising the mass meeting re. the Nkana Strike which was banned and that I was responsible for the issuing of a very inflammatory leaflet calling this meeting.
e) That although we conducted study classes for Book-keeping English, Geography etc. these were used as a means to inculcate communism into native workers namely because a very welknown communist woman was one of the teachers.

I had a long discussion with the Control Officer on the above and I did not deny my political opinions but carefully pointed out how the police had made dirty false statements against me. I shall not go into all the details of what I said but I finally asked whether there was a possibility of my being released on parole. He replied that the police were of the opinion that I was unreliable because I could never be relied on to act consistently. I pointed out that the people who signed the petition for my release thought differently. He then advised me to put in a statement in writing on the accusations levelled against me. I asked him whether there was a possibility that this would be considred and my release granted in view of the fact that Lawrence had dismissed my appeal. He replied that he new about the latter but could not promise me anything but still advised me to make another appeal. This I have done replying in writing to the various charges made. I suggest that a statement be sent from the Unions that I was not responsible for the Nkana leaflet.[8] A fact which is well known. Further that the Chairmen of the different Unions send in statements regarding the allegations that I exploited the Unions finance. The Control Officer admitted that the first three charges could not be held as reasons for interning me but obviously they were put into the police report to bias the case against me. Regarding the Nkana leaflet if the accusation made was correct then why was I not charge criminally under the Riotus Assembly Act for attempting to create hostility between black and white. With reference to the study classes the accusations are based purely on the fact that one of the teachers was a communist although it is admitted that I never conducted any of these classes, but that I was responsible for them.

My opinion is that they were not concerned about my doing any political work but objected to the trade unions as such. I was asked if I had any connection with the C.P. or any of their papers. This I of course denied. However regarding your advice and also in view of the above I am prepared to agree for the time being although I am very pessimistic about the out come.

I will probably go next week to hospital and will write to you from there. Actually I was suppose to go on Monday in view of Truter's visit this was postponed. It also appears that a number of the others in the camp will soon be released. Of course it is encouraging to hear that you people are as active as possible on the release question. I received a letter from Saffery[9] that he was of the opinion that it was not worth while approaching Hofmeyr.

The Camp received £2-10/- from a Pastor Hermon who also sent a similar amount to the nazi camp. We have not yet decided to accept as some are of the opinion that his church has nazi sympathies as obviously we do not wish to accept anything from them. The matter has been left over pending enquiries.

An internee Kluenthal was released to-day and I recommended him to look you up so that you may advise him where he could apply for a job. He is a very charming person. Prehaps the Civil Liberties Association could do something for him.

With good wishes to all my friends,

Yours Sincerely,
Max.

Document 125
INTERNMENT OF MAX GORDON (c. 1941)

We the undersigned
  ... Chairman of the African Commercial & Distributive W.U.,
  ... Chairman of the African General Workers Union,
  ... Chairman of the African Printing Workers Union,
  ... Chairman of the African Laundry Workers Union.

as responsible officials of the foregoing African Trade Unions with whose activities Max Gordon was connected in the capacity of General Secretary, and as associates of his for a number of years in the conduct of these Trade Unions hereby state as follows:

1. a) The said Max Gordon at no time misappropriated the subscriptions or other funds of our respective Unions.
 b) The said Max Gordon did not have control of finances, being assisted in disbursing money and signing cheques by other appointed and officially responsible members of each Union.
 c) Annual balance sheets were submitted and passed by the membership of each Union.
 d) At the end of the financial year immediately prior to Gordon's internment the books were reviewed by an auditor, Mr. W. D. Bramwell and certified correct.
 e) The books of our respective Unions have at no time been examined by the Department of Labour or the Police or other authorities to ascertain whether or not the said books were in order.

2. a) The said Gordon did not constantly agitate amongst the African workers but confined himself to legitimate Trade Union activities. In innumerable instances where dissatisfaction existed among employees by reason of unfair or irregular or unlawful treatment meted out to them by their employers, the said Gordon secured redress for the employees through the legally prescribed channels such as the Wage Board, the Department of Labour, the Native Affairs Department and Industrial Councils.
   The said Gordon was the author of several lengthy memoranda presented at Wage Board sittings which formed the basis for discussion and investigation into the conditions of employment in several industries.
 b) A strike of African employees took place in the Laundry Industry in December 1936. The said strike lasted only one day and resulted in the betterment of working conditions of employees who were at that time being notoriously underpaid. An agreement was entered into, the consequences being the establishment of amicable relations in the industry between employers and Native employees.
   Since that period no strikes have taken place in any of the industries in which members of our respective Unions are employed.

3. To the best of our knowledge the said Gordon has never been a member of the Communist Party and was antagonistic to its policy. At no time did he use the Trade Unions as a channel for spreading Communist propaganda but, on the contrary, confined himself to routine Trade Union activities.

4. a) In the month of April 1940 a leaflet was issued calling a meeting in connection with the strikes on the Nkana and Mufulira mines in Northern Rhodesia, which meeting was prohibited by the authorities.
 b) The said Gordon, although aware of the issue thereof, was not responsible for the

publication of the said leaflet which was issued by the United Committee of African Trade Unions. This body only partly consisted of representatives of our respective Trade Unions having, in fact, a number of other African Trade Unions associated with it. The said Committee was an independent body and in no way identical with our respective Unions. Furthermore, the said Gordon was not personally associated with this Committee.

c) There was no intention to incite hostility between black and white in the calling of the meeting. As workers, the members of the various Trade Unions represented were naturally concerned with the use of violence in dealing with strikers, white or black, whether in this country or in any other part of South Africa. No hostility was felt against the white Rhodesian mine workers because they had fared more successfully in their strike. The purpose of the meeting was also to explore ways and means of raising assistance for the strikers and their dependents and to demonstrate sympathy with the victims.

The aims of the leaflet, therefore, were confined to the calling of a meeting with the above stated objects.

5. a) No study classes were at any time conducted on behalf of the said Gordon or of the said Trade Unions. Permission was, however, granted by the said Gordon and the Unions for the conduct of classes for the benefit of Trade Union members in the offices of the said Trade Unions.

b) To the best of our knowledge no subversive subjects were taught at these classes but only those of a very elementary and general educational nature. The attendance was irregular and extremely small and ranged from illiterates to pupils who, in general, had not attained more than a Standard Four level of education.

Document 126
Letter from W. G. Ballinger to Mampurie (*Self Mampuru*)[10], 1 May 1941

COPY

HOUSE OF ASSEMBLY,
CAPE TOWN.
1st. MAY, 1941.

Dear Mampurie,

Mrs. B and myself discovered that the real grounds for Gordon's internment rests on charges made by the Department of Labour, in regard to violation of the Industrial laws of the country, and not for either subversive activities or organisation or trade unions. We were so disturbed by this revelation that the matter was reported by Mrs. B to the Native Representatives group meeting, and discussed in some detail. Yesterday Moltena, Jones and Mrs. B. saw Mr. H. Lawrence, Minister of Interior.[11] The facts that they placed before him resulted in an immediate decision to have the dossier regarding Gordon forwarded from Pretoria. The papers were telegraphed for by Mr. Lawrence.

There can be little doubt that Gordon's continued internment is in a large measure due to the somewhat aggresive manner in which his friends! i.e., the C. Press and

"Trotskyists" have handled his case. Furthermore, it appears that the statement to the effect that Gordon's internment would react adversely against the Unions which he was credited with controlling was disputed by Natives who were consulted. On the other hand the fact that Kosa and Co have carried on has impressed the authorities favourably. You will gather from the foregoing that there is some hope that Gordon will be released. If he is I trust that the authorities will not make it conditional, as they have done with Missionaries, that he refrains from working among Natives during the War.

It is now fairly certain that attempts at Peace will be made in July on the basis of recognising German or Nazi control over the European Continent, and "English speaking" hegemony over the "Western World" with safeguards for the continuance of the British Empire. In other words a truce while the New Imperialism trys to make an accomodation with the Old. The enigma is Russia, uncertain as to her friends and derided by Germany as a military force.

As formerly use your discretion in regard to my information re Gordon but inform Kosa and his group, Burford and Fanny Klenerman of developments.

Regards,
(sgd) W. G. Ballinger.

Document 127
6 Point Communist Programme (c. 1941)[12]

Smash Fascism!
The people of the world are on the march in a great crusade against Fascism.

Fascism is not something found only in Germany and Italy.

Hitler's strength has not come only from his guns and tanks and planes. It comes also, and chiefly, from his friends the Quislings, the Petains and Lavals who are found in every land where there are wealthy parasites who put profits before patriotism.

Fascism means the subjection of the many to the few – wherever there is a privileged class striving to maintain its position at the expense of the common people –
THERE HITLER HAS HIS FRIENDS.

Fascism stands for the domination of one race over all others – wherever there is racial discrimination or privilege –
THERE ARE TO BE FOUND PEOPLE WHO WANT HITLER TO WIN.

Fascism is fighting against the citadel of the working class – the Union of Soviet Socialist Republics. Wherever there are people refusing to support the U.S.S.R. in its heroic struggle for civilisation –
THERE ARE THE FASCISTS.

Fascism smashes all working-class organisations – a strongly organised working class is the main defence against Fascism.

Wherever the Fascists gain power their first attack is against the Communist Party.

Fascism wins its victories by deceit. It pretends to be anti- capitalist, anti-imperialist, and what not, in order to win the support of the people. It is only the Communist Party in all lands that has been able to expose these lies, because the Communist Party is the only consistent party of the working class.

South Africa must also play its part in this world-wide crusade against Fascism.

It can only do so effectively if the vast masses of the people of all races and colours are mobilised in the common struggle. Such a struggle calls for the co-operation, sacrifice and energetic action of all those who love freedom and hate oppression.

For this reason the Communist Party is launching this great "Smash Fascism" Campaign on the basis of six broad demands for the people.

Point 1:
DEMOCRACY FOR ALL
Successful war against Fascism demands the full mobilisation of the human and material resources of the country.

The war against Hitler and Fascism cannot be fought in a half-hearted way.

But how can this country take its proper place in the common fight when four out of every five men are denied the right to bear arms?

How can this country develop its industrial strength, either for war or for peace, when four out of every five of its men are denied the right to take part in skilled occupations?

A divided country is a weak country. How can this country present a united front against foreign foes when the small ruling class keep the people divided on racial lines, denying to the majority all rights of citizenship?

A war for democracy must be fought democratically. It demands great sacrifices of many kinds, **but not the sacrifice of democracy itself**. If, while the war is going on, we see a few getting rich whilst most people are going short, or if we see inequalities of various kinds increasing, then we can be sure that it is not being sincerely fought for democracy.

THIS WAR CAN ONLY BECOME A REAL WAR AGAINST FASCISM WHEN IT IS REALLY A PEOPLE'S WAR.

During the war new Colour Bar laws and regulations have been introduced in this country – stricter segregation in the factories, stricter segregation on the beaches, stricter residential segregation, stricter segregation in the schools. That is fascism, not democracy.

New dictatorial powers have been given to bureaucratic factory inspectors, marketing boards, etc., giving them power over the conditions under which you work and the supplies and prices of the things you need to buy. These people are not responsible to you. That is dictatorship, not democracy.

THE COMMUNIST PARTY OF SOUTH AFRICA DEMANDS –

A PEOPLE'S WAR AGAINST FASCISM;
A DEMOCRATIC SOUTH AFRICA AS THE ONLY ALTERNATIVE TO A FASCIST SOUTH AFRICA;
NO SEGREGATION OR COLOUR BARS;
NO POLL TAX, HUT TAX OR PASS LAWS;
EQUAL DEMOCRATIC RIGHTS FOR ALL;
A PEOPLE'S ARMY WITH EQUAL RIGHTS TO BEAR ARMS, EQUAL PAY AND ALLOWANCES IRRESPECTIVE OF RACE OR COLOUR, AND PROMOTION, EVEN TO THE VERY HIGHEST POSTS, TO BE BY MERIT ONLY AND OPEN TO ALL, WHATEVER THEIR RACE OR FAMILY.

Point 2:
RECOGNISE SOVIET RUSSIA
Throughout South Africa people are expressing surprise and amazement at the tremendous resistance of the Soviet people to the Nazi invader.

AMONG THE GENERAL PUBLIC THIS HEROIC RESISTANCE HAS COME AS A COMPLETE SURPRISE.

For years we have been saturated with misleading propaganda about the Soviet peoples, about their system of government, about their standard of living, about their organising ability, about their morals and their views on religion. For years, since the revolution in 1917 in fact, the relations between Socialist Russia and the people of the rest of the world have been poisoned by a lying press, a press controlled by the monopoly capitalists of the kind who made Hitler, who sabotaged peace efforts and finally plunged the world into this bloody slaughter.

We have to remember that even if the truth about Soviet Russia is leaking out in the capitalist press to-day, this is no guarantee that it will be so to-morrow. They can switch their propaganda in a day. They have done it before.

South Africa needs to know about the Soviet Union, about its people and their institutions. It needs to know about a country which in twenty years changed from a backward, poverty-stricken country into a powerful state strong enough to challenge Hitler's armies. It needs to know about a country which managed to raise the standard of living of its citizens at the same time as it built up a powerful defence force. It needs to know about a political system which brought an end to national hatreds and conflicts between different races and united them in their love for their country and in their determination to defend it.

South Africa needs to know all these things and to understand them.

YET THE GOVERNMENT OF SOUTH AFRICA REFUSES TO RECOGNISE THE EXISTENCE OF THE SOVIET UNION. SOUTH AFRICA HAS NO DIPLOMATIC, COMMERCIAL, MILITARY OR CULTURAL RELATIONS WITH THE SOVIET UNION.

Only after a tremendous outcry had been raised by the whole of South Africa at the Government's dictatorial action in banning Soviet literature was the ban lifted to a certain extent. There is still a ban on "Communist propaganda."

The Government is appeasing the most reactionary forces in this country by these actions. It would have the support of hundreds of thousands of South Africans if it ceased to appease them.

FOR SEVEN YEARS NAZI GERMANY WAS RECOGNISED. FASCIST ITALY WAS RECOGNISED.

WHY NOT THE SOVIET UNION?

Is it because there are elements inside the Government which dislike Socialism so much that they are willing to insult the government of a people fighting as much in the cause of South Africa as in their own?

THE COMMUNIST PARTY OF SOUTH AFRICA DEMANDS –

THAT THE GOVERNMENT OF SOUTH AFRICA RECOGNISE AND ESTABLISH DIPLOMATIC RELATIONS WITH THE U.S.S.R.

THAT THE GOVERNMENT OF SOUTH AFRICA RENDER THE FULLEST POSSIBLE ECONOMIC AND MILITARY AID TO THE U.S.S.R.

THAT THE GOVERNMENT OF SOUTH AFRICA REMOVE THE BAN ON

ALL SOVIET AND ALL OTHER PROGRESSIVE LITERATURE.

Point 3:
NO PROFITEERING

In this war against Nazism the tendency is to think only of getting rid of Hitler and Mussolini. But the Fascist system represented by these scoundrels is merely the expression of the rule of German and Italian monopoly capitalists who seek to dominate the world as a field of exploitation for themselves.

There is a grave risk that even if German and Italian monopoly capitalist are conquered at the tremendous sacrifice of hundreds of millions of lives, some other monopoly capitalism would be substituted.

In Britain, United States, and certainly in South Africa, the owning classes are making gigantic profits out of the war, while the common people are making unheard-of sacrifices. It is not enough to say that the wealthy classes are the heavily taxed. For instance, in Britain, taxation leaves a certain wealthy brewer with only £8,000 a year out of a normal income of £350,000. This looks like enormous sacrifice. But when £8,000 a year is contrasted with the allowance paid out to soldiers' dependents, there can be no talk of equality of sacrifice. Although taxation is heavier in South Africa than it used to be, it is still very much lower than in Britain, profits are much higher, and the rich have all sorts of loopholes for escaping taxes.

Attempts have been made to prevent profiteering. But mainly these resolve themselves in prosecutions of small traders who overcharge by a penny or so. There has been no prosecution of anybody except small men. What is happening here is that the big men are becoming richer and more powerful, and that the steadily increasing cost of living is hitting the worker and ordinary consumer.

Here is one example taken from the press of the way in which this business of "equality of sacrifice" works: Lever Brothers-Unilever accounts for 1940 show an increase of 22 1/2 per cent in trading profits AFTER ALLOWING FOR TAXATION. Lever Brothers, South African Subsidiary, operated from Durban, reported that it was making good progress in conducting the groups interest outside Europe.

Yet Lever Brothers applied to the Union government for exemption from paying the cost of living allowance to its employees.

For the big men it is "business as usual". For the masses of the people it is "we must all make sacrifices". When the Government says "We must destroy Nazism," we agree. But we say that in the face of the fact that profiteering is so obvious that everyone can see it, it is impossible to expect the wholehearted enthusiasm that characterises a people's war.

THE COMMUNIST PARTY DEMANDS –
For the efficient conduct of the war against Hitlerism, there must be NO PROFITEERING. The people of South Africa are prepared to make sacrifices, BUT THERE MUST BE EQUALITY OF SACRIFICE.

Point 4:
RAISE LIVING STANDARDS

To the man in the street it seems easy enough to understand that a worker who gets little pay can buy little food, must live in unhealthy conditions, cannot hope to provide his wife and children with food, clothing, education. But to the Government the problem is not nearly so simple. To discover why men and women live in tenements and pondokkies, suffer from tuberculosis, malnutrition, try to add to their meagre wages in a variety of legal and illegal ways, the Government thinks it necessary to appoint commission after commission, committee after committee.

At the Johannesburg sitting of the newly-appointed commission investigating the economic, social and health conditions of Africans living in urban areas, it emerged that Africans living in Orlando Township are paid wages that average £4 2s. 6d. a month. (It costs an African, at a modest estimate, **a minimum of £6 a month** to keep himself, his wife and an average of two children.)

Almost equally tragic is the problem of the Poor White worker who, in spite of all the Government's attempts to protect him from the competition with coloured, African and Indian labour, finds that as an unskilled worker he has to compete with the cheaper labour of his non-European fellow-workers, and consequently to live at a level not far removed from theirs.

No Government protection can solve the problem of the Poor Whites, any more than any number of Government commissions can solve the problem of tuberculosis, nutrition and child mortality.

Only abolition of the private ownership of the means of production – the factories, the electricity plants, the big farms – can raise the standard of living of all the people to heights as yet undreamed of. But in the meantime the Communist Party stresses the urgent need of raising wages and controlling prices to enable our people, all of them, to enjoy the benefits of living in a country which boasts that it is one of the most prosperous in the world, while at the same time it admits that the majority of its population, people of all races, suffers from malnutrition – IN OTHER WORDS, FROM NOT HAVING ENOUGH TO EAT.

THE COMMUNIST PARTY DEMANDS –
RAISE THE STANDARD OF LIVING OF ALL THE PEOPLE.
ESTABLISH A NATIONAL MINIMUM WAGE.
KEEP DOWN PRICES.

Point 5:
NO APPEASEMENT OF South African Fascists
There is in South Africa a large and powerful Hitler fifth column which extends into every branch of public life. It is to be found in Parliament, in Government Departments, in the Police, in the Army and amongst certain sections of the people. These agents of Hitler have openly proclaimed their sympathy for the cause of Hitler, and wish to introduce into South Africa the same barbarous forms of Government that exist in Germany and Italy to-day.

It is impossible to fight Hitler and Fascism successfully if movements like the Ossewa-Brandwag and the Herenigde Nasionale Party are allowed to grow and develop.

Throughout the whole period of this war, these enemies of the people have been allowed to go up and down the country conducting their treasonable propaganda. Their newspapers continue to pour out vile propaganda of racial hatred, intolerance and oppression.

The Government has taken no effective steps against these people and their organisation. **It has followed a policy of appeasement towards them.**

The Communist Party, in defence of the rights of the people, demands that immediate action be taken against the agents of Hitler and Fascism wherever they are to be found. These Fascist elements must be immediately removed from the government, the Civil Service, the Police Force, the Army and the schools and their organisations and press should not be allowed to exist. The fight against these Fascist elements demands that the broadest masses of people should be made alive to this danger in our midst. **It requires the extension of democratic rights to all sections of the people, so as to render these fifth columnists and traitors impotent and insignificant.**

The Communist Party calls upon all those who love freedom and hate oppression and intolerance to unite in a struggle against the forces of Fascism which are threatening us inside our own country.

The Communist Party calls on the Government to release or bring before a public Court all interned anti-Fascists!

Point 6:
PROTECT Trade Union Rights
Trade Unions are one of the most powerful weapons of the people in the fight against Fascism. The Trade Union movement is the bitter opponent of Fascism, because in every country where Fascist Governments have come into power it has been suppressed.

In time of war it is especially important that the freedom and independence of the trade unions should be maintained. The war has given opportunities to large sections of employers to profiteer at the expense of the people, and the trade union is the only weapon which the workers have whereby they can resist exploitation by their employers, and whereby they can secure for themselves higher wages and better conditions.

THE MORE THE TRADE UNIONS ARE PREVENTED FROM EXERCISING THEIR LEGITIMATE SHARE OF CONTROL IN MATTERS CONCERNING THE WELFARE OF THE PEOPLE, THE EASIER IT IS FOR FASCIST ELEMENTS TO IMPOSE THEIR DICTATORSHIP UPON THE REST OF THE PEOPLE.

If Fascism is to be fought successfully, the workers cannot allow their rights of organisation to be taken away from them under cover of the "necessities of war."

On the contrary, it is more than ever necessary to extend the trade union movement by organising the vast masses of workers who are at present outside trade unions because of racial discriminations.

THE GOVERNMENT MUST BE COMPELLED BY THE DEMANDS OF THE PEOPLE TO RECOGNISE THE RIGHTS OF AFRICANS TO ORGANISE INTO TRADE UNIONS.

Many attempts are being made to curtail the liberty of action of the workers in their struggle for higher wages and better conditions. A few examples are the Government's Emergency Regulations dealing with control of man-power, the "freezing" of building workers' wages, the declaration by the Government of stevedoring and the sugar plantations in Natal to be controlled industries soon after the workers had gone on strike for increased wages, the tendency among employers (with the sympathy of the government) to refuse to recognise lawfully established trade unions, and to set up "welfare" committees that function as "bosses'" unions along Fascist lines.

This attitude of the Government and the employers constitutes a serious challenge to the entire trade union movement, and if allowed to continue will result in the destruction of the freedom of the trade unions, and the establishment of "Labour" unions along Fascist lines.

The Communist Party stands for a strong, free and independent trade union movement as being one of the main bulwarks in the struggle of the people against Fascism.

The Communist Party demands that the Government recognise the right of Africans to organise into trade unions.

Document 128
A. P. Mda[13], "Report of Communist Activities among the Natives in Johannesburg", *Catholic Times*, July 1942

Introduction
The report following does not pretend to be exhaustive. It does, however, give a definite general idea of the trend of Communistic activities, on the reef and in Johannesburg particularly. It will readily be seen from this report that the Communist menace is growing in volume, and this war, as far was one can judge, is not calculated to minimize the Red menace. I consider myself quite safe therefore in saying that one of the biggest post-war problems in this country will be to counteract the destructive influence of Communism.

1. Organisation
I must say from the beginning that the Communists have shown exceptional organizing ability. This organizing power is perhaps only equalled by their zeal and fervour for the spread of bolshevistic dogma. A notable feature of their organisations is the strict adherence of the members to the Party discipline. On that score no mercy is shown to those who deviate, even by an inch, from party principles. They are simply brushed away – expelled without ceremony! Every leader and group leader knows the exact path he or she has to follow.

2. Propaganda Machine
As always and everywhere, the Communist Party of Johannesburg knows the value of the printed word, and they are exploiting this avenue of propaganda to its fullest advantage. Several attempts have been made to inflame and incite the people.

A. Leaflets:
a) For instance thousands of leaflets were distributed in 1941. These leaflets were an inflamed protest against the activities of the Police, particularly in Sophiatown and Vereeniging. They were distributed in the native townships.
b) Other thousands of leaflets were distributed in October, 1941. These praised and catalogued the achievements of Socialism in the U.S.S.R., and invited the people to join the Party of the Soviet.
c) Quite recently, several thousands of leaflets (I should say 16,000, approximately) were distributed in the Native Townships, calling people to Communist Meetings at 15 different places on the Reef, including Vereeniging. These were propagandial meetings with the ostensible object of raining condemnation of the depredatory Fascists of Japan in particular, and all other Fascists, pro-Fascists, and Fascist agents in all parts of the globe. The meetings were held on March15th, 1942.

B. The Press:
The official organ of the Communist Party is the "Inkululeko" (Freedom). It is published at No. 74, Progress Buildings, Commissioner Street, Johannesburg. It is a monthly publication and has a circulation of at least 10,000 every month. Agents sell it (very often) from house to house, particularly at Orlando. A note-worthy fact about Inkululeko is its cheapness. A copy is sold for only one penny. This paper fearlessly (and even violently) purports to champion the cause of Bantu freedom with particular reference to the Proletariat – the working classes.

3. Meetings
a) Meetings exclusively for Communist members are held in most cases weekly in certain localities where there is a group leader. Every specified area has its group leader who directs the work and discipline of the party in conformity with party discipline. Such a meeting is usually termed and "aggregate meeting." For instance, weekly meetings are held in Orlando – mostly on Tuesday evenings.
b) Then we get not only the general meetings of the Party, but also public meetings held on the Market Square in Johannesburg, or at open places in the Native Townships, as it is in the case in Orlando. Another centre of meetings, especially of the United Front, is the Gandhi Hall in Johannesburg. Public meetings are primarily propagandial in nature – occasions when the leaders parade their political knowledge, and endeavour to carry the masses with them.

4. Party in Local Politics
The organising Secretary of the Party here is a European.[14] There are, of course, agents, subsidiary organisers, and leaders in different areas.

Local Politics:
a) Advisory Boards: The Communists re taking keen interest in local organisations such as Joint Councils, Advisory Boards, etc. In the 1941 annual election of Advisory Board members for Orlando (the largest township in South Africa) 3 communist members won a resounding victory over their opponents. For the time being (and on the surface) Orlando would appear to be their stronghold. Events will prove, however.
b) The Non-European United Front which meets from time to time in the Gandhi Hall in Johannesburg (and rarely at other centres) is either pronouncedly pro-Communist, or it is leaning so dangerously to the left, that one can hardly draw a line of demarcation between it and the Red organisations. However, almost all Communist members are either its members or the exponents of its principles. Dr Dadoo is at present its particular hero and champion.
c) The Party is also adopting infiltration tactics towards the African National Congress. At least I see in its attitude one underlying aim, namely, the attempt to secure positions in the Congress, and by wire-pulling antics direct its policy, and if possible, seize power from it.

5. Leadership
The great need now is for proper Party Leaders. No effort is spared to educate and indoctrinate the leaders.

Special lectures are given at No. 74, Progress Buildings, mostly on Mondays from 6p.m. to 7p.m. Among other subjects taught are:

1. Political Economy.
2. Dialectical Materialism as expounded by Marx, Engels and Lenin.
3. The organisation and Programme of the Communist State.

6. People's Education
Rudimentary attempts are being made to educate the workers. Great care is taken at these schools to introduce Atheism by degrees. The response to the effort of educating the adult workers is not so encouraging. However, the project is being maintained, and must, as time goes, bear satisfactory fruits.

Examples of such schools are:
1. One night school at Polly Street, Johannesburg.
2. One at Market Street, Johannesburg, not far from the site of the old Malay Camp.
3. Another run by the Sophiatown Communist Party at the Independent Church.

There may be, and perhaps are, others that have not come to my notice. Subjects taught at the latter include:

Book-keeping; English; Arithmetic; Politics (I suppose party politics, etc.).

7. Communism and Trade Unionism
Experience in other countries has shown that Communism has worked its way into the Trade Unions and is using them to further its ends. The Communists first excite the workers to a revolutionary "tempo" before they get on the "move" to establish their "order."

In Johannesburg, it would be wrong to say that all the Native Trade Unions are either Red or pro-Red. But there is no blinking at the fact that the aim of the Communists is to make them veritable strongholds of bolshevistic plotting and intrigue. Yes, indeed, the trend of development is towards the left. One is impressed by the increasing presence and activity of Communist leaders at the Trade Union offices. Control must ultimately pass into their hands. You can judge that by the prominence to Trade Union News in the Communist Press. I shall name the different sections, classes and groups of Trade Unions (Native) in Johannesburg, to give you just a general idea of the potential power of the Communist Party if the Trade Unions were controlled by it, and if at the same time Native Trade Unions received statutory recognition by the amendment (amongst other measures) of the Industrial Conciliation Act of 1926. The bid for such control by the Bantu leaders of the Party is almost feverish in the intensity.

Some Trade Unions in Johannesburg:
a) No. 5, Kruis Street Offices have the following Unions falling under its influence:
1. Building Workers' Union.
2. Sweet Workers' Union.
3. Milling Workers' Union.
4. Clothing Workers' Union.
5. Tobacco Workers' Union
6. Iron and Steel Workers' Union.
7. Hides and Skins Workers' Union.
8. Rope and Canvas Workers' Union.
9. Brush and Broom Workers' Union.

b) No. 8, Kerk Street Offices: Commercial and Distributive Workers' Union.
c) No. 72, Commissioner Street Offices: Flat and Domestic Servants' Union.

d) No. 12, Kruis Street Offices: Milk, bricks, mineral, meat and timber Workers' Union.
e) No. 61, Albert Street Offices: Motor Drivers' Union.
f) Polly Street, No. 72 or 74 (Not sure of No.): Furniture Workers' Union.

Complete unity among the trade Unions has not been achieved, although efforts are being made to federate the Unions to facilitate the pursuance of a common policy of bargaining among all Native Trade Unions. Some of these Unions are still in the making; for example, I was recently asked by an Orlando Communist group leader to pay a visit to some railway workers who wished to form a Union. I would have liked to see for myself what is happening, but circumstances made it impossible for me to attend to meetings. I have, however, paid several visits to some other Trade Union Offices, particularly the one at No. 5, Kruis Street, where the leaders are quite friendly to me. Everything, however, is still in embryo, but one cannot fail to be impressed by the underlying motive and driving power behind these organisations.

Conclusion

In conclusion I wish to state that the threat of Communism is more serious to-day than it was in 1926, when it was found necessary to start the C.A.U.[15] Hence the C.A.U. will be called upon after this war to fight for dear life in defence of Christian principles amongst the Natives. If that time comes, I would strongly advise the C.A.U. a positive and (if necessary) aggressive defence rather than a negative one.

Document 129
"The Programme of the 4th International in South Africa", *Workers Voice*, 1 July (1943?)

Our Attitude to the War

1. HISTORICAL CAUSES AND NATURE OF THE WAR:–
This war is not a war for democracy. It is an Imperialist war on both sides for markets and colonies. Both the Allies and the Axis have the same Imperialist designs on Russia – restoring her to capitalism, colonising her, carving her up.

2. ECONOMIC-NATIONAL BASIS OF A JUST "DEFENCE OF 'ONE'S' COUNTRY": –

(a) The workers in Imperialist and colonial countries have really no country to defend, since they do not own the means of production and distribution and since "their" countries either oppress other countries (e.g., America, Britain, Germany, France, Italy, Spain, etc.), or else are themselves oppressed by foreign powers (e.g., India, South Africa). In addition to these facts, 90 per cent. of the South African toilers have no democratic rights to defend. Our task is to get a country by dispossessing our rulers.

(b) For the unconditional defence of the U.S.S.R. by means of the class struggle against both Axis and Allied Imperialisms. Against the anti-Communist Stalinist bureaucratic dictatorship inside Russia.

(c) For the defence of China and of other countries struggling for national independence against Axis or Allied Imperialisms.

3. SOCIAL CLASS STRUGGLE: –
"Our greatest enemy is at home." Our real foe is not the worker of Germany, Italy or Japan. Our foe is our own ruling class: the pro-British capitalists, the Nationalist and O.B. capitalists and rich farmers and their class and race government.

4. POLITICAL METHOD: –
Revolutionary defeatism – then revolutionary war – then socialist peace.

(a) Revolutionary defeatism: This means the class struggle against the boss-class and its state. In this country it means struggling for the total abolition of the Colour Bar, for land to the land-hungry, and for full national independence. This struggle will organise the socialist revolution in South Africa, which will solve these three demands.

(b) Revolutionary war: Once we have taken the country away from our rulers, we will combine with Workers' Governments in other lands to break up the external, Fascist enemy, by military means and by spreading our revolution to other countries.

(c) Socialist peace: Through a chain of revolutions capitalism and its modern form, Fascism, will be destroyed and real, lasting peace will come to all of humanity.

OUR STRUGGLE IN SOUTH AFRICA

1. THE TOTAL ABOLITION OF THE COLOUR BAR: –
a) In Economic Life: –
   i) Away with the poll tax and its shadow, poll tax receipts.
   ii) Away with the pass laws, special permits, lodgers' fees and the "pick-up" van.
   iii) Opening of all trades and professions to all Non-Whites.
   iv) Abolition of the "White Labour Policy."
   v) Abolition of the Colour Bar in apprenticeship. Reduction of the period of apprenticeship.
   vi) Abolition of industrial segregation. Improved conditions of work, proper sanitation, protection, etc.
   vii) *Trade Unionism:* The right of Africans to organise. Recognition of African unions. Abolition of Colour Bar in unions and admission of African, Indian and Coloured workers into any trade union. For the "closed shop" union.
   viii) *Hours:* Universal 8-hour day in cities, towns and on farms. Forty-hour week. Proper hours for rest and food. One month paid holiday per year for all workers, irrespective of colour or sex or age.
   ix) *Wages:* "Equal pay for equal work." A basic minimum weekly real wage, independent of "short time." Double over-time rates. A sliding scale of wages (to keep up with the sliding cost of living) for all workers, White and Non-White.
   x) Extension of the Workmen's Compensation Act to all workers, especially Africans. Social insurance for all workers. Pensions, equal for all races, from a State Insurance fund.
   xi) Abolition of land-owning, land-occupying, and trading restrictions on Africans and Asiatics.

b) In Social Life: –
   i) Abolition of residential segregation, i.e., of reserves, locations, compounds, separate townships; opening of the O.F.S. to Asiatics. No prohibited areas for Non-Whites.

ii) Abolition of the Colour Bar in education. Universal, free, compulsory, state primary, secondary, higher and technical education for all, irrespective of colour.
iii) Abolition of the Colour Bar in Health Services. State medical services, free to all races.
iv) Abolition of Colour Bars in recreation and amusement places (beaches, theatres, hotels, etc.)
v) Abolition of Colour Bar in all public services (trains, buses, rest-rooms, cafes, conveniences, etc.)

c) Political Life: Abolition of all Colour Bars in the Army, Navy.
i) Universal franchise for all over the age of 18, irrespective of income, property, education, sex or race.
ii) The right of all races to be represented by members of any race in parliament. Proportional representation, i.e., representation proportional to number of votes obtained by each party. Equal electoral districts.

d) In Military Life: Abolition of all Colour Bar in the Army, Navy and Air Forces. Equal rights, duties, pay, quarters for all races. The right of all Non-Whites in the forces to be trained fully in the use of arms, and to bear arms.

2. THE AGRARIAN REVOLUTION: –
The uncompensated expropriation of the Chamber of Mines, the big Land Companies, the rich farmers and the big banks and the division of the land among the land-less, land-hungry African, Coloured, Indian and Poor White small, poor farmers.

3. NATIONAL INDEPENDENCE: –
As for India, so for us, we have to struggle for:
i) The full national independence of South Africa from British Imperialism.
ii) The self-determination and self-rule or autonomy of each national grouping in South Africa.

The struggle for these three Pillars of our programme organises the 10,000,000 toilers for the coming social revolution which will smash up capitalism in South Africa. On the other hand, this social revolution is alone able to realise these three Pillars. *This, our, revolution is part of the permanent world revolution.*

Document 130
Communists in Conference: The 1943/44 National Conference of the Communist Party of South Africa

PLANS FOR 1944

"WE meet at a time when one of the most colossal struggles against the forces of reaction is taking place.

"Out of the bloody struggle of 1917 emerged the world's first Socialist State, and we dare to hope that out of the bloodshed and the tragedy of to-day a new order of social justice will emerge," said Bill Andrews, National Chairman of the South African Communist Party, opening the Annual Conference of the Party, held this year in Johannesburg on January 15th, 16th and 17th.

He added a reminder to the fifty-eight delegates. They met together "as a businesslike political organisation and not as a debating society." But this was scarcely needed. Most delegates had come with practical problems to discuss, with knotty points to put forward, and each was confined to a speech limit of five minutes, towards the end of the conference to be cut to a bare three minutes.

> **There were representatives of all the peoples of South Africa: Africans. Coloured. Europeans. Indians. All its languages were spoken. These delegates, men and women, came from all parts of the country – from Durban, from Pretoria, from Cape Town, from Bloemfontein, from East London, from Port Elizabeth, Pietermaritzburg and, of course, from Johannesburg itself.**

Their chairman, Mr. Bill Andrews, needs no introduction to the South African labour movement. He has been an active and leading member of it for more than forty of his seventy-three years. Even the most violent of anti-Communists has not dared question the integrity of this upright and honourable man.

The Communist General Secretary is Moses Kotane, an African whose intellectual ability and personality are respected even by the colour-prejudiced. Both he and Mr. Andrews were unanimously reelected at this Conference.

COMMUNIST DELEGATES

These delegates are men and women whose firm conviction is that progress for South Africa and racial harmony can only be achieved by the abolition of the Capitalist system of production for private profit and its replacement by common ownership of the means of production.

Each delegate is, in some degree, a personality. There is Indian trade union leader H. A. Naidoo, who built up the Natal Sugar Workers' Union; well-known Pretoria advocate George Findlay and his wife Joan, who is secretary of the Pretoria Committee of the Communist Party; Errol Shanley, secretary of Durban's Trades and Labour Council Committee and one of the Communist candidates in the 1943 general election; Bertie Louw, Coloured secretary of the Non-European Railway and Harbour Workers' Union, whose members gave him a reception at every station on the way up from Cape Town; Danie du Plessis, who was another Communist candidate for Parliament, organiser of the building workers; popular Harry Snitcher, chairman of the Cape Town District and a mass leader; Alpheus Madibe, a leader of the African peasants in the Zoutpansberg; Hilda Watts, editor of "Soviet Life" and a candidate in Johannesburg's municipal elections; John M'Tini, long-time Communist and a railway worker in Cape Town; Edwin Mofutsanyana, editor of the Communist Party's fortnightly newspaper "Inkululeko"; and Betty Sacks, editor of the Left-wing weekly "Guardian" whose circulation puts it in the country's first-ranking papers. She and Sam Kahn are the Communist Party's two first City Councillors, victories won in Cape Town's municipal elections in 1943. Both are here. And so are the District Committee secretaries, Rex Close, Mike Muller, Rusty Bernstein, Roley Arenstein and the rest. These and many others make up the personalities at this Conference.

Fraternal greetings follow the Chairman's opening remarks sent by the Johannesburg

Local Committee of the S.A. Trades and Labour Council, by the Cape Federation of Labour Unions, the Young Communist League, The Guardian, Inkululeko, Die Ware Republikein (three newspapers closely associated with the Communist Party), from the Campaign for Right and Justice, and other progressive organisations.

TO WORK

Next business is the election of a resolutions committee, and then Conference gets down to work. First report considered is introduced by a member of the Communists's Central Committee, who speaks on the Committee's report, which has already been circulated to delegates. It is entitled "The Struggle for Freedom, Equality and Security" and is, as its foreword states, "limited to points that are especially important, both for an examination of what the Party set itself to do in the past year, and from the point of view of our future work."

He describes it as an optimistic report. The world is going through a period of epoch-making change. The peoples of the world have a great destiny before them. But, he warns, at this time too much emphasis is laid on the post-war period. **"In spite of all the talk of our Government and other Governments, they are very far from keeping their pledges, as the report indicates. The Capitalist Governments will not be able to find the solution to their post-war problems. It is the Labour movement alone which can lead to peace and prosperity, to social justice for all."**

CRITICAL APPROACH

The report is then before the Conference for discussion. It deals with the war, and is more critical of its conduct than was the report presented at last year's Conference. "We must begin with the war, for it remains the dominant factor in the political struggles of the people of South Africa, as in every other country." In the past year, it points out, the initiative has passed to the United Nations on all fronts. "Yet it is only on the Eastern Front that full use is being made of this position of advantage. Above all, use has not been made of the opportunities presented by the victories of the Red Army to invade Western Europe." The Allies have the forces, but they are not being used in the way total warfare demands.

This report also deals with the danger of apathy in our own country, the strength of reaction at home and abroad, the significance of the Moscow Agreement (the report was drawn up before the Teheran Conference), the need for labour unity, the struggle against national oppression, the low level of South Africa's production and the need for rapid industrialisation, war and post-war problems, and the tasks of the Communist Party.

THE GOVERNMENT'S FAILURE

"We have to reckon with the failure of the Government adequately to prosecute the war, to mobilise the people, and with its renewed attacks on the non-Europeans," said Dr. Y. M. Dadoo. Dr. Dadoo is the leader of the Indian progressives, a man who has suffered gaol for his convictions. It was no good "merely talking" about national unity among the workers and progressives, he said. We should not attain it while we had the colour bar and colour prejudice. "My contention is that on a question like the abolition of the Pass Laws the Communist Party must go the whole hog in support of the Anti-Pass Campaign." Yusuf Dadoo suggests the Government's failure to achieve a real war effort is due to its failure to mobilise the whole labour movement. Adding a final plea for support for the Anti-Pass Campaign, he says these laws and other restrictions have prevented four-fifths of South Africa's population from full support of and participation in the war effort, telling Conference that "hindrances to the war effort won't be removed by platitudes."

Several African speakers explain that the Nazi-like restrictions imposed on the African people make it difficult for them to support the war. Edwin Mofutsanyana says there is urgent need for action. Oppression, poverty, lack of opportunity are driving young Africans to crime and gangsterdom.

Durban District secretary R. Arenstein said the Communist Party should not change its attitude of support for the Government in its prosecution of the war, should intensify criticism and "work out a militant course of action against reaction." The opening of the second front was of overwhelming importance. It would require colossal supplies, men and material. "We must rally the people for the final blow against the Nazis."

CONFERENCE PLEDGES

Resolutions arising from the report pledge Conference to undertake to work for a greater mobilisation of men and resources in developing a wider and clearer understanding of the issues involved, and by fighting against the reactionary policies and practices of our Government, which are speading apathy and disillusionment among the people; in particular against:

a) The continued and increasing oppression of the non-European peoples;
b) the appeasement of the Fascist fifth column;[16]
c) the drawing of enormous profits from the war;
d) the unequal distribution of food, and failure to keep down prices;
e) the stopping of recruiting among non-Europeans and the demobilisation of sections of the armed forces;
f) the lack of democracy in the army and unfair treatment of many demobilised men.

Resolutions dealing with the international scene pledge the Communist Party "to press for a combined and total assault on Nazi Europe from the West and on all possible fronts, in accordance with a joint strategy planned by the United Nations"; to obtain wide public support for the rights of peoples of ex-enemy and liberated territories to set up their own Governments, as pledged in the Atlantic Charter;[17] and to demand the extension of the right of self-determination to all colonial countries, particularly the right of India to independence, and further, that the leaders of the Indian Congress and all other imprisoned anti-Fascists in India be immediately released.

WORKERS AND SOLDIERS

Ronnie Fleet, another candidate in last year's general election and secretary of Johannesburg's Local Committee of the S.A. Trades and Labour Council, said the question of the returned soldiers was one of great importance. "Absorption point has already been reached in many industries," he warned. Workers and soldiers must stand together. The Trades Council Local Committee had, at its very inception, resolved to work in close collaboration with soldier's organisations.

They were supporting a demonstration of unemployed soldiers, which would coincide with the opening of Parliament. Pensions must be more adequate. Jobs must be ensured at trade-union wages. Betty Sacks, Cape Town Councillor, agrees with him, quotes instances of hopelessly inadequate pensions and hardships suffered by demobilised soldiers.

George Ponen, Central Committee member and active Durban Communist, supported the report's emphasis on the importance of labour unity. "We need unity to see that the Government carries out the pledges of the Atlantic Charter," he said, and added that the campaign against the Pegging Act, which restricts Natal Indians from buying land in so-called European areas, must be supportetd.

HOME FRONT CAMPAIGN
Conference instructs the Central Committee to campaign during the coming year for the achievement of the following demands:
   (a) Fair distribution of food at low prices;
   (b) jobs or unemployment pay for all;
   (c) housing for all at low prices;
   (d) abolition of the Pass Laws;
   (e) inclusion of Africans as "employees" under the Industrial Conciliation Act;
   (f) free compulsory education for all;
   (g) security of employment at adequate rates of pay for all demobilised soldiers and adequate pensions for all disabled soldiers and their dependants.

TRADE UNIONS
A discussion of the trade union movement is introduced by Ray Alexander, General Secretary of the Food and Canning Workers' Union and a pioneer in organising workers in the country districts of the Western Province and Namaqualand. This outstanding woman comrade is a member of the Central Committee and has been a Communist almost since childhood. Through her work she has won support and respect for the Communist Party.

The report she introduces deals with the need for the expansion of production and for the improvement of working and living conditions. On strikes, it states: "Our Party's policy is directed towards a peaceful settlement of disputes and avoiding of any strikes or any other action that will hinder the war effort. BUT WE DO NOT REGARD THIS CONTRIBUTION OF THE WORKING CLASS TO VICTORY AS A ONE-SIDED ARRANGEMENT. Workers who labour under a sense of grievance, who are not able to maintain a decent standard of living, are certainly not in a position to apply their full strength and ability to production. They will be "reasonable" provided the employers are not less reasonable. It is unfortunate that with the relaxation of tension, the employers are showing increasing signs of reverting to the policy of "reducing cost of production" by attacks on wages.

"In our opinion a great body of low-paid workers have every justification for embarking on a national campaign for wage increases."

INDUSTRIAL CONCILIATION ACT
In explaining the importance of the demand for the inclusion of Africans in the Industrial Conciliation Act, the report details the support given to this demand by the whole trade union movement as well as many other important organisations. It deals with the uneasiness of some European workers. **"This fear, however, is completely unjustified. It arises from a mistaken belief in the old bogey of the 'wage-fund theory', that is to say, the theory that a fixed proportion of the national income is available for wages, and that any increase in wages of any section of the workers must necessarily reduce the wages of the other section.**

"In demanding higher wages neither the Africans nor any other group of workers desire to lower the wage standards of another group. The labour movement dare not accept the principle which the employing class is constantly trying to get established, namely that higher wages for the labourer must mean lower wages for the artisan.

"There is, however, another and even more important consideration in the removal of the colour bar. It will undoubtedly serve to strengthen the African trade unions and, therefore, the whole of the working class. It will assist in the forging of unity between all the racial groups that make up the working class, and so enable labour to play a much more effective part in the future development of South Africa."

NEED FOR UNITY

This report concludes by urging the need for increased trade union organisation and supports the plea for one trade union centre and trade union unity. "With a united trade union movement, the workers can play a decisive part in the fight against fascism and exercise a still greater measure of influence in the post-war period, directed towards the maintenance of peace and economic and social advancement of the masses of the common people."

Delegates who contribute to the discussion include well-known trade union leader I. Wolfson, who is on the National Executive of the S.A. Trades and Labour Council. Not all non-Communists must be regarded as reactionaries, he warns, and speaks on the importance of rank and file movements in the building and engineering unions. E. Weinberg says that in the past year the Non-European Railwaymen's Union has made big advances, but the situation of the European railwaymen is a bad one. They are divided up into six groups, which are little more than company unions.

MINES, RAILWAYS AND FARMS

A. L. S. Louw, national secretary of the Non-European S.A.R. and H. Workers' Union, says there is little point in demanding the recognition of Africans under the Industrial Conciliation Act while the mines, the railways and the farms are excluded from the provisions of the Act, for the majority of Africans are in the employ of one or the other. "It is high time to fight against these barriers," he says.

Philemon Tsele, secretary of the Non-European Railway Workers in Durban, says that to-day African workers are a good business proposition for unscrupulous employers who want to make wealth out of the workers. Sam Andrews brings greetings from Paarl workers, and describes his feelings on seeing the huts and pondokkies bordering the railway line between Cape Town and Johannesburg. Houses so miserable "that I am sure people can only get in and out by crawling on their hands and knees." H. A. Naidoo says the Communist Party must not shout dead slogans of "equal pay for equal work" but must also demand equal opportunity.

AFRICAN UNIONS

George Findlay of Pretoria says there are seventeen young African unions there, run by African secretaries and linked together in an African trade union council. They are well run, and they are represented on the local committee of the Trades Council. They are making real headway. Harry Snitcher warns of the dangers of ignoring the threat to the trade union movement from the Nationalists, who are again campaigning in the trade union field and attempting to split the trade union movement.

We must demand that ALL returned soldiers are given opportunity to participate in the Government training schemes, says Danie du Plessis. We must oppose repressive legislation and restrictions on freedom of movement.

M. Mokgathe is an African who draws the delegates' attention to the bad conditions in the small towns where workers are scarcely organised. Wage Determinations must be extended to cover these country areas.

Ray Alexander replies to the discussion. Useful points have been brought forward, she says. The report deals with the problems facing the trade union and labour movement, of which the right to work is the most important. Not only the Nationalists but the employers, too, are trying to prepare people to go out and organise the workers in order to obtain control over them. "THE WORKERS THEMSELVES ARE THE BEST ORGANISERS," she says.

She concludes: "Now is the time, when Parliament is sitting, to see that the views expressed at Mr. Madeley's conference on recognition of Africans under the Industrial Conciliation Act are carried into effect. We must press for this amendment and for the extension of the Act to cover employees of the railways, in agriculture and on the mines."

NATIONAL MOVEMENTS

The need for unity is again emphasised in the discussion on the report on the national movements of the non-Europeans, which is opened by Comrade H. A. Naidoo. The report declares: "The Communist Party supports the National Liberation movement of the non-Europeans, firstly because it recognises in this movement an identity of interests in the common revolutionary struggle against imperialism and secondly, as the greatest upholder of the peoples' freedom, the Communist Party supports the non-Europeans' struggle against the colour bar and for the winning of equal rights and opportunities for all people."

Conference agrees with the recommendation of the report that "while not losing sight of the long range programme of demands for the realisation of non-European rights, a basis of joint national campaigns shall be conducted on such issues as extension of the vote, abolition of the Pass Laws and poll tax, removal of barriers which restrict freedom of movement, and abolition of the industrial colour bar."

The need for the redistribution of land among the peasants is described by R. Bernstein of Johannesburg. He and Alpheus Madibe say there is trouble again in the Northern Transvaal as a result of ploughing restrictions and great hardships among the people.[18]

The Anti-C.A.C. conference recently held in Cape Town is criticised by Cape Town's District Secretary, Rex Close. It failed to deal with practical questions, he says. A delegate from Bloemfontein says it is important that the Communist Party should send organisers out into the country, otherwise others will do so "and will mislead the people."

Not enough time has been allowed to discuss aspects of important questions affecting national problems. Delegates suggest discussion continue at a further meeting to be held next day. This is agreed.

COMMUNIST CONSTITUTION

"One of the most important tasks of Conference is to consider the draft of the Party Constitution," said the chairman. Bill Andrews, when he opened Conference, and with considerable discussion and several adjustments the new Constitution is accepted.

One or two delegates consider there should be a differentiation between long-term aims and short-term aims, and are informed by other speakers that the Party's Constitution must embody THE AIMS of the Communists. One of these reads in the Draft: "To break down race barriers and to promote unity of the workers of South Africa and throughout the world." Conference replaces "to break down race barriers" with a clearer statement: "TO WORK FOR THE REMOVAL OF ALL POLITICAL, SOCIAL, ECONOMIC AND CULTURAL COLOUR BARS WHICH RETARD THE PROGRESS AND DEVELOPMENT OF ANY NATIONAL GROUP AND DIVIDE THE WORKING CLASS . . ."

There is some discussion as to whether the National Chairman and the General Secretary shall be elected by the National Conference or the Central Committee. It is Comrade Bill Andrews who gets up and speaks vigorously for the more democratic procedure of election by Conference. Conference agrees with him.

EFFICIENCY AND ORGANISATION

A report on organisation and propaganda is introduced by Mike Harmel[19], member of the Central Committee. It deals with Party organisation, the need for the publication of more pamphlets, for more efficiency, for greater speed in dealing with issues as they arise, for a uniform system of book-keeping. Advances have been made, particularly as a result of the Party's putting up candidates in the Parliamentary and other elections, but some of the resolutions for greater efficiency made last year have not been carried out. Conference pledges itself to introduce many improvements in the coming year.

Advocate Harry Snitcher, the Communist candidate in Woodstock during the general election, says that the Communist Party has learned much from the election. It has taken the message of Communism to the people, and defeat has been turned into victory with the election of two Councillors in Cape Town and Advisory Board successes at East London, Port Elizabeth and elsewhere. Councillor Archie Muller had scored "a near miss" for the Provincial Council.

Bill Andrews, who opened the Conference, takes the chair again for its closing. His words are encouraging. He tells the delegates this is the best conference, the most practical in approach, that the South African Communist Party has yet held. There are big difficulties ahead, but he is confident they will be faced by a Party membership more mature than ever before.

CONFIDENCE IN COMMUNISM

This note of confidence and optimism was struck by all delegates throughout the Conference. It was a spirit based on a year's solid progress and a sober examination of future tasks. As is stated in the main report to Conference:

"Confidence in ourselves is fully justified by the record of our growth. We have succeeded in what to many seems an impossibility; we have brought together in our organisation men and women of all racial groups in South Africa, working together for common ends on a basis of complete equality. We have done this in the teeth of bitter opposition and in the face of the dominant prejudices of society. We say that our participation in the elections of 1942 and 1943 is only a beginning of a new period in the history of the South African people. Our experience has shown that our Party can gain the goodwill and support of large sections. Our members who have been elected to the City Councils of Cape Town and East London are the first of the future body of Communists on parliamentary and other representative organs.

"A strong Communist Party, working in close alliance with the rest of the Labour movement and the national organisations of the non-European, will create the social forces that are needed to enable South Africa to play her full part in the war, and to create the conditions for a free and full life for all her people."

"THE COMMUNIST PARTY," CONCLUDES THE REPORT, "HAS A GREAT PART TO PLAY IN THE STRUGGLE OF MAN FOR LIBERATION FROM POVERTY, INSECURITY AND OPPRESSION. WE ARE MOVING IN THE DIRECTION OF HISTORY; WE EXPRESS THE DEEP-SEATED NEEDS OF THE PEOPLE, AND MUST THEREFORE EVENTUALLY OBTAIN THE SUPPORT OF THE PEOPLE."

Document 131
"Why did the V.F.P. Strike Fail?", *Workers Voice*, 1 February 1944

On the 22nd January African workers struck in the V.F.P. plants along the Reef. The Gas and Power Workers' Union stated that 4,000 struck for higher wages, for two-weeks holiday with pay every year, and for recognition of the trade union. The workers were earning 16/- a week, living in concentration camp barracks, and were working as slaves. The company made £1 [3/5] million profit during the past year.

The Trade Union Leaders

The African workers were at once imprisoned inside the compounds by the military and police. African soldiers, from the Native Corps, were ordered to work the plants and to scab. A number of White workers, according to some reports, were not eager to go on working while their black brothers were out on strike, but the White workers got no courageous lead from their trade union officials. The leaders of the strikers lacked the militant spirit to carry on and to fight the bosses, even though the position of the African soldiers and the white workers made this fight very difficult. And so, after two heroic days, the strikers were forced to go back to work, with the empty promise that their demands would be "considered" (that is put on the shelf) after the Native Wages Commission had made its statements. This means that the strikers will get nothing or next to nothing, because the V.F.P. company is tied up with the powerful Chamber of Mines which refuses to give its workers a living wage. Surely the trade union leaders know this, know that by giving in to the V.F.P. bosses they are losing the fight? Why did they start the strike in the first place? Or was the strike started from below, with the leaders out of touch with the workers? In both cases the trade union leadership is at fault. The workers have a right to demand that the union FIGHT for their demands and does not say JA-BAAS to the bosses.

The White Workers

The trade union leadership is one reason why the strike was broken. The second reason is that WHITE LABOUR DID NOT STAND BY BLACK LABOUR. It was the duty of the White union to come out in support of the black workers. The black workers always support the whites. If the whites had given this support the strike would not only have stood a great chance of success, but would have spread to other industries, chiefly those which cannot work without electric power. No troops could do the work of the skilled White workers in the V.F.P. The company would have had to give in, not only to the demands of the black workers, but to any demands which the white workers themselves put up. By not supporting the black workers, the white workers have lost a golden chance to better their own wages, hours and working conditions.

The African Soldier
The third reason why the strike failed was because African soldiers allowed themselves to be used against their own brothers. The African soldiers were told to join up to fight fascism outside South Africa. Years ago, the 4th International said that the war was not a war against fascism, but a bosses' war for the bosses's profits. Years ago we told the African soldiers that one day they would be used against the workers inside South Africa. We told the soldier that he would be used to put fascism into practice in this country, to break strikes, to murder his own brother. Now this has hapened at the V.F.P. plants. African soldiers, workers and peasants in uniform, were used to break a strike, to lock Africans into compounds. This is a bitter lesson to the African soldier. But it will open his eyes to see the truth – that his duty lies with his brothers in the factory and mine; that his struggle is one with their struggle against the boss and the government.

Learn From Defeat!
If the workers of all colours learn these three lessons, then they will be able to go forward to new strikes with more courage and energy and sureness than during the V.F.P. strike. If these lessons are learnt then the defeat at the V.F.P. plants will be turned into great victories in strikes that will still come.

Document 132
"Our Programme", *Progressive Trade Union Bulletin*, 1, 1, February 1945

WE DEMAND:
INTERNAL TRADE UNION DEMOCRACY
All officials should be properly elected by their respective Unions and should be subject to recall by the Union. Executive Committee members should be directly elected by Council and all co-options should be placed before it for its approval or otherwise, and every Executive member should be subject to recall. It is also of the utmost importance that Economic Democracy be introduced that is that each Trade Union official be paid at the prevailing rate of workers' wages in his Union. Economic democracy is one of the most effective ways of preventing bureaucracy amongst the leaders. It will do much to stop that process by which the better paid leader places himself in a class apart from the rank and file worker in his Union; rob him of the incentive to compromise with the employer, to be the "good boy" at all costs in order to retain his privileged economic position.

REVISION OF LABOUR LEGISLATION
We demand the repeal of Emergency Regulations Numbers [-] and 145 which cripple our main working class weapon – the right to strike; and the repeal of the recent

Emergency banning of meetings of more than 20 persons – a prohibition which renders T.U. organisational work, financial and other, impossible. We demand the right to picket.

A SLIDING SCALE OF WAGES

It is a phenomenon of the present period of rapid decay in the capitalist system, and especially during the war, that all citizens, but particularly the workers who can least afford it, are confronted with a catastrophic rise in prices. Against this we can only fight with the introduction of the sliding scale of wages. This means that industrial agreements should ensure an automatic rise in wages in relation to the increase in prices. TO BEGIN WITH WE DEMAND A MINIMUM WAGE OF £3 A WEEK.

A SLIDING SCALE OF WORKING HOURS

This is the only effective guarantee of every worker's right to employment in a society based upon exploitation. Trade Unions and other mass organisations should bind the workers and the unemployed together, they should be responsible to each other. In this way all the work on hand would be divided amongst all existing workers and the working week would be reduced for each worker respectively. The average wage of every worker must, of course, remain the same as it was under the old working week. TO BEGIN WITH WE DEMAND A 40 HOUR WEEK.

DRASTIC REFORMS IN THE PRESENT INTERNAL TRADE UNION ORGANISATION

We advocate that present organisation of Unions on a craft basis, that is the organisation of Unions on the basis of trades and occupations be superceded by the organisation of Unions on a basis that will embrace whole industries. We press for the transformation of craft union organisation into Industrial Union Organisation. We press for the introduction into all Unions of Shop Stwards and Factory Committees to be elected by all the factory employees. The Factory Committees elected by all the workers in the factories directly represent and organise the wishes of the rank and file workers and introduce a counter weight to the will of the Administration (the reactionary Labour Department and the Top layers of the workers in official positions.) The Factory Committee is a center of struggle against the deadening weight of reactionary leaders. We strive to replace the present routine-functionaries, racketeers, and careerists, by new militant leaders.

PUBLIC RESPONSIBILITY for workers transport, medical services, hospitalisation, and housing, and that these services shall be on a scale large enough to meet the needs of the workers.

A LEADERSHIP OF DICTATORS AND COMPROMISERS

THERE is a growing tide of dissatisfaction among African workers with the present organisation and composition of the Non-European Trade Union Council, and particularly with its Executive Committee.

The Council leadership has developed far on the road of bureaucracy. The ordinary worker plays less and less part in its decisions, and the E.C. increasingly leans towards the methods of compromise and knuckling under to the employers. The E.C. in accordance with its character. has appropriated to itself autocratic powers. The Council has come to exist merely in an advisory capacity. At the N.E.T.U.C. Conference in

April, 1944, very significant changes in the constitution took place by which the E.C. has been able to play the dictator in the Unions. The E.C. alone makes the final decisions on all questions discussed and resolved upon by the Council, and it alone can decide whether to implement or not, any decision made by the Council.

The President of the Council has full powers to co-opt any person to the E.C. whom he thinks fit, and the Council has no power to recall any member of the E.C. The co-options are not placed democratically before the General Council for approval and discussion.

This form of organisation has led to numerous abuses which it is the duty of all militants in the rank and file of the Unions and in the Council to remove. The militants must demand a democratic constitution to place control in the hands of the rank and file.

Through its bureaucratic strangle-hold on the Unions, for example, the E.C. has not infrequently sabotaged the fight of the worker for better conditions. There is an understanding that where an official organised Union exists, no rival or additional Union shall be allowed in that Trade. But, in fact, wherever the E.C. of the Council wants to break a Union which refuses to dance to its tune, it allows alternative Unions to arise. The fate of the Unions in the Laundry Industry and Catering and Liquor Trade, etc., are sufficient illustration of this policy.

Definite allegations of tribalism in the present leadership have also been made. Porminent leaders are mentioned in particular as being tribally inclined. It is claimed that before each conference, they carefully caucus the Xosa members of the E.C. and the Council in order to make sure of a Xosa majority.

Militants must be vigilant to expose these practices. Division on tribal lines, to say nothing of national lines, is exactly what the bosses want. The Chamber of Mines has always fostered tribal distinctions in order to prevent the proper organisation of its workers. To-day it is certain that the Government will increasingly resort to this weapon to split Trade Unions and the African people as a whole.

The only effective method of meeting the Government threat to smash the Unions in this and in other ways, and of achieving the demands of the workers, is organisation on a *class* basis.

ANTI-STRIKE LEADERSHIP
An accusation brought against us Progressive Council members is that we are Troskyists. They know that not all are Troskyists. It is certainly not Trotskyism which needs watching, Trotskyism identifies itself completely with the interests of the working class. The sinister role of the Communist Party, however, needs exposure. At the moment, the C.P. has a number of members in the E.C. of the Council, and they follow the uncompromisingly reactionary policy of Stalinism. The Council leadership under the direction of the C.P. has frequently gone to the extreme of pacifying the Unions whose workers are in bad economic straits and who consequently are pressing for action. It is this type of C.P. leadership that has brought many a promising strike or Trade Union struggle to an ignominious end, as the workers involved in the Timber and Milling strikes can well testify.

The milling strike is a particularly glaring example of the way in which the Council leadership meets situations with belated protests, instead of fulfilling its function of co-ordination and rallying the Unions to defend their common interests and to make their common demands.

When the workers were advised to boycott the mills, the E.C. dissociated itself from the decision. Nor did they attempt to build up any support for Timber strikers in other Unions or in any other way, and this resulted in the isolation and arrest of 128 workers who were sentenced to ten days hard labour and lost their jobs.

T.U's AND LEGAL RECOGNITION

One of the chief obstacles that faces the Unions to-day is the fact that they are not legally recognised.They have at present only indirect powers of negotiation. Where negotiations for higher wages are concerned, it is true that the Council can submit a Memorandum to the Minister and the local Department of Labour, and that it has direct verbal representation at public sittings to settle disputes of this kind, but in connection with industrial agreements under the Industrial Conciliation Act, the Non-European Trade Unions have no access to direct representation. Thus their demands can easily be mishandled or held up by the reactionary department and the Africans have no jurisdiction or powers of redress.

Recognition of the Non-European Trade Unions under the I.C. Act, will be a tremendous advance, but it will never be achieved by the milk and water methods of the present leadership. The present leadership is thoroughly imbued with the dues-collecting mentality. As long as the dues are paid, they are satisfied. Actually, the demand for recognition is not a question of fighting an individual employer for higher wages, but a frontal attack on the entire segregation policy of the Government. The conditions of the African worker will not be improved until his Unions are recognised. His Unions will not be recognised until he has the united support of the African proletariat, and the entire African people in the common struggle for democratic rights. The present Council cannot give the fearless lead which is required. It constantly reveals its fossilised and bureaucratic character in its preference for mediation instead of direct strike action.

THE W.I.L. AND THE MILITANTS

The lead in the fight will only come from the militants in the African working class, organised as a vanguard with the full consciousness of all the political implications involved in the struggle of the African worker against his burdens. This means that the militants in the Non-European Trade Unions must now actively fight for a new and democratic leadership in the Council, which will base itself on the needs and interests of the masses of the rank and file which will counter the present mediation policy and C.P. obstructionism and sabotage, with bold class organisation aiming at recognition and full democratic rights. In this fight, the workers will find that their only ally is the Workers's International League and that helping to build up the Fourth Internationalist Workers' Party is an urgent and imperative part of their battle to overthrow the capitalist system which oppresses them.

BOSSES' WAR GAINS ARE WORKERS LOSSES

THERE is not a single African worker who has not been hard hit by the war. The increase in the cost of living and the rise in prices especially on the black market to which the African is compelled to resort in order to obtain the most vital commodities, falls particularly heavily on the African worker. In increasing numbers, workers rally to the Unions to fight for conditions under which they can live – then they discover that their Unions are unofficial, that they are hampered at every turn by laws and regulations, that the leadership is not seriously prepared to make a stand.

What is the present position with regard to the non-European Trade Unions? In war-time, there has been increasing criticism of the compound system. In a number of important industries, workers have long been housed in compounds where they are under the constant control and supervision of the employers and where access is difficult. The mine-workers, hotel, boarding-house and flat workersn brick and tile workers, municipal workers; V.F.P. workers; timber workers; railway workers – are all subject to the compound system. In addition, it has been extended in the past few years and there are indications that the ruling class will try to extend it further still, e.g. railway workers at Port Elizabeth. In certain trades, the bosses have started to capitalise on this situation by organising company unions, as on the railways and municipalities. The compound system which is designed to curb militancy and any form of independent workers' organisation at all, will have to be broken by the action of the workers themselves.

EMERGENCY REGULATIONS USED TO BREAK UNIONS
In addition to the present repressive legislation applying to the African worker, the war has unleashed a whole series of emergency regulations. The demand to break these has become very strong under the impact of war hardships. The struggle for recognition of the Unions is also the struggle for bread.

The Pass Laws (Law 40 of 1895) exclude anybody who is pass-bearing from being recognised as an employee and make him a servant under the Master and Servants' Act (Transvaal and Natal Code.) This legislation must be redrafted to grant the African worker the same status as the European. Equal pay for equal work must be the slogan of the Non-European masses through their Trade Unions. This will form part of the struggle for full democratic rights and the aboliton of all discrimination based on colour prejudice.

It should be remembered, however, that although recognition under the I.C. Act would be a tremendous step forward, the Act has severe limitations in itself. It is an Act designed to hamper workers' direct action as much as possible – it is of a compromising character – it restricts strike action and encourages the settlement of disputes in such a way that the employer is heavily favoured.

In addition, the ruling class has used its dictatorial wartime powers to launch a ferocious attack on working-class organisation in other ways. Emergency regulations have been used indiscriminately to try and break the spirit of the workers. Strikes are forbidden under War Measure Number 145 of 1942 on pain of a penalty of 5 years imprisonment or £500. fine or both, e.g. arrest of Milling and Coal workers, etc.

Organisers have been prevented from collecting Union dues under The Gold Law which forbids meetings of more than 20 on proclaimed land, e.g. Messrs. Marks, Tule and others. The Government hopes to deter the workers from organising by denying them access to funds. In the case of Pioneer Stone-Crushing Yards, again, men collecting funds were threatened with dismissal if they persisted.

BULLETIN TO DIRECT AND RALLY WORKERS
These disabilities will never be removed by the bureaucrats who at present lead the Federation of Non-European Trade Unions. They must be ousted, and the general masses of workers must be educated in Trade Unionism along class struggle lines. The African people in the townships and at the pass-offices, where scab-labour is recruited, must be educated too as to the conditions of their fellow-workers in the different idnustries.

This is one of the tasks which the Trade Union Bulletin will take up. Our purpose is to help in educating the uneducated, organising the unorganised, and to demonstrate that the struggle must inevitabley become a political struggle the moment the most elementary demand for rights are raised. The fight against the reactionary Government offensive can only be met by the lcass action of the African masses under Marxist leadership.

C.P. AIDS BOSSES

The C.P. will attempt to hinder the attainment of these aims. Ever since 1941, the Stalinists have consistently encouraged support of the war effort and have attempted to curb any manifestation of militancy by the masses. They have discouraged and sabotaged strikes. Unions dominated by the C.P.? or which the C.P. has set out to break because they express the will of the workers, have deteriorated and gone out of existence altogether, as happened with the Tin and Metal workers. The C.P. not only has failed to give the masses, which it pretends to represent, a proper lead, but has tried to destry their spirit by its hush-hush and scab tactics.

Owing to the lack of proper leadership, the African masses have been persuaded into giving unconditional support to the war and great numbers have even joined the army and given their lives for a reactionary Government and oppressing system of society. The present leadership of the Council, influenced by Stalinism, must undoubtedly be held responsible for these things, and it is clear that the workers' struggle will only advance if they are replaced by militants who truly represent the masses.

Document 133
"Editorial: The Bloemfontein Trade Union Conference and the Industrial Conciliation Act",
The Militant Worker[20], **October-November 1945**

THE all-in Non-European Trade Union Conference held at the location, Bloemfontein on August 4th, 5th & 6th, adopted a resolution to wage a campaign to change the Industrial-Conciliation Act.[21] The resolution called for the amendment of this Act so that African workers have the same rights as White and Coloured workers. A further addition to this resolution called for the scrapping of the anti-strike parts in the Act, and to enlarge the scope of the Act so that it covers farm and domestic workers. This resolution was unanimously adopted by the conference.

To carry out this resolution it was decided that the Transvaal Committee of the Council of Non European Trade Unions should undertake this campaign. Two months have already gone past and many unions are wondering why the Tvl. Council is delaying this campaign. There appear to be personal fights inside the Council, which lead to the expulsion of Koza and Poffu. It is a sad state of affairs if an important struggle is held back by bureaucratic differences between the so-called P.T.U. and the Stalinists. It is equally disgusting to see both groups using the same bureaucratic tactics against each other (swamping conference, expulsions) and that the heads of the Transvaal Council – supposed to be responsible officials, could find no other solution but to expel two Council members, and in this way only deepen the division of the workers. Further, loose, untrue statements that Koza[22] and Poffu, two old African T.U.

SMUTS' "RECOGNITION"

The position is grave for African workers and their unions. For years they have been demanding full legal recognition under the I.C. Act. And, after a long struggle, the Africans got their reply, on September 21st, from – General Smuts. In an interview with the Trades and Labour Council, Smuts said he agreed to recognise African unions BUT, he said, he was NOT in favour of African unions that are controlled by the workers. He accepted the reactionary colour-bar proposal of De Vries, a member of the S.A.T.&.L.C., to PUT AFRICAN UNIONS UNDER THE "TRUSTEESHIP" OF A BODY OF WHITES. This is not recognition! It is an insult and aims at sapping the life out of the African trade unions, destroy their independence and militancy. Smuts, explaining his reasons, said he wants to get rid of the "agitators". He wants his own good boys to run the union of Africans.

The C.M.T. completely rejects this hum-bug recognition. Every union leader, white and black, and all workers, must reject this plan of Smuts. We must carry on to win full legal recognition under the I.C. Act.

Side by side with this struggle for full recognition under the I.C. Act (which means a struggle against a colour-bar in the Act), we must support every struggle against the threat of the government to de-register unions with African members. It is the duty of the Executive of the Transvaal Council of Non European Trade Unions to regard its work as urgent, and immediately to prepare for a nation-wide campaign for recognition, and in this way to justify the trust put in it by the historic conference at Bloemfontein in August, when the representatives of 200,000 Non-European workers voted in favour of an URGENT campaign to amend the I.C. Act.

Document 134
The Impending Strike of African Miners: A statement by the African Mineworkers' Union, 7 August 1946

Rosenberg Arcade,
58, Market Street,
Johannesburg.

1. At a Conference of the African Mine Workers' Union held on the Newtown Square, Johannesburg, on Sunday August 4, 1946, and attended by over one thousand delegates, representing all Witwatersrand Gold Mines, the following resolution was unanimously carried:–

    "Because of the intransigent attitude of the Transvaal Chamber of Mines towards the legitimate demands of the workers for a minimum wage of ten shillings per day and better conditions of work, this meeting of African miners resolves:–
    to embark upon a General Strike of all Africans employed on the Gold Mines, as from the 12th August, 1946."

2. On August 7, 1946, my Union wrote to the Secretary of the Transvaal Chamber of Mines, conveying the text of the above resolution, and stating "My Union regrets that your Chamber has not deemed it fit to accede to the demands of the workers or to open up negotiations; nevertheless my Union feels that it is not yet too late."
3. Frankly, we hardly expect even a reply to this letter, as to practically every communication we have addressed to the employers over the six years of its existence, my Union has received neither reply nor acknowledgment.
4. It should not be thought that the decision to take strike action has been lightly taken, without provocation, or without due care and effort to find some alternative to action so grave and far-reaching. On the contrary, as the brief case-history below demonstrates, the African Mine Workers have been waiting a long time, in patience and humility, for a sign from the Chamber of Mines or from the Government that their plea for fair treatment, for a living wage and decent conditions of employment will be heeded. This Union has repeatedly, year after year, made representations on behalf of its members, the African Mine Workers. But unfortunately, on every occasion, our modest proposals have been to no avail, and our representations rejected or ignored.
5. In considering the many steps towards effecting peaceful settlement of the workers grievances, made by our Union, it should be borne in mind that the pay and conditions of employment of the Africans on the mines can only be described as a notorious national scandal. It is not within the scope of this statement to detail the very many hardships and injustices suffered by our members. But we cannot refrain from pointing out that while the wages of almost every other group of workers in the country have advanced, the African miner receives the same £3 monthly paid by the mines in 1900, despite the very greatly reduced buying power of the pound, the enormous profits accumulated out of this great industry, the long hours of work and the physically exhausting character of the labour performed, dangerous to life and health. Against such a background, and bearing in mind the intolerable conditions of life in the compounds, and the inadequate rations, the remarkable thing is not that the African Mine Workers have decided to strike, but that they have so long persevered in other efforts to secure redress of grievances, although our efforts have all along met with nothing but frustration and contempt on the part of the Chamber of Mines and the Government.
6. It is instructive to review briefly here some of the more important of the many approaches made by the African Mine Workers' Union, over a number of years, and taken in chronological order:

1941: In September of this year the Prime Minister was approached with a request for the extension of cost of living allowances to African Mine Workers. This request was supported by the S.A.Trades & Labour Council, and by numerous other organisations throughout the country. The Government, however, not only completely ignored our request, but, in the same year, steps were taken to haul our officials before the C.I.D., as if they were common criminals and not trade unionists engaged in legitimate trade union work.

1942: The African Mine Workers' Union put forward a request to the Minister of Labour to use his powers under Section 4 (a) of the Wage Act (No. 44 of 1937) to order the Wage Board to investigate the conditions of the African

Mine employees. The Minister refused this request without giving any reasons.

1943: It was in this year that the Government raised the expectations of our members by the appointment of the "Native Mine Wages Commission," and the Union made suitable representations to this Commission. Our hopes were, however, dashed by the open announcement of the Commission in its Report, that the report was based upon the "necessity" acknowledged by the Commission, for the maintenance of the "cheap labour" system. We wish here, as trade unionists, to express our most emphatic rejection of this system, which is injurious alike to the welfare of the workers and the progress of the country, and our consequent rejection of the report of the Commission, based upon such an unacceptable principle. Nevertheless, we must point out that certain minor improvements in the conditions of African Mine Workers were recommended in the Report. Apart from a negligible and completely inadequate increase, subsidised by the Government, the majority of the improvements recommended by the Commission have been ignored by the employers.

1944: Until this year, the continual appeals by our Union for justice and fair treatment had been met by the Government with the weapon of silence. But in 1944, the Government used its emergency war powers to prohibit meetings on gold-proclaimed land under Proclamation No. 1425. We have no hesitation in declaring that was and remains the purpose of this measure to prevent and retard the effective trade union organisation of African Mine Workers. The measure has repeatedly been invoked against our Union organisers, but never, to our knowledge, against any pro-Nazi or subversive organisation. Protests against the use of this Proclamation to restrain trade union activity have repeatedly been made, not only by our Union, but also by a number of other progressive and labour bodies, but it remains in operation against us to this day. The same year, our Union made a number of efforts to secure a hearing from both the Government and the Chamber of Mines, But were consistently treated with contempt. It came to our attention that the Chamber of Mines had issued a circular to all Compound Managers and other officials that on no account were they to meet or negotiate with Union officials.

1945: In May, 1945, we endeavoured to arrange for interviews with the Acting Prime Minister and the Ministers of Justice and Labour; In a statement submitted at the time, we pointed out that considerable dissatisfaction existed among African mine workers, and suggested steps to remedy the position. However the Ministers concerned refused to meet us. A protracted hunger strike took place among workers on the Crown Mines, in protest against cuts in their rations, and only ended after a number of men collapsed. We wrote to the Chamber of Mines, urgently requesting an audience, but were again ignored.

1946: The annual Conference of our Union, held on 14.4.1946, resolved to demand adequate food for the workers and "in accordance with the new world principles for an improved standard of living" subscribed to by our Government at U.N.O., a minimum wage of 10/-. per day. The text of this resolution was sent to the Chamber of Mines, and in reply we received the first official acknowledgment we have ever received from the Chamber, in the shape of a printed post-card from the Secretary, Mr. A. J. Limebeer, stating that our resolutions were "receiving attention." That was dated 6th May 1946, and since then we have received no further communication.

7. Following our Conference, and during April of this year, African workers on a number of shafts all over the Witwatersrand, not acting on the advice of the leadership of the Union, struck work in support of the Union demands of 10/-. a day minimum and better food. Despite the difficulties placed in our way by both employers and Government, our organisers succeeded in contacting these workers and impressing upon them the need for discipline and restraint.

8. All the above circumstances should be taken into account in assessing the motives which prompted our members into taking their historic decision of last Sunday, August 4. They are conscious that the decision was a weighty one, and that the task they have undertaken is no easy one to perform; nevertheless they believe their cause is just and that justice shall prevail. As for ourselves, their Executive, we know that we have taken every step humanly possible to prevail upon the Chamber and the Government to appreciate the seriousness of the situation. As responsible men we could not advise the workers to take any other step than that upon which they have decided, the historic ultimate weapon of the trade union movement, the withholding of the workers' labour power.

9. We believe that we are fully justified in asking all sections of and all well-wishers of the labour movement for their fullest moral and financial support for the just cause of the African mine labourers, upon whose broad shoulders so much of the wealth of South Africa has been built, and in their most moderate demands upon those who have amassed fabulous fortunes from their labour over many years.

10. In view of the record of the employers and the Government as briefly outlined above, we ask in particular that every fellow-worker and fellow-democrat should demonstrate his most active protest in the event of any attempt by the Chamber or the authorities to force the workers into submission by violence or by starvation.

11. In conclusion, may we add that we make this appeal for support in the profound and sincere belief that the cause of the African mine workers is the cause of every worker and democrat throughout South Africa.

PRESIDENT: J. B. Marks
SECRETARY: James Majoro[23]
AFRICAN MINE WORKERS' UNION.

Document 135
"National Front and Class Struggle: Report to the Central Committee of the Communist Party of South Africa", *Freedom*, 5, 4, August-September 1946

FOR some years before the war, as well as during the war, the one issue that overshadowed all other political questions was the menace of Fascism. This is the period of the United Front, of the attempt to bring into action against Fascism all sections, all classes in every country. With every advance of the Fascists, made over the bodies of countless numbers of workers and the ruins of their organisations, the extent of the danger became more evident, and the need to stem the tide of capitalist reactions more imperative. As a result the working class was forced on to the defensive; the United Front was a means of protecting the gains made in previous years, not an effort to break down capitalism.

In politics, however, as in war, a defensive operation, if correctly conducted, should open the way for attack. It was at Moscow and Stalingrad that the Nazi invaders received their death blow. With the defeat of the Fascist Powers the world has not returned merely to the position that existed before the rise of Fascism. For Fascism represents in one aspect the defensive form assumed by capitalism against the working class. The defeat of Fascism has therefore been a defeat also for world capitalism. It follows that the result of the war has shifted the balance of class forces in favour of the working class. The end of the war begins a new phase in the class struggle.

The growth in the strength of the working class movement has been reflected in the elections held in Europe since the end of the war. Towards the end of May, 1946, elections had taken place in seventeen European States, including Great Britain, but excluding the Soviet Union, Poland and Rumania, and of course, Fascist Spain and Portugal. Of 109 million votes recorded in these seventeen countries, about one-quarter went to Communist and allied parties, a very small number were cast in favour of openly reactionary candidates, and the great bulk of the remaining 70 per cent went to the Social Democrats and other liberal or centrist groups. In Czechoslovakia, Bulgaria, Yugoslavia and Albania, the Communist Party has emerged as the strongest single party; in a number of other countries it has a considerable representation in elected bodies. Of 5 233 deputies elected to constituent and legislative assemblies, 1,496 (28.6 per cent.) were Communists, as compared with the 125 Communist deputies found throughout Europe before the war.

We are justified in concluding that great numbers of people in Europe have turned their backs on the policies that led to Fascism and war. This mood is shared also by the peoples of the Far East, in Indonesia, Burma, India and China. They too are finding their path to a new society, one free of alien domination and imperialist exploitation.

THE NEXT STAGE
What is to be the next stage? In some countries, such as Poland, Czechoslovakia and Yugoslavia, we may find that the fundamental issue of political power has already been settled. Certainly, in the agrarian countries bordering on the Soviet Union, where the big estates of the reactionary ruling class have been confiscated, and where the land has been divided among the peasantry, a social revolution has taken place. Here, where the defeat of Fascism involved in effect the overthrow of the dominant sections of capitalists, the war has itself been a revolutionary process, in which power has been

transferred to the workers and peasants. In Western Europe, on the other hand, that process has still to be worked out to its conclusion.

In Great Britain, France, Italy and other Western European States, conditions are not unlike those that existed after the First World War in Germany. Governments are dominated by Social Democratic parties, but the capitalist economy and the capitalist state continue to function. These governments have applied a measure of nationalisation of industry, they have introduced reforms, but they have not altered the essential features of capitalist society. As compared with the position after the 1914-18 war, however, one important difference must be noted: the revolutionary section of the Labour Movement is not now in opposition to Social Democracy, but in alliance with it. Communists are either in the governments of Western Europe, or support these governments. The United Front of the pre-war period has become the National Front of the post-war.

Like the United Front, the National Front is based on a compromise, a shelving of differences, and agreement on a joint programme. Agreement has been reached, specifically, on a policy of suppressing Fascist organisations, restoring and extending democratic rights, bringing about social reforms, and widening the scope of State control and ownership in economic life. This is not a defensive programme, but neither is it an alliance for bringing about a change towards socialism. The National Front may therefore be expected to continue on its present basis as long as the problems that must be faced can be settled within the framework of capitalist society. When, however, problems demanding a revolutionary solution can no longer be evaded, when a settlement has to be reached by making fundamental changes in the structure of society, the National Front will reach a crisis. Either it goes over to a revolutionary policy, or it disintegrates.

Such a stage must come. For capitalism has not found, and can not find, a means of overcoming its contradictions, of reconciling the technique of mass production with private ownership and the profit motive. That contradiction is not marked to-day, when the war conditions of full employment and unsatisfied markets continue to operate, and when the process of inflation gives an assurance of profitability. At some point, however, the inevitable contraction must take place; the supply of consumers' goods will exceed the purchasing power of the people, and production will decline. In order to maintain or restore the rate of profit, the capitalist class will attempt to carry out a policy of deflation. For this purpose a frontal attack will be made on wage standards. It is both during a period of unlimited inflation, endangering the living standards of the people, and during a deflation, taking the form of depression, that the demand of the working class must come into irreconcilable conflict with the demands of the capitalist. Government must then find a working class solution or a capitalist solution. Whatever course may be adopted, the National Front must undergo a radical change.

THE CHOICE

This choice, between revolutionary struggle and submission to the capitalist class, presents itself also in the field of international politics. At the present time the great international issues are being fought out around the peace table and in the United Nations Organisation.[24] The conflict has already so weakened the ties between the United Nations that something like a war atmosphere is being created. The Imperialist States, under the leadership of the U.S.A., and using the threat of atomic weapons, are attempting to obtain a peace settlement in accordance with the interests of world capitalism. On the one hand they are seeking strategic points and markets from which to dominate the world economy; on the other they attempt to obstruct advance by the forces of progress and socialism. Since the Soviet Union is the only State capable of offering effective resistance to their demands, and because of their antagonism towards their socialist economy, the Imperialist Powers have made her their chief target of attack.

We have defined two sets of factors that may be expected to change the present political situation. On the one hand we anticipate an end to the post-war boom, and a capitalist attack on workers wages and living standards. On the other hand the imperialist anti-democratic policies of the capitalist States will bring them into conflict with the people's governments in Europe and with the liberation movements in the colonies. At the moment, under conditions of inflation, the economic factors appear less urgent than questions of international policy, and it is in this second field that the National Front is being subjected to its severest tests. How has it stood up to the strain?

In the Eastern European countries, as we have already pointed out, National Front governments are following a firm policy of uprooting Fascism and strengthening the safeguards of peace. In Western Europe, however, developments are less satisfactory. Here, where the possessors of colonies are concentrated, and where Anglo-American imperialism exercises its greatest influence, Social Democratic parties generally continue to show the subservience to the imperialistic outlook that characterised them before the war. They have failed to take steps to free their colonies, and they have followed the lead of the Imperialists in their attack upon the Soviet Union.

A renewal of capitalist aggression must be expected. The working class, to-day in the ascendancy, can face and overcome this challenge, but only by making further and greater advances towards socialism and peace. This is the task facing the National Front governments; their ability to survive will depend upon their determination to find a working class solution for their problems. If Social Democracy continues its historic role of providing a bulwark for capitalism, it will be swept aside in the people's offensive against imperialism and capitalist exploitation.

In conclusion we can say that world events have confirmed our perspective of twelve months ago, a perspective of increasing class struggle and of the end of the United Front phase of defensive action. The Browder theory of continued class collaboration has been proved to be unreal.[25] We here in South Africa will draw aid and strength from the working class movement abroad. It is for us to strengthen our contacts with them and to build up units for the World Federation of Trade Unions, the World Youth Organisation and the World Federation of Women.[26] We must learn to expose South African imperialism through them, and to obtain their support. On our part, we must expose the policies of the imperialists and their threats of war, and continue to build up goodwill for the Soviet Union and the popular governments of Europe. Above all, it is our duty to join hands with the colonial peoples in their struggle for liberation, and do all we can to assist them, in Africa and elsewhere.

Document 136
"Report on the Relationship of the Party to other Workers' Organisations in South Africa", *Freedom*, 5, 4, August-September 1946

IN his opening address at the Annual Conference of the Party in December last the Acting-Chairman, Comrade H. Snitcher, said

> The working class movement is at the cross roads. Either we follow the old paths which in the past have led to division and dissention ... or we follow the only course which has proved successful throughout the world – that is, of destroying this system of capitalism and imperialism.

There can be but one answer from Communists to the question implicit in this statement. The only justification for the continued existence of the Party, here as elsewhere, is that it is implacably hostile to the capitalist system in all it manifestations and ramifications, and is pledged to do everything possible to encompass its destruction. But, having said this, the question still remains: What shall be our immediate objectives on the road to that final goal? In the period of history and in the country in which we find ourselves what tactics will most rapidly and certainly lead us towards our main objective?

In order to answer that question we must get a clear perspective of the present alignment of opposing social forces in the world in general and in South Africa in particular.

In its report to the National Conference the Central Committee very carefully analysed the situation in South Africa, and, although considerable debate took place, the report was adopted substantially as it was drafted. The problems which then presented themselves are still with us, some of them, e.g. continued repressive legislation against non-Europeans and the food scarcity, in an even more acute form.

A PEOPLE'S FRONT

But the particular aspect of our policy which you are now invited to consider is the relationship of our party to other expressions and sections of the labour movement in South Africa. Because of its claim to be a socialist party and to represent the interests of the workers of South Africa, the South African Labour Party must be considered as an important section of the South African working class movement.

The Central Committee report to the last Annual Conference touched on this question in paragraph 33, in which it stated, "Our National Conference last year" (decided) "to organise a people's front." The Central Committee was therefore instructed to "work for the calling at the earliest possible opportunity of a People's Convention of the Communist Party, Labour Party, Trade Unions, non-European liberatory organisations, and all progressive bodies and groups, with a view to securing a united political action".

As you will remember, the Labour Party Conference passed a resolution shortly after this decision was taken by the Communist Party to call for a working class united front **"without the Communist Party"**. Nevertheless the Central Committee at its July, 1945, meeting agreed to proceed with the calling of a convention. A preliminary meeting was held in Johannesburg in September but, as you know, no progress was made.

THE S.A. LABOUR PARTY AND THE COMMUNIST PARTY

In paragraph 35 the report points out that in addition to the differences between the

Communist Parties and the Socialist Parties on the class struggle and their attitude to capitalist institutions in other countries, the South African Communist Party has to face the difference between its policy and attitude to the non-Europeans and that of the South African Labour Party. The paragraph concludes, "In the past we have tried hard to achieve unity, but the prospect of this being accomplished seems very remote".

In paragraph 36 the conclusion is drawn that

> because of this major issue dividing us, unity, or even formal collaboration with the Labour Party is outside the realm of practical politics. If what we have said ... is correct, then our line towards it" (the South African Labour Party) "should be one of exposure and attack where its policy is detrimental to the interests of the working class.

The National Conference in December, 1945, under the heading "Our Tasks in South Africa" passed a resolution stating that "The Labour Party, in violation of its socialist principles, has chosen to adhere to the colour bar policy of the capitalists. In doing this the Labour Party has failed the working people of South Africa. It has preferred to unite with capitalist parties than seek unity between all workers".

It will be noticed that the resolution does not give a directive as to the attitude of the Communist Party to the South African Labour Party, and it may possibly be assumed that conference did not fully approve of the line of criticism and attack suggested in the Central Committee's report quoted above.

Arising from the serious differences of opinion revealed by the voting of the Labour Party parliamentary representatives on the question of the Asiatic Land Tenure and Indian Representation Bill, which has now been passed by Parliament, the Central Executive Committee caused to be circulated in the press and to our members a strongly worded statement criticising Mr. Madeley, M.P., the leader of the party, and others who voted with him, and in fact attacked the general line of the Labour Party on the question of equal rights for all citizens of the Union regardless of colour, race, etc.

Whether this has gone further than was contemplated by the conference is perhaps a question which the Central Committee will wish to discuss, and on which, if thought necessary, to make a pronouncement for the guidance of the Party.

It is perhaps not without significance that in an "Appeal by the South African Labour Party to the South African Trade Union Movement", which has been reproduced in the A.E. Union Journal for May, any reference to the Socialist objective of the Labour Party has been carefully omitted. "The people throughout the world, realising the bankruptcy of the capitalist system, are moving towards Labour", is a meaningless phrase. "The spirit of racial hatred which imbues tens of thousands of workers" is referred to with disapproval. But clearly this refers to the division between English- and Afrikaans-speaking Europeans. No mention is make of the anti-colour prejudice of the Europeans. Towards the end of the "appeal" appears the following – "The only possible political home for the enfranchised workers of South Africa is the South African Labour Party."

The insertion of the word "enfranchised" is significant and can have but one meaning, nor does a later phrase about "the elimination of racial division in the ranks of workers" weaken the conclusion that the South African Labour Party is still a political party devoted to maintaining the privileged position of Europeans in South Africa and which can in no sense justify its claim to be a socialist party.

THE PARTY AND PROGRESSIVE NATIONAL ORGANISATIONS

The resolution of conference on the attitude of the Party to the national liberatory movements is clear and needs no restatement.

Considerable criticism was made by some delegates to conference of the inadequacy of the efforts made by the Party to carry out its policy. How far these criticisms were justified and to what extent these shortcomings have been overcome will be considered by the Central Committee to-day. It may be said, however, that on the whole the mandate of conference has been acted upon by our party members in a number of the most important districts, e.g. Johannesburg, Cape Town, Durban, Pretoria. Notably on the question of the Indian (Ghetto) Bill[27] and perhaps, even more dramatically, on the questions of food shortage and non-European transport. These activities have revealed our Party as the champion of the poorest paid workers to thousands of non-European working men and more particularly women and have also done much to lift a section of our membership out of the somewhat passive and even pessimistic attitude which became obvious towards the end of hostilities and continued for some months afterwards.

THE PARTY AND THE NON-EUROPEAN TRADE UNIONS

The importance of assisting in the organisation of non-European workers in trade unions is recognised by conference in three resolutions.

No. 18 deals generally with discrimination against African workers in all industries.

No. 19 stresses the paramount importance of effective organisation of **African mineworkers**.

And 20 calls upon all districts to organise a campaign to bring **farm workers** into trade unions, and to organise evening schools for them and their families.

TRADE UNION UNITY

In resolution 26 Conference stated its adherence to the policy of "building a single trade union movement with one national centre" that "recognises that for unity to be effective it must be based on equality of status and rights for all trade unionists".

And resolution 27 reaffirms the principle that opportunity to engage in any trade or profession should not be restricted on the ground of race or colour.

It would appear from the above excerpt from the decisions of conference that if the line laid down in respect to our work in the national liberatory and trade union movements continues to be carried out with intelligence, vigour and determination, the value of the Party to the workers' movements will be increasingly appreciated. This will in turn draw the best workers into our ranks and so equip the Party for even greater tasks that lie ahead.

The degree of success in these two spheres of activity have been sufficiently fruitful to justify the decision already taken, and to encourage us to continue on the lines laid down by conference and the Central Committee.

On the question of election contests, which probably were very much in the minds of comrades when seeking co-operation with the Labour Party, we have to recognise that for a considerable time this field of activity will be limited to those people who have votes. This in actual practice means (excepting in the Cape) European men and women only. Excepting an enlightened minority (a growing minority, we hope), these privileged persons are so hopelessly divided by national prejudices and so saturated with capitalist ideology and the doctrine of the Herrenvolk that only in exceptional circumstances will much headway be made in asking for their votes. This does not, of course, mean that we should abandon our policy of contesting elections for Parliament and other governing bodies. These contests can have considerable propaganda and organisational value. But it is doubtful whether the considerable sums which have been sent on some election contests have been justified by the results.

It would appear therefore that our real strength, actual and potential, is likely to remain in extra-parliamentary action. We have to face up to the fact that until the ruling caste has been compelled to abandon its present policy of racial discrimination, and to recognise the right of millions of non-Europeans to full citizen rights, there can be no important part for the Party to play in parliamentary elections.

Our work must be for a considerable time education, organisation and leadership of the dispossessed and unfranchised masses. A long, thankless and gruelling, not to say dangerous, path to tread. Only when some appreciable breach is made in the walls of the political compound which confines and imprisons nearly all non-Europeans will the Party begin to come into its own. It can only hope to do so by leading the attack on the reactionary system of indentured servile and semi-slave labour and all forms of racial and class discrimination.

As the liberatory and industrial movements become stronger, new allies will appear. But we must not wait for them. We have to pioneer the way, at whatever cost, to the complete economic, political and social equality of all inhabitants of the Union, for only thus can a truly prosperous and happy South Africa be achieved.

Document 137
Letter from the Fourth International Organisation of South Africa to (*Revolutionary Communist Party?*)[28], 6 March 1947

FOURTH INTERNATIONAL ORGANISATION OF SOUTH AFRICA.

18, Roeland Street,
CAPE TOWN.
6th March, 1947.

Dear Comrade,

You are not doubt aware of the differences existing between the Workers' Party and FIOSA, of the attempts made by FIOSA to initiate unity discussions between the two organisations, and of the correspondence with the I.S. on the question. We believe also that you have recently had talks with a prominent member of the W.P. now studying in London, on FIOSA's relations with the W.P. In order to facilitate these talks, and in order to have you the better informed of our views on the W.P., the following matters are brought to your notice which, we hope, will assist you in arriving at a correct assessment of the differences.

There is in existence in the Western Cape Province a National Liberatory organisation, the Anti-CAD Committee, now almost defunct, which is under the full control of the W.P. This body publishes a fortnightly roneoed bulletin, "Anti-CAD Bulletin", which, since its inception 4 years ago up to August of last year, was edited by the W.P. member previously mentioned. Since then it has been edited by another WPer.

In May of last year "Anti-CAD Bulletin" No. ? referred to the great strikes in America and characterised the U.S. workers' struggle as a quarrel with the Wall Street plutocrats for a bigger share of the spoil sweated out colonial slaves. This bulletin, as well as No. 108 of 26/2/47, is enclosed herewith, and your attention is particularly drawn to the one paragraph of the latter bracketed off. This, we are sure, will enable you to appreciate FIOSA's characterisation of the W.P. as a petty-bourgeois tendency which has forfeited all claim to being called socialist internationalists by treacherously identifying the interests of the workers in the metropolitan countries with those of the imperialist robbers. To further assist you, the following organs of Fiosa are forwarded under separate cover with the articles dealing with the W.P. marked:- "W.V." T.O. vol. 1 No. i; "W.V" T.O. vol. 1 No. iii; "W.V." Sept., 1946; Fiosa Internal Bulletin vol. 1 No. i.

Comradely greetings,
P. R. Meissenheimer
SECRETARY.

P.S. The P.C. of FIOSA feels that in any discussions which may take place, Cde. C. van Gelderen will most nearly represent the views of FIOSA, and should, wherever possible, be consulted.

P.R.M.

P.P.S. The firstmentioned Bulletin is now unobtainable.

P.R.M.

Document 138
Letter from the Fourth International Organisation of South Africa to the Revolutionary Communist Party, 29 August 1947

18 Roeland Street,
CAPE TOWN
August 29th 1947.

The Secretary,
R.C.P.
LONDON.

Dear Comrade,

The Fourth International Organisation of South Africa requests you to acquaint the British working class with some of the terms and the meaning of the Industril Conciliation (Natives) Bill which is due to be discussed at the next session of the Union Parliament in January, 1948, and to publicise our campaign against it as much as you can. The following are some of the clauses of the Bill.

1. No European, Coloured person, Indian or anyone who is not an African may join or organise an African Union.

2. No one may organise an African trade union unless he is specially authorised by the state.
3. No one may hold office in any African union unless he is approved and appointed by the state. The African Mineworkers Union is banned.
5. No African union may go on strike.
6. A Central Mediation Board will decide all issues regarding wage levels and wage demands.
7. This board will be appointed by the state and will consist of State Officials and representatives of the employers only. (Of course the board will be all white).
8. All African unions which are not registered in terms of the Act and continue to function are illegal and liable to prosecution.

It will be clear that far from "recognising" African Unions under a form of Industrial Conciliation machinery, the South African ruling class is out to crush the african trade union movement, handicapped as it is by being semi-illegal by not being recognised under the Industrial Conciliation Act (like European, Coloured and Indian workers). Africans are therefore not able to negotiate with the employers and resort to strike action failing settlement of disputes by arbitration, which procedure is allowed to other unions under the Industrial Conciliation Act.

It is clear that if the Bill is passed, African unions will become mere State agencies like the Nazi Labour Front and similar fascist bodies for enslaving the workers.

Although the Bill applies only to African workers it is a grave threat to the entire non European people as it is a viciously anti-colour as well as anti working class measure. Its danger to the labour movement in South Africa as a whole cannot be overestimated.

For African workers the maintenance of the status quo would be far preferable and not even the white unions will be safe if the Industrial Conciliation (Natives) Bill becomes law.

Yours fraternally,
NANNET
(Sec).

Document 139
"The coming Anti-African Bill", *Workers' Voice*, 6, 2, December 1947

The Industrial Conciliation (Natives) Bill which is to be discussed at the next session of Parliament must surely rank as the most viciously anti-Non-European piece of legislation ever to come before any Union Parliament. All other statutory acts pale into insignificance before the sweeping reaction of this Bill. Its character is oppressive and fascistic to the core. The Act of Union in 1910 wrote the colour bar into the statute books of South Africa and took away the political rights of the Non-Europeans except for restricted voting rights allowed for Non-Europeans in the Cape Province. The Native Land and Trust Act of 1913 and the anti-African Acts on 1936 deprived the Africans of their land and property rights as well as the political rights still allowed in the Cape, for which they were "compensated" by the right to elect three European Representatives to the House of Assembly and four to the Senate. The Industrial Conciliation (Natives) Act is in reality designed to suppress and destroy the rising movement of African workers to trade unionism as a means of struggle for their demands as workers. Reactionary as they were, none of these previous Acts is such a deathblow as this proposed new Bill.

Although the Bill is aimed primarily at the African people it is of vital importance to all the non-Europeans and heavily affects the white workers as well. While it is not the place in this editorial to go into detail regarding the terms of the Bill, let it be sufficient to say that if it becomes law then it will mean the end in South Africa of trade unionism for the Africans, or what little of it exists; and for the Coloured and White workers it will be a short step to total regimentation of their unions in the interests of the bosses and the State.

Far from granting recognition under a form of Industrial Conciliation Machinery, this Act seeks to deprive the African workers of the rights of free trade unions, as is traditionally understood by the working class.

For a union which must have its officials approved by the State, which is forbidden by law to strike, but must, irrespective of the demands and desires of its members, abide by the decisions of a "conciliation" board which comprises only representatives of the State and the employers, which may not be organised by Socialists and which must be constituted on racially exclusive lines, is really not a trade union at all but merely the instrument and tool of the power which deprives it of these fundamental union rights, in this case, the Union Government.

For, in effect, this is what the new Bill means for the African worker: to place him into organisations which are merely State agencies, part of the apparatus of the State of the white ruling class. State company unions are what the African unions must become, or be declared illegal and thus liable for prosecution. For unions which are not "registered" in terms of the Bill will be guilty of a criminal offence if they continue to function and exist.

It must be clear to every trade unionist that this Bill is intended to destroy completely what little power African unions enjoy, for at present, while unrecognised by the Government, they are still able to organise and co-operate and record gains for their members and indulge in strike action. Handicapped as they are by non-recognition, the Africans were nevertheless able to organise an African Mineworkers' Union which waged the biggest and most heroic strike in the history of this country. If this Act becomes law, the Smuts Government, in order to maintain "industrial peace" in the foundation of the South African economy, will prohibit the African Mineworkers' Union from existing even under the reactionary Industrial Conciliation (Natives) Bill. It is far better for the African worker to fight to retain the status quo than be "recognised" by Smuts in this form.

Let not the Coloured and White workers imagine that this is a matter which does not affect their unions. Already Smuts has indicated that he intends introducing legislation for separate unions for Coloured workers only. We know the Governments of White South Africa too well to imagine that when the time is ripe they will not apply the same drastic restrictions to Coloured workers, too.

As for the White workers, although till the last they will be bribed by higher wages and better jobs through the notorious white labour policy, and in general receive preferential treatment in order to induce them to ally themselves with the white ruling class against the non-white workers – the time will surely come when, in a period of economic crisis, the South African ruling class will not be able to afford any longer the luxury of inflated wages for the white labour aristocracy, and when this time DOES come, it will suddenly be discovered how well the new Bill will have worked for African and Coloured workers, and white workers, too, will be compelled to "enjoy" the "superior working" and "administrative efficiency" conferred by it.

We repeat: this Bill cannot be dismissed as something which affects only the African workers and which does not concern other workers – it is of vital importance to the trade unions as a whole and indeed carries serious political implications for the whole working class. When non-European trade unions are gagged and bound, non-European political organisations are in real danger of being similarly outlawed and suppressed.

The time to awake is now, before it is too late. The main burden of opposition to the Bill must come from the African trade union movement itself, the leadership of which has been too complacent thus far about the whole matter. The Non-European trade unions must take instant and united action. A national conference similar to the one held in Bloemfontein in August, 1945, should be called immediately and the best methods of struggle hammered out by the workers' and trade union representatives. The South African Trades and Labour Council should be compelled to throw in its weight and work with the African unions in this struggle, but the main force behind the struggle of the African workers should be the whole non-European people themselves.

It is quite clear that existing political bodies of the non-Europeans cannot or refuse to see the grave implications of the Bill. The African working class cannot be destroyed while these organisations slumber.

There is a real and vital need for a unified national liberatory organisation to lead the oppressed peoples in South Africa. For while it is necessary to combat the new Industrial Conciliation (Natives) Bill in the industrial and trade union field, non-European bodies must wage a determined POLITICAL struggle against it as well, for the Bill has a dual anti-working class and anti-colour nature, and is therefore of the greatest importance to the non-European national movement as a whole.

The industrial development of South Africa which draws ever-increasing numbers of African workers into industry makes it necessary for the ruling class to possess the powers contained in this Bill in order to curb and control the African workers. This self-same industrial development should forge a militant and class-conscious African leadership to lead the African people in the gigantic struggles that lie ahead. If this is not done and the Bill becomes law then the African workers and ultimately the whole working class in this country will go under.

Not only the African workers but all the workers in South Africa must be made to realise and understand the real content and meaning of the Bill, the passing of which constitutes the gravest and most sinister threat to working class liberties in this country. It inevitably brings to mind events in other countries which were preceded by Bills of just such a kind.

Document 140
"Terrorism on the Mines: Union organisers allege assaults",
The Guardian, 4 December 1947

JOHANNESBURG. – Terrorism of union organisers on the mines has reached a new peak, coinciding with the preparations by the African Mineworkers' Union for its general meeting, to acquaint workers with the terms of the proposed bill to "recognise" African Trade Unions.

A union organiser who went to the Mines to distribute leaflets alleges he was assaulted by compound police disguised in blankets.

When he ran to the office of the compound manager he was badly assaulted, for the second time, in full view of the compound manager who said: "It serves your right. They should have killed you. You b.... Communists."

When the organiser was taken to the mine hospital for treatment, he says he received an almost identical reception by the doctor who attended him.

The organiser was then escorted to the police charge office by two constables, when the compound manager denied all knowledge of the assault. The man had been badly hit on the head, arms and body.

Union organisers who go to the mines on the West Rand are manhandled and have their leaflets confiscated.

Leaflets handed out at West Springs Mine have been torn up by compound police. Leaflets have been confiscated at Brakpan. At Simmer and Jack, union organisers were recently taken to the charge office to be interrogated after the police had intervened during the leaflet distribution.

AT MARSHALL SQUARE
When representatives of the Union went to Marshall Square to protest against this interference by the police they state they were told: "The police still remember the happenings of last August."

Assaults, interception by the police and mine spies are becoming part of the daily routine of the organisers and officials of the African Mineworkers' Union.

Document 141
"Apartheid Spells Disaster", Report of the Central Committee of the Communist Party to the Party's National Conference, Johannesburg, 6 to 8 January 1950,[29]
Freedom, New Series 15 December, 1949

[....] **Disillusionment**
63. Discriminating policies, exploitation, as well as prevailing bad conditions have caused resentment and unrest among the Non-Europeans and already a process of disillusionment is beginning to set in among the Europeans. Naturally, the Europeans cannot be expected to be agitated and roused by discriminatory measures against the Non-Europeans. But they will be irritated and incensed by the rising cost of living, the acute

housing shortage, unemployment and the general mismanagement by the Nationalist Party Government. Judging by the results of a number of elections held in recent months, we can safely say that the anti-Government forces are growing.

64. As far as the Non-Europeans are concerned, protests against discriminatory policies have been ma[--]continuous. There is not a Non-European organisation [--] not protested against apartheid and other forms of discriminat[ion]. [-] churches have also protested against it and even the so-called institutions of collaboration have voiced their protest. The Natives Representative Council has been on strike ever since August, 1946.[30]

65. Incidents resulting from discriminatory conditions have in several instances led to direct action by the people affected and in some the actions took the form of pitched battles between them and the police – at Sophiatown, Newclare, Krugersdorp, Nelspruit, etc. But the fighting took place in all instances because of the provocative actions and behavior of the police.

The Boycott Weapon

66. The most significant phenomenon has been the militancy of the masses and the timidity and "hamba kahle" attitude of the leaders. Indeed, the contrast has been very glaring. Leaders have talked loudly and generally but took care not to commit or compromise themselves. Others have become quite cynical about everything. The latest refuge for the doctrinaire and drawing-room strategists is the boycott. The boycott weapon is now put forward as the only effective form of struggle against discrimination and injustices. It is not difficult to find out the real reason for this strange attitude of wanting to get away from realities.

67. We are against differential and inferior institutions and systems of representation, and we believe in the boycott as a form of struggle. But we believe that the boycott is only good if it conducted in such a way that the masses participate in it in great numbers and when it leads to mass action for positive demands. The boycott is certainly useless if it leads to disengagement and withdrawal from the struggle, if it leads to the laying down of arms by the soldiers or warriors. That the boycott campaign has been given this defeatist character is shown by the boycotters' continual, scathing, pointless and utterly destructive criticism against those who refuse to sulk and withdraw form the struggle. No, we cannot withdraw from the struggle or be a party to any propaganda or deeds the effects of which will be to sabotage and subvert the people's morale and will to fight.

68. The Nationalist Government is not as strong as it pretends. Its war record and its rabid racialism – anti-English, anti-Jewish and anti-foreigner and strongly pro-Afrikaner attitude – have made it unpopular overseas and cast suspicion on South Africa. And what is more, Dr. Malan's Government is utterly incapable of solving the problems of this country. It is doing a great harm by poisoning the relations between different sections of the population.

The Big Question

69. The big question confronting the whole labour-progressive movement in this country, particularly our Party, is how to get rid of this government. We can get rid of it if we organise the people and co-ordinate their activities against rising prices of foodstuffs, food shortages, unemployment and housing shortage; for increase in wages, pensions, more hospitals and schools, greater democracy, etc.

70. Strenuous efforts must be made to get all workers and all democrats – European and Non-European – to stand together in the fight against the fascistic policies of the Government and for its overthrow. If the leaders of the trade union movement and the leaders of the various Non-European National liberatory organisations are not prepared for any positive action against oppression, exploitation, discrimination or misconduct by the Nationalists, it will then be for our Party to face the situation squarely and once and for all decide what to do in the circumstances. The most important question today is leadership. Leadership is needed, and leadership must be given.

ORGANISATIONAL TASK

[....]

74. In order to take advantage of the present favourable conditions for the growth of the Party, we shall first have to overcome our present shortcomings. Four things are necessary if we are to do this: an all-out recruiting campaign, particularly in the larger urban centres; a careful selection and intense training of cadres; ideological education for the general membership; and the building up of factory groups.

75. Recruiting must not be left to chance, but must be organised in the same way as other Party activity is organised. It can, of course, take place only within the framework of increased public activity and propaganda amongst all sections, and no medium should be neglected in this regard. Particular attention must be paid to the recruitment and organisation of industrial workers. Our propaganda work amongst them must be intensified. Regular factory meetings must be organised on a large [-] by all districts, and a direct appeal for recruits made at all such meetings. The work must be tackled in a vigorous and imaginative fashion, with the planned co-operation of Party members already working in the different industries. Lists of names and addresses of workers of all nationalities should be compiled. Copies of "Freedom", important statements and notices of meetings should be sent to them regularly.

76. Recruiting amongst other sections of the people must be conducted, with the necessary modifications in a similar carefully planned and organised fashion with public meetings, house meetings or public lectures taking the place of the factory meeting. Care should always be taken to see that our meetings deal with those subjects which are likely to prove of greatest interest to whichever section we are making our appeal to.

77. Our recruiting should be both general and selective, i.e. we must also aim at recruiting the rank and file leaders of the people, those who have established themselves as such in the ordinary course of life. Such people are to be found in all walks of life, in every locality, in every factory and compound. We must seek to win them over to our policy and to our Party. Thousands of such rank and file leaders have been produced by the people. Their proper place is inside the ranks of the Communist Party.

African Membership

78. In order to draw maximum advantage from our recruiting we shall, however, have to solve our present organisational problems. In some districts our Party has succeeded in gaining a big influence amongst the African workers with the result

that the African membership is increasing by leaps and bounds far outstripping the rate of recruitment amongst other sections. The majority of these members are organised into groups which are exclusively African. All business is conducted in their own language, the majority of members either not understanding English at all, or only imperfectly. The same position arises in regard to Coloured and Indian members in different districts. For instance, only five out of twenty groups in the Cape District have a mixed membership, all the others being composed exclusively of one nationality. There is a definite tendency for the Party organisation to separate into groups of different nationalities, particularly outside the main urban areas.

79. What is to be done? Must we try to reserve this tendency? Or must we accept it as inevitable and adapt our organisational methods accordingly? This tendency to separate into groups of different nationalities flows from the pattern enforced upon us by segregation (separate residential areas) and, equally important, from different languages used by our members. This tendency could, therefore, theoretically be reversed by:-
a) establishing groups without regard to specific residential areas;
b) the use of interpreters.

Neither of these solutions is satisfactory. The first would destroy much of the effectiveness of the groups, take the punch out of them as it were. The second, even when practicable, would be extremely clumsy and lead to a loss of efficiency.

80. It appears inevitable then, that the Party, as it expands, will more and more take on the pattern already revealed in such striking fashion by developments in the Cape District. This development carries with it certain obvious dangers. Groups composed exclusively of one nationality will tend to devote their attention only to those matters which affect their own nationality. (In another sphere, the Durban District has revealed this tendency time and time again.) The international, class character of the Party has always been under pressure from nationalist deviations and this pressure was increased by the existence of separate groups. The problem is not insurmountable. It is time, however, that we were conscious of the problem and took steps to ensure that our members fully realise that the Party is a class organisation, embracing all races.

Ideological Work

81. The different groups should be brought together regularly at general members' meetings. Joint functions, socials and party activity should be organised for the specific purpose of bringing our members of different nationalities together. More intensive ideological propaganda must be conducted amongst the general membership, propaganda designed to spread knowledge of the basic principles of Communism and the class character of the struggle we are waging. Such propaganda must be conducted both verbally and by means of material printed in the different languages, particularly the African languages. In addition, we must place much more emphasis than hitherto on making our members understand, and conscious of, the importance of the revolutionary struggle in other lands, and of [-] achievements of the workers in the Soviet Union and the People's Democracies.

82. The racial isolation existing in the area group must not be tolerated in the factory groups, in particular, where the identity of interests and the class character of the Party must be stressed, and where the best opportunities for doing so exist.

83. The establishment of factory groups therefore becomes of prime importance as a means of strengthening the working-class character of the Party. We are weak in the sphere of factory groups, the overwhelming majority of Party organisations being area groups. Factory groups which have been established have not proved stable organisations and have soon collapsed. New methods must be found and a new approach tried. We must realise, first of all, the limitations of such groups and the often difficult objective difficulties under which they must work. We must be clear, therefore, on the nature of the tasks which we set them, and must not expect them to function in the same fashion as an area group.

84. We must guard against the danger of our members in such groups confusing the role of Party with that of a trade union. If we do not do so our factory groups will continually fall into the errors of economism (i.e. neglect their political task) and will not function as political organisations of the workers. Our factory groups must function primarily, though not entirely, as political units of the Party. One way to guard against the danger of economism would be to make members of factory groups members of area groups as well. This would enable them to appreciate more easily the political role of the Party. It would enable them to make contact with more advanced members, give them facilities for political education and bring them into contact with workers of other trades and occupations, and thereby help them to overcome the sectarian tendencies of the factory group. [....]

86. But whether we are discussing area or factory groups, the training of cadres is perhaps the most urgent organisational task facing the Party at the present time. We need hundreds more rank and file Party leaders than we have at our disposal now. We need rank and file leaders who will have a sound grasp of fundamental Communist principles and be able, in turn, to impart this knowledge to others in their own language. We need rank and file leaders who are convinced of the necessity for stable, regularly functioning basic organisations and who will know how to run these organisations properly.

87. We must give our cadres adequate Marxist education which is related to our own problems and which will enable them to dispel the misconceptions which we know exist in the minds of those amongst whom they shall have to work. We must train them to be self-reliant so that they will know what to do and where to turn when any problem, political or otherwise, arises in the areas or in the factories where they work. This education should, wherever possible, be given in the home language of the pupils concerned. We must aim at giving the member a thorough grounding so that, on his own initiative, he will be able to improve his knowledge by individual study and observation.

88. We must teach them the value and necessity of paying meticulous attention to elementary organisational functions, such as regular meetings, keeping of minutes, collection of subs., check-up on membership, regular correspondence with higher Party organs, etc. This must be done in relation to practical work. Regular meetings of group officials should be convened for the specific purpose of discussing weakness revealed in the routine organisational work of the District concerned.

89. Pupils for cadre schools or classes must not be chosen haphazardly, but only after careful study of the membership by the higher Party organisation. And once pupils have been chosen, every effort must be made to assist them to attend the class [-] school. [....]

NOTES

1 Although the WPSA went underground in June 1939, those Cape Town and Johannesburg Trotskyists who still believed in the possibility of legal activity briefly united in the joint publication of *Socialist Action*.
2 Neville Chamberlain was British Prime Minister from mid-1937 until May 1940. He was particularly associated with the policy of appeasement towards Nazi Germany. Edouard Daladier was French Prime Minister at the same period. Both were involved in the negotiation of the Munich Agreement in September/October 1938 which resulted in the dismemberment of Czechoslovakia.
3 Clement Attlee (1883-1967), a middle-class socialist educated at public school and Oxford, was leader of the British Labour Party from November 1935 to December 1955. He had fought in World War One and had been a Labour M.P. since 1922. He was Deputy Prime Minister in the wartime Churchill Coalition and Prime Minister of the Labour Government 1945 to 1951. Arthur Greenwood was Deputy Leader of the Labour Party in the late 1930s and spoke for the Party in the Parliamentary debate that preceded Britain's entry into war in September 1939. Sir Stafford Cripps was a highly successful lawyer who became a Labour M.P. in 1931. He became heavily involved in the campaigns for a Popular Front and was expelled from the Party in 1939. He served in the Churchill Coalition and, after readmission to the Party, in the post-war Labour Government. Harry Pollitt was the leading advocate of the Popular Front policy within the British Communist Party. Maurice Thorez was leader of the French Communist Party in the late 1930s. Earl Browder was an equivalent figure in the United States.
4 This statement reflects the NEUF's attitude towards World War Two before the German invasion of the Soviet Union in June 1941. Reflecting the strong Communist presence within the NEUF leadership, the NEUF changed its stance after that invasion. For documents reflecting the NEUF's revised position in 1942 see Karis and Carter (1973:389-90).
5 Dr Yusuf Mohammed Dadoo (1909-83) trained as a medical doctor in Britain, where he joined the ILP in Edinburgh and became involved in Indian anti-colonial agitation. On his return to South Africa, he became an activist in the TIC. His politics were influenced by Gandhi's notion of *satyagraha* and by an advocacy of non-European unity, and he was a founder of the NEUF in 1938. The next year he joined the CPSA and reversed his position on the war once Germany invaded the Soviet Union. He became President of the TIC in 1945, moving it away from the politics of the Indian merchant class and promoting a more confrontationist style. He and other Communists were tried for allegedly organising the 1946 African mineworkers' strike. In 1947 Dadoo, Dr A. B. Xuma and Dr G. M. Naicker signed the "Doctor's Pact" with the aim of promoting joint African-Indian action. This paved the way for the Defiance Campaign; Dadoo and Yusuf Cachalia represented the SAIC on the Campaign's Joint Planning Council. Dadoo was President of the SAIC in the early 1950s, and when the SACP was reconstituted as an underground organisation in 1953, he was on the Party's Central Committee. He was banned during the Defiance Campaign and left South Africa in 1960. In 1972 he became Chair of the SACP.
6 Max Gordon, briefly a member of the WPSA, was the leading trade unionist on the Witwatersrand in the 1935 to 1940 period. He organised mine clerks into a General Workers' Union in order to relaunch the AMWU established by Thibedi and Bunting in 1931. Over several years he established about six unions and formed a trade union federation called the JCATU. By 1940 Gordon's JCATU was the leading trade union group on the Rand, due to his careful shop-floor organisation and concern with using every legal means to secure wage increases for the workers. The other main federation was the CCATU led by former-Communist Gana Makabeni. In Gordon's representations to the Wage Board he worked closely with Lynn Saffery of the SAIRR. Gordon was one of a very small number of leftists interned during the war. He was interned in 1940 and released in 1941. After his release he went to Port Elizabeth and set up a number of trade unions but was subjected to continued police harassment and retired to Cape Town.
7 In the 1920s Fanny Klenerman worked in the Clothing Workers' Union and organised the first union of women workers in South Africa. She ran classes for workers in the ICU and members of the Jewish Workers Club. She was expelled from the CPSA in September 1931 along with other prominent trade unionists and later joined the WPSA in Johannesburg. From 1931 she owned and managed Vanguard Booksellers in Johannesburg, a radical bookshop and cultural centre. During the war she helped organise and was Honourable Secretary of the Committee for the Relief of Anti-Nazi Internees. She is referred to in paragraph e as the "welknown communist woman".
8 On 3 April 1940 Northern Rhodesian troops shot workers at Nkana mines, killing 17 and wounding 65. Dan Koza drafted a leaflet about the incident which was issued in the names of Gana Makabeni of the CCATU and A. Thipe of the JCATU. See Document 125, paragraphs 4a to 4c.
9 A. Lynn Saffery was Secretary of the SAIRR and largely responsible for its interest in the black trade union movement during World War Two. After Gordon's internment, Saffery was proposed as Secretary of the JCATU but the appointment of another white to replace Gordon was opposed by most of the other members, who chose D. Gosani.

10 Self Mampuru (1908-64) from Sekhukhuneland was an associate of William Ballinger. From 1937 to 1939 he studied co-operatives in Britain but was not successful in organising them in South Africa. Dissatisfied with the ANC's inactive leadership, in September 1943 he helped found the ADP, which lasted for about five years.
11 Ballinger is probably referring to D. B. Molteno, J. D. Rheinallt Jones and Mrs Ballinger.
12 This document represents the position of the CPSA following Germany's invasion of the Soviet Union in June 1941.
13 A. P. Mda (1916-93) was educated and began his teaching career in Catholic schools. His political career began in the late 1930s as an ANC organiser in Orlando. He was a member of the ANC national executive, one of the founders of the ANC Youth League in 1944, and in 1947 became head of the Youth League. From 1949 he never held political office but he continued to be extremely influential in Africanist circles although he did not support the PAC's break with the ANC. Although socialist in outlook, he believed that Communists in the ANC were weakening African nationalism. In 1963 he went to Basutoland.
14 Michael Harmel was Secretary of the Party's Johannesburg District Committee from 1940 to 1946.
15 Mda's exhortation about the C.A.U. is reminiscent of a passage in Van der Post's (1934:151, 156) novel, in which an African agitator tries to mobilise his listeners on a platform of "Christ, Combination and Co-operation", to join the African Workers' Union.
16 This is a reference to a remark allegedly made by Franco, the leader of the Nationalist forces in the Spanish Civil War, during their attack on Madrid. He supposedly claimed that in addition to his four military columns there was a "fifth column" involved in undercover work within the city. Subsequently, the phrase was used by anti-fascists as a general characterisation of undercover fascist sympathisers.
17 The Atlantic Charter was drawn up by British Prime Minister Winston Churchill and United States President F. D. Roosevelt in August 1941. The Charter placed a heavy emphasis on human rights and this was seized upon by black South African activists. They argued that South Africa, as a wartime ally of the anti-fascist Allies, had a moral obligation to apply the Charter to its own affairs. At its annual conference in December 1943, the ANC adopted a charter of rights entitled *Africans' Claims in South Africa* (Karis and Carter 1973:209-22), which was modelled on the Atlantic Charter. The demands included the abolition of racial discrimination, an equal franchise, no restrictions on movement and residence and a range of egalitarian economic and social reforms. The agenda subsequently made an impact at the UN and at congresses of the Pan-Africanist movement.
18 In the 1930s and '40s, the state enacted a series of measures, such as the Natives Land and Trust Act in 1936, the Betterment Act and the Rehabilitation Scheme, aimed at stabilising the economic deterioration of the reserves to ensure their viability as a base for migrant labour which was to be a permanent social class in South Africa. The effect of these measures was to increase economic stratification and rural poverty and they met with popular resistance. In the Northern Transvaal, the implementation of the Betterment Act roused much opposition from the Zoutpansberg *Balemi* Association organised by Alpheus Maliba.
19 Michael Harmel (1915-74) was one of the major CPSA ideologues from the 1940s, a strong proponent of the Party's closer ties with the national struggle and the Congress movement in the post-war period. He joined the CPSA in 1939, was secretary of the Johannesburg District Committee from 1940 to 1946 and a member of the CPSA Central Committee from 1941 to 1950. Out of the seventeen members on the Central Committee, only he and Bill Andrews opposed the Party's decision to dissolve in 1950. In the 1950s he played a leading role in the Congress of Democrats. He was on the editorial board of *Liberation*, the Johannesburg representative of *New Age* and a founder of *African Communist* in 1949. Subjected to repeated state harassment, he left South Africa in 1963. In London he edited *African Communist* and published *Fifty Fighting Years* (1971) under the pseudonym A. Lerumo.
20 *The Militant Worker* was the organ of the ephemeral Committee of Militant Trade Unionists, organised by Hosea Jaffe, then in the FIOSA.
21 The Industrial Conciliation Act was introduced by the Smuts Government in 1924 shortly before its electoral defeat. It introduced a system of collective bargaining between employers and employees which effectively gave trade unions their long-pursued objective of legal protection. The system of industrial relations was criticised by the Left as enshrining a principle of class collaboration but the legislation arguably facilitated the growth of white trade unions. Essentially, the Act was discriminatory on racial grounds. It did not apply to the agricultural, domestic and government sectors. Moreover, it did not incorporate pass-bearing Africans and indentured Indians. This was achieved by a narrow definition of "employee" so that exclusions included anyone whose contract of service came under the Native Labour Regulation Act of 1911, provincial pass laws and the Indian labour statutes of Natal. The agitation in the 1940s focused on this issue with the objective of recognising excluded groups as employees under the Act.

22 Daniel R. Koza (d. 1964) was a leading trade unionist in the 1930s and '40s. He worked with Max Gordon in the ACDWU and became its Secretary after Gordon's internment until his resignation in 1948. He was a member of the PTU in CNETU. He was involved with the AAC and the ADP. At the AAC's conference in December 1943 he represented the ACDWU. At its December 1944 conference he represented the FIOSA and argued for the full recognition of African trade unions, including the right to strike. This became PTU policy.

23 James J. Majoro, organiser and Secretary of the AMWU, was charged with sedition by the state for his role in the 1946 AMWU strike. In the mid-1940s he was Organising Secretary of the ANC in Orlando.

24 The United Nations (UN) was established in June 1945 with the aims of preventing the re-emergence of aggressor states and of preserving international peace. Unlike its precursor, the League of Nations, which the United States never joined, participation of the major powers was seen as essential to the UN's success. Nonetheless, its standards for resolving international disputes and the nature of its sought-after peace are open to controversy.

25 Earl Browder was leader of the Communist Party in the United States. Browderism refers to an interpretation of the Popular Front policy which he put forward in the early 1940s and which seemed to entail a dissolution of the Party.

26 These organisations were forums which typically involved significant participation by affiliates from the Soviet Union and subsequently from other states in Eastern Europe. The World Federation of Trade Unions became a cockpit for battles in the late 1940s between pro- and anti-Communist organisations, and with the deepening of the Cold War, it split.

27 The Indian (Ghetto) Bill was the popular name for the Asiatic Land Tenure and Indian Representation Bill introduced by the Smuts Government in 1946. In the 1930s the government restricted Indian occupancy of land in the Transvaal, and in 1943 the Pegging Act prohibited the transfer of property between whites to Indians in Durban for three years, closing off the main avenue of investment still available to Indians in Natal and the Transvaal. The Ghetto Bill extended the Pegging Act throughout Natal and the Transvaal, prohibiting, with few exceptions, the further sale of property within Natal to Indians, and introducing the notion of Indian communal political rights. It offered Indians limited Parliamentary representation through the election of three European representatives to the Lower House, two European Senators and two Indian members in the Natal Provincial Council. The "ghetto" proposals of the Bill passed through Parliament; the representative proposals met with considerable Parliamentary opposition and were eventually rejected and withdrawn. Within the SALP, the Bill produced a major crisis. Internal divisions in the SALP meant that Labour representatives were allowed a free vote and they split in public. Although aimed at the Indian economic elite, once enacted, the Ghetto Act hit the working class hard. Property prices and rents soared while Indian-owned slums in Durban and Johannesburg became increasingly overcrowded. These stressful conditions lay behind the tension erupting in the 1949 Durban Riots between Africans and Indians.

28 Documents 137 and 138 were typed and included handwritten editorial changes which I have incorporated. The Revolutionary Communist Party was a British Trotskyist organisation associated in particular with Jock Haston. It acquired some public prominence in the later stages of the war when, on flimsy evidence, it was held responsible for strikes, particularly in the coal industry.

29 This document is an extract from a Central Committee report to the CPSA at the last conference before its dissolution. Another extract is reprinted in Bunting (1981: 200-11).

30 By 1946 the NRC's failure to achieve even minor reforms was fuelling popular demands for more militant strategies and tactics of political change. The impetus for NRC representatives to adjourn finally came in August 1946 after the brutal squashing of the African Mineworkers' Strike. Yet this decision was adopted hesitantly and only reaffirmed six months later, in May 1947, after General Smuts had shown himself unwilling to consider or concede any of the NRC's demands. For an overview of the NRC's demise see Karis and Carter (1973:92-8). For two African viewpoints see Z. K. Matthew's pamphlet in Karis and Carter (1973:224-33) and Jordan K. Ngubane (1946) *Should the Natives Representative Council be Abolished?*, Pro and Con Pamphlet-No. 4, Cape Town: African Bookman; available at Southern Regional Library Facility, UCLA.

List of documents

Part One
South African socialists and the racially-divided working class
1 Keir Hardie, "Stoned in South Africa", 1907
2 Letter from the Cape Labour Party to James Ramsay MacDonald, 12 August 1908
3 Letter from F. A. W. Lucas to James Ramsay MacDonald, 15 October 1915
4 "The Great Native Strike", *The International*, 27 February 1920
5 "Trade Union Notes", *The Bolshevik*, March 1920 [Extract]
6 M. Lopes, "Socialism and the Labour Party", *The Bolshevik*, April 1920
7 "'White South Africa' Two Voices", *The International*, 27 January 1922
8 S. P. Bunting, *The "Colonial" Labour Front*, 23 October 1922
9 Letter from W. H. Andrews to Tom Mann, 26 December 1922
10 Industrial and Commercial Workers' Union of Africa Third Annual Conference, 17 January 1923
11 Industrial and Commercial Workers' Union of Africa, *Annual Conference Agenda*, 18 January 1923
12 Letter from T. W. Thibedi to E. R. Roux, 27 January 1927
13 Letter from John Gomas to C. F. Glass, 31 May 1927
14 Letter from C. F. Glass to John Gomas, 7 June 1927
15 E. R. Roux, *Black and White Trade Unionism in South Africa*, 28 July 1928
16 Letter from Clements Kadalie to E. R. Roux, 10 October 1928
17 Letter from E. R. Roux to W. G. Ballinger, 19 March 1929
18 Letter from S. P. Bunting to the South African Federation of Native Trade Unions., 20 September 1930
19 Communist Party of South Africa, Memo on S.A.F.N.T.U.
20 Letter from S. P. Bunting to the Secretary, Communist Party of South Africa, 22 September 1930
21 Letter from S. P. Bunting to E. R. Roux, 27 October 1930

Part Two
Communists and the national struggle: The Native Republic Thesis
22 Letter from Douglas Wolton to E. R. Roux, 8 May 1928
23 S. P. Bunting, Statement presented at the Sixth Comintern Congress, 23 July 1928
24 E. R. Roux, *Thesis on South Africa*, presented at the Sixth Comintern Congress, 28 July 1928
25 E. R. Roux, *The New Slogan and the Revolutionary Movement among White Workers in South Africa*, presented at the Sixth Comintern Congress, 30 July 1928
26 S. P. Bunting, Statement on the Kuusinen Thesis presented at the Sixth Comintern Congress, 20 August 1928
27 Letter from E. R. Roux to Douglas Wolton, 5 September 1928
28 Letter from E. R. Roux to the Central Executive, Communist Party of South Africa, 25 September 1928
29 Letter from S. P. Bunting to E. R. Roux, 5 December 1928
30 Letter from S. P. Bunting to E. R. Roux, 9 January 1929
31 Letter from E. R. Roux to Victor Danchin, 6 March 1929
32 League of African Rights, Petition, 1929
33 League of African Rights, Announcement of Meeting, 25 August 1929

Part Three
The Comintern and the New Line
34 Letter from the Executive Bureau, Communist Party of South Africa to the Executive Committee, Comintern
35 Letter from John Gomas to the Executive Bureau, Communist Party of South Africa, 29 October 1930
36 Letter from E. R. Roux to the Executive Bureau, Communist Party of South Africa, 18 November 1930
37 Letter from S. P. Bunting to E. R. Roux, 29 November 1930
38 "How to Build a Revolutionary Mass Party in South Africa: A Letter from the Executive Committee of the Communist International", *Umsebenzi*, 12 December 1930 and 19 December 1930
39 Statement by S. P. Bunting, October 1931

Part Four
The origins and development of Trotskyism in South Africa
40 Letter from T. W. Thibedi to the Communist League of America, 26 April 1932
41 Letter from the Communist League of America to T. W. Thibedi, 30 May 1932

42 Leon Trotsky, "Closer to the Proletarians of the 'Coloured' Races!", 13 June 1932, *The Militant*, 2 July 1932
43 Letter from T. W. Thibedi to Leon Trotsky, 10 August 1932
44 Letter from Leon Trotsky to T. W. Thibedi, 4 September 1932
45 Letter from the International Secretariat of the International Left Opposition to Cape Town comrades, 23 October 1932
46 Letter from the International Secretariat of the International Left Opposition to Johannesburg comrades, 23 October 1932
47 "International Communist League formed in South Africa", *International Bulletin of the International Communist League*, New Series, 2, September 1934
48 Lenin Club, *Draft Thesis: The Native Question* (Majority) [1934]
49 Lenin Club, *Draft Thesis: Introduction* (Minority) [1934]
50 Lenin Club, *Draft Thesis: The Trade Union Question* (No division on this question) [1934]
51 Leon Trotsky, Remarks on the Draft Theses of the Workers' Party of South Africa, 20 April 1935
52 International Secretariat of the International Communist League (B-L), Minutes of meeting, 23 April 1935
53 "Remarks of Comrade Dubois", *Internal Bulletin of the International Communist League* (B-L), no. 2, May 1935
54 Letter from the International Secretariat of the International Communist League (B-L) to the Workers' Party of South Africa and the Communist League of South Africa, 24 July 1935
55 Letter from the International Secretariat of the International Communist League (B-L) to the Workers' Party of South Africa and the Communist League of South Africa, 12 October 1935
56 "Extract of a letter of 24 October 1935 from the Communist League of South Africa", *Press Service of the International Secretariat, International Communist League* (B-L), 15 November 1935
57 Letter from the Communist League of South Africa to the Workers' Party of South Africa, 13 January 1936
58 Letter from the Communist League of South Africa to the Workers' Party of South Africa, 18 February 1936
59 Letter from the Workers' Party of South Africa to N. J. Barclay, 21 February 1936
60 Letter from the Workers' Party of South Africa to the Communist League of South Africa, 3 March 1936
61 Minutes of the meeting of the Workers' Party of South Africa, Johannesburg branch, 25 March 1936
62 Minutes of the meeting of the Workers' Party of South Africa, Johannesburg branch, 3 April 1936
63 Letter from the Workers' Party of South Africa to the International Secretariat of the International Communist League (B-L), 11 April 1936
64 Letter from the Workers' Party of South Africa to the International Secretariat of the International Communist League (B-L), 1 July 1936
65 Minutes of the meeting of the Workers' Party of South Africa, Johannesburg branch, 24 July 1936
66 Letter from the Workers' Party of South Africa, Johannesburg, to the Cape Town branch, 21 February 1937
67 Letter from the African Metal Trades Union to the Workers' Party of South Africa, 21 February 1937
68 Letter from the Workers' Party of South Africa, Johannesburg, to the Cape Town branch, 26 February 1937
69 Letter from the Workers' Party of South Africa, Johannesburg, to the Cape Town branch, 22 March 1937
70 Letter from the Workers' Party of South Africa, Johannesburg, to the Cape Town branch, 26 August 1937
71 *Spartacus Club October Revolution Celebrations*, 6 November 1937
72 Letter from R. T. R. Molefe to London comrades, 21 February 1938
73 Letter from *The Spark* to M. S. Njisane, 15 September 1938
74 Letter from the Workers' Party of South Africa, Johannesburg, to Cape Town comrades, 2 November 1938
75 A. Mon [M. N. Averbach], "The Historical Basis for the Programme of the Fourth International Organisation of South Africa", *Workers' Voice*, 1, 1, July 1944

Part Five
Building political alliances: Workers' unity and black united fronts
76 Communist Party of South Africa, *What is the Native Independent Republic?* [1934]
77 M. K., "Fascism in South Africa", *Umsebenzi*, 13 January 1934
78 "What is the Communist Party? A South African Native Republic, Lesson 3: The Native Republic 1", *Umsebenzi*, 24 February 1934
79 "What is the Communist Party? Lesson 4: What will be done in the Bantu Republic?", *Umsebenzi*, 17 March 1934

List of Documents 395

80 "The Communist Party Points the Way to Freedom: A.N.C. Leaders have no Programme of Struggle", *Umsebenzi*, 7 April 1934
81 D. I., "What the 'A.C.C.' Means", *Umsebenzi*, 26 January 1935
82 "Is there a Native Bourgeoisie?", *Umsebenzi*, 2 February 1935
83 "Native Bourgeoisie as a Class", *Umsebenzi*, 16 February 1935
84 A. Z. "Is There a Class of Native Capitalists in South Africa?", *Umsebenzi*, 13 April 1935
85 E. Roux, "The Native Exploiters: A reply to 'A. Z.'", *Umsebenzi*, 20 April 1935
86 E. T. Mofutsanyana, "The Native Exploiters in South Africa", *Umsebenzi*, 27 April 1935
87 "Lessons of the All-Bantu Conference", *The Spark*, 2, 2, February 1936
88 "No Compromise", *Umsebenzi*, 20 February 1936
89 "People's Front and the Cry for Unity in South Africa", *The Spark*, 2, 4, April 1936
90 "Hertzog's Native Bill Passed: Only 11 Oppose Reactionary Measure", *Umsebenzi*, 11 April 1936
91 John Gomas, "The Native Representation Bill is Passed: What Must be Done Now?", *Umsebenzi*, 25 April 1936
92 "Communist Party of South Africa; Plenum Held from 5th to 8th April, 1936", *Umsebenzi*, 16 May 1936
93 S. B., "Unite Against Reaction and Oppression: United Front Against National Oppression and Fascism", *Umsebenzi*, 23 May 1936
94 "The United Front in South Africa: A Reply to S.B.", *Umsebenzi*, 13 June 1936
95 "Welcome the All-African Convention! African National Convention Must Mark Beginning of National Liberation Movement", *South African Worker*, 27 June 1936
96 "C.B.I. Joins Workers' Party", *Umlilo Mollo/The Flame*, 1, 1, September 1936
97 "Advisory Board Elections: Communist Party Calls on Location Residents to Support All-African Convention for Better Conditions", *South African Worker*, 26 September 1936
98 "The All-African Convention", *Umlilo Mollo/The Flame*, 1, 2, October 1936
99 Edwin T. Mofutsanyana, "All-African Convention: Masses Must Support It", *South African Worker*, 9 January 1937
100 "15th Anniversary of 1922 Rand Strike: Communist Party Calls Mass Demonstration to Commemorate", *South African Worker*, 27 February 1937
101 Letter from the Workers' Party of South Africa to G. H. Gool, 4 March 1937
102 Workers Party of South Africa, *Liberation League* [c. March 1937]
103 *Programme of the National Liberation League of S.A. as Revised and Adopted at First Congress*, Cape Town, March 1937
104 "Boycott the Elections!", *The Spark*, 3, 4, April 1937
105 John Gomas, "Cape Town: Liberation League Activities", *South African Worker*, 17 April 1937
106 "Notes of the Month", *Umvikeli-Thebe/The African Defender*, 9, June 1937
107 "Johannesburg Municipal Elections: Communist Party Asks Labour Party for Working Arrangements", *South African Worker*, 12 June 1937
108 "African National Congress to be Revived: Leaders' Co-ordinating Committee's Work", *South African Worker*, 4 September 1937
109 G. H. Gool and J. A. La Guma, "Appeal of the National Liberation League for a National Convention of the Subject Peoples of South Africa", *The Liberator*, September 1937
110 "All-African Convention Forthcoming Conference", *South African Worker*, 13 November 1937
111 Letters from Moses Kotane to John Gomas, 14, 17, 18 and 23 December 1937
112 Note from Claremont branch of the National Liberation League of South Africa, 26 March 1938
113 National Liberation League of South Africa, *Honesty is the Best Policy* [c. 1938]
114 [*National Liberation League?*], *How to Work Among Urban Africans*
115 Hawa H. Ahmed [Halima Gool], *Address Delivered at Inaugural Meeting of the Non-European Women's Suffrage League*, Cosmopolitan Hall, Cape Town, 24 August 1938
116 Committee of Action of the Non-European United Front, *Non-European United Front*, Cape Town [1939]
117 Non-European Front of South Africa, *Statement of Passive Resistance Movement* [1939]
118 Johannesburg District Communist Party, *Call to a Non-European United Front!*
119 Non-European United Front of South Africa, *Minutes of Conference* held in City Hall, Cape Town, 8 to 10 April 1939
120 *Draft Programme of the Communist Party of South Africa* [c. 1940]
121 A. Mon [M. N. Averbach], "The Colour Bar and the National Struggle for Full Democratic Rights", *Workers' Voice*, 1, 2, November 1944

Part Six
World war and the suppression of socialism
122 "Manifesto Against Imperialist War", *Socialist Action*, August 1939
123 *Statement of Dr. Y. M. Dadoo, Secretary, Non-European United Front (Transvaal) before the Court*, 6 September 1940
124 Letter from Max Gordon to Fanny Klenerman, 21 December 1940
125 *Internment of Max Gordon* [c. 1941]
126 Letter from W. G. Ballinger to Mampurie [Self Mampuru], 1 May 1941
127 *6 Point Communist Programme* [c. 1941]
128 A. P. Mda, "Report of Communist Activities among the Natives in Johannesburg", *Catholic Times*, July 1942
129 "The Programme of the 4th International in South Africa", *Workers' Voice*, 1 July [1943?]
130 *Communists in Conference: The 1943/44 National Conference of the Communist Party of South Africa*
131 "Why did the V.F.P. Strike Fail?", *Workers' Voice*, 1 February 1944
132 "Our Programme", *Progressive Trade Union Bulletin*, 1, 1, February 1945
133 "Editorial: the Bloemfontein Trade Union Conference and the Industrial Conciliation Act", *The Militant Worker*, October–November 1945
134 *The Impending Strike of African Miners: A statement by the African Mineworkers' Union*, 7 August 1946
135 "National Front and Class Struggle: Report to the Central Committee of the Communist Party of South Africa", *Freedom*, 5, 4, August–September 1946
136 "Report on the Relationship of the Party to other Workers' Organisations in South Africa", *Freedom*, 5, 4, August–September 1946
137 Letter from the Fourth International Organisation of South Africa to [Revolutionary Communist Party?], 6 March 1947
138 Letter from the Fourth International Organisation of South Africa to the Revolutionary Communist Party, 29 August 1947
139 "The Coming Anti-African Bill", *Workers' Voice*, 6, 2, December 1947
140 "Terrorism on the Mines: Union organisers allege assault", *The Guardian*, 4 December 1947
141 "Apartheid Spells Disaster". Report of the Central Committee of the Communist Party of South Africa to the Party's National Conference, Johannesburg, 6 to 8 January 1950, *Freedom*, New Series, 15 December 1949

SOURCES

Document 2, Labour Party Papers, National Museum of Labour History, Manchester.
Document 3, item 30/69/1159, Public Record Office, London.
Documents 4–7, 38, 77–86, 88, 90–100, 105–08, 110, 135–6 and 141, British Library, London.
Documents 9–11, Tom Mann Papers 1922/23, MSS 334, Modern Records Centre, University of Warwick Library.
Documents 12, 16–37 and 39, Bunting Papers, A949, Historical Papers Library, University of the Witwatersrand.
Documents 13–14 and 111, courtesy of Doreen Musson.
Documents 15 and 76, Ralph Bunche Collection 2051, Box 62, Special Collections, University Research Library, University of California, Los Angeles.
Documents 40, 44–6, 54–55 and 63, respectively items 15533, 10565, 14385, 14384, 14386, 14387 and 14482, Trotsky Archives, Houghton Library, Harvard University.
Documents 43 and 72, courtesy of Ian Hunter.
Documents 47 and 52, Prometheus Research Library, New York.
Documents 57–62, 65–71, 73–74 and 101–02, Workers' Party of South Africa Papers, Mayibuye Historical Papers, University of the Western Cape.
Documents 75, 89, 104, 121, 129, 131 and 139, South African Reference Library, Cape Town.
Documents 103, 114, 117–18, Abdurahman Family Papers, BCZA, Manuscripts and Archives Department, University of Cape Town Libraries.
Documents 112–13, 118, Abdurahman Papers, BC506, Manuscripts and Archives Department, University of Cape Town Libraries.
Documents 123 and 133, Southern African Archives, Borthwick Institute of Historical Research, University of York.
Documents 124–6 and 134, Klenerman Papers, Historical Papers Library, University of the Witwatersrand.
Document 127, Hoover Institution Archives, Stanford University.
Document 128, courtesy of Gail Gerhart.
Document 137–8, Haston Papers, Brynmor Jones Library, University of Hull.

Select bibliography

Abrahams, Peter (1954), *Tell Freedom*, New York: Alfred A. Knopf.
Adler, Taffy (1976), "The Class Struggle in Doornfontein: A history of the Johannesburg Jewish Workers' Club, 1928-1950", University of the Witwatersrand: African Studies Seminar (August).
Adler, Taffy (1979), "Lithuania's Diaspora: The Johannesburg Jewish Workers' Club, 1928-1948", *Journal of Southern African Studies*, 6, 1, October, 70-92.
African National Congress (1977), *ANC Speaks: Documents and Statements of the African National Congress 1955-1976*, n.p.
Alexander, Neville (1986), "Aspects of Non-Collaboration in the Western Cape 1943-1963", *Social Dynamics*, 12, 1, 1-14.
Alexander, Neville (1991) [1974], "Black Consciousness: A reactionary tendency?", in N. Barney Pityana, Mamphela Ramphele, Malusi Mpumlwana and Lindy Wilson, eds, *Bounds of Possibility: The legacy of Steve Biko & Black Consciousness*, Cape Town: David Philip and London and New York: Zed, 238-52.
Andrews, W. H. (1940), *Class Struggles in South Africa: Two lectures given on South African trade unionism*, Cape Town.
Basner, Miriam (1993) *Am I an African? The political memoirs of H. M. Basner*, Johannesburg: Witwatersrand University.
Berger, Iris (1992), *Threads of Solidarity: Women in South African industry, 1900-1980*, Bloomington and Indianapolis: Indiana University and London: James Currey.
Bhana, Surenda and Bridglal Pachai, eds (1984), *A Documentary History of Indian South Africans*, Cape Town and Johannesburg: David Philip and Stanford: Hoover.
Bohmer, Elizabeth W., comp. (1986-87), *Left-Radical Movements in South Africa and Namibia 1900-1981: A bibliographical and historical study*, Cape Town: South African Library.

Bonner, P. L. (1979), "The 1920 Black Mineworkers' Strike: A preliminary account", in Belinda Bozzoli, comp., *Labour, Townships and Protests: Studies in the social history of the Witwatersrand*, Johannesburg: Ravan, 273-297.
Bradford, Helen (1985), "The Industrial and Commercial Workers' Union of Africa in the South African Countryside, 1924-1930", Ph.D., University of the Witwatersrand.
Braunthal, Julius (1967), *History of the International, 1914-1943*, Vol. 2, London: Thomas Nelson.
Bunting, Brian (1975), *Moses Kotane: South African revolutionary*, London: Inkululeko.
Bunting, Brian, ed. (1981), *South African Communists Speak: Documents from the history of the South African Communist Party, 1915-1980*, London: Inkululeko.
Carr, E. H. (1987), *What is History?*, 2nd edition, London: Penguin.
Claudin, Fernando (1975), *The Communist Movement: From Comintern to Cominform, Part One*, New York and London: Monthly Review.
Coka, Gilbert (1936), "The Story of Gilbert Coka", in Margery Perham, ed., *Ten Africans*, London: Faber & Faber, 273-321.
Cope, R. K. (1944), *Comrade Bill: The life and times of W. H. Andrews, workers' leader*, Cape Town: Stewart.
Dadoo, Yusuf Mohamed (1990), *South Africa's Freedom Struggle: Statements, speeches and articles, including correspondence with Mahatma Gandhi*, edited by E. S. Reddy, New Delhi: Namedia Foundation and Sterling Publishers and London: Kliptown Books.
Deutscher, Isaac (1959), *The Prophet Unarmed, Trotsky: 1921-1929*, London: Oxford University.
Deutscher, Isaac (1963), *The Prophet Outcast: Trotsky: 1929-1940*, London, New York and Toronto: Oxford University.
Deutscher, Isaac ed. (1964), *The Age of Permanent Revolution: A Trotsky anthology*, New York: Dell.
Dimitrov, George (1986), "The Fascist Offensive and the Tasks of the Communist International in the Struggle of the Working Class Against Fascism: Main Report delivered at the Seventh World Congress of the Communist International, August 2, 1935", in George Dimitrov, *Against Fascism and War*, New York: International Publishers, 1-94.
Drew, Allison (1991a), "Social Mobilization and Racial Capitalism in South Africa, 1928-1960", Ph.D., University of California, Los Angeles.
Drew, Allison (1991b), "Events Were Breaking Above Their Heads: Socialism in South Africa, 1921-1950", *Social Dynamics*, 17, 1, June, 49-77.
Ervin, Charles Wesley (1988-89), "Trotskyism in India, Part One: Origins through World War Two (1934-45)", *Revolutionary History*, 1, 4, Winter, 22-34.
Everett, Elizabeth (1978), "Zainunnissa (Cissie) Gool 1897-1963: A Biography", B.A. Honours, University of Cape Town.
Glass, C. F. (1930) "The Labor Movement in South Africa", *The Militant*, 29 March.
Harrison, Wilfrid H. (1948), *Memoirs of a Socialist in South Africa, 1903-1947*, Cape Town.
Herd, Norman (1966), *1922: The Revolt on the Rand*, Johannesburg: Blue Crane.
Hirson, Baruch (1987), "Not Pro-War, and not Anti-War: Just Indifferent. South African Blacks in the Second World War", *Critique*, 20/21, 39-56.
Hirson, Baruch (1988), "Death of a Revolutionary: Frank Glass/Li Fu-Jen/John Liang 1901-1988", *Searchlight South Africa*, 1, 1, September, 28-41.
Hirson, Baruch (1989a), *Yours for the Union: Class and community struggles in South Africa*, London: Zed.
Hirson, Baruch (1989b), "Spark and the 'Red Nun'", *Searchlight South Africa*, 2, February, 65-78.
Hirson, Baruch (1993a), "The Trotskyist Groups in South Africa", *Revolutionary History*, 4, 4, Spring, 25-56. Also in *Searchlight South Africa* (1993) 3, 2, April, 72-100.
Hirson, Baruch (1993b), "The General Strike of 1922", *Searchlight South Africa*, 3, 3, October, 63-94.
Hirson, Baruch (1993c), "Lies in the Life of 'Comrade Bill'", *Searchlight South Africa*, 3, 3, October, 53-62.
Hirson, Baruch and Lorraine Vivian (1992), *Strike Across the Empire: The Seaman's Strike of 1925 in Britain, South Africa and Australasia*, London: Clio.
Hobsbawm, Eric (1968), *Labouring Men: Studies in the history of labour*, London: Weidenfeld and Nicolson.
Hobsbawm, Eric (1984), *Worlds of Labour: Further studies in the history of labour*, London: Weidenfeld and Nicolson.
Hofmeyr, Willie (1983), "Rural Popular Organisation Problems: Struggles in the Western Cape, 1929-1930", *Africa Perspective*, 26-49.
Hofmeyr, Willie (1985), "Agricultural Crisis and Rural Organisation in the Cape: 1929-1933", M. A., University of Cape Town.
Hommel, Maurice (1981), *Capricorn Blues: The struggle for human rights in South Africa*, Toronto: Culturama.

Hughes, Emrys, ed. (n.d.), *Keir Hardie's Speeches and Writings (From 1888 to 1915)*, Glasgow: Forward.
Hunter, Ian (1993), "Raff Lee and the Pioneer Trotskyists of Johannesburg", *Revolutionary History*, 4, 4, Spring, 57-83.
James, C. L. R. (1937), *World Revolution 1917-1936: The rise and fall of the Communist International*, London: Martin Secker & Warburg.
Johns, Sheridan (1976), "The Birth of the Communist Party of South Africa", *The International Journal of African Historical Studies*, IX, 3, 371-400.
Kadalie, Clements (1970), *My Life and the ICU: The autobiography of a black trade unionist in South Africa*, London: Frank Cass.
Karis, Thomas and Gwendolen M. Carter, eds (1973), *From Protest to Challenge: A documentary history of African politics in South Africa*, Vol. 2, Stanford: Hoover Institution.
Karis, Thomas and Gwendolen M. Carter, eds (1977), *From Protest to Challenge: A documentary history of African politics in South Africa*, Vol. 4, Stanford: Hoover Institution.
Kline, Mary-Jo (1987), *A Guide to Documentary Editing*, Baltimore and London: Johns Hopkins University Press.
Lee, Franz J. T. (1970), "Der Einfluß des Trotzkismus auf die nationalen Befreiungsbewegungen in Südafrika", Ph.D., Johann-Wolfgang-Goethe-Universität, Frankfurt am Main.
Legassick, Martin (1973), "Class and Nationalism in South African Protest: The South African Communist Party and the 'Native Republic', 1928-34", *Eastern African Studies*, XV, July.
Lenin, V. I. (1971), "The Socialist Revolution and the Right of Nations to Self-Determination (Theses)", in V. I. Lenin, *Critical Remarks on the National Question; The right of nations to self-determination*, Moscow: Progress Publishers, 98-111.
Lerumo, A. [Michael Harmel] (1971), *Fifty Fighting Years: The Communist Party of South Africa 1921-1971*, London: Inkululeko.
Lewis, Gavin (1987), *Between the Wire and the Wall: A history of South African "Coloured" Politics*, Cape Town and Johannesburg: David Philip.
Lodge, Tom (1983), *Black Politics in South Africa since 1945*, London and New York: Longman.
Lodge, Tom (1985), "Class Conflict, Communal Struggle and Patriotic Unity: The Communist Party of South Africa during the Second World War", paper presented at the African Studies Seminar, African Studies Institute, University of the Witwatersrand, 7 October.
Macmillan, W. M. (1922), "The Truth about the Strike on the Rand", *The New Statesman*, xix, 474, 13 May, 145-46.
MacMillan, W. M. (1949), *Africa Emergent: A survey of social, political and economic trends in British Africa*, Harmondsworth, Middlesex: Penguin.
Mann, Tom (1923) "S. African Natives and Coloured Men", *All Power*, March.
Mantzaris, E. A. (1987), "Radical Community: the Yiddish-speaking Branch of the International Socialist League, 1918-1920", in Belinda Bozzoli, ed., *Class, Community and Conflict: South African Perspectives*, Johannesburg: Ravan, 160-176.
Mon, A. [M. N. Averbach] (1945), "A Comment on Trotsky's Letter", *Workers' Voice: Theoretical Supplement*, 1, 3, July.
Morkel, H. [H. J. Simons] (1942), "Why We Must Support the Government in the War Against Fascism", *Freedom–Vryheid*, 9, April, 1-3.
Musson, Doreen (1989), *Johnny Gomas, Voice of the Working Class: A political biography*, Cape Town: Buchu.
No Sizwe (1979), *One Azania, One Nation: The National Question in South Africa*, London: Zed.
Ntsebeza, Lungisile (1988), "Divisions and Unity in Struggle: The ANC, ISL and the CP, 1910-1928", B.A. Honours, University of Cape Town.
Nzula, A. T., I. I. Potekhin and A. Z. Zusmanovich (1979), *Forced Labour in Colonial Africa*, edited by Robin Cohen, London: Zed.
O'Meara, Dan (1975), "The 1946 African Mine Workers' Strike and the Political Economy of South Africa", *Journal of Commonwealth and Comparative Politics*, XIII, 2, July, 146–73.
Roux, Edward (1964), *Time Longer than Rope: A history of the black man's struggle for freedom in South Africa*, Madison: University of Wisconsin.
Roux, Eddie and Win Roux (1972), *Rebel Pity: the Life of Eddie Roux*, Harmondsworth: Penguin.
Roux, Edward (1993), *S. P. Bunting: A political biography*, edited by Brian Bunting, Cape Town: Mayibuye.
Sachs, E. S. (1957), *Rebels' Daughters*, London: McGibbon and Kee.
Sachs, Bernard (1961), *The Road to Sharpeville*, Johannesburg: Dial, London: Dennis Dobson and New York: Liberty.
Sachs, Bernard (1949), *Multitude of Dreams: A semi-autobiographical study*, Johannesburg: Kayor.
Sachs, Bernard (1959), *South African Personalities and Places*, Johannesburg: Kayor.

Saunders, Christopher C., consultant editor (1994a), *Illustrated History of South Africa: The real story*, 3rd edition, Cape Town, London.
Saunders, Christopher C., advisory editor (1994b), *An Illustrated Dictionary of South African History*, Sandton: Ibis Books and Editorial Services.
Simons, Jack and Ray Simons (1983), *Class and Colour in South Africa, 1850-1950*, International Defence and Aid Fund for Southern Africa.
Simons, Mary (1976), "Organised Coloured Political Movements", in H. W. van der Merwe and C. J. Groenewald, eds, *Occupational and Social Change Among Coloured People in South Africa*, Cape Town: Juta.
Southall, A. J. (1978), "Marxist Theory in South Africa until 1940", M.A., University of York.
Stein, Mark (1978), "Max Gordon and African Trade Unionism on the Witwatersrand, 1935-1940", in Eddie Webster, ed., *Essays in Southern African Labour History*, Johannesburg: Ravan, 143-57.
Swan, Maureen (1987), "Ideology in organised Indian politics", in Shula Marks and Stanley Trapido, eds, *The Politics of Race, Class & Nationalism in Twentieth-Century South Africa*, Longman: London and New York, 182-208.
Tabata, I. B. [1952], *The Boycott as a Weapon of Struggle*, Durban: APDUSA.
Trotsky, Leon (1973),"Closer to the Proletarians of the 'Colored' Races!" *Writings of Leon Trotsky, 1932*, New York: Pathfinder, 111-12.
Trotsky, Leon (1974) "On the South African Theses", *Writings of Leon Trotsky, 1934-35*, New York: Pathfinder, 248-55.
Trotsky, Leon (1975), *The Struggle against Fascism in Germany*, Harmondsworth, Penguin.
Tsuzuki, Chushkhi (1991), *Tom Mann 1856-1941: The challenges of labour*, Oxford: Clarendon.
Van der Post, Laurens (1934), *In a Province*, London: Hogarth.
Van der Horst, Sheila T. (1949), "Labour", in Ellen Hellman, ed., *Handbook on Race Relations in South Africa*, Cape Town, London and New York: Oxford University, 109-57.
Walker, Ivan L. and Ben Weinbren (1961), *2000 Casualties: A history of the Labour Movement in the Union of South Africa*, Johannesburg: SATUC.
Walker, Cherryl (1991), *Women and Resistance in South Africa*, 2nd edition, Cape Town & Johannesburg: David Philip and New York: Monthly Review.
Workers' International League (1946), *Internal Bulletin*, 1, 6, January, Karis and Carter Microfilm Collection, 2:DW2:85/1.
[The Star] (1922), *Through the Red Revolt on the Rand: A pictorial review of events, January, February, March*, 1st and 2nd editions, Johannesburg: Central News Agency, 1922.

Collected papers and archives

Abdurahman Family Papers, Manuscripts and Archives Department, University of Cape Town Libraries.
African Collection (South Africa), Manuscripts and Archives, Yale University Library.
Ralph Bunche Collection, Special Collections, University Research Library, University of California, Los Angeles.
S. P. Bunting Papers, Historical Papers Library, University of the Witwatersrand.
Communist Party of South Africa Collection, Hoover Institution Archives and Hoover Institution Library, Stanford University.
R. K. Cope Papers, Historical Papers Library, University of the Witwatersrand.
Ruth First Collection, Institute of Commonwealth Studies, University of London.
Clare Goodlatte Papers, South African Reference Library, Cape Town.
Fanny Klenerman Papers, Historical Papers Library, University of the Witwatersrand.
Jack Simons Papers, Manuscripts and Archives Department, University of Cape Town Libraries.
Southern African Archives, Borthwick Institute of Historical Research, University of York.
Trotsky Archives, Houghton Library, Harvard University.
Workers' Party of South Africa Papers, Mayibuye Archives, University of the Western Cape.

INDEX

Abdurahman, Dr A. 186, 193 n. 41, 293-5, 330 n. 36
Abdurahman, Mrs N. 309, 314
Abdurahman, Dr W. 33
Abdurahman, Z. *see* Gool, Mrs Z. (Cissie)
Abrahams, P. 306, 312, 313, 330 n. 40
Adams, Dr 306
Africa Club 37, 119
African Congress Clubs 217–19, 222–3
African Democratic Party 11, 34, 186, 193 n. 43
African Metal Trades Union 169–73, 176–7, 180
African Mineworkers' Strike 1946 17, 36, 327 n. 5, 369–72, 382, 389 n. 5, 391 n. 29
African Mineworkers' Union 46, 67, 369–72, 381, 382, 384
African National Congress 10, 31, 67, 193 n. 41, 270–1; and CPSA 23, 32, 100, 215-17, 236–7; and LAR 21, 103, 108; and WPSA 149, 167; criticism of 29, 89, 186, 196-9, 211, 223; decline of 30, 33; *see also* African Congress Clubs; Transvaal Native Congress
African National Congress Youth League 11, 34, 37
African People's Organisation 34, 183, 186, 193 n. 41, 293–4, 311
Ahmed, H. H. *see* Gool, H.
Alexander, N. 11
Alexander, R. 358, 360
All African Convention 27, 29, 30–2, 34, 166–7, 244–5; and CPSA 30–2, 166–7, 238–9, 246–9; and franchise 230, 235–8; conference 1937 276–9; criticism of 186, 225–9, 250–1, 262–3, 294–5
Allan, L. J. 280, 306, 308, 311
Amalgamated Society of Engineers 44, 60
Andrews, S. 359
Andrews, W. H. 19, 21, 44–5, 71 n. 9, 73 n. 26, 299, 309; and CPSA 54–5, 72 n. 15, 76, 99, 355, 360–1, 390 n. 19; criticism of 116, 121 n. 8, 182–3
Anti-CAD Movement 11, 39 n. 12, 330 n. 39, 360, 379–80
Anti-Imperialist League *see* League Against Imperialism
Anti-Pass Campaign 70, 112, 113–14, 356–7
Arenstein, R. 355, 357
Asiatic Land Tenure and Indian Representation Bill 266, 273, 377, 378, 391 n. 27
Atlantic Charter 357–8, 390 n. 17
Attlee, C. 334, 389 n. 3
Averbach, M. N. 27, 181-9, 191 n. 16, 321-6
Bach, L. 26, 121 n. 8, 190 n. 11, 328 n. 14 and 20
Bailey, Sir A. 232, 327 n. 9
Bain, J. T. 71 n. 3
Baker, C. J. 99, 103, 121 n. 8, 305, 309
Ballinger, Mrs M. 342, 390 n. 11
Ballinger, W. G. 74 n. 31, 97, 108, 164, 342–3, 390 n. 10 and 11; and ICU 19, 76; and Kadalie 64-5, 73 n. 21; criticism of 227, 264; *see also* Industrial and Commercial Workers Union
Baloyi, G. R. 305, 309, 311
Barclay, N. J. 160
Barnes, G. 47, 72 n. 14
Basch, M. 190 n. 11
Basner, H. 32, 194 n. 43
Bennet, Cde 86, 95, 99, 105 n. 13
Berman, A. Z. 100
Bernstein, R. 355, 360
Bhola, Mrs M. N. 100, 277, 328 n. 23
Black Republic thesis *see* Native Republic thesis

Bolshevist Leninist League 24, 133–4, 151–2; *see also* Lenin Club; Workers' Party of South Africa
Brookes, E. H. 66, 74 n. 33, 227, 264
Browder, E. 334, 375, 391 n. 25
Bruce, G. O. 43
Buchanan, D. M. 264
Buchner, A. I. 304, 308, 309
Bukharin, N. 20, 38 n. 6, 77, 90, 92, 105 n. 5 and 14
Bunche, R. 30, 328 n. 13
Bunting R. 99, 100, 104 n. 3
Bunting, S. P. 72 n. 15, 104 n. 3, 105 n. 14, 130; and black trade unions 16, 66–8, 389 n. 6; and LAR 103, 105 n. 19; and Native Republic thesis 21, 25, 77–80, 86–93; and E. Roux 73 n. 20, 96, 102; and Tembuland campaign 105 n. 15 and 19, 109; and working class unity 18–19, 51–4, 69–70; criticism of 55, 64, 76, 111–14, 119–20, 183, 220
Burlak, Y. 166, 191 n. 12
Burnside, D. 233, 235, 293, 327 n. 11, 330 n. 35, 334
Cachalia, Y. 389 n. 5
Campbell, J. R. 57, 73 n. 23
Cape Federation of Labour Unions 19, 58, 60, 73 n. 26, 145
Cape Labour Party 43; *see also* South African Labour Party
Carnegie Commission 288, 329 n. 33
Chamber of Mines 45, 185, 362, 369
Chamberlain, N. 334, 389 n. 2
Champion, A. W. G. 57, 73 n. 21, 207, 327 n. 1
Chinese miners 43, 71 n. 6 and 8
Cloete, Mr 307
Close, R. 355, 360
Clothing Workers' Union 20, 61–2
Coka, J. G. 29, 223, 327 n. 4
Colour Bar Act *see* Mines and Works Amendment Act 1926
Coloured Advisory Council 39 n. 12
Colraine, D. 38 n. 6, 99
Comintern *see* Communist International
Communist International 18, 20, 35, 39 n. 16; Congress, 2nd 51–4, 72 n. 16; 3rd 17, 132; 6th 77–80, 81–93, 104 n. 2; 7th 157, 192 n. 26, 196, 245; policy, New Line 22–3, 108–20, 196; People's Front 26, 28–32, 196, 231–4; *see also* Native Republic thesis
Communist League of Africa 24, 73 n. 19, 125, 129, 131–2
Communist League of America 124–7, 129, 190 n. 1
Communist League of South Africa 25, 26, 36, 154–63, 166, 192 n. 23
Communist Party of South Africa 17, 38 n. 2, 48–50, 81–3; and AAC 30–2, 166–7, 238–9, 246–9; and ANC 23, 32, 100, 215–17, 236–7; and ICU 19, 38 n. 5, 60–5, 78, 97, 236–7; and LAR 103, 108–10; and National Liberation Movement 238–40, 360; and SALP 19, 269–70, 376–7, 378; and trade unions 66–70, 145, 251–2, 378–9; and World War II 33, 34–5, 37, 343–9, 354–62; criticism of 116–19, 129–33, 137–9, 182–3, 233–4, 245–6, 349–52; membership 23, 25, 36; Native Republic thesis 20–22, 26, 30, 121 n. 10, 196–7, 202–11, 213–15; policy 28–30, 37, 95–8, 240–4, 316–21, 373–5, 384–8; *see also* Trotskyism and names of individuals e.g. S. P. Bunting; E. R. Roux
Communist Party of the Soviet Union 22, 39 n. 9

Connolly, J. 42, 71 n. 2
Cookson, H. W. 303, 307, 309, 311, 312, 314
Coughlin, Father 233, 327 n. 10
Coulter, C. W. A. 235
Council of Non-European Trade Unions 36
Crawford, A. 43, 71 n. 3
Creswell, Col F. H. P. 44, 47–8, 71 n. 8
Cripps, Sir S. 334, 389 n. 3
Cupido, J. 304, 308, 309, 313

Dadoo, Dr Y. M. 33, 309, 335–9, 350, 356, 389 n. 5
Daladier, E. 334, 389 n. 2
Danchin, V. 94, 98, 101, 102, 104 n. 3, 105 n. 18, 129, 132
DeLeon, D. 16
Dimitrov, G. 241, 243, 246, 327 n. 12
Dippa, J. 57
Dladla, C. B. I. 32, 163, 168, 245–6, 248–9, 328 n. 13
Dube, J. L. 197, 226, 228–9, 327 n. 1
Dubois, Cde *see* Fischer, R.
Dunbar, A. 164, 192 n. 32
Dunjwa, Mr 307
du Plessis, D. 355, 360
du Preez, H. B. 308, 309
Dutt, R. P. 74 n. 34

Ebert, F. 47–8, 72 n. 14
Ernstzen, Mr 310
Everson, Mr 307, 310, 314

Fester, Mr 311, 314
Findlay, G. 164, 192 n. 32, 355, 359
Findlay, J. 355
Fischer, R. 152–3, 161, 191 n. 21
Fisher, P. 251
Fleet, R. 357
Fortune, Mrs I. 308
Forum Club 36–7
Foster, Mr 312
Fourth International Organisation of South Africa 25–7, 36, 133, 181–9, 192 n. 23, 352–4, 379–81
Freedom Charter 9
Freislich, R. 163–4, 168–9, 173, 177, 192 n. 31
Furniture Workers' Union 60, 70

Gamiet, M. A. 302, 306, 311
Gandhi, M. M. K. 183, 292, 329 n. 34
Garment Workers' Union 20, 58, 70, 74 n. 36
Garvey, M. 21, 328 n. 23
Ghetto Bill *see* Asiatic Land Tenure and Indian Representation Bill
Glass, C. F. 20, 38 n. 5, 58–9, 73 n. 25, 190 n. 4
Godlo, R. H. 226, 229
Gomas, J. 21, 32, 73 n. 24, 111, 236–8, 277–9; and ICU 38 n. 5, 64; and NEUF 302, 306–7, 308, 309; and NLL 33, 266–7, 330 n. 36; and tailoring industry 20, 58–9
Goodlatte, C. R. 165, 168, 173, 192 n. 34
Gool, G. 32, 160, 192 n. 29, 193 n. 34, 329 n. 30, 330 n. 36 and 39; and NLL 33–4, 252–3, 272–6, 280
Gool, H. 33, 285–95, 304, 312, 329 n. 30
Gool, J. 193 n. 34
Gool, Mrs Z. (Cissie) 33–4, 329 n. 31, 330 n. 35–7; and NEUF 299, 302, 308, 309, 311, 313–14, 316
Gordon, M. 34, 36, 180, 332, 389 n. 6, 391 n. 22; internment 328 n. 14, 339–43, 389 n. 9
Gosani, D. 163–4, 192 n. 31, 389 n. 9
Greenwood, A. 334, 389 n. 3
Grant, E. 160, 192 n. 30
Greyshirts 158, 192 n. 27, 232, 323
Gumede, J. T. 38 n. 6, 100, 105 n. 17, 208, 327 n. 1; and LAR 103, 108, 118

Haggar, D. 100
Hanekom, D. 251
Hanekom, S. 251
Hardie, J. K. 10, 16, 42–3, 71 n. 1
Harmel, M. 361, 390 n. 14 and 19
Harrison, W. H. 95, 99, 105 n. 15
Haston, J. 192 n. 31, 391 n. 28
Henderson, A. 47–8, 72 n. 14, 233
Hertzog, J. B. M. 102, 217, 229, 332
Hertzog Bills 21, 30–2, 103–4, 108, 114–15, 118, 120 n. 4, 166, 227; *see also* Native Trust and Land Bill; Representation of Natives Bill
Hofmeyr, J. H. 235
Hoho, S. 304, 309
Hoosain, Mr 306, 313
Hull, H. K. 85, 105 n. 10, 251

ICU *yase* Natal 73 n. 21
Independent ICU 67, 73 n. 21
Independent Labour Party 160
Indian (Ghetto) Bill *see* Asiatic Land Tenure and Indian Representation Bill
Industrial and Commercial Workers' Union 17, 55–6, 61, 72 n. 18, 73 n. 21; and LAR 21, 103, 108; and Native Republic thesis 100, 196–7; and Communists 19, 38 n. 5, 60–5, 78, 97, 236–7; criticism of 29, 183, 184–5, 200–1, 206–7, 211, 223; disintegration of 23, 30, 33, 66, 167, 324; organisation of 18, 21, 60–1, 83; *see also* Ballinger, W. G.; Kadalie, C.
Industrial Conciliation Act 1924 358–9, 360, 366, 367, 368–9, 390 n. 21
Industrial Conciliation (Natives) Bill 1948 380–4
Industrial Socialist League 17, 38 n. 1 and 2, 45; *see also* Communist Party of South Africa
Industrial Workers of Africa 16
International Secretariat (Left Opposition) 26–7, 126, 131–2, 151–2, 154–7, 165–8
International Socialist League 16, 17, 44, 47–8
Ismail, A. 299, 302, 306, 311, 313

Jabavu, D. D. T. 216–17, 225–9, 237, 248, 277, 279, 295
Jabavu, J. T. 186, 193 n. 42, 327 n. 6
Jaffe, H. 330 n. 38, 390 n. 20
Joffe, L. 245–6, 328 n. 14
Joffe, Dr M. 328 n. 14
Joint Committee of African Trade Unions 34
Jones, J. D. Rheinallt *see* Rheinallt Jones, J. D.
Joseph, H. 190 n. 4

Kadalie, C. 72 n. 18, 73 n. 21, 102, 108; criticism of 57, 61, 62, 117, 207–8; relations with Communists 19, 38 n. 5, 64–5, 83, 97
Kahn, M. 163–4, 168, 173, 177, 192 n. 31
Kahn, S. 30, 330 n. 37, 355; and NEUF 302–03, 306, 310, 312, 313
Kajee, A. I. 291–2, 295
Kalk, W. 60, 73 n. 20 and 28, 98
Kentridge, M. 49, 99
Kerensky, A. 47–8
Khaile, E. J. 38 n. 5, 64, 73 n. 19
Kies, B. M. 304, 306, 308, 310, 312, 313, 330 n. 38
Kirby, Mr 314
Klaasen, A. 305, 309
Klement, R. 165–6, 193 n. 35
Klenerman, F. 36, 121 n. 8, 190 n. 4, 193 n. 36, 339, 343, 389 n. 7
Koston, P. 165, 193 n. 34
Kotane, M. 28–30, 121 n. 8, 277–9, 280; and NEUF 299–300, 302, 305, 308, 309, 311–12, 314, 316

Koza, D. 34, 36, 194 n. 43, 332, 343, 368, 389 n. 8, 391 n. 22
Kruger, J. J. 305, 308, 309, 311, 313, 314
Kruger, M. 305
Kuomintang 128, 190 n. 7
Kuusinen, O. 86, 98, 105 n. 12
La Grange, I. J. 327 n. 7
La Guma, J. 19, 38 n. 5-6, 64, 105 n. 17, 299, 329 n. 25; and AAC 32, 278; and NLL 33, 272–6, 280–1, 330 n. 36; and Native Republic thesis 20-1, 32, 98-9, 104 n. 3
Lakey, B. 281, 304, 309, 310, 329 n. 29
Land Act 1913 115, 215
Latti, A. 328 n. 14
La Vita, J. W. 309
Lawrence, H. G. 342
League Against Imperialism 38 n. 6, 99, 105 n. 17
League of African Rights 21, 23, 103–4, 105 n. 17 and 19, 108–10, 118
Lee, H. 173, 177, 192 n. 31
Lee, R. 163–4, 168–73, 176–7, 190 n. 10, 192 n. 31
Leepile, L. L. 26, 279, 329 n. 27
Lefela, J. 105 n. 14
Lefela, M. 105 n. 14
Left Book Club 37, 190 n. 4
Lenin, V. I. 18, 72 n. 16, 148
Lenin Club 24–5, 133, 134–52, 160–1, 191 n. 23; *see also* Bolshevist Leninist League; Workers Party of South Africa
Lewis, D. 85, 105 n. 10, 251
Leys, Dr N. 64
Linjiza, T. B. 57
Long, H. 233, 327 n. 10
Long, S.A. "Taffy" 85, 105 n. 10, 251
Lopes, M. 47–8, 72 n. 13
Louw, A. L. S. 355, 359
Lozovsky, Cde 92
Lucas, F. A. W. 44–5, 71 n. 7, 164
Luthuli, A. 329 n. 24

MacDonald, J. R. 43–4, 71 n. 5
Madeley, W. B. 235, 269, 327 n. 11, 334, 360, 377
Madibe, A. 355, 360
Madiseng, B. D. 125, 130, 190 n. 3
Mahabane, Rev. Z. R. 278, 327 n. 1, 328–9 n. 24
Majoro, J. J. 372, 391 n. 23
Makabeni, G. 32, 34, 73 n. 19, 104 n. 3, 130, 389 n. 6 and 8
Malan, D. F. 138, 191 n. 14, 385
Maliba, A. 125, 190 n. 3, 390 n. 18
Malkinson, S. 121 n. 8
Mampuru, S. 194 n. 43, 342, 390 n. 10
Mann, T. 18, 54, 72 n. 17
Marks, J. B. 105 n. 14, 219–20, 271, 327 n. 3, 372; and NEUF 304, 308, 309, 313
Maseko, I. M. 169, 193 n. 37
Mason, G. 71 n. 3
Matseke, S. P. 279, 329 n. 26
Mbeki, T. 38 n. 5, 57, 73 n. 21
McKerrill, D. 71 n. 3
Mda, A. P. 349, 390 n. 13
Meissenheimer, P. R. 380
Mines and Works Act 1911 191 n. 13
Mines and Works Amendment Act 1926 191 n. 13, 200
Modern Youth Society 37
Modiagotla, C. D. 103, 108, 118, 120 n. 3
Modisane, B. 190 n. 4
Mofutsanyana, E. 271, 327 n. 5; and AAC 250–1, 277, 279; and CPSA 30, 32, 105 n. 14, 223–4, 355, 357
Mokgathe, M. 360

Molefe, R. T. R. 176–7
Molteno, D. B. 253, 264, 328 n. 15, 342, 390 n. 11
Mon, A. *see* Averbach, M. N.
Moore, A. A. 97, 269, 328 n. 19
Morgan, W. H. 71 n. 3
Morley-Turner, L. 281, 329 n. 29
Moroka, Dr J. S. 278, 329 n. 24
Mosaka, P. 194 n. 43
Mpama, J. 327 n. 5
Msimang, H. S. 278, 329 n. 24
Mtini, J. 304, 310, 355
Muller, A. 361
Muller, M. 355
Murphy, J. T. 80, 105 n. 8

Naicker, Dr G. M. 389 n. 5
Naidoo, H. A. 309, 355, 359, 360
Natal Native Congress 105 n. 17
National Liberation League 27, 32–4, 239, 252–61, 266–7, 272–6, 280–4; criticism of 39 n. 12, 186; *see also* Non-European United Front
Nationalist Party 37, 296–7, 385–6
Native Administration Act 1927 96, 110, 121 n. 6
Native Advisory Boards 246–8, 264
Native Laws Amendment Act 1937 266–8, 271, 295, 328 n. 18
Native Representative Council 30–2, 37, 247–8, 252–3, 385, 391 n. 29; criticism of 262–5, 294–5
Native Republic thesis 20–3, 28-30, 32, 39 n. 8, 76–104, 116–19; CPSA policy 20–2, 26, 30, 121 n. 10, 196–7, 202–11, 213–15; criticism of 137–8, 143, 148, 152, 321-1; Trotskyists and 25-6; for opinions of specific people *see* under the name e.g. S. P.Bunting, E. R.Roux, T. W.Thibedi
Native Service Contract Act 1933 216–17
Native Trust and Land Bill 30
Native (Urban Areas) Act 191 n. 14, 266
Ndobe, B. 328 n. 23
New Era Fellowship 37, 304, 330 n. 39
Ngedlane, J. 121 n. 8
Njisane, M. S. 178–9
Non-European Trade Union Council 364–5, 368–9
Non-European United Front 27, 32, 39 n. 12, 186, 280, 296–300; and CPSA 300–1, 350; and World War II 335–9, 389 n. 4; Conference 1939 302–16; formation of 33, 295
Non-European Unity Movement 9, 11, 27, 34, 36
Non-European Women's Suffrage League 285–95, 329 n. 31
Nzula, A. 68, 69–70, 74 n. 35, 101, 103, 105 n. 14

October, H. W. 304, 309
Oliphant, S. 309, 310

Passive Resistance Movement 299–300
Paver, B. G. 327 n. 7
Petrovsky, Cde *see* Bennet, Cde
Pieterse, D. R. 309
Pim, J. H. 65–6, 74 n. 32, 327 n. 7
Pirow, O. 110, 112, 121 n. 6, 211, 235
Plaatje, S. T. 217
Polish Socialist Party 191 n. 20
Pollitt, H. 57, 73 n. 23, 334, 389 n. 3
Ponen, G. 358
Poutsma, H. J. 71 n. 3
Progressive Trade Union Group 36
Purdy, M. G. 190 n. 10

Radebe, G. 271, 279, 328 n. 22
Rand Revolt 1922 17–18, 29, 38 n. 3, 48–51, 85, 105 n. 10, 251–2, 323
Red International of Labour Unions 18, 78–9, 105 n. 6
Representation of Natives Bill 30, 196, 230–1, 234–8

Representation of Natives Act 1936 294–5
Revolutionary Communist Party 379–81, 391 n. 28
Rheinallt Jones, J. D. 65, 74 n. 32, 230-1, 342, 390 n. 11
Richfield, Mr 69, 313
Roos, T. 121 n. 6
Rose-Innes, Sir J. 229, 327 n. 8
Roux, E. R. 73 n. 20, 103, 109, 222–4; and CPSA 57, 76, 81–6, 104 n. 3, 121 n. 8; Native Republic thesis 25, 93–102, 224; and trade unionism 16, 19, 21, 30, 60–70; criticism of 111–13, 245–6
Roy, M. N. 72 n. 16
Rubusana, Dr W. B. 224, 327 n. 6
Russian Revolution 18, 20

Sachs, B. 164, 192 n. 32
Sachs, E. S. "Solly" 70, 74 n. 36, 104 n. 3, 114, 121 n. 8, 232–3
Sacks, B. 355, 357
Saffery, A. L. 340, 389 n. 6 and 9
Sampson, H. W. 47
Saperstein, J. 190 n. 11
Sapire, M. 163, 164, 174, 180
Seme, P. ka I. 32, 105 n. 17, 327 n. 1; and ACC 217–19, 222–3; criticism of 197, 202, 208, 226, 229, 278
Shanley, E. 355
Smuts, Gen. J. C. 47, 110, 232, 271, 369, 382, 391 n. 29
Snitcher, H. 310, 312, 330 n. 35; and CPSA 30, 355, 359, 361, 376
Socialist Action 332
Socialist Workers' League 36, 39 n. 13
South African Association of Employees' Organisations *see* South African Trades Union Congress
South African Communist Party 37; *see also* Communist Party of South Africa
South African Federation of Non-European Trade Unions 61, 66–9, 74 n. 29
South African Indian Congress 186, 193 n. 41, 300
South African Labour Party 44, 71 n. 4; and CPSA 19, 269–70, 376–7, 378; and Ghetto Bill 391 n. 27; criticism of 47–8, 136–7, 145, 233–4; segregationist policy 16, 293
South African Native National Congress 105 n. 17
South African Party 100, 115
South African Socialist Party 330 n. 35
South African Trades Union Congress 19, 60, 62–4, 73 n. 26, 99
South African Trades and Labour Council 70, 145, 171, 191 n. 17, 383
South African Trades Union Co-ordinating Council 19, 63
The Spark 161, 162, 178–9
Spartacus Club 24, 161, 163–5, 167, 168–9, 174–6
Spendiff, H. 251
Stalin, J. 39 n. 9, 102, 246
Stallard, F. 138, 191 n. 14
Stone, L. 306, 311
strikes 17, 20, 61, 84–5, 362–3; African Metal Trades Union 169–73, 176–7; black mineworkers 1920 17, 45–6, 71 n. 11; 1946 17, 36, 327 n. 5, 369–72, 382, 389 n. 5, 391 n. 29; Clothing Workers' Union 20, 61–2; seamen 79, 105 n. 7
Stuart, W. H. 264
Stuttaford, R. 297, 302–3
Stuttaford Bills 33, 297
Suppression of Communism Act 1950 11, 36, 39 n. 17, 74 n. 36

Tabata, I. B. 193 n. 34
Tantsi, N. B. 103
Tema, Rev. S. S. 270, 328 n. 21
Thaele, J. M. 277, 279, 328 n. 23

Thema, R. V. Selope 327 n. 7, 328 n. 21
Thibedi, T. W. 72 n. 19, 105 n. 18, 119, 124–7; and CLA 24, 129–31; and Native Republic thesis 21, 98–9, 101, 102, 104 n. 3; and Black trade unions 16, 19, 34, 389 n. 6; and ICU 38 n. 5, 57; and SAFNTU 68, 69–70, 113
Thipe, A. 389 n. 8
Thomas, C. J. 305, 310
Thorez, M. 334, 389 n. 3
Thuku, H. 83, 105 n. 9
Tinker, T. P. 21, 99
Tjelele, J. 105 n. 14, 125, 190 n. 3
Tonjeni, E. 328 n. 23
Transvaal Chamber of Commerce and Industry 200-1
Transvaal Native Congress 17, 45; *see also* African National Congress
Treason Trial 37
Tredgold, Sir C. 264
Trotsky, L. 24, 26, 34, 39 n. 9, 124, 126–31, 146–51, 165
Trotskyism 23–7, 31, 34–6, 124–89, 365; *see also* Bolshevist Leninist League; Communist League of Africa; Communist League of South Africa; Fourth International Organisation of South Africa; Lenin Club; Spartacus Club; Workers' Party of South Africa
Tsele, P. 359
Turner, L. M. 306, 308, 313
Tyamzashe, H. D. 57, 65, 73 n. 21
Tyler, C. B. 121 n. 8

United Nations Organisation 374, 391 n. 24
United Party 296
United Front Party 239–40

van Gelderen, C. 192 n. 28
van Gelderen, H. M. 159, 192 n. 28, 304, 312

Waterston, R. B. 49, 71 n. 3
Watson, A. 71 n. 3
Watts, H. 355
Weinberg, E. 359
Weinbren, B. 21, 101, 104 n. 3, 121 n. 8
Welcome, Mr 311
Wilson, Mr 310
Witte, Cde 130–1, 190 n. 9
Witwatersrand Tailors' Association 20, 58–9, 61
Wolfson, I. 270, 328 n. 20, 359
Wolton, D. 104 n. 1 and 3, 328 n. 14; and CPSA 76, 93, 98-101, 105 n. 15; and New Line policy 111–13, 119, 121 n. 8
Wolton, M. 100, 104 n. 1 and 3, 121 n. 8
Women's Enfranchisement Act 309, 329 n. 31
Workers' International League 36, 39 n. 15, 366
Workers' Party of South Africa 24–7, 35–6, 39 n. 13, 146–51, 154–74, 180, 191 n. 23, 245, 389 n. 1; and AAC 248–9; and NLL 252–3; and FIOSA 379–80; *see also* Communist League of South Africa; Lenin Club; *The Spark*
The Workers' Voice 161
World War One 16, 44
World War Two 11; and CPSA 33, 34–5, 37, 343–9, 354–62; and NEUF 335–9, 389 n. 4; and trade unions 363–8; and Trotskyists 332–9, 352–4

Xuma, A. B. 120 n. 3, 186, 193 n. 42, 389 n. 5; and AAC 226, 227, 229, 277

Zelikowitz, M. 100, 104 n. 1 and 3, 121 n. 8
Zilwane, Mr 305, 307